Believers Church
Bible Commentary

Elmer A. Martens and Willard M. Swartley, Editors

Believers Church
Bible Commentary

Acts

Chalmer E. Faw

HERALD PRESS
Scottdale, Pennsylvania
Waterloo, Ontario

Library of Congress Cataloging-in-Publication Data
Faw, Chalmer Ernest, 1910-
    Acts / Chalmer E. Faw.
        p.   cm.   —   (Believers church Bible commentary)
    Includes bibliographical references.
    ISBN 0-8361-3631-4 (alk. paper)
    1. Bible. N.T. Acts—Commentaries. I. Bible. N.T. Acts. English. New Revised
Standard. 1993. II. Title. III. Series.
    BS2625.3.F39   1993
    226.6'077—dc20   93-17294
                                                                      CIP

27897514

BELIEVERS CHURCH BIBLE COMMENTARY: ACTS
Copyright © 1993 by Herald Press, Scottdale, Pa. 15683
    Published simultaneously in Canada by Herald Press,
    Waterloo, Ont. N2L 6H7. All rights reserved
Library of Congress Catalog Card Number: 93-17294
International Standard Book Number: 0-8361-3631-4
Printed in the United States of America
Cover by Merrill R. Miller

02 01 00 99 98 97 96 95 94 93 10 9 8 7 6 5 4 3 2 1

To Mary,
for her unfailing love
and encouragement

Contents

Part 5: The Witness of a Persecuted and Scattered Church, 8:1b—9:31

Part 6: The Continuing Ministry of Peter, 9:32—12:25

Part 7: First Mission of Witness to the Gentile World, 13:1—15:35

Part 8: The Witness in Macedonia and Athens, 15:36—17:34

Part 9: The Witness in Corinth and Ephesus, 18—19

Part 10: Journey to Jerusalem and Witness There 20:1—23:35

Part 11: Witness in Caesarea, 24—26

Part 12: Witness—On to Rome, 27—28

Series Foreword

The Believers Church Bible Commentary Series makes available a new tool for basic Bible study. It is published for all who seek to understand more fully the original message of Scripture and its meaning for today—Sunday school teachers, members of Bible study groups, students, pastors, or other seekers. The series is based on the conviction that God is still speaking to all who will hear him, and that the Holy Spirit makes the Word a living and authoritative guide for all who want to know and do God's will.

The desire to be of help to as wide a range of readers as possible has determined the approach of the writers. Since no blocks of biblical text are provided, readers may continue to use the translation with which they are most familiar. The writers of the series use the *New Revised Standard Version, the Revised Standard Version*, the *New International Version*, and the *New American Standard Bible* on a comparative basis. They indicate which of these texts they follow most closely, as well as where they make their own translations. The writers have not worked alone, but in consultation with select counselors, the series' editors, and with the Editorial Council.

To further encourage use of the series by a wide range of readers, the focus is on illumination of the Scriptures; providing historical and cultural background; sharing necessary theological, sociological, and ethical meanings; and, in general, making "the rough places plain." Critical issues are not avoided, but neither are they moved into the foreground as debates among scholars. The series will aid in the interpretive process, but not attempt to provide the final meaning as authority above Word and Spirit discerned in the gathered church.

The term *believers church* has often been used in the history of the church. Since the sixteenth century, it has frequently been applied to the Anabaptists and later the Mennonites, as well as to the Church of the Brethren and similar groups. As a descriptive term it includes more than Mennonites and Brethren. *Believers church* now represents specific theological understandings, such as believers baptism, commitment to the Rule of Christ in Matthew 18:15-18 as part of the meaning of church membership, belief in the power of love in all relationships, and a willingness to follow the way of the cross of Christ. The writers chosen for the series stand in this tradition.

Believers church people have always been known for their emphasis on obedience to the simple meaning of Scripture. Because of this, they do not have a long history of deep historical-critical biblical scholarship. This series attempts to be faithful to the Scriptures while also taking archaeology and current biblical studies seriously. Doing this means that at many points the writers will not differ greatly from interpretations which can be found in many other good commentaries. Yet basic presuppositions about Christ, the church and its mission, God and history, human nature, the Christian life, and other doctrines do shape a writer's interpretation of Scripture. Thus this series, like all other commentaries, stands within a specific historical church tradition.

Many in this stream of the church have expressed a need for help in Bible study. This is justification enough to produce the Believers Church Bible Commentary. Nevertheless, the Holy Spirit is not bound to any tradition. May this series be an instrument in breaking down walls between Christians in North America and around the world, bringing new joy in obedience through a fuller understanding of the Word.

The Editorial Council

Author's Preface

This book has been several years in preparation, and during that time I have lived in five different locations. While such a protracted effort has presented its problems in terms of continuity and the availability of resource materials, it has also led to certain benefits. For one thing, this has given me more time to live with Acts in the context of the needs and interests of the local church and to try out portions of the commentary on numerous classes during these years.

This has also given me an opportunity to arrive at two or three distinctive features now embodied in this book. One was the decision to write the expository notes of the commentary in the present tense. Though the narratives of Acts are all in the past, the message of the book is so timeless that to make its action really "live" today, the present tense seemed most fitting.

Another bonus derived from this long production time has been an opportunity to move from a predominance of linguistic, historical, and geographical data, so characteristic of the commentaries of the earlier decades of this century. Instead, this finished work balances such interests with more recent studies in literary patterns and theological motives. As a result, we hope that the commentary combines something of the strengths of both approaches.

Every effort has been made to explore the original history of events and presentation of ideas. To do this, a great deal of attention has been paid to persons in the story, motives, and issues, together with considerable detail of a historical and geographical nature. Then this is set in the larger perspective of the selective processes which eventually gave us Luke-Acts as a unique Gospel-history. I have come to believe that this combination will be of greatest value for the various users of the commentary, whether they be pastors, Bible teachers, or individual students of the Word.

As I collected resource materials and produced this commentary, I have become indebted to more people than I can begin to list by name. Librarians assisted me in securing resource materials, various secretaries labored over my earlier manuscripts, and more recently, the computer word-processing people helped this octogenarian learn to use this wonderful modern device and came to his rescue in time of trouble.

I owe a special debt of gratitude to those who helped me with the text of the commentary as readers and advisers. Howard Charles was the New Testament editor for the first several years and gave both encouragement and expert advice. After he was forced by ill health to give up that responsibility, I have been blessed by the thorough assistance of his successor, Willard M. Swartley. An additional professional reader of great value has been Jacob W. Elias, with the many learned members of the Editorial Council in the background.

My cooperative lay readers have been American housewife Katy Stover, Nigerian evangelist and student Toma Ragnjiya, and Hispanic-American pastor Gilbert Romero. All these have spent hours in perceptive and helpful critiques of the manuscript from their own special backgrounds.

Then, over and beyond them all, I give ceaseless thanks to almighty God, who has given me the strength; the eternal Son, my Lord and Savior; and the Holy Spirit, who has provided the wisdom to complete this task.

Chalmer E. Faw
McPherson, Kansas

Acts

Introduction to Acts

Nature of the Book

When we start reading Acts, we soon discover that it is a continuation of Luke. Acts is dedicated to the same person, refers back to the Third Gospel, briefly overlaps with it, and then carries its story forward. We further note that the style is like that of Luke and its interests are similar. Indeed, Acts is the second half of a two-volume work.

Acts is thus a continuing *Gospel,* a proclamation of the good news of Jesus Christ that is carried on by a Holy Spirit-empowered church. While historically based, it is not history in the ordinary sense of covering the events of a period or interpreting important developments in a complete fashion. Omitted, for example, are accounts of the rapid growth of the church to the east, across North Africa, or north into present-day Albania (cf. Acts 2:9-11; Gal. 1:17; Rom. 15:19-20; traditions on Thomas and Mark in Eusebius and Jerome). Nor in the carrying of the gospel to Rome is there any attempt to record the whole movement. Instead, Acts provides a selection of narratives showing how God directed key individuals to bear witness to the Lord Jesus and plant churches in a northwesterly direction from Jerusalem to the capital of the Roman Empire.

In early chapters, Peter stands out as the agent of divine action, with John, Stephen, and Philip playing minor roles. Barnabas and Saul-Paul are introduced for their later leadership. They work together for a while and overlap with James in one midpoint story.

From chapter 13 to the end of Acts, Paul is the one chosen and endowed to channel the witness, assisted by a variety of associates.

This way of composing the book has suggested a title such as "The Acts of Peter and Paul." In view of the commissioning in 1:8, a better name might be "The Acts of the Holy Spirit," or perhaps "The Spirit-directed Witness from Jerusalem to Rome." The present title, "The Acts of the Apostles," was attached to the work about the middle of the second century. It no doubt reflects the mention of the apostles as a group through the first fifteen chapters and the fact that Paul is cast in that role for the remainder of the book.

Author

As with each of the other Gospels, no author's name is found in either Luke or Acts. Yet the early church from Irenaeus (A.D. 180) onward universally regarded *Luke*, physician, friend and colleague of Paul (Col. 4:14; Philem. 24; 2 Tim. 4:11), as the writer of both books. No other name was seriously proposed nor was this one disputed until the latter part of the nineteenth century.

This unbroken tradition of Lucan authorship is supported by two lines of internal evidence. First, we have the series of *we* passages in Acts, in which the author seems to include himself as personally present during the events related in 16:9-18; 21:1-18; 27:1—28:16. Since the last *we* passage takes the writer to Rome, where Paul's letters locate Luke, the case is strengthened (Col. 4:14; Philem. 24; cf. also 2 Tim. 4:11). Second, a long list of words and phrases in both Luke and Acts are suitable for a physician such as Luke to use. These include general concern for the sick, incidental remarks about the afflicted, references to symptoms of diseases, and stories of cures. They do not constitute a special medical vocabulary, as once thought, but are touches a concerned doctor would include in his stories.

Scholars rejecting Lucan authorship often do so by suggesting that Luke-Acts reflects a later perspective, idealizing Paul or ministering to other needs of the ongoing Christian movement. Then the *we* passages may be explained as an editor's use of a diary of a travel companion of Paul. Such theorists frequently hold that the author/editor shows literary dependence on Josephus, who wrote around A.D. 90-95.

The position of this commentary is that the traditional view of Luke as author of both volumes has more to commend it than any of the alternative explanations. Thus his name will be used throughout.

Date of Writing

Three major considerations affect the dating of Acts. First is the relationship of the Gospel of Luke to Matthew and Mark. If Luke used Mark as one of his sources, as many believe, then his writing can be dated after A.D. 66 and possibly after the destruction of Jerusalem in A.D. 70, the period when Mark's Gospel likely was written.

A second question is the relation between Acts and the death of Paul. The book closes at the end of Paul's two-year imprisonment but with no hint of his death or even of his trial before Caesar (ca. A.D. 62-63 *[Chronology, p. 309]*). Either Luke chooses not to mention these events or they have not yet happened. Was Paul aquitted, arrested again after more missionary work, and executed around A.D. 67, late in the reign of Nero? (This is supported by Clement, 1 Cor. 5; Eusebius, *Ecclesiastical History* 2.22-25; 3.1; cf. 2 Tim. 4:6-8.)

A third matter is the purpose of the book. If it functions as a defense written in behalf of Paul's trial before the emperor (in ca. A.D. 63-67), then an earlier date would be in order (so Munck, 1967: xlvi-liv). But if that is not its purpose, then a later date might be indicated: one after the early 60s, the death of Paul, and the destruction of Jerusalem, but within the lifetime of Luke. The balance seems tipped in favor of the latter. This would allow for Luke's use of Mark and can be reconciled with the silence of the end of Acts about Paul's death (see notes on Acts 28:30-31).

Purpose

In Luke 1:1-4 the writer states the purpose of producing an orderly account so that Theophilus may know the truth concerning those things of which he has been informed. While this refers primarily to the Gospel of Luke, it would also have relevance for Acts, which continues the story on into the early church.

This has often been interpreted to mean that Luke-Acts is a *defense*, first of Christianity itself, and then of Paul, who becomes the focus at the end of the second volume. The movement is portrayed as a divinely inspired faith with power to transform individuals and groups and make them loving and law-abiding. Christian leaders, though attacked and even killed, are proved by Roman authorities to be innocent of any real crime. Paul particularly is presented in a favorable light. Hence, this may be a document to be used in connection with his upcoming trial before Caesar, either as general information for the public or as an actual brief at the trial. Such a purpose can neither be proved or disproved; it remains as a real possibility.

Related to such defense is the theory, developed at length, that Luke is writing for the believers of his day who are facing trial. Thus he instructs them as to the nature of true Christian witness by accounts of Jesus and his apostles, including Paul as an outstanding example. Cassidy develops this view at length, calling it the "allegiance-witness" theory (158-170).

A second proposed aim of Luke-Acts is based primarily on its contents, which suggest an *evangelistic* goal of winning nonbelievers to Christ and of creating Christian fellowships throughout the empire. Certainly there is much to support this view, especially since there are so many stories dealing with individual and group salvation.

Along with this is the likely purpose of providing *guidance* for those already Christian. Persons are to be filled with the Holy Spirit (Acts 1:8; 2:4; 6:3-10; 9:17) and to witness to others wherever they go (3:11-26; 8:4-13; 9:20-22). True Christianity is distinguished from false (cf. 4:36-37 with 5:1-11, and 8:14-17 with 8:18-23). Partially instructed Christians are to be nurtured further in faith (18:24-28; 19:1-7). Models of initiative in the founding of churches abound in the exploits of Barnabas and Saul and then of Paul and his various co-workers (chaps. 13–19).

The purpose of the whole Christian movement, and therefore of Luke-Acts which presents it, is a *revolutionary* one. It confronts individuals, groups, and systems with Jesus, who brought a gospel of love and forgiveness and challenged the very foundations of Roman society. Furthermore, this Jesus died, was raised from the dead, and was enthroned on high as a king above all Caesars. He then baptized his followers in the Holy Spirit and sent them forth as witnesses to proclaim the same revolutionary gospel but to do so without breaking the law or resorting to violence.

For those who believe Acts to have been written after Luke's time, toward the end of the first century or in the early second, other purposes have been suggested. One is to establish Paul as a great apostle for a generation not acquainted with him. Another is to make a case for Christianity to a hostile Roman society. Still another is to revive the later church by this portrayal of early Christianity.

On the assumption, however, that Luke-Acts was indeed written by Luke, we may conclude that the purpose was first to *inform* readers of the truth about Christianity. This would serve to *evangelize* those who were unbelievers, give *guidance* to believers, and provide a *defense* of the movement, a defense which may or may not have been used in the trial of Paul. The ultimate aim, however, was the revolutionary one of *transforming* all life and bringing it under the lordship of Jesus.

The message is first to Jews; some receive it and are saved, but the majority reject it. Then a wholehearted mission to Gentiles is launched. Those of *the nations* who are won to Christ become the fulfillment of the old covenant's promises of an Israel that will cover the earth. A new people of God emerges, composed of Jews and Gentiles. This spread of the gospel (the action of *euangelizomai* throughout Luke-Acts) is the growth of the kingdom of God, a dominant theme of Acts (1:3-4, 8; 8:12; 19:8; 20:25; 28:23, 31). Acts ends by portraying Paul convincing people in Rome, the capital of the Empire, about the kingdom of God and proclaiming its good news *without hindrance* (28:23, 28). Thus Luke, in his double volume, narrates the spread of God's good news of peace from its origin in Jerusalem's temple (Luke 1:5-23) to the center of the Empire.

Sources

It is obvious that Luke was not personally present to witness most of the events described in Acts. He must therefore have had *sources* on which to depend, especially for the first fifteen chapters. There were the traditions of local churches, of Jerusalem for chapters 1-7 and 15, of Caesarea for 8:26-40 and 9:31—10:48, and of Antioch for the writing of 11:19-30 and 12:25—14:28.

Filling out these sources and adding valuable stories are memories of men like Peter, John, James, Philip, and Cornelius, whom Luke could have consulted. For portions where Paul is the central character, that apostle was a valuable source for this travel companion now turned author. Luke's reliability in handling his sources is set forth in his own statement about careful investigation (Luke 1:3). This can be checked by noting how he treats his source Mark and the source (often called Q) which Luke has in common with Matthew. In these cases he follows records faithfully but is free to shorten accounts at times and add touches of his own.

Literary Characteristics

Luke's Greek is among the best in the New Testament. His vocabulary is greater than most, with a wider range of subject matter. Moreover, he is capable of producing near-classical prose when he considers it appropriate. Luke 1:1-4 is a neatly crafted Greek sentence with balance and symmetry on a par with Hebrews 12:1-2. Yet Luke is composing a Gospel history and not a literary treatise. Most of his writing is in the common Greek of the street and marketplace. He is able to adapt his style to the cultural setting of the events he is recording. In Acts 1—12, for example, where the background is largely that of Palestine, he lets first-century Aramaic usage show through his Greek. As a result, this second volume is a document that reflects the mood and language of its changing scenes.

Along with this is his careful attention to historical and geographical detail. Here, as in the Gospel, he gives the names and deeds of the various Herods, carefully portrays their characters, and clearly sets forth the part they play as puppet rulers under Rome. High priests and members of the Sanhedrin, Roman governors and military officers, as well as local magistrates of all kinds—these all are presented with an accuracy that is amazing (see, for example, the use of the technical Greek name for city magistrates in 17:6).

What Luke does with historical information, he also does with his many place names and details of travel. There is no description of the countryside, nor is there the local color that a modern writer might give. Yet the names are there so that everything can be traced on a map or followed by memory.

The Use of Narrative Form

As Tannehill explains in considerable detail (1:2-9), Luke-Acts is an intricately constructed narrative, unified around the revelation of God's purpose for the salvation of humankind. Material is chosen with this in mind. Divine direction is shown in angel visitations, visions, answers to prayer, Spirit guidance, as well as by scriptural citations and allusions. These are highlighted as integral parts of the history and, with specially chosen characters, help provide narrative unity.

Of particular interest are the ministries of John the Baptist and Jesus in Luke and their continuation, with variations, by the various witnesses in Acts. Connections with them and with certain events and characters of the OT provide internal commentary on the story. Some of the parallels are major and obvious, being consciously emphasized by the repetition of key words and phrases. "Type scenes"— basic situations which appear several times in the narrative with a set of recognizable characteristics—are among the devices for accomplishing this. Other parallels are more subtle and require a sensitive and disciplined imagination to detect. Readers mostly see and hear what the author wants them to, and in the way he wants them to.

Along with this narrative unity, a recurring feature of Luke's stories is a touch of the dramatic. He is able to see this dimension in what happens and highlight it with great effectiveness. Omitting items that do not contribute to his purpose, he singles out specific actions and speech to convey the message, painting them with the skill of an artist. Examples of this from the early part of Acts are the falling of the Holy Spirit upon the company in the upper room and the dramatic action that follows (2:2-13), and the interrupting of Peter's speech by those cut to the heart, followed by spirited dialogue and mass conversions (2:37-41). Then from this point on, one exciting event follows another. Thus mob scenes, lynching parties, narrow escapes, sharp clashes, and surprise appearances enliven a history that might otherwise make heavy reading.

Mixed in with this is the author's sense of humor. It does not show up everywhere but now and then shines through in the turn of a phrase or the picturing of a situation, a subtle irony for the perceptive reader. In the Gospel is the caricature of the pretentious Pharisee in the temple. He preens himself in public as he "pray[s] thus with himself" (RSV), only to find that all the praise goes to a despised tax collector, awkward at praying but strong on honest contrition (Luke 18:10-13). Then there is the spectacle of a Jewish prodigal who sinks so low as to hire himself out to feed pigs; he wants to eat their food, but is denied even that (Luke 15:16)! In Acts the careful reader will find a number of such delightful touches, like the seven sons of Sceva who are beaten up by the man they are trying to help and have to run off naked (19:13-16). Another example is the city clerk who publicly chides the multitude for shouting so hard and long about something that everyone already knows (19:35-40)!

Particular Interests

In Luke's stories special attention is given to persons. They come from every major class and condition of humankind. All are important. There are the rich and the powerful, rulers of every kind, from local magistrates to governors and proconsuls. Kings and two different emperors are mentioned. Figuring in several dramatic stories are the wealthy and politically powerful Sadducees and the Sanhedrin they dominate. Along with them, middle-class people abound: businesspeople, artisans, petty officials, various ranks of the military, and hosts of ordinary church workers—the central core of society. Below them on the social scale of the times are the servants and slaves who figure in Luke's story. And there are mobs of all kinds. No one is unimportant in this Gospel-history.

Some groups of people are, however, given especially sympathetic treatment by the author. These include otherwise undervalued persons of his day like women, Samaritans, Gentiles, and all who are sick or demon-possessed. Love for these fits in well with a message of salvation for the needy of the world. Women are mentioned by name (Acts 1:14; 9:36-41; 12:12-15; 16:13-15, 40; 17:34; 18:2, 18, 26), and groups of women referred to (6:1; 13:50; 16:13-15; 17:4, 12; 21:5, 9). Samaritans, favorably mentioned in Luke 10:30-37 and 17:16, respond in large numbers to the gospel message of salvation and healing in Acts 8:5-25.

As for Gentiles, they are mentioned near the beginning of Luke-Acts (Luke 4:16-30) as divinely favored over Israelites. At the end of the first volume the mission "to all nations" (Gentiles) is proclaimed (Luke 24:47). In Acts the nations are implied in the commission of 1:8, are given center-stage prominence in the Cornelius cycle of 10:1—11:18, and figure in the founding of the church at Antioch (11:20-26). From chapter 13 to the end of the book, their conversion is a major theme. In all these cases of women, Samaritans, and Gentiles, the central teaching is that *God shows no partiality* (10:34).

As to Luke's interest in the sick and demon-possessed, there is little need for proof. The cases are too numerous to discuss here. Details of Luke's special touches are found in the notes on each section.

Luke's interest in persons shows in his concern with urban life. Whether or not he himself is a city man is not clear, but at least his concept of the spread of Christianity from one urban center to another is quite evident. The church grows from Jerusalem to Antioch, with important events in Damascus and Caesarea. Then it goes on to the cities of Asia Minor, Macedonia, Achaia, and back to Asia (Ephesus)—a movement from one urban center to another until it reaches Rome. In these various cities, Luke says a good deal about marketplaces, city streets, and crowds. Lodging becomes a matter of vital importance, and hospitality is a major virtue.

Another of Luke's interests lies in the area of money and economics. In the Gospel we clearly see this concern in the several parables about stewards, accountings, and the relations of the rich and the poor. In Acts are stories that deal with greed for money (5:1-11; 8:18-24), the economic exploitation of others, and fierce attacks on anyone who interferes (16:19-24; 19:23-41). Bribes are given and taken (24:26), and human life is endangered for profit (27:10-12).

In Acts another noticeable characteristic is the great attention given to travel. This includes both the journeys by land and by sea, with special interest in the latter. The various ports of call are carefully given and time lapses noted. Particularly in the voyage to Rome with the great storm at sea (chap. 27), Luke shows an intimate knowledge of the parts of a ship, the mechanics of sailing, and the handling of a vessel in times of crisis. In fact, his use of the pronoun *we* at certain points in the story seems to indicate that he is personally involved in some of the action (see commentary on 27:1—28:13).

The Greatest Emphasis

Permeating all these special interests and tying them together is the most basic one of them all: the divine guidance and empowerment provided by the Holy Spirit, with the accompaniment of prayer, signs, wonders, visions, angels, and prophetic utterances. God is at work on every page! To list examples and give references would result in a topical index of almost every paragraph of Acts. This is so central that there are more words for power in the book than there are for love. Concern and compassion are not lacking. Indeed, they are implied in every aspect of the gospel message. But the "acts" needed to witness to the ends of the earth are primarily manifestations of power, meeting and conquering the authority structures of the pagan world.

The missionary method found in Acts is that of (1) basic preaching and teaching, (2) accompanied by signs and wonders. Again and again people can see the gospel, the inbreaking of the new order (by miracles), as well as hear it (in spoken message). This gives the Christian evangelists two mutually reinforcing forms of witness with which to carry the message from Jerusalem to Rome.

Plan and Outline

The chapters of this commentary reflect the major divisions of Acts, worded in terms of witness, as found in the key verse, 1:8. Under each chapter heading are subdivisions into which the text most naturally divides. These will guide the reader through the movement of action and thought of the book.

A skeleton outline of Acts may be found in 1:8 with its stress on power from the Holy Spirit to witness in a series of areas. These are Jerusalem (found in chaps. 1-7), all Judea and Samaria (chaps. 8-12), and the ends of the earth (the movement in chaps. 13-28). Each successive phase in this series includes returns now and then to earlier areas, but the general direction is toward Rome.

It is the "Tale of Three Cities": Jerusalem to Antioch to Rome. The key story is the conversion of the first Gentile in 10:1—11:18. The authorization of the Gentile mission in 15:1-35 is its pivotal narrative. In it are included four major outpourings of the Holy Spirit: the "Jewish" in chapter 2, the "Samaritan" in 8:14-17, the "Gentile" in 10:44-48, and the "Johnite" or "incomplete Christian" of 19:1-17. A "heartbeat" story is the thrice-told account of the conversion of Saul-Paul in 9:1-19; 22:6-21; and 26:12-18.

How to Use This Commentary as a Study Guide

Read the text of Acts itself in more than one translation, a passage at a time, before consulting the comments in this book. Then read the commentary, checking biblical texts mentioned. Cross-references to "notes" mean the "Explanatory Notes" on the verses indicated, available in sequence following the order of Acts. The discussion of "The Text in Biblical Context" (TBC) will give you perspective, and the portion on "The Text in the Life of the Church" (TLC) will aid you in present-day application. Make use of other commentaries as well, and continue your study of each passage until you are ready to go on.

At the back of this book are "Essays," which discuss in greater depth or in more detail certain important issues in Acts. They are of two general kinds: (1) those having to do with the thought world of the book, and (2) some technical matters for those interested in them. References in the text to essays with page numbers are enclosed within square brackets in italics, such as this: [Witness in Acts, p. 321].

The bibliography lists works to which the text refers in an abbreviated style of documentation, with the author's name (if not already given) or other abbreviation followed by the page number in parentheses. Date or volume number are given before the page number if needed to distinguish the book from another listed in the bibliography. Here are samples: for (Ramsay, 1896:316), the bibliography will show you William Ramsay's book dated 1896, and the reference is to page 316; (Jeremias: 58-84); (Tannehill, 2:336-338) means volume 2, pages 336-338. Also note the later sections of the bibliography on ancient writings and the believers church.

Part 1

Beginnings in Jerusalem

Acts 1:1–26

PREVIEW

Luke begins this second volume with a carefully worded reference to his Gospel, a brief summary of the forty-day period between the resurrection and ascension of Jesus. This provides an overlap with the first volume sufficient to carry the reader into the story that follows. Emphasized above all else is the commandment to remain in Jerusalem and await the promised baptism in (with) the Holy Spirit.

Then Luke prepares the reader for the great experience of Pentecost. First he tells how Jesus commissions the apostles to receive power from on high and be his witnesses to the ends of the earth. Then he shows them returning to the upper room, where they and others devote themselves to prayer. There, in a meeting led by Peter, Judas is replaced and Matthias divinely chosen to bring the number of apostles back up to the complete number of twelve.

OUTLINE

Summary of the Story Thus Far, 1:1-5

Commissioning of the Apostles, 1:6-8

Ascension and Promise of the Lord's Return, 1:9-11

Events in the Upper Room, 1:12-26
1:12-14	Return to Prayer in Jerusalem
1:15-22	Peter's Word on Judas and His Replacement
1:23-26	Matthias Chosen to Join the Eleven

EXPLANATORY NOTES
Summary of the Story Thus Far   1:1-5

This volume, like the previous one, is dedicated to Theophilus. Commentaries on Luke (1:3) discuss the identity of this person. He is likely a man of considerable standing, with a genuine interest in Christianity, and connected in some significant way with the writing of these two volumes. One may regard him as an inquirer, perhaps sponsoring this literary production. Possibly he has something to do with the trial of Paul. We cannot answer these questions with certainty. Yet the mention of Theophilus does tie Luke and Acts together.

The contents of the Gospel of Luke are described as *all that Jesus did and taught from the beginning until the day when he was taken up to heaven* (1:1b-2a). *Began to do and teach* (RSV) may be taken as an idiom of the language meaning simply what Jesus actually did. Here it is more likely to have something of its literal meaning. In the first volume (Luke), Jesus began those deeds and words now continued in this second volume (Acts).

The author does not dwell on either the death or the resurrection of Jesus, since the reader has already had a full account of them in the Gospel. The death is simply referred to as the *suffering* and the resurrection as *present[ing] himself alive* (1:3). The focus here is on the command to await the promise of the Father (1:4) and all that this would lead to. For the present story, this is the most significant event of the forty days. The dramatic appearances of the risen Lord are summarized as the *many convincing proofs* (NIV) that he is alive. This living reality becomes increasingly important as the story of Acts unfolds, with its signs and wonders worked through the Holy Spirit, its use of the powerful name of Jesus, and the divine guidance given through prayer and angelic visits.

Only here in the NT is the period of occasional postresurrection appearances given as forty days. This matches the forty days of the Lord's temptation (Luke 4:2) and may recall the period of equal length that Moses spent on Mount Sinai awaiting the giving of the Law (Exod. 24:18; cf. Num. 14:33-34). Following the ascension, another ten-day period completes the fifty days from Passover to Pentecost.

Luke has been calling the disciples *apostles* since their call (Luke 6:13; 9:10; Acts 1:2), but now this title ("those sent out") takes on new significance in the great missionary thrust of Acts. We cannot be sure of the first occasion on which the command is given not to leave

Jerusalem but to await the promise of the Father (1:4, a repeat of
Luke 24:49). A few Greek manuscripts of 1:4 have Jesus *eating salt
with* his followers, sharing a meal; but the best texts give the meaning
of *staying with.* In any event, it is a time of close fellowship during
which the Lord charges them not to go forth without being *baptized
with (in, by) the Holy Spirit.* It is a promise first given by John the Baptist in Luke 3:16, repeated by Jesus in Luke 24:49, and now about to
happen (*in a few days,* NIV).

Commissioning of the Apostles   1:6-8

The story continues with the risen Lord meeting once more with his
chosen apostles. It is a moment of high expectation. He has spoken to
them before of *the kingdom of God* (1:3). Now they ask him if this is
the time for restoring the kingdom to Israel. They are thinking of an
earthly rule, as seen in Luke 22:24, where they all wanted to be the
greatest in the kingdom.

Jesus' answer is twofold. First, he tells them that the times for the
coming of the kingdom are in God's hands, a well-kept secret. Not
even the angels in heaven nor the Son know the day or the hour, he
has told them (Mark 13:32). Second, Jesus directs their minds away
from the matter of times and seasons and onto the task that awaits
them. The important thing right now is their empowerment from on
high and their witness to the *ends of the earth.*

Acts 1:8 has rightly been seen as the key text of the book. Here
Jesus gives the central theme of witnessing by the Holy Spirit. The
ever-widening areas of witness correspond with the three major divisions of the Acts account: *in Jerusalem,* found in chapters 1—7; *in all
Judea and Samaria,* in 8—12; and *to the ends of the earth,* in
13—28. The latter expression may not refer to Rome, though the
book ends there, but to the open-ended ministry indicated in 28:31.
As for the three concentric circles of geography, we shall note that
each successive area includes some return to earlier areas. Thus
chapters 8—12 tell of further work done in Jerusalem, and 13—28
report witnessing once more in both Jerusalem and Judea-Samaria.

In 1:8, Jesus speaks of the *power* that the apostles will receive
when the Holy Spirit has come upon them (cf. Luke 24:49). This refers to the experience they will have on the Day of Pentecost (Acts
2:1-47). The power they are to receive will be primarily for witnessing, the content and effectiveness of which will be demonstrated
again and again throughout the book (see "The Threefold Meaning

of Witness" under TLC). This ministry is a fulfillment of the prophecy of Isaiah, who spoke of Israel being called to be God's witnesses to the world (Isa. 43:10; 44:8). Paul makes this point in Acts 13:47, where he quotes Isaiah 49:6. Since the witnessing of the early church is by both word and deed, miracle-working is a major expression of this power, as seen through all of Acts.

Ascension and Promise of the Lord's Return   1:9-11

The last words spoken by the risen Lord are about the power of the Holy Spirit to make his followers into worldwide witnesses (1:8). Luke has already told of the ascension in 24:51 of his Gospel, and these two texts give the fullest account of it in the NT. It is implied, however, in many passages, both in Acts and elsewhere, which refer to the heavenly enthroned Jesus.

The apostles stand gazing upward as Jesus is taken into heaven. Then two men in white robes appear, chide them, and point them to the future (1:9-11). In similar fashion "two men in dazzling apparel" had appeared to convey a message from the risen Lord in Luke 24:4-7. Such angelic beings continue to play an important role in the lives of apostles (cf. 5:19; 8:26; 10:3; 12:7-11; 27:23).

By his threefold mention of the apostles looking into heaven as Jesus is taken up, Luke emphasizes the fact that they are eye-witnesses of the ascension. Yet they are not to continue gazing but to get on with the commission given them. Jesus will come again (1:11b), but in the meantime they are to be his witnesses. This sets their assignment of carrying the message to the world within the framework of history, between the *now* of the ascension and the *then* of the return. Here is "the era of the church," within which the events recorded in Acts will take place.

There is no indication as to when the return will take place, but the interval will give the church opportunity to accomplish its mission. The expression that Jesus will return *in the same way* as he now ascends refers both to the power and glory of God, who brings it about, and to the visible nature of the return of the Lord on the clouds of heaven (cf. Matt. 24:30; 26:64; Rev. 1:7). The term *Men of Galilee*, by which the apostles are addressed, may simply be a way of identifying them. Yet the mild rebuke that follows and the later disparaging label, *these . . . Galileans* (2:7), allow us to see a divine reminder that the apostles are provincials who have a worldwide task ahead of them.

Events in the Upper Room   1:12-26

1:12-14   Return to Prayer in Jerusalem

Only now do we learn that the ascension took place on the Mount of Olives. In Luke 24:50 the site of the ascension is "Bethany," a village on the eastern slope of the mount. The distance from Jerusalem is *a sabbath day's journey*, about three-quarters of a mile. Rabbis set this at 2,000 cubits, which a law-abiding Jew might walk on the day of rest. To make this rule, they took Numbers 35:5, on the length of pastureland around the cities of refuge, and applied it to Exodus 16:29, telling people not to leave home on the Sabbath. By the time of Jesus, it has become a common Jewish term.

The apostles now walk into the city and go to the upper room, where they have been making their headquarters (1:13). There they are joined by *certain women, including Mary the mother of Jesus, as well as [Jesus'] brothers* (1:14). This gives them a place of privacy and is suitable for prayer (cf. Dan. 6:10: the prophet went to his upper room to pray). There is no proof that this is the "large upper room" where the Last Supper was held (Luke 22:12), since a different Greek word is used there. Yet it may be the same room, and if so, certain postresurrection appearances took place there (Luke 24:33, 36; John 20:19, 26). Some also think this is a room in the house of Mary the mother of John Mark, where believers later meet (Acts 12:12), but the evidence is insufficient to prove it.

The list of apostles given here (1:13) is identical with that in Luke 6:14-16, with the omission of Judas Iscariot and some difference in order. The women who meet with the eleven remaining apostles are likely those referred to Luke 8:2-3 and 23:49. If so, then among them are Mary Magdalene, out of whom seven demons had been driven; Joanna the wife of Chuza, a steward in the court of Herod Antipas; Susanna, about whom nothing more is known; and "many others." All of them have been healed of various diseases or delivered from demons. Out of appreciation for what the Lord did for them, they followed him and his apostles about, ministering to them from their own resources. They were the last at the cross and the first at the empty tomb. Now, as dedicated and experienced disciples themselves, they are present in the upper room awaiting the fulfillment of the promise of the Father.

Jesus' own family is also present with the eleven and this goodly company of women. They include his mother Mary and her four sons, *his brothers*. According to Mark 6:3, they were James, Joses, Judas, and Simon, probably half brothers. Roman Catholic scholars, believing in the perpetual virginity of Mary, hold that they were either stepbrothers (sons of a supposed earlier marriage of Joseph) or first cousins (sons of Alphaeus and Mary of Clopas). Most Protestant scholars take the usual meaning of *brothers* here and assume them to be the half brothers of Jesus.

From John 7:3-5, we learn that Jesus' brothers did not at first believe in Jesus. The change probably came after the resurrection; 1 Corinthians 15:7 mentions a special appearance to James. This one, the eldest of the four, rises to prominence in the Jerusalem church, a presiding elder of note (12:17c; 15:13-21; 21:18-25) and traditional author of the epistle of James. The only other one known to church history is Judas, traditionally identified as the author of the epistle of Jude (Jude 1 calls him "the brother of James").

As this growing company of believers meet to await the promised Holy Spirit, they devote themselves to prayer. This is the human side of the bestowal of the Spirit. Luke has already quoted Jesus as saying that the Holy Spirit is given to those who "ask" the heavenly Father (Luke 11:13), and in Acts 10:44 he will tell how a man who *prayed constantly to God* (10:2c) has the Spirit fall upon him and his household. The Greek verb translated *devoted to* (RSV, NASB; NRSV, *devoting*) or *joined together constantly in prayer* (NIV), means "to be busily engaged in," "persevering and spending much time in" prayer. How wonderful that before long the Lord pours out the Spirit upon them in full measure!

1:15-22 Peter's Word on Judas and His Replacement

The selection of a successor to Judas is the only incident from the period in the upper room recorded in Acts. Happening *in those days* (1:15) means at some undisclosed time during the eight to ten days between the ascension and Pentecost. Perhaps it is near the end of that period, after much prayer. By now the company numbers *about one hundred twenty*. (For other examples of the use of *about* with round numbers, see 2:41; 4:4; 10:3; 13:18, 20; 19:7, 34). This total would include the eleven, the women from Galilee, the members of Jesus' family, and nearly a hundred others. Among the latter could be such persons as the seventy sent out in Luke 10, the two on the way to Emmaus (Luke 24:13), and others from among the "more than five hundred brothers and sisters" mentioned in 1 Corinthians 15:6.

In this setting of prayer and waiting, Peter, already a leader among the apostles, stands up to summarize their situation since the departure of Judas Iscariot. It is all according to God's revelation in Scripture, he says, quoting Psalm 69:25 and 109:8. Luke's view, reflected now in these comments from Peter, is that the whole Christian movement was foreordained by God, who revealed it long ago to the prophets by the Holy Spirit. Thus Peter can say that the Holy Spirit spoke beforehand by the mouth of David concerning Judas, whether or not David consciously foresaw that man's betrayal of Jesus (1:16, 20). Therefore, the words of Psalms, *let his homestead become desolate* and *let another take his position of overseer*, can be applied literally to Judas and acted upon by the group.

All this gives Luke an opportunity to explain to the reader what happened to Judas. Acts 1:18-19 are thus correctly put in parentheses in most recent translations as comments of the author and not part of Peter's speech, as the KJV might suggest. The details here differ somewhat from those given in Matthew 27:5-7. They can be reconciled, however, by remembering that it was Judas's money that was used to buy the field, and he can be said, as here in Acts (1:18), to have bought the field. Then it is possible that he fastened a rope around his neck, as in Matthew, before he fell and burst open, as here in Luke's account. This is an explanation first made by Augustine of Hippo and found in the Latin Vulgate of ancient times.

It is important to this emerging messianic group within Judaism that there be exactly twelve apostles. The Lord himself chose twelve in the first place (Luke 6:12-16), likely as a conscious raising up of a "kingdom," a new "Israel of God" (in Luke 22:29-30, the twelve are to be "judging the twelve tribes of Israel; cf. Gal. 6:16). Treachery reduced that number for awhile and was divinely punished. Now top priority must be given to restoring it and becoming once more the foundation of a new people, as the Lord intended.

So Peter takes the lead in suggesting the major qualification for apostleship. He must be one who has been in the company of Jesus from the time of his baptism by John and on to the present (1:21-22). In this way he can be a full-fledged witness with the same background of experience as Peter, James, John, and the rest. He can tell the story from the beginning, culminating in the resurrection.

1:23-26 Matthias Chosen to Join the Eleven

The statement of qualification is followed by the procedure of choosing a new apostle. First, two men are nominated, each measuring up to the standard. One of these is *Joseph called Barsabbas,* surnamed Justus (1:23). *Bar-shabba* in Aramaic means "son of the Sabbath" and may indicate that he was born on that day of the week. The same name is attached to the Judas chosen to carry the decision of the Jerusalem council in 15:22c. The name Justus is the nominee's Latin or Gentile name, meaning "just" or "righteous." At Corinth, Luke calls a Christian Titius Justus (18:7), but he is not to be confused with this man. Nor are attempts to identify him with the other Barsabbas of Acts (15:22) convincing, though there might be some reason to see this outstanding early disciple as the one chosen along with Silas to carry the decisions of the Jerusalem council. But such thinking is guesswork; such names appear frequently in the first century.

Matthias is the second nominee put forward and the man eventually chosen. He has a name which every first-century Jew would respect. It is a shortened form of Mattathias ("gift of Yahweh") and was popular as the name of the father of the great Judas Maccabeus, deliverer of his people from the Greek oppressors (1 Macc. 2ff.). Like the names Simon and Judas, it recalls the days of independence, when Jewish patriots threw off the foreign yoke in the second century B.C. Now this Matthias, like Joseph Barsabbas, has been a follower of Jesus from the *beginning*. Both may have been among the seventy sent out in Luke 10, as the fourth-century historian Eusebius thought, although proof is lacking (*Ecclesiastical History* 1.12).

The next step after nomination is renewed prayer. In Acts, this is the first of many prayers whose content is summarized. The group asks the Lord, who knows *everyone's heart*, to show which of these persons has been divinely chosen to take the ministry and apostleship left vacant by Judas. The Lord, who ordained the apostleship in the first place, is the one to complete the number.

The method used is the casting of lots. It is the way persons are chosen to perform certain duties in the temple, as seen in Luke 1:9, where Zechariah is picked by lot to burn the incense. In the OT, it is employed, after prayer, to decide who committed sin (1 Sam. 14:41-42; in Jon. 1:7, even pagans use it). In Nehemiah 11:1, lots were cast to see which one out of every ten men is to live in Jerusalem. The basic idea is that God, in control of all that goes on in the world, uses the lot to make divine choices, beyond all human wisdom or will. As stated in Proverbs 16:33, "The lot is cast into the lap [of a person], but the decision is the Lord's alone."

The common practice is to write the names of persons involved on stones and put them in a jar. This is shaken, after prayer and great ceremony. The name on the stone drawn out first is the one divinely chosen. Since this is the last mention of such practice in the NT, it is possible that it was not common in the first-century church, although it has been used by various Christian groups since then.

Matthias is never mentioned again in the NT, but that is no evidence that his election is not from the Lord, as some have maintained. The text indicates that both those involved and the author Luke regard this procedure as making sure God does approve. Matthias is just as divinely chosen as any of the other apostles, most of whom also are not mentioned by name after this.

THE TEXT IN BIBLICAL CONTEXT
One Era Ends, Another Begins

After Jesus ascends to heaven (Luke 24:51; Acts 1:9) and is exalted to the right hand of God (Acts 2:33; 7:55), the era of his earthly career ends and a new one begins. The Holy Spirit came upon Jesus of Nazareth, and he performed his works in the power of the Spirit (Luke 3:22; 4:1, 14, 18). Now he is no longer present in bodily form, and his Spirit-filled church must carry on the work.

Jesus himself foresaw and prepared for this transition when he trained his apostles and seventy others by sending them out on preliminary tours (Luke 9:1-6; 10:1-13). After his resurrection, he further instructed them for their task (Luke 24:45-49; Acts 1:4-8). This is the extension of the work of the kingdom of God, predicted by Isaiah as the work of the Messiah (Isa. 9:7), announced to Mary by the angel (Luke 1:32-33), inaugurated by Jesus (4:43; 6:20; 8:1; 10:9; 16:16; 17:20-21), proclaimed by the earliest disciples (9:2, 60), and made the subject of careful teaching by the risen Lord (Acts 1:3). It is the goal of the Lord's entire mission (Luke 22:16, 18, 30) and at the center of early apostolic preaching (Acts 8:12; 19:8; 20:25; 28:23, 31). This kingdom, the universal reign of God through the Messiah, will not be complete until the consummation of all things. Meanwhile, it will be visibly represented on earth by the church of Jesus Christ. The rest of Acts will tell how this new era gets under way.

Jesus' Ministry Moves from Earth to Heaven

According to Luke, Jesus also prepares for this move. In the passage referred to above, the Lord promises that he will be with them in their mission to give them "a mouth and wisdom" to answer all opponents

(Luke 21:15, RSV). This is amply fulfilled in Acts; the heavenly Jesus manifests himself to key individuals and inspires them to do his will. For Stephen, it comes through his vision of Jesus at the right hand of God (7:55, 59); for Ananias, through his conversation with the Lord (9:10-15); and for Saul-Paul, through encounters on several occasions (9:1-6; 18:9; 23:11). In other NT writings as well, Christ is portrayed as being with God as an intercessor for his people (Rom. 8:34; Heb. 7:25; 9:24; 1 John 2:1).

The Return of the Lord Assured in Spite of Delay

Luke envisions the return of Jesus on the clouds of glory (Luke 21:27; Acts 1:11). On the timing of this event, there appears to be a difference between Luke and the early Paul. In Luke-Acts, there will be a lapse of time sufficient to allow the witnesses to carry the gospel to the ends of the earth and the church to be firmly established. The apostles are told that the timing is God's exclusive domain (Acts 1:7). Thus the book closes with the future still open (28:30-31).

By contrast, Paul in his earlier letters speaks as though he and his generation will still be alive when the Lord returns (1 Thess. 4:17; 1 Cor. 15:51-54). This difference works itself out as the two men spend many years together (Acts 20-28; Col. 4:14) and are with each other toward the end of Paul's life (2 Tim. 4:11). They know that the parousia has still not taken place but will come in God's own good time, even if they die first (2 Cor. 1:8; 5:1-10; Phil. 1:21-25).

THE TEXT IN THE LIFE OF THE CHURCH
The Threefold Meaning of *Witness*

A key word for Acts is used in the eighth verse of this first chapter: *witness*. There are three progressive levels in its full meaning.

First and basic is to be a witness *of* something. The apostles have seen, heard, felt, sensed, and participated in the ministry of Jesus for about three years. This has included his teaching and his mighty works. Their lives have been forever changed. Everything they do or say in carrying the gospel to the ends of the earth will be conditioned by this experience.

Second, having seen and heard so much, each one of them is ready to be a witness *to* others. They can bear testimony based on personal experience. Peter and John will make both this part and the first phase of witnessing clear when they tell the Sanhedrin, *We can-*

not keep from speaking about what we have seen and heard (4:20).

The third phase is an extension of the first two and its ultimate outcome: witnessing *unto* (1:8, KJV). This means continuing to be a witness of great realities and then witnessing to others about them right on to the end of time or the ends of the earth. Sometimes this means until being run out of town, other times unto death (Rev. 2:10). This dimension is seen again and again on the pages of Acts. Here the Greek word for witness, *martus,* takes on the meaning of the English word derived from it, *martyr.*

Stephen is the first martyr mentioned in Acts (7:60), and James son of Zebedee the second (12:2). Peter almost becomes one in 12:1-12, and Paul has several brushes with death, one of the more dramatic being at Lystra, where he is left for dead (14:19). The history of Christianity is filled with countless examples of believers paying the ultimate price for their beliefs. In fact, the believers church was born out of such martyrdom, as chronicled in *Martyrs Mirror,* a monument to their triumphant faith (Braght).

Choosing Church Leaders

The casting of lots to choose a new apostle may strike us as a bit strange, but there is actually much in the story for Christians today. The prevailing atmosphere is prayer. First, they are *devoting themselves* to prayer, for eight to ten days. Out of that prayer comes Peter's inspired words on the need and the qualifications for the office. Then, in the same spirit, come the nominations, followed by specific prayer that God's will be expressed in the lot. The last act is enrolling the newly elected man as a full apostle with the others.

Quite a few groups in church history have used the lot. More modern adaptations, however, have been either the ballot on paper or some other discernment process. As sometimes practiced, members come forward one at a time and privately reveal to leaders, such as the moderator and clerk, the name(s) laid on their hearts by the Lord. Whatever the procedure, the important thing is that it be the Lord's election carried out through inspired human beings in an atmosphere of prayer.

Part 2

The Day of Pentecost

Acts 2:1-47

PREVIEW

What Jesus' return to Nazareth in Luke 4:14-30 does for the Gospel, this chapter does for Acts. It may be regarded as a frontispiece, like the one-page picture of central themes found in some books of a century or two ago. Its function is to provide a "message model" for what follows. Both here and in Luke, there is an event of great importance which focuses on fulfillment. After reading "The Spirit of the Lord is upon me because he has anointed me," Jesus went on to say, "Today this scripture is fulfilled in your hearing" (Luke 4:18-21). Now in Acts the long-promised baptism with the Holy Spirit takes place before the eyes and within the hearing of all (Luke 3:16; 24:49; Acts 1:4-8).

The story of this day sets the stage for the events and themes of the entire book: empowerment by the Holy Spirit, human response across national lines, opposition, the preaching of a gospel for all peoples, a great ingathering, and the formation of a community of believers with its many signs and wonders.

OUTLINE

The Outpoured Spirit on the Day of Pentecost 2:1-13
2:1-3	Divine Manifestations
2:4	Infilling with the Spirit and Gift of Tongues
2:5-13	Reactions of the People

Peter's Speech and the Response, 2:14-41
| 2:14-21 | Explanation of Events |

| 2:22-36 | Preaching of the Gospel of Jesus |
| 2:37-41 | Response and Peter's Concluding Words |

The New Community of Believers, 2:42-47

2:42	Summary of Community Activity
2:43	Wonders, Signs, and Holy Awe
2:44-45	All Things in Common
2:46-47	Continuing Prayer, Praise, and Growth

EXPLANATORY NOTES

The Outpoured Spirit on the Day of Pentecost 2:1-47

2:1-3 Divine Manifestations

Now is the Jewish Day of Pentecost, one of the three major festivals of Judaism at which every adult male Jew was commanded by the Law to appear in Jerusalem (Exod. 23:14-17; 34:18-23). The other two are Passover and the Feast of Tabernacles. Pentecost was originally known as the Day of the First Fruits of the Wheat Harvest, or just First Fruits (Exod. 34:22). Before long it came also to be called the Feast of Weeks (Deut. 16:10, RSV) because it was celebrated seven weeks or a week of weeks from the day after the Sabbath of Passover (Lev. 23:15). From the second century B.C. on, it was known as Pentecost, from the Greek word *pentēkostos* meaning "fifty" (Tob. 2:1; 2 Macc. 12:31-32).

Pentecost is a week-long festival, beginning soon after dawn on the first day of the week, with the offering in the temple by each male Jew of two loaves made from the new wheat. It thus marks the end of the harvest of that grain. Later it seems to have become also a celebration of the giving of the law on Mount Sinai (Knox: 80ff.; documented after A.D. 70: TDNT, 6:48-49). It is uncertain whether this is in the minds of Peter and company on this day or of Luke in recording the story.

Attendance at the festival has been estimated at 180,000, with some 120,000 of them from foreign lands (Jeremias: 58-84). Pentecost seems to have attracted as many pilgrims as Passover, and possibly more, since by this time of year navigation on the Mediterranean is opened up, causing many people to wait this late before journeying to Jerusalem by sea (cf. Acts 20:5, 16). During the week of the festival, both city and temple are crowded with *devout Jews* and *proselytes* (converts to Judaism) from every nation of the dispersion.

On the morning of the first day of the week, the group that has been meeting in the upper room are *all together in one place* (2:1). Presumably they are the 120 mentioned in 1:15. Attempts to restrict the number to the apostles only (based on 2:14, where Peter is *standing with the eleven*) do not reckon with the force of the *all* in 2:1, the many different languages spoken in 2:9-11, nor with the implication of the quotation from Joel that the Spirit is poured out on *all flesh* (2:17).

It is possible that they are still in the upper room mentioned in 1:13, since 2:2 here speaks of a *house*. However, a crowd soon gathers, and this suggests that they have moved to some larger area. This area might be either the streets outside the building or even a part of the temple where meetings are later held (3:11).

The first divine manifestation they experience is *a sound . . . from heaven*, a noise like that of a violent, rushing wind. This not only fills the house but is also heard throughout the city (2:5-6). Note, however, that this is not an actual wind but the sound of one. It is the mighty outpouring of God's presence, told in a language in which the word for *wind* also means *spirit* (Greek: *pneuma*; Hebrew: *ruakh*).

The second sign of the Spirit's coming is a visual one. People see *what seem to be tongues of fire* (NIV), flames that do not consume but, like the burning bush (Exod. 3:2-6), show God's presence. These tongues divide and come to rest on each of the 120 (2:3), presumably on their heads. The Spirit outpouring is for the whole company and at the same time very personal. As Paul says, "All these [spiritual gifts] are activated by one and the same Spirit, who allots to each one individually just as the Spirit chooses" (1 Cor. 12:11). This visual manifestation of tongues fulfills the prophecy of John the Baptist that the mighty one coming after him would baptize "with the Holy Spirit and fire" (Luke 3:16).

2:4 Infilling with the Spirit and the Gift of Tongues

What these manifestations show is that *all of them were filled with the Holy Spirit* (2:4a). This is Luke's favorite expression for the coming of the Spirit (Luke 1:15, 41, 67; 4:1; Acts 4:10, 31; 6:3, 5; 7:55; 9:17; 11:24; 13:49 *[Holy Spirit, p. 313]*). The immediate result of this filling is that they begin to *speak in other languages, as the Spirit gave them ability* (2:4b). From what follows, Luke means for us to understand that these are other human languages, each the mother tongue of people present (2:8-11; for the relationship of this to the gift of tongues found in 1 Corinthians 12-14, see the essay *[Speaking in Tongues, p. 319]*).

Scholars differ as to whether what happens here at Pentecost is a miracle of speaking or of hearing. Some who equate this with the tongues-speaking at Corinth say that members of the crowd hear a jumble of sounds and syllables and either imagine or actually do receive a message in their own language. If this is the case, then it is a miracle of hearing. Others point out that Luke clearly says, *They began to speak in other languages* (2:4), and that the hearers themselves later say, *We hear, each of us, in our own native language* (2:6). This makes it a miracle of speaking.

Luke likely regards it as a miracle of both speaking and hearing since both aspects are distinctly mentioned three times in referring to the audience (2:6-11). There is a joyous enthusiasm about their speaking, enough for the scoffers to say they are drunk (2:13). Yet what they say comes out in connected speech as the people hear them telling in their own tongues the mighty works of God (2:11b).

2:5-13 Reactions of the People

The sound of the mighty wind attracts large numbers of devout Jews from various countries of the dispersion. When they hear the speaking in tongues, they are surprised and amazed. It is so totally unexpected that they don't know what to think. To hear these Galileans speaking these various languages completely bewilders them. The Greek verb here is a strong one, meaning "blew their minds." It is incredible that people so provincial should be fluent in foreign languages! (Cf. Matt. 26:73 and John 1:46 for some current opinions of Galileans.)

The bystanders ask, *How is it that we hear, each of us, in our own native language?* They want to know by what power such a thing can happen. Peter will soon answer this in his speech. But first Luke lists fourteen nations or areas whose native languages are used by the Galileans. There may be more present, but these are representative and prove the point.

Beginning northeast of Jerusalem, Luke names Parthians, Medes, Elamites, and residents of Mesopotamia. Then he mentions Judea, where all of them are now, perhaps using the term in the OT sense of a vast central section (Gen. 15:18). Next come five groups of people from Roman provinces to the north and west: Cappadocia, Pontus, Asia, Phrygia, and Pamphylia—all known to have large Jewish populations. Two North African countries are listed: Egypt and parts of Libya belonging to Cyrene. Then the text singles out Rome, capital of the empire and destination of the witnessing in Acts. *Both Jews and proselytes* (converts to Judaism) from Rome hear and see these divine manifestations. The final two groups are Cretans from the Mediterranean and Arabs from vast territory east and south of Israel.

The content of the messages coming in tongues from this large group of speakers is one of praise to God. Over and over again in one language or another, the 120 tell of the Lord's mighty works, raising a chorus of joyous witness that continues to amaze those who hear them. *What does this mean?* they keep asking each other (2:12). No doubt some are favorably impressed. Others, however, are quick to put it down as intoxication at this festival time (2:13). They've just drunk too much *new wine,* they jeer. *New wine* it is indeed! Discerning readers of Acts will remember how Jesus himself used these very words to describe the gospel! (Luke 5:37-39).

Peter's Speech and the Response 2:14-41

This is the first of some twenty-four discourses in Acts, making up about one-fifth of the book. They provide variety and also furnish much biblical background for the story and theological interpretation of the events. Together they comprise our finest collection of early Christian preaching, known as the kerygma (*kerugma*).

These speeches are likely digests of much longer addresses. The choice of material quoted from any given one depends both on Luke's narrative purpose and what is available. Speeches vary in length and content according to the occasion and speaker. Most of them are proclamations of the gospel, and may or may not also be defenses. The longest one so far as *duration* is concerned, but shortest in the text of Acts (not one word), is Paul's sermon at Troas (20:7), lasting from evening until midnight. The longest *quoted* one is Stephen's speech before the Sanhedrin (7:2-53). Peter's message at Pentecost (2:14-40) is also lengthy and important in helping the reader grasp the tremendous significance of that day both for the newly emerging church and for the whole book of Acts.

2:14-21 Explanation of Events

As mockers hurl taunts of drunkenness, Peter stands up among the apostles and begins a defense. He addresses them with respectful words: *Men of Judea and all who live in Jerusalem* (2:14). With a touch of gentle humor, Peter mentions that it is only nine o'clock in the morning—too early to be drunk. Later Christian readers will likely see here, as in the *new wine*, a significant symbolic meaning. This is *early morning of a new day*, one predicted by the prophet Joel (2:28-32). The rabbis saw the Joel passage as referring to God's final intervention in history, now heightened for the hearers on Pentecost by the added expression *in the last days* (Acts 2:17) and the apocalyptic touches from that prophet about wonders in the heavens. These set the tone for the many *wonders and signs* (2:43; cf. 2:22) to be performed in Acts in the interval before that end comes.

There is a surprisingly broad spectrum of people in Joel's prophecy of the outpoured Spirit. It is for *all flesh*. Both males and females (*sons and daughters*) are specified, and both *young* and *old* shall be given visions and dreams. There is no distinction between the sexes as *slaves, both men and women*, are to receive the Holy Spirit. Here the reference to *all flesh* signals the removal of social class discrimination. This is later found in Christian fellowships where both sexes, slaves, servants, young and old, and all other levels of persons and major groupings of people, such as both Jews and Gentiles, are included (e.g., Gal. 3:28; Col. 3:11).

2:22-36 Preaching the Gospel of Jesus

After further words on the fulfillment of Joel's prophecy, Peter begins a new point: *Israelites, listen to what I have to say* (2:22a). He has come to his major theme. It is about *Jesus of Nazareth* and the good news that has come through him. Here may already be a hint of his messianic role. Where the NRSV has *Nazareth*, the Greek has *the Nazorean* or *Nazarene* (cf. 24:5; Matt. 2:23; note similarity in sound and perhaps in meaning between the Aramaic word for Nazareth and the Hebrew word translated *branch* in Isa. 11:1). Peter introduces Jesus as *a man attested to you by God with deeds of power, wonders, and signs* (2:22b). Not only that, it was God's definite plan that he be delivered up and sentenced to death. And, Peter says, **You crucified and killed [him] by the hands of those outside the law** (2:23).

This is what *humans* did to Jesus. What *God* did was the miracle of miracles! God changed everything by raising Jesus up out of the grip of death—an event, like the outpouring of the Spirit, foretold in Scripture. Peter finds a prediction of the resurrection in Psalm 16:8-11, where David, called *a prophet* (2:30), must be speaking of the Messiah and not of himself. David says, *He was not abandoned to*

Hades nor did his flesh experience corruption. This could only be true of Christ, Peter argues. And of this resurrection, he and the others are witnesses! (2:32). Moreover, they are witnesses of his ascension into heaven (1:10-11), where he is *exalted at the right hand of God* (2:33a).

Thus, as the enthroned Lord, Jesus fulfills the *promise* of the Father and pours out the Holy Spirit on his witnesses, as the hearers can now *both see and hear* (2:33). Then, in what proves to be the final point of the quoted speech, Peter turns to David once more, citing Psalm 110:1 to show that Jesus has now been made *both Lord and Messiah* (2:34-36). The reasoning is the same as before. Since David cannot be speaking about himself, he must be predicting the Christ. This is one of the major emphases of the address. Along with it, Peter makes clear the guilt of Israel by saying that *this Jesus whom* **you** *crucified* has become *both Lord and Messiah*/Christ.

Taken as a whole, Peter's message on this day makes three great affirmations which set the tone for the remainder of Acts. (1) The outpouring of the Holy Spirit is the genuine fulfillment of OT prophecy (2:14-21). (2) This Spirit has been bestowed by Jesus, who was attested by God with deeds of power, crucified, raised from the dead, and made both Lord and Christ (2:22-36). (3) The promise of salvation and the outpoured Spirit through Jesus are for all who will repent and believe: both Jew and Gentile, near and far, for all generations (2:38-40).

2:37-41 Response and Peter's Concluding Words

Peter pauses after the first two major points in his speech, and his hearers cry out in pain. They are *cut to the heart* to think that they have had a hand in crucifying Jesus, now Lord of the universe! Not only to Peter but to all the apostles (probably still standing in front—see 2:14), they plead in anguish, *Brothers, what shall we do?* (2:37b).

The answer is swift and to the point. With the force of a John the Baptist (Luke 3:3) and out of the depths of his own experience with Jesus (Luke 4:8), Peter shouts, *Repent!* And also like John, he adds, *And be baptized every one of you* (2:38a). But the new era has dawned and the *name* now is that *of Jesus Christ.* Then through him their *sins may be forgiven;* not only that, but they also *will receive the gift of the Holy Spirit!* (2:38b). This is the first mention in Acts of doing things *in the name of Jesus.* From now on, this will be the authority and power for *healing* (3:6, 16; 4:7; etc.), for *salvation* (4:12); for *teaching* (4:17-18; 5:28, 40), for *preaching* (9:27), and for *casting out demons* (16:8; 19:17). *[The Name of Jesus, p. 318.]* Other examples of *baptism* in Jesus' name will be found in 16:8 and 19:13.

Then Peter makes the statement that covers the rest of Acts and reaches down to our own times and beyond. It is the promise of the Holy Spirit *for you, for your children, and for all who are far away, everyone whom the Lord our God calls to him* (2:39). This gives meaning to the prophecy of Joel that the Spirit will be poured out on *all flesh* (quoted in 2:17). The offer of baptism in the Holy Spirit goes down through history *(for you* and *your children)* and out to the ends of the world *(for all who are far away)*. The condition for receiving this blessing is to be called by the Lord God, that is, to be a believer who responds wholeheartedly to the divine invitation.

At this point Luke summarizes the rest of Peter's remarks as testifying and exhorting, with one main thrust: *Save yourselves from this corrupt generation* (2:40, NRSV, CF). In view of the dynamics of salvation, this means *Let yourselves be saved.* Then, without any mention of the size of the crowd or the procedures followed in handling conversions, the author tells of an incredible number of people who receive the word and are baptized. About *three thousand new believers* are added to the church at one time! Here is a 2,500 percent increase over the original 120, without doubt the most spectacular growth Christianity is ever to experience.

The New Community of Believers 2:42-47

2:42 Summary of Community Activity

This is the first of a series of such summaries of the growth and success of the church. Others to come are Acts 4:32-35; 6:7; 9:31; 12:24; 16:5; 19:20; 28:31. Their narrative function is to mark the endings of specific sections and accent the Lucan emphasis: *the word of God prevails and the church grows* (CF). The present summary is multiple in nature, first indicating four areas of activity, then the working of divine powers (2:43), and finally the communal sharing, worship practices, and growth of the group (2:44-47).

Luke lists four major features of the new congregation's life. First is *the apostles' teaching,* to which believers devote themselves. This is the instruction that the leaders provide daily for the whole church—words from Jesus, messianic passages from the OT, and

Spirit-inspired lessons of their own. Such teaching is an important ongoing task as the Lord is adding daily to their number (2:47b). Second, there is the *apostles' . . . fellowship.* Here the Greek word *koinōnia* is used, a "common union" with the Lord and with one another, a new experience for converts in such great numbers.

The third and fourth aspects of their life may be regarded as part of this koinonia, the *breaking of bread and the prayers.* "Breaking bread" is the term used for beginning a Jewish meal and, through Jesus, has become especially meaningful. The term is used when Jesus feeds the multitude (Luke 22:19), at the Last Supper (Luke 22:19), and at Emmaus after his resurrection (Luke 24:30, 35). Hence, it reminds all believers of the gracious presence of Jesus. This act will occur again in Acts 20:7 and 27:35, at times of special importance. Some scholars take 2:42 to mean the celebration of the Lord's Supper by the Jerusalem church. Others see it as fellowship meals with a special Christian emphasis, as in 2:46, breaking *bread at home* and eating *food with glad and generous hearts.* The fourth activity of the new church, *the prayers,* is most likely a reference to appointed times of united prayer among the believers. This was practiced in the upper room in 1:14. There may also be a secondary reference to believers' attendance at regular prayer times in the temple (cf. 3:1).

2:43 Wonders, Signs, and Holy Awe

So great is the presence of God upon the new church that a holy awe pervades their lives. And the *signs on the earth below* predicted by Joel (quoted in 2:19) become a reality among them as miracles begin to happen, *done by the apostles.* No specifics are given in this general statement, but in the light of 3:1-10 and subsequent wonders and signs, there is little doubt about either the fact or the powerful effect of these mighty deeds. This will continue to be a noteworthy feature of early Christianity as the church grows and spreads. In 4:31, the place of prayer is supernaturally shaken, and a fresh infilling of the Holy Spirit takes place. In 5:1-10 a man and wife are struck dead for trying to cheat on their commitments, and in 5:11-16 great fear comes upon people both inside and outside the fellowship. It is a time of divine visitation that makes everyone aware that the Lord is mightily at work both for judgment and grace, a time of high-voltage Christianity that puts the fear of God in saint and sinner alike!

2:44-45 All Things in Common

This powerful sense of divine presence and outpoured love through the Holy Spirit creates a new attitude toward personal property. As Luke puts it in the parallel passage (4:32), *No one claimed private ownership of any possessions, but everything they owned was held in common.* They are shaken loose from possessiveness and self-seeking. No longer is it "I" and "mine" but rather "we" and "ours" as the Spirit creates a higher unity to which all belong. They begin to share *all things in common* in a new and exciting sense of community. With almost reckless abandon, they start to sell off property and pool the money to help those in need (2:45).

We are not told how many of the participants are longtime local residents and how many are visitors from abroad. Apparently the sharers stay on in Jerusalem. Nor does Luke at this point indicate what kinds of possessions are sold or that holding all things in common is a rule for all members of the community. Here he focuses on the powerful work of the Holy Spirit in bringing all this about, and on the results of it in their life and witness.

The Western text moves *day by day* from 2:46 (where it describes attendance at the temple) to 2:45 and attaches it to *distribute*, thus suggesting a *daily* distribution to needy believers. *[Greek Text, p. 311.]* This would accord with Jewish custom in rabbinical times of collecting food on a tray from house to house each day and distributing it to the needy (cf. 6:1, *daily distribution*), and likewise with a weekly basket for food and other gifts. Hence it appears that believers are forming a separate community with organized mutual aid (cf. 4:34); yet one wonders if some of the help reaches poor persons in general: *to all, as any had need* (2:45); and *good will of all the [Jewish] people/the world* (2:47, NRSV/Western text; cf. 3:6; Metzger: 303-304; Cadbury and Lake, 4:29; 5:140-150, K. Lake's note on 2:44-45; 4:32-35; 6:1-6).

2:46-47 Continuing Prayer, Praise, and Growth

Luke is careful to point out that, as the true heirs of Israel, the new believers faithfully attend times of temple prayer. According to Josephus (*Ant.* 14.4.3), these are twice daily, one early in the morning and the other at three in the afternoon (cf. 3:1 for the 3:00 p.m. service). This gives them an opportunity to worship the Lord as they and their ancestors have been doing for centuries. Now also they can share their new faith with the crowds that gather in the temple courts (some results of this ministry will be detailed in chaps. 3—5). Faithfulness to Jewish customs is not confined to the beginning of the church but will be seen again and again throughout Acts.

Along with participating in the temple prayers, this new Christian fellowship has the practice of meeting from home to home and sharing meals in a spirit of great joy (2:46). The word *generous* here means openness and frankness in their relationships, the mark of selfless dedication to the Lord. As they break bread in their homes, they can be sure that Jesus is right there with them (Marshall: 83). They are not simply eating together, but also *praising God* in thanksgiving for their food and fellowship (2:47a). Such joyous group spirit is attractive, a magnetic force, which Luke calls *having the goodwill of all the people*. The result is an amazing daily ingathering as the Lord uses such vital testimony to add to the number of those being saved (2:47b).

THE TEXT IN ITS BIBLICAL CONTEXT
Harvest Festival and Sinai Combined

As noted before, this feast grew out of a firstfruits harvest festival and then later became also a celebration of the giving of the law on Mt. Sinai (documented after A.D. 70). Scholars differ as to what part these two aspects played in the thinking of the first participants or in Luke's record. But there is no doubt that there are significant parallels with each that the modern reader will want to consider.

As for *harvest*, there is an abundant ingathering on this day of about *three thousand persons* (2:41). It is an event never to be forgotten in the history of the church, a firstfruits of the new era. On this day God comes with power to enlarge and weld together a body of believers, filling them with power to carry out their worldwide mission.

At the same time, the great events of Sinai are echoed in the experience of this day. First, there is a loud noise from heaven (Acts 2:2), matching the great trumpet sound which came out of the thunder and lightning on the mount and kept growing louder and louder (Exod. 19:16, 19). In the midst of this, the Holy Spirit is given at Pentecost (2:4), paralleling the descent of the Lord on Mt. Sinai to speak to and through Moses. Those receiving the revelation testify to it (2:4-12) and usher in a new era in the history of divine revelation, much as Moses did for Israel in his day. On both occasions, there is a focus on the Lord's salvation and the offer of a new relationship between the Lord and people (2:21, 38-39; Exod. 19:4-6).

Moreover, the speaking in tongues at Pentecost, inspired by the Spirit, matches and even outdoes an experience of the seventy elders appointed soon after Sinai. These leaders were filled with the spirit which the Lord took from Moses and put upon them (Num. 11:16-17, 25). Two of them in particular not only prophesied but kept on until Joshua urged Moses to stop them. Moses refused to do so, saying, "Would that all the Lord's people were prophets, and that the Lord would put his spirit on them!" (11:29). Now in the church's Pentecost, the fervent request of Moses is fulfilled. God's Spirit has indeed been put upon the people, and all of them are becoming prophets! This is as Joel prophesied and as quoted by Peter in his speech (Acts 2:17-21). Even Joshua's temporary opposition is matched by the scoffers at Pentecost who say the people are drunk with new wine (2:13).

The Reversal of Babel

According to Genesis 11:1-9, God rebuked human *self*-exaltation by confusing the languages and making it impossible for people to understand each other's speech, resulting in a dispersion of the tribes. Now at Pentecost, in the gift of tongues, Spirit-filled people are able to speak in languages they have never learned, which people from the dispersion can understand. The result of this miracle is an outbreaking of *God*-exaltation as these inspired believers tell of the mighty works of the Lord (Acts 2:11). Yahweh, who imposed the curse, has now removed it. Human language barriers will no longer prevent the spread of the gospel *to the ends of the earth!* (1:8).

Beginning of the Witness to the Roman World

By causing peoples from various parts of the empire to hear the good news preached in their own mother tongues, the Lord has now prepared the way for the fulfillment of the commission in 1:8. Here is evidence that the gospel is being taken home by visitors from parts of the world not mentioned in Acts. This includes Eastern areas of Parthia, Media, Elam, and Mesopotamia, as well as North Africa, and the provinces of Pontus and Cappadocia along the Black Sea. This Pentecostal witness thus fills out Luke's selective history, in token fashion at least. Then provinces to be evangelized later by Paul have some advance exposure to the gospel in this way. These include

Phrygia, Pamphylia, and Asia (Ephesus). Finally, here may be a clue to the planting of Christianity in Rome before either Paul or Peter reach that city. The Jews and proselytes from there (2:10) can take back some beginnings of the faith.

The Trinity and the Holy Spirit

With Peter's statement in 2:33, the giving of the Holy Spirit throws further light on how Luke understands the relationships within the Godhead. Luke has already told of the Spirit-filled John the Baptist witnessing the coming of the Holy Spirit upon Jesus at his baptism (Luke 1:15; 3:22). John predicted that this mightier one would some-day baptize his followers with the Holy Spirit and fire (3:16). Luke has also noted how Jesus returned from baptism "full of the Holy Spirit" (4:1) and went on "in the power of the Spirit" (4:14) to Nazareth. There he proclaimed that the Spirit of the Lord was upon him, that he was "anointed" thereby to preach the gospel (4: 18). Throughout the rest of Luke's Gospel, this Jesus continued to embody the Holy Spirit by word and deed. After his resurrection, he told his apostles that they should await the "promise of the Father" in the outpouring of the Spirit (Luke 24:49; Acts 1:4-8). Now finally, at Pentecost, *it happens*, as announced by Peter in his speech (2:33).

Jesus, having been exalted to the right hand of God and having received from the Father the promise of the Holy Spirit, has now poured out what the people have *seen* (the manifestation of tongues of fire and witnessing) and *heard* (the proclamation of the mighty works of God in the languages of the dispersion). The whole Trinity is involved in this miracle of Pentecost and will see that the commission of 1:8 is fulfilled.

The Wound That Brings Healing

Repentance is necessary before the crowd can experience salvation and the infilling of the Holy Spirit. This is dependent on their keen awareness of sin. Peter shows them how they all have been guilty of crucifying their Lord and Messiah. Then the realization hits them, and they are pierced to the heart with conviction (2:37).

Peter is conscious of how he fell to his knees in total repentance when first called to discipleship (Luke 5:8) and how he went out and wept bitterly when he realized how he had denied his Lord (22:61-62). Now Peter leads his hearers to the foot of the cross. There they see the one who, in the words of Isaiah 53:5, "was pierced for our transgressions, crushed for our iniquities, . . . and by whose wounds we are healed" (NIV). Little wonder that the response is overwhelming! Later Peter will take a similar approach in his temple address of 3:12-36 and again win large numbers to the Lord.

Join the Righteous Remnant

Peter's added words of appeal to his audience to save themselves *from this corrupt generation* (2:40) sound an invitation as old as Genesis 6. There Noah was commanded to build an ark to save his family from the "wickedness" that was "great upon the earth" (6:5), a civilization corrupt and "filled with violence" (6:11). No break with the world could have been more complete than that. It was found again in the call of Abram to leave his country, his people, and even his father's household to go and start a family holy to the Lord (Gen. 12:1-3). Thus the attempt to avoid contamination by the world continued: in the giving of the law, the battles against the Canaanites and other pagans of the land, as well as in the preaching of the great prophets.

Isaiah most clearly defined the righteous remnant who would return (10:20-23; 11:10-16; 37:31-32; 46:3-13). Jeremiah renewed the call (23:1-6; 31:7-14), and it formed the basis of both Ezekiel's vision of the valley of dry bones (Ezek. 37) and the gloriously reconstructed temple and worship (40–48).

More recently John the Baptist had appeared in the wilderness to call out a righteous remnant, told to "escape from the wrath to come" (Luke 3:1-18). Jesus continued the same message but with a broader scope and more discipling and teaching. Like John and the prophets before him, he had a strong sense of impending destruction from which only a few would be saved, and that only through repentance and complete commitment to the kingdom of God (Luke 13:3). Thus Peter, standing at the beginning of the era of the newly outpoured Spirit, continues the call of God to come out from a dying generation and join the ranks of those who will truly live.

Embodying the Renewal in a Community

There are no close scriptural parallels to the new community created by the Spirit on the Day of Pentecost. The OT tells of occasional revivals. Under Hezekiah the idols were removed from Jerusalem

and a new covenant made with God (2 Chron. 29:1-26). Under
Josiah the book of the covenant was found in the temple. When it
was read to the king and the people, widespread reforms resulted
(2 Chron. 34:1—35:19). The nearest thing to a Pentecostal
experience came in the days of Ezra (Neh. 8:1-8). At the Feast of
Tabernacles, a mass meeting of the people was held, and Ezra read
from the Law from daybreak until noon. There was much praising of
the Lord, with shouts of "Amen! Amen!" from the crowd. The reading
continued each day, leading first to a moving public confession of
sins (Neh. 9:1-37). This was followed by the binding of the community in a new covenant and the creation of a people holy unto the
Lord, separated from evil and bringing their offerings to God (Neh.
9:38—10:39).

For a parallel to the *community* aspect of the church following
Pentecost, one must turn to Qumran along the Dead Sea and read
the story of the group called Covenanters or Essenes, known from
the Dead Sea Scrolls. Flourishing during the century before Christ
and continuing to influence Jewish life and thought in NT times, they
had a strong sense of separation from the world, even from the rest of
Judaism. They believed themselves to be the righteous remnant and
were saving themselves from a corrupt world.

Yet the Day of Pentecost in Acts 2 is, even more than the OT or
Qumran revivals, an occasion of divine visitation, noteworthy for the
outpouring of the Spirit, widespread repentance, and glorious
ingathering. The new community created out of it, unlike that at
Qumran, remains in the mainstream of life and continues to
permeate and influence it. Its total impact is more far-reaching and
enduring than either that of Qumran or the OT examples, with results
so powerful that they are alive among us today.

THE TEXT IN THE LIFE OF THE CHURCH
Conversion and Baptism in the Holy Spirit

Acts presents no one pattern for conversion or baptism in/by/with
the Holy Spirit, and today the same diversity exists. As Bauman
points out (63-73), factors such as the thoroughness of instruction,
the extent of admitted need, the expectations and spiritual vitality of
the congregation, as well as the willingness of persons to lay hold on
God's promises—these all make for a variety of genuine experiences.

In our day we see different ways of regarding the relationship
between conversion and the baptism in the Spirit. Some say conver-

sion and receiving the Spirit are synonymous. According to this view, no further experience is needed except growth in the grace of the Lord Jesus Christ.

In a second view, the Spirit is present throughout the experience of conversion and is available for the asking. But one must claim that baptism in the Spirit in order to receive the reality of the Spirit's presence and power. This is the position of many evangelicals open to Holy Spirit renewal (e.g., Bauman: 78-79). In a variation of this view, if one does not specifically claim the baptism in the Spirit at the time of conversion, it can occur later, and at that time various gifts and manifestations may be experienced.

A third major position is that one becomes a Christian through the new birth and forgiveness of sins and then has a "second blessing" or work of grace by receiving the baptism in the Holy Spirit, again with or without speaking in tongues. This is the view of many in the charismatic or neo-Pentecostal movements of our times. A variation of this is the classical Pentecostal position, that speaking in tongues *must* accompany the baptism in the Spirit.

In Acts, baptism in the Holy Spirit, whenever and however it occurs, is the initial experience of Spirit-power in one's life, with the result that the individual is *filled with the Holy Spirit* (2:4) and united with believers in *fellowship* (2:38-47; cf. 1 Cor. 12:12-13). Then, from time to time, those already so baptized need refilling (e.g., 4:8), not because they have lost any of the Spirit, but because new occasions require an updating of that fullness. In Ephesians 5:18b, Paul uses the present imperative tense to say, "*Keep on being* filled with the Spirit." This results in a continuing transformation into Christlikeness (2 Cor. 3:18). In Acts, fullness of the Spirit is always associated with *speaking the word with boldness*, a manifestation of the Spirit-power to witness mentioned in 1:5-8 (Bauman: 75). And this fullness comes through concerted Bible study, prayer, earnest seeking, and the bestowal of the Spirit through the laying on of hands.

Tongues-Speaking Today

A new interest in the gifts of the Spirit, including tongues, has arisen. This happened especially in the Pentecostal movements emerging in the early years of the twentieth century and in the rise of the charismatic renewal in the second half of that century among traditional denominations. Those who highly value the gift of tongues and those who have little use for it—both need to share understanding and acceptance in those churches where the gift of tongues is exercised.

Fine Christians are at both extremes of this issue, as well as a good many others for whom it is a matter of indifference or something to be left to individual choice. Some may even claim to have the gift when they don't, matched by others quick to be unduly judgmental. What must be avoided is polarization. It is not an issue that should be allowed to divide churches or lead to censure or ridicule. Continuing Pentecostal experience is scriptural and is intended to be a means of enriching the individual and building up the body (cf. Acts 2:39; 1 Cor. 12–14). Spiritual leaders do well to learn how to deal lovingly and creatively with those whose practices vary in this regard. [Speaking in Tongues, p. 319.]

Pentecost for First Century Only?

A larger issue than that of tongues-speaking is whether the total Pentecostal experience was intended for first-century believers only or has value for Christians *of all times.* Some would argue that it was intended to help the early church get started but that today it is not so necessary. Especially is this so, some would point out, since we now have a written NT instead of oral traditions or scattered documents, as earlier Christians had.

Against this view is the meaning of Peter's statement in 2:29 that the promise of the Pentecostal outpouring was for later generations as well, and also for those afar off. Nor is there any indication either in Acts or other parts of the NT that the era of great spiritual experience was to come to an end before Christ's return.

Furthermore, the lesson of church history is that each new dynamic movement starts with some kind of spiritual outpouring. Catholic renewal experiences like that of Francis of Assisi, the various branches of the Protestant Reformation, the Anabaptists, Quakers, New Baptists (later known as Brethren), the Wesleyan and Baptist revivals, as well as the Pentecostal churches of our own century—these all have begun with new infillings of the Spirit. Many times the early fervor is lost, but then God raises up new Spirit-led persons to restore the vision. In fact, each generation is in need of revival of its own, and there is no better scriptural resource for this than Acts.

Communal Living

The community of the Spirit described in 2:42-47 and in the companion summary in 4:32-35 has had great influence on the history of the church and is much alive today. In the Roman Catholic tradition, monastic and semimonastic orders have modeled themselves, in part at least, on these texts. Many other attempts at communal living did not last beyond the first generation of those concerned. In the believers church tradition was the ministry of Jacob Hutter, an Anabaptist of the sixteenth century. From him come Hutterian communities, now including the Bruderhof movement begun by the Arnolds in 1920 (*ME*, 5:406-409).

This emphasis of the early church is picked up by the present Reba Place Fellowship, of Mennonite and Brethren origins, and its Shalom Circle of Communities. There are a number of other Spirit-oriented communal groups. It is their conviction that true Christianity never abandoned either this doctrine or its practice. With great dedication such groups engage in Christ-centered sharing of property and works of service, based on a study of the Word and enlivened with prayer and the praise of God.

On the other hand, the great majority of Anabaptists and Brethren have not followed the way of close-knit communal groups. Possessing many of the same ideals, they have preferred to live and do business in society. Yet they hold private property as a sacred trust to be shared both within and outside the church family in many forms of relief work and mutual aid.

Evangelism by Attraction

The impact of the newly Spirit-filled Jerusalem church upon the people around them (2:47; cf. 4:12-16; 6:7) might well be a model for congregations everywhere. Here transformed persons show such mutual love and are used of the Spirit for such wonders and signs that they draw others in large numbers. It is an evangelism of attraction. Nothing is so appealing to hurting, spiritually hungry outsiders as a body of people just like themselves, but who have now been genuinely changed into victorious, joy-filled Christians. God uses such believers, along with miracles, to add daily *those being saved!*

Part 3

The Witness of the Early Jerusalem Church

Acts 3:1—5:42

PREVIEW

Now that the vibrant new community of faith is started, Luke goes on to give a series of stories to illustrate their continuing witness and impact upon the world about them. Peter plays the lead role, with John, the other apostles, and the church as a supportive cast. The Lord's *wonders and signs* continue with aid in healing, meeting opposition, and answering prayers. The section is a connected series of events involving the apostles, the people, and the Sanhedrin. It is composed of three major movements: First is the healing of a cripple, which leads to opposition by the authorities and results in release by the Sanhedrin (3:1—4:31). Second is an interlude on communal giving, introducing the generous Barnabas and, by contrast, a tragically hypocritical couple (4:32—5:11). Then there is another victorious round with the Sanhedrin (5:12-42). This final narrative reduplicates the first one as it moves from *arrest* to *hearing* to *release* (Tannehill, 2:46-50).

This section is united to the one which precedes it by frequent references to the *name of Jesus*, a practice resumed in chapters 8—10 but less frequent thereafter. This shows that it does not reflect so much changing habits of expression as the deliberate emphasis of the author to provide narrative unity. The text is enriched by complex echo effects, recalling earlier characters and events in a set of similarities, differences, and fulfillments that deepen the reader's experience of the story. For example, the beginning of the apostles' mission echoes the early days of Jesus' ministry: prayer and the coming of the Spirit (cf. 1:14 and 2:1-4 with Luke 3:21-22), followed by an inaugural speech (cf. 2:14-36 with Luke 4:16-22), healing of a

60

helpless man (cf. 3:1-8 with Luke 5:17-26), subsequent opposition by religious leaders (cf. 4:1-31 with Luke 4:28-29; 6:11), leading to proclamation of the saving power of Jesus (cf. 3:11-16; 4:8-12 with Luke 5:26; 6:20-21).

OUTLINE

Witness of a Great Miracle, 3:1—4:31
3:1-10	Dramatic Healing of a Cripple
3:11-26	Peter's Witness to the Gathering Crowd
4:1-4	Peter and John Arrested and Held Overnight
4:5-22	Trial Before the Sanhedrin
4:23-31	Triumphant Prayer Meeting

Continuing Life Within the Community, 4:32—5:16
4:32-37	Believers Share Their Possessions
5:1-11	The Tragic Case of Ananias and Sapphira
5:12-16	Continued Miracle-Working and Growth

Another Encounter with the Sanhedrin, 5:17-42
5:17-21a	Imprisonment and Release of the Apostles
5:21b-26	Return of Apostles to Teaching in the Temple
5:27-32	Re-arrest, Trial, and Answer of the Apostles
5:33-39	Advice of Gamaliel
5:40-42	Release of Apostles and Continued Teaching

EXPLANATORY NOTES

Witness of a Great Miracle 3:1—4:31

3:1-10 Dramatic Healing of a Cripple

It is the *three o'clock* afternoon prayer service in the temple, the Jewish *ninth hour*, counting from 6:00 a.m. (3:1, RSV). As shown in 2:46, the growing group of believers continue their attendance at these services. Luke turns the spotlight on two of their leading apostles, Peter and John. They enter through a gate called *Beautiful*, likely the one Josephus called the Nicanor Gate, covered with Corinthian bronze and "far exceeding in value those plated with silver and set in gold" (*War* 5.5.3). (Another possibility is the Shushan Gate, the outer one on the east side of the temple.) The Nicanor Gate is the major entrance for Jewish worshipers as they pass from the Court of the Gentiles to the inner, more sacred areas, an ideal place for beggars to ask alms of people going in to worship.

Near the gate the apostles see a man crippled from birth. People are carrying him in and laying him where he can attract the attention of passersby. Apparently he is looking down out of long habit as he asks them for money, and Peter commands him to look up (3:4). The eye contact is important. But then the helpless man is told that there is no money. Expecting a nice gift, no doubt he is disappointed. At that very moment, Peter offers him something far better. He seizes the cripple's right hand and says, *In the name of Jesus Christ of Nazareth, stand up and walk!* (3:6). Luke tells how at once the man begins to feel strength coming into his feet and ankles. Legs that have never supported his weight now straighten up, and he soon rises to full height. And then, wonder of wonders, he begins to leap in the air and praise the Lord! (3:8).

As Peter and John proceed through the Court of Women, this newly healed forty-year-old goes with them, leaping and bounding for joy. Then they apparently go in and finish the prayer service, returning eastward to the Portico (or Colonnade, NIV) of Solomon. Other people begin to follow in growing numbers. Those who knew this hopeless beggar marvel that he is now perfectly healed. They are *filled with wonder* (*thambos*, a strong word ranging in meaning from astonishment to outright fear) and *amazement* (*ekstasis*, beside themselves in a mind-boggled state; 3:10).

The crowd increases as they gather in the Portico, a covered walk forty-five feet wide with two rows of stone columns twenty-seven feet high and roofed over with cedar (3:11). Though named in honor of Solomon, it is of more recent construction, modeled on the *stoa* (porch) of Greek temples and ideal for holding public meetings. In 5:12 it becomes a place where people are converted in great numbers.

3:11-26 Peter's Witness to the Gathering Crowd

The former cripple stays close to Peter and John as people quiet down. They want to hear what the apostle is saying (3:12). There is enough of a crowd that the authorities will later complain, with obvious exaggeration, that *all who live in Jerusalem* have heard the gospel (4:16). Luke reports Peter's speech at some length, about two-thirds as much as the coverage he gives the one at Pentecost. Like that day, Peter has a surprised and attentive audience. In place of over a hundred Spirit-filled people shouting the praises of God in languages they had never learned, there is now a miraculously cured lame man jumping about and blessing the Lord.

Again the air is electric with expectation. This time also Peter addresses them formally, *You Israelites*, and hastens to answer their unspoken question (3:12a). If you are thinking about the power that could raise this cripple, he tells them, be assured right from the start that it was not from *us*, nor was it by *our own power or piety*. Focus rather on the *God of Abraham . . . Isaac, and . . . Jacob, the God of our ancestors, who glorified* his suffering servant (cf. Isa. 52:13).

Peter identifies this *servant* as Jesus and begins to zero in on the fact that *you* (his audience) had a hand in crucifying him (3:12b-15). First you *handed him over*. Then when there was a chance to have him released, you *rejected* him and asked for a *murderer* instead (3:14). After that *you killed* this servant, the very *Author of life* (3:15). But God raised him from the dead, and *we* who stand here *are witnesses* of that fact (cf. 2:22). Now here is the answer to the question of power. It is *faith* in the *name* of this risen Lord that has brought about the obvious healing of this man (3:16).

At this point Peter is ready to make his evangelistic appeal. He mentions the crucifixion theme again and explains that they really *acted in ignorance*, but there is hope for them through *repentance* (3:17-26). God has already foretold these events through the prophets so that evil can be overcome through the sufferings of Christ (3:18). All of them can now *repent*, people as well as rulers, have their sins blotted out, and get ready for a messianic time of *refreshing* (3:20). Actually, on one level they *did* know what they were doing when they crucified Jesus, but in terms of understanding God's purposes and the depths of their own sin, they did *not* know. Luke has already quoted Jesus as praying, "Father, forgive them; for they do not know what they are doing" (Luke 23:34). This is the *ignorance* in which they acted.

Repentance is the way out, the only real hope (3:19). Then God can send the appointed Messiah. His name is *Jesus*, now ascended to heaven (1:10-11), where he will remain until all is fulfilled (3:21). The *times of refreshing* refer to a coming period of *universal restoration* foretold by the *holy prophets*. This was predicted by Moses, Peter says, who pointed to a prophet like himself (Deut. 18:15, 18-19), now known to be Jesus, to whom all must listen or be *rooted out of the people* (3:21-23).

Peter's final appeal (3:24-26) is also based on the Hebrew Bible, where all the prophets after Moses are referred to as prophesying about these days. (In the speech itself, there may have been many other quotations at this point). In closing, Peter says, **You** *are the descendants of the prophets and of the covenant*, and *to you God first sent his servant, to turn you from your wickedness* (3:26).

4:1-4 Peter and John Arrested and Held Overnight

Just then three groups of authorities bear down on the apostles and cut short the meeting (4:1). There is no mention of a call to repentance, just a hostile confrontation by *priests* from among those on duty in the temple, the *captain of the temple* police, and some *Sadducees*. The *temple police* (5:26) are Levites serving their term of duty and charged with keeping the sacred precincts orderly and undefiled. Such a crowd would make them fear a riot, and they must report this to the authorities. The Sadducees, in league with the high priest, are annoyed by the preaching of the resurrection, which they reject (Luke 20:27; Acts 23:8), and are threatened and angered at being accused of killing the Messiah (Acts 2:23, 36; 3:14-15).

Without further ado, the temple police arrest the two apostles and, since it is evening, throw them into the common lockup overnight (4:3). Luke takes this occasion to note that many hear the message and become believers, and the total of *men* reaches a remarkable 5,000, likely more with women and children (4:4, RSV; obscured in NRSV). This figure may, as Marshall suggests (99), include not only Jerusalem but the country region round about. Not all this increase, of course, is due to the one speech. There has been great growth since the last such notice (2:41).

4:5-22 Trial Before the Sanhedrin

The next day the supreme council or Sanhedrin meets, what Luke calls the *rulers, elders, and scribes* (4:5). Some antecedent to this body was likely organized by Ezra after the exile (cf. Ezra 5:5; Neh. 2:16; etc.). By Peter's time it is modeled after the group of seventy elders who assisted Moses (Num. 11:16-24; Mishnah Sanhedrin 1.1, 6). This court has come to exercise wide-ranging powers, functioning as the final authority in religious matters and handling many domestic political cases as well. The high priest presides over the assembly, with former high priests, members of privileged families, and noted jurists on the court with him. In earlier days the Sanhedrin was made up chiefly of Sadducees, but around 67 B.C. Pharisees gained in power. Now both parties are found in some strength in the Sanhedrin (cf. Acts 5:34-40; 23:6-10).

The present meeting seems to be a specially called one. The councillors sit in a semicircle, with the presiding officer (high priest) and his clerks in prominent positions. From A.D. 6 to 15, *Annas* has been *high priest* with present influence and prestige shown by continued use of his title. With him are his son-in-law *Caiaphas*, now high priest (A.D. 18-36; John 18:13, 24); *John* (perhaps Annas's son Jonathan, who follows Caiaphas as high priest); and *Alexander*, otherwise unknown but also a member of the powerful *high-priestly family* (4:6; Luke 3:2). All are linked with the temple and are determined opponents of the new messianic movement centered in Jesus.

They order Peter and John to stand out in the middle and put to them the question of authority (4:7). Are these two operating by the power of the devil, as Jesus' accusers claimed that he was (Luke 11:15-19)? Like the other challenge hurled at the Lord during his last week of teaching (Luke 20:2), they want to know who gave these men the right to disturb the smooth flow of temple life.

Peter has already told the crowd the source of his authority in the name of Jesus (Acts 3:12-16), and now he speaks up boldly to the high court. Luke reports that as he does so, he is *filled with the Holy Spirit,* meaning no doubt that this already Spirit-filled apostle is given a special endowment of wisdom for this occasion. Jesus had promised that his followers would be given "a mouth and wisdom" which none of their adversaries would be able to withstand or contradict (Luke 21:14-15, RSV).

Addressing the council respectfully as *rulers of the people and elders* (4:8), the apostle calmly reasons with them about the good deed he and John have done for a hopeless cripple. Then he becomes more direct: *Let it be known to all of you, and to all the people of Israel,* that this man was healed *by the name of Jesus Christ of Nazareth, whom you crucified, whom God raised from the dead* (4:10). Going beyond their question, Peter continues his forthright testimony by citing a Scripture they well know and applies it to Jesus (cf. Mark 12:10; 1 Pet. 2:7). The stone *rejected by you builders . . . has become the head of the corner* (4:11, RSV; Ps. 118:22).

Nor is this all. In strong, unyielding terms Peter declares that it is only in the name of Jesus that *we must be saved* (4:12). This is a key statement for the whole book of Acts. From the beginning Jesus' name has been appealed to and used for all kinds of mighty works:

preaching, teaching, healing, and both public and private evangelism [*The Name of Jesus, p. 318*]. Now Peter maintains that it is the only name by which human beings, if they are to be saved at all, *must be saved*. It is clear that by *salvation* is meant a whole range of divine actions, from rescue in time of danger (27:20, 31), deliverance from punishment (16:30; 27:43), to various kinds of healing (14:9; 3:1—4:37), and most importantly, eternal salvation (2:21, 47; 11:14; 15:11, 16:31).

Peter's assertion arises from the conviction that God has exalted Jesus to the right hand of all power, a position that cannot be shared with anyone else. It follows that only in the name of Jesus can all these blessings come. Since the Sanhedrin has no knowledge of nor belief in this exaltation of Jesus, they cannot accept the apostle's statement, though believers can. Nevertheless, Peter's word contains a solemn warning to the supreme council that if they persist in repudiating Jesus, there is no further hope for them personally nor for Israel. In Jesus the Messiah, their salvation is inextricably bound up (see TBC, "Salvation Only in the Name of Jesus").

Amazingly, Peter's emphatic claim does not infuriate the council but surprises them and fills them with new awe. They are greatly impressed by the *boldness* and *courage* (NIV) of these *unlearned and ignorant men* (4:13, KJV). Here Luke uses terms that express the contempt of aristocrats for commoners, yet Peter and John are not illiterates. They have taken the common synagogue classes and thus are only comparatively *uneducated and ordinary*.

What is more, the apostles remind the rulers of another uneducated man who also spoke in such a bold, unanswerable manner. As Luke puts it, *they recognized them as companions of Jesus* (4:13). This can mean that some of the councillors remember seeing them in the company of the Lord during that last week. Or perhaps their Galilean accent reminds them of Jesus. More likely, however, it is their similarity in style and impact. Like Jesus, these two exercise the healing powers of God and present a forthright message of salvation to match it. They also use the *name of Jesus* in everything they do or say, confirming the impression of a close relationship.

The major problem for the council is how to deal with such witnesses. They are immensely popular with the people, and right beside them in court stands the proof of a mighty miracle, the newly healed cripple. In no way can the Sanhedrin deny that the power of God has been working through these unauthorized preachers. So in order to talk over the matter privately, the council orders the accused to leave the room (4:15). Once alone, the court voices the big question: *What will we do with them?* (4:16).

All who live in Jerusalem know that a notable sign has been performed in the name of Jesus. Hence, the Sanhedrin can do nothing but call the apostles back in and lamely warn them not to speak any more in this name! This they do, only to receive another surprise. Instead of meekly complying, these Spirit-filled witnesses throw down the gauntlet in the conflict between the council and the Lord Jesus Christ. *You must* judge, Peter and John answer, *whether it is right to listen to you rather than to God!* We ourselves are under obligation to tell openly and fairly what we have *seen* and *heard* (4:19-20).

There is nothing left for the Sanhedrin to do but add more threats to the warnings they have already given (4:21). What these might be, Luke does not say, nor are they any longer important. Finding no way to punish the apostles, the council has to release them. People are praising God for the healing of this cripple, whose age Luke now gives as over forty years; thus he is widely known in the area (4:22). The present embarrassment of the high court is similar to that in the days of Jesus when the authorities wanted to destroy him but "did not find anything they could do, for all the people were spellbound by what they heard" (Luke 19:47-48).

4:23-31 Triumphant Prayer Meeting

Luke now brings the story to another major climax, matching the dramatic ingathering and founding of the new church community in 2:41-47. This is the prayer meeting that follows the release of Peter and John by the Sanhedrin (4:23). Instead of being cowed by threats and warnings of the authorities, these believers simply raise their voices in prayer and praise to the *Sovereign Lord* (4:24-30).

They cite a portion of Psalm 2 about the heathen raging and use it as a prophecy of what Herod and Pilate did to Jesus, seeing in that attack the *predestined* work of the Lord. Luke makes it clear that both the *Jews*, represented by Herod, and the *Romans*, through the procurator Pilate, have been responsible for the death of Jesus. As Jesus' followers interpret the psalm, the *nations* or *Gentiles* who raged against Jesus were the Romans who sentenced and executed him. And *the peoples* who *imagine vain things* were the Jewish adversaries who accused him to the Romans. Moreover, the *kings of the earth* who took their stand against him would include Herod Antipas. Pilate represented *the rulers . . . gathered together against the Lord and against his Messiah.*

It is therefore not a case, as some scholars have maintained, of Luke blaming the Jews alone for the crucifixion. For both Luke and the early believers, that was a crime shared by the leaders of both ethnic groups. Yet God, with infinite wisdom and power, has used their evil actions to fulfill his own *predestined plan* (4:28; for earlier mentions of God's foreknowledge and plan for the death and resurrection of Jesus, see 2:23; 3:18).

This understanding of the situation leads the Jerusalem believers to make two requests. Instead of asking that God lessen or remove the threats against them, they pray that they may be given *all boldness* to speak the word. They have already been bold. Now they want more! Their other request is that the Lord will continue to heal and perform signs and wonders (4:29-30).

The climax comes as a mighty Amen to their prayers. The place is shaken as the Holy Spirit comes down afresh, fills every one of them with the new boldness they request, and shakes the foundation of the place where they are meeting. This kind of divine response occurs again in the experience of Paul and Silas at Philippi (16:25-26).

Continuing Life Within the Community 4:32—5:16

4:32-37 Believers Share Their Possessions

After this dramatic account of prayer power in the new fellowship, Luke gives the reader another summary of church activity (cf. 2:42-47). This one underscores the unity, communal sharing, powerful witness, and popularity of these believers. In so doing, it provides a background for introducing Joseph Barnabas for the role he will play in the next eleven chapters of the book.

The members of the church are *of one heart and soul* because all are centered on Jesus, who unifies deep within. Thus dedicated to Christ and one another, no one claims *private ownership of any possessions*. All things belong to the Lord and are on loan to them for the good of the community. Thus Luke can say that everything they own is *held in common* (4:32).

This enables them to testify to the resurrection of the Lord *with great power*. They can rise above selfish material interests so that spiritual realities take first place in their testimony, and the grace of God is manifest in them all (4:33). Such a situation may well be an answer to their prayer for *boldness* (4:29). One manifestation of this is the way they begin to sell off their property and bring the proceeds to the apostles to be distributed to the needy in their midst. The result is that no one among them suffers serious want (4:34-35; see notes on 2:44-45; 6:1).

In this context Luke introduces Joseph, surnamed Barnabas, who sells a field and brings the money to the church (4:36-37). This man is a good example of the community practice. His commendatory name, Bar-naba (nebu'a), given by the fellowship, is an Aramaic phrase whose exact form is no longer known. But its meaning, son of encouragement, fits the man so well that Luke mentions it here for the reader to keep in mind from this point on (for examples of his unique caring qualities, cf. 9:27; 11:23; 15:37).

Though of the tribe of Levi, which furnished most of the temple workers, this man's family emigrated to Cyprus. There he grew up, later to return to Judea. Nothing further is known of his early life. Perhaps he was one of the seventy sent out in Luke 10:1, or among the 120 in the upper room and on the Day of Pentecost, but this cannot be proved. Clement of Alexandria (third cent.) made the former claim, and the latter one is often connected to it. We do know that he was a relative of John Mark of Jerusalem (Col. 4:10) and therefore had close ties in the holy city.

Luke presents Barnabas here not only as a fine example of generosity in the early church but also as a sharp contrast to Ananias and Sapphira, the cheating couple to be mentioned next (5:1-11). Apparently there is no longer any restriction against a Levite owning property (as in Num. 18:20 and Deut. 10:9). Even as early as Jeremiah (seventh cent. B.C.), that prophet from the tribe of Levi (Jer. 1:1) was told to go and buy a field (32:7). Whether the property now sold by Barnabas is in Cyprus or Judea, we cannot know, although the context would seem to favor the latter.

5:1-11   The Tragic Case of Ananias and Sapphira

A more complete picture of the early Christian community is now provided by this story of human weakness and loss. Among the many who participate in the joy of sharing, this one couple demonstrates a totally different spirit. The husband bears the fairly common name of Ananias (cf. 9:10; 23:2) and has, with his wife's knowledge, kept back part of the money received from the sale of some property (5:1). He brings the rest and lays it at Peter's feet as though it were the whole amount (5:2). That leader is aware of the deceit and asks, Why has Satan filled your heart to lie to the Holy Spirit? (5:3). Compare John 13:2, where the devil "put it into the heart of Judas" to betray Jesus.

Peter next reveals both the freedom of the community and the nature of the couple's sin. While the property remained unsold, it was theirs, and even after that they may do with the money as they wish. The community is dedicated to sharing, but this is to be voluntary. The grievous sin of Ananias and Sapphira is that they have conspired together to bring *part* of the money as though it were the whole proceeds, and to enjoy the remainder in private for themselves. It is a lie not only against human beings but against *God!* (5:4).

Peter has been criticized by some modern thinkers for what takes place next, and Luke has been blamed for including it in Acts. Some call it a "punitive miracle" on the apostle's part and say that it does not belong in the NT where the central teaching is love. Yet Luke includes it with a full understanding of its meaning. What *does* happen, according to the text?

It is a direct act of God. Peter is simply the Lord's spokesman. As soon as he exposes their guilt, the weight of Ananias's sin is too much for him, and he collapses at the apostles' feet. Such immediate and drastic death as "the wages of sin" (Rom. 6:23) sends a shock through the community which Luke describes as a *great fear* seizing all who hear it (5:5). Some scholars explain what happened as a massive heart attack brought on by the sudden exposure. Burial takes place soon. The *young men* who carry out the body are probably not some special funeral crew but an informal group within the community (5:6). In the tense moments that follow this event, even Sapphira is not notified (5:7). Judgment has fallen quickly, with no time for repentance.

Three hours go by before Sapphira appears, still ignorant of what has happened (5:7). Peter proceeds to interrogate her, now without her husband, to determine what she knows about the conspiracy (5:8). When she shows that she has shared in the lie from the beginning, Peter has one nagging question: Why? How can it be that she and her husband would agree together to *put the Spirit of the Lord to the test?* This echoes the word of the Law against putting God to the test (Deut. 6:16) and Jesus' quotation of that command in answering Satan in the wilderness (Luke 4:12).

Then, with a word of knowledge similar to that spoken to Ananias, the apostle tells Sapphira that she too will be carried out and buried (5:9). Like her husband, she collapses under the weight of her guilt and is soon taken away and buried next to him by the same young men (5:10). Again Luke observes that *great fear seized the whole church and all who heard of these things* (5:11). There must be no trifling with the Holy Spirit. It is high-voltage Christianity, powerful for good (as in 2:43-47) when channeled according to God's will, but destructive when short-circuited by human greed.

At 5:11 is the first time Luke uses the word *church* for the new community of believers. As in 15:22-29, this word appears here in a context of discipline, recognition of God's moral law and the Spirit's action, and defining limits to acceptable conduct in the group (cf. Matt. 16:18-19; 18:15-20; the Western text *[Greek Text, p. 311.]* adds *church* at Acts 2:47, followed by KJV; see notes on 20:17 about *church*).

5:12-16 Continued Miracle-Working and Growth

Here is another summary, the third in the series. It is similar to the former ones (2:42-47; 4:32-35) but contains two new features. One of these is the report that *none of the rest dared to join them, but the people held them in high esteem* (5:13). This is followed by the seemingly contradictory statement that *more than ever believers were added to the Lord, great numbers of men and women* (5:14). If everyone is afraid to join them, how can they be growing so fast? The answer is in the heightened reverence with which the public is beginning to regard them. On one hand, with such drastic divine judgment at work within the community, few want to enter it lightly. Yet the high standards of the group make it attractive, a guarantee of the presence of God, and therefore greatly to be desired. Thus a vital impact is being made on outsiders by their outreach meetings in Solomon's Portico (see on 3:11) in connection with the daily prayer times and their continued preaching of the gospel.

The second feature stressed in this summary is the great healing ministry that takes place throughout the area (5:15-16). Sick people of various kinds, including some oppressed by demons, are carried out into the city streets and laid there awaiting healing by the apostle Peter. So great is the attraction of this display of divine power that people flock in from surrounding villages and towns. Their hope is that at least the *shadow* of Peter will fall on them and they will healed.

Some interpreters call this superstition and out of character for the followers of Jesus. Others say it is the superficial belief of the masses and Peter does not necessarily approve of it. A comparison with the accounts of Jesus, however, shows that this is not too different from some of the Lord's own methods. One woman was healed by simply touching the fringe of his garment (Luke 8:44), and in some cases people were healed at a distance with no touch at all (Luke 7:2-10; cf. Mark 7:24-29; John 4:46-54). Luke, who records those healings, sees here also the power of God operating by faith. Now he simply states, *They were all cured* (5:16). Moreover, in 19:11-12 Luke tells how Paul is used of the Lord to perform *extraordinary miracles* of healing as *handkerchiefs and aprons* are carried from him to the sick in Ephesus.

Another Encounter with the Sanhedrin 5:17-42

5:17-21a Imprisonment and Release of the Apostles

Luke now records another round of conflict between the church and the supreme council. Some scholars regard this as a doublet or variant account of the story in 4:1-31 rather than a sequel. Acts, however, presents it as ongoing history with some similarities but containing the significant new testimony of the learned councillor Gamaliel.

The high priestly leaders in the Sanhedrin are alarmed as the healing power of the Holy Spirit brings in more and more people from the surrounding country (5:16). The new believers movement grows ever stronger. Luke calls it a *jealousy* which causes them to reach out and *seize the apostles* (5:18). No numbers or names are given, so we cannot be sure just how many or who among the apostles are meant. Peter is one of the them, and there are more than two, for Luke speaks of *Peter and the apostles* (5:29). John is probably one, and it could be that most of the twelve are meant (cf. "the whole band of apostles," Bruce: 119).

Whatever the number, the apostles are arrested and put overnight in the local lockup (5:18; likely the same as in 4:3). Then something new happens. On the former occasion (4:3-7), the authorities themselves had the apostles brought out. Now an *angel of the Lord* comes by night and opens the prison doors (5:19). Noting that *angel* in Greek is *messenger,* some commentators have taken this to mean a human being, perhaps a friend of the apostles. But the added words, *angel of the Lord,* are against this, as well as the command in 5:20 to go and preach. It seems clear that Luke means an actual supernatural angel, as in 12:6-11, where Peter is again involved.

Boldness is what the church prayed for after the former deliverance (4:29). Now the Lord's angel tells them to go right back into the temple and demonstrate it in strong proclamation of the gospel. They are to tell *the whole message about this life.* Jesus is the life, and believers are to be alive with this new and eternal dimension of living.

5:21b-26 Return of Apostles to Teaching in the Temple

So the apostles, no doubt tingling with excitement over their divine deliverance, enter the temple at daybreak. They resume their public witnessing, presumably again in Solomon's Colonnade (5:21a). Meanwhile the high court reassembles, knowing nothing of what has happened. They send for the prisoners and are surprised and angered to hear the report that the prison doors are open and the apostles gone (5:21b-23). No mention is made here of stern measures taken against the prison guards. Yet emotions may be strong enough that, were the authorities following strict Roman rules like Herod Agrippa in 12:19, they might order the guards killed for negligence. All they do on this occasion, however, is to stand around *perplexed about them, wondering what might be going on* (5:24). It is bad enough to have prisoners who defy orders, but to have them vanish right out of prison is just too much!

5:27-32 Re-arrest, Trial, and Answer of the Apostles

While the authorities are thus puzzled and confused, a man comes with the report that the apostles are, at this very moment, in the temple courts teaching the people! (5:25). The only thing they can think to do is to send the *temple police* to bring them in for trial. But they must do so without violence. These apostles are so popular that any officers using rough treatment on them might be stoned by the people (5:26). In Luke 19:48 the author tells how Jesus also is protected for awhile by his popularity.

As they stand now before the council, the apostles are confronted by the high priest himself, who charges them with defying orders by filling Jerusalem with their teaching! (5:27-28). And the serious part of it is that in this teaching they have been publicly accusing the authorities of murdering the Messiah! (as in 2:23, 36; 3:13-15; 4:10; 5:28). It is a tense moment. They have been duly warned, and now they can be convicted and severely punished. Peter, as always, speaks up for the group. Putting in positive form what he formerly posed as a question for the council to face (4:19-20), this bold apostle now declares for all time: *We must obey God rather than any human authority!* (5:29).

Then, not at all intimidated by the accusation of the high priest, he repeats his accusation. God has raised from the dead and exalted this Jesus whom *you had killed by hanging him on a tree* (5:30). Thus God confirms that Jesus is indeed the Messiah. Moreover, lest they dismiss all this as the product of a vivid imagination, Peter adds, *And we are witnesses to these things!* (5:32). While answering the Sanhedrin in this forthright fashion, he also outlines for believers of all times their mission of preaching repentance and forgiveness to Israel with the Holy Spirit as their co-witness (5:31-32).

5:33-39 Advice of Gamaliel

Such powerful witness (5:29-32), though convincing to the reader of Acts, makes the Sanhedrin furious. Many of the councillors want to kill the apostles outright (5:33). Then help comes from an unexpected source. A member of the council, known to history as Gamaliel I, grandson and disciple of the much-loved Hillel, stands and counsels moderation (5:34-39). Like his grandfather, he is known for his humane position on the Law. Such was the respect a later generation held for him that it was said, "When Rabban Gamaliel the Elder died, the glory of the Law ceased and purity and abstinence died" (Mishnah Sotah 9.15; *Rabban* means "our teacher," to distinguish him from an ordinary *rabbi*, "my teacher"). This is the Gamaliel under whom Saul of Tarsus studied (22:3).

With obvious authority, the learned rabbi, *respected by all the people,* orders the apostles removed while he addresses the members (5:34). The point he makes is that those involved in movements not according to the will of God come to naught and therefore can be left to run their course. To illustrate this, he takes two examples from recent history. The first mentioned is *Theudas.* Gamaliel tells how he arose as a leader of about 400 men, *claiming to be somebody,* but was killed and his followers disbanded (5:36).

Exactly who is meant here is not clear; the only Theudas we know from Josephus is from a period about ten years after this incident in the Sanhedrin (*Ant.* 20.5.1). Some scholars think that either Luke or Gamaliel is in error and cast doubt on the whole story. Such a conclusion is unnecessary. There were scores of uprisings in those days, with as many as four leaders named Simon and three called Judas in a forty-year period. A name like Theudas, which Bruce calls "sufficiently common" (125, n. 47), might refer to two men separated in time. A less-likely possibility is that Josephus was mistaken about the date of the uprising of Theudas (Marshall: 122).

The second-named leader, Judas the Galilean, is easier to identify. Josephus mentions this Judas leading a revolt in A.D. 6 (*War* 2.8.1; *Ant.* 18.1.1), when Judea was made a Roman province and a census was held to determine the amount of tribute to be levied. Judas's uprising was crushed by the Romans, but his cause lived on with the Zealots and other revolutionary groups (ABD, 6:1045ff.). Gamaliel is right about his followers being scattered at the time, but he underestimated the long-range results of the resistance movements, which continued for many years. His main point, however, is that God is in control of all things, and that only those doing the divine will are able to succeed. This is not only good Pharisaic teaching but also in harmony with the beliefs of Luke and other Christians. Hence, Gamaliel strongly advises the council to have nothing to do with the apostles. If their enterprise is purely human, it will fail; but if it is of God, no one will be able to stop it. In fact, the council might even be guilty of *fighting against God!* (5:38-39).

5:40-42 *Release of Apostles and Continued Teaching*

The council takes the advice of the conciliatory Gamaliel even though Pharisees like himself are in a minority on the Sanhedrin at this time. So all the high court can do is to flog them soundly and set them free (probably "forty lashes minus one"; cf. 2 Cor. 11:24; Deut. 25:3). Again they uselessly command these believers not to speak any more in the name of Jesus! (5:40; cf. 4:21).

This gives Luke the opportunity of concluding his long section (chaps. 3—5) with another summary. Now it is the joy of these returning witnesses that they are *considered worthy to suffer dishonor for the sake of the name* (5:41). This is not whistling in the dark nor a sick enjoyment of persecution but goes back to Jesus himself (Luke 6:22-23) and becomes the hallmark of true Christianity (cf. Matt. 5:11-12; 2 Cor. 6:10; 1 Pet. 1:6-9). It is written of Jesus that, on the night before his crucifixion, he gave his teaching "that my joy might be in you, and that your joy may be full" (John 15:11). Jesus "for the joy that was set before him endured the cross" (Heb. 12:2).

Such a movement is unstoppable! Thus Luke can close this phase of his history with the observation that the believing community completely ignores the command of the Sanhedrin. Indeed, they go right on with their twofold thrust: (a) invading *the temple* with the gospel of Jesus as Christ and (b) continuing to teach and practice it *at home*, or *from house to house* (5:42, footnote). On this triumphant note, Luke concludes a phase of his story.

The victory is a twofold one, with alternating depictions in the structure of the narrative. *Internally,* the church has faced and solved the problem of the believers' economic livelihood by practicing voluntary sharing and distribution according to need (2:44-45). As a result, all are supplied with the necessities of life (4:34-35). When economic deception threatens, Peter's bold Spirit-inspired confrontation protects the honesty and health of the community. The later serious complaint, that Hebrew widows are given preference over their Hellenist counterparts (6:1), is handled promptly and with Spirit-directed wisdom (6:2-6).

Externally, the Christian community has met and prevailed over political opposition. The authorities arrest their leaders (4:3; 5:18) and try them before their highest court (4:5-20; 5:27-39). They cannot convict them of crime and therefore release them (4:21; 5:40). In all this, the apostles are divinely led (4:8-12; 5:19-20) and, instead of being stopped by the authorities, actually succeed in converting large numbers of people (5:14), including many priests (6:7).

THE TEXT IN BIBLICAL CONTEXT
Unstoppable Witnesses

The OT has many stories of messengers of Yahweh who persisted in their work in the face of severe opposition. Jeremiah was hounded by enemies all his life. On one occasion four officials had him thrown into a foul cistern, where he would have died had not a human "angel" of the Lord rescued him (Jer. 38:7-13). Once delivered, he continued prophesying throughout the siege and destruction of Jerusalem and unto his death as an exile in Egypt (chaps. 38—47).

Daniel was forbidden to pray to any other god but the king (Darius) and was cast into a den of lions overnight for disobeying. But he too was saved by the intervention of an angel and went right on witnessing for God (Dan. 6:1-28). Nehemiah was another one opposed by a powerful group of leaders (Neh. 2:10, 19; 4:1-3; 6:1-7). Yet he kept on at his task of rebuilding the walls of Jerusalem until it was completed to the glory of God. "Should a man like me run away?" he asked (6:11a). These and many others would agree with the apostles: *We must obey God rather than any human authority!*

Salvation Only in the Name of Jesus

How true to Jesus' own teaching was Peter's claim that there was no other name by which people could be saved? (4:12). And, in any event, was it not an arrogant statement to make and without proof? In answering these questions, we need first to realize that, in Greek as in Hebrew, *salvation* includes both spiritual redemption and healings of various kinds. In his Gospel, Luke does not seem to have recorded any direct statement by Jesus claiming to be the only Savior. But Luke certainly implies this with the many stories about Jesus' unique birth, his unusual powers of healing, his casting out demons and raising the dead, as well as his resurrection. That Jesus is the only way to the Father is made much more explicit in the Gospel of John, in passages like 10:7-9 and 14:6.

The rest of the NT shows that faith in Jesus as the only way to salvation and wholeness becomes standard belief for Christians. Paul, for example, believes it strongly, as his letters reveal (Phil. 2:9-11; Col. 1:15-18). The author of Hebrews also leaves no doubt on this matter (1:2-4; 4:14-15; 5:8-10; 10:12-14). In Revelation, Jesus Christ holds the keys to Death and Hades (1:18), is the only one worthy to open the scroll of the future (5:1-5), and is himself the "King of kings and Lord of lords" (19:16). Therefore, when Luke quotes Peter as proclaiming that Jesus is the one and only Savior, he is simply stating the prevailing Christian view.

On the question of whether or not this is an unreal or arrogant claim, we need to note the OT view of God and move from it to the NT belief in the Son of God. For the Jews, Yahweh is the one and only God (Exod. 20:3; Deut. 5:7), to be totally loved and worshiped (Deut. 6:4-5). Now these Jewish believers are witnesses to the resurrection of Jesus and convinced of his exaltation on high at the right hand of God (Acts 2:32-33). Hence, it is little wonder that they take a similar view of his exclusive claims upon them. There is no arrogance in this confession of faith, since both their Lord and they pay for it with their very lives. To them, it is fact and not fantasy, a reality to be humbly proclaimed. And even to this day, it is the faith of all Bible-believing Christians that Jesus *is* the only Savior.

Judgment on God's People

The parallels between the Ananias and Sapphira story (5:1-11) and that of Achan in Joshua (chap. 7) are quite clear. In both cases there were greed and deceit, with the consequent swift and total judgment of God. This was to wake up the believing community and bring it into a closer relationship. Even earlier than Achan in Israel's history, Miriam was struck with leprosy for conspiring with Aaron against Moses (Num. 12:9-17). A bit later, Korah, Dathan, and Abiram, with their wives and children, were swallowed by the earth because they rose up against Moses (Num. 16:1-33). After each of these incidents, the chosen people were awed by the presence of the living God, repented, and were eventually cleansed as a preparation for greater things to come.

The Law was strict about the life of the people, especially in Leviticus (chaps. 17—20). In many cases wrongdoers are to be "cut off from their people" or killed outright. The basic reason for this was to keep God's people as a holy nation because God is holy (Lev. 19:1-2; 20:7). With the coming of Jesus, however, his followers are not to take the law into their own hands and kill the offending parties. God is the only one who has the authority to do this (cf. Rom. 12:19). That is what happens with Ananias and Sapphira. And that same sense of the wrath of God is found in Jesus' teaching. In the Gospel of Luke, Jesus stressed the sureness of God's judgment, as in the four "woes" (6:24-26), the repeated warning that those who do not repent will perish (13:3, 5), and the reminder of destruction upon the wicked like that of the great flood and of the fire raining upon Sodom and Gomorrah (17:26-30).

THE TEXT IN THE LIFE OF THE CHURCH
Miracles of Healing

There are not many healings as spectacular and complete as that of the lame man at the temple gate (3:1-10). Yet there have been remarkable miracles down through church history and still among us today. What is needed is neither skepticism about genuine divine healings on one hand, nor exaggeration or exploitation of them on the other. In these days of great advances of medical science, we need not create a false conflict between praying for healing and the work of the physician. Actually, all true healing is from God, whether directly through prayer ministries, or through medicine, or a combination of the two (cf. Sirach 38:1-15). The church should not shrink from the command of the Lord to "proclaim the kingdom of God and to heal" (Luke 9:2). Jesus commands the seventy, "Whenever you enter a town, . . . cure the sick" (10:8-9). This is the practice of the missionaries in Acts.

One danger in basing such a ministry on the success stories in the Gospels and Acts is the feeling that unless the cure is total and spectacular, then it is not of God or worth doing. Nothing could be farther from the truth. It is the nature of Luke's and other NT writings to record some dramatic cures. In actual everyday prayer ministries today, people may not be totally restored to physical health but still greatly helped spiritually, mentally, and emotionally. In such cases there is real healing even though there is not what may be called a complete physical cure. Thus all prayers for healing are answered, some more dramatically or more completely than others. Yet all of them bring glory to God and are eminently worth undertaking.

Everyday Witnessing

The fearless and effective sharing of the good news by the apostles in 3:12-26 and 4:8-12 is clarified by Peter's statement in 4:20: *We cannot keep from speaking about what we have seen and heard.* This simple formula puts evangelism within the reach of every Christian. It tells of a *compulsion* to speak: the power of the Holy Spirit. And it indicates the *content* of that speaking: the things that have been *seen and heard.* For Peter and John, this is a great deal: the whole life of Jesus, his death and resurrection, and the outpouring of the Spirit at Pentecost—these are enough to talk about for a long time!

Laypersons may not feel that blessed with experience, but the formula is the same. They need only tell what the Lord has done in their own lives and in the lives of those they know about. This would include great evidences of God's grace and power of which they learn in the Bible, other books, teachings, sermons, and testimonies. Such evangelism by sincere and dedicated believers is often more effective than the efforts of professional clergy.

Power in United Prayer

A dynamic prayer event happens back in the church after the return of the apostles (4:23-31). This speaks directly to our needs today. First, *they raised their voices together*, indicating both spontaneous and united praying. This is full of praise, recounting the power of the Lord in creating the universe, and rehearsing the Holy Spirit's revelation in the written Word. They see God's purposes being fulfilled in the gathering of forces against them. Near the end of the prayer, they voice their one simple request. Moving powerfully within God's will, they ask the Lord to look upon these threats and grant them *all bold-ness* in witnessing. They are already filling Jerusalem with their message. Now they want to do more. Hence, God wonderfully answers their prayer by shaking the house in which they are meeting and once more pouring out the Holy Spirit upon them all!

Generosity Personified

The Spirit-filled Barnabas, introduced in 4:36-37 (further depicted in 9:27 and chaps. 11—15), is the kind of church leader any Christian group would be glad to have. Generous and forthright in his giving and an encourager of others, he exemplifies the character and conduct that spell complete commitment to the Lord's work. Such a person gives life to popular expressions like "actions speak louder than words" and "I'd rather see a sermon than hear one." Indeed, this Mr. Encourager of the early church may well be regarded as the patron saint of the believers church tradition, where one's talk should be shown by one's walk.

Obeying God Above All

The strong statement in 5:29 that we ought to obey God rather than human authorities has played an important role in the Anabaptist-Brethren tradition. Perhaps its most frequent application has been in nonresistance to war, but it has also figured in other nonconformist issues. Again and again this verse has been quoted to enable the conscientious objector to stand firm in obedience to God, whether in court or in everyday life.

In this case, obeying God means taking seriously the strong statements of Jesus about loving one's enemies and turning the other cheek (Luke 6:32-36). All killing is wrong and war is a monstrous evil to be resisted even at the risk of one's life. Thus specific civil disobedience in the light of biblical teaching has been a continuing part of this witness. To avoid abuses and extremes, such activism is usually kept in balance with texts on paying tribute to Caesar (Luke 20:22-25) and cooperating with the government as possible while showing love (Rom. 13:1-10; 1 Pet. 2:11-17). One should disobey only when political authorities are in conflict with the commands of the Lord, and even then with much heart-searching, prayer, and counseling together.

Many church groups and individuals have sensitivities on

freedom of speech, war, civil rights, and other social issues. They will need to be constantly discerning the points of conflict between the gospel and current political and social practices. Then in faithfulness to their Lord, they will be the church in acting boldly to meet human needs and in making their protests known to authorities in the tradition of the prophets and apostles. They also need to be willing to suffer the consequences of their position. Issues such as the payment of taxes to support huge military preparations, discriminatory employment practices, amnesty for political prisoners, and many others—these all will come under consideration. Appropriate Christian action needs to be taken as occasions arise.

The Gamaliel Principle

This approach, derived from the advice of that rabbi to the Sanhedrin in 5:35-39, has been an important one in wise churchmanship from that day to our own. It means being careful in evaluating various movements both inside and outside the church. We need to discern between good and evil and understand the various mixtures. Then waiting is often necessary to see whether any particular line of action *is of God* or not (5:39a). The church must have faith that, through the workings of the law of sowing and reaping, divine purposes will ultimately prevail.

An extension of this principle, beyond that practiced by Gamaliel, is the approach of Paul in dealing with some preachers who seriously opposed him (Phil. 1:15-18). Instead of being jealous or hurt because of certain ones whose motives he seriously suspected, Paul simply rejoiced and said he would continue to rejoice "that in every way, whether in pretense or in truth, Christ is proclaimed" (1:18). Such an approach is anchored in the faith that if Christ is really preached, he will take care of himself in spite of human weaknesses, and Christ will prevail. This is akin to Paul's affirmation that "God causes all things to work together for good to those who love God" and that Christians are really "more than conquerors through him who loved us" (Rom. 8:28, NASB; 8:37a). Such an optimistic trusting in the Lord has helped relieve many a tense situation in the history of the church.

Part 4

The Martyr-Witness of Stephen

Acts 6:1—8:1a

PREVIEW

In chapter 6, Luke continues the story of the fast-growing Jerusalem church with the apostles still in charge, but with different leaders ready to appear. The section as a whole (chaps. 6—7) continues the conflict between the new movement and the temple authorities. A minor theme is the resolution of yet another crisis within the community of faith. Both problems are prefaced by reassuring references to the continuing growth of the church (6:1, 7). Enough time has elapsed for an entirely new situation to arise, one that could split the church along cultural lines if not handled properly. It is the second threat to the internal life of the church, the first being the deceit injected by Ananias and Sapphira (5:1-11).

In solving this new crisis, the apostles delegate leadership responsibility for the first time. Thus the seven emerge, with Stephen first-named and occupying center stage for the whole section. Luke briefly sketches this man's unique ministry and then at some length gives a digest of his speech, the longest in the book of Acts. The short career of Stephen, strategically placed here, highlights the theme of conflict with the temple authorities, so much a part of Acts. The defense, really a brief for the whole new messianic movement centering in Jesus, serves to clarify fundamental differences between it and official temple-centered Judaism (7:2-53). It therefore provides a backdrop for the great missionary efforts to come. With its emphasis on a pilgrim people worshiping in a portable tabernacle rather than a static temple, the speech shows the Christian church as the one agency through which God can work to evangelize the world.

The atmosphere is electric with excitement as Stephen hurls

strong prophetic charges at his accusers and goes down under a pile of stones as the first known Christian martyr. That martyrdom, added to the crucifixion of Jesus, sets the pace for the sacrificial leadership to be represented by Peter, Paul, and his associates.

Earlier in the account, Luke also introduces Philip, who will take the gospel into Samaria and send a convert to faraway Ethiopia (Nubia; Acts 8:27). Then, at the end of the account of Stephen, he brings on stage the man Saul, destined to become the leading figure in the long second section of Acts.

OUTLINE

Appointment of the Seven, 6:1-6

Continued Growth of the Church, 6:7

Stephen's Ministry and Arrest, 6:8—7:1

Stephen's Final Speech, 7:2-53
7:2-8	God's Work with Abraham and Family
7:9-16	God's Work Through Joseph—Rise of Opposition
7:17-43	God's Work Through Moses—More Opposition
7:44-50	The Tabernacle and the Temple
7:51-53	Charge of Present Rebellion

Stephen's Witness in Death; Saul Introduced, 7:54—8:1a

EXPLANATORY NOTES

Appointment of the Seven 6:1-6

Luke's expression *now during those days* (6:1) suggests an indefinite passage of time. The church is growing rapidly (cf. 4:4; 5:14) and has run into problems in the distribution of food and other supplies to all the needy. Not only is there the sheer weight of such a job, but now the charge of discrimination rears its ugly head. The murmuring (RSV) here recalls the rebellion of the Israelites in the wilderness (Exod. 15:24; 16:2; 17:3; Num. 14:2; 16: 41; Deut. 1:27). It calls for the immediate attention of the twelve, the leaders of the entire church (see on 1:26).

Hellenists are complaining that their widows are not getting a fair deal in the *daily distribution of food* (see notes on 2:44-45; 4:32-35).

These are not Greeks but Jews whose main language is the common or Koine Greek of the day. They may also speak Aramaic or Hebrew but, either because of being born abroad or having important cultural ties there, prefer Hellenistic speech and certain aspects of its lifestyle and manners.

For the history of this situation, one must go back to the deportations of 597 and 586 B.C., when worshipers of Yahweh were exiled to Babylon and other countries to the north, south, and east. While a few returned to the homeland under the more lenient rule of the Persians, most of the dispersed Jews remained abroad, especially in the major cities. Then with the conquests of Alexander the Great (331 B.C.) and the spread of Greek language and culture throughout those lands, Jews also, though loyal to their religion, spoke Koine Greek more readily than their native Hebrew. By the middle of the third century B.C., the chief Greek translation of the OT (the Septuagint or LXX) was in existence and, in the course of time, was extensively used in the synagogues of the dispersion (or diaspora, as the widely scattered settlements were known). By NT times these dispersed Jews were quite different in culture and speech from those born and educated in the homeland.

It was common for Jews living abroad to spend their last days in Jerusalem, and the number of Hellenists' widows living there was proportionately large, as Haenchen points out (261). Luke makes it clear that a great many foreign-born Jews were present for the ingathering on the Day of Pentecost (thirteen such nations are listed by name in Acts 2:9-11 as representative of a larger group). Presumably many of them were among the 3,000 added to the church that day, to say nothing of the big increase when, according to 4:4, the number of males alone reached 5,000!

These then are the *Hellenists* who have become so numerous that their widows cannot be fully taken care of by the usual food distribution. They are complaining that the widows of the *Hebrews* in the church are getting a better deal. Like *the twelve* themselves, the widows of the Hebrews were born in the land and speak the local Aramaic or Hebrew as their first language. While the line of demarcation between the two is not hard and fast, since many on both sides are bilingual, they do represent two different cultural groupings.

The apostles dare not neglect their main task of witness, so they decide to find help. When they say, *Select from among yourselves seven men* (6:3), they may be suggesting that some Hellenists be chosen. Those finally chosen all have Greek names, yet such names also appear among Aramaic-speaking Jews (Munck, 1967:57). The Hellenists among the seven would be better able than anyone else to care for the needs of the group who feel they are being discriminated against. This is a delegation of responsibility and workload, like Moses' appointment of seventy elders to assist him (Exod. 18:13-27).

The new leaders, nominated by the group but appointed by the apostles, are to be *seven* in number. This is common among Jews in appointing boards for special duties (Marshall: 126) and appropriate because Jerusalem has seven wards (Cadbury, 5:149). They must all be highly qualified (6:3). For one thing, they are to be persons of good reputation and therefore to be trusted. Beyond that, they must be *full of the Spirit and of wisdom* (cf. Num. 11:17, 25, where elders are endowed with some of the spirit that is on Moses). The role played by the Holy Spirit in their work is most important. Luke continues to emphasize this feature with regard to Stephen (6:5, 10; 7:55). The *wisdom* here is not just the practical good sense which the job requires, but a wisdom from above given by the Spirit (6:10).

Of the seven men chosen, only two figure in the history that follows. First mentioned is *Stephen*, whose name in Greek means "wreath" or "crown"—an appropriate name for the first Christian to be "crowned" with martyrdom. Luke says nothing of his background, but he can hardly say enough about his Spirit-filled character and ministry. He is a prime example of the kind of witness Jesus wanted his followers to be (1:8), a Pentecost person, *full of grace and power* in performing miracles (6:8). His opponents can *not cope with the wisdom and Spirit* with which he is speaking (6:10, NASB).

Philip, the second one listed, carries the popular Greek name of the father of Alexander the Great (fourth cent. B.C.). He is not to be confused with the apostle Philip (Luke 6:14; Acts 1:13). This Philip is best known for miracle-working and widespread conversions (8:4-40). He is therefore later called *Philip the evangelist* (21:8), a good designation to use today. Like Stephen, he will figure prominently in the dramatic stories to follow.

The other five men, *Prochorus, Nicanor, Timon, Parmenas, and Nicolaus* also have recognizable Greek names, but nothing is known about them for sure. They no doubt have ministries of their own of which we are ignorant. Tradition has it that Prochorus later served as a scribe for the evangelist John, became bishop of Nicomedia, and was martyred at Antioch (Bruce: 129). Nicolaus, a *proselyte* (Gentile convert to Judaism), is identified by Irenaeus (*Against Heresies* 1.26.3) as the founder of the heretical sect of Nicolaitans (Rev. 2:6,

15), but this may be due to similarity of names and have little or no historical value.

The apostles *appoint* the seven *to this task* (6:3), *to wait on tables* (6:2). It is not clear just what is meant. Traditionally these have been taken to refer to the tables at which people eat and the serving (RSV) to refer to actual waiting on such tables or supervising such work. There is a strong possibility, however, that the reference is to money tables. The term is used in Mark 11:15 to refer to the place where money is counted and disbursed. Acts (4:35, 37; 5:2) speaks of funds being brought and laid at the apostles' feet. Thus the task of the seven is to assist the apostles in social services.

Nowhere are the seven called deacons. That name comes from the Greek root *diakon-*, as in *diakonia* (6:1, distribution, service), *diakonein* (6:2, to serve), and *diakonos* (Rom. 16:1, deacon, minister). This word points to the intended work of the seven, and traditionally they are regarded as the first to hold the office of deacon. On the other hand, Stephen and Philip demonstrate a ministry that goes much beyond what is suggested for deacons in the NT letters (Phil. 1:1; 1 Tim. 3:8-13).

Continued Growth of the Church   6:7

At this point Luke emphasizes once again the rapid growth of the church (cf. 2:41, 47; 4:4; 5:14) and will continue that theme (9:31; 12:24; 16:5; 19:20; 28:31). The exciting new development this time is the conversion of *a great many of the priests*, no doubt meaning those functioning in the temple. Estimates of the total number of Jewish priests run as high as 18,000, including Levites and others serving on the rotation system of those days (Marshall: 128; cf. Luke 1:8). With the believers in Jesus preaching daily in the temple courts (2:44; 3:1-26; 4:1; 5:25), priests can hear the message and be gathered in. Perhaps the church's good organization to care for human needs impresses them. Yet the conversion of priests is surprising because they come from a background of denying the resurrection (4:1-2; 23:8). Since there is no hint that these converts give up their former duties, the new movement now has members serving the Lord as witnesses right within the Jewish house of worship!

Stephen's Ministry and Arrest   6:8—7:1

Whatever his duties in the daily distribution to widows, we are told first (6:8) of Stephen's doing *great wonders and signs* among the people, just as the apostles have been doing (2:43; 3:1-10). Like them (4:10), he makes a powerful witness for the Lord. In addition to his ministry among believers, he preaches in the so-called *synagogue of the Freedmen* (Libertines, KJV, wrongly suggests something immoral). Here are many who have gained their release from slavery or are descended from such persons. As an eloquent Hellenist, Stephen witnesses to Cyrenian and Alexandrian Jews, as well as some from the provinces of Cilicia and Asia (6:9). Luke doesn't make it clear whether these are all in one synagogue or in two or even five (in one —Bruce: 133; Hemer: 176, "most likely." In two, one for the Freedman, Cyrenians, and Alexandrians; and another for the Cilicians and Asians—Marshall: 129).

What we do know is that his foreign-born Jewish hearers disagree with his type of message and resist him vigorously. But they are unable to *withstand* his powerful presentation and must resort to underhanded means of getting men to lie to the authorities about his teaching (6:11-13). According to Mark 14:55-59 and parallels, false testimony was also used to condemn Jesus. In both cases some true statements having to do with the eventual destruction of the temple are deliberately twisted to sound like rebellion and blasphemy. In Stephen's case, his accusers quote him as saying that Jesus will destroy the temple and change the customs of Moses (6:14).

Luke captures the vivid drama. The accused witness is hauled before the high court, and all eyes are turned on him as these false charges are read. But instead of cowering, Stephen stands in the opening of the semicircle with a face shining like an angel (6:15). Of no other human being in the Bible is this comparison made. Perhaps the nearest parallels would be the glowing face of Moses at Mount Sinai (Exod. 34:29-35) and the altered appearance and dazzling white clothing of Jesus on the Mount of Transfiguration (Luke 9:29). It is the heavenly radiance of one uniquely blessed by God (Ps. 34:5; Isa. 60:5). As Stephen thus stands before them, the high priest asks the simple question they all must consider, *Are these things so?* (7:1)

Stephen's Final Speech 7:2-53

The high priest's question sets the stage for Luke's long report of how Stephen defends not only his own Spirit-inspired ministry but also the whole Christian movement. Stephen says that he (and therefore the church) is not the only one who can be charged with blasphemy.

They, the Jewish establishment, can also be so charged, as their history shows.

7:2-8 God's Work with Abraham and Family

To present this case, the accused begins respectfully, *Brothers and fathers, listen to me.* It is an old story with which all the learned councillors are familiar. Yet the emphasis is uniquely new. The *God of glory* called Abraham out of Chaldea to Haran and then to Canaan, with no land of his own. Thus God created a pilgrim people who would be *resident aliens* on foreign soil (in Egypt). Later they would return to Canaan to worship God and receive the covenant of circumcision (7:2-8).

7:9-16 God's Work Through Joseph—Rise of Opposition

Then Stephen quickly moves to Isaac, Jacob, and *the twelve patriarchs.* The latter, *jealous of Joseph,* sold their brother into slavery. Only by the grace of God was he spared and the whole family saved from famine. Thus God met rebellion among the chosen people and turned it into a fulfillment of divine purposes (7:9-16).

7:17-43 God's Work Through Moses—More Opposition

The speech goes on at once to Moses and deals with his career in some detail. Much emphasis is given to the opposition he encountered from *his kinsfolk* (7:25), who misunderstood him and caused a long delay in the deliverance of Israel from Egypt (7:23-29). Forty years later God called this Moses to lead God's people out of bondage (7:30-34). Then, after doing so, he prophesied the coming of a prophet like himself (in 7:37; Stephen means the Messiah; cf. 3:22; Deut. 18:15). Moses received *living oracles* (the Law) from God while part of the *congregation in the wilderness* (7:38). But, insists Stephen, *our ancestors* were unwilling to obey him and *pushed him aside. In their hearts they turned back to Egypt* and *reveled in the works of their hands* (7:39-41). As a result, God gave them over to gross idol worship, which eventually led to their exile *beyond Babylon* (7:42-43, quoting Amos 5:25-27).

7:44-50 The Tabernacle and the Temple

Then Stephen turns to a theme begun in the review of Abraham's pilgrimage (7:3-5) and hinted at in mentioning the *congregation in the wilderness* (7:38). It is the second major emphasis of the speech: that God *does not dwell in houses made with human hands* (7:48). In support of this thesis, Stephen quotes Isaiah 66:1-2. As he puts it, God gave the pattern for the *tent of testimony* (the tabernacle), and though Moses had it constructed, it was not a human building. Joshua brought it into the land, and it served as the sufficient house of worship to the time of Solomon (7:44-47). The implication is obvious: their charges about the *temple* are beside the point, since God's original plan was not the temple at all (see 2 Sam. 7:4-7), but the tabernacle.

The speech proper ends at this point. It enunciates some of Luke's major themes in Acts and accomplishes at least four purposes:

1. It is an adequate defense of Stephen and all he stands for. He has not spoken against the Law of Moses. In fact, he is a defender of the Law. Moreover, Stephen's criticism of the temple has scriptural support, as he proves in his comparison of tabernacle and temple.

2. It is an attack on unbelieving Israelites for their failure to accept the revelation given in the Scriptures and for their consequent rejection of the Messiah with his new way of worship.

3. It correctly defines the true Israel as a pilgrim people not tied to the temple but free to worship God everywhere that the proclaiming of the word takes them.

4. It lays the groundwork for the view that, since unbelieving Israelites have rejected the gospel preached to them, the door is now open for the evangelization of the Gentiles—a dominant theme through the rest of Acts.

The speech is indeed hotly polemical but must be considered as intra-Jewish polemic, in the vein of OT prophetic judgment against Israel. It does not give scriptural license for anti-Semitic feelings or actions today. Further, it ends with a prayer that this sin, the martyrdom of Stephen, not be held against them (7:60).

7:51-53 Charge of Present Rebellion

Then, as Luke reports it, at this point Stephen concludes with a direct attack on these leaders of Israel for their own rebellion against God (7:51-53). He calls them *stiff-necked*, as God had earlier called the people at Sinai (Exod. 33:5). They are *uncircumcised in heart and ears*, unclean and pagan within, and *forever opposing the Holy Spirit* (7:51). They have shown this by betraying and murdering the very Messiah the prophets predicted! (7:52). They are thus true sons of their ancestors who killed these prophets and supreme hypocrites for not keeping the divine law of which they are the guardians! (7:53).

Jesus has earlier accused the Pharisees of the same sins of prophet-killing (Luke 6:23; 11:47-51; 20:9-14) and hypocrisy (Luke 11:46, 52; 20:47). Stephen is not condemning all Israelites, but only those leaders among them who oppose Jesus, the Messiah. Jesus himself was a Jew, as were all his original disciples. So are Stephen and the rest of the seven. Stephen's defense is not anti-Semitism any more than was the preaching of Amos and other OT prophets, who announced God's judgment on Israel, Judah, and also pagan nations. It is the Spirit-inspired proclamation of one who loves Judaism enough to expose the false leadership of the times and to point to the true fulfillment of OT faith in the Messiah whom God has sent.

Stephen's Witness in Death; Saul Introduced   7:54—8:1a

Luke pictures the blind fury that seizes the council as they rush at Stephen with gnashing teeth (7:54). The verb for *enraged* is a strong one, like being *cut to the heart* (KJV; cf. 5:33) They grind their teeth in anger (cf. Job 16:9; Ps. 35:16). There is no mention of a formal vote of the Sanhedrin, in accord with Jewish law, nor a trial before the governor, as the Romans required for capital crimes (cf. Luke 23:1-25; John 18:31). It is more like an unrestrained lynching, with *witnesses* required to be present and cast the first stones (Deut. 17:7), in case an accounting should ever be necessary (Acts 7:58). Hemer observes that such a lynching might easily happen during the troubled last years of Pilate (176-177, n. 23). Bruce wonders if the Sanhedrin is exceeding its authority (179).

In sublime contrast to this furious attack, Stephen remains calm, caught up in a vision of *the glory of God and Jesus standing at the right hand of God!* (7:55). Why Jesus is said to be *standing* beside God, rather than *sitting*, as in all other NT references (Mark 14:62; Luke 22:69; Col. 3:1; Heb. 8:1; 12:2), has been widely discussed. While it might be simply a variation in wording without significance, Luke may be suggesting that the Lord is standing as a witness to Stephen's faithfulness in martyrdom. The proper posture of a witness is standing, not sitting. This could be a fulfillment of the promise that Jesus will acknowledge before the Father those who have confessed him on earth (Luke 12:8-9). Another view is that the Lord is welcoming this martyr into heaven, as Bengel (1687-1752) and many interpreters after him believe. Whatever the case, Luke underscores the event by first stating it and then having Stephen tell his attackers about it. In sharing his vision, Stephen calls Jesus *the Son of Man*, thus claiming authority for him as the heavenly judge (7:55-56; cf. Luke 5:24; Rev. 1:13).

This is the ultimate blasphemy! All restraint is gone as the enraged crowd stops up their ears and, with loud shouts, hustles him out of the city to kill him (7:57-60). The Law prescribed that blasphemy be punished by stoning, done outside the city to avoid defilement from a dead body. Everyone present is expected to take part in the deadly deed (Lev. 24:16; Num.15:35). So, like Jesus (Heb. 13:12), Stephen is killed "outside the city gate," and his executioners are representatives of Israel.

At this point Luke subtly introduces the one who will soon rise to be the leading missionary in the rest of Acts. He is a *young man* with the familiar Hebrew name of Saul (also called Paul, 13:9), apparently a budding leader. At his feet the murdering crowd throw their coats (7:58b). Saul approves of Stephen's death (8:1) and casts his *vote against* believers who are *being condemned to death* (26:10).

Yet there is no convincing evidence that Saul himself is a member of the Sanhedrin. That would require him to be a true elder in age, married, the father of at least one son, and a jurist who has served on a succession of lower courts. Luke does not picture Saul thus, and nowhere do Paul's writings indicate that he has a family with a son or attained this high office. Likely he is present as a rabbinic disciple (22:3), fanatic in hating the new heresy (Gal. 1:13-14), perhaps already in touch with the high priestly group and authorized to play a key role in such operations (cf. 9:1-2). As a Hellenist from Cilicia, he might be one of the Cilicians who could not stand up against Stephen's witness in their synagogue (6:9).

Saul's presence on this occasion helps answer the question of where Luke got his information for the final speech and death of Stephen. That Paul later remembers the martyrdom is shown by his statement in 22:20. He says he was standing by and approving, in fact holding the garments of those who killed him (cf. 8:1). His travel companion Luke may thus have received a complete eyewitness account of the event. The death of Stephen makes a deep impression on Saul the persecutor and may have been one of the factors that later led to his conversion. The violence with which he sets about to destroy the church (8:3), persecuting believers all the way to

Damascus (9:1-2), may be the reaction of a man "under conviction." Stephen dies with the name of Jesus on his lips (7:59), and this same Jesus later appears to Saul on the road (9:5). It is almost certain that Luke is making a connection between the two events.

As the deadly stones beat upon the standing Stephen, he implores the Jesus of his vision (cf. 7:55-56) to receive his departing spirit (7:59). Then bowed to earth and dying, he breathes a final prayer of forgiveness for his murderers (7:60), clearly in the spirit of Jesus, who prayed for *his* murderers, that God would forgive them for they didn't know what they were doing (Luke 23:34). Saul, mentioned once again for the reader's benefit, is standing by and approving *of their killing him* (8:1a).

THE TEXT IN BIBLICAL CONTEXT
Appointment of Spirit-Endowed Persons

The choice of seven men *full of the Spirit and of wisdom* echoes various Septuagint accounts of Joseph and Moses (6:3). In Genesis 41:33, Joseph advised Pharaoh, on the basis of his dream, to "select a man who is discerning and wise" to supervise Egypt's food production and distribution. The king acted on this advice and appointed Joseph himself, described as "one in whom is the spirit of God" (41:38). Stephen and associates are also linked to Joseph by the nature of their tasks as administrators of food.

In Deuteronomy 1:13-15, Moses told how he had asked the Israelites to choose tribal leaders who were "wise and reputable" to serve as under-shepherds of the people and judge rightly among them. This was done, and Moses installed them in that office. Later Moses prayed for an assistant and was told by the Lord to take Joshua, "in whom is the spirit," and have him stand before the priest and the congregation. Then Moses "laid his hands on him and commissioned him" (Num. 27:16-23). This act was recalled by Moses in Deuteronomy 34:9, where he spoke of Joshua as being "full of the spirit of wisdom," the very words used to describe Stephen in Acts (6:3, 10). The parallels between the appointment and consecration of the seven and that of both the tribal leaders and Joshua are apparent: their endowment with Spirit and wisdom, their responsibilities as supervisors, and their consecration through the laying on of hands.

Martyrdom of the Prophets, Jesus, and Stephen

Luke legitimates the new Christian movement by portraying Stephen as one in the noble line of martyrs from Abel and the prophets to Jesus (Luke 11:49-51; Acts 6—7). Still to come will be the apostle James the son of Zebedee (Acts 12:2), with both Peter (12:3-19) and Paul (14:19; 21:31; 23:12-35) almost killed. In all cases they are men who do not court death but who are able to face it when it occurs.

Particularly significant are the *parallels* which Luke draws between the martyrdoms of Jesus and Stephen. Both are filled with the Spirit (cf. Luke 4:14; Acts 6:5) and yet violently opposed by their own people (in Luke 4:29, Jesus' townsmen tried to kill him; in Acts 6:9, fellow Hellenists viciously attack Stephen). In neither case are their opponents able to stand up against them (cf. Luke 20:1-40; Acts 6:10-14). In both instances the opponents accuse them of *blasphemy* (Luke 5:21; 22:71 ‖ Acts 6:11-13). They are linked closely together in the charge of speaking against the temple and threatening to change the customs of Moses (Luke 21:5-6; 23:2; Mark 14:58; Acts 6:13-14). Neither of them shrinks from the attack but with dignity faces his accusers (Luke 23:3 ‖ Acts 7:2-53).

What really precipitates the death of Jesus is not the trial but cries of murder from the crowd (Luke 23:18-23). Stephen is not formally tried at all but rushed upon by an angry mob (7:54-58). Both forgive their murderers (Luke 23:34 ‖ Acts 7:60). And at the end, Jesus commends his spirit to the Father (Luke 23:46), paralleled by Stephen who prays the risen *Lord Jesus* to *receive* his *spirit* (Acts 7:59).

Worship Beyond the Limits of a Temple

Stephen speaks of the tabernacle as the divinely appointed place of worship and proclaims that God does not dwell in houses made with human hands (7:44-50). He is sounding a note as old as the preexilic Hebrew prophets. Micah foretold that Zion would be plowed like a field and the temple made a heap of rubble (3:12). Jeremiah preached that if the people went on sinning, the house of God would become like Shiloh, an object of shame and cursing (7:12-15; 26:6). And Ezekiel, in one vision after another, tried to help the people make the transition from worship in a specific house to the worship of a God who was also present in exile with them (chaps. 1—3, 12). For Israel to become "a light to the nations" (Isa. 42:6; 49:6) and draw others to God, the people would need to understand that God is not tied to a building but is free as a mighty Spirit to be worshiped everywhere (cf. 1 Kings 8:27; Isa. 66:1-2).

Out of the bitter experience of the exile, Israel partially learned this lesson. Somewhere in the course of time, the synagogue, a decentralized institution for both worship and teaching, came into being, and Judaism survived the dispersion. The later revival of a temple-centered worship and the restoration of a priestly hierarchy posed problems for those who had come to worship God anywhere.

Jesus began by preaching in the synagogues (Luke 4:15). When he did come to the temple, he drove out those who cluttered it with their selling (Luke 19:45-46). Though he used the temple as a place for teaching (Luke 19:47—21:38), he predicted its destruction (Luke 21:5-6) and prepared his followers to go to all nations without it (Luke 24:47; Acts 1:8; cf. Swartley: 188-190).

Thus Stephen's teaching about a pilgrim people (7:3-6), the tent in the wilderness (7:44-45), and the true worship of a God whose throne is heaven (7:48-50)—these all prepare the reader for the dispersion of the church to come (chaps. 8—28). Believers fulfill Jesus' command to witness to the ends of the earth, using not the temple but the synagogue as the springboard for their endeavors.

THE TEXT IN THE LIFE OF THE CHURCH
The Choice and Work of "Deacons"

Though the seven are never called *deacons*, the work for which they were chosen, that of caring for the needy, is a function usually associated with that office. Consequently, most denominations have taken them to be the first deacons and have used this Scripture along with 1 Timothy 3:8-13 as the basis for their call and ministry.

While the office of deacons varies from one communion to another, three basic aspects of the account of the seven have persisted. One is that deacons and deaconesses (and their spouses in churches which consecrate married couples to this ministry) are to be persons *of good standing* (6:3). From 1 Timothy come similar phrases: "above reproach" (3:2) and "well thought of by outsiders" (3:7). Both their character and conduct must be in line with their calling for them to inspire confidence and be able to function effectively.

A second qualification is the spiritual life of the deacon and deaconess (and spouse). The original seven are to be *full of the Holy Spirit* (6:3, 5, 8, 10). They are to have a spiritual ministry to persons, which may include menial tasks such as physical preparations for baptism and communion, or handling relief and welfare supplies, but also ministries of word. They are earnestly to ask for every measure of infilling of the Spirit, as Jesus taught (Luke 11:13), and put to work every evidence of the Spirit's presence demonstrated by Stephen (6:5-10, faith, grace, power, and wisdom). Thus equipped, deacons and deaconesses can add greatly to the church's effectiveness by assisting pastors in worship, visitation, and healing ministries.

The third contribution of our text to the deaconate, both historically and in contemporary practice, is the consecration of such persons by the laying on of hands. For Stephen and his companions, this was done by the apostles and accompanied by prayer (6:6). Today there is little variation in practice on this point, except that many groups now install deacons for short-term service instead of life and are careful to make a distinction between such commissioning and lifetime ordination. Even where lifetime service is envisioned, there has usually been some difference between the consecration service for a deacon and that for a minister.

Martyrdom Through the Centuries

From the first-known martyr to the present, there have been uncounted multitudes whose discipleship has cost them their lives. Especially memorable have been those who, like Stephen, were able to make a public witness and thus strengthen their contemporaries and even later generations.

A most remarkable collection of stories about such witness unto death, from the first century up to and including the earliest Anabaptists, is *Martyrs Mirror*. It was published in Dutch in 1660 by Thieleman J. van Braght, under the title *The Bloody Theater or Martyrs Mirror of Defenseless Christians Who Baptized Only Upon Confession of Faith*. Then it was translated into German by Peter Miller and widely circulated in that language. The major printing (1748-49) was done by the Ephrata Society of Pennsylvania, of Brethren origin, at the request of Franconia Conference Mennonites.

The result was a folio volume of over 1500 pages, the largest book printed in the American Colonies. With its moving accounts of how men and women endured incredible hardships, torture, and death for their Lord, it has inspired generation after generation to courageous witness. The first English edition appeared in 1837, and Joseph F. Sohm's English translation is still in print. The book's influence is seen in the willingness of many in the Anabaptist-Brethren tradition to accept death rather than to compromise with evil. It also aroused opposition, and some of the original 1,300 printed copies of the German edition were seized by the American

Revolutionary forces and used as cartridge wadding during the war.

Nor is martyrdom all a matter of the past. It has been estimated that more people have died for their faith in Jesus Christ in the twentieth century than in any previous one. And for every one who has died, there have been scores of others, with the same devoted spirit, willing to risk death for the Lord.

A good example of a twentieth-century Christian martyr is Kornelius Isaak. In 1958, he and two other Mennonites of Paraguay set out to contact the Moro Indians, who for years had been stealthily murdering various outsiders. They wanted to make friends of them as they had already done with the Lengua and Chulupie tribes. After a 200-mile ride in their jeep, they found signs of the Moros and hung gifts for them on a stick standing in the ground. After some days these gifts were taken, and they thought that a breakthrough had been made. But when they gave out other gifts, they were suddenly surrounded by a crowd of Moro tribesmen. They so wounded Kornelius with a spear that he eventually died. His last hours were spent praying for those who killed him.

The Paraguayan government was informed of the incident and sent soldiers to the area with strict orders to shoot any Moro they saw. But Kornelius's companion, David Hein, heard of this and asked in the Christian congregation for volunteers to go back with him to head off the soldiers. Three young Indians volunteered and went with him to the Moro people in time to prevent disaster. As a result, their former enemies became their friends and were ready to hear the gospel of Jesus Christ, who gave his life for all. Kornelius Isaak had not died in vain (Lehn: 108-109).

Part 5

The Witness of a Persecuted and Scattered Church

Acts 8:1b—9:31

PREVIEW

Luke makes it clear that, though Stephen is dead, the church goes on. Harassed by a great persecution that drives many believers out of Jerusalem, Spirit-filled leaders now carry the gospel to new and unexpected places. Entirely without human planning, the message reaches Samaria, and the witness moves on to the second phase of the program outlined in 1:8. There is a double irony in this thrust that we must not miss. First, the apostles are not the ones who carry out this work, even though Jesus commanded them to do so (1:8). Instead, the pioneer missionary to Samaria is the recently appointed Philip. Yet the apostles are not bypassed; Peter and John do follow Philip and complete his work (8:14-25). They become the stabilizing, verifying, and unifying force in the mission that moves out ahead of them. The second ironical feature is that the move out from Jerusalem is brought about as the result of persecution. It is not in any way a planned human effort (Tannehill: 102-103).

The Spirit directs Philip into a new ministry. Like Stephen, he goes beyond food distribution and begins proclaiming the word. Moreover, Philip and other nonapostolic persons scattered by persecution carry out the work of Jesus and the apostles before them. They are *proclaiming the good news about the kingdom of God* (8:12; cf. Luke 4:18, 43; 9:6). Philip also performs miracles, just as did Jesus and the apostles (cf. 8:7 with Luke 4:33-36; 5:18-26; Acts 5:16; 9:33-35).

Thus the fiery attacks intended to wipe out the new movement make it grow instead, and this second-named member of the seven becomes a key figure. His efforts are later matched by unnamed evangelists fleeing the same scourge of persecution (11:19-21). Into the formerly hostile territory of Samaria goes Philip, and also through him the gospel reaches faraway Ethiopia (Nubia).

Then Luke relates an even more exciting and incredible story: how the risen Lord intercepts the persecutor Saul outside Damascus, makes a believer of him, and gets him ready for great things to come. Nowhere in Acts is Luke's storytelling ability, with dramatic turns and subtle nuances of thought, more in evidence than in this sequence. Nor is there any more important personal account than this, in which the central figure of Acts 13—28 is recruited for the Lord and launched on his lifelong mission.

OUTLINE

Hellenist Christians Scattered by Persecution, 8:1b-3

Philip's Witness in Samaria, 8:4-13
| 8:4-8 | Widespread, Successful Ministry |
| 8:9-13 | Encounter with Simon the Sorcerer |

Mission of Peter and John to Samaria, 8:14-25
| 8:14-17 | Giving of the Holy Spirit |
| 8:18-25 | Simon's Request, Peter's Rebuke, Back to Jerusalem |

Philip's Witness to the Ethiopian, 8:26-40
8:26-31	The Meeting on the Gaza Road
8:32-35	Philip's Exposition of Scripture
8:36-39	Baptism and Departure of the Ethiopian
8:40	Philip's Trip to Caesarea

The Conversion of Saul, 9:1-19a
| 9:1-9 | Saul Met by the Risen Jesus |
| 9:10-19a | Ananias Ministers to Saul |

Saul's Witness in Damascus, 9:19b-25

Saul's Witness in Jerusalem, 9:26-30

A New Era of Peace and Growth, 9:31

EXPLANATORY NOTES

Hellenist Christians Scattered by Persecution 8:1b-3

Luke ties together the death of Stephen and the persecution that follows with a simple observation: *And Saul approved of their killing him* (8:1b). NASB says Saul *was in hearty agreement with* what happened: Saul does not cast the stones, but he is totally behind the lynching. Moreover, he is undoubtedly the one who directs the *severe persecution . . . against the church* that follows immediately (8:1b).

All except the apostles were scattered throughout the countryside of Judea and Samaria. This sounds like only the twelve, of the thousands of Jerusalem Christians, were left there. Yet there are clues that a strong church continued on in the city (8:14, 25; 9:26-31; 11:2-18; 12:5, 12-17). Here the inclusive *all* means something like "considerable numbers of." We are not told who these are. Yet the Hebrew apostles are not driven out, and Hellenists like Philip and the unnamed witnesses of 11:19-20 *are* expelled. It therefore appears that the ones scattered are chiefly such foreign-born, Greek-speaking believers.

Meanwhile, proper funeral honors are given Stephen (8:2). The oral law prohibits public mourning for executed persons (Mishnah Sanhedrin 6.6). Thus it is evidence of both true courage and much caring on the part of believers that such a *loud lamentation* and burial be made for Stephen.

Now Luke names the chief persecutor, the young man he has already mentioned twice (7:58; 8:1). *Saul*, who has supervised the stoning, begins to enter *house after house* to ferret out believers, seizing both men and women, imprisoning them, trying to make them *blaspheme* by confessing Jesus as Lord, and voting for the death penalty at their trials (8:3; 26:9-11). Motivated by a violent zeal for the traditions of the fathers (Gal. 1:13-14), his aim is to stamp out the new movement completely.

Philip's Witness in Samaria 8:4-13

8:4-8 Widespread, Successful Ministry

Luke now tells of an evangelizing dispersion of the church, with Philip as his leading example (8:4-40). He goes to Samaria and begins preaching the gospel. Evidence is divided between this being *a city of Samaria* (RSV; NIV; cf. 8:8) and *the city of Samaria* (KJV, NASB, NRSV; support of earlier manuscripts). Though the OT capital of the province is usually known in the first century by its Roman name *Sebaste*, the old name also continues to be used (Hemer: 25-26), and it is difficult to be certain about which one is intended here. If it is not Samaria, then it may be *Gitti*, said by Justin Martyr to be the birthplace of Simon Magus (*Apology* 1.26.2), or simply some unnamed city.

More important is the fact that ever since the days of Ezra, there has been hostility between Jews and Samaritans. Luke earlier recorded an incident in which Samaritans refused to let Jews (Jesus and his disciples) stay in their village overnight. Some of Jesus' disciples wanted to call down fire out of heaven against the Samaritans (Luke 9:53). Yet Jesus demonstrated restraint toward the Samaritans (Luke 9:54-56) and used them as examples of true gratitude and love (Luke 10:30-37; 17:11-18). Now a follower of Jesus is bringing these longtime enemies the good news of God's love on terms equal to that of Jews.

Philip's approach is first of all preaching, and this is accompanied by miraculous *signs* (8:6-7). It is the way Jesus did it (Luke 4:31-34), and this same combination of proclamation and miracle-working was continued by the early Jerusalem Christians (2:43; 3:1-26; 6:8). With Philip, people can see the effects of the gospel as well as hear it. Even the most unlearned among them can grasp this demonstration of Christ's presence! Among the Samaritans, it is first the casting out of evil spirits and with that, various healings (8:7). Many signs and wonders have been mentioned thus far in Acts, but this is the first time the casting out of demons has been specified. It was the earliest of the miracles of Jesus reported in the synoptic Gospels (Mark 1:22-27; Luke 4:31-36). Now also here in Samaria, loud cries of departing spirits rend the air and proclaim the working of divine power. After that, Luke tells of the many paralytics and lame being restored to health. Little wonder that there is *great joy in that city* (8:8)!

8:9-13 Encounter with Simon the Sorcerer

At this point Luke introduces Simon, powerful in the eyes of *the people of Samaria*, one who has practiced magic in this city and has impressed everyone (8:9). Acts tells us nothing of the nature of his magic but a great deal about his reputation and self-image. He has been putting himself forward as *someone great* and, in turn, has been acclaimed by the people as being *the power of God that is called Great* (8:10). According to these statements and later traditions about him, this man has come to regard himself as divine, a manifestation of deity able to amaze the people and keep them under his control, but not necessarily the Messiah. In later church lore, he will be looked upon as the founder of Gnosticism, who leads many astray with his sect called the *Simonians* (Irenaeus, *Against Heresies* 1.23). In Philip's time, however, he is simply a popular sorcerer claiming magical powers and divinity for himself (8:9-11, KJV).

Simon is impressed by the large crowds that respond to the evangelist Philip and are baptized by him (8:12). So great is the power moving through Philip that, as Luke puts it, *even Simon himself* believes and is baptized. However mixed his motives, this sorcerer becomes a believer and follows Philip around, amazed at the miracles he is able to perform (8:13). This is the first of a series of encounters in Acts between preachers of the true gospel and magic. The others are the sequel in 8:18-24, the dealings of Paul with Elymas Bar-Jesus in 13:6-12, and the apostle's later conflict with exorcists and magicians at Ephesus in 19:11-20. In each case, it is spiritual warfare between Jesus, powerful with true gospel miracles; and evil, the source of magic.

Mission of Peter and John to Samaria   8:14-25

8:14-17 Giving of the Holy Spirit

News reaches Jerusalem of the Samaritan ministry of Philip. The church promptly sends their two leading apostles to see if this is truly the working of the divine will. What they discover is that the disciples in Samaria have been baptized in the name of Jesus, but the Holy Spirit has not yet fallen on them (8:14-16). They have not had the experience of those on the Day of Pentecost upon whom the Spirit did fall, with the manifestation of speaking in other tongues and boldness in witnessing (chap. 2; 4:8). Subsequently, many were receiving and being filled with the promised Holy Spirit (2:38; 6:3, 6). So Peter and John lay hands on the Samaritan converts, and they too receive this added blessing (8:17). Perhaps, in this case at least, only apostles have the authority to do this.

8:18-25 Simon's Request, Peter's Rebuke, Back to Jerusalem

Simon sees something happen when the apostles lay hands on the converts and bestow the Holy Spirit. He wants the power to confer the same experience (8:18). No mention is made of manifestations like tongues, prophecy, or exuberant praise of God, but in the light of the parallel accounts in 10:44-46 and 19:6, they seem to be implied here. At any rate, he sees and probably hears enough for him to try to buy the same apostolic authority (8:19).

Peter's response is swift and emphatic. With prophetic zeal he consigns both the sorcerer and his money to destruction. The Holy Spirit is *God's gift* and can never be bought or sold! (8:20). For Simon even to think of buying God's gift shows that he is of an alien spirit and has *no part or share in this*. In spite of his profession of the gospel and baptism, his heart is not right before God (8:21). What he needs, Peter tells him, is to repent of his wickedness and pray that *if possible* he may be forgiven (8:22). Simon is *in the gall of bitterness and the chains of wickedness*, one who has turned away from God and run after idols (Deut. 29:18; cf. Heb. 12:15).

Simon is alarmed enough by the apostle's rebuke to ask for prayer (8:24), but beyond that there is no indication of his repentance and forgiveness. All we have are the statements of the church fathers centuries later who remember him as the great heretic and enemy of the faith. His name lives on in the name for the sin of *simony*, the buying or selling of church offices or privileges, common in medieval times.

Once they are finished with the situation in the city where Philip has been evangelizing, Peter and John begin their return to Jerusalem. They seem to be in no hurry, however. While in Samaria they go about preaching the gospel in a good many villages in the area (8:25). This helps complete the work begun by Philip in fulfilling the second phase of the Lord's command to be witnesses *in all Judea and Samaria* (1:8).

Philip's Witness to the Ethiopian   8:26-40

8:26-31   The Meeting on the Gaza Road

Philip's ministry now takes an unexpected turn. As so often in Luke's writings, the Lord intervenes and changes human plans through a vision or, as in this case, by the word of an *angel*. The command is to go south to the road leading from Jerusalem to deserted Gaza, razed in 99 B.C. (8:26; Josephus, *Ant.* 13.13.3). The city was rebuilt in 57 B.C. on a new site. It is strange that a popular evangelist is sent to a *wilderness* area where people are scarce. But likely Philip by now is used to the Lord's surprises.

The angel only speaks. Philip simply arises and goes (8:27).

Instead of a crowd of people, he finds just one man, an *Ethiopian*, from what is known as Nubia (Cush in OT; extending from Aswan in Egypt to Khartoum in the Sudan). Instead of being despised or deprived, he is, to Luke's first-century readers, a fascinating individual (Willimon: 71). He belongs to that group known as court officials or eunuchs (2 Kings 20:18; Isa. 39:7; Jer. 38:7) and may or may not be an actual eunuch. What Acts emphasizes is his high position as the chief treasurer for the queen mother of his nation.

Nubian kings are regarded as offspring of the sun-god and are too sacred to do the actual ruling. Such duties are left to the monarch's mother, always called by the hereditary title *Candace*. As her chief treasurer, this man is both rich and powerful. He represents his country and is now returning from Jerusalem, where he has gone to worship Yahweh, the God of the Jews (8:27). If he is an actual eunuch, it is doubtful that he can be a proselyte of the faith. Therefore, he likely is a God-fearer or inquirer. If so, he is the first of a series of such persons in Acts: Cornelius (10:2), Lydia (16:14), and the many *devout Greeks* of Thessalonica (17:4) and other cities.

Philip is first aware of a richly furnished covered *chariot* with a driver in the front seat and the finance minister seated comfortably behind, busily reading a biblical scroll (8:28). The *Spirit*, now directing Philip (8:29) after the angel's initial command (8:26), tells the evangelist to *join* the carriage. To do so, he actually runs up alongside it, close enough to hear the man *reading* aloud (8:30). Philip recognizes it as from Isaiah (53:7-8) and boldly asks him if he understands what he is reading. It is possible that the Ethiopian has heard believers in Jerusalem discussing the messianic meaning of this very passage, and now here is a stranger to explain it to him. So he eagerly invites Philip up into the back seat of the chariot with him. It is obvious by the way Luke writes this that the Spirit is guiding every move they make (8:29, 39, framing the whole encounter).

8:32-35 Philip's Exposition of Scripture

This Isaiah passage (52:13—53:12), from the well-known Servant Songs, is claimed as a key prophecy of the afflictions of the Messiah. Jesus said, "Thus it is written, that the Messiah is to suffer" (Luke 24:46; cf. 22:37; Acts 3:18). In his Gospel, Luke does not highlight the redemptive suffering servant aspect of Jesus' work in the way Mark does (10:45 || Matt. 20:28). Now he uses these verses as clearly pointing to the Lord.

The Ethiopian's question of whether this text might be referring to the prophet himself (8:24) is a logical one, especially since Jeremiah describes his own sufferings in similar terms (11:18-20). For Philip, this provides a wonderful opportunity to begin here and tell about Jesus and his gospel. Luke omits the actual exposition. Yet it seems clear that Philip takes the words *like a sheep led to the slaughter* (8:32) and *his life is taken away from the earth* (8:33) to tell of Jesus' trial and crucifixion and then of salvation through him. After that, in view of what happens, Philip must have added a great deal more, such as instruction in repentance, baptism, and the Christian life.

8:36-39 Baptism and Departure of the Ethiopian

Luke moves at once to the dramatic outcome of the encounter. However adequate or inadequate the preparation for discipleship might be, the sight of water brings it to a culmination. The official himself sees it, is eager to be baptized, and orders the chariot to stop (8:36-38a). While it might seem surprising to find water along this desert road, either the Wadi el-Hasi northeast of Gaza or the wadi in the valley of Elah of that area (1 Sam. 17:19, 40) might have contained adequate pools. The Ethiopian's question, *What is to prevent me from being baptized?* sounds like an early baptismal formula (8:36; Munck, 1967:78). The words of Acts 8:37, found in the KJV and in the NRSV footnote, are not supported by the most ancient manuscripts. They are an early addition by the Western text *[Greek Text, p. 311]*, supplying proper words to ask a candidate for a profession of faith in Jesus Christ as the Son of God.

Luke seems to make a point of them going *down into the water* before baptism and *up out of the water* afterward, but says nothing more of the ritual itself except that Philip does the baptizing (8:38-39). Since *baptizō* usually means to "dip" or "wash," some form of immersion administered by the evangelist seems likely. Philip, however, could use pouring after they step into the water.

Soon after the two emerge from the water, they part company. The Spirit of the Lord catches up Philip out of the Ethiopian's sight, and they never see each other again (8:39). But the baptized chief treasurer goes on his way, rejoicing in his newfound faith. Joy is an important fruit of the Spirit (Gal. 5:22), evidenced again in Acts after another unusual person is brought into the kingdom (16:34).

Tradition has it that the Ethiopian later becomes a missionary among his people (Irenaeus, *Against Heresies* 3.12.8). Though there is no record of an Ethiopian church for another three centuries, it may well be that the roots of the Ethiopian Coptic Church go back to this incident. Certainly Luke has placed this baptism strategically between those of the Samaritans and of Cornelius and his household, as examples of the *unhindered* outreach of the gospel (28:31; Willimon: 72). Moreover, he has recorded here a series of divine promptings, by angel and by Spirit, paralleled in only one other story, that of Cornelius (Haenchen: 315). Thus the evangelistic thrust is moving from Jew to Samaritan and now to the boundaries of the world. Psalm 68:31b is being fulfilled: "Let Ethiopia hasten to stretch out its hands to God."

8:40 Philip's Trip to Caesarea

As Philip later tells this story to Luke, he describes it as being taken on his way by the Spirit. Either in his mind or that of the author who records it, there may be memory of the way Ezekiel was lifted up by the Spirit and brought from the River Chebar to the east gate of the house of the Lord (Ezek. 11:1). However it happened, Philip is presumably so filled with the Spirit that he is hardly conscious of anything else until he later has *found himself* at the town of *Azotus*.

Azotus is the ancient Ashdod, rebuilt by the Romans in about 55 B.C. It was situated three miles from the coast, some 20 miles north of Gaza and halfway between it and Joppa. Northward from along the coast, Philip begins preaching the gospel in all the towns and villages until he reaches Caesarea (8:40). In that city Luke, on his way to Jerusalem with Paul and his party, stays at the house of Philip and has an opportunity to hear from him an eyewitness account of this whole incident (21:8-10).

The Conversion of Saul 9:1-19a

While Philip is doing his work, Saul the persecutor has continued to ravage the church. With a *meanwhile*, Luke makes the transition and resumes the account begun in 8:1-3. It is an incredibly dramatic story, one that holds the reader in its grip as it ushers in a new chapter in the mission to the ends of the earth. So important is it that Luke has it reported twice more before his book is finished. This first account is the only one told in the third person by the author. In all three tellings, the risen Lord is central, with Saul and Ananias the principal human characters. Together these accounts comprise a series in which Saul's new mission is related in three different ways. First, the Lord speaks to Ananias about the call and future work of this former persecutor (9:15-16). In 22:14-15 Ananias is the one to tell Saul that the Lord has chosen him to be a witness to all the world. Then in 26:16-18 the Lord again speaks, this time directly to Saul, to reveal the purpose for which he has been chosen, together with an assurance of his divine protection.

9:1-9 Saul Met by the Risen Jesus

Since the events of 8:1-3, Saul has increased his attack on the disciples of Jesus. Some time has gone by, and now he is branching out beyond Jerusalem. *Still breathing threats and murders* in his attempt to root out this heresy completely, Saul goes to the high priest for authority to journey north to the large city of Damascus. There he intends to arrest such disciples and bring them to trial in Jerusalem (9:2). The high priest was present at the execution of Stephen and is no doubt eager to supply Saul with letters to outlying synagogues, enabling him to carry on this work. As head of the Sanhedrin, the chief priest's jurisdiction includes such communities outside Jerusalem (Josephus, *Ant.* 14.10.20-21).

The reason Saul chooses Damascus in which to continue the persecution is that many of the Hellenistic believers seem to have gone there to seek refuge when they were scattered (see on 8:1). Josephus gives a figure of ten thousand Jews in the city (*War* 2.20.2). Perhaps New Covenanters or non-Qumran Essenes have found refuge there (Rowley; ABD, 2:8-10, on the Damascus Rule, CD; or is Damascus a cipher for Babylon, from which Essenes migrated in the Maccabean period?). At any rate, this would be the kind of place in which Saul can expect to find a good many followers of Jesus.

Luke says that the letters Saul is carrying authorize him to seize men and women *who belonged to the Way*. This is the first mention in Acts of *the Way* being used by believers to describe their movement. It is found again in 19:9, 23; 22:4; 24:14, 22; their gospel is called *a way of salvation* (16:17) and *the Way of the Lord/of God* (18:25). It is a good self-designation for the followers of Jesus, who called himself "the way, and the truth, and the life" (John 14:6; see notes on Acts 19:9). Saul would bring them bound to Jerusalem (9:2). Thus the whole procedure is being carried out legally, with due arrests and proper transfer of prisoners to headquarters to be tried.

Then heaven intervenes and the well-made plans of the persecutor suddenly collapse. Saul is near Damascus when a strange *light from heaven* blazes forth, and he falls to the ground (9:3-6). The light exhibits divine power. In the third telling of the story, it symbolizes the salvation which Paul will someday preach, *to open their eyes so that they may turn from darkness to light* (26:18). This echoes Isaiah 42:6 and 49:6, "the light to the nations." In addition, the light symbolizes glory, as in Luke 2:9: the "glory of the Lord" shone all around the shepherds, and they too were struck down with fear.

Then comes *a voice*. At his baptism Jesus heard a voice (Luke 3:22), and again on the Mount of Transfiguration (Luke 9:35)—what the rabbis called a *bath-qol* (lit., "daughter of a voice"). But now it is different. This is no joyous proclamation of the Messiah, but a sharp confrontation calling for a decision. The risen Jesus has caught up with his persecutor at last and is pressing for an answer to a question that will change his life. *Saul, Saul,* the voice calls in his native Aramaic (cf. 26:14, NRSV note), *why are you hounding me this way?* The Greek verb means to pursue with intent to harm.

Saul, on the ground and now blinded by the dazzling light, can only ask who is thus probing his very soul (9:5). He addresses him as *kurie*, which can mean either a polite *sir* or, in view of their later relationship, *Lord*. The answer is as simple and to the point as Saul's question. *I am Jesus!* the voice replies. According to the later words of Barnabas, no doubt based on Saul's report, this erstwhile persecutor actually sees the Lord as well as hears him (9:27).

Whether or not Saul at first acknowledges the lordship of Jesus, he cannot question the authority of this new presence. *Get up and enter the city, and you will be told what you are to do* (9:6)—these are all commands that must be obeyed. There is now someone in control of his life who can order him to do things beyond his choosing. Little wonder that in the years that follow, he often speaks of himself as the *slave* of Jesus! (cf. Rom. 1:1, NRSV note; 1 Cor. 7:22b; Gal. 1:10, note; Phil. 1:1, note; Tit. 1:1, note; the Greek *doulos* is really *slave* rather than *servant*). Right from the start Saul learns to follow the Lord's commands. In the OT, patriarchs, prophets, and kings were called "slaves of Yahweh." In the NT, such slave language indicates a "special and honored relationship" to Christ and "full dependence" on him (*ABD*, 6:62, 72).

Luke's comment in 9:7 that those traveling with Saul hear the voice but do not see anyone seems at first glance to contradict what he says in 22:9 about the same event, that they see the light but do not hear the voice. Probably they hear a sound but not the words expressed, and, if so, both statements are true.

The stricken man does not realize the full effect of the bright light until he gets up and tries to walk. Then he discovers that he is totally blind and must have someone lead him by the hand (9:8). Luke paints a dramatic picture of this fiery persecutor now rendered so helpless that he must depend on others like a child!

It is a short distance into Damascus, and Saul's companions take him to a place only revealed later (9:11). He is so upset that for three days he can neither eat nor drink (9:9). In his helplessness he is now ready for the saving work of the Lord. Though the story to this point is often referred to as the conversion of Saul-Paul, it is actually only the beginning. The Lord has struck him down and made him ready, but the real work is yet to come.

Now Luke introduces God's agent in completing the transformation of the man of destiny. Ananias is a true unsung hero, otherwise unknown. All we can be sure about him is that he is a Jewish *disciple* or follower of Jesus. There are two other men in Acts with the same name (the husband of Sapphira in 5:1-11 and the high priest in 23:2; 24:1). *Ananias,* the Greek form of the Hebrew *Hananiah,* is quite common, appearing for at least fourteen persons in the OT. It means "the mercy of the Lord" and is especially appropriate here. This particular Ananias seems to be a long-time resident of Damascus, perhaps even a native, and not a recent fugitive from Jerusalem. He has only a secondhand knowledge of Saul (9:13), and later he is said to be respected by all the Jews of the city (22:12). He might even be the leader of the Christian group in Damascus since he is chosen to receive a vision and to give this important ministry to Saul.

As Luke tells it, the story begins simply enough, like something out of the life of an OT prophet. The Lord calls his name, and he responds with the well-known *Here I am, Lord* (9:10b; cf. 1 Sam. 3:2-10). Then Ananias is told in this vision to *go to the street called Straight.* This causes no problem because Ananias knows it well: the wide east-west thoroughfare running through the center of the city and lined with many shops and dwellings. (The street still exists in the twentieth century under the name of *Darb al-Mustaqim*). He is to go to the home of a man by the name of *Judas,* obviously a Jew and possibly an acquaintance of his.

Up to this point the instructions are quite routine, nothing unusual. But then the Lord drops a bombshell. Ananias is told to inquire there for *a man of Tarsus named Saul!* And what is more, says the Lord, this man *is praying* (9:11). Not only that, but he too has been given *a vision*. Remarkable as it may seem, here is a vision within a vision. In Saul's visit from the Lord, Saul has seen Ananias himself come in, *lay his hands on him*, and pray for his healing (9:12). This is just too much. Imagine! The feared and hated persecutor is in town and right now may be setting a trap for him, Ananias, at the house of Judas. "No, it can't be!" his spirit cries out within him. So he speaks up and, like many a prophet before him, voices his misgivings. Addressing the Lord, he mentions all the evil Saul has worked against *your saints in Jerusalem*. Ananias already knows that Saul's present trip to Damascus is to continue the same attacks against *all who invoke your name* (9:13-14).

But, says Luke, the Lord answers him firmly with one word: *Go!* There is no arguing, just this simple imperative. But with it comes the helpful explanation that Saul is a chosen *instrument* of God to carry the gospel before three kinds of people of the world: *Gentiles, kings,* and *the people of Israel* (9:15). The *Gentiles* constitute the major mission field for Paul. The *kings* are rulers representing the emperor, like Agrippa II (26:1-12), Felix (24:1-21), Festus (25:1—26:32), and possibly minor authorities like Sergius Paulus (13:7-12) and Gallio (18:12-17). *Israel* refers to the many Jews to whom Saul-Paul is careful to address first with the gospel in every city before offering it to Gentiles. The divine election for such a task will be treasured by Paul. In later years he says that he was set apart from his mother's womb to preach the gospel to the Gentiles (Gal. 1:15; cf. Rom. 1:1-6).

Then the voice tells Ananias something else that helps him decide to go. The Lord will show Saul how much *he must suffer* to fulfill his ministry. This seems to settle the matter. God is in control, and from now on this erstwhile persecutor must bear his share of hardship. Ananias is human enough that somehow this appeals to him and relieves his mind. It shows that Saul is indeed going to become a believer, because suffering for Jesus is one of the hallmarks of true disciples (Luke 6:22-23; 9:23-24; Acts 14:22; 1 Thess. 1:6-7; 1 Pet. 4:12-16). After this statement there is no further hesitation. Ananias goes!

With great economy of words, Luke writes, *So Ananias went and entered the house* (9:17a). There is no word about distance or of the thoughts racing through his mind on the way. Before readers know it, Ananias is in the house of Judas laying his hands on the praying persecutor. He is no longer archenemy Saul but now *Brother Saul*—in this context two of the sweetest words in the NT! Healed of his hostility and terror, Ananias is a new man himself and can identify with this Christian-in-the-making. He explains how the same Lord

Jesus who appeared to Saul outside Damascus has now sent his servant Ananias to cure his blindness and bestow upon him *the Holy
Spirit* (9:17).

What happens next is a double miracle. Something like scales fall
from Saul's eyes, reminiscent of the film that scaled off the eyes of
Tobit when his son Tobias healed him (Tobit 3:17). Then, rising up
with sight restored, this man from Tarsus is baptized and receives the
promised Holy Spirit (9:17d-18). Luke adds one further detail: he
takes food and is strengthened, important after three days and nights
of fasting (9:19).

Saul's Witness in Damascus 9:19b-25

Contrary to a widespread notion, *Saul* does not become *Paul* upon
conversion, and the latter is not therefore a "Christian" name given to
him at that time. Luke first speaks of him as Paul only after many
years (13:9). He has most likely had both names from birth, Saul as a
true Hebrew (Phil. 3:5) and Paulus as his Roman family name. At any
rate, during these years of working in predominately Semitic areas,
Luke calls him by his Hebrew name and later, as he moves into the
wider Roman world, he is known as Paul (see notes on 13:9).

It is natural now, as a believer, that Saul seeks out fellow believers
in Damascus (possibly in company with Ananias) and begins to fellowship with them *for several days* (9:19b). And *immediately*, as the
author puts it, he begins to testify to his newfound faith in the local
Jewish synagogues, proclaiming *Jesus* as *the Son of God* (9:20). This
text and 13:33 are the only two in Acts in which the expression *Son
of God* is used of Jesus (plus the Western text of 8:37 *[Greek Text,
p. 312]*). Since both are from reports of the preaching of Paul and the
expression is common in the apostle's writings, it is evident that Luke
here accurately reports his central message. In further confirmation,
this title is prominent in both Paul's account of his call in Galatians
1:16 and his consecration as an apostle in Romans 1:1-4. The vision
of the risen Lord outside Damascus convinces him that Jesus is
indeed the Son of God, and that becomes the focus of his earliest
preaching.

The first reaction to such forthright proclamation is amazement at
the radical turnaround of this former persecutor (9:21). The severity
with which he previously set about to destroy the church is matched
by the zeal with which he now preaches the new faith. No wonder
Luke can record that he becomes *increasingly more powerful* as he

confounded (*baffled*, NIV) his Jewish opponents with his proof of Jesus as the Messiah (9:22).

As with Stephen before him (6:8-14), Saul's strong witness arouses bitter opposition (9:23). Luke does not tell us how long his ministry lasts, nor does he refer to Saul's sojourn in Arabia (Gal. 1:17). He may have no knowledge of it or may omit it because it involves no evangelistic thrust toward Rome. Taking this account together with Paul's record in Galatians (1:17-18), we see that the *some time* of 9:23 includes three years. Part of that time is spent in Arabia, the Nabatean kingdom ruled by Aretas IV.

The sequence of events is something like this: Saul witnesses in the synagogues for a while and succeeds in making *disciples* (9:25a). Then he goes into Nabatean territory for both spiritual retreat and evangelistic work. The latter infuriates other Jews in that area, and Saul returns to Damascus. Jews plot against Saul and likely complain about him to King Aretas, who by now has one of his governors in control of Damascus (no Roman coins found there dated A.D. 35-61: ADB, 2:8). Saul is in danger again and must be let down over the wall by some followers to escape with his life, from Jews and Aretas (9:23-25; 2 Cor. 11:31-32). [*Chronology, p. 309.*]

Saul's Witness in Jerusalem 9:26-30

Though not specifically stated, it seems that Saul goes directly to Jerusalem after his escape (9:26). There, as at Damascus, he tries to join the followers of Jesus, but he is in for a rude awakening. No one will believe that he is a genuine disciple because the last time they saw him he was trying to destroy the church (8:3; cf. 9:1). The fear of the apostles is a repetition of the fear shown by Ananias in 9:13-14. It is hard for humans to adjust to the Lord's surprises!

At this point, Luke tells how Barnabas, introduced in 4:36-37 as a cooperative and generous member of the Jerusalem church, saves the day. This time he shows warmth and courage by bringing to the apostles the man whom all others fear. Barnabas simply tells them the story of the Damascus road and Saul's subsequent ministry in that city (9:27). The dangerous newcomer is allowed to go *in and out among them* (9:28; for further examples of Barnabas affirming and upbuilding others, see notes on 11:22-30; 12:25; 13:1-3; 14:12; 15:36-39).

In the parallel account in Galatians 1:18, Paul makes the point that he associates mainly with Cephas-Peter during this visit, has a brief contact with James the Lord's brother, and is there only fifteen days. During this time Saul makes his mark on the church with his bold preaching and presents his case among Hellenists in the synagogue (Acts 9:29). Like Stephen before him (6:10-14), and as he himself experienced it in Damascus (10:23-25), this arouses such bitter opposition that his life is again in danger (9:29). Once more he must be rescued by fellow believers, and this time he is personally escorted to the coast at Caesarea for safety and sent to his home in Tarsus of Cilicia (9:30). There, years later, Barnabas will find him and bring him to Antioch for a whole new phase in life (11:25-26).

A New Era of Peace and Growth 9:31

With Saul's career now launched, Luke inserts another of his short *summaries* (9:31). It serves as a transition between the events of the gospel's expansion in chapters 8–9 and the completion of the witness to Judea in 9:32—12:24. The point is that now, with the conversion of the one great opponent, the church of Jesus Christ enjoys a period of peace and continues to grow. The area of this new development is specified as Judea, Galilee, and Samaria, the very provinces of the earthly ministry of Jesus.

THE TEXT IN ITS BIBLICAL CONTEXT
A Dispersion That Spreads the Faith

The comparison of the scattering of the Christians under the persecution by Saul with the dispersion of the Hebrew people by the Babylonians is instructive. God's people were originally called to be a blessing to all the nations of the earth (Gen. 12:2-3) or, as Isaiah put it, "a light to the nations" (Isa. 42:6; 49:6). But this did not happen while they stayed in their own land. They suffered disaster, were carried into captivity, and dispersed into many strange lands. Then they began to fulfill their God-given destiny. There synagogues sprang up, to which Gentiles could be attracted and become believers, either as proselytes or God-fearers (cf. Acts 10:2). These synagogues, in time, provided the bases for the preaching of the gospel as we find it in Acts. The command to spread the word was not sufficient. It took the severe lessons of deportation and exile to bring about the fulfillment of the promise.

In similar fashion, then, the great commission of Jesus that his followers be his witnesses to the ends of the earth (1:8) did not happen soon nor easily. It also required violent action by the enemies of the faith, who drove many of the believers out of Jerusalem and set the stage for them to do the work they were commanded to do all along.

Miracle Overcoming Magic

As seen in the story of Philip and Simon the sorcerer, there are some similarities between works of magic and the true miracles of the Lord. Moses found this to be true as he and Aaron confronted Pharaoh in Egypt (Exod. 7:8-12). The king's magicians were able to do exactly what Aaron did, throwing down their staffs and having them turn to snakes. The only difference was that Aaron's serpents swallowed up those of the sorcerers. So also Simon of Samaria has been amazing his people for years with his works of magic, some of which may have been healings.

Both magic and miracle are demonstrations of a power not commonly possessed by humans. Both are therefore convincing to people who witness them. There are, however, three fundamental differences between them. (1) Magic tends to be self-serving, either performed for money, a part of one's job, or to gain attention from people or power over them. A true miracle, on the other hand, is basically for the benefit of others. (2) In the long run, magic is nonproductive so far as human welfare is concerned and may even exploit people. By contrast, true miracles contribute to the good of persons and society. (3) Magic may be learned, bought or sold, and passed on from one individual to another. Miracles are the work of almighty God, gifts and not human achievements, and the power to perform them is not subject to trade or exchange.

The two are actually direct opposites. *Magic* is the attempt of human beings to *gain control* over natural or supernatural powers, while *true miracle* is the result of putting oneself *under the control of God* for divine purposes. These fundamental differences can be seen in each of the passages of Acts where the battle between them is joined (8:9-24; 13:6-12; 19:11-20). Quite similar to this also is the basic clash between the gospel and misguided business interests, as related in 16:19-21 and 19:23-41.

The Norm for Christian Conversion?

The account of Saul's conversion and call outside the city of Damascus (9:1-9) has often been taken as a model for all Christians.

Countless evangelists have used it so forcefully that they have sometimes created the impression that all persons must come into the kingdom in the same dramatic way. Actually, there is no one pattern of conversion and call in the NT or in Acts. People have their own experiences, from the mass convictions and baptisms at Pentecost (2:37-41) to the quiet acceptance of the Ethiopian (8:36-38), from the dramatic falling of the Spirit on the house of Cornelius (10:44-48) to the gentle opening of the heart of Lydia and the baptism of her household (16:14-15). The norm is not to be found in any of the externals but in the results of a transformed life. Moreover, conversion is just the beginning of a much longer series of experiences, as the many years of maturation in the life of Saul-Paul show (from 9:8 to 11:26).

THE TEXT IN THE LIFE OF THE CHURCH
Radical Turnaround Can Be Real

Conversion should not be made to fit the mold of Saul's. Yet the truth in his experience needs to be burned into the consciousness of all Christians. The Lord has the power to change the *direction* of a person's life completely. Early Anabaptism broke with the established churches at this point, with the baptism of adults as a celebration of the regenerated life. Thus conversion, the "new life in Christ by the power of the Holy Spirit, was the real center of their identity" (C. J. Dyck, "Anabaptism," in *BE*, 1:29).

Added to this must be the realization, however, that complete *change of character,* especially in a case as radical as that of Saul, often takes much time. It is many years before the newly converted persecutor is able to write and exemplify in life the love chapter (1 Cor. 13) or many of the great passages in the epistles of Romans, Philippians, and Ephesians. Continuous living in the Spirit is marked by training, testing, and toughening in the hard realities of life.

Throughout the history of the Christian church, God has continued to intervene in the lives of people and turn them around for his kingdom's work. One such recent experience is that of James Dennis, son of an alcoholic father in southeastern Georgia. He had lived with violence and hatred, then God encountered him and gave him new life in and through Jesus Christ. Today he is a pastor of Diamond Street Mennonite Church in Philadelphia. Thank God, who continues to defeat the powers of evil and turn people *from darkness to light and from the power of Satan to God, so that they may receive forgiveness of sins and a place among those who are sanctified* (Acts 26:18; *Together,* Aug. 1992).

The Perennial Need for Helpers and Encouragers

The somewhat parallel stories of Ananias (9:10-18) and Barnabas (9:26-27) show that those who stand by and work with the newly converted are of utmost importance. Without an Ananias to minister healing, the giving of the Holy Spirit, and a Barnabas to befriend this chosen vessel of the Lord—without these it is difficult to imagine how Saul-Paul would ever have started as an apostle. God thus uses men and women who are enablers to take diamonds-in-the-rough and help them not only to survive but eventually to shine for the gospel. Particularly important has been this function in the Anabaptist-Brethren tradition, with its radical break from the world. Again and again the Lord has raised up an Ananias who has dared to approach and help a formerly hated or feared individual to begin on the road of discipleship. And when times of crisis arise, how often has God sent a reconciler like Barnabas to save the situation!

Part 6

The Continuing Ministry of Peter

Acts 9:32—12:25

PREVIEW

Peter appeared last in 8:28, when he and John returned to Jerusalem after preaching among the Samaritans. Luke now continues the story of the apostle by telling of his journeys outside Jerusalem, going *here and there* among the Christians (9:32). Peter will be the central figure in most of the accounts from this point on to the end of chapter 12.

This section completes the Judea-and-Samaria phase of the witness outlined in 1:8. One story follows another in quick succession, filled with miracles and surprises. They reemphasize the wonders and signs first performed by the apostles in Jerusalem (2:43) and most vividly represented by Peter's healing of the lame man (3:1-10). After ministering with some spectacular healings in two outlying centers, Peter becomes the Lord's instrument for winning the first named Gentile to the new faith (10:1—11:18). Luke presents this as the pivotal event of this period, a drama in seven scenes with enough internal repetition to impress the message deeply on the mind of the reader. Narrative unity is maintained by a subtle interlacing of motifs and significant symbolisms. Angel visitants and visions give it a divine dimension, yet such promptings always call for human response. The characters in the story are at all times alive to meanings and the need to make decisions. Here Jew meets Roman, and a surprise breakthrough by the Holy Spirit surprises them all as it ushers in the era of Gentile Christianity.

Immediately following that, the author tells of the first real Jew-Gentile congregation, that in Syrian Antioch. Many subtle features link it with the Jerusalem congregation. It goes through a period of rapid advance similar to the initial growth in Jerusalem, with the same language used of the Lord adding people to the church (cf. 2:41, 47; 5:14). The dedication of the Jerusalem disciples to the teaching and fellowship of the apostles (2:42) is matched by Saul-Paul and Barnabas in their nurturing ministry for a whole year (11:26). Then the sharing of wealth within the community at Jerusalem finds its counterpart in Antioch, both within their own fellowship and in the relief they send to the mother church at Jerusalem—another tie between the two congregations. As a new development both ethnically and geographically, Antioch becomes the springboard for future missionary activity (cf. chaps. 13ff.).

Then Peter comes back onto center stage in a thrilling series of episodes: imprisonment, threatening death, incredible escape, and a final scene in which divine judgment is meted out on a proud oppressor (12:20-23). Though not connected with the events that immediately precede or follow it, this is the second of three rescues from prison in Acts (cf. 5:18-20; 16:23-29). With the others, it is linked with the sea rescue of chapter 27. Many words and expressions echo the arrest and trial of Jesus (Luke 22:47-54) and the earlier experiences of the apostles in Jerusalem (Acts 3—5).

OUTLINE
Healing of Aeneas at Lydda, 9:32-35

Raising of Dorcas at Joppa, 9:36-43

Conversion of Cornelius and Household, 10:1—11:18
10:1-8	Scene 1. Cornelius's Vision
10:9-16	Scene 2. Peter's Vision
10:17-23a	Scene 3. Cornelius's Men Meet Peter
10:23b-33	Scene 4. Peter Meets Cornelius
10:34-43	Scene 5. Peter's Sermon
10:44-48	Scene 6. Coming of the Holy Spirit and Baptism
11:1-18	Scene 7. Witness to the Jerusalem Elders

The Jew-Gentile Church in Antioch, 11:19-30
11:19-26	Founding of the Church
11:27-30	Famine Relief Mission to Jerusalem

Peter's Imprisonment and Deliverance, 12:1-19
  12:1-5   Arrest of Peter and Prayers for Him
  12:6-11   Peter's Deliverance by an Angel
  12:12-17   Peter's Return to the Praying Church
  12:18-19   Punishment of Sentries and Departure of Herod

The Death of Herod Agrippa I, 12:20-23

Church Growth; Return of Barnabas and Saul, 12:24-25

EXPLANATORY NOTES
Healing of Aeneas at Lydda   9:32-35

Peter is doing evangelistic work in the western areas of Judea, visiting groups of believers with teaching and healing. He comes *down* to Lydda, a town on the plain of Sharon ten miles southeast of Joppa (9:32). In OT times it was known as Lod (1 Chron. 8:12; Ezra 2:33; Neh. 11:35), a part of Samaria after the exile and then returned to the Jews in 145 B.C. While ministering in this town, Peter comes across a man with the well-known Greek name of Aeneas (9:33). Many early readers of Acts will remember the name as that of the hero of Virgil's epic poem *Aeneid*, a survivor of the Trojan War.

This Aeneas at Lydda is a paralytic, one who has been confined to his bed for eight years (9:33). Luke does not say whether or not he is a believer. Peter simply assures him that Jesus Christ is healing him and, like the cripple at the gate of the temple (3:7), the man rises immediately (9:34). The unusual expression that Peter uses, *Make your bed*, or *take care of your mat* (NIV), might also be translated *set your table* (eat). In any case, the once-paralyzed man is now completely healed, and this so impresses the local residents that people turn to the Lord in great numbers (Luke's *all* in 9:35 needs to be taken like the one in 8:1 as an expansive way of saying *many*). Again the divine purpose prevails.

Raising of Dorcas at Joppa   9:36-43

The scene now shifts to Joppa (the present Jaffa) on the Mediterranean coast some 20 miles away. The focus is on a believer there called *Tabitha* (Aramaic) or *Dorcas* (Greek). The English meaning of both names is *gazelle*, as supplied by the NRSV note, and the Hebrew equivalent *Zibiah* is in 2 Kings 12:1. She is known in the church fellowship at Joppa for her good works and many acts of charity (9:36).

The story begins after this admirable lady has died from some illness and is laid out for burial (9:37). The local believers, however, are not ready to give her up, and they send to nearby Lydda because they have heard of Peter's miracle-working ministry there (9:38). At their request, he comes at once, and they take him to the upper room, where weeping neighbors surround the corpse. These are mostly *widows* who in times past have been blessed by the expert needlework of Dorcas and are now displaying coats and other garments she has made for them (9:39). Added to the faith which made the church send for the apostle is now this mute plea to him for help.

Following the example of his Lord, Peter first has everyone leave the room (Mark 5:40). Then, after praying for her on his knees, he turns to her and commands her to arise, using her Aramaic name. His words are almost identical with those of Jesus in the case of Jairus's daughter. The Lord said, "*Talitha cumi* (girl, arise)," and Peter (assuming he speaks in Aramaic) says, *Tabitha cumi* (Tabitha, arise). Luke now adds, as vivid little touches, that she opens her eyes, looks at Peter, and sits up (9:40). Like Jesus, Peter takes her by the hand and lifts her up to new life. Then he dramatically calls in the local believers and widows to present the newly revived sister of mercy (9:41).

This is the first recorded example of raising the dead by a follower of Jesus. It fulfills a command of the Lord found in Matthew 10:8 and is in harmony with the promise in John 14:12 that those who believe in him will do his works and even greater ones. Later in Acts is the record of Paul's recovery from a condition in which he is left for dead (14:19-20) and an account in which he himself raises a person presumably dead (20:10).

Just as at Lydda (9:35), so here also a miracle worked through Peter so impresses those who hear of it that they become believers. As in 5:12-14 and 8:6, the Lord's wonders and signs are powerful instruments of evangelism (9:42). Therefore, Peter stays on in Joppa for a time and is on hand at the house of Simon the tanner for the next divine call (9:43). Tanning is one of the unclean trades. Some commentators (e.g., Harnack: 85) have taken Peter's lodging there as a sign of growing freedom from Jewish restrictions and hence a preparation for the Cornelius story that follows. On the other hand, it is doubtful that Peter the fisherman ever had such strict scruples or that Luke is trying to make a point of laxity on his part (Marshall: 180).

Conversion of Cornelius and Household   10:1—11:18

The scene suddenly shifts to Caesarea. In a series of dramatic episodes, Luke presents a major breakthrough that makes the rest of the book possible. By this time other Gentiles may have become believers: the Ethiopian in 8:38, possibly some Gentile converts of Saul initial ministry (9:20-30), or even some early ones at Antioch (11:20-21). Yet Cornelius is the showcase example, told in great detail, and one that is accepted by the church in Jerusalem. It becomes widely known that a Roman army officer is divinely led to embrace the Christian faith. This brings within sight the mission to the ends of the Roman Empire. To make this event live in the mind of the reader, Luke manages to repeat the more essential parts. Thus all of 10:9-48 is retold in condensed form in 11:4-16. One important feature, the divine message to Cornelius through an angel, is mentioned no less than four times (10:3-6, 22, 30-32; 11:13-14)! Variety and change of pace, along with surprise events and providential timings, keep the reader intrigued to the end. The outline into seven scenes is from Haenchen, elaborated on by Willimon (95-99).

10:1-8 Scene 1. Cornelius's Vision

It all begins in Caesarea, mentioned in 8:40 as the destination of Philip and in 9:30 as the place from which Saul was sent off to Tarsus. There, amid lavish palaces and public buildings, a large amphitheater and a huge temple dedicated to Caesar, the Roman governors and Herodian kings have their headquarters. It is a relatively new city, built by Herod I about fifty years earlier and now the capital of the province.

The spotlight is on Cornelius, a minor military officer, risen from the ranks, now captain over a hundred men, and a Roman citizen by virtue of his rank. He is one of six centurions serving in the *Italian Cohort*, originally recruited from Italy but now stationed in provincial Caesarea as a peace-keeping force (10:1).

Though a military man from an alien nation, he is *a devout man*, fearing God—a Gentile attracted to Judaism because of its monotheism and high ethical standards, worshiping God, but not a full proselyte or convert to Judaism. Along with that, he is known both for his generous giving and his faithful prayer life (10:2). While he is engaged in the latter, a life-changing vision comes to him, an experience which Luke now tells in great detail and will refer to three more times before he ends the account (10:22, 30-32; 11:13-18).

In broad daylight, at three o'clock in the afternoon, Cornelius *clearly sees an angel of God* come in and call him by name (10:3). The language Luke uses makes it plain that this is no mere psychological experience but an actual angelic presence (10:3). The common human reaction to the divine is great fear (Luke 1:12, 29-30; 2:9c; et al.) or *terror*, as in the case of Cornelius. With trembling he asks what this is all about, and the angel praises him for his almsgiving—the second time Luke emphasizes his piety. His *prayers* and *alms* are ascending as a *memorial before God* (10:4; cf. Lev. 2:2, RSV, "offering" is a "memorial" on the altar; Lev. 1:4, "burnt offering," Hebrew: 'olah, lit. "what ascends"). It must be reassuring to Cornelius to hear that his life and witness are known in heaven!

Then the divine messenger gives him specific instructions, including the name and address of a stranger to contact (10:5-6), much as the Lord did to Ananias in 9:11. There Saul was a feared persecutor, here Peter is unknown. In both cases adventure awaits in the house of a stranger. Wasting no time, Cornelius calls two of his trusted slaves and a God-fearing soldier from the ranks, shares the whole story with them, and sends them off to Joppa on this mysterious quest (10:7).

10:9-16 Scene 2. Peter's Vision

With the three men sent on the way, Luke now turns the reader to Peter, another pious man, who is just going up on the housetop for midday prayers at the home of Simon in Joppa (10:9). It is not one of the appointed times for such devotions but appropriate anyway, for a good Jew is to pray three times a day (Ps. 55:17; Dan. 6:10), and housetops are where one can find privacy. Peter is there praying and, as the noon meal is delayed, grows hungry. While in this condition, he is caught up in a divine ecstasy or *trance*, somewhat like a vivid dream (10:10; cf. 11:5; 22:17-21). To his amazement the heavens open and a great sheetlike apparition comes down before him full of strange creatures (10:11-12). Most mysterious of all is the Lord's command to rise, *kill and eat* (10:13).

All kinds of four-footed creatures and reptiles and birds are there, but obviously unclean. Even in a trance Peter proves himself scrupulously Jewish as he bluntly says, *No . . . , Lord!* This happens again, and this time there is an answer that will be lodged in his consciousness for a long time to come: *What God has made clean, you must not call profane!* says the voice (10:15). *Profane* or *common*

(RSV) means "unclean," as seen in 10:14 and 28, where it is applied to Gentiles. The whole procedure is repeated once more, and the sheet is taken back up into heaven (10:16). The threefold action is a mark of divine certainty in both the OT (cf. Num. 22:23-28; 24:10; 1 Kings 17:21) and the NT, as seen in the three predictions of Jesus' death (Luke 9:22, 44; 18:32), his three actions in prayer in Gethsemane (Mark 14:35-41), and the threefold restoration of Peter (John 21:15-17).

10:17-23a Scene 3. Cornelius's Men Meet Peter

God's timing is perfect. Just as the men from Cornelius arrive at the gate and call out to the house, Peter is puzzling over the meaning of his strange vision (10:17-20). It is no easy matter to deal with. Then, while he is turning it over in his mind, imagine his surprise when he looks out and sees two slaves and an armed Roman soldier there shouting his name! As a Galilean lad, he grew up not far from Sepphoris. In 4 B.C. the Romans burned that city and enslaved its inhabitants. At that time they also crucified 2,000 other Jews (Josephus, *War* 2.5.1-2; *Ant.* 17.10.5-10). No doubt Peter was conditioned to fear and to hate Romans. Such a feeling is further intensified as he recalls how Roman soldiers killed his Lord (Luke 23:33-36; cf. Acts 2:23, RSV, where he calls those soldiers *lawless men* by whose hands the Messiah was slain).

Then in the midst of such musings, the Holy Spirit tells Peter about the three at his gate, commands him to go down, greet them, and even to *go with them without hesitation*—on a trip not yet proposed to him! *The Spirit* has sent them, he is told (10:19-20). Still not knowing what this is all about, the apostle goes out to the men, tells them he is the one they are looking for, and asks the reason for their coming (10:21). The three men inform Peter (and readers once more) of Cornelius's devout character and heavenly vision, as they recount the story from the beginning (10:22). Then Peter the Jew does a surprising thing. He invites these Gentiles in to be his guests overnight! (10:23a). They even eat together. This is the first in a series of unclean-making contacts with the uncircumcised and will later be called into question by the elders at Jerusalem (11:3).

10:23b-33 Scene 4. Peter Meets Cornelius

Nothing is said about that night together, what fellowship they have, or the things they discuss. It is suddenly morning. Peter and the three Gentiles are on their way to Caesarea, accompanied by some local believers whom Peter wisely invites to go along (10:23b). Only later does Luke tell the reader that these are Jewish Christians he is taking with him (10:45), and still later that there are six of them to serve as witnesses (11:12). The next thing the reader knows, the group of ten have spent a day on the road together and *the following day* complete the 30-mile journey. Cornelius is waiting for them when they arrive, surrounded by relatives and close friends, all of them undoubtedly sympathetic to his point of view and fully aware of his vision and his sending for Peter (10:24).

Luke introduces the apostle's entrance into the house with the formal *and it came to pass* (CF; common in OT narratives but not reflected here in NRSV). It indicates a turn of events to be especially noted. To Peter's complete surprise and embarrassment, Cornelius treats him as some kind of divine visitor and falls at his feet in worship (10:25). With a touch of Jewish horror at being treated thus by any human being (cf. 14:11-18), the apostle commands him to arise. *I am only a mortal*, he declares (10:26; cf. 14:15). Imagine a Roman officer behaving like this and a Galilean fisherman giving him orders! Peter's meaning is that they should meet as equals, each serving the other under the one true God (Luke 9:48; 22:26; cf. John 15:15).

Luke pictures them carrying on animated conversation as they move into the house together and meet the others (10:27). There are two sides to this story. It is the conversion of Cornelius and company—and of Peter as well! To the assembled group, the apostle voices his amazement at all that is happening. They know how unlawful it is, he says, for a Jew *to associate with* or enter the home of any *Gentile, one of another nation* (RSV; in Hebrew and Greek, *nation* or *Gentile* translate the same word). But now *God has shown* him that he is not to call *anyone profane or unclean* (10:28).

What started out as unclean animals (in the vision) is now understood to symbolize unclean human beings, *Gentiles*. Yet there is a connection: the Pharisaic food laws make it difficult for Jews to associate with Gentiles. Peter is verbalizing the change taking place in his own attitudes. It will be years before his mind is completely transformed, as Paul's later encounter with him shows (Gal. 2:11-21). However, this is a significant start, sufficient to prepare him for surprises awaiting in the house of Cornelius (10:44-48) and for the stand he will make at Jerusalem (11:1-18; 15:6-11). This much cleared, he tells of his willingness to come and his eagerness to find out just *why* he was sent for (10:29).

Luke has the centurion reply by going back and recounting his vision of four days earlier. It is the third telling of this significant event and, while it omits a few words at the beginning, it is a faithful recap (10:30-32). The value of this repetition is its refrainlike proclamation that all this is of God and therefore right. Cornelius concludes by saying that he followed the heavenly command and Peter was good enough to come. They are all together now and ready to hear what he has come to tell them (10:33). The warm intimate contact here in the home gives a hint of the joyous new possibilities for community among believers of various backgrounds.

10:34-43 Scene 5. Peter's Sermon

The apostle's first words are a stunning confession, actually the theme of the whole book of Acts: *I truly understand that God shows no partiality* (10:34). For in every branch of the human family, God accepts anyone who (1) truly reverences God (including repentance and willingness to change) and (2) *does what is right* (is forgiven and bears the fruit of repentance; 10:35). What a basis for worldwide evangelism!

Then, in this digest of Peter's speech, Luke presents the high points of the kerygma or proclamation of the gospel of Jesus Christ. It began in Galilee with the Lord's baptism and anointing with the Holy Spirit, manifested in his *doing good and healing,* and moved swiftly on to his death, resurrection, and command to witness (10:36-42). Within this framework, the sermon emphasizes that God is the one who sent Israel this message of salvation by Jesus Christ, *Lord of all,* who was *preaching peace* (10:36). This summary word *peace* is rich in scriptural concepts. In Isaiah *shalom,* "peace," is equated with "good news" and "salvation" (52:7), and the ends of the earth shall eventually see it! (52:10).

Nor is this a proclamation of the gospel in word only. True to Luke's opening sentence of Acts (1:1), Peter speaks of what Jesus did as well as what he taught (10:38). Moreover, the apostles are witnesses of all these things and especially chosen to bear testimony of them to the people (10:39-42). The focus is on Jesus, *ordained by God* to judge *the living and the dead.* And the scriptural proof is the prophets who proclaimed Jesus and, through him, faith and *the forgiveness of sins* (10:43).

10:44-48 Scene 6. Coming of the Holy Spirit and Baptism

Peter is still preaching when heaven intervenes. It is the most breathtaking surprise of the book. At this moment the Holy Spirit literally falls on these Gentiles! (10:44). And it is not on Cornelius only, but on *all who heard the word.* The six Jewish believers are completely stunned to hear these Gentiles praising God in *tongues* as the 120 did on the Day of Pentecost (10:45-46). God really is in control and bringing about a revolution in human history!

Once Peter catches his breath, he voices the conviction of everyone present (and of Luke and every reader). These people, though Gentiles, have been accepted by the great God of the universe and sealed by baptism in the Holy Spirit just as much as the apostles have! They are just as truly believers as anyone on the Day of Pentecost. The wind has blown where it wills (John 3:8), and all must face the new reality. *Can anyone withhold the water?* (10:47; cf. the similar formulaic question in 8:36). So Peter promptly has them baptized in the name of Jesus Christ. What has happened is so wonderful that he cannot leave at once but stays on *for several days* enjoying the fellowship now created by the Spirit—and no doubt transgressing some food laws (10:48).

11:1-18 Scene 7. Witness to the Jerusalem Elders

The first six scenes tell the action and now, in the final episode, comes the reaction. Word gets back to Jerusalem before Peter does. Just as echoes of the strange new workings of the Spirit in Samaria reached the mother church almost at once (8:14), so also here *the apostles and the believers . . . in Judea* receive word that Gentiles have now become believers (11:1). So Peter faces a serious problem when he returns. Luke says it is *the circumcised believers* who confront him with the question. *Why did you go to uncircumcised men and eat with them* (11:3)?

This is the first mention of such a circumcised group of disciples. In Acts 15:5, Luke speaks of believers as belonging to *the sect of the Pharisees* and in 21:20 as *zealous for the law.* Though they criticize Peter for eating with Gentiles, the real problem is the deeper one of circumcision, as can be seen from the account in 15:1-5. For them the rite of circumcision was given as an eternal sign and seal of God's covenant, never to be broken (Gen. 17:9-14), and therefore Peter's action is against the will of the Lord and quite inexcusable.

The apostle's reply to such charges is classic. Instead of arguing the case in any way, he simply tells the story of what has happened. This gives Luke a chance to brief the reader once more on the essential facts and make it clear that opening the door to Gentiles is God's action, not Peter's. The recap, as reported, is about one-fourth the length of the original story, but in the actual telling no doubt included all the details necessary for a full understanding. The statement that the Holy Spirit fell as Peter *began to speak* (11:15) does not contradict the account in 10:34-44 if it is remembered that *began to* is a fairly common Semitic idiom meaning simply that he was not yet finished (Bruce: 235, n. 13; Marshall: 197).

Peter's addition in 11:16 of the Lord's word of promise from Acts 1:5 that they would soon be baptized with the Holy Spirit prepares the group for his next statement: God gave these Gentiles the same gift as he did the apostles at Pentecost. Most of the hearers remember this well. So, to clinch the argument, Peter simply asks, *Who was I that I could hinder God?* (11:17). The whole presentation is convincing and, for the present at least, they are all silenced and even praise God for what he has done. They realize that the way is now open for even Gentiles to repent and find eternal life (11:18).

Though Luke has the Cornelius cycle of stories end on this positive note, the issue is far from settled. It will come up again forcefully in Acts 15. In fact, it will continue to be a problem for a long time to come, as can be seen in 21:20-36 and in Galatians 2:11-21; 5:2-12; 6:12-17.

The Jew-Gentile Church in Antioch   11:19-30

11:19-26 Founding of the Church

Luke now takes the reader back to the situation recorded in 8:4, where those driven out of Jerusalem after the death of Stephen *went from place to place, proclaiming the word*. Here he begins a story parallel to that of Philip (8:5-40). This time unnamed Hellenist (Greek-speaking) believers make their way up the coast to Phoenicia, some going by way of the island of Cyprus in the Mediterranean and others continuing on to Antioch of Syria. The work of these refugees in Phoenicia is reflected in the later existence of a church there (15:3; 21:2-4). As good Jews, they at first evangelize only among fellow Jews (11:19).

Luke is not too specific, but some of these same persons, or others originating in Cyprus or Cyrene in northern Africa, break across religious and ethnic lines when they reach Antioch and witness as well to *Greeks* (11:20, NRSV note; Metzger: 389, Greek-speaking persons, a mixed population of Jews and Gentiles). The response is unusually good, the first known large ingathering among non-Jews. What happened in a small way at the house of Cornelius is now start- ing to become a movement, thoroughly in line with the commission of 1:8 and something Luke sees as *the hand of the Lord* (11:21). The work of converting Gentiles, along with Jews, will indeed become a major activity in Acts, from chapter 13 to the end.

Luke's first readers will know about this Antioch on the Orontes, third largest city of the empire, with a population of half a million, including many Jews. Founded around 300 B.C. and capital of the old Seleucid empire, it is now the seat of the Roman provincial administration of Syria. There could be no more strategic place in the eastern part of the empire for the new faith to gain a foothold. Though located 22 miles up the river, Antioch has a harbor on the Mediterranean that is the center of travel and trade between the east and the west. Like every great Roman city, it is known for its lax morals, but now it begins to hear a new message. In time it will become the capital of Gentile Christianity. Here will arise the con- troversy whose solution determines the future of the faith (15:1-35), and here Saul-Paul's major missionary journeys will begin (13:2; 15:39-40; 18:23) and most of them end (14:26-28; 18:22).

For the third time in this section of Acts, Luke tells of the supervi- sion of the Jerusalem church over new evangelistic ventures in outly- ing areas. In 8:14, that church sent Peter and John to oversee matters in Samaria. In 11:2-18, they questioned Peter about his receiving Cornelius and household into the faith. Now to investigate the new developments here at Antioch, they send Barnabas (11:22). He is a man already known to the reader as generous (4:36-37) and a helper of the newly converted (9:27). Luke introduces him once more. Being from Cyprus, he is able to identify with this new movement which some of his fellow countrymen have fostered. More than that, he is a man of the future for what he will do in mission work with Saul-Paul (chaps. 13—14) and for his help in making the council of Jerusalem a success (15:1-4).

Luke then adds to the reader's knowledge and appreciation of Barnabas an account of his joy over the Gentiles being converted. He is portrayed as the ideal person to exhort and encourage them because of his character (*a good man*) and his spiritual qualifications (*full of the Holy Spirit and of faith*). This is followed by a typical Lucan statement about a large number being added to the Lord

(11:23-24; cf. 2:41, 47; 5:14).

During this large ingathering among Gentiles, the idea comes to Barnabas that he should look up the young convert, Saul of Tarsus. Ten or more years have gone by since he was sent off to his home in Tarsus (9:30), and Luke seems to have no informatiom about his activities during these "silent years" of his life. The fact that there are enough Gentile Christians in Cilicia for the Jerusalem council to include them in the letter of 15:23 may well indicate that Saul has been busy making converts in his own province.

At any rate, Barnabas is led of the Lord to go and hunt for Saul (11:25). The Greek verb here is the one used of Joseph and Mary searching everywhere for the boy Jesus (Luke 2:44) and, in the secular literature of the day, of tracking down runaway slaves or criminals. Finding Saul apparently takes some time, for Luke repeats the idea in 11:26, *and when he had found him.* Once Barnabas locates him, then, he persuades him to come to Antioch. There a great future awaits him, as the reader either already knows or has learned to expect from Luke's narrative style.

For a whole year Barnabas and Saul work together at Antioch, with major emphasis on instructing the new group in the way of the Lord (11:26). Saul's rabbinic skills combined with Barnabas' ability to strengthen persons result in a robust interracial church. Here the Jew-Gentile issue will later be raised and debated with some vigor (chap. 15; Gal. 2:11-14).

Luke reports that in Antioch, for the first time, the disciples of the Lord are called *Christians* (11:26). The meaning of this name and the reasons for its use have been much discussed. There are two general views. One is that the people of the city give them this designation, and the other holds that they themselves choose it. In favor of the former, the majority view, is the fact that the *-ianos* suffix often means "party of." Thus it would be a likely name for outsiders to give Jesus' disciples to distinguish them from (other) Jews who reject Jesus as Messiah but with whom the disciples otherwise have so much in common. Christians are the Christ-party, those who identify Jesus as the Messiah-Christ and base their whole faith on him. Such a name might be one of reproach, or simply a factual description of what the church stands for.

On the other hand, some scholars have pointed out that the verb translated *were called* (*chrēmatisai*) literally means "to do business." Thus it might have been chosen by Christ's followers to indicate the banner under which they do business or operate. Though no final judgment can be made, it is clear that the believers accept the name and regard it as one under which they can glorify God (1 Pet. 4:16). It is used in only one additional text in the NT: Acts 26:28, where Agrippa II will call Paul's line of persuasion *Christian*. This naming shows that *Christ* is becoming a proper name and not just a title (Munck, 1967:106).

11:27-30 Famine Relief Mission to Jerusalem

Luke uses the general phrase *at that time* to indicate that during the year Barnabas and Saul are working together at Antioch, Christian prophets come to the city from Jerusalem with a message (11:27). Peter, quoting Joel, has spoken of prophecy as one of the gifts of the Spirit and given his own prophecy of future spiritual endowment (2:18, 39). Thus from that Pentecost onward, there have been believers with prophetic messages for the church. Such messages would often combine predictions of events to come with exhortation, as here. (For a more detailed discussion, see 1 Cor. 12:10; 14:1-5, 22-33. The rank of a prophet is next to that of an apostle, according to 1 Cor.12:28; Eph. 4:11).

The chief spokesperson of this group is one named Agabus, who will enter the story again as a prophet in 21:10-14. The burden of his message on this occasion is the prediction of a worldwide famine (11:28). While there is evidence of recurring famines during the reign of Claudius (A.D. 41-54), in 45-46 an unusual period of drought and failure in the annual inundation of the Nile causes a famine in Egypt, which cuts short the supply of grain for Rome. At the same time, Syria-Palestine is experiencing drought (Josephus, *Ant.* 20.2.5), so Luke's phrase *famine over all the world* is an apt description, as they see it.

The Antioch Christians take this prophecy seriously and decide to send relief (probably in the form of money) to the believers in Judea, where the crop failures are known to be the most severe (11:29). Jerusalem has been looking after the young church spiritually (11:22-24), and now the daughter congregation sends material aid to the mother church. Paul later will urge this kind of mutual sharing to the benefit of both givers and receivers (2 Cor. 8:13-15; 9:11-14). It is only logical that the bearer of these gifts be Barnabas, their respected leader from Jerusalem, and his junior partner Saul (11:30). How skillfully Luke prepares the reader for the partnership of these leading personalities of chapters 13—14! This is the first mention of the *elders* at Jerusalem, who from now on function alongside the apostles (15:4, 6, 22-23; 16:4; 21:18) as the administrators of the church. In this case, they seem to be continuing the work of the seven in the distribution of relief (cf. 6:3-6).

This relief mission to Jerusalem provides opportunity for Barnabas and Saul to confer with the church leaders there. The report of the visit is completed in 12:25 (see the notes on that verse).

Peter's Imprisonment and Deliverance 12:1-19

12:1-5 Arrest of Peter and Prayers for Him

Luke now resumes the narrative series about Peter which he interrupted after 11:18 to tell the story of Antioch (11:19-30). *About that time*, he says, *Herod the king* begins an attack on the leaders of the church (12:1). This is *Herod Agrippa I*, grandson of Herod the Great (Luke 1:5) through Aristobulus and therefore a nephew of Herod Antipas, tetrarch of Galilee during Jesus' ministry (Luke 3:19; 9:7). Born in 10 B.C., he has been brought up largely in Rome, a boyhood friend of Claudius and later a friend of Gaius Caesar, who as Emperor Caligula in A.D. 37 has made him a puppet king. By the time of our story, Agrippa has helped Claudius become emperor, and Claudius has added Judea and Samaria to Agrippa's territory (A.D. 41-44). Now his rule almost equals that of his grandfather. Like all Herods, he is vain and corrupt. He maintains his present position by courting the Jews, who tolerate him because he is descended from the revered Maccabean-Hasmonean line of kings through his grandmother Mariamne.

In his effort to please the Jews, he kills James the son of Zebedee *with the sword* (12:2). This is the first of the apostles to be martyred (in about A.D. 44). Discovering that this illegal and high-handed act of murder (cf. Haenchen: 382) wins him further favor, Herod sets out to kill off other church leaders. He next seizes the prominent apostle Peter (12:3). Since the days of Unleavened Bread (Passover) have begun, he cannot put his prisoner on trial at once, so has him thrown in prison under heavy guard. After the festival he intends to bring him out and deal with him as he did with James (12:4). This is not a general persecution of the church like that under Saul (8:1-4; 9:1-2) but one aimed at select leaders.

By the mention of Unleavened Bread, Luke is reminding his readers that it was at this season that Jesus was arrested and crucified (Luke 22:1, 7). But, unlike his Lord, Peter is spared for the time being, and earnest, continuous prayer for him is made by the church (12:5). Peter is probably imprisoned in the fortress of Antonia (the majority view) or perhaps in Herod's palace. More important to the story is the number of soldiers guarding him. Four are on duty at a time, one on each side of him and two at his cell door, with changes every three hours, especially at night. The fact that he has already escaped from prison once (5:19) may have led to the unusual precautions now. At any rate, Luke has prepared his reader for a supreme contest between the praying church and the wicked king doing his utmost to destroy Peter.

12:6-11 Peter's Deliverance by an Angel

Again Luke shows that God's timing is perfect. On the very night when the king is to bring Peter out for trial and execution, the prayers of the church are answered! During the darkest hours, the apostle is sleeping between two guards and bound to each with chains. Two other armed soldiers block the door of the cell (12:6). There is no human way for Peter to escape.

Then an angel of the Lord appears in a bright light and frees the prisoner with a single blow. The dazed man is awakened, his chains are struck from his wrists, and he is ordered to dress, all in quick order (12:7-8). The guards at the door give no trouble as the apostle follows the angel out of the prison. The outer gate is mysteriously opened as by an unseen hand, and they are soon on the city streets (12:9-10). Luke records the lively orders of the angel and the feelings of the gradually awakening Peter, as apparently later reported by Peter himself. It is a real deliverance, not a mere vision or psychological experience (12:9). The apostle puts into words what Luke has woven into the narrative all along: that the Lord has indeed rescued him from the hand of Herod and from the expectations of his enemies, fellow Jews (12:11).

12:12-17 Peter's Return to the Praying Church

Luke next turns from miraculous deliverance to an inside view of one of the praying groups. Here is the delightfully human church caught by surprise, a story of real people told with feeling and humor. In it, Peter, having fully come to himself after his bewildering rescue, seeks refuge in a home he knows, that of Mary, mother of John Mark (12:12). Prayer for his release is still going on inside while he stands at the outer gate knocking and apparently calling for someone to come and let him in.

On duty is a servant girl, or perhaps a member of the household, named Rhoda ("rosebud" or "little rose," an apt designation for a lively maid). She hears the knocking and comes running (12:13). Recognizing the familiar voice, she suddenly realizes that their prayers have been answered. Peter is here! *Overjoyed, instead of opening the gate,* she leaves the church's leading apostle standing there and runs to tell the others (12:14; cf. Luke 24:41, the disciples "were disbelieving" "in their joy" at the sudden appearance of the risen Lord).

The humor of the situation reaches its peak as these praying Christians tell her she is crazy! When that doesn't seem right in the face of her insistence that Peter really is there, they say it must be his angel (12:15). Belief in guardian angels, who apparently can assume the form of the person being protected, is common among the devout of this time (Gen. 48:16; Dan. 3:28; 6:22; mentioned by Jesus in Matt. 18:10 and accepted in Heb. 1:14).

Luke extends the ironical scene. Peter, the very man for whom they have been praying, is left standing out in the street, knocking and calling loudly. Finally members of the group come and open to him, amazed that their prayers have been so miraculously answered! (12:16). Even after he is inside, the apostle has difficulty getting them quieted down so he can tell of the Lord's great work. At the end he tells them to report this to James and other members of the church. Then out the door he goes! (12:17).

Thus Luke informs his readers that this praying group is only one among many and that James, the Lord's brother, has risen to a position of leadership. His key role becomes evident at the council of Jerusalem (15:13-29) and continues for many years (21:18-25; cf. also 1 Cor. 15:7; Gal. 1:19; 2:9, 12). Also underscored here is the need for Peter to leave at once, presumably for parts unknown. That Herod is angry at his escape is seen in the episode that follows (12:18-19). Luke's next mention of the apostle will be his appearance at the Jerusalem council in 15:7-11.

12:18-19 *Punishment of Sentries and Departure of Herod*

The morning after Peter's deliverance, a great commotion occurs among the prison guards. They can't imagine what has happened to their chained and closely watched prisoner (12:18). Since he is obviously at large somewhere, he must be found at once or there will be serious trouble! Herod Agrippa sends out a search party, perhaps several of them, but with no success. The next thing to do is to call in the sentries on duty that night and question them carefully. They are as surprised as anyone over the escape and can add nothing to the investigation. This puts them under the penalty prescribed by Roman law that any guard who allows a person to escape must suffer the same punishment as that to be meted out to the prisoner (cf. the later Code of Justinian 60.4.4). Fear of such a fate will put terror in the heart of the Philippian jailer in the story of 16:27-30.

The threat is now carried out by Herod Agrippa as he orders that the guards on duty when Peter escaped be put to death. Agrippa has intended that fate for the apostle as soon as Passover ended (12:4). Though their death is not actually mentioned, no doubt the order is carried out and the men are killed. Then, after this matter is taken care of and his work in Jerusalem apparently finished for the present, the king returns to headquarters in Caesarea, where he remains for awhile (he in 12:19, NRSV note, RSV, Greek—meaning Herod, not Peter as in NRSV text).

The Death of Herod Agrippa I   12:20-23

For this one episode of Acts, there is a parallel account in the writings of Josephus (Ant. 19.8.2). Thus we have both a Christian and a Roman interpretation of the last days of the king. Each is told from its own perspective. For Luke, this is the judgment of God upon an enemy of the faith who sets out to destroy a leading apostle, and as a consequence he meets a sudden and horrible death. In the Josephus account, Herod Agrippa I is a Roman puppet king who, in the act of honoring the emperor with festal games, impiously accepts divine worship for himself. A victim of fate, he is seized with violent pains and dies after five days of intense suffering.

As indicated by Luke, the historical situation is that of an angry struggle between Herod Agrippa and the Phoenician cities of Tyre and Sidon over grain supplies they receive from his province of Galilee. The Phoenicians seek to resolve the crisis by suing for peace through Blastus, Herod's chamberlain or trusted personal servant (12:20, NIV). So the king sets a day on which to give them an elaborate royal audience, possibly the emperor's birthday (Bruce: 256). Josephus mentions the celebration of games and the large crowd of administrative officials present at Caesarea. Both writers tell of

Herod's pompous display, his royal robes made, according to Josephus, "entirely of silver of altogether wonderful weaving." The robe is shining and glittering in the sun with resplendence that inspires "a sort of fear and trembling in those who gaze at them." Luke suggests Herod's showmanship in sitting upon his throne, a raised seat of honor in the arena.

Then Herod addresses the assemblage with a flowery oration (12:21). In both accounts it is the flattery of the crowd that goes to his head. *The voice of a god, and not of a mortal!* they shout (12:22). Josephus says they invoke Herod as a god, saying that henceforth they "acknowledge him to be of more than mortal nature." Worst of all, Herod does not rebuke them for their impious flattery. We are disgusted by the sheer hypocrisy of it all. After his death, reports Josephus, the majority of the people revile him, remove the statues of his daughters, and put them up in brothels.

Both sources tell how Herod is struck down by a serious illness. Luke attributes it to an angel of the Lord, not in visible form as in 12:7-11, but in direct divine retribution like the smiting of Nebuchadnezzar and Belshazzar (Dan. 4:28-33; 5:22-30). Josephus appeals to the Roman mind by telling how Herod first sees an owl sitting on a rope above his head, a bird which on an earlier occasion had been the messenger of release but if seen again would be an omen of death (*Ant.* 19.8.2).

Luke describes the attack as Herod being *eaten by worms* (12:23). Josephus speaks of it as "a severe pain in the belly" which begins with a violent attack and keeps Herod in pain until his death five days later. *Worms* were known to be the final devourer of mortal bodies (Isa. 51:8; 66:24; Mark 9:48) and the cause of the death of other tyrants like Antiochus IV (2 Macc. 9:5-29, "the Lord . . . struck him") and Herod the Great (Josephus, *Ant* 17.6.5). Thus Luke's mention of this from his sources may mean either that Agrippa belongs in that company of kings aspiring to be gods or that this is an actual physician's diagnosis. There have been several modern attempts to determine the nature of the attack, such as internal rupture, appendicitis leading to peritonitus, or a cyst produced by tapeworm (Neill: 152).

Church Growth; Return of Barnabas and Saul 12:24-25

Luke now rounds out this phase of the history with another of his summaries on the growth of the church. There are no details given in this shortest and last one of the series (12:24)

Then Luke prepares the reader for the events to follow (chap. 13) by recording the return of Barnabas and Saul *from Jerusalem* to Antioch after fulfilling their relief mission at Jerusalem (12:25, RSV, rather than NRSV *to Jerusalem*; cf. 11:29-30). Perhaps during this visit to Jerusalem of 11:30—12:25, some of the conversations of Galatians 2:1-10 take place (on this matter, see TBC of part 7 on 13:1—15:35, "Relationship of Acts 15 to Galatians 2"). If so, the leaders at Jerusalem recognize Paul as being sent to take the gospel to the Gentiles without requiring circumcision of them. Paul promises to "remember the poor." He is "eager" to do just that, as the present famine relief visit proves. This agreement may be behind the collection mentioned openly in the letters and barely noticed in Acts (see notes on 20:1-3; 21:24; 24:17).

Of importance for the ongoing story is the report that they bring back with them to Antioch a young man, *John,* whose other name is *Mark* (12:25). *John* is from the Hebrew *Yohanan,* meaning "Yahweh has shown grace," and is a common name among Jews of the time. *Mark* is one of the most common of Latin names, *Marcus,* by which the young man will usually be known in the larger Roman world. This practice of having two or more names in such a multicultured society has already been seen in 1:23, where Joseph (Hebrew) was also called Barsabbas (Aramaic) and Justus (Latin). Another fact about John called Mark is that he is a "cousin" of Barnabas (Col. 4:10) and the son of *Mary* of Jerusalem (Acts 12:12). Those family connections no doubt have something to do with his being taken along with Barnabas and Saul, as do the duties he will perform on that journey (see notes on 13:5).

THE TEXT IN ITS BIBLICAL CONTEXT
Jew Meets Gentile, and God Prevails

The dramatic significance of Peter being sent to Cornelius can hardly be overstated. It is one more step in the fulfillment of prophecies like those of Isaiah 42:6 and 49:6. The Servant of the Lord (*Israel,* and then *Jesus* as the embodiment of the best in Israel) is to become "a light to the Gentiles." "The ends of the earth shall see the salvation of our God" (Isa. 52:10). Foreigners and others outside the covenant will be gathered into the house of the Lord (Isa. 56:1-8). Yet such ingathering is in direct contrast to the exclusive spirit of Ezra and Nehemiah (as in Neh. 13:23-31) and the cluttered Court of the

Gentiles, which kept the temple from being a house of prayer for all nations (Luke 19:45-46 ‖ Mark 11:15-17; cf. Swartley: 169-171).

Peter confesses that he has prejudices against all things profane or common and unclean (including uncircumcised people; 10:14, 28). Such thinking has come to him quite honestly from home train-ing, the reading of the OT in the synagogue, and the influence of Jewish society about him. Among all the uncircumcised, for him the worst are the Romans. They are the ones who conquered Israel, desecrated the temple, introduced many unclean pagan practices, and in the crucifixion of Jesus, have aided the enemies of the faith by killing the Messiah. Then among the Romans, it is the *military* which he fears and hates the most, since their main reason for being in the land is to keep down Jewish hotheads like himself.

So what does the Lord do? He sends Peter to a *Roman military man*, and an officer at that! True, Cornelius is an upright and devout person, the only kind that would have a chance of being accepted into the Christian fold. Even then there are some deep-seated suspicions to be overcome, and the genius of this story is seen in the step-by-step fashion in which God deals with Peter's prejudices.

Intercessory Prayer

Prayer has always been a vital part of the lives of God's people. Both OT and NT have many stories of praise, thanksgiving, and earnest petition. Intercession is also found, but for the most part, it is *individual*. Examples are Abraham pleading for Sodom and Gomor-rah (Gen. 18: 22-33), Amos beseeching the Lord to spare Israel (Amos 7:1-3), or Jesus praying for Peter that his faith not fail (Luke 22:32). There are surprisingly few examples of *group intercession* for persons in great need or undergoing trial, such as in 12:5-17. The church prays continuously and earnestly for the release of Peter. Such intercessory prayer may be implied in 4:23-31, where the church prays for more boldness in witness. Yet the account does not explicitly say that they intercede for the apostles while they are in prison or on trial.

Perhaps the closest biblical parallel is that of Esther 4:15-17, where all the Jews fasted for three days and nights and presumably prayed as they did so. Meanwhile, Esther went in to petition the king on behalf of her people. There must have been hundreds of other occasions of corporate intercession for persons being put to the test or in trouble, but few accounts of such are to be found in the Bible.

Thus Luke's description of the church at prayer for Peter is as significant as it is unique.

God's People and a Wicked King

Luke's theme of a divine purpose which prevails in spite of the overwhelming power of a wicked ruler is a continuation of the record of the OT. Abram, chosen of Yahweh to father a great nation, had four eastern kings and their armies delivered into his hand by God (Gen. 14:13-16). When all escape seemed impossible, Moses and the fleeing Israelites were miraculously rescued from the hosts of Pharaoh (Exod. 14:10-31). Similarly, in the days of Hezekiah, all Jerusalem seemed doomed to destruction by the hordes of Sennacherib. The Lord sent an angel to put the enemy to flight by slaying 185,000 of them in one night (2 Kings 18:13—19:37). Though the nations rage and the kings of the earth set themselves against the Lord and his Anointed, God laughs at them from heaven and holds them in derision (Ps. 2:1-4).

Luke underscores this theme in the Song of Mary, "He has brought down the powerful from their thrones, and lifted up the lowly" (Luke 1:52). Now in Acts he dramatizes it unforgettably in the story of the wicked King Herod (a name which conjures up memories of both his grandfather Herod I and his uncle Herod Antipas). Here is a puppet king who struts like a tyrant, reaches out to kill off the chief apostle of the Lord's Anointed, accepts divine honors, and ends up eaten by worms, dying an ignominious death (chap. 12)!

THE TEXT IN THE LIFE OF THE CHURCH
Going About Doing Good

A vital part of the believers church tradition has been an emphasis on doing the works of Christ and his followers, especially deeds of compassion. Help for refugees, feeding the hungry, hospital and rehabilitation programs of various sorts, counseling centers—these and other projects have been distinctive and precious aspects of the witness. Sometimes those engaging in such activities have been labeled do-gooders, a term of reproach from some who put the emphasis elsewhere in their ministries. Coupled with this is often the charge that such people are guilty of "work's righteousness" or trying to earn their way into the kingdom.

Such criticisms need to be taken seriously and examined carefully for whatever truth they may contain. Peter, in his kerygma (gospel proclamation) to Cornelius, says that Jesus *went about doing good* (10:38). On one hand, this seems to make the Lord himself the role model for do-gooders. The same verse states, however, that Jesus' good works were the *result* of his being *anointed . . . with the Holy Spirit and with power.* Jesus' place in the kingdom was already assured, and this was the fruit of his relationship with God, not a means of obtaining right relationship.

So far as the larger theological question of the place of grace, faith, and works in salvation is concerned, the statement in Ephesians 2:8-10 is most helpful. There Christian readers are told that they are saved "by grace" "through faith," and not by their own doing; so "no one may boast." Entrance into the kingdom is the *gift* of God. Yet, once believers are in the kingdom, they should understand themselves as God's workmanship, "created in Christ Jesus for good works," the service which the Lord has "prepared beforehand" for Christians to do after conversion. Such works may then, in turn, be the means of winning others to the kingdom, as was the case with Jesus and has always has been with his true disciples.

Christian and the Antioch Experience

The fact that the name *Christian* is first used in the Antioch situation has some interesting implications for the church today. Although little is known for sure about the circumstances, the designation is meant to identify these people. And what is that identity? (1) They are *international and interracial* in character. They have crossed the Jew-Gentile barrier and are no longer a narrow ethnic clique. (2) They are also the product of recent evangelistic efforts. This means there is an *eagerness* about them to hear the gospel, coupled with the *zeal* of the newly converted. (3) That they continue to grow in numbers is a sign that they are also *witnessing* Christians themselves, sharing the good news with others. (4) In addition to all this, the story of their sending relief money to the needy in Judea shows that they are *caring and generous.* Taken all together, what better description could there be of a truly *Christian* church than one which embodies these four characteristics?

Mutual Aid and Relief

The fourth item listed above, that of sending relief to Judea, rings a loud bell in the Anabaptist-Brethren tradition. From their very beginning, the believers church groups have been moved to share with others in need. Often it has taken the form of *mutual aid*, in which they help other members of the fellowship or neighbors outside the church in time of disaster. Houses and outbuildings have been rebuilt after a fire or tornado, corncribs filled, silos replenished, and household food restocked. Needy families have found kind hands bringing in supplies of all kinds.

Relief goods and money have been sent by individuals, congregations, and whole denominations to persons at a distance, whether the need was due to famine, the ravages of weather or natural disturbances, or the result of war. Particularly significant has been the witness of the historic peace churches in sending aid and personnel to nations regarded as "enemies," thus fulfilling the command to "love your enemies," do good to them, and feed them (Luke 6:27-29; Rom. 12:20-21). Especially meaningful have been many projects of reconstruction where material aid and Christian presence have combined to bind up the wounds of war and open ways to reconciliation.

Divine Guidance Today

Both the story of Cornelius and that of the deliverance of Peter from prison raise the question of direct divine guidance in our day. Can Christians now expect to receive visions, hear messages from the Lord, and have angels visit them to bring direction or deliverance? Two general groups would say no. One would be the so-called rational or humanistic school of thought that regards these as mythological aspects of the ancient story, to be left behind as Christianity advances. The other school of thought believes in the validity of such divine experiences but would tend to confine them to the first-century church. (See Part 2, TLC, "Pentecost for First Century Only?" p. 56, for a discussion of such "dispensationalism.")

A third position is one more in harmony with believers church thinking. It says that such methods of divine guidance can happen in our times and, on occasion, do happen. According to this view, the NT is the rule of faith and practice for Christians. Thus activities of the Holy Spirit and direct expressions of the divine are operative in our times as well as in the early church. This, however, is no blanket endorsement of all kinds of ignorance or gullibility. As in the days of Jesus, believers must take care today not to go to extremes by demanding signs or reveling in the miraculous (Luke 11:16, 29; John 4:48). Yet basic spirituality and divine workings have not changed through the centuries. On occasion the Lord, in harmony with divine purposes, does give audible or visual signs in our day—guiding, protecting, and delivering persons in unexpected ways. Moreover, there would be even more of this sort of experience on the part of believers today were it not for widespread skepticism (cf. Luke 4:24; Mark 6:6; Matt. 13:58b).

Part 7

First Mission of
Witness to the
Gentile World

Acts 13:1—15:35

PREVIEW

At this point Luke begins a significant new phase of the witness *to the ends of the earth* (1:8). He has traced the spread of the gospel into Judea and Samaria; has brought Saul-Paul, the man of the future, well on his way as a Christian leader; and has described the founding of the church at Antioch, the base for future missionary activity. Now the reader is ready for a bold new thrust and will not be disappointed.

Here is the first intentional mission in Acts, one directed by the Holy Spirit and therefore part of the master plan. Yet there is throughout a built-in tension. This is due partly to uncertainty as to how the work may be accomplished. Then, in addition, there is great opposition to be met. The section we are considering includes the traditional first missionary journey of Paul, plus the council of Jerusalem that follows it and deals with problems it raises.

Some remarkable events take place in these chapters. Barnabas and Saul are formally called and consecrated for a mission which takes them to into essentially non-Jewish lands (13:1-3). They are accompanied by young John Mark, destined, according to tradition, to play a significant role in the writing of the NT (13:5-13). On this journey they meet and overcome an antagonistic magician and have contact with the first high Roman official of Acts (13:6-12). Saul, called by his Roman name *Paul* from 13:9 on, becomes the central character for the rest of the book.

Here is the first example of Paul's preaching in the synagogues of the dispersion (13:16b-41). In this encounter we see the pattern of response found from this time on: favorable reception by some of the Jews and many of the God-fearers and Gentiles, with bitter opposi-

146

tion from the majority of the house of Israel (13:14-51). Then chapter 15 tells how the mission of Paul and Barnabas to the Gentiles is finally validated by the Jerusalem elders. This is a continuation of the supervision of Jerusalem over the spread of the gospel to outlying areas, as already seen in the case of Samaria (8:14-25), Caesarea (11:1-18), and Antioch (11:22-26). The great significance of this action will be discussed in the notes on 15:1-35.

Structurally, chapters 13 and 14 are a major narrative segment, carefully crafted by Luke with an introduction (13:1-3) and conclusion (14:27-28). Close examination also reveals that this section has significant parallels to the early ministry of Jesus as well as to that of Peter in Acts 2—4. In all three missions, there is first a *commissioning* by the action of the Spirit (Acts 13:1-3; cf. Luke 4:18-21; Acts 2:1-4), a *public proclamation* (Acts 13:26-41; Luke 4:21; Acts 2:14-16), and a *scriptural quotation* to interpret it (Acts 13:47; Luke 4:18-19; Acts 2:17-21). In all three narratives, these events lead to *opposition* (Acts 13:45-52; Luke 4:24-30; Acts 4:1-3) and a mention of the *inclusion of Gentiles* as a part of God's plan (Acts 13:46-48; Luke 4:25-28; Acts 2:39; 3:25-27). Then, strangely enough, there is the healing of a lame man in each larger context (Acts 14:8-10; Luke 5:17-26; Acts 3:1-10).

OUTLINE
Mission from Antioch and Return   13:1—14:28

Commissioning of Barnabas and Saul, 13:1-3

Witness of Barnabas and Saul on Cyprus, 13:4-12

Paul and Barnabas at Pisidian Antioch, 13:13-52
13:13-16a	In the Synagogue
13:16b-41	Paul's Message
13:42-43	Favorable Response
13:44-50	Opposition, a New Church, Departure

Further Witness in the Galatian Highlands, 14:1-23
14:1-7	Paul and Barnabas at Iconium
14:8-20a	Paul and Barnabas at Lystra
14:20b-23	Derbe; Backtracking to Pisidian Antioch

Return to Syrian Antioch and Report, 14:24-28

The Council of Jerusalem 15:1-35

Dispute over Circumcision for Gentiles, 15:1-5
15:1-2   Dissension in Antioch
15:3-5   Witness on the Way and Dialogue in Jerusalem

Jerusalem Meeting of Church Leaders, 15:6-21
15:6-12   Peter's Testimony to the Apostles and Elders
15:13-21   Barnabas and Paul Report; James's Key Speech

What Seems Good to the Spirit and the Church, 15:22-35
15:22-29   The Decision of the Council
15:30-35   The Letter Delivered to Antioch

EXPLANATORY NOTES

Mission from Antioch and Return
13:1—14:28

Commissioning of Barnabas and Saul 13:1-3

Barnabas and Saul have returned from Jerusalem (12:25) and are two among the five leaders in this fast-growing Christian church. They are called *prophets*, gifted charismatic leaders endowed by the Holy Spirit to speak for God about both present and future matters (see notes on 11:27-30), and *teachers*, Spirit-led interpreters of the Word whether written or oral (cf. Rom. 12:6-8; 1 Cor. 12:28; Eph. 4:11). While some of them may function more in one capacity than the other, as a group they minister in both areas (13:1).

The first-named, *Barnabas*, is by now well known to the reader. *Symeon* (or Simon) *who was called Niger* may be the Simon of Cyrene, father of Alexander and Rufus, who carried the cross of Jesus (Mark 15:20), but this cannot be proved. The name *Niger* (Latin for "black") may or may not have anything to do with the man's color. The third-named, *Lucius of Cyrene*, has sometimes been identified with the man Paul mentions in Romans 16:21 as his "relative," or with Luke himself, said to have been from Antioch; but both these possibilities are purely conjectural. The fourth leader listed is surprising in this company. *Manaean a member of the court of Herod the tetrarch* (RSV), bears the common Hebrew name "Menahem." He is actually a foster brother of Herod, *brought up with* Herod (NASB,

NIV). What a tribute to the powerful grace of God that a man with his background is now a prophet and teacher in the church at Antioch! Like the first leader, the fifth, *Saul*, is well known to the reader. Luke places him last likely because he is the most recent to move into this position of prominence (cf. 11:26).

Either on a regular worship occasion with fasting involved or during a special time of seeking the Lord's will, the Holy Spirit speaks to the group. The message, probably given through one of the inspired prophets, tells the church to set apart for a special Spirit-directed mission their revered leader Barnabas and his co-worker Saul (13:2). The rest of the church continues to pray and fast. Finally, after consecrating them with the laying on of hands (cf. 6:6), the church sends them off (13:3).

Witness of Barnabas and Saul on Cyprus 13:4-12

The Holy Spirit sends the two men (13:4) and young John Mark (13:5b) down to Seleucus, the port of Antioch, fifteen miles away. There they board a ship for Cyprus, Barnabas's home country (4:36), and dock at Salamis, a Greek city on the east coast of the island. In that city they find an influential Jewish colony some centuries old and proclaim the gospel in more than one of its synagogues (13:5).

The role of John Mark is not entirely clear. He is called an *attendant* or *helper* (NASB, NIV), which may mean a personal servant who carries luggage, buys food, arranges for lodging, and the like. Or possibly he helps with the instruction of converts or does the baptizing. Texts like John 4:2; 1 Corinthians 1:14-17; and Acts 10:48 show that this rite is often performed by assistants.

Evidence that John Mark serves by instructing converts may be found in the fact that Luke uses the same Greek word here (*hupēretēs*) in the singular that he does in Luke 1:2 in the plural to designate "ministers of the word" (RSV). There they are grouped with "eyewitnesses" as sources of the gospel. Thus Mark may be one who has been taught by the apostle Peter to memorize accounts of the words and deeds of Jesus and to pass this tradition on to converts (Swartley: 27-37). This intriguing possibility throws light on why he later quits the team (13:13) but still later accompanies Barnabas on his mission to Cyprus (15:39). Eventually Mark comes to be valued by Paul (Col. 4:10), and sometime after that Paul urges him to come and assist that apostle because he is "useful" to Paul in his "ministry" (2 Tim. 4:11).

Luke tells nothing of the missionary efforts of the team between Salamis and Paphos at the western end of the island. Presumably they carry on their work in whatever synagogues they find, continuing the pattern already set of taking the gospel to the Jews first and then to God-fearers and Gentiles as they respond. (See Rom. 1:16 for a theological statement of Paul's approach and Acts 13:46 for the way it works out in actual practice.)

The author now focuses on *Paphos*, really "new Paphos," nine miles south of the old city and the current seat of Roman provincial government of the island. There the worship of Aphrodite, the Greek goddess of love, has its center. But uppermost in Luke's mind is not a reference to that pagan cult but the presence of a Jewish magician, who provides the first real opposition to these Christian missionaries. He is known both by his Semitic name *Bar-Jesus* (son of Jesus/Jeshua/Joshua) and a popular title *Elymas*, explained as *magician* (13:8), perhaps related to the later-attested Arabic '*ālim*, meaning "sage."

As Elymas appears in the story, he is attached to the court of the chief Roman official of the island, the proconsul *Sergius Paulus*. At least two men with this name are known in the history of the times, a "Lucius Sergius Paulus" mentioned in an inscription as one of the caretakers of the Tiber under Claudius, and a "Sergius Paulus" spoken of by Pliny as a natural scientist. Neither of these can be proved to be the proconsul of Cyprus. Since the name is quite common, there is no reason to doubt the accuracy of the reference here.

Luke's point is that here is another Roman who, like Cornelius (10:2-8), sends for someone to come and explain the word of God to him (13:7). Unlike the situation with Cornelius, however, this time an adversary tries to defeat God's purposes. Elymas comes against Barnabas and Saul and tries to keep the proconsul from believing them (13:8). By this he shows himself indeed a *false prophet* (13:6b). Then Saul, from now on called Paul, is *filled* anew *with the Holy Spirit* for the occasion, takes charge, and attacks this enemy of the Lord. In 4:8 Peter was similarly filled in order to answer his opponents; both instances are fulfillments of the Lord's promise of sufficiency in the Holy Spirit (Luke 12:11-12).

The language Paul uses, like that of Peter with Simon the sorcerer (8:20-23; 13:9-11, KJV), is both blunt and effective. Elymas is of the devil, full of all evil, twisting the straight paths of the Lord (13:10). He is attempting to undo what John the Baptist and Jesus have done to straighten what was crooked (Luke 3:4-6). Then, along with this verbal blast, Paul pronounces a curse upon the magician. The Lord will strike him blind for awhile, and he will grope about for people to lead him by the hand (13:11). The parallel to Paul's own experience outside Damascus (9:8-19) is too obvious to miss. In a subtle way, Luke may be suggesting that the punishment is redemptive and that the man is eventually restored. At any rate, the miracle has a powerful effect on the proconsul, and he becomes a believer at once (13:12). With this climactic touch, the author closes the incident and in 13:13-14 moves on to the next phase of the missionary journey.

The fact that from 13:9 onward, through the rest of Acts, Luke uses the name *Paul* for Saul, shows that in all likelihood he has had both these names from birth. *Paulus*, well documented among the records of the times, would be his Roman cognomen or family name. *Saul* is his personal Hebrew name, derived from King Saul, like himself a member of the tribe of Benjamin (cf. 1 Sam. 9:1-2; Phil. 3:5). As a Roman citizen, he would also have a praenomen or first name like Gaius or Julius—a name no longer known. The widespread notion that *Paul* is a Christian name given to him at conversion has no biblical support, especially since Luke begins to use it only now, some thirteen years after that event. *[Chronology, p. 309.]*

The context in Acts suggests that at this point Paul has moved out beyond predominantly Semitic territory into the wider circles of the empire, where his Roman name is more appropriate. For example, he can be right at home with the proconsul who has the same family name, *Paulus*. More important, however, is the fact that from now on Paul seems to become the leader of the team. Whereas it was *Barnabas and Saul* who took the relief to Jerusalem, returned to Antioch, and were set apart by the Holy Spirit (11:30; 12:25; 13:2), from this point on both the names and their order are changed (except Barnabas first in 14:12-14; 15:12).

Paul and Barnabas at Pisidian Antioch   13:13-52

13:13-16a   In the Synagogue

Luke makes it clear that Paul now takes the lead. It is *Paul and his companions* who set sail from Paphos to Perga in Pamphylia. Barnabas, though included, is not even mentioned (13:13). Paul is the one who will address the synagogue in 13:16-41, and from this time on it is *Paul and Barnabas*, in that order, who carry on the ministry (13:43, 46, 49) and who go to Jerusalem to settle the dispute over circumcision (15:2). For the remainder of this journey, it is only at

Lystra that Barnabas, for the brief time he is taken to be the father of the gods, is given any prominence and mentioned before Paul (14:12-14). Otherwise he is secondary.

At Paphos the three missionaries, under Paul's leadership, find a ship bound for the southern coast of the mainland of Asia Minor. The Roman province is *Pamphylia*, an impoverished, malaria-ridden lowland lying between the sea and Mt. Taurus. Its religious capital is *Perga*, where the party is headed (13:13a). They may either dock at Attalia and walk the twelve miles to the city or sail up the Cestus River to a port east of there.

Here at Perga a breakup of the team occurs. John, called Mark, leaves and returns home to Jerusalem (13:13b). No reasons are given, but from 15:38 we gather that it is not a happy situation. Paul regards Mark's desertion as turning back from a God-given mission. Factors involved may be such things as homesickness, hard or unsatisfactory work, personality clashes with Paul, or, as Swartley suggests, dissatisfaction with Paul's plans (29-30). According to the latter theory, Mark was not anticipating a mission to the Gentiles of Asia Minor in the first place. So perhaps he now is returning to report to Peter that Paul not only intends to carry out such a mission but plans to take in Gentiles without circumcision. This is a policy not yet authorized by the Jerusalem church.

The two remaining missionaries do not remain long in Perga but make their way up onto the 3,800-foot-high plateau and proceed to Pisidian Antioch (13:14a). This city is actually in the southwestern part of the long province of Galatia, and its population is basically Phrygian. The Romans, however, call it "Antioch near Pisidia" because its earlier location made it a buffer against the warlike tribes of that area (Hemer: 228, citing Strabo). Founded in the third century B.C., the city has grown to medium size. It was made a colony under the Caesars and therefore maintains an imperial presence and has descendants of war veterans in its population (see notes on 16:12 for more about Roman colonies). The basically Phrygian stock has been overlaid with elements of Greek culture and Roman colonial manners. Within the city a strong Jewish community has sprung up. Two main roads connect it with other centers, making it a good place in which to establish a Christian fellowship.

13:16b-41 Paul's Message

Luke now introduces the first of three representative speeches from Paul's active ministry. This one is an example of his approach to Jews and God-fearers in the synagogues of the dispersion. A second one in 17:22-31 is his message to cultured Greeks in Athens, and in 20:18-35 we find his farewell address to leaders of a Christian community.

Paul and Barnabas lose no time at Antioch as they enter the synagogue on the Sabbath (13:14b). After the preliminary worship, the local elders invite them to speak, and Paul rises to the occasion at once (13:15). Unlike Jesus in the synagogue at Nazareth (Luke 4:20), he *stands up* to speak (13:16a), probably because here Hellenistic traditions are strong and the habits of Greek orators are followed even in Jewish assemblies. With his opening words, he includes his two types of hearers: *You Israelites* (the Jews) and *others who fear God* (devout Gentiles). He is careful to affirm community relationships and bind his audience to him as speaker. To do this, he presents a story familiar to these synagogue worshipers as he traces God's dealings with his people from of old (cf. Stephen's address in 7:2-52).

Paul begins with God's choice of Israel, their growth in Egypt, and the mighty deliverance from that land (13:17). Then he moves on to the wilderness wanderings and the destruction of the seven nations of Canaan (named in Deut. 7:1) to give the Israelites the Promised Land (13:18-19). It is a message on the election and salvation of Israel. Next he takes them down through the era of the judges to Samuel (13:20) and from him to David (13:22). From David's line God has brought to Israel the promised Savior, Jesus of Nazareth (13:23). The theme word is *promise,* and the gospel is the way God has in Jesus fulfilled what he *promised* (13:23).

At 13:26 Paul addresses them again by name to get their attention for his important proclamation (kerygma). What the Scriptures foretold about Jesus, he says, has now been fulfilled by his death and resurrection (13:28-37). This was preceded by the preaching of John, a baptism of repentance to all the people of Israel (13:24). In Jesus the *forgiveness of sins is proclaimed* (13:38), and *everyone who believes* is offered freedom from *all those sins* from which the law of Moses could not liberate them (13:39). Now, after making this appeal for acceptance of the gospel, Paul concludes with a severe warning. They must not scoff at the offer of the Lord or they will perish with all those who do so (13:40-41).

13:42-43 Favorable Response

The message is well received. As people gather around afterward, they ask Paul and Barnabas to continue with this kind of preaching the following Sabbath (13:42). Many of them even express interest in becoming followers (13:43a). The latter are of two kinds: *Jews and devout converts to Judaism*, or *proselytes* (KJV). At this point Luke mentions no Gentiles among the new converts. They will come into view the following week (see on 13:48). The people responding on this Sabbath are said to be *many*, with no estimate as to numbers. More important is the fact that the missionaries spend some time instructing them and encouraging them to continue in the grace they have now received (13:43). They become the nucleus of a new fellowship of believers here at Pisidian Antioch.

13:44-52 Opposition, A New Church, Departure

A week later the synagogue is filled to capacity. As Luke puts it, *almost the whole city gathered to hear the word of the Lord* (13:44). Again Paul is the speaker. But this time he meets determined opposition. Such success has aroused what the writer calls *jealousy* on the part of those Jews who do not believe (13:45a). They are offended, not that their synagogue is now crowded, but that these visiting rabbis are proclaiming a Messiah killed by Jews like themselves and raised from the dead by God. Moreover, in his name these outsiders are making many converts. Thus Paul meets contradiction and revilings, perhaps early in his message (13:45). There is no report of what he says, simply that he and Barnabas grasp the situation and speak out boldly.

What they now say becomes the watchword of their mission and the theme that Luke will underscore through the remainder of Acts: *It was necessary that the word of God should be spoken first to you Jews. Since you reject it, . . . we are now turning to the Gentiles* (13:46). They back this policy with a quotation from Isaiah 49:6, about the Servant being a light for the Gentiles to bring them to salvation, a verse that has been rightly called "the great commission of the OT." This program, to the Jew first and then to the Gentiles, continues to be central to Paul's evangelism for the rest of his active career (18:5-6; 26:23b; 28:23-28; cf. Rom.1:16; 2:9-11).

Such a pronouncement fills the Gentiles of the city with understandable joy (13:48a) and leads to a considerable ingathering from among them. Luke reports that *as many as had been destined for eternal life became believers* (13:48b). This means more than just being disposed toward eternal life, as some interpreters have it. Instead, the author claims, the new believers are those actually *destined* to it in the sense of having their names inscribed in the book of life (Luke 10:20; cf. Exod. 32:32; Ps. 69:28; Isa. 4:3; Dan. 12:1; Rev. 13:8; 20:12-15; 21:27; see Bruce: 283, n. 72). They are the ones who have responded to God's call in faith, have repented, been baptized, and are thus ordained to live forever. As happens other times in Acts, from a core of enthusiastic believers, the word of the Lord now goes out over a whole area (13:49; cf. 5:16; 9:35, 42).

Yet there is a price to pay. As the Lord predicted, his apostles are persecuted, delivered up to synagogues and to prisons, mistreated and hated for his sake. But they are not to worry, for they are given a mouth of wisdom and protected (Luke 21:12-19). Here in Antioch, the unbelieving Jews stir up *the devout women of high standing*, some no doubt influential in their own right. They, with some of the city leaders, take action against Paul and Barnabas (13:50). Luke gives no details, calling it a *persecution* during which prominent citizens drive the apostles out of their region. Paul and Barnabas, however, are not discouraged. They simply remove their sandals and shake away the dust of the city as a sign of judgment against them, as Jesus taught his followers to do when rejected (Luke 9:5; 10:11). Moreover, they leave behind them freshly converted disciples who, like all new Christians, are *filled with joy and with the Holy Spirit* (13:52; cf. 2:44-47; 8:8, 39b).

Further Witness in the Galatian Highlands 14:1-23

14:1-7 Paul and Barnabas at Iconium

After a journey of some seventy-eight miles to the east and a bit south, they come to a vast plain known for its beauty and agricultural fertility, upon which is situated Iconium (13:51). Highways from Syria to Ephesus pass through the city, and it enjoys extensive trade. The local inhabitants regard themselves as Phrygians and speak that language along with the almost universal Koine Greek. There are enough Jews to support a fair-sized synagogue, here the apostles begin a new work (14:1).

Again, as at Antioch (13:15), they give the exhortation. Paul is not singled out as the speaker this time but likely is. The first service is successful, and *a great number of both Jews and Greeks* become be-*lievers* (14:1b). Luke handles the rise of opposition with a single statement, making explicit what was implied at Antioch (14:2). It is not all the Jews but some determinedly *unbelieving* ones, notably synagogue *rulers* (14:5), who stir up the Gentiles with poisonous charges. One might expect that with such division and bitterness, the apostles would leave at once. But the text surprises the reader: *So/therefore* (NRSV/NASB) they stay on *for a long time!* (14:3a). Some scholars (e.g., Haenchen: 421-423) claim this is so unreasonable that there must be some mistake. Yet it is quite in harmony with the spirit of the earlier Jerusalem believers, who pray for still more boldness in the face of persecution (4:29). This is also true to the courage Paul later demonstrates at Lystra (14:20), Philippi (16:35-40), and Ephesus (19:30).

Their boldness is blessed of the Lord, who bears witness to *the word of his grace* by performing many miracles through them and making such an impact that the new faith becomes an issue in the whole city (14:3). The people are divided (14:4). Though there is a strong group of people whose minds have been *poisoned* against them (14:2), they do not drive the missionaries out, and the latter enjoy a long period of active work. Whereas at Pisidian Antioch it was largely Jews who opposed the Christian evangelists, here there is also a strong Gentile element against them. Eventually the situation at Iconium becomes unmanageable. Even the rulers of Gentiles and Jews lead their unbelieving peoples in a lynching plan to *mistreat* and *stone them* (14:5). Paul and Barnabas decide it is time to move on to proclaim the good news in Lycaonia (14:6-7). Apparently by now the new church at Iconium is strong enough to survive without them.

14:8-20a   Paul and Barnabas at Lystra

Lystra is about eighteen miles south of Iconium, a small rural settlement on a fertile plain where ancient Lycaonian is used and only a minority speak the Koine Greek. It is a separate administrative area as well, a colony like Antioch, with its own Roman establishment. Luke brackets it with Derbe as the area in which the apostles now take refuge and preach the gospel (14:6-7).

Here are echoes of the ministry of Jesus (Luke 5:18-26) and even stronger ones of Peter's miracles (Acts 3:1-10; 9:32-35) as Paul begins by healing a man *crippled from birth* (14:8-10). It is a dramatic moment. A crowd soon gathers, and people talk excitedly in their own local language. To them these strangers are gods who have come among them in human form. Ovid (*Metamorphoses* 8.626ff.) tells a local legend about *Zeus* (the Roman Jupiter) and *Hermes* (Mercury) *in human form* visiting an old couple and rewarding their hospitality. Now *the crowds* think these two deities must be here again, performing this miracle (14:11). Perhaps because of his stature and bearing, Barnabas is taken as *Zeus,* the father of the gods; and Paul, *the chief speaker,* as *Hermes* his messenger (14:12). What comical irony we see when the priest of the temple of Zeus, located outside the city gates, comes up leading a pair of oxen decorated with woolen garlands for sacrifice! (14:13).

The humor of such a situation is evident to the reader, but to the mystified apostles there is nothing funny about it. As good Jews and Christians, they are shocked at being worshiped as gods and rush in among the people tearing their garments and shouting loudly. They are not deities but only human, and such actions must stop at once (14:14-15a). Yet the pagan proceedings seem to continue (14:18) while Paul manages to quiet the crowd and deliver a brief gospel message (14:15-17).

Luke summarizes here the first example of the apostle's approach to a thoroughly Gentile audience, to be compared to that used with another totally non-Jewish group at Athens (17:26-30). First comes an exhortation to turn from vain idols to the worship of the living God (14:15; cf. 17:22-25). But Paul makes allowance for their different religious background and does not harshly condemn them. He points out that in times past God has permitted all nations to go their way (14:16; cf. 17:30). Even in their pagan existence, Paul declares to this agriculturally minded group, God was making a witness through the natural order of things: rains, harvests, and bounteous living (14:17). Though rare in the NT, the theme of nature as witnessing to the goodness of God is often found in the OT (cf. Rom. 1:19-21; Ps. 145:15-16; 147:8-9; Jer. 5:24). Paul likely continues beyond this brief digest. The groundwork is laid for the point made in 17:30-31: now that Christ has come, God will no longer overlook their ignorance, and people must repent to have a share in the eternal kingdom.

Strangely enough, the speech seems to fade out without any kind of a conclusion. There is no report of a call to repentance, no statement about a response. How and in what numbers did the church begin, as evidenced in 14:20 and 16:1-2? Instead of telling us these things, Luke recalls once more the scene of the priests wanting to sacrifice to them and how they can hardly keep the people from worshiping their visitors (14:18).

Then suddenly the scene changes as angry enemies arrive from Antioch and Iconium. Paul and his entire ministry are almost wiped out! Some of the persecutors have come 100 miles to vent their wrath on the hapless evangelists. To do so, they stir up the local people to fever pitch to attack Paul with stones. They crush him to the ground until they are sure he is dead and drag out his body like a corpse (14:19). Those who earlier were eager to worship the apostle as a god are now bent on killing him. (In writing later to people of this region, Paul suggests that fickleness is a trait of theirs: "so quickly deserting the one who called you," Gal. 1:6.)

Once more, however, the Lord intervenes. The new *disciples* come and surround the man left for dead until he is revived enough to get up and go back into Lystra, where he has just been murderously attacked! (14:20a). Nothing is said here about prayers for revival, but the quick recovery suggests a miracle of resurrection like that in 20:9-12. Paul's return to the city where he was brutally attacked not only speaks of his courage but lets the reader know that the Lord is in control.

14:20b-23 Derbe; Backtracking to Pisidian Antioch

The next morning Paul, now divinely restored, is able to walk the thirty miles southeastward to Derbe with Barnabas (14:20b). They find a medium-sized settlement on the same Lycaonian plain as Lystra, a frontier town along the eastern boundary of Galatia (a site now known as *Kerti Huyuk*). Either Luke has at hand no details about the ministry here, or there is nothing new and interesting to report. All he writes is that the apostles make *many disciples* and so are able to leave the beginnings of a substantial church (14:21a). Later Paul will revisit the congregation, accompanied by Silas (16:1), and a Gaius from Derbe will be a member of the delegation that takes the offering of the Gentile churches to Jerusalem (20:4).

Luke's interest at this point is to get the missionaries back to home base as quickly as possible. He tells how they return to Lystra, Iconium, and Pisidian Antioch in that order (14:21b), with only a general statement about their activities in these church centers. The purpose is to strengthen and confirm the new converts in the faith, a practice Paul will continue from this time on (cf. 15:36; 16:1-5; 18:22-23; 19:21; 20:2).

In this instance it takes courage to go back to the very cities where opposition has been so bitter and strong! Even if new magistrates have been appointed in these places, it is still a dangerous thing to do (Ramsay, 1896:120). They tell these new believers that it is costly to be a Christian. Tribulation and persecution are to be expected, as Jesus predicted (Luke 10:3; 21:12-19; John 15:18-25) and as fellow believers before them discovered (Acts 4–5; 7:54-60; 8:1-3; 9:23-25, 29-30; 12:1-5). As Paul and Barnabas reflect on their experiences on this journey, with deep feeling they include themselves in a parting statement: *through many tribulations we must enter the kingdom of God* (14:22b).

In each new congregation, they appoint *elders* who serve as leaders (14:23a). This is the first mention of such officers outside the Jerusalem church, and some scholars have doubted the authenticity of this reference. Yet we know that appointing elders becomes a practice of Paul, for such leaders of the church, obviously put in office by the apostle, will be found at Ephesus (20:17; 1 Tim. 5:17). In Titus 1:5, Paul instructs his representative on Crete to appoint elders in every congregation in that area as well. Luke would therefore know what he is talking about when he states that Paul and Barnabas appoint elders in these South Galatian churches. *With prayer and fasting*, they commit them to the Lord (14:23b). The service of consecration likely includes the laying on of hands and prayer, as in 6:6; 8:17; and 13:3.

Return to Syrian Antioch and Report 14:24-28

The tempo of narration picks up even more as Luke, in one sentence, tells how Paul and Barnabas travel back down through Pisidia, a wild area with little opportunity for evangelism, and arrive in Pamphylia, 100 miles from Antioch of Pisidia. To do so they descend from an elevation of 3,800 feet to near sea level (14:24). Though nothing is said about missionary activity as they entered this province a year or more before (13:13), they now pause long enough to preach the gospel and make a few converts in the city of Perga. Built on an ancient site some twelve miles from the coast, it has an overlay of Greek and Roman culture with a large theater and stadium. Like Ephesus, it supports a grand temple of the goddess Artemis and has become a "cathedral city" of that deity (to be discussed in connection with 19:22-27). Nothing is said here of the church that results from the apostles' efforts, but centuries later a thriving one exists there. In Byzantine times it becomes the seat of the archbishop of the province.

From Perga, Paul and Barnabas lose no time in going on to the port city of Attalia (in our day called *Antalya*). There they find a ship bound for Seleucia (13:4) and make their way as rapidly as possible to Syrian Antioch, where they have been commissioned for their work (14:26; cf. 13:1-3). Then, as a conclusion to the section and balancing the introduction in 13:1-3, Luke tells of the Antioch church once more assembled as a congregation (14:27a; cf. 13:2a). This time it is to hear what God has *done through* these whom the church has earlier set apart and consecrated by the command of the Holy Spirit (14:27b, NIV; 13:2b). Singled out for special mention as a result of the mission is the way the Lord has opened *a door of faith for the Gentiles* (14:27b). This and the statement in 14:28 that the apostles stay on for a considerable time in Antioch provide a suitable transition to the narrative Luke will relate next.

The Council of Jerusalem
15:1-35

In the plan and purpose of Acts, this narrative marks a major turning point. The mission to the Gentile world has been launched, and a number of non-Jews have converted to the faith. Christians have founded new congregations—like the two Antiochs, Iconium, Lystra, and Derbe—where a freer attitude toward the law is in evidence. But as yet there has been no thorough discussion and agreement on the issue of what is involved in the conversion of Gentiles by the leaders of the church. Only now, as depicted in this pivotal account, does such a consultation takes place. As a result, the westward thrust of Christianity can go forward as something agreed upon and approved. Because of these decisions and their implementation wherever the gospel is preached, the believers in Jesus Christ tend toward becoming a distinct church rather than a sect of Judaism restricted by that religion's limitations in evangelizing the world (cf. 24:5; 26:5; and 28:22; where Christianity is still called a *sect*).

The outcome of this council has a threefold significance for the ongoing movement. First, it clears the way for an unhindered proclamation of the gospel to both Jews and Gentiles. Second, it frees the church from the restrictive prescriptions of Judaism and allows it to become a worldwide faith in its own right. Third, it preserves the unity of the church both in evangelism and in table fellowship wherever believers of various backgrounds meet (cf. Gal. 2:11-14, where eating together is clearly the issue, and Acts 15:20, 29, where provisions are made to make it possible).

Luke's literary artistry can be seen in the overall outline of this series of episodes. A teaching that originated in Jerusalem (15:1a) has become a problem in Antioch (15:1b-2), and now it is to be resolved in Jerusalem (15:22-29). Its solution is to be applied back in Antioch (15:30-35), where the story starts (15:1a).

Dispute over Circumcision for Gentiles   15:1-5

15:1-2 Dissension in Antioch

There is no break in the story at 15:1, just an interval of time that leads to another example of the watchful eye of the Jerusalem church over developments in outlying areas. In 8:14-25, that congregation sent Peter and John to check on the new evangelistic work among the Samaritans. Then the unexpected conversion of Cornelius and household needed the approval of *the apostles and the believers* in Judea (11:1-18), and the Jerusalem church sent Barnabas to investigate the unusual developments at Antioch (11:22). Now the long arm of Jerusalem is seen in the coming of some unauthorized Judaizers, who apparently are simultaneously believers and Pharisees (cf. 15:5). They are teaching (formally, or in casual discussions and arguments) that circumcision is necessary for salvation (15:1). Luke's report is too brief for us to reconstruct what actually takes place. All we can say is that there is a series of disputes serious enough to require a consultation on the matter in Jerusalem.

If these events are those spoken of in Galatians 2:11-14 and Peter is in Antioch at the time, as the traditional view has it, the dispute is a deep and bitter one, casting doubt on the salvation of uncircumcised Gentile Christians (see TBC, "Relationship of Acts 15 to Galatians 2"). The harmonious Jew-Gentile fellowship of the Antioch church is threatened. If these Judaizers are right, Paul and Barnabas are completely mistaken in their evangelistic approach to non-Jews. Even if this Jerusalem council is not the encounter Galatians 2:1-10 reports, it is enough of a crisis to warrant sending Paul and Barnabas and others to the apostles and elders at Jerusalem to settle the matter as soon as possible (15:2).

15:3-5 Witness on the Way and Dialogue in Jerusalem

On the way to Jerusalem, they follow the coast southward

through Phoenicia and turn southeast across Samaria. As they travel, they proclaim the good news of the Lord's work among Gentiles that has recently taken place in their ministry. In reverse order they cover territory evangelized by the unnamed refugees of 11:19 and by Philip in Samaria (8:4-13). The Christians of these areas rejoice that the gospel is opened to non-Jews (15:3).

After arriving in Jerusalem, the two missionaries have further opportunity to tell their story (15:4a). The church and its leaders welcome them and hear what God has done with them—but there is no mention of enthusiasm or joy (15:4b). Instead, the reader is introduced at once to the opposition party. Like those who came to Antioch, these believers who are also Pharisees require that Gentiles be circumcised and instructed to obey the law of Moses before they can become Christians (15:5).

Jerusalem Meeting of Church Leaders 15:6-21

15:6-11 Peter's Testimony to the Apostles and Elders

Luke gives no information as to the number of persons involved in the council, nor of the times and places of their meetings, but passes quickly to the major speakers and their points of view. There is an informality in which no particular individuals seem to be designated to lead out, but weighty persons speak up as the Spirit directs. Thus, in this continuous unified gathering, *after . . . much debate*, Peter rises to tell of his experience in the conversion of Gentiles (15:6-9) and to give his opinion on the matter at hand (15:10-11). He reminds them of his Spirit-led encounter with Cornelius and his household, perhaps dwelling at length on this story now known to most of them.

Luke, in his brief summary of the speech, spares his readers the details of a narrative already thoroughly covered in 10:1—11:18 and reports only the major emphases of the apostle's presentation. *God* is the one who chose him to be the first to bring the gospel to the Gentiles, and *God* bore witness to this by pouring out on them the Holy Spirit, just as at Pentecost (15:7-8; cf. 10:45-47; 11:17). What God was showing unmistakably by this sign is that in the matter of salvation, there is no distinction between Jew and Gentile. All must come *by faith* for *cleansing* (15:9).

Then Peter turns directly to the circumcision party and confronts them with the question *why? Why* do you keep opposing God by your legalisms? You're trying to load new converts with a law which neither we nor our ancestors have ever been able to bear! (15:10). The why? is as piercing as the one he asked Ananias in 5:3, about his lying to the Holy Spirit. *Putting God to the test* recalls his own rhetorical question in 11:17: *Who was I that I could hinder God?* Years before, Peter had heard Jesus say of the Pharisees that they lay on burdens hard to bear (Luke 11:46). Now he hurls the same charge at these *believers who belonged to the sect of the Pharisees* (15:5).

Peter concludes with a theological summary of the whole matter, a position Luke wants to underscore, one true to the teachings of Paul. It is that both Jews and Gentiles must be saved by the grace of God through faith (15:11). In fact, if the encounter of Galatians 2:11-21 has already occurred, Peter has recently learned or confirmed this lesson the hard way. On that occasion Paul accused him of hypocrisy, building up again what he had torn down (i.e., salvation by works of law). Paul told him to his face that "a person is justified not by the works of the law but through faith in Jesus Christ" (Gal. 2:16). So, on this understanding of events, it is a chastened and corrected Peter who now drives this message home to the leaders of the whole church. He puts the burden on Jewish Christians first as he declares, *We believe that we [Jews] will be saved through the grace of the Lord Jesus, just as they [the Gentiles] will* (15:11). Once more a strong stand on the part of this influential apostle commands silence, if not universal assent (15:12a; cf. 11:18).

15:12-21 Barnabas and Paul Report; James's Key Speech

As the assembly pauses to absorb what Peter has told them, Barnabas and Paul, fresh from their own ministry in mixed Jew-Gentile communities, rise and speak, perhaps each in turn. Note that Barnabas is now mentioned first, probably because they are in Jerusalem where he has always been the senior and Paul the junior member of the team (9:27-30; 11:30; 12:25). Though these two have already told their story to *the church* (15:4), they now have the opportunity to go over it again for this special meeting. They simply bear witness to the miraculous signs which God has worked through them among the Gentiles and let the record speak for itself. It is obvious that *God* (15:8) is the one who has led non-Jews to become believers, and that without circumcision!

The final speaker and the one who carries the most weight is James, the Lord's brother. With Peter so often away from Jerusalem (cf. 8:14-25; 9:32—11:48), the leadership of that church has passed to James (cf. 12:17), and he will continue to exercise it for years to come (21:18). James is uniquely fitted to take charge at this point (15:13) because he is a careful believer who commands the respect of the conservatives with his strict piety. Yet he is also open to Peter and now the message of Barnabas and Paul. Familiarly referring to Peter by his Hebrew name, *Simeon* (a Semitic form of the current *Simon*), he reviews that apostle's testimony (15:14). James finds Peter in agreement with *the words of the prophets* (15:15) as found near the end of the oracles of Amos (9:11-12) in the section on Israel's restoration. It is a well-chosen Scripture which speaks to the present as the time when the rest of the world will seek Yahweh—those Gentiles called by the Lord's name (15:16-18). Then on the basis of this convincing text, James renders his judgment.

James's judicious proposal is twofold and becomes the basis for the decision of the council. First is the recognition that, as the Scripture says, many Gentiles are turning to God, and they should not be hindered from doing so (15:19). This will require a change in the thinking of the Judaizers, but they can be assured that the new converts will be careful at three points of the law and thus not cause offense. Second, James recommends that the apostles and elders *write* a letter to the *Gentiles*, charging them to abstain from three practices common in pagan society (15:20; cf. 15:29; 21:25).

Gentiles are asked to abstain from *things polluted by idols*, eating anything sacrificed to an idol. This restriction is necessary lest some converts bring into the body of Christ defilements that cannot be tolerated by any believers, especially those of Jewish background (cf. Rom. 14:2, 15; also a "stumbling block" to converts of pagan background: 1 Cor. 8:7). They should not eat food available in the markets after being routinely sacrificed to idols, as Paul will tell his Corinthian converts (1 Cor. 8:1-13; 10:14-22).

Another area of contamination from paganism to be avoided has to do with the sexual immorality or *fornication/unchastity* (15:20, NRSV/RSV). This is common in current society, especially found around temples where religious prostitution is practiced. It is also prevalent among Greek and Roman families (cf. 1 Cor. 6:13-20; 1 Thess. 4:3-8) and may violate the Levitical degrees of relationship (Lev. 18:6-18; 1 Cor. 5:1-5).

James mentions a third kind of defilement, likely related to the first (cf. 15:29); he calls them to stay away from eating *whatever has been strangled and from blood* (15:20). This has long been a deeply held scruple of all good Jews, based on Genesis 9:4 and elaborated into many dietary laws. Since that verse says the life is the blood, to eat meat not properly prepared is a grave offense against God.

If Gentile Christians are careful about these and similar matters, they will help create unity among believers of both Jewish and Gentile backgrounds. Finally, James reminds the group that the laws of Moses are expounded every Sabbath in synagogues throughout the dispersion (15:21). By this he may mean that every Gentile has ample opportunity to learn about these essential teachings. Or he may be saying that Christians of non-Jewish background should be careful not to give offense to the many followers of the Mosaic law in the cities where they live.

What Seems Good to the Spirit and the Church   15:22-35

15:22-29   The Decision of the Council

The carefully worded proposal of James finds acceptance by *the whole church*. They decide to choose from themselves men who will carry a letter to Gentile Christians expressing the decisions of the assembly. This seems to be done without a vote—a consensus reached in the *Holy Spirit* (15:28) and regarded as final. The plan is to send living representatives to carry the *decrees/decisions* (16:4, KJV/NRSV) on *essentials* (15:28) and interpret them in person to the various churches. The two chosen are *Joseph called Barsabbas* and *Silas*, who will accompany Paul and Barnabas back to Antioch to begin the presentations (15:22).

Joseph has sometimes been taken to be the brother of the Judas Barsabbas of 1:23, but there is no convincing evidence for this view. Silas, the second-named, will become Paul's companion on his next missionary journey (15:40—18:17). His full Roman praenomen is "Silvanus," by which he is called in Paul's letters (1 Thess. 1:1; 2 Thess. 1:1). Like Paul, Silas is a citizen and is entitled to those privileges (16:37). Both Judas and Silas are able and well-respected Christian *leaders*, the kinds of persons who will be good interpreters of the broader view of salvation they are to represent (15:22b).

The letter to be taken and read to Gentile Christians, as now quoted by Luke (15:23-29), begins with the customary mention of senders and receivers. The latter are specified as the Gentile Christians of Antioch and of the province of Syro-Cilicia, of which it is the capital. Paul has apparently started churches in areas of Cilicia (cf. 9:30; 11:25; 15:23, 41). No mention is made of Galatia and Pamphylia, most recently evangelized (13:4—14:25), but they may be regarded as church extensions of Syro-Cilicia, since the decisions are delivered to them as well (16:4).

Then, after the statement of senders and receivers, comes the simple word *greetings* (cf. James 1:1, also attributed to James). The letter proper begins with a carefully worded review of the problem caused by some unauthorized persons who have been troubling Gentile Christians and unsettling their minds (15:25). This situation has led to the sending of chosen men, along with the beloved Barnabas and Paul, to convey the action of the Jerusalem council (15:26). The role of these two is further emphasized as they are praised for the completion of their dangerous mission for the Lord (15:27). Their testimony (15:4, 12) has made a deep impression on the assembled elders. Judas and Silas are then named as the ones who will further interpret the decisions *by word of mouth* (15:28).

The *decisions* (16:4) of the council are now tactfully introduced as the product of the Holy Spirit, who has moved the assembly to make them. Furthermore, they are proposed as minimal requirements, *essentials* (15:28). Then the three major areas in which Gentiles are to exercise care, already enumerated in 15:20, are listed simply in a slightly different order that groups together the items having to do with eating (15:29). The brief letter closes with a final appeal to abstain from these matters of defilement and offense, and a *farewell* (15:30), as brief and to the point as the *greetings* with which it began (15:23). Again, as with the speeches of Acts, one may suspect that we have here a digest of a longer letter, which Luke has skillfully summarized in the present form.

As a result of this council, (1) a rupture in the church has been averted, with the easing of tensions for both the Jewish and Gentile wings; (2) a basis for unlimited evangelization of Gentiles has been achieved; and (3) the supervisory control of the Jerusalem church over satellite congregations continues. This is God's gift to the fast-growing movement of Christianity at this particular time.

15:30-35 The Letter Delivered to Antioch

The delegation from Antioch, now increased by the addition of Judas and Silas, are sent off with God's blessing by the leaders at Jerusalem and make the trip down to their city. There they call the whole church to listen to the letter and the personal interpretations they give to it (15:30). The congregation of Antioch, with its strong Gentile element, rejoices at the *exhortation*, which gives approval to their open style of evangelism and enables them to go on being the exciting church they are (15:31). The two official spokesmen, Judas and Silas, are especially active in instructing the members as to what this will mean for them from this time on. As Luke states it, they are *themselves prophets,* able to exercise the gift as explained in 1 Corinthians 14:1-5, 22-33 (see notes on Acts 11:27-30). They spend time encouraging and strengthening the believers (15:32).

We are not told how long it takes to heal the rupture in the fellowship caused by the events of 15:1-2 and Galatians 2:11-21. The two deputies eventually go back to Jerusalem, from which they were sent (15:33). Some ancient Greek texts have a brief statement that Silas stays on in Antioch (to be on hand for the action of 15:40). This is 15:34, now omitted as secondary by most translations (in NASB in brackets, in NRSV note). If Silas does leave, as the approved text says, then he returns in time for Paul to choose him for the journey. To prepare the reader further for the next story, Luke adds the editorial note that Paul and Barnabas themselves remain in Antioch for a considerable time, engaged in preaching and teaching (15:35).

THE TEXT IN BIBLICAL CONTEXT
Continued Spiritual Warfare

When Paul meets Elymas the sorcerer (13:6-12, KJV), the struggle between true Christianity and various forms of magic is resumed. As it was with Simon of Samaria, so now it is again a matter of *miracle* against *magic* (see TBC on 8:9-13). The new element in the present story is the magician's fierce opposition to the word of faith, his attempt to defeat the work of the apostles and *turn the proconsul away from the faith.* Such spiritual warfare has its background in the battles between the followers of Yahweh and the false gods (1 Kings 18:20-40; 2 Kings 18:3-6; 23:4-20; Isa. 44:9-17; Dan. 3:1-30; 6:6-24). In the NT these gods appear as demons (1 Cor. 10:20-22, cf. Deut. 32:16-17), to be cast out by the people of God (Luke 4:41; 8:26-33; 9:1, 42; Acts 8:7; 16:18; 19:12b).

Paul later clarifies the spiritual battle: "Our struggle is not against enemies of blood and flesh, but against the rulers, against the authorities, against the cosmic powers of this present darkness, against the spiritual forces of evil in the heavenly places" (Eph. 6:12). Then in Revelation 12—13, the endtime battle with Satan and all his demonic manifestations is graphically depicted. Therefore, in the passage at hand, the heat with which Paul confronts Elymas Bar-Jesus is not so much a matter of human anger as it is an expression of divine wrath.

Superior Benefits of the Gospel

Paul gives a key statement in 13:39. The gospel frees believers from everything from which they could not be delivered by the law of Moses. This is in harmony with his more extensive teaching on sin in Romans (5:13, 20; 7:7-23). There he teaches that the law can convict one of sin, but it cannot free a person from sin and may even cause one to sin all the more!

In Matthew 5:21-48 Jesus illustrates deep human weaknesses from which the commandments are helpless to redeem one: hostility, lust, deceit and the need to swear, the urge to retaliate, and the tendency to hate. In Mark 7:21-23 the Lord gives an even more extensive list of inner defilements: evil thoughts, fornication, theft, murder, adultery, coveting, wickedness, deceit, slander, pride, and foolishness. Paul speaks of similar "works of the flesh" from which the law cannot redeem a person, but Christ can (Gal. 5:19-21). Only by the transforming power of the Holy Spirit can such ingrained sins be overcome (Rom. 7:24-25; 8:1-3, 10-17).

To the Jew First, Then to the Gentile (cf. Rom. 1:16)

Paul's policy of taking the gospel to the Jews first and then to Gentiles, proclaimed in 13:46, calls for further exploration. The origin of this approach is in the call of Abraham and his line to be God's own people (Gen. 12:1-8), confirmed (Gen. 15:1-21) and made the basis of much of OT thought and action. Thus the Jews were given the law, bound by the covenant, admonished by the prophets, and promised the kingdom in the coming of the Messiah. Jesus, himself a Jew, came to them; his original followers were also all of that background. Moreover, his earliest disciples were not sent to the Samaritans or Gentiles but to Israel (Luke 9:1-6; 10:1-12; especially clear in Matt. 10:5-6). Only at the end of his career does the Lord give the command to go to all nations (Matt. 28:16-20; Luke 24:47; Acts 1:8).

Jews are the ones who have the Scriptures, the belief in God, high ethical standards and quality of life, as well as the expectation of a coming Messiah (see Rom. 9:4-5). Furthermore, they have the synagogue, found in most major cities of the dispersion and providing a forum for the presentation of the gospel. Therefore, it is not only fitting, but also highly practical, that the good news of Christ be presented to them first. Associated with the Jews in each of these synagogues are proselytes and devout Gentiles, God-fearers, who also hear the message about Jesus. Since the latter are often more responsive than are the traditional Israelites, they become a substantial part of the newly formed church. Then after the break with the synagogue occurs in many centers where Paul evangelizes, Gentiles generally are won to the fellowship.

The very success of this ministry, however, leads to strife and eventual division. Most of the Jews do not accept Jesus and force Paul to leave the synagogue and begin a separate church group. This happens at Pisidian Antioch (13:45-50) and in later missions at Thessalonica (17:5-9), Corinth (18:6-8), and Ephesus (19:8-10). Such a split is always painful. Yet it does have the beneficial result of leaving Christians free to evangelize persons of all backgrounds, affirming the body of Christ as open to include believers from all races, nationalities, and ethnic origins (cf. Gal. 3:28 and Col. 3:11 for Paul's proclamation of such unity in and through diversity).

Paul comes to see a divine purpose in the rejection of Christ by the majority of Jews because it opens the door to the Gentiles in a way that would otherwise not happen. Then eventually, in the long purposes of God, the Jews may become jealous of the entry of the Gentiles and themselves turn to Christ (Rom. 11:7-15). For the present, Christian missionaries must be content to "save some" of the Jews (Rom. 11:14), but in the end "all Israel will be saved" (Rom. 11:26-27, perhaps meaning "all the elect, Jews and Gentiles" or "Israel as a whole"; cf. Gal. 3:29; 6:16). How much of this has been revealed to Paul by the time of this first tour is not clear, but Luke knows this pattern together with Paul's later theological interpretation by the time of the writing of Luke-Acts. Thus Luke interprets the missionary tour with this emphasis on going to the Jew first and then to the Gentile.

Relationship of Acts 15 to Galatians 2

The traditional view that these are two different accounts of the same event is supported by the fact that in both of them the same people are present, the same topic discussed, and essentially the same principle accepted (that Gentiles need not be circumcised).

There are, however, some important differences between them and a number of unresolved problems to be faced in equating the two. Acts 15:22 suggests a public meeting, but Galatians 2:2 indicates a private one. In the Acts account, certain conditions are imposed on the Gentiles, but in Galatians there seem to be none. It is hard to see how the events of Galatians 2:11-14 could take place *after* the decisions of the Jerusalem council reflected in 2:1-10. Those who equate Acts 15 and Galatians 2:1-10 tend to regard the confrontation of Galatians 2:11-14 as happening *before* the visit of 2:1-10. Another difficulty is the numbering of Paul's visits to Jerusalem after his conversion. In Galatians it sounds like 1:18-20 is the apostle's first visit to Jerusalem (cf. Acts 9:26-30), and the trip of 2:1-10 his second. In Acts, chapter 15 is Paul's third visit to Jerusalem, following the second visit of 11:30 and 12:25.

Many of these difficulties disappear, however, if the trip to Jerusalem of Galatians 2:1-10 is equated with that in Acts 11:30 and 12:25. It solves the problem of the number of visits Paul makes to the holy city and assumes that the council of Acts 15 is not mentioned in Galatians. This might be because Galatians was written earlier than the council and/or because Paul is basing his ministry on the agreement reached on his second visit more than on the later decisions of the council.

The tentative solution to the Gentile question proposed in Galatians 2:1-10 may also account for the vacillation reflected in the sequel account in 2:11-21, with Paul confronting Peter to make the case for Jewish Christians and Gentile Christians eating together. In this episode, Peter's actions do not seem to be consistent with his experience of Acts 10. The council of Acts 15 is then called to settle the matter, with Peter now reciting how God gave the Holy Spirit to Cornelius and company. This view of the sequence of events also fits with Paul being told of the council's decree in Acts 21:25 as though for the first time—is James just reminding him, or was he not at the council? If not, that may explain why Paul rejects other food scruples (Col. 2:20-23, rules in addition to the Jerusalem decisions?) and does not absolutely forbid food offered to idols (1 Cor. 10:27-29; cf. Acts 15:29). Barnabas and Silas may have more to do with the council itself and presenting its letter of decisions than Paul does (Acts 15:12, with Barnabas named first; 15:32, 40; 16:4).

On this matter we can no longer be certain. It is the position of this commentary that the truth lies either in the traditional view of equating Acts 15 with the Galatians 2 visit, or in the alternative view that sees Acts 11:30 and 12:25 identifying the Jerusalem visit during which the events of Galatians 2:1-10 take place. (For details of this debate, see Cadbury and Lake, 5:195-212; Knox: 40-53; Dibelius: 93-101; Haenchen: 455-472; Marshall: 242-247.)

Council Decisions More Than Mere Compromise

At first glance the *decisions/decrees* issued by the Jerusalem consultation may seem to require each side of the controversy to give up some of its basic convictions in order to preserve unity in the church. This would be compromise. However, the church leaders are actually making sure that the Gentile mission can go forward by asking all converts to affirm basic Christian morality and show consideration for the scruples of the conservative Jewish element.

Two of the restrictions should cause no problem among most true believers. One is that they abstain from *fornication/unchastity* (NRSV/RSV) or sexual immorality. Some enlightened Gentiles may already hold this as important even before accepting the gospel and would readily agree to it as a requirement of the church. This decree possibly prohibited marriage within the prohibited degrees of relationship (Lev. 18:6-18; 1 Cor. 5:1), which the rabbis said was forbidden for *porneia* (*fornication*, Acts 15:20, 29); mixed marriages with pagans (Num. 25:1; 2 Cor. 6:14); and religious prostitution and participation in pagan worship, which is spiritual adultery (Hos. 2; 1 Cor. 6:15-20; Rev. 2:14; Metzger: 431).

The general command to avoid the pollution of *idols* (15:20) is something most new converts would see as necessary. The specific restriction against food *sacrificed to idols* (15:29; 21:25) might cause some discussion and difference of opinion, as later at Corinth. Yet most of them would agree with Paul's convincing teaching on the subject (1 Cor. 10:14-33; Rom. 14). Certainly Judas and Silas, sent to interpret the decision, are prepared to make explanations similar to this and prevent any serious division on this point.

The other decree on diet, to avoid eating *what is strangled* or what has *blood* in it, causes the most difficulty and requires the greatest change in the eating habits of Gentile Christians. Yet, with "kosher" Jewish butchers and markets in most cities of the Graeco-Roman world, this would not likely cause serious hardship. Paul was even willing to eat vegetarian to avoid offense (1 Cor. 8:13).

The agreements reached in Jerusalem do more than any mere compromise could do. They provide a basis for an ongoing world mission with the minimum of tension or division. True, the Jew-Gentile question will continue for a generation or more, but a significant step forward has been taken. While there are no close biblical parallels to this situation, the same kind of divinely inspired wisdom that helped resolve the Hebrew-Hellenist dispute of Acts 6 is in evidence here, with similar successful results in the spread of the gospel.

THE TEXT IN THE LIFE OF THE CHURCH
The Emergence of Spirit-led Leadership

Deeply rooted in the believers church tradition is the practice of having persons rise from among the laity and become set-aside and Spirit-endowed leaders of the church. This is what occurs in Antioch when the Holy Spirit directs the choosing of Barnabas and Saul for a work to which they are to be called (13:1-3). Instead of the congregation deciding on their own that they would like to send missionaries out to a given area and then electing them by popular vote, they are in prayer and fasting as the *Spirit* speaks and chooses. This divine directive is then accepted by the whole body, and the two persons chosen by the Holy Spirit are put before them for consecration. Such a procedure keeps human factors to a minimum, so that the choice is not based on popularity, political influence, or family backing, but on divine election. Nor is it, as in some Christian bodies, a matter of apostolic succession nor an appointment made by a central office.

Reaching Unbelievers with Limited Preparation

The experience of Paul and Barnabas with the worshipers of Zeus at Lystra (14:15-18) has been paralleled many times in the work of missionaries of various denominations. H. Stover Kulp, a pioneer of the Anabaptist-Brethren tradition who labored among the illiterate people of northeastern Nigeria, was asked how he presented Christ to those with so little background. His reply, remembered by the author, showed real understanding of the Acts 14:15-18 story:

> Since our meetings were usually out under a tree, I would reach down, pick up a twig, and ask where it came from. On being told that it came from a branch overhead, I would ask where the tree itself came from, and the answer would always be *God*. In similar fashion I would trace the origin of other objects and get the same reply. Then I would have them tell me if they had *ever seen* or *heard* God. After much discussion I would be told, "No, we have never seen God with these eyes nor heard him talk with these ears." I would thank them for their good answer and tell them how true it is, but that a long time ago God sent his Son and people *could see* him with their eyes and *hear* him with their ears, and what is more, it is written down in a book—which I would then show them. Eagerly they would listen as I read to them some of the deeds and sayings of Jesus in

their own language. From that I would tell them of our Bible classes and services and invite them to enroll in literacy classes and send their children to the school. Eventually, many of them would give their hearts to the Lord and become Christians.

Inequality and Prejudice in the Body of Christ

Peter's statement in 15:9 that God makes no distinction between Jew and Gentile is coupled with the decision of the council to insure equal status for Gentiles within the church. This calls each generation to reexamine themselves at this point. The late twentieth century and early twenty-first are still wrestling with distinctions arising, among other things, from race, ethnic origin, education, economic level, and gender. Usually people will grant that different persons have *salvation* but at the same time be reluctant to treat them as full brothers and sisters in the body of Christ, with equality in every way.

In the believers church tradition, in addition to the prejudices listed above, there are often two other more subtle kinds of bias. One of these arises out of the kinship structures within the church. Old established family lines with certain well-known names sometimes have an advantage over newcomers with strange-sounding names. Different waves of migration have also been known to cause divisions. Persons from other states and especially other countries even within the same denomination have at times found full acceptance difficult. One middle-aged wife who had moved from a distance into such an ethnically solid church community tearfully explained that, though a member in good standing, even after twenty years she was not made to feel at home!

The other area of concern in such denominations is what might be called ethical edginess. The laudable emphasis of the Anabaptist-Brethren on strong family life, clean living, economic sufficiency, and peace has sometimes made them overly critical of followers of Jesus without these same standards. Like the Judaizers in Acts 15, they find it hard to accept as equals in the church those whose gifts may differ and whose personal habits are not like their own, even though such people have experienced conversion and are led by the Spirit. We need to uphold strong biblical teachings with love and understanding and to maintain the unity of the body. The gift of the Spirit should be decisive, not works or ethics. Never should we let our social concerns or high moral standards mute our testimony to God's saving grace!

Personal Presence for Interpretation and Reconciliation

The wisdom shown by the Jerusalem apostles and elders in sending two of their representatives with the decisions of the council is one well understood in the subsequent history of Christianity. This is especially true in the believers church tradition, where decrees from central bodies are not always appreciated unless they are personally interpreted. In Acts this was the principle behind sending Peter and John to confirm the work of Philip in Samaria (8:14-25) and dispatching Barnabas to assist with the new work at Antioch (11:22-24). Among Anabaptist-Brethren churches, many misunderstandings have been averted by sending not only decisions but also conciliatory persons into situations that otherwise might prove divisive.

In the same spirit, the Jerusalem Council also sends a well-worded letter with persons who are to present the decrees. It is written not to Gentiles alone but to Christians of all backgrounds and reflects the kind of sweet reasonableness that one would expect among persons who have experienced the grace of the Lord Jesus. Yet it is not a permissive document, but one meant to be obeyed. Even so, the readers are treated with great respect. The assumption is that Gentile and Jewish Christians will *want* to cooperate and work together harmoniously. Thus also, in the history of the church, there have been many delicate situations in which legalism or harshness would have only brought disaster. Christian groups, at their best, have learned from this and other examples, that a courteous yet firm document in the hands of the personal representatives is a great help in preserving harmony in the body of Christ.

Part 8

The Witness in Macedonia and Athens

Acts 15:36—17:34

PREVIEW

After the decisions at Jerusalem, the way is clear for further mission work in Gentile areas. Luke tells how Paul takes the initiative by suggesting to Barnabas that they return and strengthen the churches established on their previous journey. This results in a sharp controversy and the regrouping of teams, as Paul takes Silas (representing Jerusalem) and later picks up Timothy (of Jew-Gentile descent and from the newly evangelized churches). Barnabas chooses John Mark, takes him along to Cyprus, and is never mentioned again.

Whereas in the previous section (chaps. 13—15), Paul and Barnabas worked together much as equals, first one taking precedence and then the other, from this point on to the end of Acts, it becomes primarily *Paul's* mission. His companions fade more and more into the background and, beginning with chapter 17, Paul is alone or with others who either remain unnamed or are with him only temporarily.

Here are echoes of the earlier journey as Paul and his new partners move in a westerly direction. This one also begins from Antioch with the support of that church (cf. 15:40; 13:3; 14:26). While there is no mention of the Holy Spirit sending them out, as in 13:2-3, the Spirit does meet them along the way and guide them in negative fashion (16:6-7) until they reach Troas. There in a vision, Paul receives divine authority for going forward into Macedonia (16:8-9).

This is a new and greatly expanded missionary enterprise in the general direction of Rome, where the witness is to find its fulfillment (1:8; 28:30-31). This section takes the apostle and his companions into the centers of ancient Greek political power and culture, now under Roman control. First comes Macedonia, the home of the illustrious King Philip and his even more famous son, Alexander the Great. After that the witness is taken to Athens, the cultural capital of the Greeks.

The reader will be treated, in these various missions, to an interesting and exciting variety of experiences: clashes with local authorities, encounters with Roman nationalism, a night in jail, a couple of narrow escapes and sudden flights for safety, and an attempt to present Christ to a sophisticated group of philosophers.

This section and the one following (chaps. 18—19) give Luke an opportunity to present a series of four "type-scenes" (repeated patterns) dealing with *public accusations* against Paul and his mission. Taken together, they provide illustrations of the problems Christianity creates for the culture about it (Tannehill, 2:201-3). Gentiles are the accusers in the first and fourth of these, and Jews in the second and third. The two charges found in chapters 16—17 are that the apostles are (1) importing Jewish customs that undermine practices that supposedly made Rome great (16:20-21) and (2) upsetting society by claiming another king than Caesar (17:5-7). (The third and fourth, in 18:12-13 and 19:25-27, are discussed in the next section). There also are many minor literary patterns, echoes of earlier emphases, and similarities in structure. These are mentioned in the notes as they occur.

OUTLINE

From Antioch to Troas, 15:36—16:10

15:36-39	Separation of Paul and Barnabas
15:40—16:5	Paul Visits Galatia Again, with Silas
16:6-8	Journey of Paul, Silas, and Timothy to Troas
16:9-10	Paul's Vision and Call to Macedonia

Witness of Paul and Silas in Philippi, 16:11-40

16:11-12	Journey of the Four to Philippi
16:13-15	Witness to the Women and Conversion of Lydia
16:16-18	Deliverance of a Demonized Slave Girl
16:19-24	Public Disturbance; Apostles Imprisoned
16:25-34	Earthquake at Midnight; Jailer Converted
16:35-40	Magistrates' Accountability; Apostles Depart

The Witness in Thessalonica, 17:1-9
17:1-4   Journey to Thessalonica; Synagogue Ministry
17:5-9   Disturbance; Release of Paul and Silas

The Witness in Berea, 17:10-14

The Witness in Athens, 17:15-34
17:15   Journey to Athens
17:16-21   Encounters with Jews and Philosophers
17:22-31   Paul's Message at the Areopagus
17:32-34   Responses to Paul's Message

EXPLANATORY NOTES
From Antioch to Troas   15:36—16:10
15:36-39 Separation of Paul and Barnabas

After a brief time at Antioch, Paul, still taking the initiative, suggests to Barnabas a return to the churches recently founded in the southern part of the province of Galatia (15:36). Since they spent some time with each of these congregations on their way back to Antioch of Syria (14:21-23), this would be a third visit to most of them, something beneficial for new Christian fellowships facing opposition. The return is all the more urgent if, as many scholars believe, the crisis reflected in the letter to the Galatians has already arisen. Whatever the situation, there is still enough to deal with to justify Paul's proposal.

Barnabas is willing to go but strongly desires to give his cousin John Mark another chance and to take him along (15:37; Col. 4:10). This is what one would expect from the man who sponsored the newly converted Saul of Tarsus when everyone else was afraid of him (9:26-27). It is also the spirit with which he greeted the new Christian fellowship at Antioch, searched eagerly for this same man Saul, and brought him there to work as his partner (11:22-26).

Now Barnabas's suggestion touches a sensitive nerve, and Paul strikes back with a resounding no! Apparently their relationship has not completely healed from disappointment over Mark's defection in 13:13, or perhaps from confrontations like that of Galatians 2:11-21 over whether Jewish and Gentile believers may eat together (cf. esp. Gal. 2:13; Acts 10:28). There may even be a bit of rivalry over leadership. At any rate, Paul *kept insisting* that they should not take Mark (15:38, NASB). The result is a *sharp contention* (RSV) which leads to a permanent separation of these longtime partners. Barnabas takes his young relative with him, and they go to Cyprus, his former homeland and the area of their earlier ministry (15:39).

15:40—16:5 Paul Visits Galatia Again, with Silas

Paul chooses Silas and they leave, now carrying out the proposal he made to Barnabas of returning to the Galatian area and strengthening the churches there. No doubt they are duly consecrated and sent out as were the original two, with fasting, prayer, and the laying on of hands (13:3), spoken of here as *the believers commending him to the grace of the Lord* (15:40). So much is Paul now the leader that Luke simply writes that *he* goes through *Syria and Cilicia*, although Silas is obviously with him as the bearer of the decisions of the council. *Strengthening the churches* now includes sharing with them the good news that from this time on Gentiles can be received into the kingdom as first-class citizens, equal to converted Jews (15:41).

They probably travel north from Antioch and westward across Cilicia to Tarsus, Paul's hometown. Then northward they climb up through the pass in the Taurus Mountains known as the Cilician Gates. From there a westwardly route veering slightly to the south takes them first to Derbe and then to Lystra. Again Luke says little about Derbe (cf. 14:20-21), but they undoubtedly visit the Christians there and deliver the decisions of the council (16:4). The real emphasis is on Lystra, that backward Lycaonian town where Paul almost lost his life on the earlier visit (14:8-20). There they not only find an ongoing church but stay long enough to recruit *Timothy*, a young *disciple* (16:1) destined to play an important role in the life and ministry of Paul from this time on.

Luke introduces Timothy here as the product of a mixed Jew-Gentile home, with a Greek father and a Jewish mother (16:1). The use of the aorist tense of the verb suggests that the father has died (16:3; Marshall: 259). The mother, Eunice, and the grandmother Lois have taught Timothy the Scriptures from childhood, and by now the three are believers (2 Tim. 1:5; 3:15). Paul is impressed that Timothy has qualities that would make him a good third member of the team, possibly to *assist*, doing the work earlier performed by John Mark (see on 13:5). He is *well spoken of* by believers of both his hometown and Iconium, only eighteen miles away (16:2). A good reputation is highly important (cf. 1:21; 6:3; 1 Tim. 3:7).

There is one serious difficulty, however. Paul cannot take this uncircumcised son of a Gentile father (whom the Jews know would not circumcise his son) and have him well received by Jews with whom he will minister. For Timothy to have full credentials with all groups, he must be circumcised, which Paul has done (16:3). Some scholars like Haenchen (478-479) see this as inconsistent with Paul's teaching (Gal. 5:2-6) and out of harmony with the decisions of the Jerusalem council. But this is not circumcision as a *requirement for salvation*. It is equipping an already-saved man for effective work among people of all backgrounds. Furthermore, if Timothy is counted as a Jew because his mother is Jewish, this circumcision is consistent with Paul's rejection of the rite for Gentiles (Munck, 1967:155).

Luke makes no mention of the now-enlarged team's visits to Iconium and Antioch, but these would be included in towns mentioned in 16:4, where they share the decisions of the Jerusalem council. Then before he tells of the three leaving the area, the author gives another brief summary of the daily growth of the church (16:5). Similar to earlier summaries in 6:7; 9:31; and 12:34, this one refers primarily to the Galatian churches and tells how they are *strengthened in the faith* and increasing *in numbers daily*.

16:6-8 Journey of Paul, Silas, and Timothy to Troas

The team has now covered the areas previously evangelized and continues on in a northwesterly direction into new territory. The *region of Phrygia and Galatia* through which they pass seems to be all one area. Phrygia is the older ethnic label; its southeastern part lies in the newer Roman province of Galatia, and the northwestern part in the province of Asia. But they are *forbidden by the Holy Spirit to speak the word* and to evangelize while passing through *Asia* at this time (16:6), so they continue in a northwestern direction toward *Mysia* (16:7a). This revelation may be one given to Paul or to the team through the prophet Silas (cf. 15:32).

Then after two hundred miles or so of walking toward the northwest, they start to go into the province of Bithynia, an attractive area to the north with several cities where the gospel might be preached. But again the Spirit, this time called *the Spirit of Jesus*, says no! (16:7). They are actually trying to enter Bithynia when they are stopped by the Spirit, and this has led to speculation. Some think it may be a matter of local circumstances, like Haenchen's suggestion (486) that they are stopped by bad political relations between that country and Galatia. While this is possible, it is not *Luke's* story. He is interested in showing how God is directing his men toward the ministry which they are to do.

Prevented from entering Bithynia, they must still go through Mysia, a wild and lonely country. The term used is *passing by* in the sense of neglecting, *passing through hurriedly* (16:8, CF). This brings them to Troas on the coast of the Aegean Sea. Ten miles south of ancient Troy, it has become the chief port of call for ships plying between Asia Minor and Macedonia. In the early years of the first century, it was made a Roman colony by Caesar Augustus and known officially as Colonia Augusta Troas.

16:9-10 Paul's Vision and Call to Macedonia

After two negative leadings of the Spirit, Paul may be wondering if he has now reached a dead end and must go back (Neill: 180). But while here at Troas, he is given a positive word in a night vision. Paul sees a man of Macedonia standing before him, recognizable perhaps by his garb, and if not, at least by what he says. He begs the apostle and his men to come over to his province and *help* them (16:9). The nature of the help will be seen in the events that follow—clearly understood by Paul as taking the gospel to that area.

Ramsay, and others after him, have the theory that this *man of Macedonia* might be Luke himself. Luke now enters the story (16:10, *we*), goes to Macedonia with the team, and apparently remains there. Although Ramsay's theory is attractive, there is no proof for it. What we do know is that Paul wastes no time in following the vision. On the assumption that the use of *we* at this point includes the author (see page 18, on "Author"), there now are four who *immediately* want to sail to Macedonia to obey the call to preach the *good news* there (16:10). This use of the first-person plural subject continues through 16:17 and is resumed in 20:5, to occur off and on until 28:16. Thus Luke modestly makes his presence known as one of the persons present during the events recorded in these sections.

The Witness of Paul and Silas in Philippi 16:11-40

16:11-12 Journey of the Four to Philippi

Paul, Silas, Timothy, and Luke soon find a ship in the Troas harbor and sail for Macedonia. As personally on board, the author notes at the end of the first day's voyage the mountainous island of Samothrace, rising some five thousand feet above the sea. At the end of the second day, with favorable wind, they make the port city of *Neapolis*, altogether about 125 miles from Troas (16:11). (In 20:6, with an adverse wind, it takes *five* days to return over the same expanse of water!) Neapolis, the modern Kavalla, is the gateway to Philippi, some ten miles inland. It is also the eastern end of the Egnatian Way, the Roman road which links the Adriatic and Aegean Seas.

Three or four hours of walking bring the party into Philippi, *a leading city of the district of Macedonia* (16:12). By this time it is an old city, begun early in the fourth century B.C. and first known as Krenides, the "place of springs." Then in 356 B.C. Philip of Macedon took control and named it Philippi, after himself. High above the city stands the acropolis (chief fortification on a hill) with the rest of the settlement spread out at its base. Along the west side is the river Gangites, and near it the large open area where, in 42 B.C., Mark Antony and Octavian Caesar (later called Augustus, Luke 2:1) defeated Brutus and Cassius for supremacy. After those battles, the Romans made the city a colony and officially named it Colonia Julia Augusta Philippensis.

The population in Paul's day consists of Thracians from the local area, Greeks brought in when it was further settled, and finally Romans, introduced after it became a colony. Thus the local religion is a mixture of the worship of the old Thracian gods and goddesses, the Greek Athena, and the Roman gods of Jupiter, Mars, and the emperor. Also present are the mystery cults of Cybele, Isis, and others.

Philippi is not *the* leading city of this district (16:12, RSV and NIV), but rather *a* leading city (NRSV). Amphipolis is the capital of this "first district" which includes Philippi, and Thessalonica is capital of all Macedonia. There are variant Greek texts, and some scholars read *a city of the first district of Macedonia* (Metzger: 444-446). More important for Luke's narrative, however, is the status of the city as *a Roman colony*. As already noted in connection with 13:15 and 14:5, these are outposts of imperial authority, "little Italys" with many veterans of the wars and their descendants. Latin is spoken by the higher officials, and an air of Roman superiority pervades the place. In no other city of Acts outside of Rome are these aspects more in evidence than here in Philippi.

16:13-15 Witness to the Women and Conversion of Lydia

There is apparently no synagogue *inside* Philippi, perhaps because of Roman dislike of Jewish *customs* (cf. 16:20-21) or the lack of ten adult male Jews to begin one. But there is a *place of prayer*, possibly a synagogue, outside the city on the banks of the river Gangites (or Ganga), away from the anti-Jewish Roman settlement and at a place where water is available for ceremonial washings (cf. Ps. 137:1). Paul and company find it and appear on the Sabbath for worship, along with a group of *women* who gather there regularly (16:13).

The atmosphere is informal as they sit down and talk with the small company of devout followers of Yahweh. Paul is the speaker and makes at least one convert, a woman called Lydia, whose heart *the Lord opened* to hear the gospel message (16:14). They learn that she is a dealer in purple goods from *Thyatira,* a city known for its textile manufacturing, capital of the district of Lydia in the province of Asia. She may be an agent for one of the companies there. Apparently named after her district of origin, Lydia is obviously well-to-do, as shown by her living quarters, which are big enough to house them all (16:15b, 40). More important is her religious situation. Luke calls her a *worshiper of God.* This term *worshiper/devout* is used in 13:43 to modify *proselytes,* Gentile converts to Judaism, but Lydia is not called a proselyte. Like Cornelius (10:2), she is likely a devout inquirer, worshiping at Jewish services without becoming a convert.

The narrative passes swiftly from her opened heart to her baptism, leaving the impression that it happens that first Sabbath (16:15). This would echo the Ethiopian's experience of immediate baptism in 8:36 and be matched by that of the jailer (16:33; cf. Neill: 182). On the other hand, the use of verbs in the progressive sense—*was listening . . . eagerly to what was [being] said* (16:14)—might be taken to mean it does not all take place on one Sabbath (Lenski: 658). Her *household,* also *baptized,* would be family members, domestic servants, and/or business associates. This also repeats the experiences of Cornelius and his people (10:47-48), and of the jailer and his family in 16:33, providing a series of three such group baptisms.

Whatever the timing on this occasion, Lydia demonstrates that she is genuinely converted not only by her confession of Jesus but by opening her *home* to these traveling evangelists. Hospitality is one of the graces of true Christianity (Rom. 12:13; 1 Tim. 3:2; Heb. 13:2; 1 Pet. 4:9; 3 John 5-8). Hers is an especially persuasive appeal. She puts her discipleship on the line and tells them that if they regard her as truly *faithful to the Lord,* they will come. They may be reluctant, or

Luke uses a touch of dry humor: *And she prevailed upon us* (15:15). At any rate, her spacious accommodations now become their lodging place and perhaps the headquarters of the new church (cf. 15:40).

16:16-18 Deliverance of a Demonized Slave Girl

On a later trip to the place of prayer, the evangelists are met by a slave girl oppressed by a demonic *spirit of divination* (15:16). It is called a *spirit of Python* (Greek text), after the snake that guards the sacred shrine at Delphi, where divine oracles are given. The Greeks speak of persons under its power as ventriloquists, giving forth utterances beyond conscious control, the same word used of the witch of Endor (1 Sam. 28:7-25, Greek). This particular slave is being exploited by owners making money from her (16:16), rough men capable of attacking Paul and Silas and dragging them into the marketplace (cf. 16:19).

Being attracted to the evangelists, the girl begins to follow them about and publicly advertises their ministry: *These men are slaves of the Most High God, who proclaim to you a way of salvation* (16:17). This is the way certain demonized persons announced Jesus, recognizing him more readily than did normal people and acknowledging his power over them. Hence, Jesus rebuked the demons and cast them out (Luke 4:35, 41; 8:29; and par.). After *many days* Paul is so thoroughly *annoyed* by the slave girl's unsolicited publicity that he turns and addresses the evil spirit and orders it to come out *in the name of Jesus Christ.* The effect is immediate, and she is delivered once for all of her demonic burden (16:18). Nothing more is said about the girl, whether she becomes a Christian or not or ever finds her way into the Philippian church. Luke turns attention to the effect this deliverance has on her owners.

16:19-24 Public Disturbance; Apostles Imprisoned

The owners are outraged by this merciful act, which robs the girl of her ability to tell fortunes and cheats them of a nice income. So they seize Paul and Silas, the two leaders, manhandle them, and hustle them into the marketplace. There, in what is known as the agora or forum, where both the courthouse and prison are located, the two men are brought before the city officials for trial (16:19). The charge against them is that they are Jewish troublemakers advocating customs unlawful for Romans to accept or practice (16:20-21).

Two aspects of it stand out in Luke's striking summary. One is the strong anti-Semitism that puts their being Jewish as the first change against them. The other is the tough Roman nationalism apparent in the accusers' smug reference to themselves as *us Romans*. They do not mention their real grievance against the apostles, the loss of profits from this closing down of a questionable business. Instead, they cloak it under emotionally charged religious and racial accusations. Added to this is the fact that just the previous year (A.D. 49) the Emperor Claudius expelled all Jews from Rome, the impact of which is no doubt sharply felt in this Roman colony *[Chronology, p. 309]*. That is why Paul and Silas can be so viciously attacked even though there is nothing against Rome in the things they have been doing—attending Jewish worship, making converts to Christianity, casting out a demon.

There seems to be no real trial, no attempt to hear what the accused have to say. Their guilt is assumed, and immediate punishment is inflicted. Even the magistrates join in and tear the clothes off them while they give orders to the lictors (men with rods for beating prisoners) to strip them and flog them soundly (16:22). This may well be one of the three beatings with rods which Paul later mentions in 2 Corinthians 11:25. It is a cruel whipping which breaks the skin and raises inflamed welts on the backs of the victims. In this case, it is all the harder to bear, because it is both undeserved and highly illegal, as they later maintain (cf. 16:37).

Not content with simple imprisonment, the authorities consign Paul and Silas to the *innermost cell* of the prison (16:24). They instruct the jailer to keep them safe, and this he does by shackling their feet in stocks, wooden fasteners bolted to the wall. This is either in the dungeon or the most remote inner cell. The jailer is likely a centurion, disciplined, trustworthy, and eager to carry out these orders to the letter.

16:25-34 Earthquake at Midnight; Jailer Converted

Hours go by as God's messengers sit uncomfortably bound in the darkness, their backs sore and bleeding. Yet, instead of groaning or vowing revenge, they are praying and singing psalms to their Lord in sounds that carry throughout the prison. The present participle for the praying and the imperfect tense for the singing of hymns show continuous, simultaneous witnessing. Here are seen in action the Christian ideals of praying and rejoicing under all circumstances (cf.

Phil. 4:4; 1 Thess. 5:16; Rom. 5:3; James 1:2; 1 Pet. 5:6).

Then, without warning, an earthquake strikes. It is so powerful that the prison foundations are badly shaken, doors fly open, and individual fetters come unfastened (16:26). Earth tremors are quite common in this area, yet the timing and effects of this massive one are seen as a divine answer to prayer, both by the prisoners and by Luke himself. God has intervened to make sure that the work goes forward! Just how an earthquake can dislodge bars from doors, bolts from walls, and loosen each prisoner's bonds has been questioned by some. For the persons involved, however, nothing is impossible with God (Luke 1:37; cf. Neill: 184, discussing possibilities in this case).

The shaking of the earth awakens the jailer, possibly in his house above the prison, and he rushes down to find the doors flung open. He assumes the prisoners have escaped in the darkness. As a Roman officer strictly charged with the care of all prisoners, there is only one thing to do, and that is to commit suicide. He knows that any guard who permits a prisoner to escape will have to bear that person's punishment (12:19; 27:42). Drawing the short sword which every centurion carries as part of his equipment, he is about to kill himself when Paul intervenes (16:27-28). Out of the darkness the apostle shouts that all of them are here. So, trembling with fright, the jailer calls his assistants to light torches, and in the smoky gloom, he sees Paul and Silas calm and composed. He rushes to them and falls at their feet (16:29). They are obviously men with miraculous powers, and he needs their help.

What must I do to be saved? he cries in desperation (16:30). This echoes the similar question asked by those cut to the heart by Peter's Pentecost speech (2:37). But what does the jailer now mean by his question? The prisoners have not escaped, so he has already been saved from his Roman superiors. Yet here is a force beyond any he has encountered before. How can he be saved from such tremendous power, such a God? Though he does not know the Christian meaning of salvation, these evangelists see that he is ready for that experience and answer that he must *believe on the Lord Jesus,* he and his whole *household* (16:31). The story is as abbreviated here as it was in the case of Lydia (16:14) and the Ethiopian (8:35). Luke has already written enough in Acts about what it means to be a Christian that he can move swiftly to the climax of the story. No detail is given about them going *up into the house,* nor of the instruction Paul and Silas give those present (16:33).

What is mentioned is the care with which the now-converted jailer has the wounds of the apostles washed and dressed (16:33a). Many hours have gone by since the severe flogging, and this good Samaritan type of ministry (Luke 10:34) is remembered and recorded here with great appreciation. Then the jailer and his whole household are *baptized* (16:33b). Luke gives no information as to the place or form of baptism, nor of any problem in finding sufficient water at this time of night. It is the *fact* of baptism that is stressed, that it is of the whole group, and happens *without delay*.

The concluding scene shows the jailer taking the evangelists up into his house, where food has been prepared, and feeding these men who haven't eaten since the morning before (16:34a). There are echoes here of the early Jerusalem Christians, who broke bread in their homes and partook of food *with glad and generous hearts* (2:46). Paul later breaks bread on board ship and urges all to eat and regain strength (27:33-36). For now the jailer with his household is rejoicing over becoming a *believer in God* (16:34b), just like the Ethiopian who went his way rejoicing after his baptism (8:39).

16:35-40 Magistrates' Accountability; Apostles Depart

Day comes quickly as the jailer finds *police* at his door (the lictors who earlier did the beating; cf. 16:22-23). They give the simple command to let the prisoners go, without any reason for this unexpected order (16:35). Perhaps the magistrates know of the earthquake and want nothing to do with the men responsible for it. More likely, they consider that a beating, an overnight in jail, and a command to leave the city are enough punishment for such a minor misdemeanor. The jailer quickly reports the release order to Paul and Silas, possibly expecting them to be happy over the cheerful word to *come out now and go in peace* (16:36).

Paul, however, refuses to leave under these conditions. He tells the police that he and Silas are Roman citizens who have been illegally beaten and thrown into prison. They all know that this is a grave offense that could lead to severe punishment. So Paul gives an emphatic no! to any attempt on the part of the authorities to get rid of them privately. He asks that they come personally and set them free (16:37). Luke does not say why the evangelists have waited this long to declare their citizenship. But it should be obvious that the events of their arrest (16:19-23) happened so swiftly that there was no opportunity to make any defense and that, had they tried, they could not have been heard above the noise. Now, however, in the calm of the morning after, they can make their point. Not only is Paul interested in establishing their own status as citizens but also in protecting the newly established church from harassment.

The police respond immediately and hurry back to inform the magistrates of the new development. This puts fear into the city officials, for they know that to mistreat a citizen is punishable by death (16:38). On the other hand, falsely to say *Civis Romanum sum* (I am a Roman citizen) is also a capital crime, so Paul and Silas must be able to make good on their claim. The same issue will come up again in 22:25-28 and there too be settled by simple affirmation. It becomes a battle of wills, and in both instances Paul wins out.

The Philippian *magistrates* come and *apologize* to the missionaries (*appease them*, NIV; *appeal to them*, NASB), making a formal request that they leave the city (16:39). They probably feel they no longer want to be responsible for persons capable of bringing such wrath upon officials. Paul, on the other hand, is apparently satisfied and makes no further demands; he and his party prepare to leave. They are in no hurry, however, and return to the house of Lydia, where the Christian group is assembled. There Paul can give them a final exhortation, and the three missionaries leave with dignity. Luke apparently remains in Philippi, since the *we* passages have already come to an end in 16:17 and will not be resumed until 20:5.

The Witness in Thessalonica 17:1-9

17:1-4 Journey to Thessalonica; Synagogue Ministry

The party of three pass through Amphipolis and Apollonia on their way to Thessalonica (17:1), traveling on the Egnatian Way (see on 16:11). Since these towns have no synagogues and are spaced a day's journey apart (thirty to thirty-five miles), they are listed simply as overnight stops. Like Philippi, Thessalonica is an old city given new life under the Greeks and Romans. In 316 B.C. it was named from Thessalonike, wife of King Cassandra, daughter of Philip of Macedon, and stepsister of Alexander the Great. Before long it became the chief seaport of Macedonia and was made the seat of administration of the province two years after the Romans took over in 148 B.C. By the time of Paul, it is a thriving walled city, with the Egnatian Way running through it from southeast to northwest. Just north of that highway near the middle of the city is the agora (forum).

Three features of the place are important for understanding the story in Acts. First, the ruling authorities are called *politarchs*, a name found only in Macedonia and ascribed to them by Luke (17:6, 8, note). Not until the nineteenth century were inscriptions found to confirm this title and prove the author's accuracy here. Second, the city has a large synagogue, providing a base for Paul's preaching and teaching (17:1). Third, extensive dockyards provide *ruffians* to be easily found and incited to mob action in the marketplace (17:5).

Luke's story of the mission is brief and highly selective. Paul goes into the synagogue and for three successive Sabbaths presents the gospel from the Hebrew Scriptures (17:2). Since readers have already been given an example of such preaching in 13:16-41, all that is needed now is a short summary. Here again the kerygma consists of showing the necessity of Christ's suffering, followed by his resurrection (17:3; cf. Luke 9:22; 17:25; 24:26, 46; Acts 3:18-20), and the proclamation that such a Messiah can be none other than Jesus of Nazareth (Acts 9:22; 13:23-38). This is the crucial issue for Jews, and *some of them* are convinced (17:4). Though a minority, they are enough to provide a Jewish Christian base for the new group of believers.

Most who accept the gospel, however, are *devout Greeks,* God-fearing Gentiles like Cornelius (10:1-48) and Lydia (16:14-40), *a great many* of them. Then Luke mentions a third group worth noting in the Thessalonian situation: *leading women,* including both upper-class women of influence and possibly also wives of leading men of the city. They are *not a few* in number, that is, *quite a few* (17:4). Although they also belong to the devout Gentile class, they are distinctive enough to be mentioned separately. There is a clear contrast here with Pisidian Antioch, where *women of high standing* were used to stir up opposition against the apostles (13:50). The Philippian church had notable women like Lydia and her friends (16:13-15, 40), and a good many *Greek women and men of high standing* will be mentioned among the converts at Berea (17:12). Hence, this would seem to be a special characteristic of the Macedonian congregations.

This first phase of the mission in Thessalonica, within the synagogue, is said to last only three weeks (17:2). But the situation reflected in Paul's two letters to them suggests a much longer stay in the city. In 1 Thessalonians 2:9-11, he speaks of a period of toiling with his hands to support himself, and in 4:1-12 he refers to instruction which would need to be given over a considerable time. Moreover, a reasonably long ministry is suggested in the greatly telescoped text of 17:5-9. The seeming discrepancy is resolved, however, when it is noted that these verses in Acts indicate the length of time spent in the synagogue, after which the new Christian fellowship leaves and moves to the house of Jason, where the work continues.

17:5-9 Disturbance; Release of Paul and Silas

After an interval perhaps of weeks, unbelieving Jews from the synagogue, like those in Pisidian Antioch (13:50), are *jealous* and take action against this newly proselyted group of Christians. They find *ruffians* in the marketplace who are easily persuaded to stir up a mob and attack the headquarters of the group (17:5). Their aim is to seize Paul and his men and bring them to justice before the *politarchs*. But, not finding them at home, they drag Jason and some other converts into court. This is the same kind of rough treatment that Paul and Silas received at Philippi (16:19-24).

The charge against the men is that they have taken in these well-known disturbers of the peace (17:6). The colorful rendering of the NRSV, that they are people who have been *turning the world upside down,* is attractive but introduces an idiom not found in the Greek. It is more accurate to say, *causing trouble all over the world* (NIV) or *upsetting the world* (NASB). Judging by what follows, it seems likely that Jason is a man of some importance, and for him to be harboring such dangerous men is serious business.

Even more threatening is the charge that they are *all* proclaiming *another king named Jesus* (17:7). This would include Jason and the other converts, as well as the evangelists. Just what *decrees of the emperor* they are violating is not clear, unless it is mistakenly thought that Christians are predicting a change in rulers, something strictly forbidden by several imperial edicts. Actually, there is an element of truth in the charge, just enough to make it effective. These new believers are indeed worshiping Jesus instead of Caesar and regarding Jesus as Lord, a title to be applied only to the emperor. What their attackers do not understand is that they are not advocating the overthrow of the Roman government, but obedience to it as long as it is in harmony with God's law (Rom. 13:1-7; 1 Pet. 2:13-17). They have brought a peaceful revolution accomplished by the transformation of lives (Luke 3:10-14; 12:25-27; Acts 2:38; 9:1-18; Rom. 12:1-2).

The uproar of the mob and these emotionally charged accusations are enough to upset both people and rulers and force some kind of action against the Christians (17:8). Again, there is no formal trial, but this time the magistrates are much more restrained than at Philippi (cf. 16:22-24) and arrange a settlement by which the accused may go unmolested if Jason and the church will post *bail* (17:9). Luke says nothing of the terms of this "peace bond," but it is likely a sum of money guaranteeing that the party will leave town at once and not return in the foreseeable future. This explains the problem Paul later has of desperately wanting to return to Thessalonica but being unable to do so without bringing persecution upon the church (cf. 1 Thess. 2:17-20 and his statement, "We wanted to come to you, . . . but Satan blocked our way").

The Witness in Berea 17:10-14

Luke's story of the mission in Macedonia, like his treatment of the journey into Galatia, follows a pattern of accounts of decreasing lengths. In each case there is first a long, fairly detailed narrative (on Philippi in 16:11-40; cf. Pisidian Antioch in 13:13-52), then a shorter one or two accounts (on Thessalonica, with which compare Iconium and Lystra), and now this four-sentence report of events at *Berea* (matching an even briefer one about Derbe).

In spite of the peaceful settlement with the Thessalonian authorities, Jason and company take no chances and send the missionary team off by *night* to their next place of service. They travel west along the Egnatian Way for a short distance and then turn south on the road from Thessaly, climbing in elevation until they reach *Beroea* or *Berea* (NIV), forty-five miles away. There they find themselves in a summer resort area with pleasant streams and distant snow-capped mountains, a town that still exists, known as *Verria* and famous for its fine climate.

They seek out the synagogue (17:10) and are met by a *receptive* group of *Jews* (lit., *more noble*, RSV), who welcome their message eagerly. With no large commercial trade or tough Roman establishment as in the previous two centers, Berea is an ideal place for evangelistic work. Luke tells how they study the Scriptures daily in their zeal for the gospel (17:11). The result is a large ingathering of both men and women, mostly Gentiles who are devout and of high social standing (17:12). Little wonder that Christians through the centuries have used the name Berea for Bible classes, congregations, and religious institutions. Even the unbelieving Jews of the city seem to cause no trouble. Here at last would appear to be the fulfillment of the Macedonian mission!

Luke does not say how long such a favorable situation continues. Characteristically, he jumps to the conclusion of the matter. Enemies of the faith from Thessalonica hear of their success. The kind of people who stirred up the crowd in that city (17:5) now come to Berea and launch a bitter persecution (17:13), an echo of 14:19, when the angry Jews from Antioch and Iconium traveled all the way to Lystra to put an end to the evangelistic work. Again the Christian believers rally around the evangelists (cf. 16:40; 17:10) and get them out of danger. This time Paul is in the most risk, and his converts send him off before he is mobbed.

The best Greek manuscripts say they send *Paul off as far as the sea* (17:14, CF), but this is a bit strange when 17:15 says he is personally escorted all the way to Athens. The Byzantine text underlying KJV reads, *to go as it were to the sea.* This allows for the possibility that Paul's friends pretend they are taking him to the coast in order to throw off pursuers but actually send him southward toward Athens (for example, Bruce: 347). Since such a strategy cannot be proved, it is best to take the text as translated in NASB, NIV, and NRSV simply to mean that the Christians act quickly enough to get Paul out of Berea on his way to the sea and from there to Athens. All texts agree that Silas and Timothy, not being objects of the attack, can safely remain behind awhile to care for matters so abruptly brought to an end (17:14).

The Witness in Athens   17:15-34

17:15 Journey to Athens

Paul is quickly escorted to the sea by converts and then on to Athens two hundred miles to the south and slightly west by some unmentioned route. Luke says nothing of the mode of travel nor details of the journey, but a sea voyage is the most likely. His main interest is to get the apostle to the cultural capital of Greece as swiftly as possible and record his ministry there. Some scholars have conjectured that because Paul is taken there personally, he must be suffering another attack of illness (as in Gal. 4:13-14). But the unusual devotion of the Berean Christians would account for this loving service and make such a theory unnecessary. It is safer to travel as a group, and with Silas and Timothy left behind, others conduct Paul.

Paul puts his friends under strict orders (a *command*, RSV) to arrange for *Silas and Timothy* to come to him *as soon as possible* (17:15). These two do later rejoin Paul at Athens, and he sends them back to Macedonia—Timothy to Thessalonica and Silas likely to Philippi (1 Thess. 3:1-6). After that they will return to him yet another time after he has begun his work in Corinth (18:5).

17:16-21 *Encounters with Jews and Philosophers*

The author assumes that his readers know the city of Athens, the cultural center of the Greco-Roman world. Here, for over five centuries, its art, architecture, philosophy, and scientific studies have come to be recognized as among the highest achievements of the Western world. Though in Paul's day the city is no longer of political importance and is living on past glories, it is still revered for its former magnificence. The Romans have left it free to carry on its own traditions and institutions.

Yet the wonderful sculpture and architecture of the city, though without equal in the world of his day, mean only one thing to Paul: *idolatry*, and that on a wide scale. It is not that he is unfamiliar with Greek art. Having spent his early life in Tarsus, a Greek university city, and having returned there for several years as a mature man (cf. 9:30; 11:25), he is at home with structures of beauty and grace. But as a Jewish Christian, he sees behind all this cultural achievement a worship of false gods, *idols*. Instead of being filled with admiration for the great works of art he sees on every hand, he is *deeply distressed* (17:16, NIV, NRSV), *his spirit . . . provoked within him* (RSV, NASB).

All this happens while Paul is alone, looking around and waiting for Silas and Timothy to join him. Then Luke uses the strong *therefore* (CF; Greek: *men oun*) to introduce his attending the local *synagogue* and engaging in discussions there (17:17a). Perhaps in his mounting indignation over all the false gods, he goes to the synagogue to vent his feelings about idolatry to fellow believers in the one true God and stays on to preach Christ. Out of this ministry likely come some of the converts mentioned in 17:34. During the weekdays the apostle spends time in the ever-busy agora or marketplace, the center of city life. Here—amid shops, public buildings, and porches—he has many opportunities to meet Gentiles of all kinds and to address crowds. Here Socrates once engaged in public dialogue and, after him, centuries of other philosophers and wandering teachers.

During these days it is possible that Silas and Timothy have joined him and have been sent back to Macedonia (1 Thess. 3:1-5; see notes on 17:15), but Luke says nothing of this. The important thing now is Paul's contact with some Epicurean and Stoic philosophers, representing the two most influential schools of Greek thought of the times

(17:18). Epicurus (ca. 300 B.C.) taught that happiness is the highest good and is to be attained by living a life free from excesses of all kinds, getting rid of fear and of love for others. By Paul's time, however, this philosophy is often equated with the seeking of pleasure, a reputation that has persisted to our own day.

Stoicism, begun by Zeno (ca. 300 B.C.), taught that there is a great Purpose shaping all nature and humankind toward good ends. As people conform to this Purpose, they fulfill their destiny. What actually happens to a person is not as important as the pursuit of goodness for its own sake. From this view has come the popular use of the term *stoic* today to indicate the grim endurance of any kind of hardship.

Both of these philosophies, at their best, have points in common with Christianity. But as Paul's encounter with their followers shows, there are also some basic unbridged differences. With real contempt they call Paul a *babbler* (lit., *seedpicker*, a bird that feeds on fragments, a person who has no original ideas but passes on secondhand scraps of information). Others remark that he seems to be a *proclaimer of foreign divinities*, for they have heard him speak of *Jesus* and *Anastasis* (Greek for *resurrection*). No doubt they think this must be another pair of male and female gods (17:18).

The debate is no casual matter for these philosophers. They take Paul and bring him to *the Areopagus*, where they may further investigate his views (17:19). This literally means *the hill of Ares*, the Greek equivalent for the Roman god of war, Mars (hence the *Mars' hill* of KJV). In earlier times the supreme judicial and legislative body of the city met here. By Paul's time, this Areopagus council, stripped of its civil powers but continuing to control religion and education, no longer meets on the hill. Instead, it assembles in an open building at the marketplace known as the *Stoa Basileios* (according to most scholars). What now takes place is not so much a trial as an open hearing so this group in charge of public lecturers may scrutinize the new teaching.

Meeting in council, the authorities inquire about the strange new religion and ask Paul to explain it to them (17:19-20). At this point Luke adds a comment about the habit of Athenians and their many visitors of spending their time obsessively talking about the latest novelties (17:21). Other Greeks said this about them as well. For example, Demosthenes, the orator of Corinth, criticized the Athenians for running around looking for what was *new* instead of guarding their liberties (*Orat.* 4.10-11, cited by Neill: 190).

17:22-31   Paul's Message at the Areopagus

This speech and the short message at Lystra (14:15-18) are the two examples in Acts of the apostle's approach among people with no Jewish background or knowledge. This one, by far the longer of the two, provides a theological base for the coming ministries at Corinth and Ephesus, where the apostle goes far beyond the synagogue in the delicate task of appealing to Greek culture. As Tannehill suggests (2:212-213), we have here a universalized version of preaching *the whole counsel of God,* which Paul will tell the Ephesian elders has been his aim in the Greek mission (20:27, RSV).

Luke now paints the scene of Paul standing *in front of the Areopagus,* before the council and others gathered here. He addresses them as do the orators of the day, *Athenians/Men of Athens* (NRSV/RSV), and proceeds to make an observation that will lead into his message. He compliments them: *how extremely religious you are in every way* (17:22). In view of what follows, this seems to be truer to his intention than *superstitious* (KJV), since it is their yearning for God that he goes on to emphasize. To illustrate this point, he tells how, among their many objects of worship, he has found an altar inscribed *to an unknown god.*

No altar with this exact inscription has been found, nor is it quoted by the ancients. But church fathers and pagan writers mention Athenian altars "to unknown gods" or "unnamed gods," and such an inscription has been found at Pergamos. One pagan writer does tell of a sacrifice to "the god concerned in the matter," to cleanse the Athens from pestilence and pollution (Cadbury, 5:240-246, note by K. Lake). Possibly Paul does see an inscription *to an unknown god,* or with similar words (Bruce: 356; Marshall: 286). Some commentators, however, conclude with Jerome that Paul takes the liberty of changing the reference to fit his monotheistic message: from "unknown gods" to *an unknown god* (ABD, 6:753-755). Whatever the case, Paul is not implying that they have already been unknowingly worshiping such a god, but rather that what they do not know about the supreme deity, Paul will now make known to them.

Like a philosopher, the apostle begins with the First Cause, *the God who made the world and everything in it.* He proceeds to show that such a one does not live in temples made by hands and does not need people to serve him (17:24). This echoes a point made by Stephen (7:48-50). Thus he skillfully summarizes the best in Jewish and Christian thought in language acceptable to the Epicureans: God is self-sufficient. Then he makes a statement which the Stoics can approve, a free quotation of Isaiah 42:5b to the effect that God gives all humankind their life and breath (17:25). Since this, like all the speeches in Acts, is a brief digest, Paul no doubt elaborates further on these opening statements about God in his actual message.

Next Paul emphasizes the unity of humankind by creation, drawing heavily on Genesis 1 and 2. He uses terms that would appeal to the Stoics, who also stress this (17:26). Then he notes God's sovereign management of the world. This shows the goodness of the Lord, who allots to the nations their times of existence (as in Dan. 2:36-45; cf. Luke 21:24b) as well as their boundaries (Deut. 32: 8). All of this is designed to inspire people to seek after God with the hope of finding him. While talking the language of the philosophers about the human search for the infinite, Paul is really making the biblical appeal to *search for God* (Isa. 55:6; 65:1; Ps. 14:2; Prov. 8:17). On the human side, people *grope for* God, and this comes close to revelation, for God is available, *not far from each one* (17:27). The Stoics can also accept such teaching. However, for them there is no personal God, while for Paul this is the living Lord of Israel, always near at hand (Ps. 145:18; Jer. 23:23-24).

To clinch his argument, the apostle now quotes from the Greek poets. First comes a line adapted from Epimenides of Crete, that in God we *live and move and have our being* (17:28a). The second is found in several writers and in *Phaenomena* by Aratus of Cilicia (Paul's home province), who borrowed it from *A Hymn to Zeus* by Cleanthus, stating that we are indeed *God's offspring* (17:28b). Paul does not mean that Zeus is the same as the Christian God, nor that we are children of God in the way the poets view it. These quotations are points of contact from which he can proceed to preach the good news in Jesus.

From this point on, Paul begins to show the difference between the gospel and Greek philosophy. If we are God's children, then the divine nature cannot be represented in *gold, or silver, or stone* (17:29), a truth proclaimed in Scripture (Deut. 4:28; Ps. 115:4-8; Isa. 40:18-20; 44:9-20) and accepted by the more enlightened philosophers of the day. Moreover, God is willing to overlook the *ignorance* and idolatry of the past if people will now *repent* (17:30). This is necessary because (1) there is a *day* on which God *will have the world judged,* (2) through a *man whom he has appointed* and (3) approved as Lord and Judge by *raising him from the dead* (17:31). While Jesus' name is not mentioned in Luke's summary, there can be no question that he is the one with whom all must come to terms.

17:32-34 Responses to Paul's Message

The reported speech ends on this note of *the resurrection of the dead*, and to this Paul receives two main responses. As on the day of Pentecost, there are some who *scoff* (cf. 2:13), but *others* are open (cf. 2:12) and say they want to hear more about it (17:32). Many educated Greeks of the times believe in the immortality of the soul, but they think absurd the claim that a dead person once actually came to life again. Typical of this view is the statement put in the mouth of the god Apollo in the drama *Eumenides* by Aeschylus, celebrating this very Areopagus: "Once a man dies and the earth drinks up his blood, there is no resurrection" (Bruce: 364-365). Of all the Greeks, the more materialistic Epicureans are most likely to sneer at Paul's mention of a Christ risen from the dead.

Those who wish to hear Paul again are more polite, whether believing or not. There seems to be no further presentation of the gospel in the Areopagus. The sincere among them, as well as any converts from the synagogue and the marketplace (17:17), now *join* him and begin a small fellowship of *believers* (17:34). Luke mentions only two such by name. *Dionysius the Areopagite* is a member of the council and becomes the first bishop of Athens, according to later tradition. Then Luke lists a woman *named Damaris*. Chrysostom (*On the Priesthood* 4.7), seems to misunderstand this passage and takes her to be the wife of Dionysius. Ramsay regards her as likely a notable foreign woman, since no ordinary Greek female would attend the Areopagus meeting (1896:252). Perhaps she is a convert from the synagogue, as Bruce suggests (364). Luke then mentions *others* and abruptly ends his account of the mission at Athens, important for the cultural encounters and the speech, but not pivotal for Paul's continuing mission.

THE TEXT IN BIBLICAL CONTEXT
Uncertainty and Faith in Fulfilling a Call

Paul received a distinct call to come to Macedonia and was sure that God meant for him and his party to preach the gospel there (16:9-10). Yet when they arrived at Philippi, the first city, they found only a handful of people available and made few converts (16:13-15). This was soon followed by a vicious attack, a night in jail, and a hurried exit from the city (16:16-40). Must Paul not have wondered what God was really doing in calling him to Macedonia?

This is reminiscent of Abram's call to go "into a land that I will

show you" (Gen.12:1) and his unquestioning response: "By faith . . .
he went out, not knowing were he was to go" (Heb. 11:8). The initial
Macedonian mission was followed by years of hardship, uncertainty,
and the testing of Paul's faith before the work was done.

Thus Paul and his team were not to have an easy time in fulfilling
what they were sure was the call of God. Only after the perspective of
time can the apostle see that the enterprise has been successful.
Within the following year, he will come to understand that the new
church he planted in Thessalonica has survived and become dear to
him (1 Thess. 1:2—3:10). Then later, while raising his offering among
the Gentile Christians to take to Jerusalem, he can praise all the
Macedonian churches for being unusually generous in giving both
themselves and their means in the midst of great affliction (2 Cor.
8:1-5). Still later, in his letter to Philippi from prison, he can speak of
them as one of his most beloved congregations and rejoice greatly in
them (1:3-8; 4:1, 10-18).

Prayer and Praise in Life's Darkest Hours

Paul and Silas pray and sing hymns at midnight (16:25). This echoes
two striking OT stories that both had been brought up on: the
deliverances of Daniel and of his three friends from similarly
desperate situations. Daniel had the practice of praying to Yahweh
on his knees three times a day, and for doing so was thrown into a
den of lions (Dan. 6:10-12). Thus, like Paul and Silas, he was locked
in a fearsome place overnight with little hope of escape. Though no
mention is made of his praying and singing at that time, it may be assumed that he did not cease to look to the Lord all that night. The
deliverance, though not accompanied by an earthquake, was just as
dramatic, for the mouths of the lions were sealed shut (Dan. 6:22).

In the case of Daniel's three friends, there was a still more unusual
deliverance. Though thrown into a blazing hot furnace for defying
the emperor's command to bow down and worship his statue, they
were able to walk about untouched (Dan. 3:19-25). Even those who
threw them in were killed by the heat. Again, nothing is said about
them praying during the ordeal, but no doubt they, like their friend
Daniel, were faithfully lifting their petitions to the Lord. Two additional features marked their experience. Though assured ahead of
time that their God was able to deliver them, they replied that even if
he did not, they would not change their convictions (3:17-18). A
fourth person (probably an angel of the Lord) could be seen even by

the unbelieving Nebuchadnezzar to be walking with these three faithful witnesses (3:25).

Kings in Conflict

Paul and Silas are accused of proclaiming Jesus as king in an empire where all recognize Caesar as the supreme ruler (17:7). This sounds a note common in the OT and reaching a climax with the early Christians. It is essentially the conflict between the worship of the one true God and of any earthly ruler. Samuel was reluctant to anoint a king over Israel because it could mean the rejection of the Lord as their supreme ruler (1 Sam. 8:6-8). From that time on, the "good kings" acknowledged the rule of Yahweh over them with themselves as stewards (cf. 1 Sam. 10:25). The "bad kings" often behaved as though God were not in control of their lives or their nation. Manasseh and Amon actually brought in the worship of foreign gods (2 Kings 21:2-9, 20-22). During the exile, however, under the yoke of foreign rulers, the problem came into sharpest focus. The classic case is that of Daniel and his three friends, who struggled to maintain the supremacy of Yahweh in the face of commands to worship the emperor (Dan. 3:1-30; 6:1-28).

Matthew, the book placed first in the NT canon, most effectively dramatizes this conflict and the victory of the heavenly king. The magi come seeking the one born "King of the Jews," whom the earthly king Herod tries to kill. But God provides his escape and his return to preach the kingdom of heaven after that earthly king is dead (Matt. 2). Luke's handling of the theme comes at the end of Jesus' active ministry as the members of the Sanhedrin accuse him before Pilate. They present Jesus' statements about being the Christ (22:67-69) as him setting himself up in opposition to Caesar (23:2-5). Then the Roman governor pronounces him innocent of that charge and wishes to release him, a position he finds confirmed by Herod Antipas (23:4, 14-16).

Thus when Paul and Silas are accused of proclaiming a new king, they are simply sounding the deep biblical conviction that God is King above all kings and that the Son of God is—what he will later be called—"King of kings and Lord of lords" (Rev. 19:16). Paul himself affirms this to other Macedonians when he writes that God has highly exalted Jesus and given him "the name that is above every name," that before his name "every knee should bend" (Phil. 2:6-11).

THE TEXT IN THE LIFE OF THE CHURCH

Rough Treatment from the Authorities

The persecution of Paul and Silas and the beating they received by order of the magistrates at Philippi (16:20) was a kind of treatment often inflicted on the early Anabaptists. Menno Simons wrote about some of the so-called Christian authorities of his day:

> When I think to find a magistrate who fears God, who performs his office correctly and uses his sword properly, then verily I find as a general rule nothing but a Lucifer, an Antiochus, or a Nero, for they place themselves in Christ's stead so that their edicts must be respected above the Word of God. (298-299)

While the forms of persecution have changed from century to century and culture to culture, illegal action against Christians still continues. And often it is those in high office who permit such outrages or subtly encourage and engage in them.

Witnessing Through Suffering

Believers singing hymns and praying while their backs are bruised and bleeding is no new phenomenon in Christian history. Said Tertullian of this passage, "The legs feel nothing in the stocks when the heart is in heaven" (*To the Martyrs*, quoted in Bruce: 337). Again and again in *Martyrs Mirror,* reflecting the sufferings of true witnesses from earliest times on through the rise of the Anabaptists, the ability of Christians to keep on praising the Lord even under torture made a profound impact upon their persecutors. The latter would gain a new respect for persons who demonstrated the unconquerable joy of suffering for Christ (cf. Rom. 5:3; 1 Pet. 5:5).

Which King to Serve?

Early Anabaptists and Brethren were strong on the kingship of Jesus. Wrote Menno Simons, "That Christ is the King of all the earth is abundantly testified to by the Scriptures. . . . He testifies of Himself that He is the mighty King, saying: All power is given unto me in heaven and in earth" (35).

The critical question of which king to serve is well illustrated by the story of John Naas, Brethren leader in Germany and colleague of Alexander Mack. John was a large, athletic man, a head taller than most of his contemporaries, attracting attention wherever he went. A recruiting officer of the King of Prussia, who ruled Crefeld, where Naas was preaching, seized him and urged him to enlist in the army. When he refused, he was tortured and finally hung upside down by his left thumb and right big toe. When he still would not give in, he was finally released and dragged by force to the royal presence.

The king asked why he would not yield. He replied, "Because I cannot, as I have long ago enlisted in the noblest and best army and I cannot become a traitor to my King." "Who is your captain?" asked the king. "My Captain," answered John Naas, "is the great Prince Immanuel, our Lord Jesus Christ. I have espoused His cause and cannot and will not forsake Him." "Neither will I then ask you to do so," answered the King of Prussia, handing him a gold coin in recognition of his fidelity. After that, the ruler released him and permitted him to continue his evangelistic work (Brumbaugh: 103-105).

Bible Study, Berean Style

Because of the character of the people of Berea as *more noble* or *more receptive* than others and giving themselves to the daily examination of the Scriptures, this name has become a symbol for eager, thorough, and regular Bible study. Berea might well be taken by the believers church tradition as a model. This kind of study of the Word gave rise to the Anabaptist and Brethren movements and, at their best, has characterized them to this day. The original Bereans did three things that distinguished them: (1) They *received* or *welcomed the word eagerly*, as taught by the apostles. (2) They *examined the Scriptures* daily to test these teachings. (3) They believed and acted upon what they learned (16:11-15).

For the early Anabaptists, the Bible was the final authority for doctrine and life, for worship and service, and for church regulations and discipline. They held to *sola scriptura* (Scripture alone), in contrast on one hand to those who appealed to church tradition, and on the other hand to those who looked to dreams, visions, and special revelations. They regarded the NT as the fulfillment of the Old. The OT is the shadow, and the NT brings the reality. The OT lays the groundwork for the building to which the NT witnesses. Where the two testaments differ, they held the NT to be the perfect revelation for which the OT was a preparation (Wenger, in Bender: 167-179). The late A. C. Wieand, cofounder of Bethany Bible School (Theological Seminary), often stated a Brethren formulation of this same principle: "We take everything in the OT in the light of the New, and everything in the NT in the light of Jesus Christ."

In order to base all individual and corporate Christian life on the Bible, Anabaptist-Brethren people need a Berean type of study of the Scriptures characterized by the three points listed above.

Part 9

The Witness in Corinth and Ephesus

Acts 18—19

PREVIEW

Luke takes Paul from Athens to Corinth without a break in the narrative. Yet one may note significant differences in Paul's ministry from this point on. First, though his work both in Corinth and Ephesus begins in the synagogue, as before, it soon extends beyond that institution and continues on until it makes a greater impact on each city than has been true of any previous ministry. Furthermore, Paul is no longer the typical itinerant missionary, driven from one place to another against his will. Now he is more like a pastor, able to engage in extensive teaching and nurturing. In Corinth also he ceases to serve as the leader of a well-defined team and works more with people whom he meets locally. Silas and Timothy soon disappear from the scene, and he associates with fellow artisans, Aquila and Priscilla, in both Corinth and Ephesus.

Luke structures Paul's ministry at Corinth around four episodes (18:1-4, 5-8, 9-11, 12-17), held together with narrative links and featuring three type-scenes. The latter three consist of important pronouncements by Paul (18:6), by the Lord (18:9-10), and by Gallio (18:14-15). Here we find Paul working at his trade (18:3), receiving a reassuring vision from the Lord to face this tough urban situation (18:9-10), and being acquitted in a Roman court after an attack on his life (18:12-17).

The account of Paul's work at Ephesus is presented as the climax of his mission as a free man. Luke dramatically frames it between four preliminary events and a powerful concluding message. The opening scenes are an early visit to the city (18:18-21), a trip to headquarters and return on a new missionary journey (18:22-23), the launching of the gifted Apollos (18:24-28), and the outpouring of the Holy Spirit on a group of twelve (19:1-7). On leaving Ephesus, Paul says farewell to the Ephesian elders (20:17-35).

The structure of the ministry itself is threefold, comprised of three major episodes. First is a three-month period of preaching in the synagogue (19:8), followed by two whole years in a rented lecture hall (19:9-10). Next comes a longer story of encounters with demon exorcists and workers of magic (19:11-20). Finally, after an interlude about travel plans (19:21-22), comes the longest, most detailed and dramatic account of all—the story of a riot and how it is resolved (19:23-41). The total effect of Paul's Ephesian mission is summed up in the statement: *all the residents of Asia, both Jews and Greeks, heard the word of the Lord* (19:10).

OUTLINE

EXPLANATORY NOTES
Ministry in Corinth   18:1-17
18:1-4 Paul's Beginnings There

Paul apparently travels to Corinth alone, fifty miles west and slightly south from Athens (18:1). There he finds himself in the commercial crossroads of Greece, the new Corinth rebuilt by Julius Caesar in 46 B.C., after the Romans had destroyed it. By this time it has attracted so many of the worst elements of the empire that the expression "to Corinthianize" has been coined to describe a life of debauchery. High on the Acro-Corinth, 1,800 feet above the city, stands a temple to Aphrodite, goddess of love, where a thousand religious prostitutes help resident males celebrate immoral rites. However, Corinth's importance as a Roman colony, capital of Achaia and hub of travel and trade, makes it, in spite of its corruption, a good place to plant the gospel.

Sometime after arrival here, Paul finds Aquila and Priscilla, a congenial husband-and-wife team of artisans from Rome, moves in with them, and works with them in their shop as tentmakers (17:3). Aquila ("eagle" in Latin) is a Jew from Pontus, along the southern coast of the Black Sea. He found his way to Rome and there married Priscilla (familiar form for *Prisca*, 1 Cor. 16:19), presumably a native of Italy. They were driven out of the capital by the Emperor Claudius and sought refuge in Corinth (18:2; likely in A.D. 49 *[Chronology, p. 309]*). The historian Suetonius tells how the emperor banished all Jews for "indulging in constant riots at the instigation of Chrestus" (*Life of Claudius* 24.4). While there can be no certainty, many scholars conclude that the reference is to *Christus*, the Christ, whose name would be pronounced the same. If so, it was likely the repeated story of unbelieving Jews causing riots over the conversion of some of their number to Christianity, in this case resulting in all of them being expelled.

On this supposition, Aquila and Priscilla are already believers when Paul meets them. This view is supported by the fact that Luke assumes that they are Christians and does not record their conversion (cf. 18:18, 26). Interestingly enough, only here in Acts, where they are introduced, and again in 1 Corinthians 16:19, where Paul speaks of the church in their house, is the husband's name mentioned first. Otherwise, Luke and Paul always mention Priscilla (or Prisca) before Aquila (Acts 18:18, 26; Rom. 16:3; 2 Tim. 4:19). This may indicate that she is the one who takes the lead in Christian ministry (cf. esp. 18:26). There is some evidence also that she may be from a higher social class than her husband (cf. Bruce: 369 and note).

Tentmakers use either goat's hair (called *cilicium*, from Cilicia, Paul's home province) or leather, and thereby they produce sails, curtains, tents, and other marketable articles. Most recent scholars (like Haenchen, Neill, Bruce, and Marshall) understand the term to mean "leatherworkers" and picture them dealing with tanned hides as well. Paul, in the role of a rabbi, would not be allowed to take pay for his teaching and would have been apprenticed in early life to this trade. His feelings about supporting himself by his own hands are strongly expressed in 1 Thessalonians 2:9, written here in Corinth, and again in a letter to Corinth, where he states his aim of making "the gospel free of charge" (1 Cor. 9:18).

Paul begins his work as always in the local Jewish synagogue (18:4). The only exception to this was Lystra, where apparently no such institution was found (14:8-18). Philippi had *a place of prayer* outside the city, possibly a synagogue (16:13, 16). Corinth, with its large Jewish population, has a good-sized synagogue where Paul can present the gospel to both Jews and Greeks (God-fearing Gentiles). In Acts 13:16-41, Luke has already given a sample of the general content of Paul's teaching to this kind of group. Although not stated, it is reasonable to assume that Priscilla and Aquila are working with him in this ministry in view of their prominence in the church that later grows out of it (cf. 18:18, 26).

18:5-11 Withdrawal from Synagogue; Continued Ministry

Finally, sometime while Paul is still involved in his synagogue ministry, Silas and Timothy arrive from Macedonia (18:5a). (See notes on 17:15; they were sent back to that province from Athens, Timothy to Thessalonica, and Silas likely to Philippi). Their coming is a source of strength and encouragement to the apostle, both for their help at this strategic time and for what they bring with them. Coming from Thessalonica, Timothy has good news about the faithfulness of that church to the Lord and their loyalty to Paul even under great persecution (1 Thess. 1-3). So great is the apostle's relief that now he can "really live" since receiving this word! (1 Thess. 3:8, NIV). Silas, presumably coming from Philippi, may well be the bearer of the gifts mentioned in Philippians 4:15 and 2 Corinthians 11:8-11. Their presence and these gifts now enable Paul to devote *himself entirely to preaching*, proclaiming that the long-awaited Messiah is none other than Jesus of Nazareth (18:5, NEB).

The result of such forthright preaching is bitter opposition from unbelieving Jews and a prophetic sign of judgment upon them from Paul, a replay of his experience at Antioch of Pisidia (13:45). This time, however, instead of shaking the dust off his feet against them (as taught by Jesus in Luke 9:5; 10:11), he shakes out his garments at them as Nehemiah did to the opposition in his day (Neh. 5:13). Paul hurls two strong statements at them. First, their blood will be upon their own heads (18:6b). Like Ezekiel, he has warned the Jews of God's coming judgment and is no longer responsible for them. Their destruction is no longer his responsibility but theirs (Ezek. 33:1-9). Paul takes this prophetic role seriously and later tells his own Ephesian elders that he is innocent of all bloodguiltiness since he has declared to them *the whole purpose of God* (20:26-31). Second, Paul proclaims to these Jews at Corinth, as at Pisidian Antioch (13:46), that since *they* have rejected the gospel, he will now turn to the Gentiles (18:6c).

In this case, the Gentiles begin to meet right next door to the synagogue! The house is owned by *Titius Justus*, a God-fearing uncircumcised man like Cornelius, who has now become a Christian (18:7). Though some texts spell his name *Titus*, the reading given here is preferred, and he is not to be confused with Paul's coworker Titus (known from Paul's epistles; cf. notes on 20:1-3 and see a Bible dictionary). Paul's act of taking his group of new believers to a place so close to the synagogue is surely as galling to the Jews as it is convenient for those now leaving that institution. Then, to make matters worse, *Crispus* is among the new converts. He is the former elder of the synagogue, in charge of buildings and arrangements for all services (18:8a; Paul personally baptizes him, according to 1 Cor. 1:14). With such prominent people joining the movement, it is not surprising that *many of the Corinthians* now become believers and are baptized (18:8b).

At this point the narrative moves to *one night* sometime later, when the second major incident of the mission in Corinth takes place—a nocturnal vision. At Troas, Paul heard a *man* speak to him by night, calling him to Macedonia (16:9). Now it is *the Lord* who has a message. This also becomes the second declaration of the Corinthian story, the first by Paul (18:6) and this one by deity (18:9-10). It is a timely word of assurance in view of the hostility the apostle has already faced and will continue to encounter. He is told (1) not to be afraid, but (2) to speak out, for (3) the Lord is with him to protect him from all harmful attacks. These words are like those given to the prophet Jeremiah to strengthen him for a lifelong ministry against much opposition (Jer. 1:5-8). The point of it is that the Lord has many people to call in the city (cf. the *many Corinthians* of 18:8b who already believe). Therefore, Paul should keep on witnessing boldly (progressive present tense of the verb). Though enemies oppose him, they will not really harm him so as to put him out of action.

18:12-17   The Trial Before Gallio

Then Luke includes one more anecdote about the mission in Corinth. He prefaces it with a statement covering the entire year-and-a-half stay in the city, a literary device already used in 14:6 and 16:12. By his reference to Gallio, he has provided a clue to the date of Paul's ministry here. From an inscription at Delphi mentioning the proconsul, we gather that Paul's eighteen-month stay extended from A.D. 50 (possibly autumn) to the spring of 52 (on the inscription and the process of dating, see Bruce: 371-373 and note; Haenchen: 535ff.; Marshall: 297 [Chronology, p.]).

Marcus Annaeus Novatus is known as Gallio because he was adopted by Lucius Junius Gallio when he moved from his native Spain to Rome. He is the son of the widely acclaimed rhetorician, Seneca the Elder of Cordova, and brother of the even more famous Seneca the Younger, Stoic philosopher and tutor of Roman emperors. He is known among his contemporaries as a man of great wit and charm, having served as a praetor (lower official) and now *proconsul,* on his way to becoming a consul (senior magistrate). Luke presents the story that follows, telling of Paul's escape from the clutches of unbelieving Jews, no doubt as a fulfillment of the promise of protection given by the vision (18:9). This important Roman official's lack of interest in prosecuting him foreshadows later delays in Roman prosecution which make it possible for him to go *to the ends of the earth* before being convicted (cf. 1:8; 24:26-27; 25:12; 26:32; 28:30-31).

Proconsul Gallio is seated on the *tribunal,* a stone platform in the city marketplace, a place that can still be visited in our day (18:12). Paul is brought in by his angry Jewish opponents and charged with promoting worship that is *contrary to the law* (18:13). This is obviously their own Jewish law, as seen by Gallio's response in 18:15. They may have in mind the fact that Paul has made converts from the synagogue like Titius Justus, Crispus, and others, and has filled them with his own teachings. This accusation of violating the laws of Moses is the forerunner of others to come (21:21, 24, 28) as well as of a series of occasions on which Paul will be answering such charges (22:3; 24:14; 25:8; 28:17). Paul's accusers claim that such violators of Jewish law are no longer entitled to the protection given Jews by imperial edict (cf. Bruce: 374; Marshall: 297).

As Luke narrates it, before Paul can ever open his mouth in defense, Gallio takes over and rules the Jewish assailants out of court (18:14). In one swift pronouncement, he shows that they have no basis in Roman law for their action but are merely raising matters pertaining to their own peculiar doctrines and should settle it themselves (18:15). In dismissing the case so abruptly (18:17), the proconsul may be betraying his own anti-Semitic bias (Haenchen: 536, 541), especially noticeable in his utter indifference to the beating then given to Sosthenes, the successor of Crispus as ruler of the synagogue (18:8, 17).

It is not clear *what* men now brutally attack this official. Most interpreters take them to be Gentiles, loafers and loiterers, "the crowd of bystanders" (Bruce: 278; Tannehill, 2:228). Marshall (299), however, entertains the possibility that this Sosthenes is the Christian mentioned in 1 Corinthians 1:1 and associated with Paul in the writing of that epistle. If this is the case, he may already be a sympathizer with Paul, now set upon by his *fellow Jews* when they see they are ruled out of court by Gallio.

Journey Toward Syria; Stopover at Ephesus 18:18-21

Paul stays on in Corinth *for a considerable time* after the Gallio incident (18:18a). This likely means that he extends his ministry for an undesignated period as a result of the victory over Jewish opposition. Eventually, however, he says his farewells and leaves for the eastern end of the Mediterranean, making significant stops along the way.

Priscilla and Aquila go with him as far as Ephesus. At Cenchreae, a port village for Corinth, the three pause, likely to visit Christians (Rom. 16:1-2 mentions a church). While there Paul cuts his hair in what appears to be a temporary Nazirite vow (18:18b), perhaps in thanksgiving for safety at Corinth or in anticipation of the long journey to Jerusalem. The proper ending for such a ceremony would be shaving the hair off completely and offering it in the temple at Jerusalem (Num. 6:18). Luke makes it clear here and later (21:23-26) that Paul is still a good Jew with a high regard for the law and a sincere devotion to God, who is directing his mission *[Luke and the Jewish Law, p. 317]*.

It is not Paul's intention to spend much time in Ephesus on this trip, important city though it is. He is hastening to Jerusalem, both to complete his vow and to keep in touch with that important church center. So he stays only long enough to see Priscilla and Aquila settled at Ephesus and to make an opening presentation to the local synagogue with the idea of returning later (18:19). Ephesus is the most important city of the Roman province of Asia, with a fine harbor on the Cayster River, a natural port of call for ships plying between eastern cities and Rome. Obviously it is a strategic place for planting a church. Paul's brief discussion in the local synagogue meets with a favorable response, and he is invited to stay longer (18:20). This assures him of a good reception when he returns later (19:1—20:1). His companions, Priscilla and Aquila, stay on in the city, start a Christian fellowship in their home (1 Cor. 16:19), and before Paul comes back, will be instrumental in bringing the gifted Apollos to fullness in the Lord (cf. 18:26).

Visit to Jerusalem; Return to Ephesus 18:22-23

Nowhere else in Acts does Luke have Paul cover as much ground in so few words as here. Either his information is scanty or so little of importance happens. Paul takes a ship to Caesarea and from there goes overland to Jerusalem. Actually, the word *Jerusalem* is not found in the best Greek manuscripts but is supplied here in verse 22 by NRSV from the use of *church*, a clear reference to the mother congregation. The verb forms here for *went up* and *went down* often describe travel to and from the holy city. This means that each missionary journey eventually ends in Jerusalem (cf. 15:2-4; 20:16; 21:17). The Western text of verse 21 (in the notes of some versions) has Paul say he wants to *keep the approaching festival in Jerusalem* (probably Passover; Bruce: 378). If so, then this trip may give him a chance to complete his vow (18:18) and would parallel the one later for Pentecost (20:16).

After Jerusalem, Paul goes down to Antioch (18:22b), the second city of importance for the church and the place where each missionary journey begins (cf. 13:3; 15:40). But Luke still gives no detail, simply writing that Paul spends some time in that city, perhaps, as Neill suggests (200), a matter of several months as a sort of "breathing space" between journeys. Then Luke briefly records the beginning of the third missionary journey, with Paul *strengthening* former churches and engaging in a long ministry at Ephesus. One wonders if he is alone as he returns to that city by way of Galatia and Phrygia. Yet later Luke names *Gaius and Aristarchus* as his *travel companions* (18:23; 19:29). This is his fourth visit to some of these churches (cf. comments on 16:6) and enables him to bring much-needed counseling and new life to believers who have been going through the serious crisis reflected in the letter to the Galatians.

Apollos at Ephesus; On to Corinth 18:24-28

This paragraph is unique in being the only one from chapter 16 to the end of Acts in which Paul is in no way involved and not even mentioned. Here Luke deals with events around Ephesus while the apostle is away. He introduces the gifted Apollos, who receives further training by Priscilla and Aquila, preparing him for a powerful ministry in Corinth. The passage is a companion to the story of twelve *disciples* of John, who are brought to a fullness of experience by Paul with proper baptism and an outpouring of the Holy Spirit (19:1-7).

Apollos was born and brought up in Alexandria, important seaport and university city of Egypt. With a library containing perhaps 700,000 papyrus scrolls on a variety of subjects, it has long since supplanted Athens as the intellectual center of the empire. Here the Greek translation of the OT, the Septuagint, was produced. In this city also, as part of its large and flourishing Jewish population, the noted philosopher and interpreter of biblical themes, Philo Judaeus, lived and worked from 20 B.C. to A.D. 45. How much of this rich cultural background Apollos has absorbed can no longer be determined, but Luke's coupling of the name Alexandria with a description of his abilities suggests that it may be considerable.

What impresses the synagogue attenders in Ephesus is the eloquence of this man and his great knowledge of the Scriptures (18:24). His indoctrination in the gospel of Jesus is accurate so far as it goes. This plus his *burning enthusiasm* (lit., "boiling" or "seething" in spirit) mark him as a Christian leader with great potential. His only limitation is that he has had only the baptism of John (18:25). One wonders what Luke means by this or what it takes to equip Apollos fully for his ministry. Comparison with other passages in Luke-Acts suggests that he is in the situation of Luke 3:16. There John the Baptist says that his role is to baptize with water and to introduce the "more powerful" one who will baptize with/in the Holy Spirit. This distinction is so important that it is repeated in Acts 1:5; its fulfillment by Jesus and the Spirit occurs in Acts 2, on the day of Pentecost.

Therefore, the total statement about Apollos means that he has been baptized in water and is well informed of Jesus' deeds and words to a certain point. What he lacks is both instruction in and experience of the rest of the story, notably Acts 1 and 2, including baptism in the Holy Spirit. This is confirmed by the companion story of 19:1-7, in which Luke tells of the outpouring of the Spirit upon others who also have only the baptism of John.

So Priscilla and Aquila take Apollos and bring his knowledge of Christianity up to date. They teach him the way of the Lord even *more accurately* and apparently supply the baptism he lacks (18:26b). The fact that Priscilla's name is mentioned first makes it probable that she takes the lead in this special instruction. Such updating enables Apollos to go to Corinth with a strong letter of recommendation from the believers in Ephesus and to carry on a powerful ministry there (18:27-28).

Evidence of the effectiveness of his work is found in Paul's references to Apollos in 1 Corinthians (3:4-9; 4:6). There he is not only regarded as an equal but as one whose eloquence has given rise to an "Apollos party" (3:4). His role in the early stages of that church is defined as one who built on the foundation that Paul laid (3:5-9). Luke's account agrees with this by mentioning his great *help* to the Corinthian Christians (18:27) and the powerful way he witnesses to the Jews of that city about the messiahship of Jesus (18:28). In this latter ministry, he is reminiscent of Stephen (6:8-10) and a worthy successor of Paul (9:22; 13:16-44; 17:2-4; 18:5).

Paul's Ministry in Ephesus 19:1-10

Luke now resumes the story of Paul's return to Ephesus on the most direct road, *through the upper country* (RSV; or *interior regions*, NRSV). Here in this city with a population estimated at a third of a million, the apostle begins the longest ministry of his career. Dating from before 1300 B.C., the city of Ephesus has become the political and commercial capital of the province of Asia, known for its three temples and proudly called *the temple keeper* of the empire (19:35). Most famous of these shrines is that of Artemis, a structure so ornate as to be ranked as one of the Seven Wonders of the World. Then among all these pagan elements, Paul finds a large colony of Jews. They will furnish him a base for his own evangelistic work and, as elsewhere, provide him protection until his own group has to go on their own. In the center of the city is a large theater, able to accommodate twenty-five thousand people, an arena that will play a part in the story of Paul's ministry here (19:28-41).

19:1-7 Paul and the Disciples of John the Baptist

Before proceeding with Paul's major ministry at Ephesus, Luke includes an interesting story which, like that of 18:24-28, also deals with *some disciples* of John the Baptist. Both this account and the previous one about Apollos show something of the vitality and persistence of the John the Baptist movement and may indicate Luke's interest in showing the superiority of Christianity to that movement in his own day. These men, *about twelve* in number (19:7), are called *disciples*, a common name for Christians. In view of their lack of knowledge of the Holy Spirit, however, most scholars doubt that they should be considered such (e.g., Marshall: 303-304: they simply "appeared to be" Christian believers). Perhaps, like Apollos, they know some things about Jesus, but not the full story (18:25).

Paul asks them point-blank if they received the Holy Spirit when they believed (19:2a), perhaps sensing that they are in need of further help. They reply that they haven't even heard *that there is a Holy Spirit* (19:2b), much less that an outpouring of the Spirit has happened. Paul reminds them that John, their teacher, prophesied clearly that the Messiah would baptize in the Holy Spirit (Luke 3:16; Acts 19:4). They are pre-Pentecostal disciples of John, baptized upon repentance for the remission of sins, prepared for the one to come after John (19:3-6). Paul tells them they must now believe in Jesus, the one to whom John pointed. They do so and are baptized in that name (19:5). Then Paul lays his hands on them, as Peter and John did with the Samaritans (8:17), and the Holy Spirit comes upon them. As a sign of the Spirit's work, they begin to speak in other tongues (19:6), like those on the day of Pentecost (2:4), like the Samaritans (see notes on 8:18), and Cornelius and company (10:46).

19:8-10 Ministry in Synagogue and Hall of Tyrannus

In Ephesus, Paul is able to teach in *the synagogue* for three whole months (19:8). This is in contrast to three Sabbaths in the synagogue in Thessalonica (17:2) and short times in Berea (17:10-14), Athens (17:17), and Corinth (18:4-7). But, as in other places, there finally comes a parting of the ways, and Paul takes his disciples and withdraws. The resistance is similar to that at Corinth, where they *opposed and reviled him* (18:6). Here they *spoke evil of the Way before the congregation.* Luke is unique in reporting that Christianity is, simply, *the Way.* This term occurs here in Acts for the second time (cf. 9:2; 19:23; 22:4; 24:14, 22). *The Way* emphasizes the *way of salvation* (16:17), the true *way of the Lord/of God* (18:25-26), new relationship with God (Heb. 10:20), and righteous lifestyle (Ps. 1:6). It recalls Jesus' statement that he himself is "the way, and the truth, and the life" (John 14:4-6; cf. Mark 10:52). Likely *the Way* is one of the earliest names used by believers to describe themselves.

As at Corinth (18:7), Paul makes an orderly exit from the synagogue and moves with his converts to a new location. The strong verb used of his departure indicates a *sharp separation* between the unconverted left in the synagogue and the *disciples,* converted *Jews and Greeks,* now torn away to start a new congregation. Furthermore, they move to a rented lecture hall where the apostle can hold daily meetings (19:9). Nothing is known either of the building nor of the Tyrannus for whom it is named, but likely he is a local teacher or philosopher who holds meetings there part of each day, leaving the rest of the time open for Paul's missionary efforts. This view is supported by words the Western text adds, that Paul teaches there *from eleven o'clock in the morning to four in the afternoon* (19:9, NRSV note), including siesta hours during the heat of the day. This schedule enables Paul to work early and late at his tentmaking and still have up to five good hours each day for presenting the gospel.

Such arrangements provide the apostle ample opportunity to make an impact on Ephesus greater than any other mentioned in Acts. Moreover, he leads in evangelism for the next two years, and Luke states that *all the residents of Asia, both Jews and Greek,* have a chance to hear *the word of the Lord* (19:10). This widespread impact is an emphasis of the author's account of the Ephesian ministry, not mentioned at any other place—a further proof that he sees this as the climax of Paul's missionary endeavors. Likely during this time, the seven churches of the province of Asia are founded (Rev. 1:4). An impressive example of far-reaching results is the case of Epaphras of Colossae, who apparently is converted by Paul in Ephesus, returns to his home area, and founds and serves the three congregations of Colossae, Laodicea, and Hierapolis (Col. 1:7-8; 4:12-16; Philem. 23).

Triumph of Miracles over Magic at Ephesus 19:11-20

19:11-12 Deeds of Power Through Paul

Luke's language is exact. During the course of Paul's work in Ephesus, God does *extraordinary miracles through* him (19:11). To the people, these are the accomplishments of the apostle, proving him to be a mighty healer who can cast out evil spirits. But for Acts, these signs and wonders are the doing of *God*. In his letters, Paul verifies the fact that miracles do accompany his work (Rom. 15:19; 2 Cor. 12:12; Gal. 3:5). This is to be expected. Jesus himself predicted that unusual powers would work through his witnesses (Mark 16:17-18; John 14:12), and after Pentecost such wonders are done through the earliest believers (Acts 2:43; 3:1-10). Here at Ephesus they are called *dunameis* (from which comes *dynamite*), "mighty acts." This term is used for Jesus' *deeds of power* in expelling demons and healing (2:22; Luke 10:13; 19:37), and sometimes for believers' deeds (8:13; 19:11; cf. Luke 10:17-20, with other words).

The kind of wonders performed here, taking handkerchiefs or aprons from Paul's body to heal the sick (19:12), reminds one of how people brought their sick out so that the shadow of Peter might fall on them and cure them (5:15-16). Nor was this far different from the healing power that went out from Jesus, enabling him to heal through the touch of his garment (Mark 5:28-29) and deliver people from demons and cure them even at a distance (Mark 7:24-29; John 4:46-54). In Paul's case, the articles used would be the sweat-rags normally tied around his head and other cloths fastened at his waist in his daily work. Whereas in 5:15-16 the wording leaves the possibility that the healings were due to the expectations of the people, here Luke leaves no doubt that miracles really happen from the touch of these articles. Such wonder-working makes a powerful impact upon the people of Ephesus.

19:13-16 Paul and the Jewish Exorcists

One result is that it inspires imitators. Luke illustrates this with a humorous story. Jewish outsiders, known as the *itinerant* seven sons of a high priest Sceva, have picked up the name of *Jesus* from Paul's ministry and are using it to cast out demons (19:13-14). The term used for them is *exorkistēs* (exorcist), and they *adjure*, as with an oath—terms never used in the NT for Jesus and his disciples. Pagan and Jewish sources verify that non-Christians used the name of Jesus in exorcism (cf. Mark 9:38-41). No Jewish high priest by the name of

Sceva can be identified. Perhaps this Sceva is a relative of a high priest or the exorcists are self-appointed pretenders (magicians? Cf. 19:19), using the title to enhance their reputation, much as Simon the Sorcerer put himself forward as *someone great* (8:9).

Whatever their initial success, however, they soon run into trouble. As often happened to Jesus (e.g., Luke 4:34), the evil spirit talks back to them. Quite unexpectedly, this particular demon retorts, *Jesus I know, and Paul I know; but who are you?* (19:15). Nor is that all. To their dismay, the possessed man leaps upon all seven of them and beats them up so badly that they run away *naked and wounded!* (19:16). However amused Luke's readers may be by the thought of such a sight, the residents of Ephesus are *awestruck* and the name of Jesus is *praised* (19:17). Once more the Christian gospel has over-come evil adversaries (cf. 8:9-24; 13:9-11).

19:17-20 Burning the Books of Magic

Then Luke gives an impressive account of the impact of Paul's miracle-working and the dramatic defeat of the unbelieving sons of Sceva. First, some of his own Christian converts are deeply touched and come confessing and renouncing the magical practices in which they have been engaged (19:18). Such confessions are likely made before the whole congregation (Haenchen: 567), and divulging these secrets renders them ineffective from this time on (Bruce: 391). Not only that, but a number of repentant believers, possibly joined by non-Christians as well, bring their parchment scrolls and magical writings and burn them in public. The bonfires are piled high; manu-scripts and magical sheets worth 50,000 days' wages go up in smoke! Many examples of such magical "Ephesian letters" may be seen today in museum collections (Bruce: 391), mute evidence of the thriving business of occult arts in Ephesus. After such a powerful defeat of this satanic work, Luke can write triumphantly, *So the word of the Lord grew mightily and prevailed* (19:20).

Paul's Plan to Go to Jerusalem   19:21-22

Then the author briefly charts Paul's travels to the end of the book. In fulfilling the commission of 1:8 and his own ministry foretold in 9:15, the apostle now is led of the Spirit to plan a trip back through Macedonia, on to Jerusalem, and from there to Rome (19:21; and on to Spain, he hopes, Rom. 15:24, 28). The reason for this roundabout journey can be seen from a study of Paul's letters (1 Cor. 16:1-9; 2 Cor. 8-9; and Rom. 15:25-28). Paul has added to his original plan to carry the gospel to Rome a more immediate second plan of gathering an offering from the Gentile churches around the Aegean Sea, including Galatia (cf. Gal. 2:10). Accompanied by local representatives, he wants to take it as aid for the saints in Jerusalem. To do this, he must go *through Macedonia and Achaia* and travel from there with that group to complete the mission, a journey to be narrated in 20:1-21:16.

To prepare for his visit, Paul sends two *helpers* on ahead to Macedonia, the well-known Timothy and a man named Erastus. The latter is probably not to be identified with the Corinthian city treasurer mentioned in Romans 16:23 but rather with the Christian associate by that name in 2 Timothy 4:20. The apostle himself remains behind to finish his work in Ephesus (19:22).

Silversmiths Stirring Up Confusion at Ephesus 19:23-41

Luke's concluding narrative from Paul's Ephesian ministry is the longest and most detailed single account in the book having to do with his work. But, interestingly enough, the apostle is not the center of the story at all. He is referred to only twice: once in a remark about his powerful preaching (19:26) and again as he tries to become part of the action but is prevented (19:30). Yet the whole narrative is convincing evidence of the total impact of his work on both the business and religious life of the city.

19:23-27 Concern and Speech of Demetrius

The action begins with a business man bearing the common Greek name *Demetrius*, a silversmith of leadership ability. He has noted the teaching of Paul against worshiping gods made with hands and has seen in it a threat to the local business of making *silver shrines* of the goddess Artemis. To meet this crisis, he has called a meeting of his fellow artisans and lays the case before them (19:23-26).

In some places, *Artemis* is the equivalent of the Roman *Diana*, goddess of the hunt. In Ephesus, she has taken on many of the features of the Asiatic Great Mother, is represented by a female figure with many breasts, and is a patroness of nature and fertility. In her worship are wild orgies and sexual excesses. The shrines these silversmiths fashion are small models of the great temple, one of the Seven Wonders of the World. No such silver shrines have survived because the silver is the first to be plundered in ancient times. Yet terra cotta shrines of this temple do exist.

The reported speech of Demetrius begins with a frank statement about the wealth of the silversmiths being at stake (19:25b). Then he tells of the impact of Paul's preaching, underscoring what Luke has already made clear to his readers in 19:10, that all Asia has been influenced. Now the emphasis is on how the gospel has drawn people away from the worship of Artemis (19:26). Demetrius goes on to say that the consequence of this will first be the collapse of their trade—his primary concern. Second, their world-famous temple will suffer, and with it, Ephesus itself will lose its supreme position as the center of such worship! (19:27).

19:28-34 Mob Action and Confusion

This latter emotionalizing, patriotic appeal now stirs the crowd to fever pitch and sets the stage for one of the most dramatic scenes of the book. Luke tells the story with much relish and humor. The crowds are *enraged* by the silversmith's words and raise a shout that attracts a crowd and sends all of them moving toward the big midcity theater. On and on they surge, a milling mass shouting at the top of their lungs, *Great is Artemis of the Ephesians!* (19:28). On the way some of them grab two of Paul's associates, Macedonians *Gaius and Aristarchus*, and drag them along (19:29).

Gaius cannot be identified for sure, since the *Gaius* mentioned later as Paul's companion is from Derbe in Lycaonia (20:4). There a Western text attempts to reconcile the references by calling him a *Doberian* from Macedonia. But with a Roman name as common then as John is today, there can be no certainty. *Aristarchus*, however, surely is the dauntless companion who makes the journey to Jerusalem (20:4), continues with Paul, is present with him on the voyage to Rome (27:2), and is later found by his side in prison (Col. 4:10; Philem. 24).

Paul hears of the commotion and wants to get into the theater and face his accusers. But he is wisely prevented from doing so both by his own people and by some high *officials of the province,* called *Asiarchs,* civic benefactors and magistrates (19:30-31, NRSV note; ABD, 1:495-497). Thus, even in the madness of the mob, there are islands of sanity and good judgment. Confusion continues to reign within the spacious arena, however, as some people yell one thing and some another, most of them caught up in the hysteria, with no idea of what is going on! (19:32). At one point in the proceedings, a Jew named Alexander stands up, backed by his fellows, and attempts to make a defense so that his people will not be blamed for something this sect of messianists is doing. But once he is recognized, he is shouted down by the merciless crowd, pagan and probably also anti-Semitic. The chant that has been filling the city rings on and on for two full hours: *Great is Artemis of the Ephesians!* (19:33-34). The situation seems completely out of hand.

19:35-41 Dispersal of the Mob by the City Clerk

Then a man comes forward who has been trying for some time to bring order, the *town clerk*. As chief magistrate of the city of Ephesus, he is responsible to the Romans for keeping the peace. When silence finally settles upon the vast crowd, he begins to reason with them. Softly stroking their city pride, he asks them who could possibly be ignorant of the greatness of Ephesus as *temple keeper of the great Artemis* and of the *statue that fell from the sky* (19:35). The city is famous for its great temple to Artemis and caring for a meteorite that once fell in this region—now enshrined in a temple, sacred, and to be worshiped as though it were a statue of the goddess Artemis. (Ephesus is also known as an early center of emperor worship, with imperial temples, but this is not mentioned.)

A murmur of assent goes through the crowd at such wisdom. The clerk has them listening intently. Since this is so, he continues, there is no need to shout or do anything rash (19:36). He then points to Gaius and Aristarchus and, without examining them, gives reasons for letting them go. It is not as though they were some kind of temple robbers or blasphemers! (19:37). Beside that, the whole attack on Paul is wrong. Instead of stirring up a mob, let Demetrius and his men bring the matter to the courts, where just complaints can be processed. *The courts are open!* There are judges (Roman *proconsuls*) to settle such cases (19:38). And if there are any further questions concerning the city as a whole, citizens can bring them to the *regular* meetings of the general *assembly* for decisions (19:39).

Then the town clerk closes with the problem that the total situation creates for the city of Ephesus. This is the danger that their Roman overlords will accuse them of rioting over a matter that cannot be defended—protecting the silversmith business (19:40). Thus they might lose "their existing privileges of self-government" (Munck, 1967:196). After such a skillful and level-headed presentation, the city official manages to dismiss the crowd (19:41). On this note of victory for Paul and the gospel, Luke concludes his account of the mission in Ephesus.

THE TEXT IN ITS BIBLICAL CONTEXT
Tested and Proved Innocent by Secular Authorities

Twice in this section of Acts, Paul and his gospel of Christ are accused before civil magistrates and both times are allowed to go free (18:12-17; 19:37-41). This follows a pattern familiar in the OT in the case of Joseph (Gen. 41:41-57), Moses (Exod. 12: 31-36), Daniel (3—6) and his three friends, and Esther (6—7). Then in the NT, Jesus was thrice pronounced innocent by the highest magistrate in the land, though eventually condemned and crucified (Luke 23:4, 15, 22). Peter and John, on trial before the Sanhedrin, were found not to have committed any crime and finally released (Acts 4:5-22; 5:27-40).

Thus again and again, unbelieving human authorities show the Lord's chosen witnesses to be right in spite of the evil opposition brought against them. This then becomes the theme underlying the long series of trials Paul endures in Acts 21—26, is implied in the final trip to Rome (27:1—28:16), and gives meaning to the last paragraph of the book (28:30-31). The same pattern provides evidence for Cassidy's thesis (159-170) that one of the primary purposes of Acts is to inspire believers to be faithful in their witness and allegiance to Jesus Christ, even in the face of conflict and persecution.

The Series of Spirit Outpourings

The outpouring of the Holy Spirit on the twelve whom Paul meets in Ephesus (19:1-7) is the fourth in a series of such occasions specifically detailed in Acts. First is the long-promised experience of being *baptized* or *filled with the Holy Spirit* on the Day of Pentecost (cf. Luke 3:16; 24:49; Acts 1:5, 8; 2:1-47). This episode defines the phenomenon by an account of the manifestations, two different immediate reactions, Peter's speech of explanation and proclamation, and the long-range results—a large ingathering and the new community created by it.

The second outpouring of the Spirit occurs in chapter 8, what we refer to as the "Samaritan Pentecost," even though Luke does not use that term. It is highly significant because it marks the invasion of the Spirit in the next area of witness after Jerusalem and Judea, the Samaria spoken of in 1:8. It also records the wonderful way the Spirit deals with persons who have long been regarded with contempt and often as outright enemies. Luke sees no need at this point to report all the manifestations of the day of Pentecost. His emphasis is rather on the working of signs and wonders and the conversion of large numbers of these people. An added feature is the episode of Simon the Sorcerer, showing the superiority of true miracle over magic, and containing a rebuke of the magician for attempting to buy the power to bestow the Spirit.

The third in the series might be called the "Gentile Pentecost." It is as dramatic as the first one and gives an account of the way the Spirit falls upon Romans, pagan in origin and members of the most feared and hated of all nations (10:44-47). Like the outpouring in Samaria, it symbolizes another stage in the fulfillment of the commission of 1:8, this time to *the ends of the earth*. Speaking in tongues and praising God mark it as being like the first Pentecost (cf. 11:17). Its effect is to open the door of the gospel to Gentiles as equals with Jews (15:7-11) and to make possible the rest of the book of Acts.

The fourth and final one, in this section (19:1-7), may be called the "incomplete believers Pentecost." These are persons who know only the baptism of John and perhaps a few things about Jesus, but have no knowledge or experience of the Holy Spirit. After they are baptized in the name of the Lord Jesus, the outpouring of the Spirit upon them is accompanied by speaking in tongues and prophesying. This is symbolic of the fulfillment that can come to persons of all backgrounds whose religious preparation is insufficient.

By including these four baptisms in the Spirit: for Jews, Samaritans, Gentiles, and partially prepared believers, Luke is saying in effect that there is powerful renewal available in Jesus for all who are truly open to it.

Final Story of Victory over Magic

Another important series reaches its climax in Paul's ministry at Ephesus: the conflict between miracle and magic. The three episodes have already been discussed in the notes (8:9-24; 13:8-11; 19:13-20). They are instances in which the true faith encounters the dealing in false spiritual powers, at present often called the occult. It is a form of spiritual warfare necessary if Christ is to be declared supreme over all powers. All three accounts tell of the victory of the gospel over magic and over the sorcerers, false prophets, or practitioners involved.

In the first case the magician is converted, although with doubtful results (8:9-24). In the second instance the sorcerer is blinded and left in the hands of God (13:8-11). The last account is twofold: (1) the story of some demon exorcists wrongly using the name of Jesus (19:13-16). Their defeat leads to (2) the wholesale burning of books of magic (19:17-19). Here the would-be exorcists are beaten, stripped, and put to flight. The whole city is purged of magical practices by divulging their secrets and destroying their papyrus scrolls. The final result in all these accounts is that the gospel of Jesus is victorious over every enemy, and the leadership of God's people is kept in the hands of true faith. (See BCBC commentaries on Colossians and Ephesians for discussion of Jesus' victory over evil powers.)

THE TEXT IN THE LIFE OF THE CHURCH
The Unsalaried Ministry

Paul's work as a tentmaker (18:3; cf. 1 Cor. 9:1-23; 1 Thess. 2:9) is in harmony with the lifestyle of Jesus and of the other apostles. It is a pattern that has persisted among many denominations through much of their history. Among the believers churches, there are still groups that help their ministers with gifts from time to time (cf. Phil. 4:14-18; 1 Cor. 9:3-14) but do not pay a regular salary. This position is based on the conviction that all Christians are really ministers and that the pastor should not be exempt from earning a living through usual trades any more than other members.

They noticed that Jesus told his disciples, "You received without payment; give without payment" (Matt. 10:8). Paul said the gospel should be given "free of charge" (1 Cor. 9:18) and that he and his ministry companions "worked night and day" so as not to "burden" any of those hearing the gospel (1 Thess. 2:9). Moreover, this system worked reasonably well as long as such churches were rural. Leaders' large families could help on the farm, and they could manage a reasonable living and still proclaim the gospel.

With the industrial revolution came the move to cities and the growing conviction that the pastor should have a higher education. The "tentmaking" ministry ideal became more difficult to maintain, whatever the trade practiced alongside leadership ministry in the church. Along with texts quoted above, believers found other passages that justify paying the set-aside minister.

Paul makes it clear that he has the right to be paid if he so desires: "The Lord commanded that those who proclaim the gospel should get their living by the gospel" (1 Cor. 9:8-14). While he does not ask for pay from the new converts at Corinth, he does receive gifts from established but poor churches of Macedonia (Phil. 2:25; 4:10-18; 2 Cor. 8:1-2). Jesus instructed his followers as they went out, "The laborer deserves to be paid" (Luke 10:7).

Thus, in modern times, both out of necessity and with the sanction of Scripture, the majority of Anabaptist-Brethren specialized ministries are salaried. Along with it, however, is still the strong conviction that both clergy and laity should do a great deal of volunteer work and make the gospel as free as possible.

Going All the Way with Jesus

Priscilla and Aquila bring Apollos to a more accurate knowledge of Jesus (18:24-28), and Paul leads about twelve persons to baptism in the name of Jesus and a fullness of the Spirit (19:1-7). These efforts provide inspiration for something central and precious in the Anabaptist-Brethren tradition. This is the earnest desire to go all the way with Jesus. Thus sixteenth-century Anabaptists restudied the Word and, on the basis of it, emphasized discipleship for responsible adults, with baptism as its sign and seal. In doing so they were saying in effect that the Lutheran, Calvinist, and Zwinglian reformations did not go far enough. They set out to go beyond them by teaching regeneration and rebaptism for all new believers. As a result, they ran into trouble with both church and state and were severely persecuted.

Then the process was repeated in the early eighteenth century when the New [Ana]Baptists under Alexander Mack and others sought a deeper walk with Jesus than they could find in any of the reform movements of their day. They combed the NT for the commandments of the Lord and, by the power of the Holy Spirit, set out to keep them. The present five groups of Brethren are heirs of that tradition, and at their best, are still eager to "go all the way with Jesus." Renewal movements since then have had similar zeal, each with its own set of understandings: the Wesleys not too long after the Brethren, Finney and Moody in the nineteenth century, the Pentecostals from 1901 on, and the various Holy Spirit renewal groups since that day on up through the twentieth century and beyond—all of them may be regarded as worthy successors of Priscilla, Aquila, and Paul in their updating efforts at Ephesus.

Peaceful Alternatives to Violence

The calm, judicious manner with which the city clerk of Ephesus quieted the frenzied mob is a model for an approach found in the Anabaptist-Brethren way of life (19:35-41). These believers have a high regard for orderly behavior and an ability to bring the force of personality to bear upon explosive situations. People of this tradition have demonstrated spiritual gifts for defusing tension and bringing sanity. Not all the confusion has been outside the church. There have been many occasions of sharp contention within various denominations where poise and graciousness have preserved the peace.

Many examples of this are known for each of the several believers church groups. One that happened in a remote mission school might be cited as typical. The author was teaching in the early 1970s at the Theological College of Northern Nigeria, a Christian institution training church leadership persons for some twenty different tribes representing nine Nigerian churches. One day as I was attempting to call my class of twenty-five together after the midday break, I was met by excitement. A thief had been discovered going through the single men's dorm. Some members of my class had been among those who caught him and held him under guard awaiting the police. Tribal custom encouraged the beating or even killing of a thief caught in the act, and several of these students wanted to do this right then, rather than have class.

Sensing that this matter was too important to ignore, I let them talk. The discussion became hot, but the men stayed in class. Finally a youth from one of the most primitive of our hill tribes rose calmly to his feet. He had learned the way of peace as a part of becoming a believer and was a good-enough student to command respect from his peers. Soon he quieted the class and gained their attention. "My brothers," he said, "we are the people of God. We have been sent here to learn to be ministers of the gospel of Jesus, not to beat or kill people. I suggest that we calm down, finish the lesson of the day, and then go, befriend this troubled man. Who knows? Perhaps we may even lead him to salvation." So sensible and so truly Christian were these words that the group gradually settled down and some even apologized for acting as they did. The syllabus lesson for the day was soon forgotten, but the impact of this simple witness for peace lived with them from that day on.

Part 10

Journey to Jerusalem and Witness There

Acts 20:1—23:35

Having closed out Paul's ministry at Ephesus with the riot scene (19:21-41), Luke now tells of the apostle's last journey to Jerusalem. There is an overall pattern of farewell teachings and final encounters which end in conflict and trial before the authorities, reminiscent of Jesus' final visit to Jerusalem (Luke 9:51—23:56). In the case of Paul, the narrative ends with him as a prisoner, not with crucifixion, though death is always a possibility (Acts 21:13, 31; 23:12). Many of the parallels between the two journeys will be noted in the commentary.

Paul has been planning this trip. For a year or more he has been raising an offering from among the Gentile churches to take to Jerusalem (Gal. 2:10; 1 Cor. 16:1-5; 2 Cor. 8-9; Rom. 15:25-27). Now, after one last visit to Macedonia and Greece (Acts 20:1-4), he is ready to go. Yet the relief money is scarcely mentioned in Luke's account. Before Felix, Paul simply says that he came to Jerusalem to bring *alms* to his *nation and to offer sacrifices* (24:17).

What Luke emphasizes in his account of the journey is a combination of strengthening and farewell to Christian groups along the way. Paul encourages and bids good-bye to the disciples at Ephesus (20:1), goes through Macedonia, giving *much encouragement* (20:2), spends three months in Greece (Achaia), apparently also fortifying them (20:3a). Then, with seven named companions, he sets out for Jerusalem, and pays a farewell visit to Troas (20:7-12). At Miletus he meets the elders of the Ephesian church and delivers a long message of encouragement and farewell (20:18-35), an example of the kind of exhortation he likely gives at each place.

Paul and his party go on to Tyre, where the farewell lasts a week

(21:3-6), followed by a day with the believers at Ptolemais (21:7) and several days at Caesarea (21:8). For this entire journey, from 20:5 to the arrival in Jerusalem in 21:18 (except for the meeting at Miletus), Luke uses the *we* style. This not only indicates his own presence in the party (see Introduction) but, as Tannehill points out (2:246-247), increases the imaginative participation of the reader in the narrative.

Soon after arrival in Jerusalem, however, the atmosphere changes. After a brief welcome, Paul is presented with a problem, that of proving his innocence of a serious charge by the Jewish wing of the church—that he has been teaching Jews of the dispersion to forsake the laws of Moses (21:20-21). This is the third in a series of church conflicts arising from the Jew-Gentile mission. The first was on the baptism of Gentiles (11:1-18) and the second on the problem of requiring such converts to be circumcised (15:1-31). Here are echoes of the Jerusalem council. Present, for example, are James and the elders, representing the law and challenging Paul and his work among the Gentiles. To vindicate himself, Paul performs a ritual in the temple which puts him into a great deal of trouble. By the end of this section, he is transferred to Caesarea as a prisoner of Rome under heavy guard (23:12-35).

The narrative in the whole section flows along from one exciting event to another. A man falls out of a window (20:9-12), a sharp disagreement arises among Christians about Paul going to Jerusalem (21:12-14), a case of mistaken identity proves almost fatal (21:27-31), two mobs reach riot proportions (21:30-31; 22:22-24), and Paul narrowly escapes death through the efforts of a teenager (23:12-22).

OUTLINE

From Ephesus to Jerusalem 20:1—21:16

Farewells in Macedonia, Greece, and Troas, 20:1-16
20:1-3	Paul's Visit to Macedonia and Greece
20:4-16	From Macedonia to Troas and Miletus

Farewell to the Ephesian Elders, 20:17-38

Farewells at Tyre, Ptolemais, and Caesarea, 21:1-14
21:1-6	Visit with the Christians at Tyre
21:7-14	Visits at Ptolemais and Caesarea

From Caesarea to Jerusalem, 21:15-16

Encounters in Jerusalem 21:17—23:35

Report to Jerusalem Church; Request of James, 21:17-25

Paul's Arrest at the Temple, 21:26-40
21:26-30	Purification Ritual and Mob Scene
21:31-40	Rescue by the Roman Tribune

Paul's Defense in Jerusalem, 22:1—23:10
22:1-21	Paul Addressing the People
22:22-29	Further Dealing with Mob and Tribune
22:30—23:10	Paul Before the Sanhedrin

A Night Vision of Reassurance, 23:11

Dealing with the Plot Against Paul, 23:12-35
23:12-22	Discovery of the Conspiracy
23:23-35	Paul's Transfer from Jerusalem to Caesarea

From Ephesus to Jerusalem

20:1—21:16

Farewells in Macedonia, Greece, and Troas 20:1-16

20:1-3 Paul's Visit to Macedonia and Greece

The near-riot and general hubbub in the theater at Ephesus are enough to convince Paul that his ministry there is over. He assembles the church, *encouraging them* and *saying farewell* (20:1; cf. 20:18-35 for a sample of parting exhortation). From 2 Corinthians 2:12-13, we learn that Paul travels the Aegean Sea to Troas, where he fails to meet Titus as hoped. From there he crosses over into Macedonia (20:1b) and finds Titus. With others, this assistant has been working with the well-off believers in Corinth for over a year trying to raise the relief offering for Jerusalem (2 Cor. 8:6-24; 9:1-5). In Macedonia, Paul spends time visiting the churches and giving the believers *much encouragement* (20:2).

It becomes necessary, however, for Paul to go south to Corinth in *Greece* (20:2c), perhaps taking Titus with him, to finalize the offering matter. Altogether this consumes another three months before he and the church representatives can start out on the trip to Jerusalem (20:3a). But again his plans are changed when he discovers that the unbelieving Jews of Corinth have made a plot against him. Instead of sailing directly *for Syria* as planned, he and his men return *through Macedonia* (20:3bc). There he assembles a group of travel companions, presumably representatives of the congregations mentioned with their names, entrusted with the relief money for the saints in Jerusalem (24:17; cf. 11:29-30). The seven named are *Sopater* (short for Sosipater; cf. Rom. 16:21) of Beroea/Berea, *Aristarchus* and *Secundus* of Thessalonica, *Tychicus* and *Trophimus* of Ephesus. Galatia is represented by *Timothy* of Lystra and *Gaius* of Derbe.

A Western text reads *Gaius the Doberian* after a small town in Macedonia, perhaps identifying him with the Gaius of 19:29 and making him the representative of Philippi. Since he is linked with Timothy here, more likely Derbe and not Doberus is meant (Haenchen: 52-53; Marshall: 324). No delegate from Corinth is mentioned; perhaps either Paul himself or Titus or unnamed brothers serve as representatives of Corinth and share in auditing the accounts of the gifts (24:17; Gal. 2:10; Rom. 15:25-33; 1 Cor. 16:1-5; 2 Cor. 8-9; Bruce: 406). Luke, included in the *we*, may represent Philippi (Marshall: 324). *Seven* are named to represent the churches and carry their offerings (cf. 6:3; Swartley: 110-132). Paul may intend to demonstrate fulfillment of prophecy by showing the treasures of the nations flowing into Jerusalem through the Gentile mission (Isa. 60:1-6; 61:6; Hag. 2:7; Munck, 1977). These brothers "are messengers of the churches, the glory of Christ" (2 Cor. 8:24).

20:4-16 From Macedonia to Troas and Miletus

The meeting place for the delegation is Troas, and some go ahead to wait there for Paul and his group. Luke is with the apostle in Philippi, where they stay until after Passover (*the days of Unleavened Bread*) before making the five-day trip to Troas. There the whole group assembles and spends seven days with the local church (20:6). At the end of this stay, on the evening of the *first day of the week* (Sunday), the church meets *to break bread* (20:7a). This is one of the clearest NT references to the Christian practice of meeting on resurrection day instead of on the old Jewish Sabbath (Sunday services seem also to be implied in 1 Cor. 11:20; 16:2, "collections" on "the first day of every week"; Rev. 1:10, "the Lord's day"). The meeting place is either a home or a hall with a large upper room and windows. Evening services are common, in view of the fact that many believers (slaves?) have to work during the daytime.

The breaking of bread here is a part of the meeting, some form of communal meal or "love feast." Yet its repetition in 20:11 suggests it is also a symbol of *farewell*, echoing Luke 22:19; Jesus performed a similar act at the Last Supper. On this last night together, Paul is *talking to them* (NASB; rather than *holding a discussion*, NRSV) and continues on in a farewell mood until midnight (20:7). Weariness and fumes from the *many* (oil) *lamps* bring on uncontrollable drowsiness in a young man named Eutychus, sitting high in a window. He falls to the ground three stories below and is *picked up dead* (20:9).

Paul hurries to the spot to revive Eutychus. He bends over and embraces the body, much as Elijah and Elisha did in restoring the dead (1 Kings 17:21; 2 Kings 4:34-35). Here are echoes of the raising of Jairus's daughter: Jesus spoke a word of life beyond death, took her by the hand, and raised her (Luke 8:52-55). One also thinks of the raising of Tabitha at Joppa: Peter went to the body, commanded her to arise, and lifted her up, once more alive (Acts 9:40-41). Some scholars take Paul's statement *his life is in him* (20:10) to mean that he is simply unconscious. But scriptural parallels and the simple statement by the physician Luke point to actual death and resurrection; *life is in him* then refers to his newly revived self. In this case it would be another fulfillment of Jesus' command to raise the dead (Matt. 10:8; cf. also Acts 14:19-20). They take *the boy away alive* and are *comforted* while Paul stays on conversing with the church people until daybreak (20:11-12).

Writing as a participant on the trip, Luke includes details that may seem unnecessary, like that of the main party going on ahead by ship while Paul walks overland (20:13). Incidentally, this twenty-mile walk after an all-night vigil shows remarkable stamina on the part of a man who, just a year or two before, was "so utterly, unbearably crushed" that he "despaired of life itself" (2 Cor. 1:8) and whose "outer nature" was "wasting away" (2 Cor. 4:16)! Luke's detailed travel notes continue as he records stops at Assos and Mitylene, with landfalls at both Chios and Samos, all names known to seafaring readers of the times (20:14-15). Paul's haste is because he wants to reach Jerusalem in time for Pentecost. With this in mind he does not go inland to visit Ephesus, but sends for the elders of that church to meet him at Miletus (20:16-17).

Farewell to the Ephesian Elders   20:17-38

As Paul's ship lies at harbor in Miletus, messengers hasten (by sea or land?) to Ephesus, some thirty miles away, and soon the apostle has his church leaders gathered around him. This arrangement may be due to the need to hurry on to Jerusalem (cf. 20:16) and possibly some lingering danger of a mob at Ephesus (cf. 20:1a). Here now is the only extensive message of Paul to Christians to be found in Acts, a farewell speech comparable to that of Jesus in Luke 22:14-38. It is his final parting with leaders of the church where he last worked extensively, and it is placed here, not at the end of his active ministry (Tannehill, 2:252-253). Luke may personally be present for the occasion and therefore able to preserve this eyewitness account and first-hand summary of the speech.

The message moves forward from Paul's opening statement about his past ministry (20:18-21) to his immediate plans (20:22-23). Then it interweaves references to his own exemplary work among them with warnings and exhortations as they face opposition in the more distant future (20:24-35).

The opening sentences (20:18-21) contain ideas repeated later in the speech in reverse or chiastic order. Here he speaks of how he has been (a) ministering in humble service, (b) proclaiming the whole gospel, and (c) preaching repentance to both Jews and Greeks. He goes on to develop the same ideas in reverse order: (c) preaching the kingdom to all (20:25), (b) proclaiming the whole purpose of God (20:26-27), and (a) dedicated self-supporting ministry (20:33-35).

Paul is presenting himself here as a pastor in addition to his usual role as a missionary and teacher. He has *lived among* his people from the very beginning (20:18), his quality of life reinforcing his words. It has been a life lived *with all humility* (20:19; cf. work with his hands, 20:34) and *with tears* (cf. 20:31). This echoes experiences like those of 2 Corinthians 1:8-11 and 6:3-10, written from Ephesus during his time there and telling of a serious crisis and many sufferings. Yet in spite of all this, he did not shrink from proclaiming the message to them (20:20; cf. 20:27), both in public and from house to house, giving a witness of the necessity of repentance and faith to both Jews and Greeks (20:21, 24).

Then Paul turns to his immediate future as he goes to Jerusalem, *captive to the Spirit,* or *bound in the Spirit* (20:22, RSV). This echoes Luke 9:51, "Jesus set his face to go to Jerusalem," and leads into Paul's warning that these elders themselves will one day experience *savage* opposition (20:29-30). In Paul's case, the Holy Spirit testifies that imprisonment and persecutions await him (20:23). This is the first time the reader is given this information, illustrated in the following story (21:4, 10-11). Such predictions parallel the trials and death of Jesus that awaited him on his last journey.

The danger, however, does not frighten Paul because his life is given over to the Lord and thus no longer to be held onto as something *dear* (NASB) or of *value* (NRSV) to himself. In fact, this journey gives him an opportunity to finish the course which he has begun (20:24). It is, however, a genuine farewell. He knows that none of them will see his face again in this world (20:25), a conviction that likely came to him as he was bound in the Spirit to make the trip and told that trials and imprisonment await him (cf. 20:22-23). This word then sticks in their memory as the saddest news of all (cf. 20:38).

Returning now to his three years of pastoral work among them, he touches once more (cf. 20:19-21) on the theme of his dedicated service. As he had earlier testified to the unbelieving Jews at Corinth (18:6), he regards himself as under the charge that God gave to Ezekiel (33:1-9): a prophet who does not preach the whole message of judgment and grace is guilty of the blood of the people. On this basis, Paul is *not responsible for the blood* of any of them, for he was careful to declare *the whole purpose of God* (20:26-27). As Tannehill points out (2:257), for Paul this counsel or plan of God undoubtedly also refers to the salvation of all humankind on a world-embracing scale and is not confined to Jews only.

Then Paul addresses the *elders* (20:27; cf. 20:17) as leaders of the flock of God, exhorting them to be good *overseers* of the church and to *shepherd* believers. Here are strong echoes of the Hebrew prophets where the LXX (Greek OT, Septuagint) uses the same Greek root for the work of the shepherd (Jer. 23:2; Ezek. 34:10; Zech. 10:3; 11:16). Paul calls their *flock* the *church of God*, recalling the LXX "assembly of God" (Deut. 23:2-3; Judg. 20:1; 1 Chron. 28:8). They must remember that this church has been bought by the blood of God's own Son (20:28). Moreover, it is going to be under attack, both from outside and from within. There will be men *like savage wolves* (NASB), heretics who will distort the truth and entice the faithful from the gospel of Jesus (20:29-30). This prophecy is accurate, as shown by the problems which church leader Timothy faces later in that same church (1 Tim. 1:3-11; 2 Tim. 2:16-18; 3:1-9) and the state of affairs there when Revelation 2:4-5 is written.

Paul once more emphasizes his servant role at the end of his speech (20:18-21, 33-35). Possibly holding out his rough and calloused hands, he reminds them how he supported himself and his colleagues by manual labor (20:34), an example of how Christians should work and help the weak (20:35a). Then, Luke reports, he climaxes it all with an otherwise unknown saying from Jesus that *it is more blessed to give than to receive* (20:35b). This word, though not found in any of our gospels, is true to other teachings of Jesus (Luke 6:38; 11:11-13; John 13:34) and is found in slightly different form in the Didache (1.5; The Teaching of the Apostles, dated ca. 120).

After this moving farewell, the whole group of elders along with Paul and his party, kneel down where they are and pray. This is accompanied by much *weeping* at the thought that they will never see him again (20:37-38, cf. 20:25). They show their warm Christian love for him by hugging and kissing (20:36), a practice in harmony with the apostle's own teaching on holding others deep in the heart and showing mutual affection (Phil. 1:7-8; Rom. 12:10). In this mood the Ephesian elders reluctantly escort Paul to the ship and see him on board for his long journey to Jerusalem (20:38b).

Farewells at Tyre, Ptolemais, and Caesarea 21:1-14

21:1-6 Visit with the Christians at Tyre

Again Luke provides a firsthand touch as he writes of their parting at Miletus: After we had torn ourselves away from them (21:1, NIV). once more he gives details of the voyage south along the western coast of Asia Minor and around toward the east. The first port they touch is the small island of Cos, south of Miletus. The next day they turn southeastward, round Cnidus, and head eastward to the city of Rhodes on the island with the same name. Now sailing along the underbelly of Asia Minor, they keep on to Patara (21:1) and, according to a Western Text, to Myra, another fifty miles. At one of these ports, they find another ship, likely a large merchant vessel that no longer hugs the coast, and in it they sail across that part of the Mediterranean straight for the Phoenician coast some 400 miles away (21:2). Luke uses the correct nautical term when he tells of them sighting Cyprus (the southwest tip) on their left (21:3, NIV).

A few days later they land at Tyre, where their ship is to discharge its cargo (21:3b). Paul knows of disciples there, a church founded when Hellenist Christians were driven out of Jerusalem after the death of Stephen (11:19). He and Barnabas visited there on their way to Jerusalem (15:3). Now he seeks them out for an extended farewell visit (21:4a). In spite of some haste to get on to their destination, the party stays around a whole week, enjoying the hospitality of this loving group of believers.

At Tyre a conflict arises that will not be easily resolved, the clash between the Spirit-led determination of Paul to go to Jerusalem and the attempts of his friends to change his mind. This echoes the struggle Jesus had with himself in Gethsemane, asking that the cup of suffering be removed from him but finally accepting God's will (Luke 22:42). Here unnamed believers, led by some prophet speaking through the Spirit, urge Paul not to go on to Jerusalem (21:4b).

No doubt there are meetings and perhaps much preaching by Paul. All that Luke mentions is this message by the Spirit and a touching scene on the beach where men, women, and children kneel with the apostle and his party in prayer. The author reminds the reader of his presence by five uses of we in this one verse (21:5). Then come the farewells, perhaps as on the docks at Miletus (20:37), accompanied by much kissing and weeping (21:6a). This is followed by the actual leave-taking as seen by Luke and party, who board the ship and watch the others return to their homes (21:6b).

21:7-14   Visits at Ptolemais and Caesarea

Forty miles down the coast, the ship puts in at *Ptolemais*, a port in southern Phoenicia (21:7a). This is the city known as Acco in the OT (Judg. 1:31) and Acre in the Middle Ages. Its present name is Akka. There Paul and his party find Christians also, a group brought to the Lord at the same time as those of Tyre (11:19). One day is all they spend with this church before they board ship for another forty-mile voyage down the coast to Caesarea (21:8a). Christians have been there at least since Philip arrived and made converts (8:40). Cornelius and household later became disciples (10:44-48), and more came to the Lord as a result of the work of the fleeing Hellenists (11:19-20). Caesarea is the headquarters of the Roman governors of Judea and an important coastal port. It will become a strategic center of Christianity for centuries to come. (For more on Caesarea, see notes on Paul's two years in this city, chaps. 23—26).

The place of lodging for the party is the home of *Philip the evangelist* (21:8b), the second named of *the seven* consecrated in 6:5. He also has carried the gospel to Samaria (8:4-13) and won the Ethiopian treasurer to the Lord (8:26-38). Since he is mentioned as reaching Caesarea in his evangelistic work, perhaps he has settled down. He does have a family there. When Paul and his men visit him in his home, he has four unmarried daughters, all of whom have the spiritual gift of prophecy (21:9). But Luke takes the reader quickly to the point of the story, the visit of the prophet Agabus and the showdown on the matter of Paul going to Jerusalem (21:10-14).

This is the same Agabus who earlier came to Antioch from Jerusalem and had predicted a great famine. That message led to the sending of relief funds to the mother church by the hand of Barnabas and Saul (11:28-30; 12:25). Now once more he enters the life of Paul by joining the ranks of those who would caution the apostle about going to Jerusalem. Like some prophet from the OT, he makes his point with a visual aid, a symbolic action (cf. 1 Kings 11:29-40; Isa. 20:2-6; Jer. 13:1-11; 19:1-15; 28:1-17). Taking Paul's belt, he ties himself up with it to show what will happen to the apostle. The message is clear. He does not say that Paul should not go, but that if he does go, he will be bound and imprisoned, the very thing Paul had already told the Ephesian elders (20:23). Here are echoes of Jesus' prediction that he will be "betrayed into human hands" (Luke 9:44). In Paul's case, however, the Romans deliver him from the Jews. In Jesus' case, the Jews turn him over to the Romans to be killed.

After the symbolic act and words of Agabus, the whole group,

Paul's party, and the local Christians together, use this occasion to urge the apostle not to go on to Jerusalem (21:12). Like Jesus on his last trip to the holy city, Paul will not be persuaded by well-meaning companions to shrink from his divinely directed duty. His reply reflects a fine sensitivity to both the friends' pleas and God's leading. *What are you doing, weeping and breaking my heart?* Luke remembers the moment well. *I am ready,* replies Paul, *not only to be bound but even to die in Jerusalem for the name of the Lord Jesus* (21:13). It is Spirit-inspired friends against Spirit-led leader, and someone has to give! As the author puts it, since Paul is not to be swayed from his divine purpose, *We remained silent.* Reaching the same conclusion that Jesus did in Gethsemane (Luke 22:42b), the group finally agrees, *The Lord's will be done* (21:14). From this time on, no one tries to turn Paul back from the trip for which he was *bound in the Spirit* (20:22, RSV).

From Caesarea to Jerusalem 21:15-16

Jerusalem is some sixty-four miles away, and the party now sets out on foot, or by horseback (as suggested by Haenchen: 607; and Marshall: 341; following Ramsay, 1896:302). Accompanied by some of the Caesarean Christians, they take the overland route to the home of *Mnason,* where lodging has likely already been arranged. These fellow believers from Caesarea come along not only to make sure that the party is well taken care of but, like Paul, also to celebrate Pentecost (cf. 20:16). Luke speaks of Mnason as an *early disciple* from *Cyprus* (21:16). One is reminded of his countryman Barnabas, also a disciple in the first years of the church, a broad-minded Hellenist from Cyprus who, like Mnason, is most generous and hospitable. Not all Jerusalem Christians would welcome a large party of Gentiles into their house like this. They apparently make their headquarters with Mnason while they are in the city.

Encounters in Jerusalem

21:17—23:35

Report to Jerusalem Church; Request of James 21:17-25

Paul now seeks the blessing of the apostles and elders of Jerusalem. This is in line with Luke's purpose to have the leaders of that church approve each new thrust of the Gentile mission. One of his main reasons for going to Jerusalem, that of delivering the offering from the Gentile churches (Rom. 15:25-31), is not even directly mentioned at this point (cf. 24:17). In its place is the story of how Paul submits to James to prove that he does not teach *Jews living among the Gentiles to forsake Moses* (21:20-25). Eventually Paul suffers great persecution because of this.

Luke seems to indicate two different meetings with the Jerusalem Christians. In 21:17, the party is given a warm reception. On the following day, they meet with James and the elders (21:18-25). Because 21:22 seems to imply that a large segment of the church does not yet know of Paul's arrival, Haenchen plausibly suggests that this first meeting is a welcome given them by primarily Hellenistic churchmen like Mnason and others (607).

The next day in meeting with *James* and *all the elders,* Paul takes the initiative and relates the great things God has accomplished among the Gentiles through his ministry (21:19). Likely at this time, Paul and his companions present the substantial offering raised among the Gentile churches for the mother congregation. The response of the latter may be included in the statement that, as a result of his report, *they [the Jerusalem Christians] praised God* (21:20a).

Luke, however, chooses not to mention the offering here. That Paul and his party do deliver the gifts is made clear later, where Paul calls them *alms for my nation* (24:17). Is it because the offering is not as much appreciated by the Jewish Christians as Paul and his Gentile representatives hoped it would be? Or is the opposition to Paul so threatening that this great demonstration of love and unity is passed over as unimportant? Bruce (429, n. 28) suggests that perhaps the Jerusalem Christians look upon the money as something due them in the light of the command and agreement of Galatians 2:10, or as the equivalent of the annual half-shekel paid into the temple each year by Gentile proselytes.

Whatever the original circumstances, James and his followers have another matter on their minds, so pressing that Luke can tell the story without mentioning the offering except for a possible hint in 21:24. As the account now has it, Paul tells story after story about the conversion of Gentiles. The Jerusalemites listen politely and praise God for this great work (21:20a). Then they respond with a scathing rebuttal, letting the apostle know of a rumor that has reached many thousands of believing Jews *zealous for the law*. They have heard that Paul is destroying the law of Moses by teaching Jewish converts in Gentile areas not to *circumcise* their male children or observe other *customs* of the law (21:20b-21). From Paul's letters (1 Cor. 16:1-4; 2 Cor. 8—9; Rom. 15:25-27), one might expect this to be a moment of triumph for Paul and the Gentile mission. Instead, there is serious criticism of the apostle. To prove his innocence, he is drawn into a series of attacks that put him in jeopardy from this time on.

In Jerusalem now comes the culmination of the series of accusations that Paul is upsetting the world (17:6; 18:13; 19:25-27). But this very fact is used of God to enable Paul to carry the witness to the centers of power, first in Jerusalem and then in Rome (Tannehill, 2:266-267).

James and his men already have a plan for solving the problem they raise, and they proceed to outline it to Paul (21:23-24). He must demonstrate that the charges are false by taking part, as a Jew, in a purification ritual. They have four Jewish believers who have undertaken a temporary Nazirite vow involving the shaving of the head (see on 18:18). These men are likely poor and unable to pay the expenses (21:24). As an added act of piety, Paul is to cover their dues from his own funds (Ramsay, 1896:310) or as part of bringing *alms* to his *nation* (24:17). The details of the ritual are no longer clear, especially about the kind of impurity dealt with (for three possibilities, see Marshall: 345 and note). Yet Paul is willing and takes the necessary steps to carry the plan to a successful conclusion (21:26).

James also tells Paul of the letter on minimal requirements for Gentile believers as though he has not heard of it (21:25). This decree shows that the Jerusalem leaders are trying to accommodate the Gentile mission (cf. notes on chap. 15 and the following TBC, "Relationship of Acts 15 to Galatians 2").

Paul's Arrest at the Temple   21:26-40

21:26-30   Purification Ritual and Mob Scene

According to the most plausible theory (Haenchen: 611-612), Paul is allowed to participate in the temple ritual by being cleansed of the defilement of coming from Gentile territory. This is accomplished by a ritual sprinkling with water on the third day and then again on the seventh. In Luke's abbreviated account, the apostle arranges to enter the temple with the four men and undergo the initial purification. At this time he announces that the ritual will be terminated on the seventh day. Then he will have his final sprinkling, and the men will have their heads shaved as part of their Nazirite vow, Paul paying the expenses. A sacrifice will be made for each of them (21:26). But according to the story, this never happens. When the seven days are *almost completed*, everything goes wrong. Some Jews from Ephesus (*Asia*), knowing Paul by sight and seeing him *in the temple*, jump to the conclusion that he has brought the Gentile *Trophimus* into that sacred place. Earlier they have seen the two together in the city (21:29). They promptly lay hands on Paul and stir up a mob while shouting lies about him (21:28, 30).

Paul cannot be too surprised, since such irrational group action has happened in almost *every* place where he has ministered (13:50; 14:5-6; 16:19-39; 17:5-9, 13; 18:12-13; 19:23-41). In fact, from the time of his conversion onward, he has been victimized by similar vicious attacks (9:23-25, 29). In the present case, he is dragged outside the temple gates, where the mob is free to kill him without defiling the sacred precincts (21:30). An inscription from Herod's temple, written in Greek, gives warning of the death penalty for any Gentile who enters the Court of Israel (May: 114). No doubt this would also apply to those who take *Greeks into the temple* (21:28).

21:31-40 Rescue by the Roman Tribune

Responding to this *uproar*, the Roman army enters the story. Luke presents a varied picture of the military. On one hand, he praises individual centurions for their great faith (Luke 7:9), their favorable response to Jesus (Luke 23:47), and their conversion to Christianity (Acts 10:1—11:18). On the other hand, he quotes Jesus as predicting that the Roman military will mock, insult, and kill him (Luke 18:32-33). Luke also shows how the Roman governor gave in to the masses and had the Lord crucified, but only after thrice declaring him innocent (Luke 23:4-25). In Peter's speeches, Luke recalls the part the soldiers had in the crucifixion of Jesus (Acts 2:23) and lists Pilate as one arrayed against the Lord (4:27).

Though a citizen, Paul has been both beaten and jailed by Romans officials and then grudgingly released (Acts 16:22-24, 38). In general, Luke shows how relations between Paul and Roman officials "end in a friendly way" (Ramsay, 1896:304-310). Now in Jerusalem, he is both rescued by the Roman military and made a prisoner of it. From this time on in Acts, he is never again a free man.

The fortress of Antonia stands just outside the temple area to the northwest, connected by two flights of stairs with the Court of the

Gentiles. Here the Roman garrison is quartered and their guard can look over and quickly detect any disturbance in the temple courtyard. Word is sent immediately to the officer in charge, called *the tribune*, with a rank comparable to that of a major or colonel today (21:31). At Jerusalem his *cohort* consists normally of a thousand men, 760 of them infantry and 240 cavalry. Claudius Lysias (cf. 23:26) acts at once, taking with him at least two hundred men (*centurions*, plural). With this impressive military presence, he stops the murderous beating of Paul (21:32).

The tribune comes up, personally arrests the victim, and has him bound with chains (21:33a), on the assumption that he is the leader of a violent band called the *assassins* (cf. 21:38). Though no doubt happy to catch this dangerous criminal at last, he must observe Roman law and question the prisoner (21:33b). So great is the uproar, however, that he cannot make out anything said, so he orders his soldiers to pick up Paul bodily and carry him in their arms into the barracks (21:34). The cries of the crowd recall bloodthirsty shouts, "Crucify him!" which Luke records from another Jerusalem mob years earlier (Luke 23:21).

On the way into the barracks, Paul finds an opportunity to get the tribune's attention and, in the good Greek of one whose early life was spent in the university city of Tarsus, asks if he may say something to the officer. The Roman thinks he is the rough uncultured man from the wilds of Egypt and is surprised that he can talk Greek (21:37). Isn't the prisoner the leader of a band of *four thousand assassins* known to have had designs against Jerusalem? he wonders.

Though the numbers vary, the rebel leader sought may be the false prophet from Egypt about whom Josephus writes. He led several thousand followers to the Mount of Olives and said he would order the walls of Jerusalem to fall down as he attacked. Felix met them with Roman soldiers and destroyed, captured, and dispersed them, but *the Egyptian* fled (*War* 2.13.5; *Ant.* 20.8.6).

Now Paul has an opportunity to tell the tribune who he really is. First he is a *Jew*, a *citizen* of the free city of Tarsus, capital of Cilicia. Its university is known as a stronghold of Stoicism, and estimates of its current population run as high as half a million. Thus Paul can call it *an important city*. He is not yet claiming Roman citizenship (cf. 22:25-28). But he is asking for the right to speak to the crowd (21:39). The tribune gives him permission.

Paul picks a suitable spot on the staircase, high enough to be out of reach of the mob, yet low enough to put him in eye contact with his hearers. Standing erect in spite of his severe beating and motioning with his hand, he gives his captors and the audience another surprise. Instead of using Greek, the common language around the eastern Mediterranean, he addresses the crowd in *Hebrew!* Many scholars take this to mean the Aramaic dialect of the day, and that may well be what Luke means here and later (21:40; 22:22; 26:14). However, the discovery of the Dead Sea Scrolls, written in biblical Hebrew, show that language to be in use during Hellenistic times. Hence, a strong minority of scholars have come to take Luke's *hebraïdi* here quite literally. According to this view, Paul is speaking *in the Hebrew dialect* (NASB). Whatever the case, when the people hear the apostle use their native tongue and not Greek or Latin, the languages of their Roman overlords, they become respectfully quiet (21:40; 22:2).

Paul's Defense in Jerusalem 22:1—23:10

22:1-21 Paul Addressing the People

This speech and the comparable ones before Felix (24:2-23) and Festus with Agrippa (26:2-32) follow an ancient pattern for defenses. There is first an introduction (technically called the *exordium*), whose purpose is to render the audience well disposed, attentive, and receptive. This is followed by the *body* of the speech, which usually contains three elements: the statement of facts, the proof, and the refutation. Then the final part is the *peroration*, or closing word, which brings the whole defense to a conclusion.

Paul puts his audience at ease, not only by his use of their mother tongue, but by addressing them respectfully, *Brothers and fathers*, the way Stephen also had begun his speech years before (7:2). Then in dignified fashion he asks them to listen to his defense (22:1). They become even quieter when they hear Paul speaking in (a dialect of) Hebrew (22:2). As he had told the Roman officer (21:39), he says he is a foreign-born Jew. Yet he hastens to add that he was *brought up in this city* and educated by the celebrated Rabban *Gamaliel* (22:3a; see notes on 5:34 about this greatest and best-loved teacher of the law). The verb *having been brought up in this city* suggests that he came from Tarsus to Jerusalem at a relatively early age and received most of his education here. This statement is intended to gain him a good hearing, and so are the following two points.

First, like his hearers, Paul has had a strict upbringing in the law and is *zealous for God* (22:3b). Second, he has demonstrated his zeal for the traditions of the fathers by vigorously persecuting the movement connected with *this Way* (of Jesus, 22:4). Then, to clinch the point and establish his credibility among them beyond question, he cites the historical fact that can be verified with the high priestly group: he received letters from the top authorities to carry the persecution on to Damascus (22:5; cf. 9:2).

Paul has already been narrating facts as he moves into the body of his speech with what might be called the proof of his case. This is the story of his conversion some twenty years earlier, the first retelling of this pivotal event in his life. The threefold occurrence of this narrative in Acts is an indication of its key importance. Moreover, it is strategically placed: the first time (9:1-19) at the beginning of Paul's career as a believer, as a foundation, and the last two times (22:4-16; 26:9-18) at the beginning and end of the defense sequence, framing this phase of the apostle's witness. The narrative here and in Acts 26 differs from the one in Acts 9 in that they are presented by Paul himself in the first person and in each case are a part of a defense.

The first part of the present account follows that of Acts 9 point by point: the approach to Damascus, the great light, his falling to the ground, the voice of the risen Lord asking *why* he is persecuting him, Saul's question as to the identity of the voice, with the answer that he is Jesus of Nazareth whom Saul is persecuting (22:6-8). The only added detail is that this happened *about noon* (also in 26:13), a touch making the reader aware of this as a genuine divine light that outshone the sun. But in this retelling there is one seeming contradiction. In 9:7 Luke writes that Saul's associates stood speechless *because they heard the voice but saw no one*. Now, however, Paul is quoted as saying that these men *saw the light but did not hear the voice* (22:9). The discrepancy disappears, however, when one takes it to mean that they heard the *sound* of the voice but did not understand the *words*.

Then, because this story tells Paul's own experience, he gives only what the Lord said to him and not what was said to Ananias. Accordingly, the instructions he received are enlarged to include the command to go on into Damascus and await further orders (22:10). Since this account is part of a defense before angry Jews, Paul makes a point of introducing Ananais as *a devout man according to the law and well spoken of by all the Jews living there* (22:12). It is important for both the Jerusalem crowd to hear and later for the world to read this in Acts: what happens at the time of Saul's conversion is within the plan of the eternal God of the Jews.

Paul omits all mention of the vision of Ananias that brought them together (9:10-17) but does include the coming of that devout Jew to miraculously restore his sight (22:13). Nor is anything said about Saul receiving the Holy Spirit, since this is a message to Jews. Instead, Ananias tells him how the *God of our ancestors has chosen* Paul to *see and hear the Righteous One* (the Messiah) and to be his witness to all the world (22:14-15). This holy commission is then accompanied by the cleansing waters of baptism (22:16; cf. 9:18b).

In Luke's digest of the speech, Paul skips over his entire ministry in Damascus, including his narrow escape from there (9:19b-25). He moves on at once to his experience when he showed up in Jerusalem some time later. Paul omits the events of 9:26-30 and tells instead of an otherwise unknown vision in the temple. From 2 Corinthians 12:1-10, we learn that he had many such *exceptional . . . revelations.* In this *trance, Paul sees him,* the *Righteous One* (the Messiah: 3:14; 7:52; the risen Jesus: 22:8, 14). Jesus tells Paul to leave Jerusalem quickly because unbelievers there will not accept his testimony (22:18). Paul reminds Jesus of his former persecution of believers (22:19-20)—a good point for his hearers to ponder once more (cf. 22:3-5). Yet Jesus still orders Paul to leave the city. The reason now given, however, unlike the situation described in 9:36, is to fulfill his mission as a *witness to all the world* (22:15). Paul is being sent *far away to the Gentiles* (22:21). This points readers to the end of the book, in Rome. On that note the reported speech ends.

22:22-29 Further Dealing with Mob and Tribune

Mention of being sent *to the Gentiles* turns an attentive crowd once more into a howling mob, venting its wrath with cries of murder (22:22). As a defense, the speech is a failure, serving to sharpen the problem rather than solve it. Yet from Luke's standpoint, this is but the first of a series of such defenses that will have a powerful cumulative effect (Tannehill, 2:278-279). The reader must press on, caught up in the excitement of the account. The cries of the people become *a roaring* (literally, both the sound and the meaning of the Greek participle *kraugazontōn,* at the start of 22:23). They then wave their garments in the air to rid them of dust, a sign of intense hatred for Paul and horror at his remarks of going to the Gentiles.

The hubbub is so great that the Roman tribune must once more intervene to rescue Paul from death (22:24). The soldiers sweep down, bring the apostle into the barracks, and prepare to flog him. This brutal practice is the Roman way of beating the truth out of a prisoner, illegal to use on a *citizen* but, for all others, standard procedure. The tribune is not present at the time, just one of the centurions, and his men have Paul stretched out and tied down to receive the lash. The scourge is a fearful instrument made of leather thongs to which rough pieces of bone and metal are fastened to cut the skin. If a man does not actually die under such treatment, he is almost sure to be crippled for life. Paul has earlier undergone Jewish beatings (2 Cor. 11:24-25) and even lashings of the Roman rods (16:22-23), but neither was as cruel as this.

Once more Paul takes the initiative (cf. 21:37). As Marshall (358) puts it, he now "plays his trump card." A series of laws over many years has made it illegal to beat or even chain a Roman citizen without trial, with serious penalties for anyone not obeying. So now Paul asks the centurion, the ranking officer present, whether it is lawful to scourge a Roman citizen, an uncondemned one at that (22:25).

The military is taken by surprise and reacts immediately. The centurion in charge hurries to his superior officer and breathlessly asks what they are about to do to this *Roman citizen* (22:26)! His question brings *the tribune* to Paul's side at once to ask him outright if he is indeed a citizen. The prisoner's answer is simple: *Yes.* No doubt Paul is glad to be able to bring this up before the whipping rather than after it, as at Philippi (16:37-39).

Then with some delight, Luke records a conversation showing that Paul has more claim to Roman citizenship than does this high-ranking officer (22:27-28)! Tribune Lysias bought his citizenship for *a large sum of money* (a practice common under Claudius Caesar, chiefly a matter of bribing key people). But Paul, whom he is about to have flogged, was *born* a Roman citizen! This means that his father must have been a citizen. How he became one is not known. It may have been from services rendered by an ancestor to a high-ranking Roman, or, as Ramsay argues, in 171 B.C., when Tarsus was made a free city (1907:185).

Surprising as it may seem, all that Paul apparently has to do is to claim to be a citizen, solemnly affirming, *Civis Romanum sum (I am a Roman citizen).* As pointed out in connection with 16:37, this is true because the danger of falsehood on the one side is equally balanced by the penalty for mistreating a citizen on the other. Thus the soldiers who are about to flog Paul quickly withdraw, afraid to lay hands on the man. Fear also grips the tribune for a moment, since he has ordered this citizen to be bound (22:29). Disaster is averted, and surely all involved have a sense of relief.

22:30—23:10 Paul Before the Sanhedrin

The tribune still doesn't know why the Jerusalem crowd is so intent on killing Paul. Understanding nothing of what the apostle said in his speech and learning little from the cries of the mob, he still wants to know the accusations against the man (22:30a). So he decides to seek the help of the supreme Jewish council (Sanhedrin). Some scholars (like Haenchen: 645) think it unlikely that the Roman tribune has either the authority to call the Sanhedrin together or the right to attend it himself (cf. the implication of 23:10). However, both these objections are overcome if, as Marshall suggests (361), it is not an *official* meeting of that body, but a consultation to help the officer determine the nature of the charge to send on to his superiors.

The following day Paul is released and ordered to stand before the whole Sanhedrin (22:30b). This is the first in a series of defenses before the highest religious and political authorities of the region (chaps. 23—26): the Sanhedrin, two Roman governors, and King Agrippa. Here is the gospel making its appeal not only to individuals but to the cultural and political structures of the times. In this appearance before the council, Luke does not report a full-fledged defense speech but an interrupted exchange designed to make two points: First, Paul is living in obedience to his heavenly call (23:1; cf. 26:19). Second, the real issue at stake is *the hope of the resurrection of the dead* (23:6).

Without mentioning the opening procedures, Luke at once presents the apostle, standing before the Sanhedrin, addressing them cordially as *Brothers,* and pleading a *clear conscience* so far as the charges against him are concerned. He has followed God's commands faithfully to this very day (23:1). This is too much for the quick-tempered high priest, and he orders the apostle to be slapped on the mouth (23:2). Ananias (not to be confused with Annas of 4:6) was appointed high priest in A.D. 47 by Herod of Chalcis, brother of Herod Agrippa I, and held the office until 58/59. He was well known for his greed and vicious character (Josephus, *Ant.* 20.9.2; Bruce: 449-450). Imagine such a person ordering Paul to be struck across the mouth for claiming a clear conscience!

Paul's quick retort, *God will strike you, you whitewashed wall!* further heightens the tension. Paul is like the prophet shouting "Jereboam shall die by the sword!" (Amos 7:11). He is like Elijah confronting the king, "Because you have sold yourself to do what is evil in the sight of the Lord, I will . . . cut off from Ahab every male!" (1 Kings 21:20-21). Now the apostle lashes back at evil power with the sword of divine judgment. The imagery of the *whitewashed wall* is likely from Ezekiel 13:10-11: false prophets are accused of covering over a rickety wall with whitewash to prevent it from falling. It is similar to Jesus' term, *whitewashed tombs,* outwardly beautiful but inwardly full of dead men's bones (Matt. 23:27). Paul's prophecy will be fulfilled in A.D. 66, some ten years later. Ananias is assassinated by Jewish zealots, who see him as a friend of the Romans.

For the present, however, the council is shocked by the boldness of the retort. Some react with anger that Paul would dare to insult *God's high priest* (23:4). They use words like those of the temple police who struck Jesus on the face and asked him, "Is that how you answer the high priest?" (John 18:22). Jesus asked them to point out where he was wrong or to admit their faulty trial procedure in striking him (John 18:23).

Paul responds with the puzzling statement that he does not know the high priest is the one who ordered him to be slapped (23:5). Since this is an unofficial session, perhaps the high priest is not so easily identified, or Paul's poor eyesight is hindering him. More likely, however, this is biting irony on the part of both Paul and Luke. It is hard to recognize as high priest anyone who can order a defendant to be so cruelly and unlawfully struck! Even so, once the high priest's identity is brought to his attention, Paul apologizes by quoting from the law that one should *not speak evil of a leader* of the people (Exod. 22:28). Luke is making two points here. First, Paul is badly mistreated by this Jewish high priest. Second, in spite of it, and contrary to the charges made in 21:28, he respects the sacredness of that office. In other words, Paul is definitely not anti-Jewish.

Now, with the air so tense that a wrong word could ignite an explosion, Paul again seizes the initiative. He cries out that he is a Pharisee and the son of Pharisees and that it is for *the hope of the resurrection of the dead* that he is being tried (23:6). This immediately divides the house (23:7). The majority are Sadducees, who deny a resurrection. But a strong minority are Pharisees, for whom the ancestral hope of Israel is tied up in belief in resurrection, whether in angelic form or as immortality of spirit (for more on 23:8-9, see "Resurrection" under TBC).

As Tannehill (2:287) points out, there is much more here than a tactical move on Paul's part. Instead of being a cheap way of getting out of a bad situation, as some critics maintain, it is a theme to which Paul will be returning again during the defense sequence (24:15, 21). Thus it is the central point in his climactic speech before King Agrippa (26:6-8, 23) and a vital part of his presentation to the Jews in Rome (28:20; cf. 4:1-2, 10). Luke would regard it as a stroke of divine genius, a fulfillment of Jesus' word that "the Holy Spirit will teach you at that very hour what you ought to say" (Luke 12:12).

As a result, a great debate takes place, with Paul's fellow Pharisees standing up and declaring, *We find nothing wrong with this man* (23:9ab). This is what King Agrippa will later declare (26:31-32) and what the author wants his readers to realize from this point on in Acts. It is also the very conclusion that Pilate and Herod Antipas had earlier reached with regard to Jesus (Luke 23:4, 14-15, 22). In the course of the debate, the Pharisees put in question form what the reader knows to be true: *What if a spirit or an angel has spoken to him?* (23:9c). So violent is the division between the two parties that the Roman tribune, present at the trial, has to intervene. With ironic humor Luke tells how these august councillors are about to tear Paul apart. Soldiers have to come, take him by force, and bring him back into the barracks to protect him (23:10).

A Night Vision of Reassurance 23:11

At the height of a controversy with the Jews in Corinth, the risen Lord appeared to Paul in the night and assured him that, while he might be attacked, he would not be harmed. Therefore, he should not be afraid but speak out, since the Lord had many people in the city yet to be converted (18:9-10). Now also the apostle needs some special word from the Lord to let him know what is happening. Paul has been severely beaten by an angry mob (21:30-31), later cursed and again threatened with death by the same mob (22:23), tied up for a crippling flogging (22:25), and almost torn to pieces in the Sanhedrin (23:10). Thus Paul might well be wondering about the purpose of his coming to Jerusalem. What is God allowing to happen, and what will it lead to?

In this vision, as in the former one, he is told not to be afraid. He has testified *in Jerusalem,* meaning that ordeal is now over, and that the next step is to go on and *bear witness also in Rome* (23:11). Though the message is minimal, it does let the apostle know that his life will be spared all the way to Rome, regardless of what happens and how much time it will take.

Dealing with the Plot Against Paul 23:12-35

23:12-22 Discovery of the Conspiracy

Luke now goes into a surprising amount of detail describing Paul's escape from death at the hands of some determined enemies and his transfer to Caesarea. There are several interesting parallels here with the equally detailed account of the sea voyage to Rome in Acts 27 (Tannehill, 2:294). In both cases the apostle is under armed guard as he is taken from one Roman jurisdiction to another. In both narratives the dangers are vividly depicted with high drama and suspense. The Greek verb *diasozō* (*bring safely through*), used in each case, is found only here in Acts (23:24; 27:43-44; 28:1, 4). In both accounts there is a reassuring vision from the Lord that he will eventually witness in Rome (23:11; 27:23-24).

The morning after Paul's vision, more than forty of his Jewish enemies band together to have him killed. Unable to get to him openly because of Roman protection, these assassins bind themselves in a mutual pact to do away with the apostle. They will neither eat nor drink, they say, until he is destroyed (23:12). This plot now becomes the behind-the-scenes threat running through the next three chapters of Acts, hovering over Paul like an evil presence for more than two years (cf. 24:2-9; 25:3, 7, 18).

The conspirators would never manage to survive this long under such an oath were it not for a long-standing rabbinic interpretation eventually releasing them from it (Mishnah Nedarim 3.3; cf. Mark 7:11-13 for similar casuistry, and Matt. 5:34-37 for Jesus' teaching against rash vows). They cannot do their work, however, without help from higher up. They go to key Sadducean leaders in the Sanhedrin, reveal their plans to them, and enlist them in a plot to have Paul summoned for further examination by the council. The plotters intend to ambush and kill Paul on the way (23:14-15).

At this point appears a relative of Paul whom we otherwise know nothing about. Although the apostle mentions "relatives" Andronicus, Junia, and Herodion (Rom. 16:6, 11), there is no information about his sister whose son is present in Jerusalem on this occasion. He is young enough that the tribune takes him *by the hand* (23:19), yet old enough to pass on accurately details of the plot and make a wise suggestion to that officer (23:20-21). Perhaps he is an alert and adventurous teenager.

Luke gives no clue as to how the lad hears of the conspiracy nor where he lives in relation to the Roman garrison. It is enough to know that God uses this young man to save Paul's life. With considerable detail the author tells how the youth goes to the barracks, gains entrance, gives details of the plot to his uncle, who then calls a centurion and has him take the youth to the tribune (23:17-19). There is an air of intrigue about the story, as well as urgency. *Tomorrow* the murderous plot will be launched (23:20)! This forthright youth does not hesitate to tell the commander what he should and should not do (23:21). Surprisingly, the officer takes his advice! The two of them now join Paul in a quiet counterplan (23:22).

23:23-35 Paul's Transfer from Jerusalem to Caesarea

The tribune wastes no time. By 9:00 p.m. that day, two of his centurions have their 200 infantrymen ready to start. With them are an equal number of *spearmen* (javelin throwers) along with 70 cavalrymen—a bodyguard of 470 heavily armed soldiers! Since this is almost half the total garrison, some have thought that Luke exaggerates the numbers. But the fact that the 200 foot soldiers travel only overnight and then return (cf. 23:32) makes it not improbable. As an added convenience, the tribune furnishes *mounts* for Paul, more than one horse or mule to provide for a change and to insure that he reaches Caesarea comfortably (23:24). All these provisions are an indication of how seriously the commander is taking the threat of the assassins. For Paul, Luke, and all Christian readers, the account shows the abundant protection which the Lord gives those who are fulfilling the divine will.

Along with this armed escort, the tribune sends a letter to the governor explaining the whole matter (23:26-30). It has the distinction of being the only secular letter in the NT. Though Luke has included the text, he does not claim that this is a word-for-word copy, since he has no way of knowing that. Thus he introduces it as *a letter to this effect* (23:25). Here for the first time, the tribune's name, *Claudius Lysias*, is mentioned. Since Lysias bought his citizenship under the Emperor Claudius (22:28), it is reasonable to suppose that his personal name came from that ruler (Bruce: 446, 459; Marshall: 361).

After the author's name, customarily put first in ancient letters, comes the name of the addressee. In this case it is the governor of Judea, accurately called *his Excellency*. Antonius *Felix* is a freed Greek slave now risen to high rank. He has served first in a lower position in Samaria and was then made governor of the province in A.D. 52. He tried to hold the rebels of Judea in check but acted with such cruelty that he was later removed from office (24:27). The historian Tacitus wrote that "he exercised royal power with the mind of a slave" (*Annals* 12.54). Paul is now sent in chains to this man.

As Luke reports, the letter contains a brief account of the events of the past few days (21:31—23:22). It is carefully written to show that the tribune has followed correct Roman legal procedures and that the prisoner is a Roman citizen whose life is in danger but against whom there are no substantial charges. The discerning reader will smile at the way Luke has Claudius Lysias omit his almost disastrous blunder of preparing to flog this citizen (22:25). He states that first he learned of Paul's citizenship and then came and rescued him! (23:27). The author, as so often, is using subtle humor to make a point. In this case he shows how a Roman official needs to project a public image better than his actual performance.

This exposure of weaknesses of those in political power will be repeated in subsequent accounts of the governors Felix and Festus and of King Agrippa, showing that Roman justice itself is flawed. Such repetitions with variations are a characteristic of OT narratives, often subtle but with cumulative power. In spite of his tendency toward cover-up, however, the tribune Claudius Lysias has Paul's best interests at heart and is doing all he can to see that the apostle receives a favorable hearing in Caesarea.

The soldiers, accompanied by cavalry and lancers, then follow instructions and escort Paul by night some 35 miles to *Antipatris* (23:31). There, over halfway to Caesarea, they leave the party and by daylight return to Jerusalem. From this point on, Paul and the 200 horsemen and 70 javelin throwers travel northward through open country, far enough on their journey that they need no longer fear attack from the assassins. By evening they have covered the last 27 miles to Caesarea, capital of the province, and have delivered Paul and the letter to the governor (23:32-33).

Though corrupt and inept as a ruler, Governor Felix does know correct legal procedure and begins by asking Paul about his province of origin (23:34). Since the prisoner is not from Judea where the governor presides, but from Cilicia, some distance away, he is sent to the palace built by Herod the Great and now serving as headquarters of the Roman administration. This is the Roman *praetorium* (*headquarters*), one of a network of such buildings scattered over the empire. At such places the official business of the emperor and his subordinates is handled. Here a special Roman prisoner like Paul will be kept under guard for trial, in this case until his accusers arrive from Jerusalem (23:35).

THE TEXT IN BIBLICAL CONTEXT
The Trials of Paul and Jesus

There is striking similarity between Paul's last trip to Jerusalem with its ensuing trials and Jesus' last journey to that city with the experiences that befell him there. Paul himself and those around him must have sensed this. Then Luke highlights these parallels and makes his account more dramatic and meaningful as a result. Probably he also has in mind the value such a narrative will have for Christian readers who likewise will be facing trial. (For a discussion of this aim, see Introduction, "Purpose," p. 19.)

Among these similarities are, first, the fact that both Jesus and Paul are impelled by the Spirit to go to Jerusalem (cf. Luke 9:51; Acts 19:21; 20:22; 21:13). Second, both of them persist in spite of attempts of well-meaning friends to turn them back (cf. Mark 8:32-33, which Luke knew; Acts 21:4, 11-14). Third, they both run into incredible opposition, persecution, and death or near death, foreseen and predicted ahead of time (cf. Luke 9:21-22; 9:43-45; 18:31-34; chaps. 22—23; Acts 21:37—23:31). Fourth, each makes a lasting witness by this journey. Finally, by triumphing over foes, each leaves a timeless legacy through words and deeds.

Nevertheless, there are important differences. Jesus was and is the Son of God and Redeemer of the world, and Paul is one of his apostles. The mission of Jesus is the salvation of humankind, and that of Paul the completion of his work in bringing the offering to Jerusalem and making a final witness there. For Jesus, this climactic period of testimony and trial lasted only a week; for Paul, it stretches out over several years. Jesus is crucified, but Paul is simply beaten and made a prisoner. His death is not recorded. Yet in Luke's handling of the two narratives, parallels stand out beyond all differences, with great significance.

Jerusalem Mob Scenes in Perspective

With 21:30-31 and 22:22-24, we come to the last of the series of mob scenes in Acts. The most extensive and detailed of them was the one recorded in 19:23-41 (you may consult the notes on that text).

For composing such narratives, Luke had some significant background. He had already written his version of the crowd crying out for the death of Jesus (Luke 23:18-23). To the synoptic tradition (Matt. 27:17-23; Mark 15:11-14), Luke added the detail that after Pilate offered to chastise the prisoner and let him go, the mob "all cried out together, 'Away with this man and release to us Barabbas.' " So now, in recording the reaction of the crowd to Paul's speech from the staircase, he quotes their enraged cries, "Away with such a fellow from the earth! For he should not be allowed to live" (22:22b).

Several descriptions of crowds in the OT could have furnished both imagery and language for Luke's mob narratives. The story of the Israelites worshiping the golden calf at the base of Mount Sinai has a graphic picture of "people . . . running wild" in their frenzy (Exod. 32:25), a feature prominent in these scenes in Acts. Another narrative depicting hysterical crowd action is found in 1 Kings 18:25-29. It was not a lynching mob, as in the stories of Acts, but one showing irrational and dangerous behavior. The prophets of Baal worked themselves up into a frenzy from morning till night, shouting and cutting themselves as they "raved on." Korah, Dathan, and Abiram assembled a more hostile crowd to confront Moses and Aaron and angrily denounce them to their faces (Num. 16:1-19).

What these narratives show is the tendency of a crowd to be easily inflamed by agitators and carried away by their emotions to the point that they no longer function rationally. Under such conditions they lose all control of themselves, disregard the rights of others, reject authorized leadership, and unless stopped, work great destruction.

Resurrection: The Sadducee-Pharisee-Christian Debate

Luke points out that the Sadducees do not believe in the resurrection (Luke 20:27; Acts 23:8). Holding to a strict interpretation of the Torah, Sadducees can not deny the existence of angels, which do appear in the Pentateuch. Yet they are cool to elaborate beliefs about angels and demons that flourished among the Jews in the late postexilic period, and they do not see belief in resurrection in the books of Moses (though others might: Heb. 11:19). As Viviano and Taylor say, Sadducees reject any belief in "individual personal survival beyond death in an afterlife in terms either of resurrection or of immortality." The Greek of 23:8 is best understood: *The Sadducees say that there is no resurrection, either (in the form of) an angel or (in the form of) a spirit; but the Pharisees acknowledge both* (based on Viviano: 498, giving *amphotera* the usual sense of *both* rather than *all three*, as in NRSV).

The Pharisees are spiritual descendants of Ezra, interpreting and developing the Law, in sharp theological and political conflict with the Sadducees from Hasmonean times (second cent. B.C.). Injustice may seem to prevail for a time in this life, but the Pharisees believe God will eventually set things right, even after saints are martyred (cf. Dan. 12:2; Rev. 6:9-11). They hold to a resurrection of the earthly body and a future world where persons are rewarded or punished according to their behavior in this one. The Sadducees, however, believe Sheol is the end. Pharisees understand existence in this future world to be angelic (Dan. 12:2-3; 2 Macc. 7:9; Mark 12:25 and parallels) or as spirit (immortality of the soul: Wisd. 3:1-4; cf. Josephus, *Ant.* 18.1.3); Pharisees accept both kinds of afterlife.

More than that, Pharisees also believe that a time is coming when the glories of David's kingdom will be restored on earth by the Anointed One (Messiah) from David's line. It would be an earthly paradise in which the pious dead would arise and share with the living these earthly glories in the messianic age (cf. 1 Enoch 1—36).

In debating with the Sadducees on the resurrection, Jesus cites texts familiar to the Pharisees and, in general, allies himself with their point of view (Luke 20:34-38). Then he himself is raised from the dead (Luke 24:1-45). This ushers in a whole new era of belief as the early Christians make the resurrection of Christ and his heavenly enthronement the reason for their existence and the basis for their ministry (Acts 2:24-36). The Christians' belief in the resurrection goes beyond that of the Pharisees in that they already have living proof of it in the resurrection of Christ, the "first fruits" of the final resurrection (1 Cor. 15:20-28).

As shown by Paul, believers have an eschatology tied to Christ, through whom God will one day judge all (Rom. 2:16). Believers look for the return of the Lord, the resurrection of those who have died in him, and their meeting with living saints, all caught up in the air to reign with Christ forever (1 Thess. 4:13-17; 2 Tim. 2:12). The Spirit will change the earthly body of believers to an imperishable (angelic) resurrection body, as God "has chosen" (1 Cor. 15:35-53). This is different from the belief by Greeks that souls are by nature immortal—a belief that apparently influenced some Pharisees (Acts 23:8).

Thus, there are some significant differences between the belief in the resurrection held by the Pharisees and that of Christians. Yet there is enough similarity between them to give meaning to Paul's statement that he is on trial for the *hope of the resurrection of the dead* (Acts 23:6b). The two groups are united in something that both hold dear: Pharisees for the restoration of the kingdom of David with all its glories, and Christians for the triumph of Christ's rule and their future as transformed beings reigning with Christ. Both groups stand for reform and together pose a threat to the Sadducees in power. In the dissension that arises between them and the Pharisees, Paul is rescued by the Romans and completely escapes judgment by the Sanhedrin (Acts 23:7-10).

THE TEXT IN THE LIFE OF THE CHURCH
Preaching by Example 20:33-35

Believers church groups have a strong emphasis on *leading by example* as well as by word. This accompanies their centuries of experience with the unsalaried ministry (discussed in the previous section in connection with 18:3). At the close of his address to the Ephesian elders, Paul stresses the modeling role of church leaders (20:33-35). His work to support himself is an example to the whole flock. The absence of coveting (20:33), combined with hard manual labor—these are ways all of them can help the weak and learn the blessedness of giving (20:35).

Anabaptist-Brethren believers, being earnest in the Word and pious in their way of life, have always stressed the importance of witnessing by quality of character and conduct. Ministers and deacons and their wives, followed closely by dedicated laity, have let their light shine through deeds of kindness and acts of generosity. Each of the denominations in this cluster of churches will recall countless examples of this. In fact, these people have not been distinguished so much by educational degrees or by numbers of persons who have gained recognition in the life of the nation. Yet they have had a remarkable record of impacting the everyday life of their communities by honesty, hard work, and simple goodness—the qualities called "blessed" in Acts 20:35.

Christian Hospitality 21:1-14

While every grouping of people in the history of the world has no doubt shown hospitality to its own, there is a unique dimension to Christian hospitality. It is the presence of the risen Lord himself in every true believer and in the midst of every group of two or more gathered in his name (Matt. 18:20). To have fellow Christians in one's home is a rich experience, and so is being guests in their home. Hospitality blesses both parties, beginning with provisions for physical comfort and safety and extending to mutual social and spiritual strengthening. Hence, it is easy to understand why Paul and his party, though in a hurry to get to Jerusalem (20:16), spend a week at Troas (20:6) with fellow believers and another week at Tyre (21:3-6). This is followed by a considerable period of time with Philip and his four daughters at Caesarea (21:8-14). Then in Jerusalem the home of Mnason of Cyprus is open to them (21:16). Little wonder then that in Romans 16:3-16, Paul can speak with such affection of close personal relations with so many Christian friends!

Stories of warm hospitality among the Anabaptists and Brethren abound, from the earliest days in Zurich, Switzerland, on across central Europe into the Netherlands, later in the North American colonies, as well as in other countries where they have settled. These range all the way from relaxed gatherings in homes for social and spiritual nourishment to the sheltering of Christian brothers and sisters in time of persecution, migration, or other great need. They have not been the only ones to practice hospitality, but theirs has had a family warmth of its own. A more recent adaptation of this ministry is one that many members and friends continue to enjoy, the Mennonite-Your-Way plan; travelers may arrange for bed-and-breakfast along with Christian fellowship in believers' homes as they journey about the United States and Canada.

When Spirit-Led Christians Differ 21:4, 11-14

Among the Anabaptists and Brethren are several different denominations with diverse leadership, organization, and practice. There have been many occasions when sincere Spirit-led believers have not only differed but also parted company over differences. Issues at stake have varied, all the way from doctrine and church polity to matters of dress, waves of migration, and personal ambitions of leaders. Not all differences have led to division, and each of the several denominations has in its fellowship various shades of opinion and practice. So the handling of disagreements among earnest Christians continues at several levels and with differing results.

The issue at hand when Paul and his party stop at Tyre and again at Caesarea is not a matter of doctrine nor a controversy that would lead to division. It concerns God's will for a dedicated apostle of the church and has consequences affecting the whole Christian world. No general rules can be deduced from it to apply to all cases of difference among Spirit-led Christians, but there are some important considerations worth noting. (1) Paul and his party listened to the voice of the Spirit as mediated through fellow Christians (21:4b). (2) They were moved by the symbolic action of a Spirit-filled prophet who foretold what would happen (21:10-11). (3) They expressed their sincere opinion in the light of these leadings (21:12). (4) They gave heed to the deeply held contrary conviction of the person in question (21:13). (5) They reached unanimity when they finally submitted to the one willing to be sacrificed, saying, *The Lord's will be done* (21:14).

Part 11

Witness in Caesarea

Acts 24—26

PREVIEW

The *imprisonment and persecutions* (20:23) that begin in Jerusalem follow Paul to Caesarea where, as this section opens, he waits under Roman guard in Herod's praetorium (23:35). One trial follows another after an interval of two years and a change in governors. Thus is fulfilled the promise of 9:15 that Paul will *bring my name before Gentiles and kings and before the people of Israel.* The section reaches a climax in the statement of King Agrippa that the apostle is innocent and could be set free had he not appealed to Caesar (26:32). But, having thus appealed, he will go on to Rome by divine will and continue his ministry there.

In terms of the whole book, this portion provides a vital link between Paul's encounters and witness in Jerusalem and his final trip to the capital of the empire. Here Luke continues to use his story to establish the lawful character of Christianity. Paul is the central character, controversial but effective as he stands before the heads of government, an unjustly accused prisoner who keeps on spreading the message. Just as at Antioch, Iconium, and Lystra (13:13—14:20); Philippi, Thessalonica, and Berea (16:16—17:13); Corinth and Ephesus (18:12-17; 19:23-41); so now in both Jerusalem (21:27—23:22) and Caesarea (24:1—26:32), Paul is accused and attacked but proven innocent of any crime. This shows that Christianity is not against the law either of the Jews or the Romans. Such an affirmation will strengthen the cause of the church in relationship to any society in which it will exist until the end of the age. (See Introduction under "Purpose" for the "allegiance-witness" theory of Cassidy.)

Two matters of historical interest today are completely passed over in this section: (1) whether or not Paul wrote any of his extant letters from Caesarea, and (2) what investigations and gospel writing Luke might have engaged in during these two years. Few if any recent scholars trace our NT Pauline epistles to Caesarea, although this city may be a possibility for that writing and offers much less travel difficulty for the movements of persons mentioned in Philippians and Colossians. There is much room for scholarly conjecture regarding Luke using Paul's Caesarean imprisonment time to be gathering material for his Gospel and certain Palestinian parts of Acts. With no concrete evidence to go on, however, this will have to remain but an attractive possibility.

The section continues without *we* passages but with enough interesting detail to suggest a narrator close to the situation and perhaps an eyewitness to much of it. For example, there are such matters as the smooth tongue of the lawyer Tertullus (24:2-8), Paul's gracious and persuasive reply (24:10-21), the deliberate delaying tactics of Felix (24:26-27), the trickery of the chief priests in trying to get Paul sent back to Jerusalem (25:3), the apostle's decisive appeal to Caesar (25:12c), the conversations of Agrippa and Festus amid the pomp and circumstance surrounding the final defense (25:14—26:27), and Paul's personal encounter with the king, culminating in the latter's pronouncement (26:28-32).

OUTLINE

Paul's Trial Before Felix   24:1-27

24:1-9	Introduction and Accusations by Tertullus
24:10-21	Paul's Defense
24:22-23	Adjournment; Delay by Felix
24:24-26	Visits of Felix and Drusilla with Paul
24:27	Paul Left in Prison Two years

Paul's First Trial Before Festus   25:1-12

| 25:1-5 | Coming of Festus and His Visit to Jerusalem |
| 25:6-12 | Paul's Defense and Appeal to Caesar |

Paul's Hearing Before Festus and Agrippa   25:13—26:32

25:13-22	Report of Festus to Agrippa and Bernice
25:23-27	Public Presentation of Paul to the King
26:1-23	Paul's Defense; Third Account of His Conversion

26:24-29   Interruption by Felix; Three-Way Conversation
26:30-32   Agreement on Paul's Innocence

EXPLANATORY NOTES
Paul's Trial Before Felix 24:1-27
24:1-9 Introduction and Accusations by Tertullus

Paul's enemies waste no time in following him to Caesarea. Just five days after the apostle arrives, the high priest Ananias, some members of the Sanhedrin, and the lawyer Tertullus show up at the governor's palace to press charges (24:1). Ananias is no doubt stung by the exchange he had with Paul in the council (23:2-4), embittered by the confusion the apostle caused in the meeting (23:6-10), and frustrated by the prisoner's transfer to Caesarea under Roman protection. Now he is more determined than ever to destroy this *pestilent fellow* (24:5).

The governor calls the court to order and has Paul brought in to face his accusers. The prosecuting attorney Tertullus, bearing a common Roman name, is likely a Hellenistic Jew who has received careful legal training. He rises to address the group, beginning, as taught, with flattery of the governor. As Luke reports it, his praise is so overdrawn that the reader will recognize at once how wide of the truth it is. While some Jewish leaders have enjoyed the *peace* of which Tertullus speaks (24:2b), the governor's corrupt and brutal methods have left most of his subjects dismayed (Josephus, *Ant.* 20.7-8). Nor is anything known of *reforms* brought about by Felix. The *utmost gratitude* of the Jewish nation for such an official is pure oratorical fiction (24:3). Then, as an accomplished speaker, Tertullus promises to be brief as he nods to the governor and appeals to his *customary graciousness* (24:4).

After this beginning, the attorney gets down to the charges against Paul. They are basically two. First, Paul is *an agitator among all the Jews,* a danger to society (24:5). This is like the charge against Jesus that he was "perverting the nation," one who "stirs up the people" (Luke 23:2, 5). Paul is said to be *a ringleader of the sect of the Nazarenes,* the only place in the NT where that term is used to designate Christians. In Acts 2:22 *Nazarene* is used for Jesus and was probably a nickname given to his followers (cf. Matt. 2:23; *[Designations, p. 310]*). The lawyer apparently expects Felix to know of the group and to be aware of their dangerous activities.

Second, Paul *tried to profane the temple* (24:6). This represents a shift from the earlier accusation that he simply taught against the people, the law, and the temple (21:28). Now he is portrayed as a threat to the peace of the empire which the Roman governor cannot ignore. The translation *pestilent fellow* (24:5) does not mean some annoying eccentric, but the Greek connotes one who transmits a plague, a fomenter of revolution among Jews *throughout the world.* To this, Tertullus adds the reasonable proposal that Felix examine Paul himself and discover that all this is true (24:8). After the attorney for the prosecution steps down, the members of the Sanhedrin who have come along add their voices to the accusations that have been made (24:9).

24:10-21 Paul's Defense

Then Paul rises to his feet as the governor motions for him to speak. Like Tertullus before him, he begins on a positive note but avoids undue praise as he carefully confines himself to a statement of his happiness at the chance of defending himself before one who has been governor so long (24:10—about nine years). The implication is that Felix is therefore experienced enough in affairs of the province to judge the case wisely.

The apostle demonstrates even more skill than Tertullus. To build his case, Paul repeats in similar words the attorney's point, *You will be able to learn* (24:8, 11). He cannot be starting a revolution, he argues, having been in the city only twelve days (24:11) and never disputing or stirring up a crowd as alleged (24:12). Paul refutes the earlier charge of defiling the temple by declaring that he came there *to worship* (24:11), *to bring alms and to offer sacrifices* (24:17). He was in the temple *completing the rite of purification,* and all this *without any crowd or disturbance* (24:18).

The idea that he has taken Gentiles into the temple is a totally false supposition (cf. 21:28-29), and those Jews from Asia who made such charges should be here now in court to present their evidence (24:19). There is only one statement that might incriminate him, he says, and that is his declaration that he was on trial for his belief in *the resurrection of the dead* (24:20-21). By saying this, Paul does two things: (1) He ignores the Sadducees and appeals to Pharisees who may be in the high-priestly delegation. (2) Now he reminds the governor of what his successor Festus will later point out: he is not being charged with any real crimes but with disagreements over religion and particularly over the resurrection of a certain man named Jesus (cf. 25:18-19).

24:22-23 Adjournment; Delay by Felix

Paul apparently makes his case with the governor that he is not a criminal, and the latter concludes that there is no hurry about putting him on trial. At least the threat of death is lifted for the present. As Luke explains it, Felix is fairly well informed about *the Way* (cf. 9:2; 19:9, 23; 22:4 for the use of this term for Christianity). Thus he sees that Paul is not a dangerous man and the Way is not a politically subversive movement. He also needs more evidence than what has been presented before he can proceed with the case. So Felix adjourns the hearing until Lysias himself can come and tell him what actually happened (24:22-23). He is hoping for a bribe (24:26), and postponement may be his way of putting pressure on Paul to come up with the money, either from his friends or from his own significant financial resources, likely inherited (Ramsay, 1896:310-312). Felix wants *to grant the Jews a favor* (24:27); this makes it clear that he neither cares to condemn the apostle nor take the political consequences of offending the high priest and his supporters (Tannehill, 2:301).

Felix is willing, however, to˙hear Paul's message and holds repeated conversations with him (24:24-26). This gives Luke an opportunity to present the apostle as a witness to governors and kings, as the earthly Jesus had promised (Luke 21:12-13) and the risen Lord later confirmed (Acts 9:15). The governor has Paul put in custody under the direction of a centurion, as befits an uncondemned Roman citizen being held for further questioning (24:23). Josephus tells of similar treatment given to Agrippa in Rome, handcuffed to soldiers but given a daily bath and a comfortable bed. Friends were allowed to visit and brought gifts of food and other necessities (*Ant.* 18.6.6-7). While Paul may not receive all these considerations, he is treated well by the governor.

24:24-26 Visits of Felix and Drusilla with Paul

Therefore, with mixed motives Felix, accompanied by his Jewish wife, summons the apostle and listens to him speak about his Christian faith (24:24). Drusilla is the governor's third wife, daughter of King Agrippa I, a lady not yet twenty years of age. Felix has lured her away from her former husband by a magician. He may want her present to get her reactions as a Jewess, or she may be there simply out of some interest or curiosity of her own.

What they hear from the apostle is unsettling to the governor, a searching discussion of *justice, self-control, and the coming judg-*

ment (24:25a; cf. Rom. 2:15). One who has been so brutal in his tactics is embarrassed to hear *justice* preached. Talk of *self-control* may rankle a man with a record of violent action and one marriage after another. And the idea of a *coming judgment* for such a man of the world is just too much. Something about it frightens him, and he dismisses Paul in order to let his mind cool off (24:25b).

In spite of misgivings, Felix keeps coming back (nothing further is said, however, of Drusilla). Probably knowing that Paul has the means to support himself in prison has reinforced the governor's idea that he may get a handsome bribe out of him (24:26). In any case, he keeps the apostle in prison and visits him from time to time. Paul no doubt continues with his reasoning about the gospel while Felix keeps the relationship alive in his quest for money. With Paul refusing to bribe and the governor refusing to believe, a stalemate develops. Two whole years go by, and then Antonius Felix is removed from office for causing bloodshed among the Jews during an uprising in Caesarea. This becomes a blot on his record, and he narrowly escapes severe punishment by his superior officers (Josephus, *War* 2.13.2—2.14.1; *Ant.* 20.8.5-9).

Luke, after including earlier favorable references to the governor's many years of experience as a judge (24:10) and his rather accurate knowledge of Christianity (24:22), concludes his account with three *negative* aspects of his character and administration. (1) Felix is impressed with Paul's preaching on justice, self-control, and judgment and yet avoids any opportunity for repentance, showing him to be basically unjust (24:25). (2) He confirms this by desiring a bribe (24:26). (3) He fails to fulfill his promise of deciding Paul's case (24:22) because of pressure from the powerful Jewish leaders, whom he hopes to please (24:27).

The result is that Paul is needlessly kept in prison for two years. What does he do during this time? Attempts to trace some of his extant writings to this period have not gained wide acceptance. Yet there is no reason for believing he is idle or not writing letters, even if they do not survive. Likely Luke does much of his research for writing his Gospel during this time (cf. Luke 1:3) and perhaps for those parts of Acts dealing with events in Judea and Samaria. Bruce conjectures, "Luke no doubt made full use" of this time and "it is highly probable that by the end of these two years he had collected and digested the non-Markan material in his Gospel, as well as part of the early narrative of Acts" (473-474, note 18). This cannot be proved, but it does raise the possibility that the seemingly wasted period of Paul's

Caesarean imprisonment turns out to be important for the production of the NT and thus for the long history of Christianity.

Paul's First Trial Before Festus 25:1-12

25:1-5 Coming of Festus and His Visit to Jerusalem

Luke introduces the new governor, Porcius Festus, in 24:27 and tells how, three days after arriving in Caesarea, he makes a trip to Jerusalem (25:1). No reason is given for the visit, nor does history supply us with that information. In fact, Festus holds office scarcely more than two years and makes little impression on his contemporaries. He would not be mentioned here were it not for his part in the trials of Paul. Festus seems to be a conscientious ruler who may be making a visit to Jerusalem as one of the chief trouble spots he knows he will need to deal with in the course of his administration.

What Festus does find in the holy city is the same group of high priests and other Jews of high rank as those mentioned in 23:14, still determined to do away with Paul (25:2). As Luke records it, there is a revival of the assassination plot of 23:12-15, with plans for an ambush during the transfer of the prisoner to Jerusalem, at their request. The theme of granting a *favor* by Felix in 24:27 is repeated now as requesting a *favor* (same Greek word) on the part of the chief priests in the collaboration against Paul (25:3).

The governor, however, refuses the request and quite logically suggests that, since he is returning to Caesarea soon, he will try the case there where the accused is imprisoned (25:4-5). The fact that he says *if there is anything wrong about the man* (24:5) may indicate that there is some doubt in his mind about the charges. He tests their seriousness by telling the prosecution to make the trip to Caesarea. There also he would be in his own headquarters and not as open to manipulation by the Sanhedrin.

25:6-12 Paul's Defense and Appeal to Caesar

Festus stays in Jerusalem a little over a week and then returns to Caesarea. Paul's enemies are on hand, eager to pursue their case, even the very next day! The governor assembles the court and summons the principals for a hearing (25:6). Luke pictures the accusers gathering around Paul and hurling various charges at him, all of them unfounded. Then the apostle is allowed to make a defense, only one sentence of which is recorded in our text: a denial of committing any crime against the law, the temple, or the Roman establishment (25:8). The account of the trial is thus abbreviated because the author has already informed the reader at length of the two sides of the case (cf. 24:2-21).

Then Festus does a surprising thing. Although he earlier refused to have Paul transferred to Jerusalem for trial (25:3-5), now he asks the apostle if he would like to go to that city and face these charges before him (25:9). Perhaps the best explanation of this change of mind on the part of the governor is that of Tannehill (2:306-307). According to his understanding, Festus' first response to Paul's opponents (25:3-5) is that of a political novice meeting with the high priests and their allies for the first time. He does not understand the hidden motive in their request, thinking that the main concern is to have the trial as soon as possible. Thus he suggests that the accusers accompany him to Caesarea and hold the trial there. As a quick student of political power, however, he soon learns of the importance of the high priests to Rome and sees the advantage of granting their request to have Paul put on trial in Jerusalem (25:9)—with the chance of him being turned over to a Jewish court.

The governor is in for a surprise as the apostle refuses to budge (25:10-11). On one hand Paul knows by now that he will receive no justice at the hands of Festus. Even more important in his mind, the divine directive is for him to witness for his Lord in Rome (23:11). So he stands on his dignity as a Roman citizen and, with considerable boldness, tells the governor that he has done no wrong to the Jews *as you very well know* (25:10). He is willing to suffer death if he has committed a capital offense, but there is nothing in the charges against him. Moreover, he says, *no one can* **turn** *me* **over** *to my enemies*, using a verb from the root word for *favor* (24:27 and 25:2), an expression repeated by Festus in 25:16.

In order to go forward on his mission and not back to Jerusalem or into a Jewish court to be unjustly treated, Paul appeals to *Caesar* (RSV renders the Greek correctly; NRSV has *emperor;* 25:11). This is a formal, legal request, the right of every citizen of the empire when threatened with gross mistreatment. Such a right was first instituted in the days of the republic as an appeal to the people in the face of any unjust magistrate. Then under the empire, the request was to be directed to Caesar himself. Such an appeal is final. Once made, it cannot be reversed by any authority along the way, as will be seen from the statement of King Agrippa in 26:32.

Paul has long planned to go to Rome (19:21b; Rom. 1:10-15;

15:22-33), and though this would be an appeal to the notorious Nero, it is better than to be delivered as *a favor* into the hands of the Jews. A quick conference with his legal advisers convinces Festus that this is correct procedure, and he makes the final pronouncement, *You have appealed to Caesar; to Caesar you shall go* (25:12, RSV). The emphasis is on the word *go*, the climactic last word in the sentence. The discerning reader will understand here not only the judgment of an earthly governor but especially the fulfillment of God's will for Paul. The decisive step has been taken. On to Rome and the tribunal of the emperor he will go!

Paul's Hearing Before Festus and Agrippa   25:13—26:32

25:13-22 Report of Festus to Agrippa and Bernice

Luke now prepares his readers for Paul's climactic defense speech (26:2-23) by telling of the arrival of King Agrippa and his sister Bernice and the briefing Festus gives them about the prisoner. The occasion is a welcoming of the new governor by the royal couple (25:13). Marcus Julius Agrippa, ·known to history as Herod Agrippa II, son of Herod Agrippa I (12:1-23), was only seventeen when his father died in A.D. 44 (12:23) and too young to be appointed to his office. So from 48 to 53 he was given a small kingdom in the area of the Lebanon mountains, exchanged in 53 for a larger one consisting of the former territories of Philip and Lysanias (cf. Luke 3:1). Three years later he picked up additional cities and villages around the Sea of Galilee.

Agrippa has been given the right of appointing Jewish high priests in Jerusalem and is in charge of certain ceremonial clothing worn on the Day of Atonement. Though only in his late twenties when he makes the present visit to Caesarea, he has already built quite a reputation as a politician and something of an authority on Jewish matters. He has spent his earlier life in Rome. Now his experience with the Jews makes him a ruler whose advice Festus is glad to have with regard to the puzzling case of Paul.

Bernice, just a year younger than her brother the king, has been in and out of one marriage (to her uncle Herod of Chalcis) and is at present living with Agrippa II in what wagging tongues claim to be incest. This is not too unlikely in view of her later affairs with Titus before he becomes emperor. She actually plays little part in the proceedings at hand other than adding to the pomp with which she and the king enter the audience hall (25:23). She is mentioned here, as was her older sister Drusilla, wife of Felix (24:24), as part of Luke's eyewitness reporting and in line with his general interest in women as part of the story. Both Agrippa and Bernice will go on later to distinguish themselves in the vain attempt to prevent a war between the Jews and Rome, suffering attacks and house-burning from Zealot extremists.

On the present occasion, Festus lays the case of Paul before these two in private in such a way that his own handling of it appears faultless. One is reminded of the way Claudius Lysias glossed over his personal blunders in his smooth letter to Felix (23:26-30). Luke's ironic humor shows through once more in the way he quotes the governor's explanation. The latter takes credit for the suggestion that the accusers accompany him to Caesarea to meet Paul face-to-face (25:5) and also for the wise counsel that Romans do not hand over a defendant before he has had *an opportunity to make a defense* (25:16). The discerning reader notes, however, that Festus tried to favor the Jews by asking Paul if he wanted to go to Jerusalem to be tried before him there (25:9), with the unspoken risk of being turned over to a Jewish court. Only *after* Paul appealed to Caesar does Festus stand firm against the Jewish requests.

Thus, instead of an inexperienced and floundering new governor, Festus makes himself appear as Caesar's mature and able representative who treats the case with utmost care. He does confess a typical Roman bewilderment at handling the matter of a man who is said to have died but is now alive (25:19) and gives that, instead of pressure from the high priests, as the reason for his being willing to have Paul tried in Jerusalem. Significant for Paul's ongoing trial is the fact that the accusation of his having desecrated the temple (24:6) has now been dropped, apparently as a result of the apostle's convincing defense of 24:12-13.

The governor's language in summarizing Paul's situation is formal and accurate. He refers to the emperor as *his Imperial Majesty* (25:21, 25), a correct rendering of the Greek term as used among the Romans. The prisoner's status is that he is *kept in custody* (25:21) until he receives that ruler's decision, a situation that will continue to the end of Acts. King Agrippa's interest has now been aroused, like that of Herod Antipas with regard to Jesus (Luke 23:8). He readily agrees to hear Paul himself, and Festus assures him that he will have the opportunity on the very next day (25:22).

25:23-27 Public Presentation of Paul to the King

On the day of the hearing, the military establishment is assembled, represented by no less than five tribunes who with their troops are stationed in Caesarea at the time. Leading citizens of the city are also on hand, most of them, like Festus, of Gentile background. The vast assembly with all the pomp and celebration, is reminiscent of a similar gathering for King Agrippa's father, Herod Agrippa I, in this same city many years earlier, an occasion described briefly by Luke but known to us in some detail from Josephus (see notes on 12:21-23). At that time the king himself made the speech and ended in disaster. On this occasion the king is to listen to the Lord's ambassador speak and will end by sending him on to Rome in the triumphant work of the heavenly kingdom.

In presenting Paul to the king, Festus enhances the picture of the pressure he is under by the exaggerated statement that he was asked by *the whole Jewish community* to deal with the prisoner (25:24). He also omits his own unwise suggestion that Paul stand trial back in Jerusalem. He wants this vast assemblage to know that he, the governor, quickly determined the prisoner's innocence of any crime and has called the present hearing to have something definite about him to send on in writing to the emperor (25:25). Then, turning to the king, Festus pays him a nice compliment by saying, *I have brought him . . . especially before you . . . so . . . I may have something to write* (25:26). The governor is sure Agrippa II knows enough about matters of this kind that a hearing in his presence will bring results.

26:1-23 Paul's Defense; Third Account of His Conversion

This last major speech by Paul serves as a climactic review and interpretation of his whole mission. It begins as his defense while on trial (cf. 26:1-2, 6) but moves on to a missionary witness. Moreover, the role of Agrippa also shifts. At first he is the authority who can help Paul by recognizing his innocence. By the end of the speech, Agrippa represents all who know and believe the prophets (26:27-29), who as Jews or God-fearers may still be reached with the gospel. This final address is almost entirely autobiographical. Paul begins with his early life in Judaism (26:4-5), stating that he is being tried for the hope in the resurrection of the dead (26:6-8). He goes on to tell how he persecuted the followers of Jesus, then gives his second account of his conversion (26:12-18; cf. 22:6-16), for the reader the third and last narration of that event (cf. 9:1-19). In closing, Paul emphasizes his preaching for repentance and belief in the Messiah, in Damascus, Jerusalem, and elsewhere, resulting in his arrest and present testimony (26:19-23).

The scene opens as Paul receives word from Agrippa that he may now speak. He does so with an outstretched hand (26:1). As when he stood before Festus (24:10), he begins with a courteous compliment, this time expressing his gratitude for a chance to defend himself before one with such an extensive knowledge of Judaism (26:2-3). Paul now stresses his own Jewishness, not his connections with Tarsus or his Roman citizenship. He appeals to the knowledge which the Jews of Jerusalem, including those present, have of his early life as a member of the strict party of the Pharisees (26:4-5). The king knows something of this most popular of all Jewish groups and of their belief in the resurrection of the dead. Thus the apostle can show how in proclaiming the resurrection, he is standing squarely within the teachings of Judaism. Not only that. He is on trial, he says, for the hope of a messianic kingdom (26:6).

The irony is that he is being attacked by his fellow Jews for this very position! (26:7). Some scholars say that the hope in the resurrection is not as important to early Judaism as Paul is implying. They need to note that Paul is not thinking just of individual life after death but of corporate renewal under the reign of a Davidic Messiah according to the divine promise to Israel. That this is the perspective of Luke-Acts is seen in Luke 1:33, where it is declared that Jesus will rule over the house of Jacob forever and of his reign there will be no end, a rule dependent upon the resurrection of both the Messiah and his people. In Luke 2:37 the prophetess Anna is presented as worshiping night and day in expectation of the fulfillment of the same hope. Then in Acts the note is sounded by Paul in 13:32-33, that *what God promised to our ancestors* has now been fulfilled by the resurrection of Jesus. He makes this point again in the defense before Agrippa, using the same Greek words (26:6).

Paul's vivid account of his earlier persecution of Christians (26:9-11) helps prepare the king for the dramatic turnaround that is to come. He adds two items not mentioned in earlier accounts: his voting against believers when they were brought to trial (26:10) and his raging attempts to make them *blaspheme*, by denying their faith in Jesus (26:11).

The story of Paul's conversion and call is much like 9:3-9 and 22:6-11, but with some added touches. This time the light that flashes is said to be brighter than the sun (26:13), a supernatural light from heaven, but there is no mention of him being struck blind. Instead, the light is connected with his commission to *open the eyes* of both Jews and Greeks (26:17-18). Moreover, Saul-Paul is not the only one to fall to the ground, but all who are with him fall (26:14). The voice speaks to him *in the Hebrew language,* his mother tongue (see notes on 21:40 on whether this is Aramaic). The risen Lord is reaching down into the deepest level of his consciousness. To the question of *why* he is persecuting Jesus (cf. 9:4; 22:7) is now added the statement that it must be painful for him to kick against the ox goads (26:14). Oxen were urged to unusual exertion by sharp prongs, and the voice reminds Saul of such proddings by the Lord, stirring up conscious memories. Then, like the prophet Ezekiel (2:1), he is told to rise and stand on his feet while the Lord speaks to him (Acts 26:18).

In the first two accounts of the conversion, the risen Jesus told Saul to go into the city and he would be shown what to do. In this telling, however, the Lord gives him instructions while still outside the city (26:16-18), combining the essential features of his commissioning from Ananias (22:14-16) and the elaboration of it in the vision at Jerusalem (22:17-21). The present account emphasizes the full ministry of salvation which the new convert will be given, a matter of great importance for his present testimony before King Agrippa.

Then in 26:19-23, Paul gives a condensed version of his activity around Damascus (9:19-25) and Jerusalem (9:26-30). This likely is short because there is little in it to strengthen the case for his Jewish faithfulness other than the key statement that he was *not disobedient to the heavenly vision.* Instead, he carried out the command of the God of his ancestors to call both Jews and Greeks to repent, *turn to God,* and *do deeds consistent with repentance* (26:20). Moreover, he says, in carrying out this divine directive, he was attacked by the Jews in the temple (26:21; cf. 21:27-30).

What he is preaching to everyone is just what Moses and the Hebrew prophets themselves proclaimed, that the Messiah must suffer, die, and rise again as the basis for a mission to all nations (26:22-23). With *help from God,* Paul testifies *to both small and great,* with inclusiveness not only of ethnic and geographic divisions but also of all social ranks—especially significant before this politically elite group. These closing words (26:23) closely parallel the risen Lord's statement that Scripture is now fulfilled in the suffering of the Messiah, his resurrection from the dead, and the proclamation of the gospel to all nations (Luke 24:44-48).

26:24-29   Interruption by Felix; Three-Way Conversation

Once again Luke ends his report of Paul's speech on the note of the resurrection and his mission to the Gentiles. In 17:32 at Athens, it was his mention of the resurrection of the Messiah that caused some to mock, and in 22:21-23 the Jerusalem crowd went wild with the report of his call to preach to Gentiles. Here the author dramatizes these two great interconnected themes of the book of Acts, rendering them powerful and unforgettable. In the present case the response of the governor reaches ironic heights. He calls Paul *insane,* driven out of his mind by *too much learning* (26:24). This does two things for the story: (1) it shows how impressed a Roman governor is by Paul's intellectual ability and (2) underscores again how incomprehensible are the ways of God to the unbelieving human mind. Similarly, in 2:13 scoffers say the new believers are drunk, and in 4:13-23 Christian leaders confound the highest local authorities (note Paul's explanation of this in 1 Cor. 1:18-23). The careful reader will see through the irony here that the gospel of salvation for all humankind is not madness at all but *sober truth,* as Paul soon explains (26:25).

Turning toward the king as the three of them continue to talk, the apostle remarks that he can speak freely to him about such things for he is well acquainted with the Christian movement (26:26a). After all, *this was not done in a corner* (26:26b). There have been mass conversions around Jerusalem (2:41, 47; 5:14; cf. 5:28) and determined efforts of rulers including Agrippa's own father to combat the church (Acts 4—5; 9:2; 12:1-23). Certainly the king is well informed!

Then Paul boldly appeals to King Agrippa, calling him by name and asking him if he believes the prophets. Before his majesty can reply, the apostle answers his own question in the affirmative (26:27). This direct bit of witnessing catches the ruler off guard and evokes a response whose meaning has been variously interpreted. The KJV of 26:28, *Almost thou persuadest me to be a Christian,* is based on late Byzantine texts that indicate more readiness on the part of Agrippa than the context warrants. To be preferred are translations that make this a question: *Do you think that in so short a time you can persuade me to be a Christian?* (NIV). *In a short time you think to make me a Christian?* (RSV). *Are you so quickly persuading me to be a Christian?* (NRSV). Evident here is surprise mingled with sarcasm and possibly some annoyance.

Regardless of the exact meaning of the king's retort, Paul's evangelistic purpose is clear. He will go to any length to convert the ruler, as well as all those present (26:29). Luke records it as something not only for Agrippa to face but also for every reader to consider. (Incidentally, this is only the second use of the word *Christian* in Acts, one of three in the entire NT—cf. Acts 11:26; 1 Pet. 4:16.) Then Luke closes his record of the speech with the apostle glancing down at his manacled wrists and saying that he would like for them all to be Christians like him *except for these chains* (26:29c), a touch of wry humor for the benefit of hearers and readers alike.

26:30-32 Agreement on Paul's Innocence

Luke concludes his section on the experiences of Paul in Caesarea with a scene involving the king and the governor, a fulfillment of Jesus' prophecy that his disciples "will be brought before kings and governors" for his sake and there testify (Luke 21:12-13). The witness before these officials has now been made, and the results are favorable to the defendant, as Jesus has predicted: "None of your opponents will be able to withstand or contradict" (Luke 21:15). Paul has been presented as a faithful follower of Jesus, carrying out the mission of the prophets of old by proclaiming the purpose of God for saving the world through repentance and the forgiveness of sins.

The closing episode, as Luke depicts it, is a casual one. Agrippa, Festus, and Bernice walk out together, commenting that Paul is doing nothing worthy of death or imprisonment (26:30-31). The king reminds them that Paul could have been freed if he had not appealed to Caesar (26:32; cf. 25:10). The reader may be saddened by this fact, but cannot cherish regrets for long, for it is precisely as the apostle continues in chains that he is guaranteed a journey to Rome, his witness is carried forward, and the central purpose of Acts is fulfilled.

THE TEXT IN ITS BIBLICAL CONTEXT
False Accusations 24:5-8; 25:7

Paul's experience of being falsely accused and Luke's reports of it reflect a long history of charges against God's true witnesses. Most memorable from the OT are those brought against Joseph (Gen. 39:7-20), Moses (Num. 12:1-9; 16:1-7; 21:5), a number of the psalmists as reflected in the laments (such as Ps. 35), Job (8:2; 11:2-4; 15:2-13; 22:5-11), Amos (7:10), Jeremiah (11:19; 18:18; 26:8-11; 38:4-5), Daniel and his companions (Dan. 3:8-15; 6:13-15), and Mordecai (Esther 3:2-6). Luke had already incorporated selected aspects of these in his account of the trials of Jesus (Luke 23:2-10) and of Stephen (Acts 6:11-13).

Underlying all of the charges are two common features. First, they are all based on *a semblance of truth*. Jesus did deal with tribute to Caesar and did speak as the Messiah, providing his enemies with some basis for the accusations made in Luke 23:2, and he did teach large crowds throughout Galilee and Judea as they said in 23:5. Moreover, Stephen did represent a movement that would eventually dispense with certain aspects of the law of Moses and alter the attitude toward the temple, giving some grounds for the charges in Acts 6:13-14. Paul also has preached extensively among the Jews and been mobbed outside the temple (Acts 21:27-36), circumstances that provide some basis or excuse for the charges of agitation and of temple defilement—if one blames the victim (24:5-6).

Second, all these accusations spring from *jealousy* and manifest malicious *distortions of the truth*. Jealousy was a common element in the charges against OT witnesses and continues to be a major factor in Luke's accounts of charges against Jesus, Stephen, and now Paul. Because of jealousy, Jesus' skillful answer of "render to Caesar . . . and to God" (Luke 20:25, RSV) was deliberately twisted to mean refusal to pay taxes to the emperor, and the Lord's ministry to the multitudes was distorted into subversive action among the people (Luke 23:2, 5).

The fact that Stephen may have referred to Jesus' prediction of the destruction of the temple (Luke 21:5-6) is twisted to mean that Jesus himself will destroy it and change the customs of Moses (Acts 6: 14). With similar malicious intent, Paul's mission efforts in reaching his own people and his defense speech in Jerusalem are misinterpreted and exaggerated to mean agitation *among all the Jews throughout the world* (Acts 24:5). His orderly consecration and conduct in the temple (21:26) are combined with a misunderstanding about Trophimus (21:29) and made out to be a defilement of the sacred precincts (24:6). Although scribes and Pharisees have been making converts of Gentiles (*proselytes*, 2:10; 6:5; 13:43; cf. *devout*, 10:2, 7; 17:4; cf. Matt. 23:15), the mob goes into a frenzy when Paul merely mentions being sent to the Gentiles (22:21-23).

Thus it happens that a kernel of truth may be used by enemies of the faith as a basis or trigger for their exaggerated attacks, all with the intent of discrediting or destroying God's true witnesses. On the other hand, as such stories were remembered and passed on in the tradition, there may have been a tendency to heighten the evil of the adversaries in order to stress the innocent suffering of the faithful.

Defense by Telling One's Story 24:10-21; 26:2-23

Instead of dealing in abstract propositions to defend himself, Paul uses the Hebrew Bible approach, the telling of a story, in this case about himself. This is the way Judah met the accusations of what he thought was a merciless Egyptian tyrant charging him and his brothers with being spies (Gen. 44:18-34). Without missing one essential detail, he told about his aged father, the events leading up to the present moment, and his own involvement in it, with a closing offer to put his own life in jeopardy to save their youngest brother.

In similar fashion, the prophet Amos simply told of his call by the Lord when the priest Amaziah sent reports of Amos's prophecies to the king and commanded him to stop preaching (Amos 7:10-17). He was no prophet at all, he said, but a humble shepherd and a tender of sycamore-fig trees (NIV), drafted into this ministry by the living God. Before he was done, however, he had a word of judgment for Amaziah and all of Israel.

Jeremiah likewise, when threatened with death for his preaching in the temple, answered by telling how he was called by the Lord (Jer. 26:12-15). He added that he was in their hands, to do with him as they pleased. Yet he stipulated that if they put him to death, they would surely bring God's judgment upon themselves and their whole city.

The defense speeches in the early chapters of Acts vary in nature. Peter appeals to the mighty works of God and gives an affirmation of faith (4:8-12; 5:29-32). Stephen launches into a recital of sacred history sharply edged with judgment (7:53). In Paul's defense speeches, the personal element reaches its height in retelling his conversion and divinely ordained ministry to the Gentiles (22:3-21; 26:2-23). Thus in the trial before the Sanhedrin, he begins with his life *in all good conscience* and ends by taking the position of a Pharisee on the resurrection of the dead (23:1-6, RSV). Like the prophets of old, he *lays his life on the line* by speaking freely of what the Lord has revealed to him and putting himself in the hands of his judges with his *apologia pro sua vita* (defense of his life).

Delays and Postponements 24:27; 25:6-12

For his stories of postponements and long delays in the fulfillment of the divine plan, Luke was able to draw on several striking models from the Hebrew Scriptures. Just as Paul is left in the prison at Caesarea for two years to no purpose other than the greed of the governor, so Joseph had been forgotten by Pharaoh's cupbearer and left to languish in jail for a similar length of time that seemed wasted (Gen. 40:12—41:9).

With Moses, the deliverer of his people, we find a much longer postponement of the divine plan as related to life of a single individual. In that case God's servant was made to suffer and be seasoned by delay for two long, forty-year periods (Exod. 2:11—4: 31). Jeremiah was yet another OT character to agonize even more personally through years of disappointing mishaps. Starting out under the good King Josiah, he suffered under his corrupt and greedy son Jehoiakim. Under that king, he was persecuted (Jer. 12:6; 15:15-18), plotted against (11:18-23; 18:18), imprisoned (20:2), declared worthy of death (26:10-11, 24), and had the record of his life's ministry cut into pieces and burned (36:20-26). Yet, like Paul centuries later, he persisted in his witness, was imprisoned again (37:17-21), and eventually met his death for his convictions.

THE TEXT IN THE LIFE OF THE CHURCH
The Defense of an Unpopular Position

Christianity was born into an unfriendly world. From the very beginning, it has had to survive both the opposition of its enemies and the weaknesses if its friends. The reformation movements of the Anabaptists and Brethren were no exception. Conrad Grebel, Felix Manz, and their followers in Switzerland, as well as Menno Simons and Dirk Philips in the Netherlands, made the ability to meet persecution one of the tests of faith. As a result, not only were the ranks of the believers kept relatively pure, but members developed skills for defending their beliefs and practices in a hostile society. Almost two centuries later, Alexander Mack and his people in western Germany prepared all converts for baptism by teaching them to "count well the cost," using Luke 14:25-33, with special emphasis on verse 28. The Brethren also widely quoted passages such as 1 Peter 3:15-16, urging believers always to be prepared to give a defense for the hope that lies within them, but to do so with all gentleness and meekness.

Tried and Punished, Though Declared Innocent 26:31-32

Often in early Anabaptist history, persons were caught, accused, and condemned to die for adhering to the true faith. Many of these were recognized by their persecutors as *innocent* of any crime. Like Paul, who was sent to Rome eventually to die though declared not guilty by King Agrippa and Festus, they too were willing to make the supreme sacrifice for their Lord.

Such were Gotthard of Nonenberg and Peter Kramer of the duchy of Berg in 1558. As faithful ministers of Christ, they were apprehended and brought to Winnick for trial. The steward in charge vented his arrogance upon them and left them in prison a long time. Again and again they resisted attempts to get them to renounce their faith. On trial also, they overcame the subtle wiles used against them. Finally, being sentenced to die by the sword, they were again abused by the steward, but they remained firm. The executioner, however, was reluctant to do his work and with tears urged them not to be afraid because Christ himself was thus bound innocently.

The two men testified powerfully before their death, and the people about them said, "What a marvelous thing we behold there: these men so willing to go to death, when they could easily obtain their liberty!" The executioner vowed never again to be instrumental in the death of such men. And even the steward was so impressed that he ordered the people not to hurry away but to help bury these pious men who died innocently, having had to suffer because they embraced a faith which the lords and princes could not understand. The writer of *Martyrs Mirror* (Braght: 590-591) concludes with the statement that they were buried "and the seed of their blood did not remain without fruit in that place."

Part 12

Witness—
On to Rome

Acts 27—28

PREVIEW

In this concluding section of Acts, Luke tells how Paul finally reaches Rome, gateway to *the ends of the earth* (1:8). It is an exciting story of a sea voyage, a shipwreck, life on an island, progress by foot to the city, and final witness to the Jewish leaders there. Nowhere is Luke's skill as a writer more in evidence. The style is for the most part that of the *we* narrative, indicating personal participation on the part of the author. Vivid details and dramatic action abound. In the opinion of many scholars, the story of the storm at sea ranks among the most vivid, a worthy successor to comparable accounts in Homer and Virgil.

In this section, motifs from the earlier parts of Acts continue, now caught up in some uniquely new forms of witnessing. The result is a powerful blend of the familiar and the excitingly new, an effective final thrust on the part of the author. As on earlier occasions, Paul is given a divine vision which he shares with others (27:22-26), visits Christians along the way (27:3; 28:14), crosses language and cultural barriers by performing a miracle (28:4-6), retells earlier experiences (28:17b-20), and appeals to Scripture in dealing with Jews (28:26-27). Yet there are new and fresh ways of witnessing.

Altogether Acts refers to ten or eleven sea voyages (e.g., 9:30; 11:25-26; 13:4, 13), only one of any length (20:6—21:6), and now this is the last. It is told dramatically and with attention to interesting detail. The entire voyage testifies to the power and providence of God, both the mighty storm and the miraculous deliverance. Paul's inspired knowledge of sea travel saves the ship (27:10-12). His timely breaking of bread gives all on board new courage (27:33-36). From a

280

shipwreck comes a healing ministry that spreads out over a whole island (28:7-10).

Some scholars have been so impressed by the great detail of the sea voyage that they tend to think of it as a separate account into which the story of Paul has been fitted. Yet there is no need to discredit the narrative as we now have it. This is but another example of Luke's versatility as a writer, an interesting variation of the theme of witnessing, one which adds substantially to the appeal of Acts to both ancients and moderns. Another thread runs through the whole trip to Rome and gives it a distinctive flavor: the friendly relationship of the centurion Julius with Paul and his general helpfulness to Paul. This feature of divine providence is then later counterbalanced by the mixed reception given the apostle after arrival in the city and the uncertain future which he faces there.

OUTLINE
Voyage to Rome 27:1—28:16
From Caesarea to Crete, 27:1-12
27:1-8	Sailing Difficulties
27:9-12	The Decision to Continue

The Storm, 27:13-26
27:13-20	Driven by the Northeaster
27:21-26	Paul's Words of Assurance

The Shipwreck, 27:27-44
27:27-32	Fourteenth Night and Crisis on Board
27:33-38	Breaking Bread at Dawn
27:39-41	Grounded on a Sandbar
27:42-44	Escape to Land

Wintering on the Island of Malta, 28:1-10
28:1-6	Paul and the Deadly Viper
28:7-10	Ministry of Healings

From Malta to Rome, 28:11-16

Paul's Witness in Rome 28:17-31
First Session with the Jewish Leaders, 28:17-22

Second Meeting with the Jews, 28:23-28

Two Years of Unhindered Witness, 28:30-31

EXPLANATORY NOTES

Voyage to Rome
Acts 27:1—28:16

From Caesarea to Crete 27:1-12

27:1-8 Sailing Difficulties

The previous narrative ends with the king and governor referring to Paul's appeal to the emperor (26:32b). Now the decision has been made that the apostle, along with some other prisoners, is to be taken to Rome in the custody of a *centurion . . . named Julius* (27:1). This man is a member of *the Augustan Cohort,* a division known to have been in Syria during the time of Emperor Augustus and presently serving not too far from Caesarea. He has with him many if not all his hundred soldiers, men who will play an important role at a crucial point in the journey (27:31-32).

Their first ship is a coastal vessel from *Adramyttium* near Troas, likely returning home, carrying both cargo and passengers as it stops at each port along the way. Though not mentioned, Caesarea is surely where the party embarks. Then, almost as an afterthought, the third Christian passenger is mentioned, *Aristarchus* of Thessalonica (27:2). He is already known to the reader as one drawn into the mob scene at Ephesus (19:29) and who then accompanied Paul to Jerusalem along with other representatives from the mission churches (20:4). Later he is mentioned in Philemon 24 and in Colossians 4:10 is called Paul's "fellow prisoner." These are clues that he may have been with Paul throughout this whole time and now voluntarily continues with him through the first imprisonment, perhaps as his personal servant.

Ramsay argues that on board ship both Aristarchus and Luke are passing as though they are Paul's slaves. Thus they not only supply comfort and friendship to the apostle but also add to the respect the centurion and others have for him (1896:316). This is a more likely possibility than the theory, sometimes proposed, that Aristarchus is on his way to his home in Macedonia and leaves the ship at Myra (cf.

Marshall: 404, for an assessment of probabilities).

It is a long day's voyage of sixty-nine nautical miles from Caesarea to *Sidon*. There the ship stops and Julius allows Paul to go ashore to visit his Christian *friends*, the first mention of the respect and kindness with which the centurion treats the apostle. Sidon is near Tyre, where Paul and his party stopped for a week on the way to Jerusalem some years before (21:3-6). The present visit, like that one, is another in the long series of farewells which began in 20:7.

From Sidon the ship continues north along the Phoenician coast and then turns westward past Cilicia and Pamphylia. They avoid Cyprus, keeping to its *lee* side, away from the prevailing westerly winds (27:4). It is a slow journey, taking, as the Western text has it, some fifteen days before they reach Myra, at the southernmost tip of Asia Minor (27:5). Here they must seek a larger vessel, one capable of traveling the great and dangerous Mediterranean.

Myra has a harbor important for east-west Mediterranean traffic, and there Julius finds a grain ship on a regular route from Egypt to Italy. It is a vessel large enough to carry a full load of wheat along with 276 passengers and their luggage (27:6, 37-38). For centuries such ships have been carrying wheat and other grain to Rome—a veritable lifeline for the capital city and the surrounding country. Thus it is not too hard for the centurion to find a vessel from Alexandria. The captain intends to keep well to the north to be sheltered by the coast of Crete (Ramsay, 1896:319), attempting to make the long journey before the shipping lanes are closed for the winter.

Once aboard this Egyptian ship, Paul and his party are transported in a westward direction toward *Cnidus*, another 170 miles away. This requires some ten to fifteen days of slow, tedious travel against the westerly winds, tacking with sails and rudder, and they arrive there *with difficulty*. From there they cannot keep going west because the northerly wind from the Aegean threatens to force them into the north coast of Crete, which has few harbors. So they wisely turn southward, seeking shelter in the *lee* side of *Crete*. They round the eastern tip at the city of *Salmone* and sail along the southern coast (27:7). Even the protection of the land does not help them much as they creep slowly on to a point about halfway across this 160-mile long island. Here they find an open bay called *Fair Havens*, difficult to manage in such windy weather. Since the place is *not suitable for spending the winter* and travel conditions have become so hazardous, they are faced with a dilemma (27:8).

27:9-12   The Decision to Continue

At this point Paul speaks up and gives the first of several bits of warning and advice for the voyage. No vision or direct word from the Lord is mentioned, but the reader knows by now to respect the apostle's word on future events and will see here again the working of the divine will. What Paul foresees is much loss of *cargo, ship,* and *lives* if they now go on across the tempestuous sea (27:10). A later word will modify his warning somewhat to specify the loss of the ship but no loss of life (27:22).

This prediction of Paul is confirmed by later events, but at the time puts a strain on his relationship with the centurion Julius. This military man, friendly though he has been, does not regard the apostle as an authority on seafaring matters and listens to the pilot and owner of the ship instead (27:11). They, understandably, favor going on and getting the grain to Italy as quickly as possible. Probably no vote is taken, but the consensus among the ship's crew and passengers backs their view. Knowledgeable seamen among them have in mind the harbor at *Phoenix,* some fifty miles further west along the southern coast of Crete, where their ship can *winter* in safety (27:12).

The Storm   27:13-26

27:13-20   Driven by the Northeaster

At first the majority in favor of going on seem to know what they are doing. A gentle breeze propels the ship along the southern coast of Crete *close to the shore* (27:13). To this extent, human wisdom prevails. Then the divinely inspired insight of the apostle begins to be manifest as a tempest sweeps down upon them from the direction of the island. Luke's first-century readers would know the name of this dreaded wind, *Euraquilō,* or *Northeaster,* the scourge of all sailors of this part of the Mediterranean. A fierce gale powerfully turns the ship to the southwest, and all the pilot and crew can do is to let it drive them in all its fury (27:15). Instead of following the southern coast of Crete toward Phoenix, they are forced by this *hurricane* (NIV) out into the Mediterranean.

Soon they sight the *small island* of Cauda (some texts have Clauda) off to their right. They are some twenty-three miles from Crete as they skirt its lee side and are helplessly driven out upon the high seas. Luke mentions the small boat towed behind the ship, a *lifeboat* (NIV), which is now with great difficulty hauled up and made secure on deck. His use of the *we* for this action (27:16) may mean that he helps personally with this operation. Then they run ropes or cables down under the ship to hold it together—another dangerous task. The fear is that they will be driven south to the *Syrtis*, an area of quicksands and shoals off the north coast of Libya, still 380 miles away but a threat nonetheless. To slow down the ship they lower the *sea anchor* (27:17) to drag in the water, or perhaps reduce the amount of sail exposed to the wind (cf. Ramsay, 1896:329-330; Cadbury, 4:333).

This is just the first day of the tempest. On the second, still taking a *violent battering from the storm* (NIV), the people on the ship begin to throw cargo overboard (27:18). Precious grain is dumped into the raging waters, reminiscent of the storm in the book of Jonah (1:4-5): "The ship threatened to break up. . . . They threw the cargo that was in the ship into the sea, to lighten it for them." As the third day dawns, there is still no relief. By now waves are sweeping over the deck, and life on board is becoming more and more precarious. The *tackle* of the ship is by now useless and is hoisted by hand into the sea (27:19). This probably includes the huge spar, a wooden or metal pole used as a mast. Luke says they did this *with their own hands*, or perhaps *with our own hands* (KJV), as though they have no hoists to use. In any case, the author is close at hand and keenly interested in the operation.

From the fourth day to the fourteenth, Luke does not record the passage of time (cf. 27:27). It is one continuous effort to stay alive in this battle with the elements. The *sun* and *stars* are blotted out by the darkened skies, and there is no good way to reckon time as one dreary night follows another. The winds, with hurricane force, lash and drive relentlessly. All hope of survival is gone (27:20). Even the Christians on board are not sure of their lives, except for Paul, who has been promised that he will witness for Christ in Rome (cf. 23:11).

27:21-26 Paul's Words of Assurance

The desperate struggle to keep from being swept overboard and the inconvenience of eating on a sea-swept vessel result in their being *without food for a long time* (27:21). And then Paul once more rises to the occasion and comes forward with a word of guidance, this time based on a direct vision from the Lord. But first he reestablishes his own credibility by chiding them for disregarding his warning and embarking on such a foolhardy venture. It is an I-told-you-so type of rebuke, followed by encouragement and a promise. The good news is that there will be no loss of life among them, just the ship (27:22). The basis for that assurance is a night vision and a message from his God. Like Jonah of old, he speaks of the Lord he worships, who will deliver them (cf. Jon. 1:9). In Paul's case, the *angel* of the Lord speaks the word of promise, a repetition of the word he received in Jerusalem (23:11), to take courage because he would bear witness before the emperor in Rome.

Added to that is the assurance of God's gracious deliverance of those *sailing with you* (27:24), a favor granted to the Gentile companions of Jonah also. For three righteous men, the lives of the 273 others of unknown spiritual condition will be spared, much like what might have happened to wicked Sodom had ten righteous persons been found in that city (Gen. 18:32). This is reason for *courage,* the apostle says, because he has *faith in God* that the prophecy will be fulfilled (27:25), even to the detail of running *aground on some island* (27:26). They soon can verify this prediction, when they are beached on the island of *Malta* (27:44—28:1).

The Shipwreck 27:27-44

27:27-32 Fourteenth Night and Crisis on Board

On and on the voyagers drift, perhaps unaware that they are no longer headed toward the shoals of the Syrtis but have veered, first to the west and then in a northwesterly direction far out of danger of the African coast. They are being driven across the middle of the Mediterranean straight south of the Adriatic in an area sometimes called the sea of Adria (or Hadria). Two weeks have gone by since the Northeaster first struck them. Now at midnight, some 475 nautical miles from Cauda, the sailors sense that they have come into shallower water and must be nearing some landmass. One ancient manuscript, perhaps preserving the original reading in 27:27, has the words *the land resounding,* indicating that the sailors can actually hear the breakers beating upon the shore. *Soundings* are immediately made by lowering a lead weight at the end of a long line and then measuring it. First results show a depth of 20 fathoms (120 feet) and then 15 fathoms (only 90 feet), indicating that they are rapidly approaching dangerous shallows (27:28).

In the darkness of the night, they can see no land but they dare not wait. Hastily they let down four anchors from specially made openings in *the stern* (rear) of the ship, both to prevent the ship's bow from swinging around and to put them in position to run straight for the shore once daylight comes (27:29). The graphic way in which such details are told suggests that Luke himself is on deck with the sailors, observing everything and even helping when needed.

The vessel has been anchored on the shallow bottom, and everyone is waiting for daylight. But all is not well. A noise is heard toward the bow of the ship, and Paul at once suspects what is going on in the dark. Pretending to be lowering anchors there as well as from the stern, the sailors are making sure *they* get out alive by lowering the lifeboat into the water (27:30). So the apostle intervenes again, this time with more insistence than ever. With the ring of divine authority, he tells his superiors that unless the sailors *stay in the ship*, no one can be saved (27:31). By now the centurion has complete trust in Paul's judgment and commands his soldiers to cut the ropes of the lifeboat and let it loose in the sea (27:32). Thus once more Paul comes to the rescue of the entire vessel.

27:33-38 Breaking Bread at Dawn

As Luke narrates it, Paul's crowning act of leadership, however, occurs before dawn on this ship anchored precariously in strange waters. As first rays of light stream across the vessel, the apostle stands on deck and addresses his fellow voyagers, both passengers and crew. He reminds them of their long struggle with the elements and the anxiety that has caused them to go *without food* (27:33). Now they must eat, he says, and build up their strength to *survive*.

Then Paul adds a note of hope, reaffirming the earlier promise of no loss of life (27:22-25) with the assurance that not one hair of their heads will perish (27:34). This is for all of them, Christian and non-Christian alike, thus opening to all a promise given by Jesus to his disciples for a time of persecution (Luke 21:18). But knowing that exhortation alone would not be sufficient to penetrate the despair, Paul performs what for believers has become a sacramental act. As Jesus did in the feeding of the multitude (Luke 9:16), at the Last Supper (Luke 22:19), and again at Emmaus (Luke 24:30)—so now Paul takes bread, blesses it, breaks it, and begins the eating (27:35).

This is enough to get everyone started, and before long all of them are taking in food with new courage (27:36). At this point Luke provides his readers with a count of persons on board the ship—a surprising 276 (27:37). Yet such a large passenger list is not unusual. Josephus tells of a shipload of six hundred, which, by coincidence, also met disaster in the sea of Adria (Adriatic Sea) around this time

(A.D. 63, according to his *Autobiography* 3).

The hearty meal *satisfied their hunger* and does wonders for the morale of the whole company. With new strength, they throw more *wheat* into the water, completing what they *began* to do earlier (27:18), hoping to make it easier to bring the ship to shore (27:38).

27:39-41   Grounded on a Sandbar

Full daylight reveals a strange island, unknown to even the most widely traveled seamen among them (27:39). They see a bay with a beach, giving them hopes of running the ship ashore with safety (27:39). This is the place presently called St. Paul's Bay, some distance from Valleta, which they would surely have recognized in their day. What they do see is a *bay* with a sandy *beach*, onto which they plan to run their ship. To do this they unfasten the four *anchors* which they previously let out from the stern (cf. 27:29) and cast them away as useless. Then they untie the lashings of the *steering* paddles (rudders) and hoist a small sail in the foremast to guide the ship (27:40). (Luke uses the technical word for this *foresail*, the earliest known use of it in Greek literature, though common enough in Latin).

As the ship moves in closer to the beach, an unexpected problem arises. Unknown to them, a channel has cast up a sandbar or reef hidden from the surface (lit., *a place where two seas meet*, CF). Here the vessel runs aground and sticks in the muddy clay. This renders the bow immovable (27:41), and the stern of the ship is exposed to the pounding of the surf. The vessel begins to break apart, and all on board are forced to scramble for their lives or perish at sea.

This time *the soldiers*, not the sailors (cf. 27:30), decide to act on their own. They plan to *kill* all the *prisoners* so that none may escape and make them subject to the stern rule that guards must pay with their own lives for persons left in their charge (cf. 12:19; 16:27; and notes thereon). Julius himself sees what is happening and prevents disaster by stopping the soldiers. He orders all persons who can swim to go overboard at once and head for land. Nonswimmers are to get hold of pieces of the fast-splintering ship and ride to safety on them (27:43). Thus Luke can record, as one of those involved, *And so it was that all were brought safely to land* (27:44), fulfilling the Lord's promise that not one of them would be lost (27:22). Moreover, the general theme of *save* and *salvation* through this story has been brought to a climax. It stresses the primary meaning of health and safety and also suggests to godly readers a secondary, symbolic meaning of eternal salvation for all of humankind who will respond (Luke 2:30-32; 3:6; cf. Tannehill, 2:336-338).

Wintering on the Island of Malta 28:1-10

28:1-6 Paul and the Deadly Viper

Some time after coming ashore, the shipwrecked party learns that this land is part of the island of *Melita*, present-day *Malta* (28:1). The Semitic name given by early Phoenicians means "of refuge" or "safety," and Luke may intend his readers to realize how appropriate that is to the present situation. Not only is the land itself a haven of refuge from the storm, but the local inhabitants prove most friendly. With *unusual kindness*, as the author puts it, they build a large *fire* to warm the sea-drenched refugees, and it is well that they do so, for it has begun to rain and turn *cold* (28:2).

Luke portrays Paul as always active and helpful, now gathering an armload of sticks to add to the briskly burning fire. But death threatens again as a poisonous snake slides out from the *brushwood* he is holding and clamps its jaws on his hand (28:3). There is no way of knowing the species of this reptile since there are no longer snakes on the island. But the *natives* (lit., *barbarians*, meaning non-Roman) recognize it at once as deadly and exclaim among themselves in amazement. Seeing that Paul is a prisoner, they take him to be *a murderer* being punished for his crime. Though he has been saved from death at sea, now *justice* (a kind of nemesis) has at last caught up with him! (28:4). An ancient poem in the Greek *Palatine Anthology* (7.290) tells of a murderer who did in fact escape from a storm at sea, was shipwrecked on the Libyan coast, only to be killed by a viper (Bruce: 522, note 11).

Imagine the people's surprise when Paul, suffering no pain or fear, calmly shakes the snake off into the fire as though nothing happened! (28:5). Then, thinking that justice may be delayed, the people wait for him to swell up and drop over dead. But this does not happen. He carries on as spry as ever. Little wonder that these simple islanders no longer take him as a criminal but see him as a god! (28:6). While opposite in order, this situation is like that at Lystra. There the backward villagers first take him as divine and want to worship him, only to change later and try to kill him as their enemy (14:11-19).

28:7-10 Ministry of Healings

Luke describes the three-month stay on the island in language that recalls the account of Jesus' healings at Capernaum near the beginning of his ministry (Luke 4:38-40). In both cases, the healing of an individual, a relative of the host, is followed by the healing of "all" or *the rest of the people* in the region, and both contain references to the laying on of hands. Such similarities show that Jesus' powerful ministry of restoration is continuing through his witnesses.

Paul, now in full favor, is introduced to the *leading man of the island,* a wealthy landowner with the Roman name of *Publius.* Inscriptions show his title to be one roughly equivalent to that of governor. Since his estate is near the place where the shipwrecked party came ashore, it is convenient for him to welcome the refugees to his home. We cannot tell whether the whole crowd of 276 persons are housed on his property, or simply the leaders among them, including Paul and Luke. But it is indeed a most hospitable act, one which enables these needy people to begin a life on the island. Perhaps, as Haenchen pictures it (716), Publius shelters the whole ship-wrecked community for three days until they can find lodging on their own in various parts of the island (28:7).

The important thing is that Paul is instrumental in healing the governor's father, who is likely living with him on the estate. He is having a bout with *recurrent fever* (NASB) and *dysentery.* Such attacks are common enough to be known at that time as "Malta fever" and are virulent enough to be distressing and often fatal. The germ is carried along in goat's milk and causes severe gastric disturbance. As a physician (Col. 4:14), Luke is no doubt acquainted with the seriousness of the disease and is happy to tell of its cure, on this occasion, not by medication but by the laying on of hands and prayer (28:8). After many healings already recorded in Acts, primarily by Peter, Philip, and Paul (cf. esp. 5:15-16; 8:7-8; 19:11-12), the reader is prepared to see once more, as part of the good news, the power of God to restore a person to health quickly and completely.

As so often happened in the healings of Jesus and the apostles, one remarkable healing miracle leads to many others. The ills of large numbers of people tend to surface, and multitudes crowd in to take advantage of the opportunity to be cured (Luke 4:41-42; 6:18-19; Acts 5:15-16; 8:7; 19:11-12). Thus, over the three-month period, others from outside the estate of Publius come to Paul and are healed (28:9). One wonders if Luke himself, as a physician, does not also get into the act of helping cure some of the people. Marshall (418) thinks that this may be inferred from his use of *us* in connection with the *gifts* received for such services (28:10, RSV). These rewards may be called *honors* (NRSV) or *marks of respect* (NASB). Included would be various expressions of thanks, freewill gifts, and even medical fees showered on them during that time. When they finally have an opportunity to leave by ship, the grateful islanders provide supplies that will add to the comfort of the travelers as they go on their way (28:10b).

It is interesting that nothing is said about evangelizing on Malta during these three months. Perhaps there is a language barrier, although 28:4 and 6 report a bit of what the *natives* say. Luke does not mention anyone coming to the Lord nor any group of believers. It is witnessing primarily by personal presence and by the healing power they channel.

From Malta to Rome 28:11-16

The winter months spent on the island are from about mid-November till mid-February, after which the shipping lanes are open again. Other grain ships, faring better than the one carrying Paul, have likewise wintered at Malta. One of them, also from Alexandria, is found by the centurion, and passage is booked for Paul and company and possibly other prisoners (28:11; cf. 27:6). Their destination is Puteoli, on the Bay of Naples. There is no mention of the rest of the large group involved in the shipwreck. From this point on, the focus is on Paul and his associates, as it was before the sea voyage.

Curiously enough, Luke includes a feature of this ship that has little importance for the story except as evidence of its authenticity and as personal interest for some readers. The *figurehead* on the prow sports the faces of the twin gods, Castor and Pollux, sons of Zeus, known in Latin as the *Gemini*, one of our constellations. Sailors worship them as patron gods and believe they bring good fortune to ships, especially in storms. They supply the name for the vessel that carries the apostle and his party on toward Rome.

The ship journey from Malta to Puteoli takes the group by way of Syracuse, where they spend three days (28:12), likely because the winds from the south fail them temporarily. Most ancient readers will know this port as the large one on the east coast of Sicily. The city was founded in 734 B.C. as a Corinthian colony and came under Roman control in 212 B.C. It is mentioned here only as a recognizable stopover on the journey. After they *weighed anchor*, they come to Rhegium, at the toe of Italy. Some later manuscripts (Metzger: 500-501) suggest that skillful tacking this way and that by the navigators against (northwest?) winds enables them to make the passage (28:13). The following day a south wind comes up and propels them on to Puteoli.

At this principal port of southern Italy, sheltered in the vast Bay of Naples, they come to the end of their sea voyage (28:14). At Puteoli the grain ships from Egypt regularly put in to discharge their cargo. Usually coming in fleets, they are given priority over all other vessels, their topsails carried aloft to signal their approach. Though he has never been here before, Paul soon locates *believers*, who in turn invite him and his party to spend a full week with them in fellowship, reminiscent of other such visits (20:6-12, 17-38; 21:4-6, 7-14). The centurion Julius is most accommodating and apparently stays with them before his party pushes on to their destination (28:14ab). Now Luke shows obvious relief that they have reached the Italian mainland: *And so we came to Rome* (28:14c). There is still some distance to go, but the worst is over, and from here on they enjoy Christian companionship.

Luke relates one more incident before Paul and his party reach Rome. It also reflects the love, thoughtfulness, and hospitality of the Christians. During the week at Puteoli, word reaches the community of believers in Rome that the apostle is finally in Italy and on his way to the city. They know Paul as the one who wrote them the well-known epistle of Romans some five years earlier. His arrival has long been awaited. In response, a group of Christians come down the main road from Rome, some reaching the *Forum of Appius* 43 miles south of the city. Others wait at *Three Taverns,* another well-known meeting place 33 miles from Rome. Paul has already written to and warmly greeted more than a score of fellow believers in that metropolis (Rom. 16:3-16, assuming Rom. 16 is an integral part of the epistle; on this question, see Cranfield, *Romans,* 1:5-11, in the ICC series). Thus the reunion with some of them is indeed sweet, as well as the meeting with others. Luke reports that when Paul meets these fellow Christians, he *thanked God and took courage* (28:15).

At last Paul and his party enter the city of Rome itself, escorted by the friends who have come out to greet them, with Julius still in charge (28:16). The centurion gives Paul over to the authorities, though nothing is said about this in the standard Greek texts. Some Western manuscripts have Julius put his prisoner in the hands of a certain Roman officer who can no longer be identified for sure, either a prefect of the praetorian guard or his assistant. This official permits Paul to live by himself outside the camp. Such readings fit with our present text in stating that the apostle is allowed to live *by himself* in the custody of a *soldier* who guards him. He is not free to move about but can do the work of a witness by having people come to see him. This is the situation as it is described at the end of Acts (28:30-31). Though Luke's last *we* occurs in 28:16, it is logical to assume that he stays on in Rome with Paul for some time since he is present, presumably in Rome, at the time of the writing of Colossians (4:14) and Philemon (24).

Paul's Witness in Rome

Acts 28:17-31

First Session with the Jewish Leaders 28:17-22

Luke has told of Paul being escorted to Rome by a group of Christians, and he says nothing more about the church there. Nor is there any further mention of the apostle's involvement with Roman officials. Instead of an expected culmination of Paul's witness at this gateway to the *ends of the earth* (cf. 1:8) or final trial before Caesar (cf. 23:11; 25:12), the closing scenes of Acts have to do almost exclusively with his message to the Jews. These are represented by certain of their leaders before whom the apostle now presents his case.

Such a focus at the end of the book shows how important Luke considers this kind of witness to be. Nor is it totally unexpected, since it parallels Paul's last visit to Jerusalem. There he also had no further dealings with the church after an initial session, but immediately became involved with Jewish matters (21:17-36). Both that occasion and this one illustrate the fact that the mission in Acts is not to those who already believe but to outsiders: *to the Jews first* and, after them, *to the Gentiles* (1:8; 13:46), a theme restated at the end of this section (28:24-28; cf. Rom. 1:15-16).

At their first meeting in his private dwelling, Paul gives the Jewish leaders a summary of his arrest, trial, and appeal to Caesar as recorded in chapters 22—26. By this he establishes his innocence of any crime and shows how his presence in Rome is really due to his loyalty to Judaism, despite the opinion of the majority of his people. Luke thus once more gives readers a convincing defense of the apostle and at the same time provides a concise summary of these five chapters of Acts.

Several important aspects of this first encounter stand out. Though he has been manhandled and almost killed by the Jerusalem mob and harshly dealt with by the Jewish authorities, Paul shows no bitterness. There is no mention of the high priest's treachery and continued attempts to take his life. Nor does he reflect critically on his treatment by Felix and Festus. In fact, he praises the Romans for seeking to free him (28:18). He is not bringing charges against the Jews, having been *compelled to appeal to Caesar* to save his life (28:19, RSV). In fact, he is on a pro-Jewish mission, bound as a prisoner for the messianic *hope of Israel* (cf. notes on 23:6; 26:6-7).

Judging by Luke's brief summary, at this preliminary get-acquainted meeting, the apostle makes no reference to Jesus nor to his own mission of taking the gospel to the Gentiles. In their reply, the Jewish leaders are also free from hostility, as they tell of receiving no official letters about him or verbal charges against him from Judea (28:21). Indeed, they are eager to hear more about the sect which he represents since it does seem to be quite controversial (28:22).

Second Meeting with the Jews 28:23-28

We can see the sincerity and openness of the Roman Jews in what happens in the second meeting, held again at Paul's lodging at an indefinite time later (28:23a). Haenchen (723) pictures this taking place at the inn where Paul has rented a room, possibly in the guest chamber (Williams: 278). Jews turn out in large numbers and give the whole day to listening to the apostle. The theme is the *kingdom of God* (28:23b), linking this occasion to important scenes in the ministry of Jesus and to the story of Acts as a whole (Luke 4:43-44; 8:1; Acts 1:3, 8; 8:12; 14:22; 19:8; 20:25). Within that theme, Paul's central thrust is an exposition of the law and the prophets to prove that Jesus is indeed the Messiah, the king of that kingdom (28:23c).

The response of these leaders is divided, like that of Jews in every previous contact in the synagogue (13:43-46; 14:1-4; 17:4-5; 18:5-8; 19:8-9). Some are *convinced* (NIV, NRSV), and others refuse to believe (28:24). Since the verb describing those receptive to the gospel is in the imperfect tense, indicating progressive or incomplete action, it is possible that only a beginning has been made. This is best expressed by the NASB: *were being persuaded,* a rendering supported by Tannehill (2:347).

The disagreement between the two groups of Jews seems to increase as the day wears on, leading Paul to make a final statement. He takes a powerful text from the prophets to show out of their own Scriptures the nature and tragic results of their unbelief. Quoting Isaiah 6:9-10, he identifies with that spokesman of the Lord as he tells his people of the irony of listening but not hearing, of looking but never perceiving (28:26). The tension is great whenever God's own people close their hearts to their mission of being a light to the nations, here and throughout all of Acts. The irony is that such Israelites defeat their own destiny, for if they would but *listen, . . . understand, . . . and turn*, God *would heal them!* (28:27).

Does this mean that the rejection of Christ by the Jews is total and that, since there is no longer any hope of convincing them, the church must concentrate exclusively on the Gentile mission? Conzelmann (227) and others after him have taken this position. Yet from the beginning of the gospel, Luke has proclaimed that the good news of great joy is for "all peoples," both the Gentiles and the Jews (Luke 2:30-32), and "all flesh shall see the salvation of God" (Luke 3:6).

Furthermore, throughout his career, Paul has borne witness to and gained converts from among both Jews and Gentiles (Acts 9:15; 13:43-48; 14:1; 17:4; 18:4-8; 19:8-10; 22:15; 26:16-18). The condemnation here is upon *unbelieving* Jews. Believing Jews will be accepted as they always have been. Paul is faithfully continuing the message that Christian evangelists have been preaching for years. And he will keep on with this message to the end (cf. 28:30, where he welcomes *all* who come to him, both Jew and Gentile). For Luke, both believing Jews and Gentiles constitute the true people of God (see Jervell and the essay on this *[Luke and the Jewish Law, p. 317]*).

Two Years of Unhindered Witness 28:30-31

Luke concludes Acts by sketching in briefly the ministry Paul has in Rome for the next couple years. He says nothing about his trial before Caesar or his eventual death, just an open-ended witness from his rented lodging (28:16, 30). Many theories have been advanced to explain the omission of further information. Did Paul's accusers fail to appear before the two-year limit? Was Paul released to continue his missionary work for some years and then executed in Rome during the reign of Nero? Some have thought that Luke planned a third volume—which he either wrote only to have it lost, or failed to write for any one of a number of reasons. The most likely explanation, however, is that the author intended to end Acts as he did and had no further writing in mind. The aim expressed in 1:8, that of witnessing to the *ends of the earth*, has been potentially fulfilled, with Rome considered the capital of that earth.

As Tannehill demonstrates (2:353-355), here is both a *closure* of previous themes of Luke-Acts (salvation offered for all, with most Jews rejecting the offer) and a significant *openness* to Paul's future ministry. The apostle's death has already been foreshadowed in his farewell speeches (20:22-38; 21:11, 13) and need not be recorded. Thus the ending does not highlight the harsh injustice of his execution (likely during the reign of Nero) at the hands of the Romans, who have already pronounced him innocent. Nor does it dwell on his martyrdom as a heroic act. Instead, Luke directs attention to the ongoing task of the church and its opportunity to witness to the Gentile world.

Luke concludes then by telling how Paul's witness continues *quite openly* (RSV, NEB) and *with all boldness*. The last word of the book, *unhindered* (RSV; *akōlutōs, without hindrance*), has been called by B. S. Easton (10) that "crisp adverb" which gives an artistic and impressive ending to a magnificent work. Though God's *messenger* is bound, the *message* of God "is not fettered" (2 Tim. 2:9, RSV), ever open-ended to the future!

THE TEXT IN BIBLICAL CONTEXT

The God of Sea Travel and Storms

The ancient Hebrews were afraid of the sea. They were primarily people of the land and not sailors like their neighbors the Phoenicians, the Greeks, and the later Romans. For them, the winds and the waves held many terrors. In the thinking of the Canaanites before them, the sea was the home of primeval monsters that had opposed God in creation. And for the Hebrews as well, "deep waters" was an expression for life-threatening experiences, and the sea was the enemy of all humankind (Ps. 18:16; 32:6; 46:3; 69:1-2; etc.). On the other hand, God had created the waters and all that was in them and was in control of them along with all the natural elements. God had parted the Red Sea to permit the Israelites to pass through and be saved (Exod. 14:21). A bit later, at the Lord's command, the same sea came sweeping back to destroy their enemies (14:27-28). Thus also the Son of God rebuked the storm on the Sea of Galilee and saved his disciples (Luke 8:22-25).

The one biblical parallel to Paul's voyage on the Mediterranean is that of Jonah on the same Great Sea. It is a story that Paul and his companions were brought up on, and every aspect of it was well-known. There too a violent storm arose and threatened to break up the ship. Even seasoned sailors panicked in their fear, threw cargo overboard, and cried out for help (1:4-14). Then their prayers also were answered after they followed the directions of the man of God on board. The Lord, who had sent the great storm in the first place (1:4), caused the raging sea to grow calm (1:15d) and eventually saved them all (1:16-17).

Also part of the heritage of Paul and his Christian friends would be Psalm 107, whose fourth stanza tells of those who go "down to the sea in ships, doing business on the mighty waters." Like Jonah, in the deeds of the Lord, they see the stormy wind and the waves that mount up to the heavens and then plunge into the depths. Then they cry to God in their trouble, the storm is stilled, and finally the Lord brings them "to their desired haven" (107:23-32). In all likelihood Paul and the other believers recall this Psalm many times during the fortnight of valiant struggle with the tempest. It would reinforce the vision the apostle had and contribute to the calm with which he assures those on board that not one of them would be lost.

The Spiritual Leader Competent in Practical Affairs

Paul displays a surprising ability to take command of the situation in time of storm, without special knowledge of ships and sea travel. This is true to the biblical revelation. When people excelling in practical affairs are at their wits' end and need help beyond their own wisdom and strength, they will sometimes look to spiritual leaders. There are three outstanding examples of this in the OT.

Joseph, a dreamer of dreams, one who rose from slavery by the grace of God and his own ingenuity, was made overseer in charge of the buying and selling of grain throughout all Egypt and the satellite nations (Gen. 41:41-47). *Moses*, though brought up in the court circles of Egypt, had forty years of hard experience as a shepherd in the desert wastelands, where he had a memorable encounter with God at the burning bush (Exod. 2:15—4:17). Then he returned to Egypt as a stranger and a believer in an unseen God, to stand before the mighty Pharaoh, lead a multitude of slaves out of captivity, forge them into a nation, and administer both spiritual and temporal affairs for another forty years (from Exod. 4:18 to end of Deuteronomy). Then *Daniel*, like Joseph an interpreter of dreams, also rose to high position in a pagan empire and eventually appeared as a chief adviser to three successive kings (Dan. 1:17-21). Thus also Paul, led by the Spirit of God, stands out as the one sane and practical man on board ship, giving advice that saves the lives of all.

THE TEXT IN THE LIFE OF THE CHURCH
The Gospel and the Nitty-Gritty of Life

Some may wonder why Luke, the gospel writer, puts so much detail in his book about winds, seas, harbors; the gear, tackle, and cargo of the ship; how a vessel can run aground, the breakup in the surf, and scores of other "nonspiritual" matters. Aren't these items best left to the secular historian or some specialist in sea travel? The answer is one familiar to members of the believers church tradition. For the true believer, *God is in every aspect of life and no detail is unimportant.* The entire creation is alive with evidences of God's work, and the life of the Christian is filled with events touched by the divine. All of it can be a part of the gospel.

There are two conditions, however, for this to be true. One is that all these details *be part of the divine thrust.* Because Paul is engaged in a mission for the Lord, many little things that happen to him on the way are important and worth recording. Luke is not telling about other ships cruising the Mediterranean—just these. The second thing true for such details to be mentioned as part of the sacred record is that they *be kept in balance, always secondary* to the main theme. Luke is not interested in details of sea travel for their own sakes. Instead, these features add color and credibility to the way the Lord brings the ship through safely without the loss of life, according to divine promise. So always in the chronicles of the faith. The minutest details can witness to the Lord's love, wisdom, and power and are therefore of interest to those dedicated to Christ's mission.

The Ongoing Ministry of Evangelism

Acts, with its open-ended closing, extends a challenge to the life of each generation of Christians that follows. Marks of a vital continuing witness are these:

1. *A willingness to be self-supporting.* Paul lived *at his own expense* (28:30a), carrying on his ministry free of charge. This has been standard among Anabaptist-Brethren congregations. In earlier times, even ministers helped financially by their people received only

occasional assistance—love offerings or donations in kind—rather than regular pay. In recent years when salaries are common, *willingness* to do all one can to bear one's own expenses has been present.

2. *An open invitation to every one.* Paul *welcomed all who came to him* (28:30b). In the first century, this meant Gentiles as well as Jews, the rich and the poor, males and females, and persons from all ethnic groups. In recent centuries, although most members of the believers church have been of European stock, their evangelistic thrust has not been limited to such people. Moreover, their relief work has extended to all those in need regardless of race, creed, or social background. Then in later years new ventures in international witness have opened up, some in connection with former mission fields, where nationals have taken over most of the ministries, and some in totally new areas.

3. *Preaching and teaching the gospel.* Paul went on *proclaiming the kingdom of God and teaching about the Lord Jesus Christ* (28:31a). The Anabaptist-Brethren witness has been strong on both preaching and teaching the Word. The proclamation occurred both in the meetinghouses and out in public places, fervent and often quite fruitful, with many being won to the faith in this way. The teaching often took place in the home or in special Bible study groups, again a straightforward presentation of Jesus and the meaning of discipleship. Such teaching took place before and after baptism. The new convert was expected to go on growing in grace and the knowledge of God throughout life.

4. *New openness and boldness.* Paul's continuing ministry was *with all boldness and without hindrance* (28:31b). Here the record of Anabaptist and Brethren traditions has been uneven. There was great Spirit-filled boldness in the early days of each tradition, followed usually by some slackening off as a denomination became more accepted or acculturated. An effective boldness was also sometimes lacking when a group considered itself a hopeless minority or a righteous remnant striving to survive. At other times groups would catch fire with the Spirit and manifest great courage in going forth to proclaim the Word. Many have been influenced by Holy Spirit renewal movements of the latter quarter of the twentieth century. These may hold the key to a new forward thrust inspired by and modeled after the book of Acts.

God's Call and Empowerment

God continues to call people into his kingdom work in ways similar to his call and empowerment of Paul's life. We think of well-known persons, Augustine, Billy Sunday, Chuck Colson, and we praise God for calling these into kingdom work and empowering their ministries by his grace.

The *Mennonite Historical Bulletin* tells how God transformed the life of Stephen Grellet, who like the apostle Paul already had an admirable moral commitment. While Paul was Pharisee of the Pharisees and had positive moral convictions based upon the Torah, Stephen Grellet was born into a wealthy upper-class Roman Catholic French family in 1773. Because of his military resistance to the French Revolution, he was forced to flee for his life. Arriving in the United States in 1793, Grellet met Quakers and through that acquaintance experienced a dramatic encounter with God. As a former "disciple of Voltaire," he now became a disciple of Christ. He embraced the Quakers' simple lifestyle, teachings of nonresistance, and plain language, and he committed himself to seek and do the truth.

Grellet became a great itinerant preacher, leaving his family, church, and job to travel and witness to people throughout North America and Europe. During one of his evangelistic trips into Russia in 1819, he met Mennonites and then traveled to many colonies, preaching the word and strengthening Mennonite brothers and sisters in the faith. (From J. Kevin Miller's introduction to and citation from *Grellet's Memoirs,* in "The Russian Mennonites in 1819," *MHB* 50, no. 1 [Jan. 1989]: 1-4.)

Let praise arise to God in celebration of the divine purpose, expressed well by the hymn text by Arthur Campbell Ainger in 1894:

> From utmost east to utmost west,
>   Where . . . [human] foot hath trod,
> By the mouth of many messengers
>   Goes forth the voice of God.
> Give ear to me, ye continents,
>   Ye isles, give ear to me,
> That the earth may be filled with the glory of God
>   As the waters cover the sea.
>
> (*The Mennonite Hymnal,*
> Scottdale, Pa.: Herald Press, 1969:605)

Outline of Acts

Part 1: BEGINNINGS IN JERUSALEM
Acts 1:1–26

Part 2: THE DAY OF PENTECOST
Acts 2:1–47

Part 3: THE WITNESS OF THE EARLY JERUSALEM CHURCH
Acts 3:1—5:42

Part 4: THE MARTYR-WITNESS OF STEPHEN
Acts 6:1—8:1a

Part 5: THE WITNESS OF A PERSECUTED AND SCATTERED CHURCH
Acts 8:1b—9:31

Part 6: THE CONTINUING MINISTRY OF PETER
9:32—12:25

Part 11: WITNESS IN CAESAREA
Acts 24—26

Part 12: WITNESS—ON TO ROME
Acts 27—28

Voyage to Rome   27:1—28:16

Paul's Witness in Rome 28:17-31

Essays

CHRONOLOGY OF ACTS   Luke gives an elaborate set of public figures by which to date the beginning of the ministry of John the Baptist (Luke 3:1-2). Yet he is not primarily concerned with chronology as we know it today. His interest is in telling the story within a historical framework, with only an occasional reference to contemporary history. His point is that *this was not done in a corner* (26:26).

Acts refers to five events that can be dated with some accuracy, and two are of major importance. The famine of 11:28 likely occurred about A.D. 46-48, during the governorships of Cuspius Fadus and Tiberius Alexander (Josephus, *Ant.* 20.5.1-2). The edict of Claudius (18:2) is not given a date in any contemporary history, but a fifth-century historian assigns it to the emperor's ninth year, or 49. The governorship of Felix (24:27) is known to have begun in 52, but there is no certainty as to when it ended.

Remaining are two historical events which can be rather accurately dated and thus are the most valuable in determining the chronology of the Acts: (1) the death of Herod Agrippa I (12:23) in 44, and (2) the proconsulship of Gallio (18:12), with reasonable assurance dated from July of 51 to June of 52. The former date (for Herod Agrippa) has been known for many years, but the latter has come to light only in the twentieth century, with the discovery of an inscription at Delphi in Central Greece which mentions Gallio as proconsul of Achaia in the eleventh year of the Emperor Claudius. This date can vary only a few months one way or the other.

Scholars work with these reliably fixed dates, with hints from Luke as to intervening periods (such as *a year and six months*, 18:11; *two years*, 19:10; *three months*, 20:3), and with Paul's references in Galatians ("after three years," 1:17-18; "after fourteen years," 2:1). There are difficulties (see Bible dictionaries under "Chronology"), but this gives us enough to put together a plausible outline:

Day of Pentecost (Acts 2), A.D. 29-30
Conversion of Saul-Paul, 33-35
Death of Herod Agrippa I (12:23), 44
The famine relief (11:27-30), 45-46
Paul's first missionary journey, 46-48
Council of Jerusalem (chap. 15), 49
Jews expelled from Rome (18:2), 49
Paul's second missionary journey, 50-52
Gallio proconsul of Achaia (18:12), 51-52
Paul's third missionary journey, 53-57
Paul's last visit to Jerusalem, 57
Imprisonment in Caesarea (24:27), 57-59
Voyage to Rome and shipwreck, 59-60
End of the two years (28:30), 62-63

DESIGNATIONS OF EARLY CHRISTIANS   The *brethren* (which includes both women and men) is the first-mentioned and one of the most frequent names for Christians in Acts. It first occurs in 1:15 (RSV) and, in the Greek, is used some 23 times after that, although NRSV almost always changes it to *believers*. The word points toward relationships within the group: brotherly and sisterly love, mutuality and sharing. Perhaps the best commentary on its wealth of meaning is the community described in 2:42-47 and 4:32-35: the new Christians showed themselves to be one family in the Lord by sharing their possessions and holding everything in common. Even in texts where this dimension is not so apparent, such a loving, caring relationship is implied, as evidenced in group solidarity or showing hospitality (cf. 1:15; 9:30; 12:17; 15:3; 16:40; 17:10; 21:17; 28:14).

Disciples (including the singular *disciple*) is found 27 times to designate followers of Jesus. Many of these are word-choice variations of *brethren*, and the meanings overlap, although where an individual Christian is meant the word *disciple* is used. Unlike *brother* or *brethren*, it is never used in direct address. This term emphasizes the divine-human relationships, in contrast to *brethren*, where human connections are primary. For example, *disciples* is appropriately used for the body of Christians spoken of objectively in 6:1, 2, 7 and again in 9:1, 19, 25-26, where Saul is in the process of breaking into the group. *Brethren*, on the other hand, is more suitable for the discussions before, during, and after the council of Jerusalem, where the term is used ten times (15:1-40).

The church is another fairly common designation for Christians in Acts, found 17 times in the singular and three times in the plural. It is a translation of *ekklēsia* (lit., "called out") and was used by the Greeks of a public assembly of citizens (as in Acts 19:39). It was also the term by which the Jews referred to Moses' congregation in the wilderness (Acts 7:38). In Acts, as a collective noun, it means either the Christian movement in general (5:11; 8:3; 9:31) or a local congregation (11:26; 13:1; 14:23).

Believer, (sing. or pl.) is always in participle form in Greek, literally "the (one or ones) believing." It is appropriately used of those who have just recently come to faith in the Lord (as in 2:44; 4:32; 19:18) or of specified types of Christians (like *circumcised believers* in 10:45, or *believers who belonged to the sect of the Pharisees* in 15:5). This designation, like *disciple(s)*, stresses one's relationship to Christ. It is found eight times in Acts. In one interesting verse, 18:27, Luke speaks of the *brethren* of Ephesus writing to the *disciples* at Corinth about Apollos, who went there and helped the *believers* (*those who through grace had believed*, RSV). This illustrates the author's use of different terms for variety's sake and with little difference in meaning.

The Way is another significant name by which early Christianity was known, a term Luke uses six times in Acts (9:2; 19:9, 23; 22:4; 24:14, 22). It is likely a name the followers of Jesus chose for themselves, based on the idea of *the way of the Lord* (Luke 3:4; Acts 18:25), *the way of God* (Luke 20:21; Acts 18:26), and *a way of salvation* (Acts 16:17). It is found only in Acts and is always used in connection with Paul: his earlier attacks on those who *belonged to the Way* (9:2; 22:4), a name given to believers in Ephesus, where Paul ministered (19:9, 23), and Paul's admission before Felix that he worshiped God according to this sect (24:14).

Four times in Acts the followers of Christ are called *the saints* (9:13, 32, 41; 26:10). This term, rather common in Paul's letters and in Revelation and found a couple times in Hebrews and Jude, does not refer to any excellence to which Christians have attained, but rather to their *call* to a life of holiness. Two times in Acts, *the saints* refers to believers under persecution, suggesting that they are precious in God's sight (9:13; 26:10). The other two are of a more general character, simply a variant of other designations (9:32, 41).

The term *Nazarenes* for Christians is used only in 24:5. It occurs elsewhere in the NT and in Matthew 2:23, where it is applied to Jesus because of his connection with Nazareth. It appears to have started as a nickname by outsiders, and may or may not have been taken up by Christians. In Acts 24:5, Tertullus, an enemy of the faith, calls the *Nazarenes* a *sect*.

Finally, *Christian*, the name universally used today to designate those who believe in Jesus, is found only twice in Acts (11:26 and 26:28). See the notes on those texts for its probable origin and meaning. It is found in only one other passage in the rest of the NT (1 Pet. 4:16).

THE GREEK TEXT OF ACTS   While other ancient writings may exist in 10 or 20 of manuscripts at the most, the NT is found in more than five thousand, in portions ranging from tiny fragments to whole books and the entire Testament. Moreover, these manuscripts are much closer to the original (the "autographs") than is the case of well-known Greek and Roman classics. Therefore, the reliability of the extant texts is not the problem, but rather the wealth of manuscript material. Though something like 95 percent of the text is in full agreement, the remaining portion is in some doubt: in it are minor variations of wording, interesting additions, and omissions. None of this is of a serious nature that affects essential teaching in any major way.

To get at these variant readings, scholars have grouped the documents into text-types or families. The oldest such group, with similar readings, is usually called the *Alexandrian* because of connection with that city where Clement, Origen, and other Greek fathers lived and worked on the Scriptures. These manuscripts were not known and classified until near the end of the nineteenth century. The actual manuscripts of this family date from the fourth century, but their texts can be traced back into the third or even second century. A few of these are in capital letters (uncials), notably codex Vaticanus and codex Sinaiticus. Many in a later cursive hand follow the same basic text. In the twentieth century, numerous fragmentary early papyri texts (second and third centuries) have been discovered, and some of them follow this text-type.

A second family of texts, dating from ancient times but only studied in the last two centuries, is the *Western* or Bezan (from Theodore Beza, who first studied manuscript *D* of this type). It is of special interest for the study of Acts. It has a fondness for paraphrase and harmonization. Some of its unique readings may date back to the second century and contain reliable information which may or may not have been a part of the original. Each such variant must be studied and evaluated on its own merits.

A third family of texts, by far the most numerous, is known as *Byzantine* because it represents a major development during the time of the Byzantine Empire. For the most part, these manuscripts date from the sixth century or later and provide a less accurate reflection of the original. Since the Byzantine text was the only one available in the sixteenth and seventeenth centuries, this corrupt tradition provided the so-called Textus Receptus of the early printings of the Greek New Testament (first by Erasmus in 1516). Thus it became the base for the earliest German and English Bibles, including the well-known and much-loved KJV (for more on text-types, see Metzger: xv-xxxi).

In this commentary we have included only those readings from the Western or Byzantine texts which throw light on the story, whether original or not. Here are some of the more interesting variants:

8:37 This *Western* addition is picked up by some *Byzantine* manuscripts, with variations; found in KJV, bracketed in NASB, omitted by NRSV and NIV but included in footnotes: *And Philip said, "If you believe with all your heart, you may." And he replied, "I believe that Jesus Christ is the Son of God."* This supplies the proper confession of faith on the part of the Ethiopian (Metzger: 359-360).

15:34 Another *Western* addition, this verse is found in KJV, bracketed in NASB, omitted from NRSV and NIV but found in footnotes. It explains how Silas could be on hand in Antioch for the trip begun in 15:40, after the statement in 15:33 that *they* (Judas and Silas) had left. The addition, with some variation in manuscripts, reads, *But it seemed good to Silas to remain there.*

16:35 After the present initial words, *When morning came, the magistrates*, the *Western* text inserts the following: *assembled together in the marketplace, and recollecting the earthquake that had taken place, they were afraid* (Metzger: 450-451, giving other Western variations). Then it continues with words translated in NRSV: *sent the police, saying, "Let those men go."* None of our present-day versions, not even the KJV, includes this obvious attempt to explain why the magistrates so completely changed their minds. Though clearly an addition to the original text, this reading is valuable as an early and perhaps accurate commentary on it.

19:9 At the end of the verse, on the matter of Paul's teaching daily in lecture hall of Tyrannus, the *Western* text, not followed by KJV or other present versions, adds what may well be an accurate bit of information: *from eleven o'clock in the morning to four in the afternoon* (Greek: *from the fifth hour to the tenth*; Metzger: 470).

24:6b-8a This *Western* reading has passed into the *Byzantine* tradition. It is an addition to the speech of Tertullus, summarizing from his point of view what has taken place; found in KJV, bracketed in NASB, and included in footnotes of NRSV and NIV: *and we would have judged him according to our law. But the chief captain Lysias came and with great violence took him out of our hands, commanding his accusers to come before you* (Metzger: 490).

28:29 This Western expansion to round out the episode was adopted by the *Byzantine* text tradition; found in KJV, bracketed in NASB, and included in footnotes of NRSV and NIV: *And when he has said these words, the Jews departed, arguing vigorously among themselves.*

THE HOLY SPIRIT IN THE BIBLE AND IN ACTS . . .

In the OT The word for *spirit* (Hebrew: *ruakh*) is sometimes used to mean *wind*, indicative of an invisible, mysterious, powerful force (e.g., Gen. 8:1; Exod. 10:13). Other times it is used for *breath*, the life force of persons or animals (e.g. Gen. 6:17; Ps. 31:6). Alongside these connotations and related to them is a third usage, for *divine spirit*, with power from outside human beings and taking possession of them. This is the sense in which *ruakh* is used about early charismatic leaders (Judg. 3:10; 6:34; 11:29; 1 Sam. 11:6) and prophets (Num. 24:2; 1 Sam. 10:6; 19:20).

In earliest uses there was little distinction between natural and supernatural forces and more emphasis on power than on moral quality. With the passage of time, possession by the Spirit of God was thought of as permanent and capable of being passed on (Num. 11:17; Deut. 34:9; 2 Kings 2:9, 15). The anointing of the king was considered an anointing with the Spirit (1 Sam. 16:13. cf. Ps. 89:20-21; Isa. 11:2; 61:1). Strangely, the eighth- and seventh-century prophets (except for Mic. 3:8) did not speak of their inspiration as from the Spirit but from the direct Word of the Lord or the hand of the Lord (Isa. 8:11; Jer. 15:17). Perhaps they were reacting against false prophets who made much of the Spirit (Isa. 28:7; Jer. 5:13; Mic. 2:11). Or they may have begun to see that the greater work of the Holy Spirit would be in the future (as in Joel 2:28-32).

During and after the exile, there was more emphasis on the Spirit as the inspirer of prophecy (Ezek. 2:2; 3:22-24; cf. Isa. 59:21), and the inspiration of the earlier prophets was now seen to have been from God's Spirit (Neh. 9:20, 30; Zech. 7:12). Most important for the NT was the tendency among prophets to see the Holy Spirit coming as the Power of the End, the hallmark of a new age. The Spirit will bring about a new creation, they said (Isa. 32:15; 44:3-4), with persons made over again by the Spirit to enjoy a more vital and immediate relationship to God (Ezek. 36:26-27; 37:1-14; Jer. 31:31-34). Moreover, the Spirit will be poured out on all God's people (Ezek. 39:29; Joel 2:28-32; Zech. 12:10; cf. Num. 11:29).

In *rabbinic literature between the testaments*, the Spirit is said to be at work in the canonical OT prophets, but the assumption is that after the last of them, there were no more such prophetic voices. The Spirit, the rabbis believed, inspired the writing of the Torah (Law), and for them this was the all-sufficient word of the Spirit to guide their lives. They taught that even in the age to come, the Law will play a more prominent role than the Spirit.

In the Gospels Here the Holy Spirit plays a more important role. John the Baptist comes as a prophet after centuries of silence, and this only by the power of the Spirit. Luke, writing many years after the event, speaks of him as *filled with the Holy Spirit* from birth (Luke 1:15b). Even his mother Elizabeth (1:41) and his father Zechariah (1:67) are reported to be filled with the Spirit for their prophetic utterances. More importantly, John the Baptist pointed to the Coming One who would baptize with the Holy Spirit and fire (Luke 3:16; cf. Mark 1:8; Matt. 3:11).

The one in whom the Holy Spirit was fully manifested is Jesus, whom believers come to accept as the Messiah. Luke and Matthew tell of his conception and birth through the power of the Spirit (Luke 1:35; Matt. 1:18). All four Gospels record a special empowering for ministry as the Holy Spirit comes upon him in objective form, and he is declared the Son of God (Mark 1:10-11; Luke 3:22; Matt. 3:16-17; John 1:33-34). Moreover, the Spirit continues to fill him and work through him from that time on. Luke tells of his being "full of the Holy Spirit" as he returns from the Jordan (4:1), coming back into Galilee "in the power of the Spirit" (4:14), and having the "Spirit of the Lord" upon him in the synagogue at Nazareth (4:18). From that time he performs one mighty work after another in the power of the Spirit. The presence of the Spirit with Jesus is again emphasized in the Gospel of John. At his baptism the Holy Spirit not only descended upon him but "remained on him" (1:32). In John, the Spirit is also evident in the close relationship between Jesus and the Father in a number of stories and discourses (e.g., 3:5-18; 4:13-14, 34; 5:17).

It is only natural, then, that as Jesus faces the end of his earthly ministry, he turns everything over to his disciples with a promise that they themselves will be empowered by the same Spirit. In Luke, leading up to Acts, the promise of the Father through John the Baptist (3:16) is repeated in 24:49 with the command that they should remain in Jerusalem until they are clothed with power from on high, a promise fulfilled on the day of Pentecost (Acts 2). Thus empowered, they are to carry the witness to the *ends of the earth* (Acts 1:4-5, 8).

At the Last Supper, the Gospel of John speaks of this endowment of the disciples with the Spirit as the coming of the "Spirit of truth," the Paraclete ("Counselor" or "Comforter" in 14:16-17, 26; 15:26-27; 16:7-15). It is accomplished, in part at least, on the evening of the day of resurrection, as Jesus stands among them, breathes on them and says, "Receive the Holy Spirit" (20:22c). The result will be continuous growth in understanding the teachings of Jesus on the part of believers (14:26; 16:13-14) and a conviction of sin, righteousness, and judgment for unbelievers (16:8-11).

In the Writings of Paul Luke gives vivid stories of the effect of the Spirit in the life of Jesus. John offers general teachings about the work of the Paraclete (Helper or Advocate). Paul's letters, however, spell out rather full teachings about the nature and work of the Holy Spirit in Christians.

The Holy Spirit brings about the new creation and adoption as children of God (1 Cor. 6:11, 17; 12:13; Gal. 3:14; 4:6; Rom. 8:14-17; cf. also John 3:3-8; 1 John 3:24). The impact of the Spirit leaves a person in no doubt that a significant change has taken place by divine action. There is a powerful experience of God's *love* (Rom. 5:5), a great *joy* (1 Thess. 1:6), an *inner awakening* (2 Cor. 3:16-17), and a *moral transformation* (1 Cor. 6:9-11). Indeed, the fruit of the Holy Spirit can be expressed as a cluster of nine new Christlike graces in the life of the believer (Gal. 5:22-23).

Beyond these are numerous gifts and manifestations of the Spirit. Altogether, three major Pauline passages list some twenty such gifts (Rom. 12:6-8; 1 Cor. 12:8-10; Eph. 4:11). These range from *ministry gifts* (or "offices") such as apostles, prophets, evangelists, pastors, and teachers (1 Cor. 12:28; Eph. 4:11) to *services* and *helps* (Rom. 12:6-8), supernatural *manifestations* like wisdom, knowledge, faith, healings, miracles, prophecy, discerning spirits, tongues, and the interpretations of tongues (1 Cor. 12:2-11) *[Speaking in Tongues, p. 319]*. All these are given as the Spirit wills, for the upbuilding of the body of Christ (the church) and the common good of believers (1 Cor. 12:7, 11; Eph. 4:12). Gifts differ according to the needs of the group, but are all manifestations of the same Spirit and are intended to bring about unity and spiritual enrichment. By them the body functions internally and makes it impact on the world about it.

In Acts Here the Holy Spirit continues the work begun in the Gospels, especially as recorded in Luke. Little is said about who the Spirit is or the relationship to the other members of the Godhead. Only 2:33 mentions Father, Son, and Holy Spirit together and that only in connection with the outpouring of the Spirit on the Day of Pentecost (see notes on this verse). The major emphasis in Acts is on the *work* of the Spirit. The apostles are to wait in Jerusalem until they are filled with the Holy Spirit for *witnessing* (1:8). From this time on, the story of this testimony by word and deed makes the Acts the inspired account that it is!

The power of the Holy Spirit is manifest in the remarkable ingathering on the Day of Pentecost (2:41), the creation of a dynamic new community (2:43-46), and the continuing witness of new believers responding daily (2:47). Then the signs and wonders begin. A spectacular healing miracle in the name of Jesus (3:6, 16) is followed by a series of incidents of fearless witness and divine confirmation (3:17—5:42). Seven new leaders emerge, all filled with the Holy Spirit (6:1-6). One of these, *full of faith and the Holy Spirit* (6:5), goes to a martyr's death, testifying powerfully to the Sanhedrin and eventually to the whole world (6:8—7:68). This leads to the second or *Hellenistic* thrust of the new movement.

The Holy Spirit continues to direct the work among the Samaritans in Acts 8 and the conversion and commissioning of the fiery persecutor Saul in chapter 9. Thus the gospel goes beyond Judea to lands of the Hellenistic dispersion. Then, in preparation for the rest of the worldwide mission, the first named Gentile (Cornelius) becomes a believer and is abundantly filled with the Holy Spirit. Even Jerusalem agrees to the genuineness of his experience (10:1—11:18).

This is followed by the founding of the first Jew-Gentile congregation (Antioch of Syria) through the action of the Spirit. This fellowship, with its handful of Spirit-filled leaders, becomes the springboard for a witness that goes on and on through the remainder of the book (11:19-30; 13:1-3). After the Spirit commands the church at Antioch to set apart Barnabas and Saul for their evangelizing work, one missionary journey follows another through Asia Minor, on into Greece, and eventually to Rome (13:4—28:28). Wonder-workings of the Spirit supplemented by inspired messages, the founding of numerous congregations, and courageous witnessing—these all continue to characterize the work to the end. Acts is the story of ever-new divine *action* which produces *faith* and results in a powerful total *witness*.

The Person of the Holy Spirit   The question of just *who* (or what) the Holy Spirit is does not arise as such in the NT, but certain facts are clear. First, the Spirit is *personal*, not just a force, yet beyond our categories of sexuality. In Hebrew, grammatically the word *spirit* is feminine gender. In Greek, *spirit* is neuter gender (but with masculine demonstrative pronoun in John 16:13, likely attracted by 14:26, *the Advocate*, masculine in gender). In English, a pronoun referring to Spirit is rarely used and varies (cf. Acts 11:15, "it," NRSV; "he," NIV. John 16:13, "he," most versions. Rom. 8:16, "himself," NIV, RSV; "itself," KJV; "that very Spirit," NRSV). In any case, grammatical gender is partly arbitrary and does not always match sexual gender (e.g., the neuter *das Mädchen* means the girl). Furthermore, our language for God and the Spirit is metaphorical, using analogies that point beyond themselves. Yet the Spirit's work shows that God's Spirit is in close, intimate, and personal relationship with believers.

As the Spirit of God, bestowed by Jesus (John 20:22c; Acts 2:33), the Holy Spirit embodies all the qualities and powers of the Father and the Son. While there is no discussion of the Trinity in the NT, the basic understandings for such a doctrine are fully present. For example, Paul includes all three in his greeting to the church at Rome when he calls himself "an apostle set apart for the gospel of *God* . . . concerning his *Son* with power according to the *spirit* of holiness" (Rom. 1:1-4). Then he ends 2 Corinthians with the trinitarian benediction, "The grace of our Lord Jesus Christ and the love of God and the fellowship of the Holy Spirit be with you all" (13:13).

More than that, in the NT the Spirit is portrayed as having intellect, emotions, and will, One who speaks (Acts 13:2; Rev. 2:7), intercedes (Rom. 8:26), testifies (Rom. 8:16; John 15:26), leads (Acts 15:28; Rom. 8:14), prophesies (Acts 20:23; 21:11), can be lied to (Acts 5:3-4), blasphemed (Matt. 12:31-32), insulted (Heb. 10:29), and grieved (Eph. 4:30). In short, in the postresurrection period of the NT, the Holy Spirit is the active Presence of the triune God in the *here and now* of Christian individuals and groups (cf. Eph. 3:14-21).

THE KERYGMA   This is an English transliteration of the Greek word meaning "proclamation" or "preaching" and may be pronounced *ke-RIG-ma*. Since the publication of C. H. Dodd's book on *The Apostolic Preaching*, this term has been widely used to indicate the pattern followed by the apostles in preaching the gospel of Christ. By studying the speeches in Acts and comparing them with the way Mark presents the message in his Gospel, Dodd and others have discovered the following major points in the kerygma (examples from the speeches in Acts given in parentheses):

1. *All that has been foretold about the Christ (Messiah) in the OT Scrip-*

tures has come to pass (2:14-36; 3:13, 24; 9:22; cf. 17:11: they searched the Scriptures to see if these things were so). John the Baptist was the herald of this fulfillment and so was sometimes mentioned in the kerygma (10:37; 13:24-25).

2. *Christ has come, performing mighty deeds that eventually led to the cross and resurrection* (2:14-36; 3:13-26; 4:10-12; 5:30-32; 10:36). This is the heart of the kerygma. Details of the preaching and teaching of Jesus are omitted, as in all the ancient creeds.

3. *The apostles are witnesses of these events, proving that they are true* (2:32; 3:15; 5:32; 10:39, 41; 13:31; 26:16, 22).

4. *Jesus is now Lord and Christ, raised to God's right hand, as evidenced by the resurrection and the outpouring of the Holy Spirit* (2:17-18, 32-36; 5:31-32; cf. Rom. 1:4; 2 Cor. 1:22; 5:5).

5. *An appeal to "repent and be baptized"* (2:38; 3:19; 5:31; 10:43; 13:38-39; 17:30; 26:18, 20).

Along with this general pattern, there are also key passages from the OT, largely from the Psalms and the prophets, which foretold the sufferings and exaltations of the Anointed One. These are called *testimonia*, selections from the Scriptures, stored up in memory or circulated in separate written form, and used to show that all that happens in the gospel story is according to God's plan.

The importance of all this is that there are embedded in Acts, especially in the speeches, genuine memories and interpretations of the meaning of the gospel of Jesus. This structure takes us behind the scenes of the witness of the early apostles and strengthens our faith in the reliability of their message. It also provides us with valuable summaries of their preaching and teaching as a guide for our own presentations today.

LUKE AND THE JEWISH LAW   Until recent years most commentators did not think the question of Jewish law was important to Luke. It was usually regarded as something in the background that emerged only as an occasional historical touch in the story. Now, however, since the publication of Jacob Jervell's *Luke and the People of God*, there has been a new look at the importance of the law in Luke-Acts and a growing consensus among scholars who see Lucan theology as fundamentally Mosaic. Jervell's theories have been subjected to careful critique by Blomberg, Wilson, and others. Now, with some variations, a fairly balanced understanding of Luke's view of law has emerged.

After pointing up several key expressions for law that are unique or almost so in Luke-Acts, Jervell characterizes the author's view as being complex but near to that of Hellenistic Judaism of the day. For Luke, the law given to Israel on Sinai, primarily the ritual and ceremonial features, distinguish Jew from Gentile (136f.). The heart of it is circumcision (Acts 15:1, 5; 16:3). The primitive church in Jerusalem adhered to the law, especially seen in their allegiance to the temple (2:26; 3:1-16; chaps. 6—7). This was already anticipated in Luke 1—2 in the accounts of ritual purity on the part of the families of John and Jesus. Unlike the other Synoptists, Luke avoids all criticism of the law by Jesus, regarding it as permanently valid. In Acts, Peter's observance of *clean* and *unclean* is noted (10:13-15, 28; 11:3), and eight times Christians are defended against charges of unbelieving Jews that they are violating the law (6:11, 13, 14; 18:13; 21:21, 28; 25:8; 28:17).

Luke is especially concerned to show faithfulness to the law on the part of Paul. In Paul's later account of his own conversion, Ananias, who ministered to him, is described as a *devout man according to the law and well spoken of by all the Jews there* (22:12). Paul himself can tell the Sanhedrin that from earliest times, both as a Jew and as a Christian, *I have lived my life with a clear conscience before God,* meaning that he has kept the whole law (23:1). In 18:18 Paul had his hair cut to engage in a temporary Nazarite vow, and in Jerusalem he consecrates himself along with four fellow Jews (21:26-27). Then chapters 21—25 and 28 highlight Paul's relation to the law. He is depicted as the great missionary among Jews. In every synagogue in the diaspora, he gathers faithful and penitent Israel and teaches them to adhere to circumcision and the law. In the final chapters, he is still the pious Pharisee observant of the law to the very end.

Luke's purpose in all this is clear. By insisting on Jewish Christians' universal adherence to the law, he shows that they are the restored and true Israel, entitled to God's promises and to salvation. Yet salvation comes not from the observance of the law, for both Jew and Gentile can be saved only *through the grace of the Lord Jesus* (15:11). More than that, Paul says, *By this Jesus everyone who believes is set free from all those sins from which you could not be freed by the law of Moses* (13:39). Thus Christians of Gentile background can be received into the church with only a minimum of restrictions, abstention in those matters particularly offensive to Jews (15:20, 29). They participate in Israel's salvation (Luke 2:30-32; Acts 3:25; 13:47; 15:14-17), joining Israel as an associate people. The latter action is in complete accordance with the law, as James proves by Scripture at the close of the Jerusalem council.

The salvation of Gentiles in Luke-Acts then illustrates what Blomberg calls Luke's most important understanding of the law (70-71): it is preeminently *prophecy* about the coming Christ and, as such, remains an eternal authority. Thus to his followers, the risen Lord interprets both the Law and the Prophets as pointing toward himself (Luke 24:25-27, 44), and the apostles continue to preach to both Jews and Gentiles (3:18-22; 8:32-35; 10:43; 13:26-43).

THE NAME OF JESUS   In the OT the *name* of God was sacred and became even more sacred between the testaments. The name stood for the person and must always be regarded as holy, never to be taken in vain (Exod. 20:7; Deut. 5: 11). Moses came to Egypt to speak in the name of Yahweh (Exod. 5:23), and in that holy name performed his mighty works. From that time forward, priests were to use that name in blessing (Deut. 10:8).

In the NT the same reverence for and powerful use of the *name* were continued, first the name of God and then, among the Christians, the name of Jesus, their Lord. According to the Gospels, Jesus himself encouraged this use. He spoke of believers gathering in his name (Matt. 18:20), receiving a child in his name (Matt. 18:5; Mark 9:37; Luke 9:48), and performing many mighty works in his name (Mark 9:39). And in *John,* Jesus is quoted as more than once urging his disciples to *pray* in his name (14:13-14; 15:7; cf. 16:23-24: Jesus is speaking of a transition time after his departure when believers will *ask anything* in his name).

In *Acts,* the reliance on the name of Jesus is rather fully developed, especially in the early chapters. Since the name stands for the totality of the risen

Lord, the apostles, after being filled with the Holy Spirit, work miracles in the name of Jesus (3:6; 4:10, 17, 30) and testify powerfully in his name (4:17-18; 5:28; 9:27). The risen Lord defines Paul's whole mission, *to bring my name before Gentiles and kings and before the people of Israel* (9:15). Most remarkable is the fact that even opponents of the faith speak of the apostles' powerful witness as made *in this name* (4:17-18; 5:28), and imitators of the Way use the name of Jesus in their attempt to cast out demons! (19:13-16). Throughout the whole history, true witnesses are happy to suffer for the name of Jesus (5:41; cf. Rom. 5:3; Phil. 1:18-19; 1 Thess. 1:6; 1 Pet. 4:13-16). Since the name of Jesus represents his whole person and redemptive power, there is salvation in *no other name* (4:12). *Everyone who calls on the name of the Lord will be saved* (2:21, quoting Joel 2:32 and applying "Lord" to Jesus). Christians are described as those who call upon the name of Jesus (9:14, 21). Baptism is in his name (2:38; 8:16; 10:48; 19:5), and in his name comes the forgiveness of sins (10:43). As a result, when works are performed in the name of Jesus and people come to belief and salvation in him, then his name is *praised* (19:17) or *magnified* (KJV).

SPEAKING IN TONGUES For the experience of speaking in other languages by the power of the Holy Spirit as recorded in Acts, see the notes on 2:1-13; 8:17-19; 10:44-46; and 19:6; with accompanying TBC and TLC. How does this relate to the total picture of tongues-speaking in the NT?

In the first place, it is quite clear that the *tongues* described in Acts 2:1-13 are other human languages and identified as such by those who heard them (2:8-11). Some scholars have suggested that it is a miracle of *hearing* rather than actual speaking in languages the people had never learned. Yet the plain meaning of *began to speak in other languages* before anyone ever hears them shows that it is indeed a miracle of *speaking* as the Spirit gives them utterance (2:4).

Acts 10:46 makes no mention of the particular language or languages spoken by Cornelius and his household. But Peter states that they *have received the Holy Spirit just as we have* (10:47) and that *the Holy Spirit fell upon them just as it had on us at the beginning* (11:15). This suggests that the Cornelius group also speaks other human languages. The fact that other languages are unnecessary for communication in the case of Cornelius is beside the point. That was also the situation in 2:1-10, as the notes on that passage show. Acts 8:18 and 19:6 give little detail, but Luke likely intends for the reader to understand a phenomenon similar to the one at Pentecost.

Yet there is an element in the Acts 2 event that must not be overlooked—the *emotional quality* of their experience. The scoffers describe the actions of these Galileans filled with the Spirit as a kind of intoxication (2:13). This is similar to outsiders who would call tongues-speaking Corinthians "mad" (1 Cor. 14:23, RSV). There must be a joyous freedom about the behavior of the Spirit-filled Christians of Acts 2. It is found again in Samaria (Acts 8:18, where Simon somehow *saw* that the Spirit was given) and recognized at once by Peter in the spontaneous response of Cornelius and his people. All these situations are not too different from the exuberance of the later believers at Corinth.

The gift of tongues described in 1 Corinthians 12 and 14 is one of nine listed as "manifestations of the Spirit" (12:7, 10). The emphasis is on unity, since one Spirit gives them all. The great central gift, then, is the Holy Spirit who, in turn, bestows the various workings or sub-gifts. One of these is "tongues." This gift is apparently not so much the ability to speak other human languages, for in this case an interpreter is necessary (14:5c, 13, 27-30). It is primarily a speaking to God, uttering mysteries which no human can understand (14:2) and at the same time edifying the one exercising it (14:4). Yet it is also a sign to unbelievers that the Holy Spirit is really at work in the group (14:22a). Such tongues-speaking is not to be forbidden (14:39b). In fact, Paul would like for everyone to have and exercise this gift (14:5a), something that he himself does even more than they (14:18).

In 1 Corinthians 14:19, Paul makes a statement that shows that there are really two principal exercises of this type of tongues, one in *private* and the other as a *public* act of worship. He says that he speaks in tongues more than his readers do, yet adds the comment, "Nevertheless, in church I would rather speak five words with my mind, in order to instruct others also, than ten thousand words in a tongue." The private use of tongues is mentioned here and possibly in Ephesians 6:18. There Paul says, "Pray at all times in the Spirit." Today this is often referred to as a "private prayer language." As a result, since others do not normally hear these private utterances, it is the *public* expression of the gift that is usually meant when people discuss glossolalia or talking in tongues.

Because public tongues are in unintelligible syllables, they need to be interpreted for others to receive benefit (1 Cor. 14:5c, 13, 27-30). Thus a separate manifestation or gift, *the interpretation of tongues*, is listed (12:10d, 30c). The Spirit, who knows both the heavenly language and that of humans (cf. Rom. 8:27), puts the meaning of the tongue in the mind of the interpreter. This interpreter may be the one who speaks in the tongue (1 Cor. 14:13), or, more frequently, another person (12: 10; 14:27-30). Then, once the message of the tongue is interpreted, it becomes like a *prophecy* (the implication in 14:5b), with all the edifying and convicting power of that kind of ministry (14:24-25). Genuine tongues-speaking may also have the added benefit of demonstrating the Spirit's presence beyond mere human thought or wisdom (possibly the reason why it can be a "sign" to outsiders, as in 14:22a).

Speaking in other human languages is one form of the gift of tongues (primarily in Acts), and private and public manifestations of tongues are two more forms. Yet a *fourth* expression may be seen in *singing in tongues*. This is likely what Paul means when he says that he will "sing praise with the spirit" (in contrast to singing "with the mind" (14:15). Examples of this are common in groups today who emphasize "charismatic" gifts of the Spirit (although in 1 Cor. 12:4, Paul counts all the gifts of the Spirit as *charismata*).

It will be seen from the larger context of 1 Corinthians 12 and 14 that, while Paul values and even encourages the exercise of "tongues," it is not for him the highest of the manifestations of the Spirit. He specifically subordinates it to the gift of prophecy (14:1-5). Tongues-speaking should not be forbidden, but it should not dominate. One, two, or at most three such expressions are enough for one meeting, and then always one at a time and with an interpreter (14:26-33). As with all the gifts, it is given for "the common good" (12:7b), that is, for the upbuilding of the church, never to cause confusion or division (14:1-12). Let everything therefore be done in an orderly fashion (14:26-33), making possible the "more excellent way" (12:31) of agape-love (chap. 13).

WITNESS IN ACTS As noted in the notes on 1:8 and found in all the chapter headings of this commentary from part 3 onward, the story of Acts is primarily one of *witnessing*. The threefold meaning of *witness* is outlined near the end of part 1 under TLC. Here we want to explore the many-faceted *character* of that witess as found throughout the book.

First, it is the *witness of ordinary people*. There are hardy Galilean fishermen, a hated tax collector, a passionate revolutionary, a traitorous Judean, several women cured of their ailments and rid of their demons—not a promising lot to start a world movement! Yet they are persons who have been involved in extraordinary experiences that have transformed their lives and made them ready.

Yes, they have all been changed by the *impact of Jesus*, another characteristic of their witness. Their reactions vary, all the way from skepticism and slowness to roller-coaster highs and lows midst occasional moments of deep insight. In it all, however, new life and hope emerge.

Then they experience the most important preparation for witness as they are *baptized in the Holy Spirit*. (For details, see part 2 of the commentary, on the Day of Pentecost and the essay on the Holy Spirit in the Bible and in Acts.) This infilling provides the *motivation* for witnessing. As Peter and John tell the Sanhedrin, *We cannot keep from speaking about what we have seen and heard* (4:20). God has commanded them to witness, and they do so because, as they say, *We must obey God rather than any human authority* (5:29; cf. also 5:42; 8:4, 26-27, 40; 11:19-21, 24; 13:2-3). Moreover, they are given a *divine power* by the Spirit (1:8). As Luke puts it, *With great power the apostles gave their testimony to the resurrection of the Lord Jesus* (4:33; cf. 6:8; 10:38). Their testimony is so wisely guided that it finds its mark. The opponents of the divinely filled Stephen *could not withstand the wisdom and the Spirit with which he spoke* (6:10; cf. 4:8-10; 9:17, 22; 13:9-12).

Along with all this, the witness of Christ's people in Acts is *based on Scripture*, the Word of God which we know as the OT. This began with Jesus himself. To explain his death and resurrection, "he opened their minds to understand the scriptures" (Luke 24:45). So his disciples continue to use the OT to prove that Jesus is the Christ (Acts 2:25-28, 31, 34-35; 4:11; 8:32-33; 13:33-35), to warn listeners against rejection and judgment (13:41; 28:26-27), and to call people to repentance (Acts 3:22-23, 25). Altogether, well over 50 OT verses are thus quoted to proclaim the messianic age and urge others to enter it (Trites: 82).

The fact that the witness is *community-based* is another important characteristic. Even before Pentecost, the 120 find strength from meeting together in the *upper room* (1:13-26). Then after a powerful infilling of the Holy Spirit, the community springs into action as it witnesses through the joyous sharing of goods and services to everyone in need. It manifests such praise, joyous good will, and miracle-working that all Jerusalem is shaken (2:44-47; 4:32-35; 5:12-16; cf. 5:28). Signs and wonders accompany this movement as it spreads out over the Roman world (6:8; 8:6, 13; 14:3; 15:12; 16:18; 19:11-12). At Antioch of Syria, the first Jew-Gentile fellowship is started (11:19-26), and this becomes the base for the ongoing missionary endeavors of Paul (Acts 13—19). These are not isolated individuals witnessing for the Lord but strong communities of the Holy Spirit which make an impact upon their contemporaries far out of proportion to their numbers.

Still another aspect of this witness is the *boldness* of the persons giving it. Luke frequently uses the noun *parrēsia* and its related verbal and adverbial forms to characterize the witness of the early Christians. The basic meaning is "forthrightness" or "outspokenness," both marks of boldness. On one occasion they prayed specifically for this quality and, as a result, the place was shaken and *they were all filled with the Holy Spirit and spoke the work of God with boldness* (4:31).

With such outspokenness, Peter and John answer the authorities (4:13), the new convert Saul witnesses for Christ in Damascus (9:27-28), Paul and Barnabas answer their opponents at Antioch of Pisidia (13:46), the same two stay in trouble-filled Iconium speaking for the Lord (14:3), and for three months Paul preaches the word in the synagogue at Ephesus (19:8). On this same note of *parrhēsia*, Acts ends as it tells how Paul goes on *proclaiming the kingdom of God and teaching about the Lord Jesus Christ with all **boldness** and without hindrance* (28:31). Even where this word is not used, it is implied in many situations of witnessing by *word* (2:23; 4:19-20; 5:20-32; 7:2-60; 8:20-24; 9:20; 13:9; 16:37; 23:3) and *deed* (9:17; 13:51a). The Christians in Acts are not timid, fearful somebodies. They are bold, resolute evangelists, proclaiming the gospel to all who will listen.

Along with this boldness is the fact that the witness of the Christians in Acts is a *convincing* one. With the guidance of the Holy Spirit, they appeal to the consciences of those about them. Their message both by word and by dead is a life-transforming one. They witness not only to the bare details of the life, death, and resurrection of Jesus but also to the life-and-death significance of these events (2:32; 3:15; 10:36-43). They see in Christ the saving act of God for all who will believe. Their passion for both the temporal welfare and eternal salvation of such people gives burning significance to their message. That is why, in response to Peter's forthright appeal, the hearers are *cut to the heart* and cry out, *What should we do?* (2:37). In similar fashion, the Christian witnesses of Acts go forth, enduring all manner of hardship and persecution for Jesus, rejoicing that they are *considered worthy to suffer dishonor* for him (5:41). Thus the story proceeds to the end of the book, full of daring adventures and effective testimony for the Lord: Peter and other apostles (chapters 3—5), Stephen (6—7), Philip (8), Saul (9:19b-30), Peter again (10—12), and Paul and his associates (13—28).

Such Holy Spirit-filled, impassioned expression produces an *enduring witness*. The Christians of Acts make a permanent impact upon their world. From the original 120 and the converts on Pentecost arises a church that soon numbers *about 5,000 males* (4:4, CF from Greek), and two and a half decades later it is still spoken of in terms of *many thousands* (21:20). From unnamed Christian refugees comes the church at Antioch which, as noted above, serves as a home base for all of Paul's missionary journeys. Other congregations also spring up in Asia Minor, Macedonia, and Greece as the powerful witness continues, each with an impact beyond anything recorded in Acts.

Finally, this witness is remembered, recorded, and thus *preserved* for multiplied millions of Christians in succeeding generations, including us today, in the book we are studying. In terms of the sheer numbers inspired and instructed by the witness, this is the most impressive of all its characteristics.

Palestine in New Testament Times

+ Means city has uncertain location

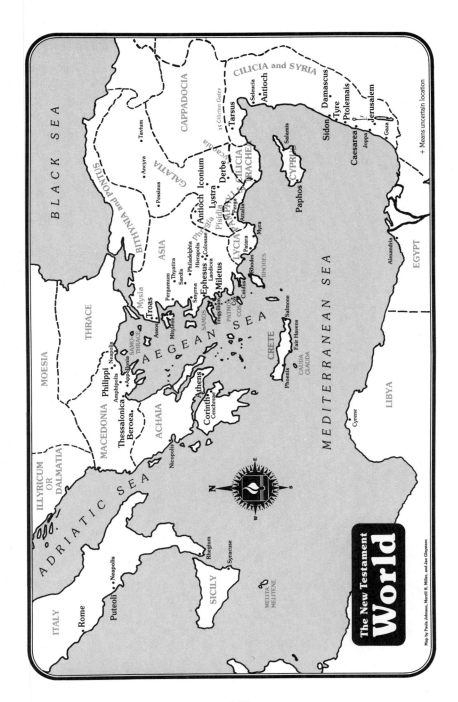

BLACK SEA

CAPPADOCIA

CILICIA and SYRIA

x Cilician Gates

Seleucia
Antioch
Tarsus

Damascus
Tyre
Ptolemais
Jerusalem
Gaza

Sidon
Caesarea
Joppa

+ Means uncertain location

Tavium

GALATIA

BITHYNIA and PONTUS

Ancyra

Pessinus

Antioch
Pisidia
Iconium
Lystra
Derbe

PAMPHYLIA

Pho
Perga
Attalia

LYCIA

CILICIA
TRACHE

CYPRUS

Salamis

Paphos

ASIA

Pergamum
Sardis
Thyatira
Philadelphia
Hierapolis
Colossae
Laodicea

Smyrna

Ephesus
Miletus

Cnidus
Cos

Myra
Patara
Rhodes

RHODES

Mysia

Troas

Assos

Mitylene

SAMOS

Trogyllium
PATMOS

COS

AEGEAN SEA

Salmone

CRETE

Fair Havens

Phoenix
CAUDA
CLAUDA

MEDITERRANEAN SEA

Alexandria

EGYPT

THRACE

MOESIA

SAMO-
THRACE

Neapolis
Philippi
Amphipolis
Apollonia
Appollonia
Thessalonica
Beroea

MACEDONIA

Athens
Corinth
Cenchreae

ACHAIA

Nicopolis

LIBYA

Cyrene

ILLYRICUM
OR
DALMATIA

ADRIATIC SEA

Rhegium
Syracuse

ITALY

Rome

Puteoli
Neapolis

SICILY

MELITA
MELITENE

N
E
S
W

The New Testament
World

Map by Paula Johnson, Merrill R. Miller, and Jan Glaysteen

325

Bibliography

(The Bibliography contains three alphabetical lists. Check second and third group if cited source is not in the first section.)

Studies Pertaining to Luke-Acts

ABD
    1992   *The Anchor Bible Dictionary*. 6 vols. New York: Doubleday.
Barclay, William
    1953   *The Acts of the Apostles* (Daily Study Bible). Philadelphia: Westminster, 1953.
Blomberg, Craig L.
    1984   "The Law in Luke-Acts." *Journal for the Study of the New Testament* 22:53-80.
Bruce, F. F.
    1954   *The Book of Acts* (The New International Commentary on the New Testament). Grand Rapids: Eerdmans.
Cadbury, H. J., and Kirsopp Lake
    1933   *Beginnings of Christianity*. Ed. by F. J. Foakes Jackson and Kirsopp Lake. Vols. 4-5. London: Macmillan; Grand Rapids: Baker Book House, 1965-66.
Cassidy, Richard J.
    1987   *Society and Politics in the Acts of the Apostles*. Maryknoll. New York: Orbis Books.
Conzelmann, Hans
    1987   *Acts* (Hermeneia). Minneapolis: Augsburg Fortress.
Dibelius, Martin
    1956   *Studies in Acts of the Apostles*. Trans. by Mary Ling and Paul Schubert. New York: Charles Scribner's Sons.
Dodd, C. H.
    1962   *The Apostolic Preaching and Its Developments*. New York: Harper and Bros.
Easton, Burton S.
    1954   *Early Christianity: The Purpose of Acts and Other Papers*. Ed. by Frederick C. Grant. Greenwich, Conn.: Seabury Press.
Faw, Chalmer E.
    1974   *When the Way Is New*. Elgin, Ill.: The Brethren Press.
Haenchen, Ernst
    1971   *The Acts of the Apostles*. Philadelphia: Westminster.
Hemer, Colin J.
    1989   *The Book of Acts in the Setting of Hellenistic History*. Ed. by Conrad H. Gempf. WUNT, 49. Tübingen: J. C. B. Mohr.

Hull, J. H. E.
1967   *The Holy Spirit in the Acts of the Apostles.* London: Lutterworth.
Jackson, F. J. Foakes
1931   *The Acts of the Apostles* (Moffatt Commentaries). New York: Harper & Row.
_____. *See* Cadbury
Jeremias, Joachim
1969   *Jerusalem in the Time of Jesus.* Philadelphia: Fortress.
Jervell, Jacob
1972   *Luke and the People of God.* Minneapolis: Augsburg.
Juel, Donald
1983   *Luke-Acts, The Promise of History.* Atlanta: John Knox.
Kee, Howard C.
1990   *Good News to the Ends of the Earth: The Theology of Acts.* Philadelphia: Trinity Press.
Knox, W. C.
1948   *The Acts of the Apostles.* Cambridge: University Press.
Lake, Kirsopp. *See* Cadbury
Lenski, R. C. H.
1934   *The Interpretation of the Acts of the Apostles.* Columbus, Ohio: Lutheran Book Concern.
McBride, Alfred
1975   *The Gospel of the Holy Spirit.* New York: Hawthorn Books.
Macgregor, G. H. C.
1951   *Acts* (in Interpreter's Bible, 9). New York: Abingdon-Cokesbury.
Marshall, I. Howard
1980   *The Acts of the Apostles* (Tyndale New Testament Commentaries). Grand Rapids: Eerdmans.
May, Herbert G., ed., with R. W. Hamilton and G. N. S. Hunt
1962   *Oxford Bible Atlas.* London: Oxford University Press.
Metzger, Bruce M., et al.
1971   *A Textual Commentary on the Greek New Testament.* New York: United Bible Societies.
Munck, Johannes
1967   *The Acts of the Apostles* (The Anchor Bible). Garden City, N.Y.: Doubleday & Co., Inc.
1977   *Paul and the Salvation of Mankind.* Atlanta: John Knox.
Neill, William
1973   *The Acts of the Apostles.* Greenwood, S.C.: Attic Press.
Ogilvie, Lloyd J.
1976   *Drumbeat of Love.* Waco, Tex.: Word Books.
Pilgrim, Walter B.
1981   *Good News to the Poor: Wealth and Poverty in Luke-Acts.* Minneapolis: Augsburg.
Rackham, R. B.
1902   *The Acts of the Apostles* (Westminster Commentaries). London: Methuen & Co.
Ramsay, William
1896   *St. Paul the Traveler and the Roman Citizen.* New York: Putnams.
1907   *Cities of St. Paul.* New York: Doran.

Rea, John
    1972   *Layman's Commentary on the Holy Spirit.* Plainfield, N.J.: Logos.
Rowley, H. H.
    1952   *The Zadokite Fragments and the Dead Sea Scrolls.* New York: The Macmillan Co.
Swartley, Willard M.
    1981   *Mark: The Way for All Nations.* Scottdale, Pa.: Herald Press.
Tannehill, Robert C.
    1986   *The Narrative Unity of Luke-Acts: A Literary Interpretation.* Vol. 1: *The Gospel According to Luke.* Philadelphia: Fortress Press, 1986. Vol. 2: *The Acts of the Apostles.* Minneapolis: Augsburg Fortress, 1990.
TDNT
    1968   *Theological Dictionary of the New Testament.* Ed. by G. Friedrich. Tr. by G. W. Bromiley. Vol. 6. Grand Rapids: Eerdmans.
Tiede, David L.
    1980   *Prophecy and History in Luke-Acts.* Philadelphia: Fortress Press.
Trites, Allison A.
    1983   *New Testament Witness in Today's World.* Valley Forge: Judson Press.
Viviano, Benedict T., and Justin Taylor
    1992   "Sadducees, Angels, and Resurrection (Acts 23:8-9)." *Journal of Biblical Literature* 111: 496-498.
Williams, C. S. C.
    1957   *The Acts of the Apostles* (Harper's New Testament Commentaries). New York: Harper and Bros.
Willimon, William H.
    1988   *Acts* (Interpretation). Louisville: Westminster John Knox.
Wilson, S. G.
    1984   *Luke and the Law.* Cambridge: University Press.
Winn, Albert C.
    1960   *The Acts of the Apostles* (The Layman's Bible Commentary). Richmond: John Knox.

Ancient Writings Cited

Aeschylus, *Eumenides*

Apocrypha

Apostolic Fathers, The

Chrysostom, John, *Homilies*

Cleanthus, *Hymns to Zeus*

Code of Justinian

Dead Sea Scrolls

Demosthenes, *Orations*

Didache, The Teaching of the Apostles

Eusebius, *Ecclesiastical History*

Irenaeus, *Against Heresies*

Josephus, Flavius (citations follow the Whiston edition)

Against Apion

Ant.: *Antiquities of the Jews*

Autobiography

War: *Jewish War*

Justin Martyr, *Apology*

Mishnah tractates, Nedarim and Sota

NT: New Testament

OT: Old Testament

Ovid, *Metamorphoses*

Pseudepigrapha

Suetonius, *Life of Claudius*

Tacitus, *Annals*

Tertullian, *To the Martyrs*

Books Relating to the Believers Church

Armour, Rollin S.
    1966   *Anabaptist Baptism, A Representative Study.* Scottdale: Herald
           Press.
Arnold, Eberhard
    1973   *A Testimony of Church Community from His Life and Writings.*
           Farmington, Pa.: Plough Press.
Bauman, Harold E.
    1989   *Presence and Power: Releasing the Holy Spirit in Your Life and
           Church.* Scottdale: Herald Press.
BE
    1983   *The Brethren Encyclopedia.* Ed. by Donald F. Durnbaugh. 3 vols.
           Elgin: Brethren Press.
Bender, Harold, ed.
    1958   *The Recovery of the Anabaptist Vision.* Especially John C.
           Wenger's "The Biblicism of the Anabaptists." Scottdale, Pa.:
           Herald Press.
Braght, Thieleman J. van
    1950   *The Bloody Theater or Martyrs Mirror of the Defenseless Chris-
           tians.* Trans. by Joseph Sohm from the 1660 Dutch ed. Scottdale:
           Herald Press.
Brumbaugh, Martin G.
    1906   *A History of the German Baptist Brethren in Europe and Amer-
           ica.* Elgin: Brethren Publishing House.
Durnbaugh, Donald F.
    1967   *The Brethren in Colonial America.* Elgin: Brethren Press.

Durnbaugh, Donald F., ed.
   1968   *The Believers' Church: The History and Character of Radical
          Protestantism.* New York: Macmillan; Scottdale, Pa.: Herald
          Press, 1985.
Friedmann, Robert
   1973   *The Theology of Anabaptism.* Scottdale: Herald Press.
Klassen, Peter J.
   1964   *The Economics of Anabaptism 1525-1560.* The Hague: Mouten
          & Co.
Kraus, C. Norman
   1974   *The Community of the Spirit.* Grand Rapids: Eerdmans; Scott-
          dale, Pa.: Herald Press, 1993.
   1979   *The Authentic Witness.* Grand Rapids: Eerdmans.
Lehn, Cornelia
   1980   *Peace Be with You.* Newton, Kan.: Faith & Life Press.
Mack, Alexander, Sr.
   1939   *Rites and Ordinances* and *Ground-Searching Questions.* (New
          trans.) Ashland, Ohio: Brethren Publishing House.
ME
   1955   *The Mennonite Encyclopedia.* Vols. 1-4, ed. by C. Krahn, 1955-
          59; vol. 5, ed. by C. J. Dyck, 1990. Scottdale, Pa.: Herald Press.
Penn-Lewis, Jessie
   1973   *War on the Saints.* New York: Thomas E. Lowe.
Radical Reformation Reader
   1971   *Concern,* no. 18. Scottdale, Pa.: Donald Reist.
Simons, Menno
   1956   *The Complete Writings of Menno Simons.* Ed. by John C.
          Wenger. Scottdale, Pa.: Herald Press.

Recommended Resources for Personal and Group Study

Barclay, William. *The Acts of the Apostles* (Daily Study Bible). Philadelphia: Westminster, 1953. Brief but strong on exposition and practical application. Rewarding for teachers and ministers.

Bruce, F. F. *The Book of Acts* (The New International Commentary on the New Testament). Grand Rapids: Eerdmans, 1954. A classic, valuable for careful study, citing primary sources and dealing with details of Acts from an evangelical viewpoint.

Faw, Chalmer E. *When the Way Is New*. Elgin, Ill.: The Brethren Press, 1974. Presents thirteen introductory lessons on the vast sweep of the Christian movement represented in Acts. Valuable for giving an overall perspective.

Haenchen, Ernst. *The Acts of the Apostles*. Philadelphia: Westminster, 1971. A critical commentary, with German scholarship and historical insights. Recommended for the mature to read along with other sources. Stimulating, forcing careful examination of the text.

Marshall, I. Howard. *The Acts of the Apostles* (Tyndale New Testament Commentaries). Grand Rapids: Eerdmans, 1980. A companion volume to Bruce, dealing insightfully with details of the original historical situation. Valuable for the serious student.

McBride, Alfred. *The Gospel of the Holy Spirit*. New York: Hawthorn Books, 1975. Retells the story in vivid narrative style, revealing a worldview excitingly relevant today. An excellent introduction to the book.

Neill, William. *The Acts of the Apostles*. Greenwood, S.C.: Attic Press, 1973. Compact, scholarly commentary, useful for its notes.

Ogilvie, Lloyd J. *Drumbeat of Love*. Waco, Tex.: Word Books, 1976. Marches through Acts with inspiring and stimulating thoughts. A delightful resource for all Christians and especially those who teach or preach.

Tannehill, Robert C. *The Narrative Unity of Luke-Acts*. 2 volumes. Philadelphia/Minneapolis: Augsburg Fortress, 1986-90. Opens up the whole new world of interweaving themes and literary motifs, a rewarding way of examining Luke's literary artistry and of gaining insights into the meanings.

Trites, Allison A. *New Testament Witness in Today's World*. Valley Forge: Judson Press, 1983. Exciting and well worth reading for an understanding of witness today.

Willimon, William H. *Acts* (Interpretation). New York: Harper and Bros., 1957. For the minister and theologian who wrestle with the book's essential messages. Rewarding stimulation on an advanced level.

Winn, Albert C. *Acts of the Apostles* (Layman's Bible Commentary). Richmond: John Knox, 1960. Provides a concise, scholarly but readable, paragraph-by-paragraph treatment. Good as an introductory study.

The Author

© Laurel Kenney — McPherson, Kansas

Chalmer Faw was born in Yakima, Washington. He received his B.A. degree from La Verne (Calif.) College in 1932, his B.D. from Bethany Biblical Seminary of Chicago in 1936, and his Ph.D. in biblical studies from the University of Chicago in 1939. In 1963 and 1964 he spent a year in postdoctoral studies at Marburg University.

Chalmer and his wife, Mary, served from 1940 to 1944 as missionaries to northeastern Nigeria, involved in village evangelism. From 1945 to 1965 he taught New Testament at Bethany Theological Seminary and became a full professor. He has served as a mentor to several generations of Bible students and church leaders.

Faw has written several other books, such as *A Guide to Biblical Preaching* (1962), *When the Way Is New* (1973), and *Our Heritage 1886-1986: History of the Church of the Brethren* (1986). Many of his articles have been published in church periodicals and scholarly journals, and he has held memberships in the Chicago Society of Biblical Research and the Society of Biblical Literature.

After their five children were grown and married, the Faws returned to Nigeria in 1965 and helped train indigenous leaders until 1976. They were involved in the Holy Spirit renewal movement in Nigeria. After their return to the United States, they engaged in an extensive traveling ministry of spiritual life renewal. In 1988 Faws settled at McPherson, Kansas, where Chalmer is a member of the local Church of the Brethren, a Bible teacher, and a freelance writer.

HELLENISTIC PHILOSOPHY

HELLENISTIC PHILOSOPHY

STOICS, EPICUREANS, SCEPTICS

A. A. Long

Second Edition

University of California Press

Berkeley and Los Angeles

Second edition 1986
University of California Press
Berkeley and Los Angeles

© 1974, 1986 A. A. Long

ISBN 0-520-05807-0 cloth
ISBN 0-520-05808-9 paper

Library of Congress Catalog Card Number 86-040066

Printed in Great Britain

Contents

Preface to the First Edition

THE purpose of this book is to trace the main developments in Greek philosophy during the period which runs from the death of Alexander the Great in 323 B.C. to the end of the Roman Republic (31 B.C.). These three centuries, known to us as the Hellenistic Age, witnessed a vast expansion of Greek civilization eastwards, following Alexander's conquests; and later, Greek civilization penetrated deeply into the western Mediterranean world assisted by the political conquerors of Greece, the Romans. But philosophy throughout this time remained a predominantly Greek activity. The most influential thinkers in the Hellenistic world were Stoics, Epicureans and Sceptics. In this book I have tried to give a concise critical analysis of their ideas and their methods of thought.

As far as I am aware, the last book in English to cover this ground was written sixty years ago. In the interval the subject has moved on, quite rapidly since the last war, but most of the best work is highly specialized. There is a clear need for a general appraisal of Hellenistic philosophy which can provide those who are not specialists with an up-to-date account of the subject. Hellenistic philosophy is often regarded as a dull product of second-rate thinkers who are unable to stand comparison with Plato and Aristotle. I hope that this book will help to remove such misconceptions and arouse wider interest in a field which is fascinating both historically and conceptually.

One reason for the misunderstanding from which Hellenistic philosophy has suffered is the scarcity of primary evidence. Nearly all the writings of the early Stoics have perished, and their theories must be reconstructed from quotations and summaries by later writers. The limitations of evidence are also a problem in dealing with Epicureans and Sceptics. In this book I have devoted little space to the evaluation of sources which technical work on Hellenistic philosophy requires. But the evidence is so scattered and so variable in quality that I have not hesitated to give references in the text for most theories which I attribute to particular philosophers. Many of the subjects which are discussed can be interpreted in different ways. I have not attempted to refer to more than a few divergent opinions, and some of my own conclusions will prove controversial. My aim throughout has been to make the best philosophical sense of the evidence, and at the same time to indicate which theories are most vulnerable to criticism. I have been liberal with quotations and the discussion of details is based wherever possible upon the extracts which I have translated.

The subject which I have treated at greatest length is Stoicism. In giving the Stoics so much space I have been influenced by two considerations: they were, in my judgment, the most important philosophers of the Hellenistic period, and at the present time their thought is less accessible to the general reader than Epicureanism or Scepticism. I have tried to keep conceptual rather than historical issues before the reader's mind in much of the book. But historical background is the main theme of the first chapter, and I have concluded the book with a short survey of the later influence of Hellenistic philosophy, which was extensive. I have also discussed some characteristics of earlier Greek thought which help to explain concepts accepted and rejected by Hellenistic philosophers.

The work of Usener, von Arnim, Brochard, Bailey and Pohlenz is indispensable to anyone who studies Hellenistic philosophy, and I have also learnt much from contemporary scholars. My thanks are also due to my pupils, my colleagues and to those who have given me many opportunities to read papers on the subject at meetings in Britain and other countries. In particular, I have benefited greatly from my membership of University College London where I taught throughout the time this book was being prepared. To George Kerferd, who commented on Chapters 2 and 3, and to Alan Griffiths, who scrutinized the whole typescript, I am especially grateful. Lastly, I thank my wife, Kay, who helped me in more ways than I can indicate with any acknowledgment.

Liverpool, 1973   A.A.L.

Preface to the Second Edition

THIS book was first published in 1974. As I remarked in the original preface, Hellenistic philosophy seemed then to need not only a general appraisal but a substantial rehabilitation. Though well looked after by a few devoted specialists, this period of Greek philosophy, broadly speaking, was depreciated and neglected by comparison with the enormous interest taken in Plato, Aristotle and their predecessors. A decade later, the fortunes of Hellenistic philosophy have changed dramatically. Through publications, seminars and international colloquia, Stoics, Sceptics and Epicureans have been talking to a wider and more discerning audience than at any time since antiquity. Much of the best work in Greek philosophy during these years has been a critical examination of the concepts, arguments and dialectical strategies of the Hellenistic schools; there is every sign, as my Bibliographical Postscript indicates, that this process of recovery and discovery will continue at an intensified rate. The old prejudices seem to have been removed once and for all. New vistas have appeared, and it is already evident that they are altering the perspectives of ancient philosophy and stimulating philosophers in general.

It would be quite impossible to do any justice to all these developments in a book of this size and purpose. I conceived it originally as an introduction, and this is what it remains. The specialist literature has now become so extensive that the book may also, I hope, serve as a suitable orientation for readers who wish to pursue the subject in depth. Rather than attempting the impossible task of revising and amplifying odd pages here and there, it seems best to let the original text stand for the present. The most useful corrective and amplification I can offer at this stage is the Bibliographical Postscript.

Berkeley, California, 1985   A.A.L.

Abbreviations

Acad.	Cicero, *Academica*
Adv. math.	Sextus Empiricus, *Adversus mathematicos* (Against the dogmatic philosophers)
Comm. not.	Plutarch, *De communibus notitiis contra stoicos* (On universal conceptions against the Stoics)
DK	*Die Fragmente der Vorsokratiker*, ed. H. Diels and W. Kranz
D.L.	Diogenes Laertius
De an.	Aristotle, *De anima* (On the soul)
De div.	Cicero, *De divinatione* (On divination)
De nat.	Epicurus, *De natura* (On nature)
De off.	Cicero, *De officiis* (On duties)
E.N.	Aristotle, *Nicomachean ethics*
Ep.	Seneca, *Epistulae morales* (Moral letters)
Ep. Hdt.	Epicurus, *Letter to Herodotus*
Ep. Men.	Epicurus, *Letter to Menoeceus*
Ep. Pyth.	Epicurus, *Letter to Pythocles*
Fin.	Cicero, *De finibus bonorum et malorum* (On the chief things which are good and bad)
K.D.	Epicurus, *Kuriai doxai* (Principal doctrines)
Met.	Aristotle, *Metaphysics*
N.D.	Cicero, *De natura deorum* (On the nature of the gods)
P.H.	Sextus Empiricus, *Pyrrhoneioi hypotyposeis* (Outlines of Pyrrhonism)
Plac.	Galen, *De placitis Hippocratis et Platonis* (On the opinions of Hippocrates and Plato)
R.E.	Pauly-Wissowa, *Real-Enzyklopädie der klassischen Altertumswissenschaft*
Rep.	Cicero, *De republica* (On the state)
Sent. Vat.	Epicurus, *Sententiae Vaticanae* (Epicurean aphorisms from a Vatican manuscript)
Stoic. rep.	Plutarch, *De Stoicorum repugnantiis* (On the contradictions of the Stoics)
SVF	*Stoicorum Veterum Fragmenta* (Fragments of the early Stoics, ed. H. von Arnim)
Tusc.	Cicero, *Tusculan disputations*
Us.	*Epicurea*, ed. H. Usener

CHAPTER ONE

Introduction

SIGNIFICANT stages in the history of philosophy are seldom identifiable with the same precision as political events, but there are good reasons for bringing the new movements of thought which developed in the Greek world at the end of the fourth century B.C. under a single description. Hellenistic is a term which refers to Greek, and later, Graeco-Roman civilization in the period beginning with the death of Alexander the Great (323 B.C.) and ending, by convention, with the victory of Octavian over Mark Antony at the battle of Actium in 31 B.C. During these three centuries it is neither Platonism nor the Peripatetic tradition established by Aristotle which occupied the central place in ancient philosophy, but Stoicism, Scepticism and Epicureanism, all of which were post-Aristotelian developments. These are the movements of thought which define the main lines of philosophy in the Hellenistic world, and 'Hellenistic philosophy' is the expression I use in this book to refer to them collectively. Their influence continued into the Roman empire and later times, but in the first century B.C. Platonism began a long revival and an interest in Aristotle's technical writings was also re-awakened. The detailed treatment of Hellenistic philosophy in this book comes to an end with these developments. They are both a cause and a symptom of an eclectic stage in Greek and Roman thought, during which the Hellenistic systems become only of secondary importance to the historian of philosophy.

In this introductory chapter our interest is chiefly in the beginning of Hellenistic philosophy, and it is useful to glance initially at the social and political circumstances which provided the framework for intellectual life at this period. Alexander's eastern empire disintegrated in the wars and dynastic struggles which followed his early death. But it prepared the ground for an unparalleled extension of Greek culture. Alexandria in Egypt and Antioch in Syria were Greek foundations, capitals respectively of the Ptolemaic and Seleucid kingdoms secured by two of Alexander's generals. The soldiers, civil servants and businessmen who settled in Asia and Egypt transplanted the social institutions of the Greek mainland. A common culture, modified by different influences in different places, and above all, a common language (the *koinê*), gave them a sense of unity. Alexandria under the Ptolemys became a new centre of arts and sciences, which had such power to attract eminent men of letters and scholars that it outshone Athens in the diversity of its culture. Athens remained pre-eminent in philosophy. But Antioch, Pergamum and Smyrna were other flourishing cities whose rulers competed with one another as patrons of poets, philosophers, historians and scientists.

For about a hundred years it was an age of remarkable intellectual achievement. The extension of the social and political horizon of classical Greece was matched by a widening of interest in subjects such as history and geography. Great advances were made in philology, astronomy and physiology. Learning affected literature, and most of the notable literary figures were scholars. One of the consequences of this scholarly activity was a narrower definition of subject boundaries. Aristotle and his immediate followers took in a very wide range of subjects under 'philosophy', including studies that we would designate scientific or literary or historical. The scope of Hellenistic philosophy is much more limited on the whole. Strato of Lampsachus (died 270/68), one of Aristotle's successors, was a philosopher whose primary interests might be called scientific. Much later, the Stoic Posidonius (died 51/50) made staunch efforts to associate philosophy with history, geography, astronomy and mathematics. But these are exceptions. The special sciences were vigorously studied in our period, but not primarily by leading members of the Hellenistic philosophical schools. In their hands philosophy came to acquire something of its modern connotations, with a division drawn between logic, ethics and general investigation of 'nature'. This distinction between philosophy and science was underlined by place as well as time. The major figures of early Hellenistic philosophy—Epicurus, Zeno, Arcesilaus, and Chrysippus—all migrated to Athens from elsewhere. Those who are most noteworthy for their scientific achievements—Archimedes, Aristarchus, the astronomer, and the medical scientists, Herophilus and Erasistratus, had no strong association that we know of with Athens.

Without Alexander there would have been no Alexandria. Many of the characteristics of the Hellenistic world can undoubtedly be traced to his imperial ambitions and their subsequent effects. Philosophy, so many have said, responded to the unsettled age of the Hellenistic monarchs by turning away from disinterested speculation to the provision of security for the individual. Stoicism has been described as 'a system put together hastily, violently, to meet a bewildered world'.[1] It would certainly be wrong to isolate Stoicism and Epicureanism from their milieu. Epicurus' renunciation of civic life and the Stoics' conception of the world itself as a kind of city may be viewed as two quite different attempts to come to terms with changing social and political circumstances. But many of the characteristics of Hellenistic philosophy were inherited from thinkers who were active before the death of Alexander. The needs of people in the Hellenistic world for a sense of identity and moral guidance can help to explain why Stoicism and Epicureanism rapidly gained adherents at Athens and elsewhere. But the Peloponnesian War a hundred years previously probably caused greater suffering to Greece than Alexander and his successors. Economically, Athens was a prosperous city at the end of the fourth century and new public works absorbed capital and energy. It is difficult to find anything in early Hellenistic philosophy which answers clearly to a *new* sense of bewilderment.

Alexander, it is true, helped to undermine the values which the declining city-states had once so proudly asserted, and Aristotle's ethics assumes as its social context a city-state like Athens. But Diogenes the Cynic was already challenging the basic conventions of classical Greek civic life many years before the death of Alexander. These three men, Alexander, Diogenes and Aristotle, all died within a year or two of each other (325-322), and this is worth mentioning because it emphasizes the need to take account of continuity as well as change in the interpretation of Hellenistic philosophy. The young Alexander was taught in Macedonia by Aristotle, and in later years Alexander, who knew the free-speaking Diogenes, is reputed to have said, 'If I had not been Alexander, I should like to have been Diogenes' (D.L. vi 32). Alexander set out to conquer the external world; Diogenes aimed to show men how to conquer their own fears and desires. Aristotle and Diogenes were contemporaries but they had little else in common. Moralist, iconoclast, preacher, these are descriptions which catch something of Diogenes' posture. He shared none of

[1] E. Bevan, *Stoics and Sceptics* (Oxford 1913) p. 32. Contrast with this kind of explanation L. Edelstein's reference to a 'new consciousness of man's power that arose in the fourth century, the belief in the deification of the human being', which he finds influential on Stoicism and Epicureanism, *The Meaning of Stoicism* (Cambridge, Mass. 1966) p. 13.

Aristotle's interest in logic or metaphysics, and attacked the city-state as an institution by advocating an ascetic life based upon 'human nature', the rationality of which was at variance, he argued, with the practice of Greek society. This repudiation of accepted customs was backed up by reference to the supposed habits of primitive men and animals.

Behind Diogenes' exhibitionism and deliberate affront to convention lay a profound concern with moral values which looks back to Socrates. The Stoics refined Diogenes' ideas, and there were men in the Hellenistic world and the Roman empire who called themselves Cynics, modelling their preaching and life on the uncompromising style of Diogenes. Unlike Socrates however he acknowledged no allegiance to any city, whether it was Sinope on the Black Sea, his native town, or Athens where he spent much of his later life. His ethical values took no account of social status and nationality, and this emphasizes the radical character of Diogenes' criticism of traditional attitudes. A study of Aristotle's painful defence of slavery in *Politics* Book I should make the point beyond doubt. What mattered to Diogenes was the individual human being and the well-being he might achieve purely by his natural endowments. This strong emphasis upon the individual and a 'nature' which he shares with humanity at large is one of the characteristics of Hellenistic philosophy. It becomes most prominent among Stoics, at the time of Rome's expansion from the second century B.C. onwards; but the early Stoics, Sceptics and Epicureans were supremely confident that a man's inner resources, his rationality, can provide the only firm basis for a happy and tranquil life. The city recedes into the background, and this is a sign of the times. But Diogenes had pointed the way before the dawn of the Hellenistic age.

When Zeno, the founder of Stoicism, and Epicurus began teaching at Athens in the last years of the fourth century the city already had two illustrious philosophical schools. A few years before 369, Plato had established the Academy, a society which seems to have had much less in common with a general centre of learning than later uses of the name might suggest.[1] Its senior members pursued a wide range of interests, but formal teaching may have been limited to mathematics and certainly is not likely to have gone beyond the curriculum, which includes dialectic for those over thirty, described in Book vii of the

[1] cf. Harold Cherniss, *The Riddle of the Early Academy* (Berkeley and Los Angeles 1945) pp. 61–72.

Republic. What the numbers of the Academy were at any one time is not known. The juniors in its early days must have been a small group of upper-class young men, not exclusively Athenians, for Aristotle who spent the years 367–347 as student and teacher in the Academy came from Macedonia. In founding the Academy Plato may have hoped among other things to educate men who could be expected to become prominent in public life. The published dialogues were his principal method of reaching a wider audience.

After Plato's death (347) the headship of the Academy passed first to his nephew, Speusippus, then to Xenocrates and thirdly to Polemo, a contemporary of Epicurus and Zeno. Aristotle remained formally a member for the rest of his life, but he left Athens for reasons which are open to conjecture on the appointment of Speusippus. He spent the next twelve years in various cities of Asia Minor and Macedonia, returning to Athens in 335. During his absence from Athens, Aristotle probably devoted much of his time to biological research, the fruits of which bulk so large in his writings. Following Alexander's accession to the Macedonian throne, Aristotle began his second prolonged stay in Athens, now teaching not in the Academy but in the Lyceum, a grove just outside the civic boundaries. Theophrastus and other Academicians, who had accompanied Aristotle on his travels, joined him there; and after Aristotle's death in 322, Theophrastus established the Lyceum (often called the Peripatos) as a school in its own right. He continued to direct its work until his death in 288/4.

The activities of the later Academy are not well documented. Aristotle often associates Speusippus with 'the Pythagoreans' (e.g. *Met.* 1072b30; *E.N.* 1096b5). The transmission of so-called Pythagoreanism is a complex and controversial subject. What seems to have happened, very briefly, is that Speusippus and Xenocrates developed certain metaphysical and mathematical principles which were not called Pythagorean by Plato. In their hands Plato's theory of Forms underwent considerable transformation.[1] They also wrote copiously on ethical subjects. Here again the details largely escape us, but it is certain that they accepted such basic Platonic notions as the necessary connexion between virtue and human well-being. Speusippus took up the extreme position of denying that pleasure in any sense or form can be something good (Aristotle, *E.N.* vii 14), and he attacked the hedonist philosopher, Aristippus, in two books. Several doctrines attributed to Xenocrates recur in Stoicism. One text is of particular

---

[1] cf. Cherniss, op. cit. p. 33.

interest: 'The reason for discovering philosophy is to allay that which causes disturbance in life' (fr. 4, Heinze). Xenocrates' name in this passage, which comes from Galen, depends on an emendation of the name 'Isocrates'. But the statement harmonizes well with the general aims of Hellenistic philosophy, especially Epicureanism and Pyrrhonism.

Xenocrates probably saw himself chiefly as a scholarly exponent of Plato's philosophy. Under his leadership the Academy professed Platonism, a systematic account of ideas which Plato himself, however positively he held them, may never have intended to be presented as a firm body of doctrine.

In the ancient biographical tradition Xenocrates is presented as a grave figure who had such an effect on Polemo, who eventually succeeded him, that the latter turned from a life of dissipation to philosophy. Polemo became head of the Academy in 314, three or four years before Zeno's arrival in Athens. With its fourth head the Academy seems to have moved away from mathematics, metaphysics and dialectic to concentrate upon ethics. Polemo is reported to have said that 'a man should train himself in practical matters and not in mere dialectical exercises' (D.L. iv 18). Plato regarded dialectic as the best moral training, on the grounds that it prepared its practitioners for an insight into the nature of goodness. But Hellenistic philosophy strove to make itself relevant to a wider social group than Plato or Aristotle had influenced. This is proved, to my mind convincingly, by the number of rival philosophers who were active at the end of the fourth century, all of them offering their own solution to the question already asked and answered by Plato and Aristotle: 'What is happiness or well-being and how does a man achieve it?' One answer, advanced by the first Sceptic, Pyrrho, was equanimity born of a refusal to make any definite judgments, but Epicureans and Stoics were the new philosophers who tackled the question most successfully. They succeeded not because they abandoned theory for practice, but because they offered a conception of the world and human nature which drew its support from empirical observations, reason and a recognition that all men have common needs. In saying this I do not mean to imply that they restricted the scope of philosophy to ethics. This is a frequent misconception about Hellenistic philosophy. Epicurus wrote thirty-seven books *On Nature*. The Stoics made contributions of great interest in logic, theory of language and natural philosophy. Both systems adopted the important assumption that happiness depends upon an understanding of the universe and what it is to be a man.

There were a number of minor philosophical movements in the early Hellenistic period all claiming descent from Socrates. We know or think we know Socrates so well from Plato that it is easy to forget the other Socratics who went their own way in the first part of the fourth century. They are shadowy figures whose views are preserved only in occasional references by contemporary writers and the bald summaries compiled in late antiquity. But they established traditions which anticipate certain aspects of Hellenistic philosophy and which influenced or even competed briefly with the new schools.[1]

I have said a little about Diogenes the Cynic, and will return to him in Chapter 4. Ancient historians of philosophy liked to concoct tidy master-pupil relationships, and they make Diogenes a pupil of Antisthenes. This man was an Athenian associate of Socrates. It is difficult to say how far Diogenes was positively influenced by Antisthenes. Perhaps twenty years older then Plato, Antisthenes himself is attacked by Aristotle for his naïveté (*Met.* 1024b33) and his followers ('Antistheneans') are criticized for their lack of culture (ibid. 1043b23). Sniping at traditional education was part of Diogenes' platform; and if Diogenes Laertius is to be trusted, Antisthenes himself claimed that virtue (*aretê*) is something practical, needing neither copious words nor learning (D.L. vi 11). In fact, Antisthenes was a voluminous writer whose style was highly regarded by a number of ancient critics. The titles of his books show that he was interested in literature, problems of knowledge and belief, and especially dialectic (D.L. vi 15ff.). The later Cynic tradition has coloured Diogenes Laertius' biography. It is reasonable, however, to suppose that Antisthenes advocated Socratic strength of mind as much by personal example as by teaching and writing. The little that we know of his logic and theories of language suggests that he was strongly at variance with Plato. But it was not for contributions to theoretical philosophy that Antisthenes became famous. His importance in this book rests on certain moral propositions in which he certainly foreshadowed and may have directly influenced the Stoics. Especially striking are the following fragments: virtue can be taught and once acquired cannot be lost (Caizzi fr. 69; 71); virtue is the goal of life (22); the sage is self-sufficient, since he has (by being wise) the wealth of all

[1] For a detailed account of the minor Socratics cf. W. K. C. Guthrie, *A History of Greek Philosophy* vol. iii (Cambridge 1969).

men (80). Probably Antisthenes, like Diogenes, dispensed with any
detailed theory which might support such statements. It was left to the
Stoics to build them into a systematic treatment of ethics.

A second Socratic, whose followers were active in the early Hellenistic age, is Aristippus of Cyrene (c. 435–355). Xenophon records
conversations between Socrates and Aristippus (e.g. *Mem.* 3.8, 1–7;
2.1) and Aristotle also mentions him (*Met.* 996a29). Aristippus' importance rests on his claim that pleasure is the goal of life. He advanced
this thesis long before it was adopted by Epicurus, and Epicurean
hedonism, though possibly influenced by Cyrenaic views, differs from
them in significant respects. By pleasure Aristippus meant bodily
gratification, which he conceived as a 'smooth movement', 'rough
movements' producing pain (D.L. ii 86). Unlike the Epicureans the
Cyrenaics denied absence of pain to be pleasure—it was an intermediate condition—and they rated pleasing bodily sensations above
mental pleasures (ibid. 89–90). Our sources do not distinguish clearly
between the theories of Aristippus himself and those of his followers,
two of whom, Theodorus and Hegesias, flourished at the end of the
fourth century. From Aristotle (*Met.* 996a29) we learn that Aristippus
scorned mathematics because it took no account of good or bad; and
it may be inferred from this that the main concern of his teaching
was ethical. Here it is possible to see the influence of Socrates, and
Socratic influence may also be evident in Aristippus' dismissal of
speculation about the physical world (D.L. 92), which he perhaps
developed into a sceptical attitude towards knowledge of external
reality.

Eucleides of Megara was a third follower of Socrates whose adherents were still prominent in the early Hellenistic period. It is
unfortunate that our knowledge of Eucleides is so slight, for he seems
to have been a philosopher of greater significance than Antisthenes or
Aristippus. The Megarian school was particularly interested in the
kind of arguments first developed by Parmenides and Zeno of Elea in
the fifth century. Parmenidean monism was also taken over by Eucleides
who held that 'the good is one thing, called under many names' (D.L.
ii 106). In the same context, Diogenes Laertius observes that Eucleides
denied the existence of that which is contradictory to the good. In
seeking to reduce everything to one thing, which is good, Eucleides
may have been as much influenced by Socrates as by Parmenides.
(Socrates' interest in teleological explanations for phenomena is well
attested in Plato's *Phaedo* 97c). But we cannot say how Eucleides

worked out the implications of this proposition. Later Megarians were largely renowned for their skill at dialectic, and they had an important influence on Stoic logic. Zeno the Stoic studied with two eminent Megarian philosophers, Stilpo and Diodorus Cronus.

To later antiquity these minor Socratic schools were of only marginal interest. It would be a mistake to regard them as insignificant in their own day. We tend to think that Plato and Aristotle completely overshadowed rival contemporary philosophers because their work has not survived or proved influential. It is unlikely that an educated Greek at the end of the fourth century would have formed the same judgment. Stilpo is reputed to have won followers from Aristotle, Theophrastus and many others (D.L. ii 113f.). Platonists and Peripatetics never exercised a monopoly in Greek philosophy, and they were soon outdone in the extent of their influence by the new Stoic and Epicurean schools.

When these schools were founded, the Academy had ceased to be outstanding in mathematics and theoretical philosophy. Its intellectual vitality was restored about the year 265 in a very different form by Arcesilaus, who turned the Academy from dogmatism to scepticism. But the Lyceum remained a vigorous society down to the death of Strato in 270/68. Theophrastus was a scholar of great versatility who maintained the research tradition established by Aristotle. He refined and expounded Aristotelian doctrines, but was also quite prepared to challenge Aristotle, as may be seen in the work which has come down to us with the title, *Metaphysics*. There Theophrastus discusses a series of problems which arise out of Aristotle's metaphysics. He made important advances in logic, and was particularly interested in the collection and analysis of data in natural history and geology. The importance of empirical checking is frequently stressed in two of his surviving works, *Inquiry into plants* and *On the causes of plants*. His ethical theory seems to have been closely based on Aristotle. Theophrastus was no radical and can hardly have found Epicurean and Stoic views on man and society congenial. Epicurus wrote a book *Against Theophrastus*, the content of which is not known, and through the writings of Theophrastus and other Peripatetics the technical works of Aristotle, which he did not prepare for general circulation, must have become more widely known.

This last point is important. Some scholars have argued that Epicurus and Zeno could have read only Aristotle's 'published' literary works and not the technical treatises which form the bulk of the work which survives today. Strabo, writing in the early Roman empire, relates that after Theophrastus' death Aristotle's manuscripts were dispatched to a man called Neleus, who lived at Skepsis, a town near Pergamum in Asia Minor (xiii 1, 54). When Neleus himself died the books were hidden in a cellar, for reasons of security, only to be recovered and edited in the early first century B.C. Too much has been based on this curious story. It has been held to show that Aristotle's technical treatises were completely unknown for about two centuries. But the conclusion does not follow. It is difficult to believe that only one version of these works was available in Athens at the time of Theophrastus. That Epicurus and the early Stoics had some knowledge of Aristotle's principal doctrines is both a reasonable and, I think, a necessary assumption. Nor is it only an assumption. We have one piece of evidence which connects Epicurus by name with Aristotle's *Analytics* and a work on Nature (see p. 29). But the decline of the Lyceum from the middle of the third century B.C. makes it unlikely that much of Aristotle's technical philosophy was known during the next hundred and fifty years.[1]

Ever since Eduard Zeller wrote his monumental *Philosophie der Griechen* over a hundred years ago, many scholars have contrasted Hellenistic philosophy unfavourably with Plato and Aristotle. But by any standards the achievement of Plato and Aristotle is virtually without parallel in the history of western thought. In assessing Hellenistic philosophy we need to remember that little of Epicurus and no complete work by an early Greek Stoic have survived. Moreover our knowledge of Carneades' sceptical methodology is also derived from secondary sources. We know the broad outlines of early Stoicism and Epicureanism. The details and the arguments are often missing. Plato and Aristotle have a head-start over the Hellenistic philosophers in terms of work which we can evaluate today.

Much of our evidence comes from hand-books written centuries after the time of the early Stoics, Epicureans and Sceptics. The absence of so much first-hand evidence makes the study of these philosophers a very different enterprise from work on Plato and Aristotle. Considerable care must be taken over comparing and assessing different sources,

---

[1] Little is known about the Peripatetic philosophers at this time. Their activities seem to have centred largely upon rhetoric, biography and works of popular moralizing. Theophrastus himself wrote on such subjects as marriage, piety and drunkenness. For the ancient evidence see F. Wehrli, *Die Schule des Aristoteles* (Basel 1944–), a series of volumes on individual philosophers.

and this preparatory work, if it is allowed too much room in the presentation and analysis of the subject-matter, can easily make Hellenistic philosophy seem tedious, inaccessible and lacking in conceptual interest. This is a false impression. We can now see that Epicurus and Zeno were philosophers whose ideas evolved gradually as a considered reaction against theories in vogue at the end of the fourth century and earlier. It is also true that they felt passionately about the truth of their own theories and the implications of them for human well-being. The same might be said of Plato. But philosophy advances by criticism, and Epicurus and Zeno were critical of current dogmas concerning the structure of the physical world, the sources of knowledge, the nature of man and the grounds of his happiness. The Sceptics challenged the basis of all objective statements, and Carneades' criticism of the Stoics provides ample evidence of his sharp mind. We can argue about the merits of the alternative Stoic and Epicurean theories, but there is no justification for regarding them as a sudden impoverishment of Greek philosophy.

The Stoics and Epicureans however interpreted the scope of philosophy more narrowly and dogmatically than Aristotle, and by the middle of the first century B.C. onwards, which is the period of our earliest secondary sources, both schools had taken up entrenched positions. But two hundred and fifty years is a long time, and our loss of philosophical writing from this period is almost total. Possibly, as is often said, Epicurus' followers were largely content from early days to accept the teachings of their founder. They certainly revered him as the saviour of mankind, but we know of developments in Epicurean logic, to take only one example, which probably occurred long after his death. The Stoics, who have far more in common with Plato and Aristotle, were more self-critical than the Epicureans, and such leading figures as Chrysippus and Diogenes of Babylon elaborated logic and other subjects in great detail, turning Stoicism into a highly technical philosophy. Stoics and Epicureans criticized each other and were criticized in turn by the Academic Sceptics. But until the time of Panaetius and Posidonius, few very significant amendments to fundamental Stoic doctrines seem to have been made, and the extent of their modifications was less substantial than has sometimes been supposed. Perhaps the new Hellenistic systems were too successful in gaining popular support to channel the development of philosophy into new directions. The Academic Sceptics, who had no 'system' to defend, were very able critical philosophers, but their influence was naturally restricted and often negative. Stoicism and Epicureanism could be understood in a rudimentary sense by almost anyone, and they could also provide intellectual satisfaction for those who wanted more than a message. The early Academy and Lyceum were less flexible in terms of general appeal. They did not make the world intelligible in a manner which could be found satisfying at many different levels.

Both the Epicureans and the Stoics were prepared to popularize their teaching. In his *Letter to Herodotus*—the name refers to a friend, not the fifth-century historian—Epicurus opens by remarking that he has prepared an epitome of his philosophy for those unable to study his technical writings (D.L. x 35). He also compiled a set of ethical maxims which set out the cardinal doctrines and were learnt by heart. But within the school itself there were those like Epicurus himself who devoted their main energies to philosophy. The Stoics assigned a special place to what they called 'suasions and dissuasions', the purpose of which was moral advice. The serious student will have been expected to advance far beyond such things, much as Lucilius, in Seneca's *Moral letters*, is conducted from the rudiments of ethics to problems about the meaning of 'good'. Under Chrysippus a course at the Stoa must have included a considerable assignment of logic and natural philosophy.

We should not think of professional Stoics and Epicureans as men in whom freedom of thought had ossified. But they became the transmitters of doctrines which provided many people throughout the Hellenistic world with a set of attitudes that religion and political ideologies might also have supported. The decline of the Greek cities accelerated the decline of the Olympian gods. Stoics attempted to accommodate the Olympians by interpreting them as allegorical references to natural phenomena. The Epicureans denied the gods any influence over the world. Eastern religious ideas infiltrated into the Mediterranean world. Some embraced them; others chose Stoicism or Epicureanism instead. Stoic and Epicurean philosophers, particularly the latter, made it their business to win supporters, but the market was open to be developed. The price which they paid for entering it with such success was dogmatism, at least outwardly, and the divorce of philosophy from scientific research. Epicurus' attitude to science was naïve and reactionary. The Stoics defended out-of-date theories in astronomy and physiology against the new discoveries of Aristarchus and Erasistratus. The Sceptics were unsympathetic to science, and only

Posidonius in the later Hellenistic period made a serious effort at re-uniting philosophy with mathematics and other scientific studies. But Epicurus and especially the Stoics were clearly interested in many problems for their own sake. The humanist focus of their philosophy is one of its most interesting features, and it leads to very different results in the two systems. In neither case is it narrowly moralistic because the ethical values of both philosophies are related to two fully developed, if divergent, conceptions of the universe.

In the period covered by this book philosophy became thoroughly institutionalized and practically synonymous with higher education. Epicureanism was the exception. For a brief period at the time of Lucretius and Julius Caesar, it was fashionable and influential in Rome. But it never achieved the public respectability of Stoicism. Philosophers were among the most eminent members of the community and some of the men who feature in this book were chosen to represent their cities as ambassadors. From the middle of the second century B.C., philosophers are found in Rome, but no school was permanently set up there. Some Romans during this period took up Hellenistic philosophy, but they made few original contributions to it. Most of the impetus and the ideas came from Athens and the eastern Mediterranean cities in which many of the Hellenistic philosophers were born.

CHAPTER TWO

Epicurus and Epicureanism

We must not make a pretence of doing philosophy, but really do it; for what we need is not the semblance of health but real health (Usener 220).

It has often been said that Epicurus was primarily a moralist, and if by this we mean someone who strives by theory and practice to advocate a particular way of life the description is appropriate. Epicurus thought that he could trace the causes of human unhappiness to mistaken beliefs in his society, beliefs about the gods, the destiny of the soul, and the objects in life which are truly valuable. Ultimately all his teaching has the aim of discrediting such beliefs and replacing them with those which he holds to be true. By his adherents Epicurus was regarded as a 'saviour', as the bringer of 'light', words which we naturally associate with Judaism and Christianity. But Epicurus was not a preacher, even if he sometimes preaches. He wished ardently to persuade, and to convince; it would be quite wrong to try to make him into a purely academic philosopher. But he was a philosopher. Arguments and evidence are the instruments by which he hoped to persuade those who would listen, and it is with the theory rather than the practical aspects of Epicureanism that I shall be concerned here. Beginning, after some introductory remarks, with Epicurus' theory of knowledge I propose to consider the details of his system in an order which seems to be both coherent and representative of his own methodology. Ethics proper is dealt with last, for other topics have ethical implications which can be noted *en passant* and moral conclusions are the ultimate goal of Epicurus' philosophy.

(i) Life and works

Epicurus was born on the island of Samos in 341 B.C. (D.L. x 14). His father, who held Athenian citizenship, had settled there some ten years earlier. The first philosophical influence on Epicurus may have come in Samos itself from Pamphilus, a Platonist (Cic. *N.D.* i 72; D.L. x 14). But Epicurus' own philosophy is strikingly at odds with Platonism, and perhaps while still an adolescent he began an association with Nausiphanes on the neighbouring island of Teos (Herculaneum papyrus 1005) which nipped in the bud any positive allegiance to Plato. Nausiphanes was a Democritean (D.L. i 15; Cic. *N.D.* i 73), and it is likely that Epicurus first became acquainted with the basic principles of atomism through the teaching of Nausiphanes. In later life Epicurus denounced Nausiphanes in highly vitriolic language (D.L. x 7–8). It is not clear what prompted these attacks, but they are typical of Epicurus' attested attitudes towards other philosophers.

At the age of eighteen Epicurus went to Athens to do his two years of military and civilian service alongside the comic poet Menander (Strabo xiv 638). We know little in detail of his activities during the next fifteen years. He may have taught for some time as an elementary school teacher in Colophon, a small town to the north-west of Samos on the Persian mainland, where his family had now taken up residence (D.L. x 1; 4). Later he established his own philosophical circle first in Mytilene (on Lesbos) and then in Lampsacus (D.L. x 15), a port near the site of ancient Troy, returning to Athens at the age of thirty-four in 307/6. Here he remained for the rest of his life. The return to Athens indicates that Epicurus was now confident of attracting followers in the main centre of philosophy. Between Athens and Piraeus Epicurus bought a house the garden of which came to stand as the name of the Epicurean school.

The community which Epicurus founded differed in important respects from the Academy and Lyceum. Its modern analogue is not a college or research institution but a society of friends living according to common principles, in retreat from civic life. Friendship has particular ethical significance in Epicureanism, and the Garden provided a setting for its realization. Women and slaves were admitted, and scraps of several private letters are preserved in which Epicurus expresses deep affection for his friends and followers. It is doubtful whether the Garden during Epicurus' lifetime offered much that might be called formal training to would-be Epicureans. Those who committed themselves to Epicurus were not so much students 'reading for a course' as men and women dedicated to a certain style of life. Seneca quotes the revealing maxim: 'Act always as if Epicurus is watching' (*Ep.* 25, 5). The similarity to George Orwell's 'Big brother is watching you' could scarcely be more misleading. Epicurus clearly inspired the strongest regard in his associates and personified the values of his own philosophy. But if the Garden lacked the formal curriculum of the Academy we can safely assume that its members devoted much time to reading and discussing Epicurus' books; his *Principal doctrines* (see below) were probably learnt by heart; some members must have been engaged in the preparation and copying of works both for internal consumption and for dissemination to Epicureans outside Athens; and Epicurus' chief adherents, such as Metrodorus, will have engaged in advanced study with the master himself.[1] Book xxviii of Epicurus' *On Nature* refers to Metrodorus in the second person, and the fragments which survive record parts of a discussion between the two philosophers on problems of language and theory of knowledge. Epicurus kept in touch with his followers outside Athens by correspondence, and the opening of his *Letter to Pythocles* is worth quoting for the attitudes it reveals of Epicurus himself and one of his disciples:

> Cleon brought me a letter from you in which you continue to show good-will towards me matching my own love for you. You are trying not ineffec-tively to memorize the arguments which are directed at a life of sublime happiness, and you ask me to send you a brief summary of the argument about astronomical phenomena so that you can easily get it by heart. For you find my other writings difficult to remember even though, as you say, you are always using them. I was delighted to receive your request and it caused me joyous expectations.[2]

Consistent with these principles Epicurus preferred the company of a few intimates to popular acclaim (Sen. *Ep.* 7, 11). He did not how-ever withdraw completely from civic life. In a letter cited by Philode-mus Epicurus says that he has participated in all the national festivals (Us. 169); his slogan 'live quietly' was not a revolutionary denun-ciation of contemporary society but a prescription for attaining tranquillity. Opponents of Epicureanism vilified the founder as a libertine and voluptuary, but this is inconsistent both with his teaching on pleasure, as we shall see, and with his own professed attitudes. He claimed to derive great pleasure from a subsistence diet which cheese would turn into a feast (Us. 181f.). On his death in 271 B.C., Epicurus bequeathed his house and garden to his follower, Hermarchus, for the benefit of the Epicurean community, and succeeding heads of the school probably nominated their own successor. On the twentieth of

[1] Epicurus probably first encountered Metrodorus, his junior by about ten years, at Lampsachus, the latter's native town.
[2] The authenticity of this letter has been questioned, but there is no reason to doubt its reliability as a statement of Epicurus' attitudes and doctrine.

every month Epicurus' memory and that of Metrodorus were celebrated at a festival within the Garden. This and other arrangements
which are recorded in Epicurus' will (D.L. x 16–21) throw an interesting
light on the character of the man himself.

Epicureanism has rightly been called 'the only missionary philosophy produced by the Greeks'.[1] Before he took up residence at Athens,
Epicurus had established a following in Lampsachus and Mytilene, and
his disciples helped to propagate the Epicurean gospel throughout the
Mediterranean world. Antioch and Alexandria are two major cities in
which Epicureanism established itself at an early date. Later, it spread
widely into Italy and Gaul. Cicero in the middle of the first century
B.C. could write, and it gave him no pleasure to do so, 'The [Roman]
Epicureans by their writings have seized the whole of Italy' (*Tusc.* iv
6–7). This was a time when Epicureanism briefly claimed the allegiance
of some prominent Romans including Calpurnius Piso and Cassius.
Julius Caesar may have been sympathetic and Cicero's Atticus was an
Epicurean. The fortunes of the movement fluctuated. Political opposition was not unknown, but the main antagonists were first rival
philosophers, especially Stoics, and later Christianity.

In the Roman world Epicureanism seems to have been at its strongest immediately before the fall of the Republic. But it suffered no
sudden decline. Seneca quotes with approval many Epicurean moral
maxims; Lucian's *Alexander*, written in the second century A.D., gives
a fascinating account of Epicurean and Christian reactions to persecution in the area south of the Black Sea. And most remarkable of
all, about A.D. 200 in the interior of modern Turkey, at a place called
Oenoanda in antiquity, an old man named Diogenes had erected a
huge philosophical inscription carved on a great stone wall. Between
1884 and the present day many fragments of his work have been
recovered, and it constitutes a summary of Epicurus' teaching which
Diogenes bestowed on his countrymen and humanity at large for their
happiness.[2] Apart from adding valuable information to our knowledge
of Epicureanism, Diogenes' inscription proves the vitality of Epicurus'
gospel five hundred years after the foundation of the Garden.

Epicurus himself was a prolific writer. Diogenes Laertius, who
records forty-one titles of Epicurus' 'best books', says that his writings

---

[1] N. W. De Witt, *Epicurus and his Philosophy* (Minneapolis 1954) p. 329. The
last chapter of this book should be consulted for a survey of the later fortunes of
Epicureanism.

[2] For the evidence see Bibliography.

ran to three hundred rolls (x 26), and that he exceeded all previous writers 'in the number of his books'. Many of these consisted of short popular tracts and letters. Epicurus' major work was the series of thirty-seven books *On Nature*, a treatise *On the criterion* or *kanón*, and a collection of ethical books which included *On lives; On the goal; On choice and avoidance*. He also wrote polemical works *Against the physicists*, *Against the Megarians*, and *Against Theophrastus*. Many of the letters, as we know from our own evidence, summarized points of doctrine or discussed these in some detail. Of all this writing only a small fraction has survived. Three letters are preserved which Diogenes Laertius included in his Life of Epicurus. The longest and most important of these, *To Herodotus*, gives a compressed and difficult summary of the main principles of atomism. Astronomical phenomena are the subject of the *Letter to Pythocles*, and the third letter, *To Menoeceus*, presents a clear if somewhat over-simplified account of Epicurean moral theory. In addition to these letters, Diogenes gives us a collection of forty *Kuriai doxai*, 'Principal doctrines', and a further set of maxims (*Vaticanae sententiae*) survives in a Vatican manuscript. Excavation at Herculaneum during the eighteenth century brought to light many charred rolls of papyrus which originally formed the library of some wealthy Roman. He was probably an adherent of Epicureanism, since most of the papyri which have been unrolled and read are fragmentary works by Philodemus of Gadara, an Epicurean philosopher and poet contemporary with Cicero. The rolls also contain fragments of some of the books of Epicurus *On Nature*. These are formidably difficult to read and reconstruct, but an invaluable supplement to earlier knowledge. Much work remains to be done on them.[1]

For our information about details of Epicurus' doctrine we are heavily dependent upon secondary sources. The most important of these is the Roman poet Lucretius, who wrote more than two hundred years after Epicurus' death. It is perhaps misleading to describe Lucretius as a secondary source. His poem, *De rerum natura*, is a work of genius which preceded the *Aeneid* and challenges it as a literary masterpiece. Lucretius, whose life and character are virtually unknown to us, was a fervid proponent of Epicureanism who presents Epicurus' teaching as the only source of human salvation. But Lucretius is no

---

[1] Nearly all the Herculaneum papyri belong to the Biblioteca Nazionale of Naples; but the British Museum has substantial fragments of Epicurus *On Nature* Book ii.

mere panegyrist. His six books set out in great detail Epicurean arguments concerning the basic constituents of things, the movement of atoms, the structure of body and mind, the causes and nature of sensation and thought, the development of human culture, and natural phenomena. At the same time, there is no reason to regard Lucretius himself as an original thinker. His work amplifies and explains points that we can find in Epicurus' own writings. Even where Lucretius reports theories, for instance the swerve of atoms (ii 216–93), which cannot be checked against Epicurus' own words, he was probably drawing on original sources which we cannot recover. Epicurus' own immediate successors were not noted for any major innovations. Certain refinements were doubtless made, and Philodemus' treatise *On signs* (preserved partially on papyrus) incorporates logical work by Zeno of Sidon (*c.* 150–70 B.C.) which may well go beyond anything worked out by Epicurus himself. But for the most part Epicurus' own writings remained canonical throughout the history of the school.

After Lucretius the best secondary sources are Diogenes Laertius, Cicero, Seneca and Plutarch. Cicero and Plutarch intensely disliked Epicureanism, and their criticism is of interest for understanding the adverse reception which the school often encountered. Seneca, though officially a Stoic, concludes most of his first *Moral letters* with an Epicurean maxim which he recommends to his correspondent, Lucilius. Sextus Empiricus, to whom Epicureanism was the most congenial of the dogmatic schools of philosophy, provides a useful supplement to our direct knowledge of Epicurean empiricism. Finally, as I have already mentioned, we have substantial fragments from the inscription of Diogenes of Oenoanda.

(ii) The scope of Epicurus' philosophy

Epicurus' philosophy is a strange mixture of hard-headed empiricism, speculative metaphysics and rules for the attainment of a tranquil life. There are links between these aspects of his thought, some of which are clearer than others. But one thing which certainly unites them is Epicurus' concern to set the evidence of immediate sensation and feeling against the kind of logical analysis which is characteristic of Platonic and Aristotelian methodology. Epicurus rejected many of the fundamental principles in terms of which Plato and Aristotle described the world. But more important than his disagreement concerning what is to be said about the world is his dismissal of certain logical and metaphysical concepts which are basic to Plato and Aristotle.

Epicurus recognized the distinction between universal and particular; but he did not regard universals as having existence in their own right, like Plato; nor apparently was he interested, as Aristotle had been, in classifying things under genera and species. He did not set up principles such as Plato's *same* and *different*, or Aristotle's *substrate* and *form*, for the analysis of objects and their properties. Philosophers who proceed in this way, he held, are merely playing with words, setting up empty assumptions and arbitrary rules. He did not deny that philosophy uses language and logic as its tools (Us. 219). But he vehemently rejected the view that linguistic analysis by itself can tell us anything about the world which is true or relevant to a happy life. The value of words is to express those concepts which are clearly derived from sensations and feelings. These latter give us our only hold on facts and the only secure foundation for language.

One might suppose from this that Epicurus would have dispensed with metaphysics altogether. In fact, his account of what exists does not stop short at the objects of which we are made aware by immediate sensations and feelings. Our senses report to us things which we call sheep, grass, cats etc., but for Epicurus all such things are compounded out of atoms and void, neither of which is something that we can sense or feel. In asserting atoms and void to be the ultimate entities which constitute the world, Epicurus is making a metaphysical statement. This is not something which he can prove or verify directly from sensations with or without the help of experiment. He has to establish it by setting up certain axioms and assuming the validity of certain methods of inference.

The first atomist explanation of things was advanced more than a century before Epicurus began his philosophical career. Epicurus clearly believed it to be a theory for which he could offer new and improved proof. But while providing an elegant and economical answer to such questions as 'What is the structure of physical objects?' or 'How are bodies able to move?', the atomist theory attracted Epicurus on other than purely theoretical grounds. If all events and all substances are ultimately explicable by reference to atoms necessarily moving in empty space, both divine causation as popularly conceived and its sophisticated equivalents—Plato's Forms and Demiurge or World-Soul, Aristotle's Prime Mover and Heavenly Intelligences—become superfluous. Epicurus held that beliefs in divine management of the cosmos and of human destiny were a major cause of human failure to live a tranquil life. On an atomist analysis of the world, supposing this to be demonstrable, consequences would follow which could not fail to affect beliefs about a man's own place in the world.

Epicurus often asserts that philosophy has no value unless it helps men to attain happiness. This applies with particular force to his moral theory, but there is no necessary connexion between atomism and hedonism. The claim that pleasure is the only thing which is good as an end is compatible with all manner of metaphysical hypotheses. Epicurus has various ways of establishing his hedonism, none of which draws direct support from atoms and void. In this he differs markedly from the Stoics whose moral theory is intrinsically related to their metaphysics. But Epicurus thought he could show the validity of hedonism by appeal to immediate experience which, less directly, he held to support atomism. If labels can be usefully applied to a philosopher, Epicurus should be called an empiricist. That at least is what he would like to be remembered as, and empiricism provides the clearest internal connexion between his different ideas.

(iii) *Theory of knowledge*

If you fight against all sensations, you will have nothing by reference to which you can judge even those which you say are deceptive (*K.D.* xxiii).

The foundation of Epicurus' theory of knowledge is sense-perception. He starts from the fact that all men have sensations (*aisthêseis*), and asserts, without proof, that these must be caused by something other than themselves (D.L. x 31). It does not of course follow from this assertion that sensations are caused by things external to the percipient, and Epicurus would acknowledge that a feeling such as hunger (a *pathos* in his terminology) has an internal cause. But he takes it as self-evident that sensations of colour, sound, smell etc. must be caused by actual objects which possess these properties. 'We must suppose that it is when something enters us from things which are external that we perceive . . . their shapes' (*Ep. Hdt.* 49). This statement at once raises questions which the Sceptics did not hesitate to ask about mirages, hallucinations and the like. But Epicurus has an answer to put forward, as we shall see later.

Suppose we accept that sensations cannot lie concerning their causes: in other words, that if I have the sensation of hearing there must be something sounding which causes my sensation. Does this support the further proposition that there is some object like a motor-car horn or a train whistle which corresponds precisely to the content of my sensation? For Epicurus the inference may or may not be warranted. That about which our sensations cannot deceive us is not a motor-car horn but a sense-impression (*phantasia*). What enters me from things outside is not a motor-car horn, if that is what I do genuinely hear, but a cluster of atoms (*eidōla*) thrown off the outer surface of such objects. Provided that these 'effluences', as we may call them, enter the sense organ without experiencing any change of structure the impression they produce on us will be an accurate image of the object.[1] If on the other hand their structure is disrupted in transit, the effluences will cause us to sense something which corresponds not to some actual characteristic of the object itself but to their own modified structure.

Sensations therefore are necessarily good evidence only of effluences. This raises the problem of how we can distinguish between those sensations which report to us accurately about objects and those which do not. For we cannot get at objects independently of effluences. Epicurus tackles this problem in an interesting way. He distinguishes sharply between the sense-impression itself and judgments, or the identification of sense-impressions with objects (*Ep. Hdt.* 50–1). Our sense-impressions are not judgments, nor are they dependent upon reason. We are not to say that this sense-impression is reliable, that one untrustworthy, for to do so presupposes an object which can test the validity of sensation, and our sole knowledge of objects is derived from sensations. Considered as an item of information about that which affects our senses every impression is of equal validity (D.L. x 31–2).

Nevertheless, sense-impressions can be distinguished from one another in terms of clarity or vividness. Sounds may be sharp or faint, visual images both clear and blurred. Epicurus was also aware of the fact that as we move away from the apparent source of many sensations our impressions change, and may decrease in clarity. Putting these facts together he concluded that sensations provide reliable evidence about objects if and only if they are characterized by clear and distinct impressions (*enargeia, Ep. Hdt.* 52, cf. *K.D.* xxiv). Other impressions 'await confirmation' by those which are clear. This conclusion could also seem to derive some support from Epicurus' explanation of the physical processes by which sensation takes place.

---

[1] Epicurus did not invent the 'effluence' theory of sense-perception. It goes back to Democritus and still earlier, in a different form, to Empedocles.

If we are near the ultimate source of our sensations the effluences which affect us are less likely to encounter disruption. It is only from a distance, supposedly, that the tower which is square looks round (Us. 247).

Epicurus does not specify conditions which establish the clarity of a sense-impression. He probably regarded this as something which would entail an infinite regress. He could take it as a datum of experience that we do distinguish within limits between that which is clear and that which is blurred or obscure. Clarity however is not a sufficient guarantee that we see things as they really are. Epicurus was grossly misled by 'clear views' when he argued that the sun is about the same size as it is seen to be (*Ep. Pyth.* 91).

Close attention to clear impressions is the first stage in acquiring knowledge. But Epicurus did not regard it as sufficient by itself. However clear our sense-impressions may be they do not constitute knowledge. They do not tell us what something is. Before judgments about objects can be made, our sense-impressions must be classified, labelled and so marked off from one another. Epicurus proposed to satisfy these conditions by what he called *prolêpseis*, 'preconceptions'.[1] These are general concepts or mental pictures produced by repeated sense-impressions which are both clear and similar in kind. They persist after particular sensations cease and constitute a record of our experience of the world. We acquire a concept or *prolêpsis* of man by repeated and remembered experience of particular men. Hence we are able to interpret new sensations by comparing them with preconceptions, and all our judgments about objects are made on this basis of recorded experiences, which we classify by using language (D.L. x 33). Epicurus agreed broadly with Aristotle who asserted that 'science comes to be when out of many ideas born of experience a general concept which is universal arises concerning things that are similar' (*Met.* A 981a5 ff.). For Epicurus, preconceptions are the foundations of judgments and language. 'We should not have named anything unless we had previously learnt its form by a preconception' (D.L. ibid.). Language is a method of signifying those preconceptions which seem to us to fit the present object of experience. Because preconceptions themselves are supposed to possess 'clarity', they establish, in association with the appropriate new sense-impressions, what it is that we see,

---

[1] Cicero (*N.D.* i 44) says that Epicurus was the first to use the word *prolêpsis* in this sense.

hear and so on.[1] Error arises when we use words which signify a preconception that does not correspond with the phenomenon (*De nat.* xxviii fr. iv col. 3). This may happen through confusing unclear with clear impressions, and Epicurus also recognized that the ambiguity of many words can be a cause of misassociating sense-impressions and preconceptions.[2]

Epicurus probably thought that all other concepts, including those which have no empirical reference, are derived from preconceptions. Preconceptions can be combined with one another, or they can be used as a basis for inference (see D.L. x 32). But, with a few exceptions, preconceptions seem to be direct derivatives of sensation, and Epicurus recommended that the meaning of words should always be established by reference to 'the first mental image' (*Ep. Hdt.* 37). In this way he hoped to forge a firm bond between statements and immediate experience, though he gave no sufficient reasons why people's preconceptions should be regarded as similar and therefore identifiable by the same words.

So far Epicurus can claim to be a rigorous empiricist. But we must now note a number of curious exceptions to the principle that our ideas about the world are all derived ultimately from sense-impressions. Apart from those effluences which cause our sense-impressions, Epicurus also supposed that there are 'images' which somehow bypass the sense organs and penetrate directly to the mind. In nature these too are atomic clusters, but their density is much finer than the effluences which affect our senses. They are *tenuia simulacra*, as Lucretius called them (iv 722ff.), and account both for dream-images, phantoms, visions of the dead, and for such ordinary objects of thought as lions. Such 'images' may be direct effluences from the surface of an object. But many of them are simply chance combinations of individual atoms; others may consist of real effluences which are compounded and then produce images of Centaurs and monsters (*Ep. Hdt.* 48; Lucret. iv 130–42). Instead of accounting for dreams and hallucinations by reference to images entirely created or brought to consciousness by some psychological faculty, Epicurus supposed that dreams and hallucinations too are explicable by the mind's contact with atoms that enter it from outside.

[1] Clement of Alexandria (Us. 255) reports Epicurus as saying that 'it is impossible for anyone to investigate . . . or to form a judgment . . . independently of preconception'.

[2] For further evidence and discussion see my article in *Bulletin of the Institute of Classical Studies* 18 (1971) 114–33.

If we ask how dreams and visions are to be distinguished from sense-impressions, the answer is not entirely clear. Lucretius looks for a distinction in terms of continuity. 'Real' sense-impressions are produced by a steady stream of effluences; but the mind can be moved by a single 'image' (iv 746), and thus presumably catch a momentary vision. Also, dream-images are said to move by a series of effluences perishing one after another; Lucretius' description makes one think of the staccato movement of early cinema. Clearly such criteria are inadequate for Epicurus' purpose. In effect he is saying that a hallucinated person really does see something which is there, but mistakenly takes it to correspond with an actual solid object (cf. Us. 253).

The gods are a further object of direct mental perception. Postponing for the present consideration of their physical structure, we may observe here that Epicurus posits a series of fine effluences from the gods which penetrate directly to the mind. The texts which describe these divine 'images' are difficult; Epicurus put forward theoretical reasons, as well as the evidence of such visions, to justify his claims about the divine nature (Cic. *N.D.* i 43–55). But he seems to have given no adequate arguments in favour of divine 'images'. It is no help to this queer thesis to invoke the supposed universality of human belief in gods. The real difficulty is however that of the grounds for verification. By the concept of 'clear' view Epicurus has a standard for verifying perceptual judgments which has some claims to be called objective. Only in a special philosophical sense could people's perception of dogs be said to depend on their beliefs. How we may conceive of gods, on the other hand, is something which cannot be assimilated to perception of empirical objects. Epicurus' theory of divine 'images' puts religious belief in the same category as empirical observation.

Some scholars have argued that Epicurus posited a special mental faculty, 'apprehension by intellect' (*epibolê tês dianoias*), which somehow guarantees the veracity both of impressions of the gods and the validity of scientific concepts. If Epicurus had held such a theory he would have been an intuitionist in much of his philosophical activity. This interpretation was defended at great length by Cyril Bailey, whose work on Epicurus and Lucretius has held authority in the English-speaking world. According to Bailey, Epicurus supposed that the 'clear' sense-impression, of which I have already spoken, is obtained by the 'attention of the senses', and correspondingly, clear visions of the gods and clear concepts concerning, for instance, atoms and void, are obtained by the 'attention' of the mind. If Bailey were merely arguing that we cannot be aware of any object or thought unless we 'attend' to something, he would be ascribing nothing remarkable to Epicurus. But Bailey meant much more than this. On his interpretation, Epicurus supposes that 'the concepts of science are built up step by step by the juxtaposition of previous concepts, each in their turn grasped as "clear"... by the immediate apprehension of the mind'.[1]

Epicurus' use of the expression 'apprehension by intellect' does not justify Bailey's view. Any explanation of Epicurus as an intuitionist is on quite the wrong tack. Probably what he means by 'apprehension', whether by the mind or the senses, is concentration or attention: we need to concentrate, if we are to grasp the images which can be received by the sense organs or the mind. I shall return to this subject in the discussion of Epicurean psychology (p. 56).

In order to use the evidence of the senses as material for establishing true propositions about the world, Epicurus assumed the validity of certain axioms. One of these has been stated already: 'Sense-impressions which are "clear" provide accurate information about the external appearance and properties of objects.'[2] These sense-impressions *confirm* or *bear witness against* the truth of judgments about objects which we may make provisionally on evidence lacking the requisite clarity. But Epicurus also allowed a weaker form of confirmation, 'lack of contrary evidence'. And this we may state as a further axiom: 'Judgments about non-evident objects are true if they are consistent with clear sense-impressions.' This second axiom is of the utmost importance to Epicurus. If positive confirmation by clear impressions were the sole ground for true objective statements, Epicurus would be unable to advance beyond the description of sensible objects. As it is, he assumes that the validity of clear impressions is such that they provide indirect evidence of things which are imperceptible, or for which a clear view is unobtainable in the nature of the case. Here is an example preserved by Sextus Empiricus (cited n. 21): If void does not exist (something non-evident) then motion should not exist since *ex hypothesi* all things are full and dense; so that since motion does exist the apparent does not contradict the judgment about that which is non-evident. (As stated, of course, the argument is invalid since it

---

[1] *The Greek Atomists and Epicurus* (Oxford 1928) p. 570.
[2] Formal statements of these 'axioms' are to be found in Sextus Empiricus, *Adv. math.* vii 212–13 (Us. 247). Epicurus writes of them more informally in *Ep. Hdt.* 51 and *K.D.* xxiv.

assumes that void is a necessary condition of movement, having fullness as its contradictory.)

Epicurus associates the axiom concerning non-contradiction with a further proposition (*X*), which may be treated as an implication of the second axiom: If more than one explanation of non-evident phenomena is consistent with observation then all such explanations are to be treated as equally valid (*Ep. Pyth.* 87). Let us state this more formally. Suppose that *p* is an evident fact, *q* a problem requiring explanation which cannot be solved directly by reference to *p*, and *s, t, u* three different statements about *q* which are all consistent with *p*. Then, independently of any other criterion or axiom, it follows from proposition *X* that *s, t,* and *u* are all equally acceptable explanations. This argument is formally valid, and Epicurus applied it rigorously to all statements concerning astronomical phenomena. In order to reject any of the hypotheses *s, t* and *u* it would be necessary to introduce some further principle of verification over and above the second axiom. Epicurus declined to do this on the grounds that it would be a departure from that which is definitely knowable, that is, the state of objects as given by clear sense-impressions.

Epicurus applies this principle regularly in the *Letter to Pythocles*, as the following excerpt shows (94):

> The repeated waning and waxing of the moon may come about owing to the rotation of this celestial body; equally it may be due to configurations of air; or again by reason of the interposition of other bodies; it may happen in any of the ways in which things manifest to us invite us to account for this phenomenon, provided that one does not become so attached to a single explanation that one rules out others for no good reason, failing to consider what it is possible for a man to observe and what impossible, and therefore desiring to discover the indiscoverable.

Up to a point this is admirable as a scientific principle. One thinks of the current debate concerning different explanations of the origin of the universe (big bang, steady state etc.) which has not yet been resolved by empirical data. Epicurus could argue, with considerable justification, that the astronomy of his own day claimed to know more than its source of evidence, the naked eye, justified. What he seems to have wholly failed to appreciate is the valid check on immediate observations which some astronomers were already trying to make by reference to systematic records and by mathematical calculations.

In application to celestial phenomena, Epicurus' use of the axiom of non-contradiction has the largely negative function of leaving open a plurality of possible explanations. But the Epicureans used the principle positively as grounds to support general statements arrived at by induction. Philodemus records this example: from the proposition 'Men in our experience are mortal' we infer that 'men everywhere are mortal'. The general statement is based on the empirical fact that we know no exception to it *and therefore* it is consistent with experience (*On signs* col. xvi). The Stoics objected to this kind of reasoning on the grounds that it presupposes the non-evident (unobserved men) to be similar in kind to the evident. The Epicureans replied that their inference does not make a presupposition that all men are mortal. It is the absence of any man known to be immortal which justifies the general inference about human mortality.

Epicurus assumes, as any scientist must, that there are certain uniformities in nature which hold for what is evident and non-evident alike. Of course, it does not follow by the second axiom that a proposition which is consistent with some evident phenomenon *must* also be true concerning something non-evident. But science cannot operate merely by propositions which are necessarily true. It must proceed by empirical generalizations which are rejected as and when new evidence refutes previous hypotheses. The Stoics held that all inferences must be established by arguments which are deductively valid. But deductive reasoning by itself can never be sufficient to establish a scientific statement. For the premises which entail a deductive conclusion about observable data must either be empirical generalizations, or be ultimately based upon statements of this form. At some point the scientist must make an inductive inference on the basis of evidence, and for Epicurus that point is reached when observation seems to support the belief that no instances are likely to be found which will contradict a general statement.

Epicurus and Lucretius often appeal to 'analogy' or 'similarity' to support an inference from the visible to the invisible. Thus Epicurus takes the (allegedly) observed fact that no parts can be distinguished in the smallest visible magnitude to support the inference that the same is true of the smallest invisible magnitude, the minimum part of an atom (*Ep. Hdt.* 58f.). The main subject of Philodemus' *On signs* is 'analogical inference', and we might suppose that this requires a further axiom for its justification. None of our secondary sources nor Epicurus himself gives any independent discussion of 'analogy', and it is not needed. The justification for inference by analogy is provided by the two axioms already discussed.[1] By the first axiom we are justified in asserting that 'clear impressions' give evidence that men are mortal. All the men of whom we have reliable experience are similar in respect of mortality. From this positive evidence Epicurus infers that men of whom we have no experience are equally similar in respect of mortality. The inference is justified by the second axiom which allows us to assert *p* if there is no evidence against it. Philodemus even states that it is 'inconceivable' that there should be something which possesses nothing in common with empirical evidence (*On signs* col. xxi 27ff.). The Epicurean test of the 'conceivable' is sense-perception and the problematic mental 'images' already discussed (p. 24).

Epicurus' method of indirect proof can be illustrated by copious passages from Lucretius. It is the poet's regular practice to refute a proposition by appeal to what is clear, what we actually see, and thus infer the contradictory of the rejected proposition. I give just one example. In Book i Lucretius argues towards the atomist thesis by stages. He begins by dismissing the proposition 'Something can be created from nothing'. For, if this were so, every type of thing could be produced out of anything; nothing would require a seed. But we see (*videmus*) that cultivated land produces better yield than uncultivated land, which proves the existence in the soil of primary bodies stirred to birth by the plough. 'If there were no primary bodies you would see (*videres*) each thing coming to birth much more successfully of its own accord' (159–214).

Like this Lucretian argument Epicurus' methodology seems imprecise and informal when judged by the criteria of stricter logic. I have no doubt that it is proper to describe as 'axioms' the two principles concerning confirmation and non-contradiction. But Epicurus does not *call* them axioms. He almost certainly knew Aristotle's *Analytics,* if a fragment of Philodemus has been correctly deciphered.[2] But although Aristotle's inductive methodology may have been an influence on Epicurus, the later philosopher did not share Aristotle's interest in logic for its own sake; and he seems to have thought that any kind of demonstrative science, based upon deductive reasoning, was mere word-play. Since most of Aristotle's *Analytics* is concerned with the analysis of deductive argument in the form of syllogisms and

[1] See Philodemus, *On signs* col. xvi ed. Ph. and E. A. De Lacey (Pennsylvania 1941).
[2] *Adversus sophistas* frs. 1, 3 ed. Sbordone (Naples 1947).

with specifying the sufficient conditions of necessary truths, Epicurus cannot have liked what he read. Above all, he rejected any kind of logical inquiry which was not applied to the understanding of empirical data. He did not, apparently, see that empirical science, if it is to be well-grounded, cannot advance very far solely on the guidance of 'clear' sense-impressions.

The reader will be able to extend the criticism of Epicurus' methodology for himself. What should be added is a warning against taking at face value off-hand remarks in ancient writers, which would imply that Epicurus had no interest in logic and scientific method. These views are to be found in many modern hand-books and they are incorrect. Epicurus, in order to shock, sometimes writes as if he despised all learning; but this is rhetoric, an expression of contempt for what he regarded as pedantic and positively harmful in the culture of his own day. Fortunately, sufficient of the twenty-eighth book of *On Nature* survives to give us a glimpse of Epicurus when he is not merely summarizing or exhorting. In this work Epicurus discussed induction, using Aristotle's technical term *epagôgê*, problems of meaning and ambiguity, the distinction between universal and particular, problems connected with the designation of individuals, and linguistic puzzles of the sort propounded by the Megarians. Unfortunately the text is too badly damaged to let us see how he treated all of these subjects in detail.[1] But it gives us sufficient evidence to judge that parts of the following statement by Cicero are grossly misleading: 'Epicurus rejects definitions [he did not]; gives no instruction concerning division [classification into genus and species]; fails to show how an argument is to be constructed; does not point out how sophisms are to be resolved nor how ambiguities are to be distinguished' (*Fin.* i 22). It is salutary to remember that Epicurus wrote thirty-seven books *On Nature*, and that we can observe Cicero's prejudice by studying fragments from just one of these.

(iv) The structure of things

The nature of the universe is bodies and void (*On Nature* i).

Epicurus claimed to be self-taught, but atomism was more than a century old in Greece by the time he re-asserted its central principles. First Leucippus and then Democritus, in the second half of the fifth century, had argued that what really exists is ultimately reducible to

---

[1] For more details see the article cited in n. 2, p .24.

two and only two kinds of thing: the full (indivisible bodies) and the empty (space). How such a thesis came to be propounded is itself a fascinating story, but it belongs to the history of Presocratic philosophy. I will touch on it here only in so far as it is essential to understanding Epicurus' atomism.

Our starting-point is once again the *Letter to Herodotus*. There, in a few paragraphs of highly succinct argumentation, Epicurus discloses the essential features of the atomist theory (38–44). The problem which that theory purports to solve may be stated as follows: What principles derived from empirical evidence are necessary and sufficient to account for the physical world as it presents itself to our senses? The answer is highly economical: an infinite number of indivisible bodies moving in infinite empty space.

Epicurus arrives at this answer by a series of metaphysical propositions, which he then uses to support inferences about the underlying structure of the changing objects of experience. (A) Nothing can come out of nothing. (B) Nothing can be destroyed into nothing. (C) The universe never was nor will be in a condition which differs from its present one.[1] The first two propositions are established indirectly by what I have called the second axiom. It would controvert experience to suppose that nothing pre-exists or survives the objects which we observe to grow and decay. Things are seen to grow *out of* something; they do not just emerge at random. Secondly, there *is* something *into* which things pass away. Otherwise there would be no limit to destruction and everything would have perished into non-being. The third proposition (C) is treated by Epicurus as analytic. Since the universe embraces all that there is, nothing exists outside the universe which could cause it to change. (He does not consider the possibility that any internal cause of change might bring about different conditions of the universe as a whole at different times.)

From (C) it follows that any explanation of things in general which holds now is eternally valid.

It is an evident fact that bodies exist; empty space must therefore also exist, since bodies must be *in* something and have something through which to move.[2] Epicurus next asserts that apart from bodies and void nothing can be conceived of as an independent entity: all

---

[1] Lucretius develops (A) and (B) at length, i 159–264; he deals with (C) at ii 294–307.

[2] For Lucretius' arguments concerning void, see i 329–97. Aristotle denied the necessity of void to explain motion, as did the Stoics.

things must be reducible to body and mind. Bodies are of two kinds, compounds and the units out of which compounds are formed. From (B) it follows that one class of bodies, non-compounds, must be limited with respect to change and destruction. Epicurus expresses this thus: 'And these bodies [*sc.* non-compounds] are indivisible and changeless, if all things are not to be destroyed into *non*-being but are to persist secure in the dissolution of compounds; they are solid in nature and cannot be divided at any place or in any manner. Hence the first principles must be bodies which are indivisible' (*Ep. Hdt.* 39–41).

Question-begging though this argument is, in Epicurus' abbreviated formulation, its main points are wholly clear. We do not see atoms, but what we see, birth and death, growth and decay, is taken to require the existence of bodies which are themselves changeless and wholly impenetrable.

What else is to be said about atoms and empty space? Epicurus proceeds to argue that the universe is 'unlimited' in itself and also in the number of atoms which it contains, and in the extent of empty space. If the universe were limited it would have extremities; but there is nothing to limit the universe. And if the universe itself is unlimited its constituents must also be unlimited. For a limited number of atoms in infinite empty space would not be sufficient to hold one another together; they could not form the plurality of compounds which we experience; and an unlimited number of atoms could not be accommodated in limited space (*Ep. Hdt.* 41–2).

Since all the objects of experience are compounded out of atoms and void, Epicurus held that the atoms themselves must have innumerable, though not infinitely, different shapes, in order to account for the variety of things. Besides shape, all atoms are necessarily subject to continuous movement, a fact which will require further discussion shortly. They also possess weight, and of course bulk or mass. All other properties of which we have experience are accounted for by the arrangements which come into being when a plurality of atoms and void combine. Atoms as such are not hot or cold, coloured or resonant, and so forth (*Ep. Hdt.* 42–4; 68–9).

It is now time to consider in more detail what Epicurus meant by the 'indivisibility' of the atom. As has been shown already, the concept of an atom is arrived at by elimination of a contradictory hypothesis, that bodies are ultimately divisible into *non*-being. If Epicurus supposed that the infinite divisibility of a body must lead to its reduction to nothing at all he was guilty of an elementary fallacy. Infinite divisibility implies nothing about reduction to sheer non-existence. Lucretius however sets out an argument for indivisible bodies which avoids this fallacy, and which, we may presume, goes back to Epicurus himself.

The argument runs thus: body and empty space are mutually exclusive, otherwise there would not be *two* kinds of real things (i.e. all things could be reduced to either body or empty space). Body therefore cannot include as part of itself empty space. Anything which does include as part of itself empty space must be bounded by that which is solid—body. Created things are of this kind, that is, compounds of body and empty space. But the particular bodies which help to form such compounds must consist of that which is wholly solid and indivisible. For nothing can be divided unless it contains within itself empty space. And nothing can contain within itself empty space unless it has components which are themselves wholly indivisible (Lucret. i 503–35).

The force of this argument turns on the assumption that empty space is a necessary condition of divisibility. The earlier atomists had spoken of empty space as '*non*-being' and of body as 'being': empty space is non-body. If we take Epicurus' reference to *non*-being as a legacy of this earlier usage his argument becomes compatible with the passage summarized from Lucretius. Just as what-is cannot be ultimately reduced to what-is-not, so body cannot be reduced to non-body, i.e. empty space.

The Epicurean atoms cannot be split into smaller bodies. They are physically indivisible. But they are not the smallest units of extension. The atom itself consists of minimal parts which are not merely physically unsplittable but indivisible in thought: nothing beyond these *minima* can be conceived of. Epicurus supposed that there is a finite number of such minimal parts for every atom. Atoms vary in size, and their size is determined by the number of their minimal parts. Again, atoms vary in shape and their shape is determined by the arrangement of their minimal parts.

This doctrine of minimal parts raises many difficulties and will only be discussed briefly here. Epicurus apparently regarded each atom as something composed of minimum units of magnitude which are not separable from one another, and therefore not separable from the whole atom which they compose (*Ep. Hdt.* 56–9).[1] The notion is obscure and may be clarified by a concrete analogy. Suppose we take a

[1] See also Lucretius i 599–634.

cubic centimetre of solid metal and mark it off in three dimensions by millimetres. Then, the minimal parts stand to the atom as each cubic millimetre to the whole cube of metal, with this proviso: each square millimetre must be taken as the smallest unit which can be distinguished on any surface of the whole cube. The Epicurean atom is the smallest magnitude which can exist as a discrete independent body. Epicurus seems to have thought that this left something to be accounted for— namely, the atom's boundary points, or the fact, to put it another way, that the atom is a three-dimensional object and as such possesses shape. He sought an explanation by reference to its having minimal parts.

In giving the atoms minimal parts Epicurus almost certainly modified earlier atomism. The atoms of Leucippus and Democritus were physically indivisible but also, in all probability, without parts, and therefore theoretically indivisible as well. Simplicius, the Aristotelian commentator, distinguishes Epicurus from the earlier atomists thus: Epicurus, he says, appealed merely to the changelessness of his primary bodies, whereas Leucippus and Democritus also referred to their smallness and lack of parts (Us. 268).

Our knowledge of early atomism is largely derived from Aristotle. Modern research has shown that he was right to connect the fifth-century atomists with the slightly older Eleatic philosophers, Parmenides and Zeno.[1] This is not the place to offer any detailed account of the Eleatics. Very briefly, Parmenides, in his poem *The way of truth*, had set out arguments of quite remarkable subtlety concerning what can be said about that which exists. He concluded that the following predicates are inadmissible: subject to creation and destruction, subject to divisibility, subject to change of place, and change of quality; what exists is 'whole, immobile, eternal, all together, one and continuous'. Zeno reinforced Parmenides' arguments by seeking to show that the proposition 'Things are many and subject to motion' leads to insoluble dilemmas. Zeno's puzzles turn chiefly on the notion of partition or divisibility. The interpretation of them is extremely difficult and controversial. One point only concerns us here. Zeno argued that if a unit of magnitude can be divided at all it must be infinitely divisible. This conclusion was unpalatable to the early atomists who wished to give an explanation of the world which would

[1] The most penetrating study of Democritean and Epicurean atomism is by D. J. Furley, *Two Studies in the Greek Atomists* (Princeton 1967). His first study deals with the notion of minimal parts.

be compatible, as far as possible, with Parmenides' logic. Hence they adopted as their primary bodies partless, and therefore indivisible, units of magnitude, which satisfied most of the predicates deduced by Parmenides to belong to what really exists. Lacking parts, the atoms of Democritus would not even be theoretically divisible.

Epicurus modified this doctrine by ascribing parts to the atom but making these parts themselves *minima*, i.e. physically and theoretically indivisible. He seems to have supposed that it is a necessary condition of the atom itself, the minimum discrete body, that it possesses parts— but parts which rule out theoretical divisibility to infinity for the atom itself. Minimal parts satisfied this condition, and they also provided a means of accounting for differences in the shape, size and weight of particular atoms. Lucretius asserts that 'things which are not augmented by parts do not have the diversities of properties which creative matter must have' (i 631–3). Finally, Aristotle had pointed out a number of difficulties in the notion of a partless atom which Epicurus' new thesis may have been intended to resolve (*Physics* vi 231b25–232a17; 240b8–241a6). We shall come back to minimal parts in the next section.

(v) *The motion of atoms and formation of compound bodies*

One modification of earlier atomism by Epicurus has just been discussed. He also differed from Democritus concerning the motion of atoms. Both agreed that the atoms are always in motion, but Democritus almost certainly supposed that the course which any one atom takes relative to any other is wholly random.[1] In fact, most of our evidence for the motion of Democritus' atoms clearly refers to motion derived from collisions with other atoms, and we can only speculate about what he might have said of the original motion of an atom. He probably did not attribute weight to the atom, and if so, cannot have used weight as a cause of motion. Furthermore, it is unlikely that he would have thought it proper to ascribe any direction to the movement of atoms since he said of infinite void that it has neither top nor bottom, centre or extremity (Cic. *Fin.* i 17). Void provided Democritus with a condition which he certainly regarded as necessary for motion, and he may have simply taken it as a fact about the atom that it does necessarily move in the void.

---

[1] This is supported by Aristotle's words, quoted by Simplicius (DK 68 A 37); cf. W. K. C. Guthrie, *History of Greek Philosophy* vol. ii (Cambridge 1965) pp. 400–2.

Against Democritus Epicurus held that weight is a necessary property of the atom. His reasons for this assertion cannot be established by any direct testimony, but they are almost certainly founded on the hypothesis that a weightless body cannot move. Aristotle devoted considerable attention to the analysis of weight as a determining factor of motion. Indeed, in the *De caelo* Aristotle defines heavy and light as 'the capacity for a certain natural motion' (307b32), and a little later says: 'There are certain things whose nature it is always to move away from the centre, and others always towards the centre. The first I speak of as moving upwards, the second downwards' (308a14). Now Epicurus recognized that in an infinite universe one cannot strictly speak of a centre, nor of up and down (*Ep. Hdt.* 60). But he thought that one could speak of up and down relative to some fixed point, and that in this relative sense the natural motion of atoms is downwards as a consequence of their weight. Any other motion than perpendicular fall requires other factors than weight alone to account for it. In all probability, Aristotle's discussion of weight as a determinant of movement influenced Epicurus' modification of Democritus.

If an atom is unimpeded by collision with other atoms its speed and direction of motion are invariant. Epicurus grasped the important fact that differences of weight make no difference to the velocity of bodies falling in a vacuum: 'When they are moving through the void and encounter no resistance the speed of the atoms must be equal. Neither will heavy ones travel faster than light ones . . . ' (*Ep. Hdt.* 61). At what speed then do free-falling atoms move? Epicurus sometimes expresses this in the graphic phrase 'as quick as thought'. But that does not help us very much. In fact, he seems to have supposed that time, like extension, is not infinitely divisible. Just as the atom is the minimum discrete body and consists of minimal parts, so time is divisible into 'minimum continuous periods' which themselves consist of indivisible temporal units, 'times distinguishable only in thought' (*Ep. Hdt.* 62). Epicurus probably supposed that the time which an atom takes to move the minimum distance, that is the minimum of extension, is the minimum temporal unit. This temporal unit, being indivisible, is not such that a movement can take place *during* it. 'Has moved' not 'is moving' is the relation which a moving body has to the indivisible units that constitute time and space (Us. 278). As Aristotle saw, such a theory turns movement into a series of jerks (*Phys.* vi 231b25–232a17). The atom has to hop, as it were, from one set of spatial units into the next. For there is no time or space in which its progression from one unit into the next can be said to occur. The minimum distance by which an atom can alter its location at any moment is the measure of any one minimal part.

Epicurus could have avoided these consequences if he had seen that the infinite divisibility of any *quantum,* whether of space or time, can be asserted without its entailing the consequence that these *quanta* are, as a matter of fact, divisible into infinite parts. He chose instead to predicate physical indivisibility of the atom and a limit to the theoretical division of its parts. Having wrongly concluded that the extremities of the atom must be accounted for by positing minimal spatial units, he accepted as a corollary the indivisibility of time and movement as well. He countered Aristotle's objection, that this makes differences of speed impossible, by arguing that apparent differences in the speed of the compound bodies which we see can be explained as a function of the collective movements at constant speed of individual atoms within each compound; the speed of a moving compound is determined by the collisions which occur between its internal atoms. The more its atoms tend to move in the same direction over a short period of time the greater the speed of the compound body. If the movement of some atoms in one direction is balanced by a movement of others in a different direction the compound body will be stationary (*Ep. Hdt.* 47; 62).[1]

Let us now return to consider the falling atom in more detail. Given that this fall is at constant speed for any atom, and in the same direction, how can a world be formed which consists of atoms in conjunction, atoms which have collided and formed compound bodies? Oddly enough, no word of the answer to this problem survives by Epicurus himself. But his theory can be reconstructed from Lucretius and other later writers. Lucretius writes as follows: 'At this point I wish you to learn this too: when bodies are being carried straight down through the void by their own weight, at an undetermined time and at undetermined places they push a little from their course—only as much as you might call a change of direction. If they were not accustomed to swerve, all things would fall down through the deep void like raindrops, nor could collision come about nor would the atoms experience blows. And so nature would never have created anything' (ii. 216–24).

This swerve which atoms make at no determined time or place has always intrigued the readers of Lucretius. It apparently builds into

[1] For a detailed treatment, to which I am much indebted, see Furley, *Two Studies in the Greek Atomists,* pp. 111–30.

the universe, as Epicurus conceives of this, a principle of relative indeterminacy. The movements of an atom, and therefore any consequences of its movement, are not entirely predictable. Our further information about the swerve in this context merely confirms Lucretius' words, and they must be taken at face value.[1] It follows then that an atom, independently of any secondary motion which may result from collisions, has both a unidirectional movement and an unpredictable tendency to deviate from this.

The atomic swerve is also important to Epicurus' theory of human action. But that will require discussion later (p. 57). The effect of the swerve with which we are concerned here is the collision between two or more atoms which it may bring about. Since every atom is solid through and through, the effect of a collision between atoms is a momentary check on atomic movement followed by a rebound (at the same speed), and hence a further change of direction. But it may sometimes happen that colliding atoms in spite of their tendency to rebound become intertwined and form a temporary and apparently stable compound. The compound so formed is in fact a dynamic entity, a collection of atoms moving both in their normal downward manner and from the effect of blows or swerves. But it will often present the appearance of something stable. Lucretius reports that the different densities of objects are determined by the relation between the atoms and void which they contain. Iron consists of close-packed atoms which are unable to move and rebound any great distance. Air, on the other hand, is composed of atoms which are interspersed with large areas of void (ii 100–8).

We have seen that for Epicurus all properties of things beyond size, shape, weight and movement are secondary. That is to say, they are properties which cannot be predicated of atoms but only of the compound bodies which atoms may form. This does not mean that colour, sound etc. are merely human ways of ordering and interpreting sense-impressions. Democritus had argued thus, but Epicurus did not agree (*Ep. Hdt.* 68–71). His discussion of secondary qualities is condensed and obscure, but seems basically to amount to this: colour, sound etc. cannot exist independently of bodies, nor are they 'parts' out of which compound bodies arise. Rather, any secondary property which is a permanent attribute of some object (compound body) is a *constituent* of the object in the sense that the object would not be what it is without this attribute. We might illustrate this point by saying

[1] The gist of what Lucretius says is repeated by Cicero, *Fin.* i 18–20.

that a man does not arise out of a combination of hands, legs, colour and so forth. He arises from a combination of atoms and void. But the effect of this combination is the production of hands, legs, pink or black colour etc., and these, or some of them, are necessary attributes of any man.

Although Epicurus' basic distinction between bodies is the simple disjunction, atom or compound, he may have supposed that certain compounds function as molecules or basic complexes which serve as 'seeds' for the production of more complex things.[1] Lucretius writes of 'seeds of water' or 'seeds of fire', and though he may mean simply 'that out of which water or fire is composed' the specific property of water or fire is something which only arises through the combination of atoms. It is probable, though not certain, that Epicurus would have regarded a pool of water as a compound of smaller compounds—molecules of water. If the molecule were broken down we should of course be left only with atoms and void. Epicurus firmly rejected the four-element theory which persists through Greek philosophy in various forms from Empedocles to Neoplatonism.

I have called the compound body a dynamic entity. This description applies not merely to its internal atoms but also to those atoms which constitute its surface. An object which persists over any length of time does not retain the same atoms throughout that time. Epicurus supposed that atoms are constantly leaving the surface of objects and having their place taken by further atoms which bombard the object and may then get caught up on its structure.[2] The notion that atoms are constantly leaving the surface of objects is fundamental to the explanation of sensation. As observed already, we sense something when effluences enter our sense organs. If these are 'real' images they are simply the outer surface or skin of objects which is 'sloughed off', to use a Lucretian metaphor, in a continuous stream of 'films'.

Epicurus took over his fundamental principles of atoms and void from earlier atomists but we have seen that he was no slavish imitator. The atomist system seemed to him to provide an explanation of the structure of things which was both compatible with empirical data and psychologically comforting, in that it did away with the need for divine causation and any form of teleology. Whether or not men find

---

[1] Good arguments in favour of this have been advanced by G. B. Kerferd, *Phronesis* 16 (1971) 88–9.
[2] See in particular *Ep. Hdt.* 48. The regular replenishment of 'lost' atoms explains why objects are not (normally) seen to diminish in bulk.

it more or less comforting to suppose that the world is determined by a supernatural being or beings, seems to be very much a matter of personal temperament. Lucretius praises Epicurus for delivering mankind from 'the weight of religion' (i 62ff.). He means popular religion, superstitious beliefs in the gods as direct arbiters of human destiny and fears of divine anger as expressed in thunder and lightning. But Epicurus cannot have taken popular superstitions as his only target. He was also concerned to reject the sophisticated theology of Plato and probably Aristotle too.

How he did so and what he put in its place will be the subject of the next few pages. Before discussing this, however, we should notice how Epicurus rejects out of hand the method of teleological explanation which bulks so large in Plato and Aristotle. Plato makes Socrates complain that Presocratic thinkers fail to show why it is best for things to be as they are (*Phaedo* 99a–d).[1] What Socrates is alleged to have found a defect—the concentration on mechanical explanations— Epicurus regarded as a positive merit. Things are not 'good for anything', he argued; this is merely a piece of learned superstition. There is no purpose which the world as a whole or things in particular are designed to fulfil. For design is not a feature of the world; it is manifestly imperfect.[2] Given the fact that the number of atoms is infinite and that their shapes are immensely various, it is not remarkable that similar combinations of things arise. Indeed, Epicurus held that the number of worlds is infinite, some of which are like our own while others vary (*Ep. Hdt.* 45). All of them however are ultimately explicable by reference to the purposeless combination and separation of discrete and inanimate physical entities moving in empty space.

Epicurus' cosmology denies the foundation of the Platonic and Aristotelian world-picture. The fossilized Aristotelianism of the schoolmen came under attack in the Renaissance, and Epicurean atomism was given a new relevance by the French mathematician and opponent of Descartes, Pierre Gassendi. The history of later science has amply vindicated Epicurus' rejection of final causes. But it is arguable that Epicurus' renunciation of teleology, in its historical context, went too far. His principle of explanation in terms of accidental arrangement of atoms will hardly serve to account adequately for such phenomena as biological reproduction. Why, to give the question

---

[1] Plato himself attacks purely mechanistic theories of causation, probably with Democritus in mind, in the tenth book of his *Laws* 889b.
[2] Lucretius attacks 'final' causes at length, v 195–234.

an Aristotelian tone, does man produce man? Lucretius, it is true, offers an answer to this question: the characteristics of a species are transmitted to the offspring through its own seed (iii 741ff.), and he repeatedly emphasizes that each thing has its own fixed place; that there are natural laws determining biological and other events (i 75–7; ii 700ff.; iii 615ff. etc.). But the basis of these laws does not seem to rest firmly on anything implied by Epicurus' atomist principles. His physical theory has to explain too much by too little. These complaints are legitimate if we judge Epicurus by Aristotelian standards. But in making them it is necessary to remember that Epicurus did not set out to be a purely disinterested investigator of things. According to his own words, 'the purpose of studying nature is to gain a sharp understanding of the cause of those things which are most important' (*Ep. Hdt.* 78). By 'most important' he means fundamental to human well-being.

The two subjects on which he thought it most important to have correct beliefs were theology and psychology. Having now discussed Epicurus' basic physical principles I turn to consider how he applied these to his treatment of the gods and the human mind.

(vi) The gods of Epicurus

That which is sublimely happy and immortal experiences no trouble itself nor does it inflict trouble on anything else, so that it is not affected by passion or partiality. Such things are found only in what is weak (*K.D.* i).

Nothing disquieted Epicurus more profoundly than the notion that supernatural beings control phenomena or that they can affect human affairs. That there are gods he did not deny. But he repeatedly and vociferously rejected the belief that gods are responsible for any natural events. His rejection of this belief is expressed most pointedly in contexts concerning astronomical phenomena.

Moreover we must not suppose that the movement and turning of the heavenly bodies, their eclipses and risings and settings and similar movements are caused by some being which takes charge of them and which controls or will continue to control them, while simultaneously enjoying complete bliss and immortality. For occupation and supervision, anger and favour, are not consistent with sublime happiness. . . . Nor again must we suppose that those things which are merely an aggregate of fire possess sublime happiness and direct these (celestial) movements deliberately and voluntarily (*Ep. Hdt.* 76–7).

The object of Epicurus' polemic in these lines is any theology which ascribes divine control to the heavenly bodies. By denying the survival of the personality in any form after death Epicurus thought he could remove the source of one basic human anxiety—fear of divine judgment and eternal punishment. And I will discuss this feature of his philosophy in the next section. But he held that it was equally false and disturbing to credit gods with any influence over human affairs here and now. Thereby he denied the foundations of popular Greek religion. The notion that human well-being and adversity are dispensed by the gods was fundamental to popular Greek religion. Language reflected the belief: a happy man was *eudaimôn*, 'one who has a favourable deity'; *kakodaimôn*, 'unhappy', literally means 'having a harmful deity'. For the majority perhaps, belief in the gods of mythology had generally been a matter of civic or private ritual rather than any inner experience. But many Greeks, educated and uneducated alike, subscribed to mystery cults which promised salvation to the initiated, and fears of pollution and divine intervention remained strong. Theophrastus' portrait of the Superstitious Man, overdrawn though it is, would lose all point if it had no basis in everyday experience.[1]

But Epicurus' attack on divine management of the cosmos was more specifically directed, we may suppose, against the cosmology of Plato and Aristotle. Plato, in his later works, constantly refers to the regularity of celestial movements as evidence of intelligent direction by divine beings. In the *Timaeus* we are told that the purpose of sight for men is to observe the 'revolutions of intelligence in the heavens, so that we may use their regular motions to guide the troubled movements of our own thinking'; we are to 'imitate the invariant movements of God' (47b–c.) This concept of divine ordination of the heavens was developed by Plato with much more detail in the *Laws*, his last major work.[2] There he defends the thesis that the heavenly bodies have as their cause virtuous souls or gods (x 899b). Their virtue is proved by the regularity of the movements which they cause. Disorderly movements, whether in the heavens or on earth, must be accounted for by a soul which is bad (897d).

Not only, according to Plato, are the stars directed by gods. Man-

[1] The reference is especially relevant because it is a contemporary one. Theophrastus' *Characters* are a set of short vignettes of character types: complaisance, boorishness, miserliness etc.

[2] The development of Plato's theology is a complex subject; for a well-balanced account see F. Solmsen, *Plato's Theology* (Ithaca, N.Y. 1942).

kind and the universe as a whole are the 'possessions' of the gods (902b–c). In the *Laws* Plato emphasizes that the control which gods exercise over men is providential. But he states equally strongly that it is absolute. Plato thought he could legislate for a reformed religion by banishing the discreditable gods of tradition and replacing them with new gods whose excellence was manifested in the mathematical perfection of celestial physics. But to Epicurus Plato's astral gods were quite as repugnant as the traditional Olympian pantheon. His refusal to regard the movements of the stars as a consequence of divine intentions is an explicit rejection of Plato's own language. In the *Epinomis,* the title of which means 'after the laws', astronomy is made the key to this new theology.[1] The heavenly bodies are there said to be the source of our knowledge of number, which itself is the foundation of intelligence and morality. This queer assertion is put forward in all seriousness, and it leads to a reiteration of the divinity of the stars. These beings possess wondrous powers of mind; they know our own wills; they welcome the good and loathe the bad (984d–985b).

Epicurus regarded such beliefs as a prime source of human anxiety. To him they seemed to compound old superstitions and to make the heavenly bodies, with their watching brief over human affairs, an object of utter terror. He can have been little less disquieted by Aristotle's theology. For Aristotle too regarded the heavenly bodies as intelligent, divine beings whose movements are voluntary. We know that Aristotle expressed such views in an early work designed for popular consumption.[2] It is also true that Aristotle's views about celestial movements developed during his lifetime and that he does not in any extant treatise make the heavenly bodies personal arbiters of human destiny. But it is a basic doctrine of his *Metaphysics* that all movement and life are ultimately dependent upon the Unmoved Mover, pure Mind or God, whose activity of eternal self-contemplation promotes desire and motion in the heavenly bodies, each governed by its own intelligence. Aristotle approved of popular

---

[1] Doubts about the Platonic authorship of this work have been expressed from antiquity onwards. If not by Plato himself, which is likely enough, it should be ascribed to a younger contemporary Academic, perhaps Philip of Opus (D.L. iii 37).

[2] Cic. *N.D.* ii 42–4. Comparison with Book i 33 of Cicero's treatise suggests the reference may be to Aristotle's third book 'On philosophy'. On Aristotle's theology see W. K. C. Guthrie, *Classical Quarterly* 27 (1933) 162–71; 28 (1934) 90–8.

beliefs in the divinity of the heavens, even though he denied their traditional mythological trappings (*Met.* 1074a38ff.). The Unmoved Mover, like Epicurus' own gods, is not personally concerned with the universe. But unlike Epicurus' gods the Unmoved Mover is the prime cause of all things. He does not determine human affairs by his own fiat. They are none the less dependent upon events, such as the sun's diurnal rotation and seasonal change, of which he is the ultimate cause.[1]

Epicurus rejects divine management of the world by an argument based upon the meaning and implications of the words 'sublimely happy' and 'immortal'. He accepts that these predicates, traditionally ascribed to the gods, express real attributes of divine beings (*Ep. Men.* 123). But he denies that sublime happiness and immortality are compatible with any involvement in 'our affairs' (Cic. *N.D.* i 51–2). In his view happiness, whether human or divine, requires for its full realization a life of uninterrupted tranquillity or freedom from pain. For the moment we must accept this concept of happiness as a dogmatic assertion, for its full analysis belongs to the field of ethics. Epicurus' argument concerning the gods' indifference to the world picks up this concept of happiness, applies it to the gods and thereby removes from them any actions or feelings which take account of human affairs. Seneca summarizes this position: 'Hence god dispenses no benefits; he is impregnable, heedless of us; indifferent to the world . . . untouched by benefits and wrongs' (Us. 364).

The argument makes three assumptions. First, that there are gods. Secondly, that the gods are sublimely happy and immortal. Thirdly, that their happiness consists in uninterrupted tranquillity. We must now consider how Epicurus justified these assumptions.

Since he was disposed to combat all beliefs about divine control of the world it may seem surprising that Epicurus accepted even the existence of supernatural beings. For, if the gods could be shown to be fictions, all activities associated with them would necessarily also be ruled out. Epicurus argued however that the universal beliefs of mankind establish the fact that gods exist. 'What people or race is there which lacks an untaught conception of gods?' (Cic. *N.D.* i 43). The argument claims that *a* belief in gods exists independently of institution-

---

[1] It was clearly Epicurean practice to attack all theological views which differed from their own; cf. Cic. *N.D.* i *passim*. Epicurus must have found much to object to in the writings of Plato's successor, Xenocrates, whose theology contained 'daimons' as well as celestial divinities and who foreshadowed the Stoics in referring the names of certain gods to natural substances.

alized religion or custom. It is therefore something *natural.* Of course the belief might be natural and false. But Epicurus uses a basically Aristotelian premise (*E.N.* 1172b35) to reject this objection: 'That about which all agree must be true.'

The same principle, *consensus omnium,* is used to establish the properties of the gods. All men are also said to have a natural belief that the gods are immortal, sublimely happy and of human shape.[1] Epicurus held that these common beliefs are 'preconceptions' derived from experience—visions which people have when awake and all the more when asleep. He argued that these visions must, like all sensations, be caused by something real, that is to say atomic configurations or images (effluences) which come from the gods themselves and which penetrate to our minds. The theory is naïve and fails to take account of other factors which might have led men to believe in gods. If as a matter of fact human beliefs about gods were as consistent with each other and as similar as Epicurus claims, the hypothesis of mental perception of divine images would offer a reason for the *consensus omnium*: we are all acted upon by the same kind of external images. But Epicurus assumes the *consensus omnium,* and then seeks to explain it in psychophysical terms.

According to Lucretius the properties of sublime happiness and immortality were inferred by men from their mental images of the gods:

> They endowed the gods with eternal life, because images of the gods were constantly supplied with unchanging form, and also because they believed that beings possessed of such strength could not be vanquished by any chance force. And they supposed that the gods enjoyed supreme happiness because no fear of death troubled any of them, and because in dreams the gods were seen to do many remarkable things without any expenditure of effort (v 1175–82).

Lucretius proceeds to argue that early men, having acquired a belief in gods, supposed them to be the agents of astronomical and meteorological phenomena through ignorance of the real cause of these things. Elsewhere he argues at length that the gods cannot have had any desire or ability to create the universe, the imperfections of which are clear evidence that it is not under divine direction (v 156–94). The gods, like true Epicureans, dwell in *sedes quietae* ('tranquil resting-places') enjoying a life free of all trouble (iii 18–24).

---

[1] Cic. *N.D.* i 45–6; see also *Ep. Men.* 123–4 which refers to the false conceptions of the 'many' about gods.

Besides the natural conceptions of mankind Epicurus himself gave other reasons for justifying his account of the gods' nature. He defended their anthropomorphic appearance by the argument that this is the most beautiful of all shapes and therefore the shape which belongs to beings whose nature is best (Cic. *N.D.* i 46–9). Not all of his statements about the gods can be reduced to the supposed evidence of natural conceptions.[1] But while recognizing that the images which men receive from the gods are 'insubstantial' and difficult to perceive, he clearly hoped to show that primary knowledge of the gods is something similar in kind to the direct acquaintance with physical objects which we obtain through our sense organs.

How is the physical structure of the gods to be conceived of and what manner of life do they lead? The evidence which bears on these questions is difficult and must be dealt with summarily here. The basic problem is the everlasting existence of the gods. Atoms and void are imperishable, for atoms possess a solidity which is impervious to all 'blows' and void is unassailable by 'blows' (Lucret. iii 806–13). But the ordinary objects of experience, because they are compounded out of atoms and void, are not of a kind to resist destruction indefinitely. So Lucretius writes:

By (natural) law they perish, when all things have been made weak by outflow (of atoms) and give way to the blows which come from outside (ii 1139–40).

Epicurus sought to avoid this difficulty by introducing a mode of being which is not a compound body in any ordinary sense. Our main evidence is a difficult text of Cicero. After observing that the gods are perceived by the mind and not the senses, Cicero writes that they do not possess 'solidity' nor 'numerical identity', like the ordinary objects of perception, but 'an unlimited form of very similar images arises out of the innumerable atoms and flows towards the gods' (*N.D.* i 49, cf. 105). Elsewhere the gods are perhaps spoken of as 'likenesses' and some gods (or all of them from one point of view) are 'things which exist by similarity of form through the continuous

---

[1] See further, K. Kleve, *Symbolae Osloenses*, suppl. xix. Epicurus (Cic. *N.D.* i 50) also inferred that there must be divine beings equal in number to mortals by the principle of 'equal balance' or 'reciprocal distribution' (*isonomia*). 'From this,' we are told, 'it follows that if the number of mortals is so many there exists no less a number of immortals, and if the causes of destruction are uncountable the causes of conservation must also be infinite.'

onflow of similar images which are brought to fulfilment at the same place' (Us. 355).[1] Scholars have questioned the accuracy of these statements on the grounds that they make the atoms which flow *towards* the gods 'images'. But these doubts may be misplaced. 'Image' (or *eidôlon* in Epicurus' terminology) is distinguished from 'solid body'. There can be 'images' in this sense which are merely patterns of fine atoms lacking the density to constitute a solid body. We may perceive Centaurs in virtue of such 'images', but they are not images contrasted with a real Centaur; for there is no solid body corresponding to a Centaur. Similarly, there is no solid body which emits images of the gods. For the gods do not possess a solid body. They are called 'likenesses', in all probability, because their nature is continuously reconstituted by a moving stream of 'images', discrete arrangements of fine atoms which possess *similar* form.

The gods then have no numerical identity. If their substance were that of an ordinary compound body they would be subject to an irreplaceable loss of atoms and hence destructible by external 'blows'. Their identity is 'formal', a consequence of the constant arrival and departure of similar forms at the points in space occupied by the gods. It has sometimes been aptly compared with the nature of a waterfall the shape of which is determined by continuous flow. Epicurus does not explain why there should be a continuous supply of atoms patterned in the right way to constitute the form of the gods. If pressed he would probably have argued that in a universe which contains an infinite number of atoms this is not impossible in principle (see p. 46, n. 1); and that our experience of the gods—the fact that we can have more than momentary visions of them—proves the continuity of their form, and therefore the supply of appropriate atoms. Moreover we think of them as immortal.

Does this strange notion of the gods' physical structure imply that they themselves make no contribution to their own unceasing existence? The evidence discussed so far could imply that the gods are simply happy beneficiaries of a constant supply of atoms which replace those they have lost. Some scholars have adopted such a view. But Philodemus, who wrote a work *On the gods* (as did Epicurus himself), parts of which are preserved on a Herculaneum papyrus,

---

[1] The word 'brought to fulfilment' (*apotetelesmenôn*) should not be emended with Kühn and Usener to *apotetelesmenous*: it is the 'images' not the gods which are brought to fulfilment; cf. *Ep. Pyth.* 115, 'by the meeting of atoms productive of fire'.

seems to have argued that the gods' own excellence and powers of
reason secure them from destructive forces in the environment.[1] It
should not be supposed that this is a laborious activity for the gods.
On the contrary, all our sources stress the fact that the gods enjoy
an existence completely free of toil. They are able, in virtue of their
nature, to appropriate the atoms which preserve their existence and to
ward off atoms of the wrong kind. This seems to have been Philodemus' view, and we may reasonably credit it to Epicurus himself.

The gods' tenuity of structure is explained by the 'images' which
form their bodies, a theory ridiculed by ancient critics (*N.D.* i 105).
We may now see why the gods are not said to have body but quasi
body, not blood but quasi blood (Cic. *N.D.* i 49). They are seen above
all in dreams and are themselves dreamlike in substance, insubstantial
like the 'images' which make up their being. It may seem strange that
Epicurus should have credited such creatures with perfect happiness,
but this becomes less odd when we study what their happiness consists in. It is something negative rather than positive. The gods have
no occupations, they can be affected by no pain, they are liable to no
change. They dwell in no world but in the spaces which separate one
world from another (*intermundia*, Cic. *N.D.* i 18). And since it is
Epicurus' claim that absence of pain is the highest pleasure, and
pleasure is the essence of happiness, the gods are perfectly happy. In
the later Epicureanism of Philodemus more positive things are said
about the gods, including the fact that they speak Greek! But Epicurus,
so far as we know, did not go in for such crude anthropomorphism.

> . . . The Gods, who haunt
> The lucid interspace of world and world,
> Where never creeps a cloud, or moves a wind,
> Where never falls the least white star of snow,
> Nor ever lowest roll of thunder moans,
> Nor sound of human sorrow mounts to mar
> Their sacred everlasting calm![2]

Human affairs are no concern of the gods. But are the gods, or
should they be, any concern of men? Epicurus seems to have held that
certain forms of ritual and private devotion are appropriate because,

---

[1] *De dis* iii fr. 32a p. 52 Diels. For further discussion of Philodemus' evidence
and theories based upon it, cf. W. Schmid, *Rheinisches Museum* 94 (1951) 97–156,
K. Kleve, *Symbolae Osloenses* 35 (1959), who attributes the gods' self-preservation
to the exercise of free will.

[2] Tennyson, *Lucretius*, based on Lucret. iii 18–23, itself a translation of Homer.

although the gods cannot be touched by prayers or sacrifices, they provide men with a model of beatitude. Whether or not a man is benefited by the gods depends upon his state of mind when he apprehends divine 'images'. If he himself is tranquil he will attain to the right view of the gods (Lucret. vi 71–8), and a passage in the *Letter to Menoeceus* (124) is perhaps to be interpreted along the same lines: those whose disposition is already akin to that of the gods can appropriate and gain benefit from divine 'images'. It is in the same spirit that Philodemus writes: 'He [*sc.* Epicurus] appeals to the completely happy in order to strengthen his own happiness' (Diels, *Sitz. Berl.* 1916, p. 895).

(vii) The soul and mental processes

Death is nothing to us; for that which has been dissolved lacks sensation; and that which lacks sensation is no concern to us (*K.D.* ii).

The first thing which Epicurus strove to establish in his psychological theory was the complete and permanent loss of consciousness at death. All his philosophy has the ultimate aim of removing human anxiety, and the therapeutic aspect of his psychology is a most conspicuous example of this. By denying any kind of survival to the personality after death, Epicurus hoped to show that beliefs in a system of rewards and punishments as recompense for life on earth were mere mythology. It is difficult to assess precisely the strength and prevalence of such beliefs in Epicurus' own time. But apart from his vehement desire to undermine them, which must be evidence that they were not uncommonly held, we find independent confirmation in literature and the popularity of 'mystery cults'.

Traces of such beliefs are already to be found in fifth-century writers. It is not likely that they declined during the fourth century. Plato, in the *Republic*, writes scathingly of those who provide books of Musaeus and Orpheus, and try to persuade 'whole cities as well as individuals' to absolve themselves from their crimes by performing certain rituals. Such men hoodwink people into believing that they will reap benefits in this world and the next, while those who fail to observe the rituals will be confronted with 'terrible things' (*Rep.* ii 364e). Cephalus, the old man who figures at the beginning of the *Republic*, is portrayed as someone who has been tormented by fears of having to expiate his offences in Hades. Plato himself condemns the quacks who try to exploit such fears by offering absolution at a fee.

But he ends the *Republic* with a myth which has judgment of the dead and rewards and punishments for earthly existence as its central feature. Similar myths are used by him in the *Phaedo* and the *Gorgias*. Both the pre-existence and the survival of the soul, after death, are central Platonic doctrines which he combines with the theory of metempsychosis.

The fear of death is common to all peoples at all times. Epicurus may have exaggerated the psychological disturbance he attributed to explicit beliefs in a destiny for the soul after death. But he did not confine his diagnosis of the fear of death to eschatological dogmas. As he himself writes (*Ep. Hdt.* 81), and as Lucretius writes at greater length, men also fear death who believe that it is the end of all sensation. Lucretius uses an argument to remove such fear which simply asserts that this is a true belief and *therefore* no grounds for anxiety: events which took place before we were born did not disturb us, for we did not *feel* them. By parity of reasoning, nothing can disturb us when we cease to be conscious of anything (iii 830–51). A little later he goes on:

If there is to be any trouble and pain for a man he too must exist himself at that time in order that ill may affect him. Since death removes this and prevents the existence of him to whom a mass of misfortunes might accrue, we may be assured that there is nothing to be feared in death and that he who no longer exists cannot be troubled (iii 861–8).

For Epicurus birth and death are limits which contain the existence of a person. *I* have not existed in another body prior to this life, nor am *I* liable to experience a further incarnation following this life. There is such a thing as *psychê*, soul, the presence of which in a body causes that body to possess life. Here Epicurus agreed with philosophical and popular conceptions. But he also insisted against Plato and other dualists that the soul cannot exist independently of the body, and that a living being must be a union of the body and the soul. Disrupt this union and life ceases. His view bears comparison with that of Aristotle who defined soul as 'the first actuality of an organic natural body' (*De an.* ii 412b5). For Aristotle too, most functions of the soul are necessarily related to the body, though Aristotle made an exception of intellect. We should not however press this comparison. Aristotle's treatment of soul proceeds by very different steps from Epicurus'. It calls for distinctions between form and matter and between potentiality and actuality which are quite foreign to

Epicurus' way of thinking; in Aristotle soul is not a kind of physical substance, as it is for Epicurus. That on which they broadly agree is the mutual dependence of body and soul.

What then did Epicurus say about the soul? Or, to put the question another way, how did he explain life? The first point is that life must be accounted for by reference to something corporeal. For that which is not body is void, and void cannot *do* anything nor *be affected* by anything (*Ep. Hdt.* 67). The grounds for denying that soul is incorporeal show that Epicurus regards the capacity to act and to be acted upon as a necessary condition of that which animates a living being. More specifically, soul consists of atoms which act upon and are affected by the atoms constituting the body itself.

'Soul is a body, the parts of which are fine, distributed throughout the whole aggregate. It resembles most closely breath mixed with heat' (*Ep. Hdt.* 63). Lucretius enables us to amplify this description. The atoms which form the soul, he tells us, are very small and they are also round. Roundness is inferred from the speed of thought: the soul atoms can be stirred by the slightest impulse (iii 176ff.). Furthermore, breath and heat (Lucretius adds air as well) are not sufficient to account for soul. That soul is warm and airy is clear from the fact that warmth and breath are absent from a corpse. But breath, heat and air cannot create the movements which bring sensation (iii 238–40). Something else is needed—a 'fourth nature', consisting of atoms which are smaller and more mobile than anything else which exists. They have no name.

How are we to conceive of the relation between the different kinds of atoms which constitute soul? As I observed earlier when discussing compound bodies, fire, breath and so forth are things which can only arise when certain kinds of atoms are combined. We are probably therefore to suppose that the atoms which can, in appropriate combinations, create the substances specified by Lucretius are in the soul combined in such a way that they form a body which is analysable as a *mixture* of fire, breath, air and the unnamed element. But the soul will not be divisible into these things. Lucretius says explicitly that 'no single element [of the soul] can be separated, nor can their capacities be divided spatially; they are like the multiple powers of a single body' (iii 262–6).[1]

This body, in virtue of the unnamed element, can produce the movements necessary to sensation. It is the unnamed element which

[1] See further Kerferd, *Phronesis* 16 (1971) 89ff.

gives the soul its specific character. Life and vital functions in general are thus explained by reference to something which cannot be analysed fully into any known substances. Epicurus wants to avoid the objection that life has been simply reduced to an appropriate mixture of familiar substances. Life requires these and something else as well. Given the primitive notions which the Greeks had of chemistry, Epicurus was wise to refrain from attempting to explain life purely in terms of the traditional four elements.

The soul then, so constituted, is the 'primary cause of sensation'. But soul by itself cannot have or cause life. It must be contained within a body. That is to say, a living being can be constituted neither out of soul alone nor out of body alone. Placed within a body of the right kind, the soul's vital capacities can be realized. From the soul the body acquires a derivative share in sensation; there is physical contact, naturally, between the body and the soul, and the movements of atoms within the body affect and are affected by those of the soul. Epicurus illustrated the relation of body and soul by considering the case of amputation (*Ep. Hdt.* 65). Loss of a limb does not remove the power of sensation; but loss of the soul removes all vitality from the body, even if the body itself remains intact. By insisting that soul must be contained in the body, Epicurus denied any prospect of sensation and consciousness surviving death.

In Lucretius (iii 136ff.) and some other sources a spatial distinction is drawn between the *animus* (rational part) and the *anima* (irrational part). The *animus* is located in the chest; the rest of the soul, though united with the *animus*, is distributed throughout the other regions of the body. These two parts of the soul do not undermine its unity of substance; they are introduced to explain different functions. That in virtue of which we think and experience emotion is the *animus*, the mind. This governs the rest of the soul. Epicurus had no knowledge of the nervous system, and we may most easily think of the *anima* as fulfilling the function of nerves—reporting feelings and sensations to the *animus* and transmitting movement to the limbs. If Epicurus had known of the nerves and their connexion with the brain he would probably have been fully prepared to accept the notion that the brain is equivalent to the *animus*.[1]

Lucretius' account of the soul inspired some of his finest poetry. It also shows much acute observation of behaviour. Before considering

---

[1] The nervous system was discovered by the medical scientists, Herophilus and Erasistratus, during the first half of the third century B.C.

further aspects of Epicurean psychology, we may pause over one or two passages in which Lucretius calls attention to the relations between body and soul:

If the vibrant shock of a weapon, forced within and opening to view bones and sinews, falls short of destroying life itself, yet faintness follows and a gentle falling to the ground, and on the ground there ensues a storm of the mind, and moment by moment an unsteady desire to stand up. Therefore it must be the case that the mind is corporeal in substance, since it suffers under the blow of bodily weapons (iii 170–6).

Furthermore we perceive that the mind comes into being along with the body, develops with the body and grows old with it. Just as young children totter whose body is frail and soft, so too their powers of judgment are slight. Then, when maturity has developed bringing hardy strength, their judgment too is greater and their strength of mind increased. Later, after their body has been assailed by the tough force of age and their limbs have failed with their strength blunted, the intellect grows lame, the tongue raves, the mind stumbles, all things fail and decline at the same time. And so it is appropriate that all the substance of vitality should be dissolved like smoke into the lofty breezes of the air (iii 445–56).

Again, if the soul is immortal and can feel when separated from our body we must, I believe, cause it to be equipped with the five senses. There is no other way in which we can imagine to ourselves souls wandering below in the realm of Acheron. And so painters and former generations of writers have presented souls endowed with the senses. But neither eyes nor nostrils nor hand nor tongue nor ears can exist for the soul apart from the body. Therefore souls on their own cannot feel, nor even exist (iii 624–33).

The psychological function on which we have most copious information is sense-perception. This is due no doubt to its importance in Epicureanism as a whole. In discussing the theory of knowledge I have already described Epicurus' concept of effluences or images from external objects which enter the sense organs, or which penetrate directly to the mind, and thereby cause our awareness of something. Perception is thus ultimately reducible to a form of touch, physical contact between the atoms of the percipient and atoms which have proceeded from objects in the external world (cf. Lucret. ii 434f.). It will not be possible in this context to discuss the treatment of specific problems of optics and other matters which Lucretius deals with at great length in Book iv. But some more general aspects of the theory need consideration.[1] In particular, it would be desirable to know how we are to conceive of the 'sense-bearing movements' which the soul bestows on the body. Lucretius states that it is not the mind which sees through the eyes, but the eyes themselves (iii 359–69), and the same holds good for the other sense organs. The eye is an organ of the body. When it is struck by a stream of effluences which have the appropriate size, we are probably to suppose that this sets up a movement of the adjoining soul atoms, which then cause sensation in the eye itself. The same internal processes will account for feelings— burns, itches and so forth. Lucretius traces a series of movements beginning with 'the stirring of the unnamed element' which passes via the other elements in the soul to the blood, the internal organs and finally the bones and marrow (iii 245–9). These stages represent an increasing disturbance of 'everything' and life cannot be maintained if the movements or sensations penetrate beyond a certain point. But 'generally the movements come to an end on the surface of the body' (252–7).

All of this still leaves the notion of sensation or consciousness very obscure. Is it simply a kind of movement, or is it rather something which supervenes as an epiphenomenon upon a kind of movement? Epicurus and Lucretius leave us in the dark here, and no wonder! For no one has yet succeeded in giving a purely mechanistic explanation of consciousness.

The treatment of thought raises further problems. In Epicurus' *Letter to Herodotus* (49–50) and in Lucretius, thought is assimilated to sense-perception so far as its objects and causes are concerned:

> Come now, learn what things stir the mind, and hear in a few words the source of those things which enter the understanding. First of all, I declare that many likenesses of things wander in many ways in all regions in all directions; they are fine in texture and easily become united with one another in the air when they meet. . . . They are much finer than those things which seize hold of the eyes and rouse vision, since they pass right through the vacant spaces of the body and stir the fine nature of the mind within and rouse its awareness (Lucret. iv 722–31).

Lucretius proceeds to illustrate these statements by reference to the perception of monsters and the dead. From this we might suppose that he is describing only certain kinds of mental perception. But he

---

[1] Epicurus himself writes about seeing, hearing and smell, *Ep. Hdt.* 49–53. Lucretius also discusses taste, iv 615–72.

goes on to argue that the thought of a lion is also produced, like the sight of a lion, by *simulacra leonum* ('images of lions'). He also asks the question, 'How is that we are able to think of things at will?' The answer which he suggests is curious:

In a single period of time which we perceive, that is, the time it takes to utter a single word, many times escape notice which reason discovers; and so it happens that in any time all the images are available, ready in every place. So great is their power of movement, so great the supply of them. . . . Because they are fine the mind can only distinguish sharply those on which it concentrates. Therefore all except those for which it has prepared itself pass away. The mind prepares itself and expects that it will see what follows on each thing; therefore this comes about (iv 794–806).

We should expect thought to be explained by reference to data, images, or what not which are somehow already present in or created by the mind. But that is not what Lucretius says. He clearly implies that the 'supply' of images is external, and that the mind apprehends just those images to which its attention is directed. Thinking, on this interpretation, is analogous to noticing something which falls within the scope of vision.

Many scholars have been reluctant to take this passage at its face value. They have presumed that Epicurus must have envisaged an internal store of images in terms of which some thought at least and memory are to be explained. It has been suggested that the effluences which are received by the sense organs or the mind cause a change in the movements of the soul atoms, and this new pattern of movement persists as a memory or thought-image. But if Epicurus held such a view no evidence about it has survived, and it is not presupposed in the theory recorded by Lucretius. According to this theory, thought is a kind of internal film-show in which the mind controls the images which it permits to enter the body. Not only thought but volition also requires the consciousness of appropriate images. Lucretius observes that we walk when 'images of walking fall upon the mind' (iv 881). Then the will rouses itself, and passes on movement to the rest of the soul so that finally the limbs are activated. In dreaming, too, passages are open in the mind through which images of things can enter (iv 976–7).

We must suppose that this is Epicurus' own theory, and it is quite consistent with the strange idea that images of the gods possess objective status. But if memory is not explicable by a storehouse of images how is it to be accounted for? The few texts which bear upon this question suggest that memory is a disposition, produced by repeated apprehension of images of a certain kind, to attend to such images as continue to exist after the previously experienced object which produced them may have perished or changed in other ways. Hence we can remember the dead.

Although Lucretius' account of thought should be given full weight as orthodox Epicurean doctrine, certain forms of thinking must have been explained in other ways. There are no images of atoms and void; there is no image of the principles of confirmation and non-contradiction. Yet these are things which cannot be grasped except by thought. Epicurus himself distinguished between what he called 'the theoretical part', and 'apprehension' whether by the senses or the mind.[1] I have already discussed 'apprehension', and rejected Bailey's claim that it guarantees the clarity of an image. What it does involve, I suggest, is the *direct* apprehension of some image. In other words, 'apprehension' covers awareness of all data, whether of the senses or the mind, which possess objective existence because they are in origin images which enter us from outside. 'The theoretical part' refers to thinking which may be presumed to function purely by internal processes. That is to say, it involves inference about things like atoms and void which are unable to be apprehended directly. How such thinking takes place in detail, and whether or not it involves images, are questions which we cannot answer categorically. It almost certainly must make use of 'preconceptions', general concepts arrived at by repeated observation of particular objects. Preconceptions however cannot be reduced to external images for there are no 'generic' images existing objectively. These must be constructions of the mind, which can be utilized in the formation of new non-empirical concepts. Epicurus may have explained them as patterns of movement in the soul, but his words on this subject, if he described it in detail, have not survived.

(viii) Freedom of action

Our next subject is one of the most interesting and controversial problems in Epicureanism. According to Lucretius and other later writers, the 'swerve' of atoms has a part to play in the explanation of 'free will' (*libera voluntas*). But what part? The answer must be sought,

[1] *De nat.* xxviii fr. 5 col. vi (sup.), col. vii (inf.), ed. A. Vogliano, *Epicuri et Epicureorum scripta in Herculanensibus papyris servata* (Berlin 1928).

if anywhere, from a difficult passage of Lucretius. It is the second
argument which he uses to prove that atoms sometimes deviate from
the linear direction of their downward movement through the void:

If every movement is always linked and the new movement arises from the
old one in a fixed sequence, and if the primary bodies do not by swerving
create a certain beginning of movement which can break the bonds of fate
and prevent cause from following cause from infinity, how comes it about
that living things all over the earth possess this free will, this will, I say,
severed from fate, whereby we advance where pleasure leads each man and
swerve in our movements at no fixed time and at no fixed place, but when
and where our mind has borne us? For undoubtedly each man's will gives
the beginning to these movements, and it is from the will that movements
are spread through the limbs.

You see, do you not, that when the barriers are opened at an instant of
time, the horses for all their strength and eagerness cannot burst forward as
promptly as their mind desires. This is because the whole stock of matter
throughout their whole body has to be set in motion, so that having been
roused through all the frame it may make an effort and follow the desire of
the mind. So you can see that a beginning of movement is engendered by
the heart, and it comes forth first from the mind's volition and then is dispatched throughout the whole body and limbs.

It is not the same as when we move forward under the pressure of a blow
from the mighty strength and strong constraint of another man. For then it
is clear that the whole matter of the body in its entirety moves and is seized
against our will, until the will restrains it throughout the limbs. So now you
surely see that although an external force pushes many men and often com-
pels them to go forward against their will and be driven headlong, yet there
is something in our breast which can fight back and resist. At its direction
too the stock of matter is at times compelled to change direction through all
the limbs, and although pushed forward is checked and comes to rest again.

Therefore you must admit the same thing in the atoms too; that another
cause of motion exists besides blows and weights which is the source of this
power innate in us, since we see that nothing can arise out of nothing. For
weight prevents all things happening by blows, by external force as it were.
But a tiny swerve of the atoms at no fixed time or place brings it about that
the mind itself has no internal necessity in doing all things and is not forced
like a captive to accept and be acted upon (ii 251–93).

This is our only detailed evidence for the relation between the swerve
and 'free' will in Epicurean literature.[1] No explicit word about the

---

[1] Cic. *De fato* 22 and *N.D.* i 69 also show that the swerve was supposed to save
'free will'. See also Diogenes of Oenoanda fr. 32 col. iii Chilton.

swerve from Epicurus himself has so far been discovered. We know however that he attacked 'the destiny of the natural philosophers' for its 'merciless necessity' (*Ep. Men.* 134). And he discussed the causes of human action in a book which is partially preserved on papyrus from Herculaneum.[1] The text contains so many gaps and defective lines that it is difficult to grasp a clear train of thought; more work may yield positive advances in our understanding of it. But Epicurus certainly distinguished sharply in this book between 'the cause in us' and two further factors, 'the initial constitution' and 'the automatic necessity of the environment and that which enters' (i.e. external 'images'). These distinctions should be borne in mind when one approaches Lucretius' text.

The first thing to notice is his context. Lucretius' main subject at this stage of his work is not psychology but the movement of atoms. He offers no formal argument to defend the 'freedom' of the will. Rather, he assumes it, exemplifies it by examples, and uses the assumption and examples to prove that atoms sometimes swerve.

The logical structure of the first paragraph might be expressed like this: (A) If all movements are so causally related to each other that no new movements are created by a swerve of atoms, then there could be no such thing as 'free will'. (B) For 'free will' entails the creation of a new movement at no fixed time and at no fixed place. (C) But there is such a thing as 'free will'. (D) Therefore the atoms sometimes create new beginnings by swerving.

In the next two paragraphs (as I have set out the text) Lucretius gives his examples to show that the will can create new beginnings of movement. First, he considers the case of the race-horses. When the barriers are raised they are free of any external constraint to move forward; and they do move forward (fulfil their desire to move) as soon as their will has had time to activate the limbs. This example is used to show that there is some faculty within the horses which enables them to initiate movement freely.

In his second example Lucretius considers a different case. Unlike the horses, which require a brief interval of time for their will's action to have an external effect, men may be pushed forward immediately by outside pressures; and such *involuntary* movements require no internal movements in the men before they occur. But men have something within them which can resist external pressures. This is a

---

[1] This is found in Arrighetti's edition, *Epicuro Opere* 31 [27] 3–9. It is just possible that the swerve is implied at 31 [22] 7–16.

power to cause atoms within the body to change their enforced direction of movement. In this case, the will initiates movement when the body is already undergoing compulsory movement. But the power which is exercised is the same as that faculty for initiating movement exemplified by the horses.

It seems clear to me that both examples are intended to illustrate 'free will', from different starting-points. And what are we to make of the 'blows' and 'weights' mentioned in the last paragraph? Lucretius does not exclude these as necessary conditions of a 'free' action. He denies only that they are sufficient to bring it about. We have already seen that the 'will' to walk requires 'images', that is, 'blows from outside' (p. 55), and nothing weightless could act or be acted upon in Epicurus' system. The weight of the mind's atoms affects its reaction to external blows. But an action caused solely by blows and weights could not be 'free'. The horses' movement and the men's resistance were 'free' in virtue of an additional third factor which Lucretius calls *voluntas*, 'will'. The will, it should be noted, is not treated as equivalent to desire. Desire is prompted by the awareness of some pleasurable object. Lucretius, I think, regards the will as that in virtue of which we seek to fulfil our desires (cf. ii 258, 265).

If we ask where the swerve features in all this, the answer seems to be that the swerve is a physical event which presents itself to consciousness as a 'free' will to initiate a new movement. Consciousness during waking states is normally continuous. But our external bodily movements are not wholly continuous. Nor are our intentions. Lucretius, I suggest, treats some animal actions as if they were relatively discontinuous events initiated by the 'will'. But they are not wholly discontinuous. Memory, reflection, habit, these and other dispositions are not ruled out as causal factors by anything which Lucretius says. A swerve among the soul atoms need not be supposed to disrupt all or even any character traits. The swerve is not treated in a context which enables us to place its precise function in the whole history of living things. But what does seem clear is its rôle as an initiator of new actions.

Once it is recognized that other causes besides the swerve are necessary to the performance of a voluntary act, certain difficulties observed by one recent writer become less acute. If the swerve, which by definition is something random and unpredictable, were sufficient by itself to explain voluntary actions, then the bonds of fate could seem to have been broken at the expense of making actions purposeless and wholly indeterminate. Sensing this difficulty, David Furley has suggested that the swerve need not be supposed to feature in the explanation of *every* voluntary action.[1] Its function, he argues, is rather to free the disposition from being wholly determined by heredity and environment. For this purpose he suggests that a single swerve of a single atom in an individual's *psyche* would be sufficient.

Furley's interesting arguments cannot be surveyed in detail here. But it is my own opinion that Lucretius' text is easier to interpret on the assumption that a swerve is at work in the freedom of particular actions. The theoretical single swerve which Furley postulates can hardly suffice to explain the 'beginnings of motion' which characterize each act of 'free' will. But Furley is right to object to interpretations which treat the swerve by itself as a sufficient condition. We know from Diogenes of Oenoanda that the swerve was held to be necessary by Epicureans if moral advice is to be effective (fr. 32 col. iii). But moral advice cannot be effective if it is to depend entirely on the possible occurrence of a swerve in the soul of the man being advised. I think we are to suppose that the swerve of a single atom is a relatively frequent event. It may occur when one is asleep or when one is awake, without having any observable or conscious effect. If however a man's natural disposition to seek pleasure or to avoid pain is roused by external or internal causes, and if at such times he is in a physical condition which makes it possible for him to act then, depending upon the kind of man he is, any swerve(s) among the atoms of his mind constitutes a free decision to act. If he is untrained in Epicurean philosophy he may decide to pursue objects which in the event cause more pain than pleasure. The true Epicurean's atoms may also swerve at a time when he walks down a Soho street, but having learnt that freedom from pain is more pleasurable than momentary sensations of pleasure he does not follow his companions into the night-club. Swerves help him to initiate new actions in the pursuit of tranquillity.

Before concluding this subject two general observations may be made. First, it may be asked whether the use of the swerve which I attribute to Epicurus is historically plausible. Furley believes not, but he omits one point which seems to me important. The so-called problem of 'free will' arises primarily out of two conceptions—

---

[1] 'Aristotle and Epicurus on Voluntary Action' in his *Two Studies in the Greek Atomists*. My brief remarks here cannot do justice to the importance of Furley's wide-ranging treatment. Much of his argument turns on similarities he has detected between Aristotle and Epicurus.

beliefs in God's omniscience and predetermination, and beliefs in the absolute continuity of physical causation. There is every reason to attribute the second of these to Zeno, the founder of Stoicism, and probably the first as well. Zeno and Epicurus were active in Athens together for thirty years, and I find it unlikely that Epicurus developed his opposition to determinism quite independently of Stoic theories. Those theories provide conditions which favour the emergence of a concept of volition which is not completely dependent upon the state of things at the preceding instant. I conjecture that Epicurus used the swerve to defend such a concept.

Secondly, the random nature of the swerve is a difficulty for Epicurus whatever its rôle in human psychology. But it seems to me logically possible to suppose that the swerve of a soul atom is not random so far as the consciousness of the soul's owner is concerned. And Epicurus attempted to solve that problem, so I think, by making the swerve a constituent of the 'will'. If it is not part of the will or cognitive faculty, but a random event which disrupts the soul's patterns of atoms from time to time, are not the consequences for morality which trouble Furley still more serious? He wants the swerve to free inherited movements of atoms and make character adaptable. But this raises new problems. A man of good Epicurean character will live in fear of an unpredictable event which may change him into a Stoic or something worse. I find it easier to posit some discontinuity between the antecedent conditions of an action and the decision to do it than discontinuity between movements on which character depends.

To conclude, Epicurus used the swerve of atoms in the soul to explain situations where men are conscious of doing what they want to do. Obscurities persist, and we cannot rule them out in order to make the theory more palatable or convincing. I pass now to a less controversial subject. Epicurus' theory of pleasure has already been referred to, and we must now consider its full ethical significance.

(ix) Pleasure and happiness

Epicurus was not the first Greek philosopher whose ethics can be called hedonist. In Chapter 1 I referred briefly to the earlier hedonism of Aristippus whose conception of the pleasant life differs sharply from Epicurus'. Unlike Aristippus, who regarded absence of pain as an intermediate condition, Epicurus claimed that the removal of all pain defines the magnitude of pleasure (*K.D.* iii), and his interest in specifying the conditions which establish a life free of trouble may well

have been roused by Democritus. The earlier atomist probably had
no systematic ethical theory, but he is credited with a conception of
happiness which consists above all in peace of mind (D.L. ix 45). It
was Epicurus' primary concern to show how this state can be attained.

Pleasure was also a topic which received considerable attention
from Plato, Aristotle and the Academy in general. It is highly probable
that Epicurus was familiar with ideas which Plato discusses in the
Philebus, and he may also have been influenced by some Aristotelian
notions, most notably the distinction between pleasure 'in movement'
and pleasure 'in rest' *(E.N.* 1154b28). The great difference between
Plato and Aristotle on the one hand and Epicurus on the other turns
on the relation they posit between happiness and pleasure. All three
philosophers are concerned in their ethics with specifying the necessary
conditions of happiness, but only Epicurus identifies happiness with
a life full of pleasure. Some pleasures for Plato and Aristotle are good,
and make a contribution to happiness; others are bad. For Epicurus
no pleasure in itself can be anything but good since the good means
that which is or causes pleasure. The fundamental constituent of
happiness for Plato and Aristotle is virtue, excellence of 'soul', which
manifests itself in the exercise of those activities appropriate to each
faculty of the personality and in moral action. (The differences between
Plato and Aristotle are less important for my present purpose than the
similarities.) But for Epicurus virtue is necessary to happiness not as
an essential ingredient but as a means to its attainment. This is the
most significant difference between Epicurus and his major predecessors:

> We say that pleasure is the starting-point and the end of living blissfully.
> For we recognize pleasure as a good which is primary and innate. We begin
> every act of choice and avoidance from pleasure, and it is to pleasure that we
> return using our experience of pleasure as the criterion of every good thing
> *(Ep. Men.* 128–9).

Subjective experience is a 'test of reality' for Epicurus, and it is on
this evidence that he based his doctrine of pleasure.

> All living creatures from the moment of birth take delight in pleasure and
> resist pain from natural causes independent of reason (D.L. x 137).

The goodness of pleasure needs no demonstration. Epicurus takes it as
an obvious fact that men, like all living things, pursue pleasure and
avoid pain. The attractiveness of pleasure is treated as an immediate
datum of experience comparable to the feeling that fire is hot (Cic.

Fin. i 30). We learn from Aristotle that his contemporary Eudoxus also inferred that pleasure is 'the good' from the allegedly empirical fact that all creatures pursue it (*E.N.* x 1172b9). Now it does not follow from the fact, if it is a fact, that men pursue pleasure that pleasure is what they ought to pursue. As G.E. Moore argued at great length in *Principia Ethica,* that which is desired is not equivalent to that which is desirable. Some scholars have indeed claimed that Epicurus is not concerned with what 'ought' to be or what is 'fitting', but only with what is.[1] But this claim is at best a half-truth. It would be a correct description of his view to say that we are genetically programmed to seek what will cause us pleasure and to avoid what will cause pain. And he probably held that no living creature whose natural constitution is unimpaired *can* have any other goals. But there is a place for 'ought' in his system because the sources of pleasure and pleasure itself are not uniform. What we ought to do is to pursue that which will cause us the greatest pleasure. 'Ought' here of course does not signify what we are obliged to do by any purely moral law. It signifies that which needs to be done if we are successfully to attain our goal, happiness or the greatest pleasure. It applies to means and not to ends:

Since pleasure is the good which is primary and innate we do not choose every pleasure, but there are times when we pass over many pleasures if greater pain is their consequence for us. And we regard many pains as superior to pleasures when a greater pleasure arises for us after we have put up with pains over a long time. Therefore although every pleasure on account of its natural affinity to us is good, not every pleasure is to be chosen; similarly, though every pain is bad, not every pain is naturally always to be avoided. It is proper to evaluate these things by a calculation and consideration of advantages and disadvantages. For sometimes we treat the good as bad and conversely the bad as good (*Ep. Men.* 129–30).

In order to grasp the implications of this important passage, we need to consider in more detail what Epicurus meant by pleasure and how he proposed to use pleasure as a guide to action. The most striking feature of his hedonism is the denial of any state or feeling intermediate between pleasure and pain. Pleasure and pain are related to one another not as contraries but as contradictories.[2] The absence

---

[1] So Bailey, *Greek Atomists,* p. 483, followed by Panichas, *Epicurus* (N.Y. 1967) p. 100.

[2] cf. Cic. *Fin.* ii 17, 'I assert that all those who are without pain are in a state of pleasure.'

of the one entails the presence of the other. If all pleasure is regarded
as a sensation of some kind, this relationship between pleasure and
pain makes no sense. For clearly most of us pass a large part of our
waking lives without having either painful or pleasing sensations.
But the periods of our waking life in which we could describe ourselves as neither happy nor unhappy, or neither enjoying nor not
enjoying something, are much smaller. Epicurus' view of the relationship between pleasure and pain should be interpreted in this light. He
has, as we shall see, a way of distinguishing the pleasures of bodily
sensations and feelings of elation from pleasures which cannot be so
described; absence of pain is not, he thinks, an adequate description of
the former. Epicurus' mistake is a failure to see that indifference
characterizes certain of our moods and attitudes towards things.

His analysis of pleasure rests on the assumption that the natural or
normal condition of living things is one of bodily and mental well-
being and that this condition is *ipso facto* gratifying. This is the
meaning of the statement quoted above: 'Pleasure is the good which
is primary and innate.' It is possible in English to speak of 'enjoying'
good health, and we may also call this something gratifying, or something a man rejoices in. Epicurus' use of the word pleasure to describe
the condition of those who enjoy good physical and mental health is
not therefore purely arbitrary. In physical terms this pleasure is a
concomitant of the *appropriate* movement and location of atoms
within the body. If these are disturbed pain follows. In other words,
pain is a disruption of the natural constitution. Pleasure is experienced
when the atoms are restored to their appropriate position in the body
(Lucret. ii 963–8).

The idea that pain is a disturbance of the natural state was not
invented by Epicurus. We find it in Plato's *Philebus* along with the
notion that pleasure is experienced when the natural state is 'replenished' (31e–32b). Plato however argued that pleasure is only experienced during the process of restoring the natural condition. According
to his theory, pleasure and pain are movements or processes. There is
also, however, a 'third' life in which any bodily processes produce no
consciousness of pleasure or pain. This 'intermediate' condition
cannot be regarded as pleasurable or painful (42c–44a).

It is interesting to find Plato attacking the theory that absence of
pain can be identified with pleasure. Epicurus of course would not
accept Plato's specification of an intermediate life. Like Plato, however, Epicurus holds that the process of removing pain results in

pleasurable sensations. He calls this pleasure 'kinetic'. Suppose that a man is hungry: he desires to eat and the act of satisfying this desire produces 'kinetic' pleasure. If he succeeds in fully satisfying the desire for food he must have wholly allayed the pangs of hunger. From this complete satisfaction of desire, Epicurus argues, a second kind of pleasure arises. This is not an experience which accompanies a process, but a 'static' pleasure. It is characterized by complete absence of pain and enjoyment of this condition. Torquatus, the Epicurean spokesman in Cicero's *De finibus*, expresses the distinction between pleasures thus:

> The pleasure which we pursue is not merely that which excites our nature by some gratification and which is felt with delight by the senses. We regard that as the greatest pleasure which is felt when all pain has been removed (*Fin.* i 37).

'Static' pleasure follows the complete satisfaction of desire. Desire arises from a sense of need, the pain of lacking something. In order to remove this pain, desire must be satisfied, and the satisfaction of desire is pleasurable. 'Kinetic' pleasure is thus (or so I think) a necessary condition of at least some 'static' pleasure, but it is not regarded by Epicurus as equivalent in value to 'static' pleasure.[1] For if freedom from pain is the greatest pleasure, we should satisfy our desires not for the sake of the pleasurable sensations which accompany eating, drinking and so on, but for the sake of the state of well-being which results when all the pain due to want has been removed:

> When we say that pleasure is the goal we do not mean the pleasures of the dissipated and those which consist in the process of enjoyment . . . but freedom from pain in the body and from disturbance in the mind. For it is not drinking and continuous parties nor sexual pleasures nor the enjoyment of fish and other delicacies of a wealthy table which produce the pleasant life, but sober reasoning which searches out the causes of every act of choice and refusal and which banishes the opinions that give rise to the greatest mental confusion (*Ep. Men.* 131–2).

Epicurus, in this passage, is not denying that drink, eating good food, sex, and so on are sources of pleasure. He is asserting that the pleasures which such activities produce are to be rejected as goals because they

---

[1] This interpretation of the relation between 'kinetic' and 'static' pleasure seems to me to suit the evidence best and to make the best sense. It has also been argued that 'kinetic' pleasure serves only to 'vary' a previous 'static' pleasure; see most recently J. M. Rist, *Epicurus* (Cambridge 1972) ch. 6 and pp. 170ff.

do not constitute a calm and stable disposition of body and mind. It is freedom from pain which measures the relative merits of different activities. This is the basis of Epicurus' hedonist calculus. His criticism of luxury and sexual indulgence is not grounded in any puritanical disapproval:

> If the things which produce the pleasures of the dissipated released the fears of the mind concerning astronomical phenomena and death and pains ... we should never have any cause to blame them (*K.D.* x).

He holds that the greatest pain is mental disturbance produced by false beliefs about the nature of things, about the gods, about the soul's destiny. Any pleasure therefore which fails to remove the greatest pain is ruled out as an ultimate object of choice by application of the rule—absence of pain establishes the magnitude of pleasure. Furthermore, the pleasure which arises from gratifying the senses may have a greater pain as its consequence. A man may enjoy an evening's drinking or the thrill of betting, but the pleasure which he derives from satisfying his desires for drink and gambling must be set against the feeling of the morning after and the anxiety of losing money.

Epicurus' concept of pleasure is closely related to an analysis of desire:

> We must infer that some desires are natural, and others pointless; of natural desires some are necessary, others merely natural. Necessary desires include some which are necessary for happiness, others for the equilibrium of the body and others for life itself. The correct understanding of these things consists in knowing how to refer all choice and refusal to the health of the body and freedom from mental disturbance since this is the goal of living blissfully. For all our actions are aimed at avoiding pain and fear. Once we have acquired this, all the mind's turmoil is removed since a creature has no need to wander as if in search of something it lacks, nor to look for some other thing by means of which it can replenish the good of the mind and the body. For it is when we suffer pain from the absence of pleasure that we have need of pleasure (*Ep. Men.* 127–8).

Epicurus' analysis of desires is consistent with the principle that freedom from pain is the greatest pleasure. The desire for food and clothing is natural and necessary. Failure to satisfy this desire is a source of pain. But, Epicurus argues, it is neither necessary nor natural to desire this food or clothing rather than that, if the latter is sufficient to remove the pain felt by absence of food or clothing (Us. 456). Hence Epicurus becomes an advocate of the simple life, on the grounds that we cause ourselves unnecessary pain if we seek to satisfy desires by luxurious means. Necessary desires, he holds, can be satisfied simply, and the pleasure which we thus experience is no less in quantity even if it differs in kind. Moreover, those who seek pleasure in luxuries are likely to suffer pain unnecessarily either as a direct consequence of luxurious living or through an inability to satisfy a desire:

> We regard self-sufficiency as a great blessing, not that we may always enjoy only a few things but that if we do not have many things we can enjoy the few, in the conviction that they derive the greatest pleasure from luxury who need it least, and that everything natural is easy to obtain but that which is pointless is difficult. Simple tastes give us pleasure equal to a rich man's diet when all the pain of want has been removed; bread and water produce the highest pleasure when someone who needs them serves them to himself. And so familiarity with simple and not luxurious diet gives us perfect health and makes a man confident in his approach to the necessary business of living; it makes us better disposed to encounter luxuries at intervals and prepares us to face change without fear (*Ep. Men.* 130–1).

Time and again in his *Principal doctrines* Epicurus asserts that pleasure cannot be increased beyond a certain limit.[1] So far as sensual gratification is concerned, this limit is reached when the pain which prompted desire has ceased; thereafter pleasure can be 'varied'—by 'kinetic' pleasure—but not augmented. This is something which needs to be grasped by the intellect, since the flesh itself recognizes no limits to pleasure (*K.D.* xviii; xx). The mind has its own pleasures the 'limit' of which is reached with the ability to calculate correctly the pleasures of sensual gratification and to assess the feelings which cause mental disturbance. Ancient critics familiar with Plato's distinction between the soul and the body criticized Epicurus for failing to draw a sharp distinction between bodily pleasures and the 'good' of the soul (Us. 430, 431). But when Epicurus distinguishes body and soul in statements about pleasure he has nothing like Platonic dualism in mind. Body and mind are in physical contact with one another; pleasurable sensations are 'bodily' events but they also give rise to pleasure or joy in the mind (Us. 433, 439). Unlike the body however the mind is not confined for its objects of pleasure to the experience of the moment:

[1] e.g. *K.D.* iii, ix, xviii, xix, xx.

The body rejoices just so long as it feels a pleasure which is present. The mind perceives both the present pleasure along with the body and it foresees pleasure to come; and it does not allow past pleasure to flow away. Hence in the wise man there will always be present a constant supply of associated pleasures, since the anticipation of pleasures hoped for is united with the recollection of those already experienced (Us. 439).

The memory of past pleasures can 'mitigate' present sufferings (Us. 437), and the same holds for the anticipation of future pleasures. Unlike the Cyrenaics who regarded bodily pleasures of the moment as the greatest, Epicurus is reported by Diogenes Laertius to have argued that the mind's capacity to look forward and back entails that both its pleasures and its pains are greater than those of the body (x 137).

The distinction between 'kinetic' and 'static' pleasures applies to both body and mind (D.L. x 136). Corresponding to the 'kinetic' pleasure of satisfying a desire for food, drink and the like, the mind can experience 'joy' when, say, meeting a friend or solving a problem in philosophy. This pleasure, consisting in motion, is to be distinguished from the 'static' pleasure of 'mental repose' which corresponds to the body's pleasure in freedom from pain.

Since pleasure is the only thing which is good in itself, prudence, justice, moderation and courage, the traditional four 'moral virtues' of Greek philosophy, can have value only if they are constituents of or means to pleasure. Epicurus settled for the second alternative. Torquatus puts his position succinctly, opposing the Epicureans to the Stoics:

As for those splendid and beautiful virtues of yours, who would regard them as praiseworthy or desirable unless they produced pleasures? Just as we approve medical science not for the sake of the art itself but for the sake of good health . . . so prudence, which must be regarded as the 'art of living', would not be sought after if it achieved nothing. In fact is is sought after because it is the expert, so to speak, at discovering and securing pleasure. . . . Human life is harassed above all by an ignorance of good and bad things, and the same defect often causes us to be deprived of the greatest pleasures and to be tormented by the harshest mental anguish. Prudence must be applied to act as our most reliable guide to pleasure, by removing fears and desires and snatching away the vanity of all false opinions (Cic. *Fin.* i 42–3).

Moderation, on the same principle, is desirable because and only because 'it brings us peace of mind'. It is a means to attaining the greatest pleasure since it enables us to pass over those pleasures which involve greater pain. Similarly, Torquatus finds the value of courage in the fact that it enables us to live free of anxiety and to rid ourselves, as far as possible, of physical pain. Justice and social relationships are analysed in the same way, but I will say a little more about Epicurus' treatment of these at the conclusion of this chapter.

Although Epicurus regarded the virtues as means and not as ends, he held that they are necessary to happiness and inseparably bound up with the hedonist life:

> Of sources of pleasure the starting-point and the greatest good is prudence. Therefore prudence is something even more valuable than philosophy. From prudence the other virtues arise, and prudence teaches that it is not possible to live pleasurably without living prudently, nobly and justly, nor to live prudently, nobly and justly, without living pleasurably. For the virtues are naturally linked with living pleasurably, and living pleasurably is inseparable from them (*Ep. Men.* 132).

This association between virtue and pleasure is striking, but it should not be interpreted as giving an independent value to prudence and the other virtues. The necessary connexion between pleasure and the virtues is due to the notion that pleasure requires for its attainment a reasoned assessment of the relative advantages and disadvantages of a particular act or state of affairs, a capacity to control desires the satisfaction of which will involve pain for the agent, freedom from fear of punishment and the like. The pleasure which men should seek is not Bentham's 'greatest happiness of the greatest number'. Epicurus never suggests that the interests of others should be preferred to or evaluated independently of the interests of the agent. The orientation of his hedonism is wholly self-regarding.

(x) *Justice and friendship*

> Natural justice is a pledge of expediency with a view to men not harming one another and not being harmed by one another (*K.D.* xxxi).

> Of all the things which wisdom secures for the attainment of happiness throughout the whole of life, by far the greatest is the possession of friendship (*K.D.* xxvii).

Aristotle asserted that 'man is naturally a political animal', and Plato held that the true good of the individual is also the good of the community to which he belongs. Epicurus took a very different view, which, though less forcefully than the Cynics, challenged fundamental values of Greek society. In his opinion human beings have no 'natural' leanings towards community life (Us. 523). Civilization has developed by an evolutionary process of which the determinants have been external circumstances, the desire to secure pleasure and to avoid pain, and the human capacity to reason and to plan. Learning by trial and error under the pressure of events, men have developed skills and formed social organizations which were found to be mutually advantageous. The only details of this process which survive in Epicurus' own words concern the origin and development of language (*Ep. Hdt.* 75–6). But Lucretius treats the whole subject at some length in Book v. Following the invention of housing and clothing, the discovery of how to make fire, and the introduction of family life, he writes, 'neighbours began to form friendships desiring neither to do nor to suffer harm' (1019–20). From this supposed historical stage in human culture Epicurus traces the origins of justice.

He describes justice as 'a kind of compact not to harm or be harmed' (*K.D.* xxxiii), prefacing this statement with the words: 'It is not anything in itself', an implicit attack on Plato's theory of the autonomous existence of moral values. Several longer statements on justice are preserved in the *Principal doctrines*, and a selection of these will serve to illustrate Epicurus' position:

Injustice is a bad thing not in itself, but in respect of the fear and suspicion of not escaping the notice of those set in authority concerning such things (*K.D.* xxxiv).

It is not possible for one who secretly acts against the terms of the compact 'not to harm or be harmed', to be confident that he will not be apprehended. . . . . (*K.D.* xxxv).

Evidence that something considered to be just is a source of advantage to men, in their necessary dealings with one another, is a guarantee of its justice, whether or not it is the same for all. But if a man makes a law which does not prove to be a source of advantage in human relationships, this no longer is really just. . . . (*K.D.* xxxvii).

The just man is most free from trouble, but the unjust man abounds in trouble (*K.D.* xvii).

This concept of justice, which recalls Glaucon's analysis in Plato (*Rep.* ii), is not the 'social contract' of Rousseau. Epicurus is not saying that people have an obligation to act justly because of an agreement entered into by their remote or mythical ancestors. The 'contractual' element in his concept of justice is not advanced as a basis of moral or social obligation. Epicurus' justice requires us to respect the 'rights' of others if and only if this is advantageous to all parties concerned. Justice, as he conceives of it, does imply recognition of the interests of others besides oneself. But the basis of this recognition is self-interest. The 'compact' of which he speaks has self-protection as its basis. It is an agreement to refrain from injuring others if they will refrain from injuring oneself.

Epicurus' comments on the fears of apprehension which beset the unjust man show clearly that justice is desirable for the freedom which it brings from mental distress as well as physical retaliation. This is wholly consistent with his calculus of pleasures and pains. Injustice is bad not in itself but because of the painful consequences which it involves for the unjust man. In a book of *Problems* Epicurus raised the question: 'Will the wise man do anything forbidden by the laws, if he knows that he will escape notice?'; and he replied, 'The simple answer is not easy to find' (Us. 18). Epicurus' comments in *K.D.* xxxv imply that the problem is a purely academic one. No one in practice *can* be confident that his injustice will be unnoticed; as Lucretius puts it, 'fear of punishment for crimes during life' is the real hell, and not the Acheron of myth (iii 1013–23). Realizing this the wise man acts justly in order to secure tranquillity of mind.

In Epicurus' eyes political life is a rat-race or 'prison' from which the wise man will keep well clear (*Sent. Vat.* lviii).[1] He diagnoses political ambition as a 'desire for protection from men', and argues that this in fact can only be secured by a quiet life in retirement from public affairs (*K.D.* vii, xiv). But Epicurus' rejection of political life as a context for the attainment of happiness was not based upon misanthropy. On the contrary, he held that friendship is 'an immortal good' (*Sent. Vat.* lxxviii). So today, 'opting out' *and* communal life are practised by many who find society at large 'alienated'. Torquatus, in Cicero's *De finibus*, asserts that 'Epicurus says that of all the things which prudence has provided for living happily, none is greater or more productive or more delightful than friendship' (i 65). Once again we notice that the value of something other than pleasure or happiness is referred to this end. But Epicurus, when writing of friendship, uses almost lyrical language at times, as when he says:

[1] See also D.L. x 119 and Lucretius' brilliant denunciation of *ambitio*, iii 59–77, related to the fear of death.

'Friendship dances round the world, announcing to us all that we should bestir ourselves for the enjoyment of happiness' (*Sent. Vat.* lii).

There is no doubt that Epicurus practised what he preached. The Garden was a community of friends, and Epicurus clearly derived intense happiness from friendship. We are told that he was famous for his 'philanthropy' to all (D.L. x 10), and on the day of his death, when racked by pain, he wrote to Idomeneus that he was happy, with the joyous memories of their conversations (Us. 138). Some of Epicurus' remarks about friendship might imply that it is compatible with altruism and self-sacrifice. But the basis of friendship, like justice, is self-interest, though Epicurus in the same breath says that it is 'desirable for its own sake' (*Sent. Vat.* xxiii). There is probably no inconsistency here. 'He is not a friend who is always seeking help, nor he who never associates friendship with assistance' (*Sent. Vat.* xxxix). One can enjoy or derive pleasure from helping a friend independently of any tangible benefit which this brings. When Epicurus writes of the 'benefits' of friendship he does not mean the pleasure which may come from helping others but the actual practical help which friends provide for each other. Apart from this, however, friendship is desirable because 'it is more pleasant to confer a benefit than to receive it' (Us. 544). One again we are brought back to pleasure as the sole criterion of value.

There is an elegant simplicity to Epicurus' ethics, a refreshing absence of cant, and also much humanity. He was born into a society which, like most societies, rated wealth, status, physical attributes and political power among the greatest human goods. It was also a slave-based society which reckoned men as superior to women and Greeks as superior to all other peoples. The good for man which Epicurus prescribes ignores or rejects these values and distinctions. Freedom from pain and tranquillity of mind are things which any sane man values and Epicurus dedicated his life to showing that they are in our power and how we may attain them. His ethics is undeniably centred upon the interests of the individual, and some have, with justification, praised the nobility of Epicurus more highly than his moral code. Yet we must see it in its social and historical context. No Greek thinker was more sensitive to the anxieties bred by folly, superstition, prejudice and specious idealism. At a time of political instability and private disillusionment Epicurus saw that people like atoms are individuals and many of them wander in the void. He thought he could offer them directions signposted by evidence and reason to a way of being, a way of living, a way of relating to others, other individuals. Negative, self-centred, unstimulating we may regard it; we cannot say priggish or self-indulgent, and in antiquity many found liberation and enlightenment in Epicureanism. For a modern reader too there is much philosophical interest in the consistency with which Epicurus applies his basic principles. What he has to say about family life and sexual love is entirely based on the proposition that the greatest good is freedom from pain in body and mind. But consistency can be purchased too dearly; a few criticisms of Epicurus' hedonism will show this.

First, it may be objected that Epicurus misapplies the factual observations with which he starts. Unless pleasure is used analytically to mean merely that which is desired, it is difficult to agree that pleasure is the object of every desire. But such a usage of pleasure tells us nothing about what is desired or desirable, and Epicurus does not use pleasure in this empty way. He is claiming that the desire to attain a state of consciousness which we find gratifying is sufficient to explain all human action. And this seems to be patently false. Secondly, Epicurus can fairly be charged with failure to grasp the complexity of the concept of pleasure. As we say, one man's meat is another man's poison, but Epicurus seems to think that he can classify by reference to absence of pain the magnitude of any man's pleasure. This may often be good advice, but many will argue from their own experience that Epicurus' claims have no basis in fact. They will also reject his assertion that sharp pains are short and long pains mild.

Ancient critics complained that Epicurus has united under the term pleasure two quite different *desiderata,* positive enjoyment and the absence of pain (Cic. *Fin.* ii 20), and there is some grounds for the complaint. Such remarks as 'The beginning and root of all good is the pleasure of the stomach' (Us. 409) are much more naturally interpreted in the former sense, even if Epicurus did not intend this. In particular, it is difficult to make sense of the notion that absence of pain entails that pleasure can only be varied and not increased. If I derive pleasure from smelling a rose at a time when I am suffering no pain, it seems perverse to say that my pleasure is merely varied. For what I experience is something *sui generis,* a new sense of gratification which is more than a variation of my previous state of consciousness. Even if it is reasonable to call tranquillity of mind a kind of pleasure it is straining language and common sense to call it the greatest pleasure. That procedure leaves us no way to take account of experiences which cannot be assimilated to tranquillity and which do cause us intense gratification without pain.

Thirdly, under 'static' pleasure Epicurus seems to have classified two quite different things. The pleasure which follows from the satisfaction of desire is normally related closely in time to the desire. When I leave hospital, restored to health, it makes sense to say 'You must be pleased to be better'. But it makes much less sense to say this a long time later. The mental equilibrium enjoyed by an Epicurean of ten years' standing seems to be something quite different.

These and other observations could be prolonged. I have confined my comments to Epicurus' own theories, and it is hardly necessary to dwell on some of the obvious objections to egoistic hedonism as a 'moral' theory. But in this book Epicurus should have the last word, and it is eloquently expressed by his great disciple and admirer, Lucretius:

When the winds are troubling the waters on a mighty sea it is sweet to view from the land the great struggles of another man; not because it is pleasant or delightful that anyone should be distressed, but because it is sweet to see the misfortunes from which you are yourself free. It is sweet too to watch great battles which cover the plains if you yourself have no share in the danger. But nothing is more pleasing than to be master of those tranquil places which have been strongly fortified aloft by the teaching of wise men. From there you can look down upon other men and see them wandering purposelessly and straying as they search for a way of life—competing with their abilities, trying to outdo one another in social status, striving night and day with the utmost effort to rise to the heights of wealth and become masters of everything. Unhappy minds of men, blind hearts! How great the darkness, and how great the dangers in which this little life is spent. Do you not see that nature shouts out for nothing but the removal of pain from the body and the enjoyment in mind of the sense of joy when anxiety and fear have been taken away. Therefore we see that for the body few things only are needed, which are sufficient to remove pain and can also provide many delights. Nor does our nature itself at different times seek for anything more pleasing, if there are no golden statues of youths in the entrance halls holding in their right hands fiery torches so that evening banquets may be provided with light, or if the house does not gleam with silver and shine with gold and a carved and gilded ceiling does not resound to the lute, when, in spite of this, men lie on the soft grass together near a stream of water beneath the branches of a lofty tree refreshing their bodies with joy and at no great cost, particularly when the weather smiles and the time of the year spreads flowers all over the green grass (ii 1–35).

CHAPTER THREE

Scepticism

(i) Pyrrho and Timon—early Pyrrhonism

Scepticism is an ability which sets up antitheses among appearances and judgments in any way whatever: by scepticism, on account of the 'equal weight' which characterizes opposing states of affairs and arguments, we arrive first at 'suspension of judgment', and second at 'freedom from disturbance' (Sextus, *P.H.* i 8).

In the first book of his *Outlines of Pyrrhonism*, Sextus Empiricus gives this definition of 'scepticism' (*skepsis* means speculation or investigation in its non-technical use). The starting-point of scepticism, he continues, is 'the hope of attaining freedom from disturbance' (ibid. 12). We are to suppose that this motive led certain men to search for a *criterion* by reference to which 'truth' and 'falsity' might be established. They failed in this quest but achieved their long-term aim, 'discovering freedom from disturbance, as if by chance, as a consequence of suspending judgment (about the inconsistency which belongs to appearances and judgments')' (ibid. 29).

Sextus was a Greek physician who flourished at the end of the second century A.D. His medical writings have perished, but he also wrote a lengthy account of Greek Scepticism, and a series of books in which he attacks the doctrines of the 'Dogmatists' from the Sceptic point of view. These works, in the form they have come down to us, occupy four volumes of the Loeb Classical Library. Sextus Empiricus' chief source is Aenesidemus, a Greek philosopher of uncertain date, whose works have not survived independently. Aenesidemus is an important figure. He was probably the first to establish in formal terms the 'modes' of judgment as we find them in Sextus and elsewhere.[1]

---

[1] The 'modes' are a series of arguments designed to show that 'suspension of judgment' should be our attitude towards all things claimed to be real or true in any objective sense. Ten of these arguments are recorded by Sextus (*P.H.* i 31–163) and Diogenes Laertius (ix 79–88); and a further set of five, probably intended to replace them, was introduced by Agrippa, a Sceptic later than Aenesidemus (Sextus, ibid. 164–86; D.L. ibid. 88–9). On Aenesidemus' date I

Aenesidemus almost certainly drew heavily upon the Academic sceptics whom I discuss later in this chapter, but in name at least his scepticism is something which has its roots in the fourth century B.C. Pyrrho of Elis, an older contemporary of Epicurus, was the founder of Greek Scepticism in its technical sense. The revival and detailed working-out of Pyrrhonist principles by Aenesidemus and his followers falls outside the scope of this book. Here I shall be concerned largely with those characteristics of Pyrrhonism which can reasonably be supposed to have developed in the Hellenistic period.

I say 'reasonably' because there is no denying the fact that reliable evidence about early Pyrrhonism is scanty and problematical. The problem, which has been much discussed, is to judge how much impetus towards the kind of scepticism documented in our late sources can be credited to Pyrrho himself. Some have said virtually none, but this certainly goes too far.[1] We should be cautious about ascribing much of the theoretical detail in Sextus and Diogenes Laertius to Pyrrho, and I do not maintain that my outline of Pyrrhonism in this chapter is a wholly accurate account of the historical Pyrrho. I have deliberately incorporated some evidence from what is probably later Pyrrhonism in order to fill out the presentation of attitudes adopted by Pyrrho. But, as we shall see, Timon of Phlius, Pyrrho's publicist and younger contemporary, provides some means of controlling later evidence, and when the sources called upon are of philosophical rather than historical significance I try to indicate the fact. The term 'Pyrrhonist' is also used, rather than 'Pyrrho' or 'Timon', in these latter contexts.

Those who are doubtful about the extent of Pyrrho's scepticism have often pointed to the fact that Cicero refers to him as a strict, dogmatic moralist (e.g. *Fin.* iv 43) but does not mention him more than once in the *Academica,* a work devoted to arguments for and against scepticism. In just one passage Cicero states that Pyrrho denied perception of 'indifferent' things by the wise man (*Acad.* ii 130). Leaving that passage aside for the moment, we may next observe that in Diogenes Laertius Pyrrho is said to have denied anything to be

am inclined to think with Brochard, *Les Sceptiques grecs* (Paris 1923) p. 246, that the first century B.C. fits the evidence best. This point has been well argued by J. M. Rist who offers an interesting interpretation of Aenesidemus' so-called Heracliteanism, *Phoenix* xxiv (1970) 309–19.

[1] The accounts of Pyrrho by Zeller and Brochard are much better balanced than the books by L. Robin, *Pyrrhon et le scepticisme grec* (Paris 1944) and most recently A. Weische, *Cicero und die neue Akademie* (Münster 1961).

morally good or bad; human behaviour is governed by convention (ix 61). This seems to chime very oddly with Cicero's Pyrrho, who asserted that 'virtue is the only good' (*Fin.* iii 12). Are we then to conclude that Pyrrho held quite contradictory positions, or alternatively that scepticism was improperly fathered upon him by later Pyrrhonists? Is Cicero quite wrong about Pyrrho?

Cicero's evidence should not be lightly discarded; he was much closer in date to Pyrrho then Sextus or Diogenes, both of whom wrote after Pyrrhonism had been revived by Aenesidemus. But if Pyrrho was not a sceptic in any recognizably philosophical sense, why did Aenesidemus and his followers call themselves Pyrrhonists?[1] A number of considerations raise doubts about Cicero's Pyrrho. For one thing, Cicero seems to know nothing of Timon's writings. Cicero's sources for scepticism were Academic writers, notably Clitomachus, Philo of Larisa and his pupil Antiochus, who reverted to dogmatism (see pp. 222ff.). The Academic sceptics did not acknowledge indebtedness to Pyrrho. They claimed Socrates and Plato as the founders of their methodology. Yet Arcesilaus, the founder of Academic scepticism, was lampooned by Timon and by the Stoic Ariston in verses which explicitly indicate a close similarity between his position and that of Pyrrho (D.L. iv 33).

I have just referred to Ariston, and mention of his name by Cicero also casts doubt upon the latter's knowledge of Pyrrho. Cicero regularly names Pyrrho alongside Ariston. We know that Ariston's most notable doctrine was the impossibility of drawing any distinction of value between 'indifferent' things, that is, things which in a moral sense are neither good nor bad. The orthodox Stoic view was that some 'indifferent' things are to be 'preferred' to others (see p. 193). It is likely that Cicero knew far more about Ariston than he knew about Pyrrho, who wrote nothing, and that he mistakenly assimilated Pyrrho's 'indifference' to externals, which was based upon problems about criteria of perception, to Ariston's advocacy of total indifference to anything apart from virtue and vice.

Cicero's evidence certainly raises problems. But perhaps it can be squared with other reports more satisfactorily than is apparent at first glance. Cicero does not say what Pyrrho meant by 'virtue' or *honestum*. We do not know whether Pyrrho thought that the word *aretê* ('virtue')

---

[1] The argument that Aenesidemus did so because he was dissatisfied with the Academy's move back to dogmatism under Antiochus of Ascalon begs the question.

had a valid usage; but suppose that he did think so, and suppose that
he used it to designate the tranquillity of mind which Pyrrhonists
regarded as the consequence of a disposition to suspend judgment.
Then, Cicero's evidence might be regarded as curiously defective
rather than totally anomalous. Pyrrho could consistently claim to be a
sceptic concerning knowledge of the external world or objective
moral standards, and at the same time maintain that 'indifference'
does not extend to tranquillity and mental disturbance. About the
respective goodness and badness of these states of mind he could
claim to be subjectively certain (so too perhaps Timon ap. Sext. *Adv.
math*, xi 20). Pyrrho's motive in advocating suspension of judgment
may well have been the practical one of freeing people from the disturbance caused by certain beliefs, especially beliefs which conflict
with each other. But this was also the professed goal of later Pyrrhonism, and the practical orientation of Pyrrho's philosophy does not
speak against his competence in arguments (cf. D.L. ix 64). The little
that is known about his life tells strongly in favour of his having, what
we may call, a professional philosophical background.

As the name of a philosophical method or particular school Scepticism originates with Pyrrho. But long before Pyrrho of course we
can find philosophers expressing sceptical attitudes. The fallibility of
sense-perception as a source of knowledge was emphasized in different
ways by Heraclitus, Parmenides, Empedocles and Democritus in the
Presocratic period. Earlier than all of these Xenophanes had written:

That which is wholly clear no man has seen, nor will there ever be a man
who has intuitive knowledge about the gods and about everything of which
I speak. For even if he should chance to speak the complete truth, yet he
himself does not know it; what occurs concerning all things is seeming (DK
21B34).

Plato in the fourth century replied that 'seeming' is only the ontological condition of phenomena. We can know that which is fully
real—the Forms—but these changeless and eternal entities are not
objects of sense-perception. Plato's distinctions between seeming and
being and between belief and knowledge can be traced to a desire to
establish a set of objects (the Forms) which are not liable to the unstable and uncertain judgments made about phenomena. Some earlier
philosophers had already faced the problem of knowledge in a different
way. Protagoras, instead of looking like Parmenides for some un-
changing noumenal subject of the verb 'exists', argued that the senses

must be accepted for what they are—sources of subjective awareness. Truth can only be relative; what is true for me—that the wind feels cold—is true; but this says nothing about the temperature of the wind in itself or how it feels to you. Protagoras did not, in my judgment, deny the existence of a world external to the percipient. He denied the validity of statements which seek to go beyond the experience of individuals.

Plato's answer to Protagorean relativism is a large and complex subject. The important point for this chapter is that certain problems of knowledge to which Pyrrho drew attention had already been recognized by earlier philosophers, who put forward different kinds of answers for resolving them. Pyrrho's scepticism has its closest conceptual connexion with Protagoras among his predecessors. But it looks forward rather than back. Both the Epicureans and the Stoics argued that objective knowlege of the world is possible. In Epicureanism the 'clear view' and its derivative, 'preconception', in Stoicism the 'cognitive impression', are laid down as valid criteria for true perceptual statements. Pyrrho's scepticism provides the basis for a penetrating criticism of such theories of knowledge, though there is no evidence that Pyrrho himself attacked Epicurus and Zeno specifically; indeed Epicurus is said to have admired Pyrrho (D.L. ix 64). The second feature of Pyrrhonism which marks its contemporary character is the ethical goal, 'freedom from disturbance'. No one had previously suggested that scepticism might be made the basis of a moral theory. This was Pyrrho's innovation, but in seeking for a means to attain tranquillity of mind he is at one with Epicurus and the Stoics.

Pyrrho was born at Elis in the north-west of the Peloponnese about 365 B.C. We know little about his life and philosophical background. He is said to have been a pupil of Bryson son of Stilpo (D.L. ix 61). This is probably a corruption for 'Bryson or Stilpo' who were both adherents of the Megarian school. There is no reason to question the likelihood of some early connexion between Pyrrho and the Megarians. From them Pyrrho would have acquired a training in dialectic and reasons for distrusting the evidence of the senses. He did not however espouse the positive aspects of Megarian teaching, which drew upon Eleatic monism and Parmenides' prescription 'judge by reason'. Stilpo also incorporated features of Cynic doctrine into his own philosophy. Anecdotes about Pyrrho suggest that he was sympathetic to the Cynic advocacy of a simple life in withdrawal from civic affairs (D.L. ix 62–9).

A second source of Pyrrho's scepticism may be found in an association he had with Anaxarchus. This obscure figure is said 'to have
abolished the criterion' by Sextus (*Adv. math.* vii 48; 87f.), and if he
was a Democritean (D.L. ix 58) he may also have adopted the early
atomist subjectivism concerning perceptual judgments. Anaxarchus
was a citizen of Abdera, Democritus' home town. Most of our information about him comes from Plutarch and Arrian's accounts of
Alexander the Great.[1] Anaxarchus became a court philosopher, and
accompanied Alexander on his eastern expedition. Pyrrho was also
a member of the party, and Diogenes Laertius says that both philosophers consorted with the Indian 'Gymnosophists' (naked philosophers)
and the Magi (ix 61). But it is impossible to know whether oriental
influences played any significant part in Pyrrho's philosophical
development. The evidence does not require such a hypothesis.

Pyrrho himself wrote nothing, possibly to avoid giving the impression of dogmatizing. Fortunately he had a follower, Timon of
Phlius, who was less scrupulous, and some fragments of Timon's
writings survive as quotations in later writers.[2] They provide the most
reliable evidence of Pyrrho's own views. Timon is a colourful figure
who defended the Pyrrhonist position in verse as well as prose. The
majority of his fragments belong to the *silloi,* 'lampoons', in which
he attacks the dogmatic philosophers. Diogenes Laertius' *Life of
Pyrrho* also draws upon Timon's work; but the best starting-point
for a discussion of Pyrrho's scepticism is a text from Aristocles' *On
philosophy*, a Peripatetic treatise written in the second century A.D.
and quoted by Eusebius, bishop of Caesaria (*Pr. Ev.* xiv 18, 758c–d).
It is unlikely that this late summary preserves Timon's precise words,
but the position attributed to Pyrrho seems entirely credible.

After observing that Pyrrho left nothing in writing, Aristocles
continues:

His pupil Timon says that the man who means to be happy must consider
these three questions: 1. what things are really like; 2. what attitude we
should adopt towards them; 3. what the consequence of such an attitude will
be. According to Timon Pyrrho declared that things are equally indistinguishable, unmeasurable and indeterminable.[3] For this reason neither our

[1] Testimonia in Diels-Kranz, *Vorsokratiker* ii 59.
[2] The evidence has been collected by Diels, *Poetarum philosophorum fragmenta* 9.
[3] These three adjectives have sometimes been interpreted in a descriptive rather
than a modal sense, 'undistinguished' not 'undistinguishable' etc. But the second

acts of perception nor our judgments are true or false. Therefore we should not rely upon them but be without judgments, inclining neither this way nor that, but be steadfast saying concerning each individual thing that it no more is than is not, or that it both is and is not, or that it neither is nor is not. For those who adopt this attitude the consequence will be first a refusal to make assertions and second, freedom from disturbance.

Pyrrho's first question is one that had been asked and answered for the past two hundred years and more. Indeed, it might well be called the basic question of Greek philosophy.[1] The assumption that the 'nature' of things, or what the world is 'really' like, can be investigated and disclosed is basic to Presocratic philosophy as it is to Plato and Aristotle. Pyrrho, with his answer to this question, is rejecting the assumption and thereby denying legitimacy to philosophical speculation. All philosophy must start from certain assumptions, at least if it is to offer any account of reality. And one of the first assumptions which a philosopher must make is that something true can be said about the world; otherwise there can be no knowledge of external reality. Pyrrho, however, claims that truth and falsehood can characterize neither our perception of things nor the (other) judgments which we make; from which it follows that what we perceive or judge cannot be an object of knowledge. Pyrrho's claim is grounded in his answer to the question: 'What are things really like?' By answering 'Unknowable' Pyrrho removes the external world as a subject of philosophical discourse. If the real nature of things cannot be known either to the senses or to reason, then there is nothing by reference to which the truth or falsehood of statements about it can be tested.

The assertion that 'things are equally indistinguishable, unmeasurable and indeterminable' is not supported by any argument in the text quoted from Aristocles. But Pyrrho's own reasoning can be reconstructed with a fair degree of certainty from the fragments of Timon and from other Sceptic sources. Pyrrho is attacking all theories of knowledge which seek, as the Stoics and Epicureans sought, to show that certain perceptual experiences provide wholly accurate information about the real nature of (external) objects. The basis of his critique is that we cannot get at objects independently of sense-perception, and

and third have a termination (*-tos*) which most frequently signifies possibility or necessity, and this interpretation suits the argument better, cf. C. L. Stough, *Greek Skepticism* (Berkeley and Los Angeles 1969) pp. 18f.

[1] 'On what things are really like', literally 'On Nature', is the standard book title among early Greek philosophers. It was also the title of Epicurus' basic work (see p. 18).

Hellenistic Philosophy

sense-perception provides no guarantee that we apprehend things as they really are. Objects in themselves are therefore not available to test our sense-perception. Sense-perception reveals 'what appears' to the percipient; but 'what appears' cannot be used as sound evidence from which to infer 'what is'.

Let us consider the last statement more closely. Pyrrho is arguing that our perceptual experience can never be sufficient to warrant indubitable statements or beliefs about the external world. He does not deny that something, say, yellow, sweet and sticky *appears* to me; and he will admit that I may be justified in saying 'This looks like honey'. But he holds that my sense-perception is quite compatible with the proposition 'This is not honey' as well as the proposition 'This does not look like honey to Pyrrho'. In the 'modes' formulated by the later Pyrrhonists we find ten types of consideration for doubting the possibility of knowledge. They concentrate upon the fact that how we perceive anything is relative to the nature of the percipient and external circumstances. Thus the Pyrrhonist adopts certain everyday assumptions for the purpose of argument, for instance that the sun is a source of heat and the shade of cold, and then refers to someone who became warm in the shade and shivered in the sun (D.L. ix 80; Sextus, *P.H.* i 82). We cannot say that he was mistaken in *feeling* hot and cold as he did. But his feelings conflict with those of other men. The Pyrrhonist concludes that the same thing may 'appear' in contradictory ways to different people, and therefore nothing which 'appears' to any man is sufficient to found a belief on what anything is really like.[1]

With regard to the contradictions in their sceptical procedures they would first demonstrate the ways in which things induce belief and then use the same grounds to undermine their credibility. They argue that those things induce belief which are agreed upon by reference to sense-perception, and things which never or only rarely change—customs, things determined by laws, objects of pleasure and wonder. Then they showed that the probabilities are equal by means of things contrary to those which induce belief (D.L. ix 78–9).

Timon, and probably Pyrrho himself, distinguished sharply between statements of the form (1) '*x* appears to me to be *y*', and (2)

[1] A. J. Ayer writes: 'It would be hard for [the sceptic] to get a hearing if the procedures which he questions never led us astray. But it is not essential to his position that this should be so. All that he requires is that errors should be possible not that they should actually occur' *The Problem of Knowledge* (Harmondsworth 1965) p. 40.

'*x* is *y*', where *x* and *y* refer to the same object. Only the second statement is banned. The first statement is perfectly acceptable to the Pyrrhonists, since it does not commit the speaker to any claim about the relationship between what he perceives and what is the case independently of his perception. There is no wish or attempt to deny that we have genuine perceptual experiences:

> We admit the fact that we do see, we recognize the fact that we do have this particular thought; but we do not know how we see or how we think. We say by way of description that 'this appears white', without confirming that it really is white (D.L. ix 103).

> That honey is sweet I do not postulate, but I admit that it appears sweet (Timon, *On the senses*, D.L. ix 105).

It is important to observe that the subject of the type of statement acceptable to the Pyrrhonists is not what later philosophers have sometimes called a sense-datum. The subject of Timon's statement 'It appears sweet' is honey, a thing or material object. There would be no point to the distinction between '*x* appears to me to be *y*' and '*x* is *y*' if *x* were merely a sense-datum. Suppose that on eating something yellow and sticky I get a sweet taste. If *what* I taste is only a sense-datum then there could be no reason to deny that *it is* sweet. What is open to question is whether the sweetness which I actually taste is a real property of the yellow, sticky object. But this is not Timon's way of proceeding. He is not suggesting that we only see, hear, taste, touch or smell sense-data; but rather, that we perceive objects—honey, coffee, dogs, chairs—as our ordinary language suggests. The problem in the form which he raises it is not the relation between sense-data and objects, but the relation between the object as perceived and the same object independently of its being perceived. In brief, he is saying that the conditions of perception are such that they introduce a relationship between the object and the percipient which cannot be assumed to hold between the object and its own properties.

That this is Timon's procedure is shown clearly by the use of the words 'the apparent' (*to phainomenon*), or as I should prefer to paraphrase it, 'the object as perceived'.[1] Thus he writes: 'But the object

[1] The Pyrrhonists use the term 'the apparent' in preference to the term *phantasia* (presentation, impression, image); in Diogenes Laertius' *Life of Pyrrho* the latter term does occur in a section (107) concerning disagreement between Sceptics and dogmatists (*phantasia* is the word used by Epicureans and Stoics). The term *phantasia* means roughly what has been called a sense-datum in modern

as perceived prevails on every side, wherever it goes' (D.L. ix 105). What Timon means with these rather cryptic words can be inferred from a passage of Sextus:

> We say that the criterion of the Sceptic school is 'the object as perceived', using this term for what is in effect its impression on the senses. For since the impression is a matter of our being acted upon and involuntary feeling, it is not open to question. Hence no one, it may be, disagrees concerning the fact that the underlying object appears to be of this or that kind; the question is whether it really is such as it appears to be (*P.H.* i 22).

(Strictly, Sextus should have pointed out that what is perceived may have no 'underlying object'.)

The Pyrrhonists are denying that perception is something intentional. I cannot help seeing this as a printed sheet of paper; for that is the content of my present visual sensation. On the basis of this evidence I am entitled to make a type (1) statement. If I go further and say 'This is a sheet of printed paper' I utter a type (2) statement. The Pyrrhonist will now object that I have postulated a relation between subject and predicate for which I have no valid evidence. I have used my experience of 'the object as perceived' to infer a definite characteristic of the object in itself. The validity of this inference cannot be proved, and my type (2) statement is therefore neither true nor false.

Since sense-perception, in the view of the Pyrrhonists, provides no grounds for judgments about things-in-themselves, we should not make such judgments. This brings us to Pyrrho's answer to the second question in Aristocles' text. Our attitude to the world should be one of suspended judgment, which is summed up by the Pyrrhonists in the expression 'no more' (this than that).[1] The effect of this formula is to leave it entirely an open question whether the subject of an objective

philosophy. Pyrrho, on the evidence of Timon and Diogenes, preferred to use the language of 'appearance', i.e. to speak of 'the same thing appearing different to different people', but from a philosophical point of view there is little reason to choose one form of expression rather than the other, cf. R. M. Chisholm's excellent article, 'The theory of appearing' (*Philosophical Analysis* ed. Max Black, Ithaca, N.Y. 1950).

[1] See Sextus *P.H.* i 188–91. In the following chapters of this book Sextus gives a further glossary of Sceptic technical terms. The terms 'no more', 'I determine nothing' etc. are not themselves to be interpreted as positive assertions. They are merely a linguistic device for expressing the refusal to make any assertions (D.L. ix 76 reporting Timon), and are said to cancel themselves in being asserted: i.e. 'I determine nothing' is taken to entail that I do not determine that I determine nothing, cf. Sextus *P.H.* i 14ff. Sometimes these slogans were interpreted descriptively as indications of the Pyrrhonist's own state of mind (Sextus ibid. 201; D.L. ix 74).

judgment is what it is said to be, or whether it has the property attributed to it. Hence, if I say 'Snow is no more white than it is not white', I am to be taken as offering no positive description or determination of any material object. The Sceptic 'determines nothing', on the grounds that determining anything entails 'assenting to something non-evident', that is, what things are like in themselves.

The judgments which the Pyrrhonist outlaws are exclusively claims to know about things-in-themselves. We might with good reason call the statement 'This appears to be honey' a judgment. Our perceptual experience typically takes such a form. We see, or there appears to us, a cat or a rose not a black shape or a red shape, though there are times when the latter expressions do describe correctly what we see. But if 'A cat appears to me' is a judgment, it is a judgment which does not, at least normally, involve any conscious inference. And though such statements can be false, either deliberately or mistakenly, we normally treat a person's claims to see, hear and so forth as authoritative. The Pyrrhonists seem to have regarded these as mere reports of perceptual experience which are to be distinguished from 'judgments'. 'The Pyrrhonist procedure is a manner of reporting on objects as perceived' (D.L. ix 78). There is no indication that the Pyrrhonists regarded such statements as amenable to truth or falsity, and every reason to think that they are excluded from the condemnation of 'asserting'. To assert, for Pyrrho, is to make a statement of the type (2) form '*x* is *y*'—this is white; by refusing to say '*x* is no more *y* than it is not' etc. the Pyrrhonist repudiates the possibility of being right or wrong about this kind of assertion.

Pyrrho's suspension of judgment concerning the nature of material objects applies equally to moral concepts. Diogenes Laertius tells us that he 'denied that anything was morally good or bad' and that custom and convention govern human actions (ix 61). An extract later from the *Life* illustrates the Pyrrhonist style of argument about the relativity of moral judgments:

Either all that is held to be good by anyone must be said to be good or not all. But all cannot be said to be good since the same thing is held to be good by one person, for instance pleasure by Epicurus; and bad by another, Antisthenes. The consequence will be that the same thing is both good and bad. But if we do not admit that everything judged to be good by anyone is good, we shall have to distinguish between different opinions. This is impossible owing to the equal weight of arguments on both sides. Therefore that which is really good is unknowable (ix 101).

In the passage of Aristocles with which this discussion began, reason as well as sense-perception is ruled out as a possible criterion of truth. Once again there is no direct evidence for Pyrrho's own arguments about this, but both Diogenes Laertius and Sextus supply arguments which were used by later Pyrrhonists. We have already seen that Epicurus, like Aristotle, based his epistemology on empirical evidence and the same is true of the Stoics. The Pyrrhonists adopted this position for their own critical purposes, and used the unreliability of sense-perception as the ground for denying reason's claims to any knowledge of the real nature of things:

> If every intelligible thing has its source and basis of confirmation in sense-perception, and the things apprehended through sense-perception are inconsistent (with each other), as we have argued, the same must be true of the intelligibles; so that the premises of the proof, of whatever kind they are, must be unreliable and insecure. Therefore demonstrative reasoning is not trustworthy (Sextus, *Adv. math.* viii 356).

The practical outcome of this attitude to reality is said to be 'freedom from confusion'. Various anecdotes are told about Pyrrho's suspension of judgment: he would have fallen into pits or would have been attacked by dogs if it had not been for the help of his friends (D.L. ix 62). Such stories should be taken with more than a grain of salt. Pyrrho's scepticism entails nothing unpractical so far as everyday life is concerned. If it did, life would be full of confusion. The Pyrrhonists do have a criterion for practical purposes, 'the object as perceived'.[1] But it is not a criterion of truth in the sense required by them. They deny that seeing is believing, that is, believing that we can see or apprehend things as they are in themselves. The object of the Pyrrhonist's attack is not common-sense attitudes to the world but philosophical claims to knowledge. Knowledge makes a claim to certainty whether it be about the nature of material objects, the structure of the universe, moral values or the existence of God. In Pyrrho's scepticism we are not debarred from saying that we see cats and dogs, or, as his language would put it, that cats and dogs 'appear' to us. But the perceptual experiences which we have do not, he argues, entitle us to say anything about the entities which we assume to exist independently of such experiences. By suspending judgment we are freed from the confusion which may arise if we hear contradictory accounts of the gods, the nature of goodness, and so forth. The Pyrrhonist

[1] D.L. ix 106; Sextus, *P.H.* i 21–4.

accepts the conventions of everyday life as a practical criterion without troubling himself over questions about their rational justification. At a time when philosophers were competing with each other in logic, or natural and moral philosophy, Pyrrho took the step of criticizing all philosophers by questioning the basis of their claims to knowledge. At the same time his critique can be given a wider ambience, taking in religion and all dogmatic prescriptions for society and the individual. Like the Stoic and Epicurean insistence on the validity of their rational explanations of phenomena, Pyrrho's antithetical scepticism is an alternative answer for men dissatisfied with the traditional values and beliefs of a society in a state of transition.

Old Pyrrho, Pyrrho, how and whence did you discover release from servitude to the beliefs and empty theorizing of sophists? How did you unloose the shackles of every deception and inducement to belief? You did not trouble to inquire into the winds which prevail over Greece, whence each comes and whither it blows (Timon ap. D.L. ix 65).

It is of course an evasive answer, especially at a time when conventions and social values were changing. What did it mean at the end of the fourth century B.C. to 'follow convention'? Pyrrho's scepticism however has the great merit of underlining the fact that our perception of objects is relative to all manner of circumstances. Knowledge of the external world is not incorrigible. There are no necessary truths about empirical objects, and David Hume was probably right to argue that no sufficient reasons can be given for inferring the nature of physical objects from sense-perception. Most philosophers today are probably content to concede that the world as perceived may not be the world as it exists in some other relation. If that lands us in dualism it is not perhaps the philosopher's task to resolve the problem. We employ physicists to tell us about the structure of matter. But matter has nothing obviously to do with the world as we perceive it. Nevertheless, there is a most important rôle for truth and falsehood in judgments about the objects of perception. We are, as a matter of fact, remarkably successful in judging distance, shape, colour and size; the mistakes we sometimes make, or may be induced to make under certain perceptual conditions, do not do much to undermine this fact. Leaving aside things-in-themselves, we have criteria for identifying and distinguishing between objects of perception with a consistency and accuracy which the Pyrrhonists overlook. If we adopt the strict Pyrrhonist requirement of matching objects as perceived with things-in-themselves, we may not succeed in giving any rational justification for objective statements. Pyrrho was quite right to see a difficulty here. But the Pyrrhonist is prepared to say 'This appears to be white', without appreciating the significance of the fact that such a sentence, as Epicurus recognized, presupposes some similar previous experience also shared by others. The Academic Sceptics under Carneades realized that conditions of truth can be laid down which need not commit a philosopher to any claims to have knowledge of things-in-themselves.

(ii) Academic Scepticism—Arcesilaus

Pyrrho died about 270 B.C. He founded no school in any formal sense, and such dissemination as his views acquired was chiefly due to hearsay and the writings of Timon. The next stage in the history of Greek scepticism is marked not by Pyrrhonists but by the Academy. The last half of Pyrrho's life overlaps the youth and middle years of Arcesilaus, who became head of the Academy about 265 B.C. Arcesilaus, like Pyrrho, is said to have denied the possibility of knowledge (Cic. *Acad.* i 45), and to a late Sceptic like Sextus Empiricus Arcesilaus' philosophical position seemed almost identical to Pyrrhonism (*P.H.* i 232).[1] It is highly probable that Arcesilaus was influenced by Pyrrho, but the intellectual background of the two Sceptics was very different. Unlike Pyrrho, Arcesilaus is a figure of the Athenian philosophical establishment, though he was to initiate radical changes in the character of contemporary Platonism.

Arcesilaus was not an Athenian by birth. He came from Pitane in Aetolia, and first studied there under a mathematician, Autolycus (D.L. iv 29). At Athens he was a pupil of a musical theorist, Xanthus, and Theophrastus.[2] But he left the Lyceum for the Academy, at a time when Polemo was its head and Crantor and Crates were prominent members. As I have mentioned in the first chapter, the Academy in the last part of the fourth century and the beginning of the third, seems to have given increasing emphasis to practical moral teaching. Crantor, for instance, wrote a 'little' book *On grief*, which is highly praised in Cicero's *Academica* (ii 135). There is no reason to think that Arcesilaus

---

[1] Ariston, the heretical Stoic contemporary of Arcesilaus, described him in a parody of a Homeric line as 'Plato in front, Pyrrho behind, Diodorus in the middle' (Sextus, *P.H.* i 234); Diodorus Cronus, the Megarian philosopher, is meant. Cf. Timon's remarks, D.L. iv 33.

[2] A. Weische, *Cicero und die neue Akademie* has attempted to find in the Peripatos a source of Arcesilaus' scepticism; but his argument is not compelling.

disapproved of practical moral teaching. Had he done so the Academy under Polemo could hardly have attracted him in the first place. But Arcesilaus was not content to maintain this tradition. On the contrary, he seems to have felt that the Academy had lost the original incentive, which it derived through Plato from Socrates, towards dispassionate and undogmatic inquiry. It was not as a moral teacher that Arcesilaus made his name, but as a dialectician. According to Cicero 'what he chiefly derived from various books by Plato and from Socratic discourses was that neither the senses nor the mind can perceive anything certain' (*De orat.* iii 67). This is hardly a conclusion which someone who had studied Plato's writings as a whole would be entitled to draw, and it is not clear that Arcesilaus actually claimed Plato's authority as the support for his own scepticism. He doubtless admired Plato's dialectical methodology, but we are also told that he was the first Academic to disturb the system handed down by Plato, and that by means of question and answer he made it more disputatious (D.L. iv 28). It was the Socratic method rather than Plato's positive philosophy which influenced Arcesilaus.

In such early dialogues of Plato as the *Euthyphro, Ion, Laches* and *Lysis,* the discussion concerns itself with attempts to answer a 'What is *x*?' question, e.g. piety or courage. Socrates' interlocutor claims to be able to answer this question at the outset of the dialogue, but under examination his suggestion is found to be unsatisfactory and alternative answers are put forward. Socrates himself makes positive contributions, but subjects them along with those proffered by others to criticism. By the end of the dialogue various candidates have been considered, but none is accepted as satisfactory. Hence Socrates concludes the *Euthyphro* by saying: 'See what you've done, my friend! You are going away having destroyed all my hopes of learning from you about piety and impiety'; or the *Lysis*: 'We have become a laughing-stock, you two, and I, an old man. As they leave, all these people will say that we regard ourselves—for I class myself as one of you—as friends, but we have not as yet been able to discover what a friend is.' Socrates' procedure in these dialogues is consistent with the portrait painted of him by Plato in the *Apology*. There Socrates disclaims the possession of knowledge, but he also asserts that recognition of one's own ignorance is better than thinking that one knows something when one doesn't. Arcesilaus' philosophical method is the Socratic procedure updated to take account of the state of philosophy in the third century B.C.

The essence of this methodology consists in taking the position of one's opponents and showing it to be self-contradictory. The most detailed argument by Arcesilaus which survives exemplifies the technique very clearly.[1]

The Stoics distinguished three epistemological states: knowledge, apprehension, and belief. They held that knowledge was peculiar to the wise man and belief peculiar to the foolish (all other men). By 'apprehension' or 'grasping' (*katalêpsis*) the Stoics meant what we would call accurate or true perception. They maintained that through the senses we receive information about the external world, some of which is absolutely accurate, and it is this absolutely accurate information which we can *apprehend*. To apprehend something is therefore to grasp it as it really is. The details of this theory will require further discussion in the next chapter. But for the present, it is enough to observe that the Stoic theory of knowledge was based on the ground that certain sense-impressions—those which can be apprehended—are 'cognitive' or self-evidently 'true'.

The Stoics did not distinguish the wise from the foolish by reference to 'apprehension'. All men, they held, are capable of apprehending things, but only the wise man's apprehension is 'secure and unshakeable by argument'. This is the mark of knowledge—not mere apprehension but apprehension which is proof against any attempt that might be made to overturn it.

To this theory Arcesilaus made the following objections. First, apprehension is not, in fact, an independent test of truth since in practice it is either knowledge (in the wise man) or belief (in the fool). This point, we may note, is based upon the Stoics' own thesis: all men are either wise or foolish. In other words, Arcesilaus is arguing that the Stoics, by their exclusive disjunction between wise and foolish, make any intermediate cognitive state redundant. 'Apprehension' is *either* knowledge *or* belief; it is not something over and above one of these, and it cannot therefore serve as the criterion of truth.

Further, Arcesilaus took the definition of apprehension, 'assent to a cognitive impression', and argued that this was vitiated on two grounds: first, what we assent to is a proposition and not a (sense-) impression (the Stoics, and other philosophers, used 'true' in a much looser sense than would be acceptable today); secondly, and more important, 'no true impression is found which is of such a kind that it

---

[1] The evidence for the next four paragraphs is drawn from Sextus, *Adv. math.* vii 150–7; cf. also Cic. *Acad.* ii 77. For the Stoic theory in detail see pp. 123–31.

could not be false'. Later Academics set out detailed arguments in support of this point (see p. 96). It forms a direct contradiction of the Stoic thesis; for the Stoics argued that the characteristic of a cognitive impression is just the fact that it is true and cannot be false.

The Stoics held that the wise man will only suspend judgment in cases where apprehension is not possible. Arcesilaus' argument leads to the conclusion that the wise man must always suspend judgment. For if apprehension is ruled out, then all things must be non-apprehensible. Only a fool would assent to what is non-apprehensible, and this amounts to holding opinions. But the wise man, according to the Stoics, does not hold opinions, for that would equate him with fools. Therefore, Arcesilaus argues, the Stoic wise man will not assent to anything but will suspend judgment.

In this argument, Arcesilaus accepts the Stoic distinction between the wise and the foolish; he also accepts their distinction between giving and withholding assent. He attacks the Stoic claim that assent can ever be well-grounded by raising objections to the notion of apprehension. And thereby he turns the Stoics' own argument into a defence of the Sceptic position.

Arcesilaus was undoubtedly concerned to attack dogmatic claims to knowledge. Stoicism, with its postulate that sense-perception can provide grounds for statements which are certainly true, offered him a ready target. But it is not entirely clear that we should take Arcesilaus to be *positively* advocating scepticism.[1] Cicero reports that he 'denied that anything could be known, not even that which Socrates had left himself' (*Acad.* i 45). By this reference to Socrates, Arcesilaus means 'knowledge that we do not know anything'. If we take Arcesilaus' statement seriously, it entails that neither the validity of knowledge nor that of scepticism can be positively established. That is to say, Arcesilaus leaves it an open question whether true or false are legitimate predicates to apply to certain statements. He denies knowledge of any criteria which are adequate to sanction the use of true and false. But it does not follow from this that some statements are not true and others not false. Arcesilaus' open-mindedness on this question emerges in Cicero's next remarks:

---

[1] Sextus asserts that Arcesilaus put forward 'suspension of judgment' as the goal of life, *P.H.* i 232. But von Arnim, *R.E.* sv Arkesilaos, gives reasons for thinking that 'the discovery of truth' would be a better description of Arcesilaus' goal, cf. Cic. *Acad.* ii 60, *veri inveniendi causa*: ibid. 76, *verum invenire voluisse sic intellegitur.*

He believed that everything lies hidden in obscurity, and that there is nothing which can be perceived or understood; therefore it is improper for anyone to make any assertion or declaration or to give anything approval by an act of assent; a man must restrain himself and check his rashness from every slip, for one's rashness would be conspicuous if something false or unknown were approved of, and there is nothing worse than assent and approval running ahead of knowledge and perception.

If nothing can be perceived or understood there are no grounds for saying that such and such is certainly the case; but it may be the case. Arcesilaus' recommendation to refrain from assent is based here on the need to avoid error. In order to assent to or approve of something we require knowledge; otherwise we may assent to what is false. But nothing can be known. Therefore we should not assent to anything, and thus we avoid the possibility of error. As von Arnim says, for Arcesilaus 'the essential mark of wisdom is not possession of knowledge but freedom from error'.[1]

The positive feature of Arcesilaus' philosophical method is the desire to discover what is true. For this purpose 'it is necessary to argue *pro* and *contra* everything' (Cic. *Acad.* ii 60).[2] An important example of this will be discussed when we come to Carneades, but the methodology goes back to Arcesilaus. Cicero, generalizing about the New Academy (i.e. the Academy from Arcesilaus to Philo of Larisa), writes as follows:

> The only object of the Academics' discussions is by arguing both sides of a question to draw out and fashion something which is either true or which comes as close as possible to truth. Nor is there any difference between ourselves and those who think that they know except that they do not doubt that their doctrines are true, whereas we hold many things to be probable which we can easily adhere to but hardly affirm as certain (*Acad.* ii 8).

As we have seen, Arcesilaus rejected the Stoics' defence of an empiricist theory of knowledge based upon 'cognitive sense-impressions'. There is no evidence that he regarded this as a doctrine with respect to which reasons of equal cogency could be advanced on both sides. His Academic successors followed up Arcesilaus' criticism of sense-perception as a source of knowledge by developing rules for assent on the basis of 'probability'. No doubt the inspiration for this stems from Arcesilaus himself, but the detailed working out of the theory is credited in our sources to Carneades. Sextus tells us that

---

[1] op. cit. col. 1166.   [2] cf. D.L. iv 28; Cic. *Acad.* ii 7f.

Arcesilaus 'says that the man who suspends judgment about everything will regulate his actions by "that which is reasonable" ' (*Adv.
math.* vii 158). By this criterion Arcesilaus may have meant that for
which good, as distinct from infallible, reasons can be given. It is not
certain however that Arcesilaus put this forward as his own view.[1]
Sextus refers to 'the reasonable' at the end of Arcesilaus' criticism of
the Stoics, and his phraseology here is for the most part Stoic. Arcesilaus may be simply applying to the Stoics the consequences of his
own critique. It will not be possible for them, if knowledge has been
undermined, to define a right act, as they did, in terms of knowledge.
They will have to say simply that it is one for which good but not
infallible reasons can be given.

   Our information about Arcesilaus is too scanty to make it profitable
to speculate further about his views. But he is an important figure in the
history of philosophy. By challenging the Stoics and other dogmatists, he restored to philosophy a critical function which it was in
serious danger of losing. Neither the successors of Plato nor the
contemporary Peripatos could consistently cast doubt upon the
foundations of knowledge while defending positivist views of their
own. Arcesilaus sharpened awareness of the problems which surround
empiricist theories of knowledge, and there are no strong reasons for
thinking that he was more sympathetic towards a metaphysical theory
such as Plato's Forms provided. It has sometimes been supposed, on
the basis of statements in St. Augustine, Sextus and Cicero, that
Arcesilaus confined his scepticism to criticism of the Stoics and other
schools, while adhering to orthodox Platonism within the Academy
itself.[2] But most scholars have rightly rejected this view.[3] Cicero,
our best evidence for Arcesilaus, presents him as a wholly honest
and consistent philosopher who regarded suspension of assent as an
honourable attitude and one worthy of a wise man (*Acad.* ii 77).
Since Arcesilaus, like Socrates, wrote nothing, it was easy for misconceptions about him to arise. It is unfortunate that we have so few
examples of his famous powers as a dialectician. Under his leadership

---

[1] Here too von Arnim seems to me to be correct, *R.E.* sv Arkesilaos col. 1167
in pointing out the Stoic context of Arcesilaus' remarks about 'the reasonable'.
Brochard, *Les Sceptiques grecs*, p. 112, sees a concession to Stoicism, inappro-
priately in my view. It is characteristic of Arcesilaus' method to draw a conclusion
from his opponents' premises.
[2] Augustine, *Cont. Ac.* i 38; Sextus, *P.H.* i 232; Cic. *Acad.* ii 60.
[3] e.g. Zeller, Brochard, Weische. An exception is O. Gigon, 'Zur Geschichte
der sogennanten Neuen Akademie', *Museum Helveticum* i (1944).

the Academy seems to have recovered some of its former prestige, and we may presume that Arcesilaus lectured on a variety of subjects. He saw his rôle as a philosopher to consist in criticism and the stimulation of argument. His epistemological doubts are only one, though a very important one, of his contributions to philosophy. Happily we know rather more about the greatest of his successors, Carneades.

(iii) Academic Scepticism—Carneades

The immediate successors of Arcesilaus in the Academy are little more than names to us. The next important phase in the history of Greek scepticism begins with Carneades who flourished about a hundred years later. A key date in Carneades' career is 155 B.C. when he was one of three philosophers chosen to represent Athens as an ambassador at Rome; the others were Diogenes of Babylon, a Stoic, and the Peripatetic, Critolaus.[1] It was on this occasion that Carneades gave his famous lectures for and against justice on consecutive days, which Cicero summarized in the *De republica* (see p. 94). By this time Carneades was about fifty-eight years old, and he died in 129 B.C.

Just as Arcesilaus devoted his attention to a sharp criticism of early Stoicism, so Carneades made it his special task to combat vigorously the theories of Chrysippus. Chrysippus' enormous contribution to Stoicism was neatly expressed in the tag: 'If Chrysippus had not lived there would have been no Stoa.' Carneades parodied this with the quip: 'Without Chrysippus there would have been no Carneades' (D.L. iv 62). On theory of knowledge, ethics, theology and causality Carneades argued at length against the Stoics, and we shall see in the next chapter that his criticism prompted some amendments to Stoic doctrine. Since Carneades' arguments are so closely tied to Stoicism, it will be necessary to anticipate over the next few pages certain subjects treated more fully later. But our chief concern here is Carneades' own philosophical position, and in particular his epistemology.

Carneades followed the fashion set by Pyrrho and Arcesilaus of not writing philosophy (D.L. iv 65). But thanks above all to Cicero Carneades is relatively well documented. His arguments were recorded and expounded by pupils the most notable of whom, Clitomachus, is reputed to have written more than four hundred treatises (D.L. iv 67). Cicero's *Academica* refers explicitly to Clitomachus for some reports of Carneades' views (cf. *Acad.* ii 98ff.), and Clitomachus is probably

[1] Cic. *Tusc.* iv 5; Plutarch, *Cato Maior* 22.

the ultimate source of most detailed evidence on Carneades. As Carneades' close and devoted associate, Clitomachus may be regarded as a most scrupulous witness to his master's views, and he succeeded to the headship of the Academy on Carneades' death.

Many ancient writers comment upon Carneades' personal qualities. He emerges as a most formidable character, renowned for his dedication to philosophy and ability in argument. He became so absorbed in his work, says Diogenes Laertius, that his hair and his nails grew long (iv 62)!

Arcesilaus' sole alternative to knowledge was suspension of judgment. He did not work out in any detail the grounds on which someone might be justified in assenting to some proposition even if its truth could never be firmly established. Carneades agreed with Arcesilaus that no proposition can be certainly established as true or false. But he also developed with considerable care a theory of 'probability', and this may be called an epistemological theory provided that we recognize it makes no claim to, indeed specifically disclaims, certainty.

Carneades developed this theory after a consideration and rejection of Stoic epistemology. An objective criterion of truth, he argued, must satisfy the conditions laid down by the Stoics. No judgment about the world can be certainly true unless (*a*) it is based upon impressions which report the facts correctly, and (*b*) the reliability of such impressions is itself correctly recognized by the percipient (Sextus, *Adv. math.* vii 161, 402ff.). The Stoics held that both of these conditions are satisfied by the 'cognitive impression' (*kataléptikê phantasia*). The characteristic of such an impression is 'complete conformity with the object' (or fact), and in assenting to it we (supposedly) recognize this characteristic. Carneades admitted the existence of sense-impressions, and he also accepted that some of them will satisfy the first condition of the criterion.[1] But this, he pointed out, is of no use unless the second condition is also met; and it cannot be met. No sense-impression, he argued, can guarantee its own correspondence with the facts. Sense-impressions do not possess characteristics which mark off one that is certainly reliable from another that is not. In no particular case is any sense-impression *self-evidently* true to the object it

---

[1] It should be noted that Carneades cannot deny (*a*) if scepticism is to be derived by help of the premise 'There do occur false impressions' (Cic. *Acad.* ii 83). The essence of his position is not 'There are no true impressions' (*contra* Brochard, p. 128). If that were the case Carneades could not establish his conclusion: 'No true impression can be distinguished *as true* from a second identical impression which is false.' Similarly Arcesilaus, Cic. ibid. 77.

purports to represent. It may and often will be true, but it cannot be known to be true.

Carneades' arguments against the Stoic criterion need not be rehearsed at greater length here. They largely turn on the impossibility of specifying that *nota*, 'distinguishing mark', supposedly indicative of the 'cognitive impression'. By reference to particular circumstances in which apparently true impressions have subsequently proved false; by posing problems about distinguishing between identical twins or eggs; by calling in dreams and hallucinations, Carneades built up his general case against the so-called cognitive impression.[1] It is sufficient for his purpose to be able to show that a single impression which seems to be entirely trustworthy may in fact be false (Cic. *Acad.* ii 84). For the cognitive impression is by definition something which seems to be entirely trustworthy, yet the possibility must always remain that an impression's character does not correspond with the object it purports to represent.

Like Arcesilaus therefore Carneades regarded knowledge in the Stoics' sense as unattainable. He was not however content to recommend suspension of judgment as the attitude to be adopted towards everything. By considering the conditions of sense-perception, Carneades arrived at a theory of knowledge which anticipates in many respects modern types of empiricism.

He divided sense-impressions into two categories: (*a*) those which can be perceived as 'true' (i.e. corresponding to some fact or object) and (*b*) those which cannot be so perceived (Cic. *Acad.* ii 99–104). It follows from our previous summary that for Carneades all sense-impressions must fall under category (*b*). To these categories also correspond two further distinctions which he adopted: (1) true and false; (2) probable and non-probable, or apparently true and apparently false. (*a*) and (1) go together, and (*b*) and (2) go together. Carneades argued that the denial of (*a*) and therefore (1) as practical possibilities, entails nothing about (*b*) and (2). Even though nothing can be perceived as true or false, some sense-impressions can be distinguished as probable or apparently true from others which are non-probable or apparently false. The justification for this admission is founded on the important observation that sense-impressions can be considered either in relation to their (external) object or in relation to the person to whom they appear. Let us call these the objective and the subjective relation

---

[1] See Cic. *Acad.* ii 49–60 in which Antiochus attempts to counter such reasoning; Sextus, *Adv. math.* vii 403–11.

respectively. Then, Carneades is arguing that, in their subjective relation, certain distinctions can be drawn between sense-impressions which cannot be drawn in their objective relation.

The basic distinction is that between probable and non-probable. What did Carneades mean by this? The Greek term which he used ('probable' (*probabile*') is Cicero's Latin translation) literally means 'persuasive' or 'trustworthy'. Cicero describes it as 'the sense-impression which the wise man will use if nothing arises which is contrary to that probability' (*Acad.* ii 99). This however is not very informative, and it is to Sextus Empiricus that we must go for more precise information (*Adv. math.* vii 166–89).

Carneades' problem is to establish a criterion which will decide between one statement and its contradictory in the absence of anything admitting of certainty. His starting-point here is everyday assumptions. We do as a matter of fact distinguish between things that appear to us clearly and things which do not. In other words, we operate in practice with a criterion of degrees of trustworthiness. If the light is poor, or if we are tired, or if our vision is confused, we are less inclined to trust our eyes than at times when different conditions are satisfied. Thus the conditions under which we receive our sense-impressions provide some means of distinguishing between sense-impressions as a whole. The first requirement of a probable sense-impression is clarity or distinctness (*perspicuitas*).

If Carneades had stopped here however he would be liable to the criticism he levelled against the Stoics and Epicureans; for, on his own terms, an isolated sense-experience can never provide sufficient grounds for our accepting it as 'true' or even probable. Carneades therefore added to the condition of 'credibility and clarity' first, the concurrence of other sense-impressions and secondly the 'testing' of each of these in turn by careful scrutiny (*Adv. math.* vii 176–83). In order to be justified in saying 'This is Socrates', we need to consider all the circumstances which characterize our sense-impression or series of impressions—the man's physical appearance, his gait, his speech, clothes, where he is situated, who he is with etc. If none of these things arouses in us a doubt of our probably seeing Socrates we are fully justified in forming this judgment.

As this example shows, the questions which the Academic sceptic is required to ask himself are going to depend on circumstances. No specific principles can be laid down in advance, but the general rule can be formulated that a judgment will be the sounder the more rigorously all the circumstances attending it are examined. Carneades compared this procedure with the Athenian practice of publicly examining the credentials of would-be magistrates and judges:

> Just as at the place of judgment there are both the one who judges and that which is being judged, and the medium through which the judgment takes place and the spatial dimensions, place, time . . . we judge the particular character of each of these things in turn: e.g. we examine whether that which is judging has sharp vision or not, whether that which is being judged is sufficiently large to be judged, whether the medium, for instance the atmosphere, is dark. . . . (Sextus, *Adv. math.* vii 183).

It is not always necessary or indeed possible to appraise all the perceptual conditions in such a systematic way. Carneades proposed that in relatively trivial matters probability can and should be established simply and quickly. Where it is a case of human well-being, however, the test of probability should be as rigorous as possible (ibid. 184).

The significant feature of Carneades' theory is his recognition that the reliance which we place upon our senses cannot be reduced to the simple terms approved by Epicurus and the Stoics. In practice we do not consciously often need to perform all the tests of probability which Carneades laid down. But that does not undermine the validity of his recommendations. He too accepted the fact that when we trust our senses, our acceptance of their evidence is generally immediate and not something which requires detailed examination. But if challenged to justify the assertion 'That is Socrates', Carneades would not appeal merely to the vividness of his visual sensations. He would point out that this apparently simple judgment is something highly complex: it involves a recognition that all the conditions which would need to be satisfied if the judgment were true are satisfied, *as far as we can observe*. We cannot, he argued, match our sense-impressions against physical objects as such; and for this reason no empirical judgment can ever be proved true or false. But we can compare one sense-impression with another; we can take account of our own previous experience and that of others; we can consider many of the factors which are involved in every perceptual experience. And on the basis of these considerations we can form some judgments about the world which, though they might in fact be false, we have every reason to accept as credit-worthy, or apparently true.

A passage from Cicero exemplifies the practical application of Carneades' doctrine:

When a wise man is boarding a ship surely he does not have it already grasped in his mind and perceived that he will sail just as he intends? How could he? But if at this moment he were setting out from here [Bauli] to Puteoli four miles away, with a good crew and an expert navigator and in these fine weather conditions, it would seem to him probable that he would arrive there safely (Cic. *Acad.* ii 100).

As we look back at such statements after two thousand years of philosophy they may strike us as somewhat pedantic, if not banal. That would be too hasty a judgment. There is no reason to think that Carneades' scepticism was intended as a recommendation to behave with exaggerated caution in everyday judgments. The scepticism of the Academics is not focused upon everyday judgments but upon philosophical theories which seek a criterion of certainty in sense-perception. In more modern terminology, Carneades is saying that the truth of empirical judgments is always contingent and never necessary. The world might, as a matter of fact, be quite different from our perception of it; but our empirical judgments can be true or false, provided that we refer truth or falsity to the world as we observe it and do not claim that our statements are true or false about the world in itself.[1]

Carneades' name, like that of Arcesilaus, is associated above all with his criticism of dogmatic claims to certainty. But whereas we know virtually nothing about Arcesilaus' arguments on any subject except theory of knowledge, there is a fair amount of evidence for Carneades' treatment of ethical doctrines, theology, and causality. On the first two topics at least, Carneades' contribution was destructive rather than constructive. This point needs stressing, for it has sometimes been maintained that Carneades had certain positive views of his own concerning ethics and theology. This would be quite inconsistent, if it were true, with his avowedly sceptical approach to problems, and there is ample evidence to refute such an interpretation. Let me take one example, from ethics.[2] In Cicero's *Academica* (ii 131) Carneades is said to have put forward the following definition of the *summum bonum*: 'to enjoy those things which nature has made primarily our own'. As Cicero observes, Carneades advanced this view 'not because he accepted it himself but in order to attack the Stoics'. The same

---

[1] On this point and on attempts to answer Carneades see Stough, *Greek Skepticism*, pp. 44–50.

[2] For a more detailed discussion see my article, 'Carneades and the Stoic Telos', *Phronesis* xii (1967) 59–90.

definition is ascribed to Carneades elsewhere by Cicero (*Fin.* v 20) 'for the purpose of disputation' (*disserendi causa*). It is a statement peculiarly suited to an attack on the Stoics since they claimed that the first human impulse is to desire 'the primary natural advantages' (i.e. a healthy body etc.), but they excluded this from the goal of mature men (see p. 187). Carneades therefore deployed against the Stoics one of their own concepts, arguing that it was inconsistent of them to accord natural advantages some value and yet to exclude them from constituents of the *summum bonum*. In another context Cicero writes that Carneades so zealously defended the statement that the *summum bonum* is a combination of virtue and pleasure that 'he seemed even to accept it' (*Acad.* ii 139). But Cicero adds the revealing comment: 'Clitomachus [Carneades' successor] declared that he could never grasp Carneades' own views' on this topic. Carneades' technique here, and in general, is the standard Academic one of exposing contradictions in the position of his opponents or adopting a contrary standpoint for purely critical purposes.[1]

A further instance of a similar kind is Carneades' criticism of Stoic theological doctrines. One technique which he used here is the *sôritês*. It takes its name from a 'heap', a term used to illustrate the difficulties of indicating precise differentiating characteristics. Suppose that someone is prepared to call a collection of thirty things a heap; subtract one thing and then another; when does the heap cease to be a heap? Clearly it is impossible to lay down precise quantitative criteria for designing a heap, yet 'heap' is a quantitative term. Carneades used this mode of argument to show the impossibility of drawing any firm distinction between that which is supposedly divine and that which is not. 'If gods exist, are the nymphs also goddesses? If the nymphs are, then Pans and Satyrs are also gods; but the latter are not gods; therefore the nymphs too are not. But the nymphs have temples vowed and dedicated to them by the state. Are the other gods then not gods who have temples dedicated to them?' (Cic. *N.D.* iii 43). If the opponent declines to accept a link in the chain then the sceptic can ask what it is, say, about nymphs which marks them off as divine from Pans and Satyrs; or what it is about nymphs that marks them off from the other gods, given that both sets of things have temples set

---

[1] It is of course possible that Carneades defended as 'more probable' one set of moral principles, cf. Brochard, pp. 160–2, who opts for 'striving to attain that which is primarily in accordance with nature'. But I find no evidence that Carneades, whatever he may have done in practice, had any positivist moral theory.

up in their honour. In the course of this discussion Cicero notes that Carneades used such arguments not to overturn religion but to show the unconvincing nature of Stoic polytheism (ibid. 44).

Like other Sceptics Carneades exploited differences of opinion between the dogmatic schools. Epicurus, as we have seen, argued that the world's obvious imperfections give clear evidence against its being under the control of the gods. The Stoics argued in quite the opposite way: the world is manifestly the work of providence, the supreme example of which is man himself, a rational being designed by the gods to live a virtuous life. Carneades held that the sufferings of the virtuous and the flourishing of malefactors prove that the gods are quite indifferent to human affairs (Cic. *N.D.* iii 79–85). Here as before Carneades is picking out a Stoic tenet, the gods' providential care for mankind, and citing evidence which seems to be wholly inconsistent with it. Man's possession of reason, he argues, cannot be used as proof of the gods' providential interest in mankind (ibid. 66–79). For reason is only a good thing, that is, something which might establish providential intentions in the giver, if it is used well; but whether reason is used well or badly by men depends on us, on how we choose to use it. The mere bestowal of reason, if in fact it is the gift of the gods, speaks rather against their providence than for it.[1]

Carneades' philosophical acumen is demonstrated particularly well in his treatment of free will. Here Cicero's *De fato* provides our main evidence. In the last chapter I discussed Epicurus' theory that the capacity of living things to initiate new movements or actions is proof of the fact that individual atoms swerve at no fixed time or place. This theory was interpreted by the Stoics at least as an admission that such movements are uncaused; and they attacked it on the ground that every movement or effect must have an antecedent cause. The Stoics were led to this notion of a necessary connexion between cause and effect by a variety of reasons. But for the present it is necessary to consider only one of these. Chrysippus argued as follows:

> If there is an uncaused movement not every proposition . . . will be true or false; for that which will not have efficient causes will be neither true nor false; but every proposition is either true or false; therefore there is no uncaused movement. But if this is so, then everything which happens happens as the result of antecedent causes; and if that is the case, then everything

[1] Traces of an attack by Carneades against the Stoic acceptance of divination are probably incorporated by Cicero in Book ii of *De divinatione*.

happens as the result of destiny; it follows therefore that whatever happens happens as the result of destiny (*Fat.* x 20–1).

Two points about this argument are to be noted. First, Chrysippus treats the proposition 'Everything happens as the result of antecedent causes' as logically equivalent to 'Everything happens as the result of destiny'. Secondly, he seeks to prove his thesis by means of the premise: 'Every proposition is either true or false.'

Carneades attacked this argument from two points of view (ibid. xi 23–8). First, he considered the statement 'No movement happens without a cause'. 'Without an antecedent cause,' he argued, does not necessarily mean 'without any cause at all.' We can say that a vase is empty without implying, as a physicist might use the word 'empty', that it contains absolutely nothing—void. We mean that the vase lacks water or wine etc. Similarly, if we say that the mind is not moved by any antecedent cause, we should not be taken to imply that the mind's movement is wholly uncaused. The notion of a voluntary movement *means* a movement which is in our power. This does not entail that such a movement is uncaused. Its cause is just the fact that it is in our power.

Secondly, Carneades argued that Chrysippus' inference of determinism from the premise 'Every proposition is true or false' is an invalid one. Chrysippus' grounds for this inference are recorded by Cicero as follows:

True future events cannot be such as do not possess causes on account of which they will happen; therefore that which is true must possess causes; and so, when they (*sc.* true future events) happen they will have happened as a result of destiny.

Here Chrysippus is continuing to use 'cause' in the sense of 'antecedent cause'. Carneades replies to Chrysippus in a most interesting way. He argues that if a prediction proves to be true, for instance, 'Scipio will capture Numantia', this tells us nothing about determinism. It is simply a logical fact about propositions that if some event *E* takes place, then it was true before the event that *E* would take place.

We call those past events true of which at an earlier time this proposition was true: 'They are present (or actual) now'; similarly, we shall call those future events true of which at some future time this proposition will be true: 'They are present (or actual) now.'

In these acute observations about truth and tenses, Carneades is making a point which has been admirably expressed by Gilbert Ryle:

Why does the fact that a posterior truth about an occurrence requires that occurrence not worry us in the way in which the fact that an anterior truth about an occurrence requires that occurrence does worry us? . . . A large part of the reason is that in thinking of a predecessor making its successor necessary we unwittingly assimilate the necessitation to causal necessitation. . . . We slide, that is, into thinking of the anterior truths as *causes* of the happenings about which they were true, where the mere matter of their relative dates saves us from thinking of happenings as the effects of those truths about them which are posterior to them. Events cannot be the effects of their successors, any more than we can be the offspring of our posterity.[1]

The 'slide' from facts about truth into beliefs about causality was made by Chrysippus and other Stoics. Chrysippus' mistake emerges with complete clarity through his attempt to establish determinism by a premise about the truth of propositions. From the proposition '*E* will take place is true' it follows that *E* must take place. But 'must' here refers to logical not causal necessity. It was a considerable achievement on Carneades' part to have distinguished these two senses of necessity and something which neither Aristotle nor the Stoics succeeded in doing.[2] From his distinction Carneades concludes that there are, to be sure, causes of such events as Cato's entering the senate at some future date. But they are not causes 'which are contained in the nature of the universe'. 'Contingent' (*fortuitae*) is his term to describe them and likewise the facts described by propositions about such things. Thus he argues that prediction can only be reliable concerning events the occurrence of which is necessary (*Fat.* xiv 32–3). It is not clear that Carneades thought that there were any such events.

Did Carneades himself accept in practice a belief in the freedom of the will? There are good reasons for thinking that his own views on this subject were positive and yet consistent with his scepticism concerning the external world. Cicero attributes to him this argument:

If all events are the results of antecedent causes they are all bound and fastened together by a natural chain. But if this is so, all things are brought about by necessity; if that is the case, nothing is in our power. Now something is in our power; but if everything happens as a result of destiny all things happen as a result of antecedent causes; therefore whatever happens does not happen as a result of destiny (*Fat.* xiv 31).

This argument relies on the premise 'something is in our power'.

[1] *Dilemmas* (Cambridge 1960) p. 21.
[2] On Aristotle's treatment of necessity in the context of determinism cf. J. L. Ackrill, *Aristotle's Categories and De Interpretatione* (Oxford 1963) pp. 132ff.

Carneades assumes the truth of this premise, and he might be merely advancing it for the purpose of refuting the Stoics. But if the premise means 'We are conscious of having something in our power', Carneades is quite entitled to assert this as a valid datum of subjective experience. It is not a claim about the nature of the external world.

Carneades, as I have mentioned, represented Athens as an ambassador to Rome along with other philosophers in 156–155 B.C. In the *De republica* Cicero used Carneades' arguments for and against justice as material in his third book. This work has reached us in a badly fragmentary condition, but fortunately Lactantius in his *Institutiones divinae* has preserved a summary of Carneades' argument against justice:

> When Carneades had been sent by the Athenians as an ambassador to Rome, he discoursed at length on justice in the hearing of Galba and Cato the censor, the greatest orators of the time. On the next day he overturned his own discourse with a speech putting the opposite position, and undermined justice which he had praised on the previous day, not with a philosopher's seriousness, whose judgment should be firm and consistent, but in the style of a rhetorical exercise arguing on both sides. This he made a practice of doing in order that he might refute those with any positive opinion (Cic. *Rep.* iii 9 [Lact. *Inst.* 5, 14, 3–5]).

Lactantius then reports certain arguments about the excellence of justice which Carneades put forward for the purpose of refuting them. The essence of this case in favour of justice was that justice is something which benefits all men; it gives to each his due and maintains fairness among everyone. Carneades, we are told, now set out to refute this position 'not because he thought that justice deserved to be censured, but to show that its defendants put up a case for justice which was quite insecure and unstable' (ibid. 11):

> This [says Lactantius] was the basis of Carneades' argument: men have ratified laws for themselves for the sake of utility . . . and among the same people laws are often changed according to circumstances; there is no *natural* law. All human beings and other creatures are directed by their own natures to that which is advantageous to themselves. Therefore either there is no such thing as justice or, if there is, it is the height of folly, since a man injures himself in taking thought for the advantage of others (*Rep.* iii 21 [Lact. *Inst.* 5, 16, 2–4]).

In this argument Carneades is attacking the claim that justice can benefit those who act justly. This of course was the position which

Plato sought to demonstrate in the *Republic*, and Carneades' argument recalls the sophistic theories about justice which Plato explicitly aimed to combat. It adds however an interesting contemporary note. By 'advantage of others' Carneades does not mean 'specific individuals within a state', but other states or peoples. He is arguing that the Romans do have justice in the form of laws and constitutional practices, but that these laws and practices work wholly in the interests of Rome and against those of non-Romans: 'What are the advantages of one's native land save the disadvantages of another state or nation? That is, to increase one's territory by property violently seized from others.' Carneades pointed out that according to imperialist ideologies those who augment the state are praised to the skies. So far as the state is concerned their behaviour is perfectly just, but it is not 'justice' in the sense laid down by the defendants of the universal beneficence of justice: it is entirely self-interest.

Carneades proceeded to develop his case by considering the behaviour of the individual:

Suppose that a good man has a run-away slave or an unhealthy and plague-ridden house; that he alone knows these faults and puts the things up for sale accordingly. Will he admit the faults or will he conceal them from the buyer? If he admits them, he is certainly a good man, since he does not cheat; but he will be judged a fool since he will be selling for a song or not selling at all. If he conceals the facts he will be a wise man because he will consult his own interests but also bad, because he cheats (ibid. 29).

In interpreting this argument we need to remember that Plato, Aristotle and the Stoics were at one in holding that both justice and practical wisdom, or prudence, are characteristic of the good man. Carneades forces his opponents to distinguish between justice and prudence. A man who deliberately allows himself to make a bad bargain cannot be called prudent: this is the essence of Carneades' argument. The argument clearly has weight only if both parties agree on the same criteria for establishing prudence. We saw in the last chapter that by Epicurus justice was commended on the ground that it is never in one's interests to run the risk of being exposed as a criminal. Plato, Aristotle and the Stoics on the other hand would reply that happiness depends on a certain condition of the soul or moral character; justice does benefit the practitioner because justice is an integral constituent of his happiness.

Carneades must have known perfectly well that his opponents

would not accept his own use of the term 'prudence' in this argument. But he could reply that everyday usage fully supported the notion of prudence which he was using. Thus his argument is a challenge to any moral philosopher who seeks to show that justice and self-interest can be combined in a coherent ethical system. In basing his arguments on ordinary language and on empirical observations which the majority of men would accept, Carneades is closer to the spirit of modern British philosophy than perhaps any other ancient thinker. Refusing to dogmatize himself, he criticized with great rigour those who were prepared to erect theories on the basis of what he regarded, sometimes with justification, as shaky and often slipshod arguments. The Stoics themselves, as we shall see, modified some of their theories in the light of his criticism, and by his follower, Clitomachus, Carneades was praised for his 'Herculean labour in ridding our minds of rash and hasty thinking' (Cic. *Acad.* ii 108). The distinctions which Carneades drew between certitude and probability, necessity and contingency, and causal and logical relations are sufficient on their own to establish his achievement as an outstanding philosopher. Had he been followed by men of comparable stature the history of philosophy might have been very different in the next hundred years.

But this was not to be. Clitomachus made it his main business to systematize and publicize Carneades' own philosophical method. The tradition was continued in the Academy by Philo of Larisa (*c.* 148–77 B.C.) with some modifications (see p. 223), but his most famous pupil, Antiochus of Ascalon, rejected the sceptical methodology of the Academy in favour of an eclectic assimilation of Stoicism to certain features of Platonic and Aristotelian philosophy. Antiochus was an influential figure about whom more must be said later in this book, and his views are discussed at length by Cicero who declared his own allegiance to the New Academy of Arcesilaus, Carneades and Philo. Under Antiochus the Academy abandoned the tradition first formally established by Arcesilaus two hundred years previously. But scepticism, if it languished temporarily, was to be revived in Alexandria under the name of Pyrrhonism by Aenesidemus, and it has been perpetuated in the writings of Sextus Empiricus.

CHAPTER FOUR

Stoicism

The remarkable coherence of the system and the extraordinary orderliness of the subject-matter have made me prolix. Don't you find it amazing, in heaven's name? . . . What is there which is not so linked to something else that all would collapse if you moved a single letter? But there is nothing at all which can be moved (spoken by 'Cato' in Cicero, *Fin*. iii 74).

STOICISM was the most important and influential development in Hellenistic philosophy. For more than four centuries it claimed the allegiance of a large number of educated men in the Graeco-Roman world, and its impact was not confined to Classical antiquity. Many of the Christian fathers were more deeply affected by Stoicism than they themselves recognized, and from the Renaissance up to modern times the effect of Stoic moral teaching on Western culture has been pervasive. Sometimes Stoic doctrines have reappeared in the work of major philosophers. Spinoza, Bishop Butler and Kant were all indebted to the Stoics. But the influence of Stoicism has not been confined to professional philosophers. Cicero, Seneca, and Marcus Aurelius were read and re-read by those who had time to read in the sixteenth, seventeenth and eighteenth centuries. These Roman writers helped to disseminate the basic principles of Stoicism to priests, scholars, politicians and others. Of course, Stoicism was pagan and Christendom abhorred the pagan. But it was easy enough to abstract from Stoicism those precepts on duty and manliness which Christianity was far from wishing to deny. In the deism and naturalism so fashionable in the eighteenth century Stoicism found a welcoming climate of opinion. Even today, the influence persists at the most mundane level. Not only the words stoic (uncapitalized) and stoical recall it. In popular language to be 'philosophical' means to show that fortitude in the face of adversity recommended by Stoic writers. This is a small, but highly significant example, of Stoicism's influence.

In modern academic circles the study of ancient Stoicism has been curiously uneven. In Europe, especially in France and Germany, major contributions have been made since the nineteenth-century revival of

Classical scholarship. In Britain and the United States Stoicism has suffered greater neglect. Until about twenty years ago, it is probably fair to say that Stoicism attracted less scholarly attention in this part of the world than any other important aspect of ancient philosophy. Now things have begun to change. The Stoics present those who are willing to take them seriously with a fascinating series of philosophical problems. But this is still not widely appreciated. The habit of thinking in terms of a Classical period of Greek culture which was extinguished by Alexander's conquests dies hard. Early Stoicism like Hellenistic culture in general has suffered in modern estimation because our detailed knowledge of its achievements is so defective.

A general characterization of the system may help to set the scene. The Stoics, as the quotation at the head of this chapter indicates, prided themselves on the coherence of their philosophy. They were convinced that the universe is amenable to rational explanation, and is itself a rationally organized structure. The faculty in man which enables him to think, to plan and to speak—which the Stoics called *logos*—is literally embodied in the universe at large. The individual human being at the essence of his nature shares a property which belongs to Nature in the cosmic sense. And because cosmic Nature embraces all that there is, the human individual is a part of the world in a precise and integral sense. Cosmic events and human actions are therefore not happenings of two quite different orders: in the last analysis they are both alike consequences of one thing—*logos*. To put it another way, cosmic Nature or God (the terms refer to the same thing in Stoicism) and man are related to each other at the heart of their being as rational agents. If a man fully recognizes the implications of this relationship, he will act in a manner which wholly accords with human rationality at its best, the excellence of which is guaranteed by its willing agreement with Nature. This is what it is to be wise, a step beyond mere rationality, and the goal of human existence is complete harmony between a man's own attitudes and actions and the actual course of events. Natural philosophy and logic are fundamental and intimately related to this goal. In order to live in accordance with Nature a man must know what facts are true, what their truth consists in and how one true proposition is related to another. The coherence of Stoicism is based upon the belief that natural events are so causally related to one another that on them a set of propositions can be supported which will enable a man to plan a life wholly at one with Nature or God.

This very briefly is the basis of Stoicism. But now we must pass from such generalities to details, beginning with a short treatment of the history of the school and our sources.

I. THE STOA, PERSONALITIES AND SOURCES

About 301/300 B.C. Zeno of Citium began, in the words of Diogenes Laertius (vii 5), to pace up and down in the Painted Colonnade (*Stoa*) at Athens, and to engage in philosophical discourse there. The Stoa bordered one side of the great piazza of ancient Athens, and from it, as one can see today, those who promenaded there looked directly at the main public buildings, with the Acropolis and its temples towering in the background. Unlike Epicurus, Zeno began his teaching at Athens in a central public place, which came to stand as the name of his followers and their philosophical system. From a decree inscribed on stone in his honour it appears that Zeno like Socrates numbered young men particularly among his adherents, and provided them with a paradigm of virtue in the life which he led (D.L. vii 10). At the time when he founded the school Zeno was in his early thirties. He was born at Citium in Cyprus about 333/2 B.C. His age on coming to Athens, like the date of his birth, is disputed by ancient sources; but the testimony of his younger follower, Persaeus (D.L. vii 28), probably gives the most reliable evidence: he arrived in Athens at the age of twenty-two (i.e. about 311 B.C.) and died in 262/1, aged seventy-two.

Such a chronology allows Zeno a decade or so in Athens before he set up as a philosopher in his own right. In other words, he came to Athens some ten years after the deaths of Aristotle, Diogenes of Sinope and Alexander, shortly before Epicurus established the Garden as his centre. What brought Zeno to Athens in the first place is not entirely clear. According to one account he began life as a merchant; was shipwrecked on a journey from Phoenicia to Piraeus; arrived somehow or other at Athens, and encountered philosophy through reading about Socrates in Xenophon (D.L. vii 2). The story continues that he was so delighted by his reading that he asked where he might find men like Socrates. At that moment Crates, the Cynic, passed by and the bookseller, in whose shop Zeno had found his Xenophon, said: 'Follow that man.' This romantic tale may be more fiction than fact. But the mention of Crates rings true. The first major influence on Zeno's philosophical development is likely to have been a Cynic one, although his aquaintance with Socratic doctrines, which the Cynics would have encouraged, may have begun before he left Cyprus (D.L. vii 31). Fragments of Zeno's *Republic* survive and they show marked Cynic elements such as the abolition of coinage, temples, marriages, and the notion that the true community must be one consisting of good and virtuous men.[1] Zeno is said to have written his *Republic* while still a young associate of Crates (D.L. vii 4), and it may have been intended as a direct attack on Plato.

The main interest of the Cynics lay in ethics (see pp. 3–4). From them Zeno inherited the notion, fundamental to all Stoicism, that the real nature or *physis* of a man consists in his rationality (*SVF* i 179, 202). Expressed in such general terms this notion was hardly revolutionary. Plato and Aristotle would agree; indeed it is ultimately Socratic in inspiration. But Diogenes, and perhaps Antisthenes before him (see pp. 7–8), gave it a particularly extreme and rigorous interpretation, an ascetic twist, which was not accepted by Plato and Aristotle. For Diogenes, a man needs nothing but physical and mental self-discipline to fulfil himself, to live according to nature (D.L. vi 24–70). Things conventionally regarded as good—property, a fine appearance, social status—all these are irrelevant if not actually inimical to human well-being (D.L. vi 72). True happiness can have no truck with anything that fails to meet the test: 'Does it accord with my nature as a rational being?' It is difficult to know precisely what Diogenes meant by reason, *logos*, but I think we can understand him to have had *phronêsis*, 'practical wisdom', in mind. He advocated a way of life in which a man so acts that what is truly valuable to him, his inner well-being, cannot be affected by conventional social and moral judgments or changes of fortune; only thus is real freedom attainable (D.L. vii 71). Such a life would be *natural* in the sense that it required nothing except minimal physical requirements from the external world. We find the Cynics appealing to the habits of primitive men and animals. This life would also be *natural* in the sense that reason is an innate human endowment which transcends cultural and geographical boundaries. Diogenes rejected all theories of human well-being which cannot pertain to all wise men whatever their ethnic and social status.

The connexion between these principles and certain Stoic ideas will appear in due course. Later Stoics were sometimes embarrassed by some of the more extreme Cynic positions which their predecessors

[1] H. C. Baldry gives a good discussion in 'Zeno's Ideal State', *Journal of Hellenic Studies* lxxix (1959) 3–15.

took over—I refer for instance to the claims that incest and cannibalism may be justifiable in certain circumstances (*SVF* ii 743–56)—but throughout the history of the Stoa we find an emphasis on *indifference* to externals (with an important qualification to be treated later), on rationality as the sole source of human happiness, on 'cosmopolitanism' and moral idealism, which all reflect Zeno's allegiance to Cynic doctrines.

Some of these attitudes are of course Socratic, and the influence of Socrates on Zeno, either through the Cynics or through books and oral tradition, is of great importance. The following basic Socratic propositions were all embraced by Zeno: knowledge and goodness go hand in hand, or the good man is wise and the bad man ignorant; from knowledge right action follows necessarily; and the greatest evil is a bad condition of the soul.

Undoubtedly Zeno's basic goal was a practical one—to demonstrate the good for man as he conceived it. But that was no novel enterprise. What Zeno may have begun to defend in the proselytizing manner of Diogenes and Crates he proceeded to develop into a coherent philosophical system. Diogenes had no sympathy for the Academy, even though he appealed to Socrates as a model.[1] But Zeno passed on from Crates to study both with Megarian philosophers, Stilpo and Diodorus Cronus, and with the Academic, Polemo (D.L. vii 2; 25).

From the Megarians Zeno is likely to have acquired a facility at logic and a general interest in linguistic theory. It is improbable that he himself developed Stoic logic in much detail; this was rather the achievement of Chrysippus. But the titles of Zeno's works include logical subjects—*Solutions, Disputatious arguments, On signs,* and *Modes of speech* (D.L. vii 4)—and he certainly used formal arguments for the presentation of some doctrines. Epictetus reports on Zeno's authority that the philosopher's speculative activity consists in 'knowing the elements of *logos,* what each of them is like, how they fit together and what follows from them' (iv 8, 12 =*SVF* i 51). One cannot be certain that these are Zeno's own words, but their sense is wholly appropriate. A further trace of Megarian influence may be seen in Stoic monism (see earlier, p. 8). That the cosmos is 'one' was asserted by Zeno (D.L. vii 143 =*SVF* i 97), and the 'unity of being', defended by the Stoics, goes back through the Megarians to Parmenides.

---

[1] Diogenes Laertius' *Life of Diogenes* contains many polemical and amusing encounters between Plato and the Cynic. Their authenticity is doubtful.

Platonic influences, apart from those which come from Socrates, can be identified more easily, but I will not enumerate them in detail here. It is sufficient to note the clear links between 'creative reason', Zeno's cosmic principle, and the divine craftsman, or soul of the world, in Plato. The theology of Plato's *Laws* with its eloquent defence of providence has affinities with Stoicism which cannot be accidental. These points of common ground, and others which will be mentioned later, exist alongside some profound differences between the Platonic and the Stoic world-picture. No doubt much of Zeno's acquaintance with Platonic doctrines was gained through his association with Polemo. But too little about Polemo's own teaching is known to make a clear assessment of his personal influence possible (see further p. 225). The influence of the Peripatetics raises further problems, though for quite different reasons. Polemo's name is linked with Zeno's, but there is no ancient evidence concerning Zeno's relationship with Theophrastus or other Peripatetics. It is probable however that Zeno knew individual members of the Lyceum, and virtually certain that he had read some of their works. I have already discussed the question of Aristotle's writings in the early Hellenistic period (pp. 9–10), and it is very difficult to believe that Zeno did not know some of them. We find Aristotelian terminology in early Stoicism and also a number of doctrines which seem to betray clear indications of Aristotelian thought.[1]

Add to all this the acknowledged indebtedness to Heraclitus (see p. 145), and we may confidently say that Stoicism from its outset drew readily upon contemporary and earlier philosophy. This is not to deny originality to Zeno. Both he and his successors advanced new theories on a variety of subjects, and the Stoic synthesis to which borrowings from existing systems contributed has a character which is entirely its own. But the Stoics' attitude to other philosophers and to Greek culture in general differentiates them sharply from Epicurus. By the time of Chrysippus at least, Stoicism had become a learned and highly technical philosophy. The view that Epicurus was only interested in a rough-and-ready philosophical methodology is mistaken, but there is no denying his unintellectual posture. The Stoics were keenly interested in literature, they established grammar for the first time on a rigorous basis, and they had a general influence on intellectual as

[1] See further J. M. Rist, *Stoic Philosophy* (Cambridge 1969) pp. 1–21 and my article, 'Aristotle's Legacy to Stoic Ethics', *Bulletin of the Institute of Classical Studies* 15 (1968) 72–85.

well as moral thinking. It was a Stoic maxim that the wise man will normally take part in politics, and Sphaerus who was a pupil of Zeno and Cleanthes acted as tutor and adviser to Cleomenes, the king who sought to reform Spartan society (*SVF* i 622–3). Cato the Younger, Seneca and Marcus Aurelius are three examples of Stoics eminent in public life. To this extent, Stoicism is much closer than Epicureanism to the spirit of classical Greek philosophy, and it can be considered as continuing rather than diverging from the Platonic and Aristotelian tradition (see p. 226).

Zeno died about 261 B.C., leaving a set of works with such titles as *Life according to nature, Emotions, That which is appropriate, Greek culture, Universals, Homeric problems* (five books), *Disputatious arguments* (two books), D.L. vii 4. He also left a reputation the significance of which is indicated by the award of a golden crown from the Athenian people, a tomb built at public expense in the Kerameikos, funeral reliefs in the Academy and Lyceum, and the high regard of Antigonus, the Macedonian Regent.[1] Of his immediate successors the most important are Cleanthes and Chrysippus. How these men whose origins were in Asia Minor came to Athens we do not know. But the old theory that Stoicism incorporates Semitic ideas cannot be defended, as it has been, merely on the provenance of its three great authorities. And there seems to be nothing in Stoicism which requires the hypothesis of Semitic influences.[2] Owing to the state of our evidence it is difficult to attain an entirely clear grasp of the innovations by Cleanthes and Chrysippus. But it is probable that Cleanthes' interests centred upon natural philosophy and theology. Chrysippus, who was head of the Stoa from about 232 up to his death in 208/4, won immense renown in antiquity as a dialectician, and reference was made in the last chapter to the saying, 'Without Chrysippus there would have been no Stoa.' This tag probably does less than justice to Zeno and Cleanthes, and Chrysippus did not claim to be the real founder of Stoicism. Rather, we are to see him as Stoicism's great scholar, a man who refined and clarified Zeno's teaching.[3] He must have made many innovations himself, particularly in Stoic

---

[1] D.L. vii 6; 10, see W.S. Ferguson, *Hellenistic Athens* (London 1911) pp. 185–7.

[2] Such points as Pohlenz alludes to—fatalism, the concept of moral obligation, the absolute distinction between good and bad (*Die Stoa* ed. 2, Göttingen 1959, vol. i pp. 164f.) do not establish Semitic influences.

[3] For a survey of modern views on Chrysippus' contribution cf. Josiah B. Gould, *The Philosophy of Chrysippus* (Leiden 1970) pp. 14–17.

logic (Cic. *Fin.* iv 9). In this field his energy was prodigious, and he wrote three hundred and eleven treatises (D.L. vii 198). For later Stoics, Chrysippus became the general canon of orthodoxy, and it is reasonable to assume that the majority of ancient summaries which begin with the words, 'The Stoics say that', report his views or views which he would have approved. Unfortunately the majority of surviving fragments are only a few lines in length, and since many of them are cited for polemical purposes by opponents of Stoicism we probably have too little evidence to form an opinion on Chrysippus' style and quality of argument at its best. But he was undoubtedly a philosopher of immense versatility.

Throughout the later part of the third century B.C. the Stoics were engaged in controversy with the Academic Sceptics and the Epicureans, but apart from Arcesilaus' arguments against Zeno's theory of knowledge (see pp. 90f.) little is known about the details of such disputes. For the second century our evidence is much better. This was the period of Carneades who debated so vigorously with the Stoics on many fronts. Chrysippus himself did not live to answer Carneades' criticism, but as a result of it Antipater of Tarsus, who was head of the Stoa after Diogenes of Babylon, Chrysippus' successor, modified the ethical theory (see p. 196) and other anonymous changes were also made. The object of these was to protect Stoicism against Carneades' objections. In fact, Antipater achieved an uneasy compromise which involved both an apparent weakening of the earlier idealism of Stoic ethics and which also failed to satisfy common sense. Early Stoicism offered a ready target to charges of setting up a goal beyond human attainment, and it is no accident to find the next important Stoic, Panaetius of Rhodes (*c.* 185–109 B.C.), developing the practical side of Stoicism in perhaps an original manner. Cicero's *De officiis* is based upon the work of Panaetius, and it provides a set of rules for conduct which are categorically stated to be a 'second-best' system of ethics, designed for the guidance of men who are not yet sages and competent to be good in the ideal Stoic sense. Panaetius spent much of his middle life in Rome. He was an intimate acquaintance of Scipio Africanus, and the spread of Stoicism among Romans of the late Republic probably owed much to his influence.

From the second half of the second century onwards Stoicism became well established at Rome. In Athens the Stoa continued to flourish as a school, and Panaetius succeeded Antipater as its head in 129. By this time however Stoicism had a number of other centres throughout the Mediterranean world. Posidonius (*c.* 135–50 B.C.) who came from Apamea, an ancient city on the Orontes in Syria, set up a school in Rhodes after studying under Panaetius in Athens; and Cicero, who visited Rhodes between 79 and 77, formed a lasting admiration for him. Posidonius is the last Stoic philosopher who is known to have shown any great inclination for original thinking. A polymath who did important work in history and geography, Posidonius remains for us a somewhat shadowy figure. He certainly rejected Chrysippus' psychology in favour of a Platonic tripartite division of the soul, and won Galen's approval for doing so (*De placitis Hippocratis et Platonis* iv and v). Following this, Posidonius modified Stoic ethics in an interesting way. We are not well informed about any other major deviations from orthodoxy. As I shall explain later, Posidonius' general conception of philosophy and his attachment to science have closer connexions with Aristotle than earlier Stoics professed. But Chrysippus' authority continued to be the strongest influence on late Stoicism.

One of the great difficulties, which has contributed to the neglect of Stoicism in modern times, is the state of our evidence. The history of the Stoa is often divided into three phases—Early, Middle, and Late—and it is the last of these, represented above all in the writings of Seneca, Epictetus and Marcus Aurelius, which is the best documented. For Early Stoicism (Zeno-Antipater) and Middle Stoicism (Panaetius and Posidonius) we must make do with quotations and summaries in later writers. No complete work by any Stoic philosopher survives from these two phases. The unfortunate fact is that our evidence is best from a period when Stoicism had become an authorized doctrine rather than a developing philosophical system. What matters above all to Epictetus and Marcus Aurelius in the second century A.D. is moral exhortation within the framework of the Stoic universe. On details of physics, logic, or theory of knowledge they have little to say. But if Epictetus and Marcus confirm rather than add to our general knowledge of Stoic theories, they do something else which is immensely valuable. Through them we learn what it meant in practice to be a committed Stoic. Thus the theory comes alive, and the dry summaries of early Stoic doctrine take on flesh and blood. None of these writers however is setting out to give an historically accurate account of early Stoicism, and in certain instances, for example their treatment of the faculties of the soul, all three diverge from Chrysippus' methodology.[1]

[1] They all tend to oppose body and soul in a manner which is Platonic rather

But if their evidence is used with care and compared with texts which undoubtedly report early Stoic views it can provide a most useful supplement to explicit reports of Zeno and Chrysippus.

Our evidence for the first two phases of Stoicism can be arranged under four categories. First, Herculaneum papyri: a few badly damaged fragments of Chrysippus have been recovered, and it is possible that further work on such material may yield new evidence, though not too much can be expected from this quarter (cf. especially *SVF* ii 131: 298a). There is also a fascinating papyrus text which preserves substantial fragments of the *Foundations of ethics* by an Alexandrian Stoic called Hierocles, a contemporary of Epictetus.[1] This illuminates the relation between ethics and psychology, and it is wholly consistent with evidence of early Stoicism.

Secondly, we have quotations. Many of these are attributed to individuals, a most important example being Cleanthes' *Hymn to Zeus* (*SVF* i 557), written in hexameter verse. The Stoic most frequently quoted is Chrysippus, and the widest selection of quotations comes from Plutarch who in his *De Stoicorum repugnantiis* and *De Communibus notitiis* repeatedly sets one passage from Chrysippus against another in order to expose apparent inconsistencies in Stoicism. By Galen too the actual words of Chrysippus and Posidonius are often cited in his discussion of the faculties of the soul (*SVF* iii 456–82). Cicero, Diogenes Laertius, John of Stobi (Stobaeus) and a number of other writers also preserve some quotations, but most of their evidence is in the form of doxography. We also find quotations which are not attributed to any individual. In his treatise *On Destiny*, Alexander of Aphrodisias, the Aristotelian commentator who flourished at the end of the second century A.D., records a number of passages, some of them quite lengthy, which are wholly Stoic in style and content. But Alexander does not identify the authors, and never refers to 'The Stoics' explicitly throughout his treatise.[2]

Thirdly, we have a copious supply of second-hand reports, the form of which may be illustrated by this passage from Aulus Gellius: 'Zeno held that pleasure is indifferent, that is, something neither good nor bad, a point which he expressed in Greek with the word *adiaphoron*'

---

than Chrysippean, cf. Sen. *Ep.* 24, 17; 65, 16; *Cons. Helv.* 11, 7; Epictet. ii, 12. 21ff.; Marcus x 11.

[1] The text has been published and discussed by H. von Arnim, *Hierokles, Ethische Elementarlehre* (Berlin 1906).

[2] I have discussed Alexander's methodology in *Archiv für Geschichte der Philosophie* 52 (1970) 247–68.

(ix 5, 5 = *SVF* i 195). Such statements are to be found in all the sources already mentioned, and other important sources of this kind are Sextus Empiricus, Clement of Alexandria, and Simplicius. Fourthly we have a class of reports often combined with one or both of the two previous categories, which are either attributed to 'The Stoics' or are inferred to be Stoic from their content and from characteristics of the authors. Cicero's *De finibus* provides a most important general statement of the main principles of Stoic ethics, without, in many cases, referring to individual Stoic philosophers. The same is true of Diogenes Laertius and Stobaeus. But such authorities, who are explicitly recording Stoic doctrines, cause less difficulties than writers who incorporate material for their own purposes without acknowledgment. The problem in the case of, say, Cicero or Stobaeus, is to decide whether some general statement should be fathered on Chrysippus or on another individual Stoic philosopher. In such cases we know that some Stoic held this view, and it will normally be a fair presumption that it belongs to Chrysippus. But from writers such as Plotinus and Philo of Alexandria it is much more difficult to dissect what is or may be Stoic material. Philo in particular is an important Stoic source, but in attempting to reconcile doctrines of Judaism with Greek thought he drew upon Plato and Aristotle as well as the Stoics; and the Stoic who may have influenced him most deeply was probably Posidonius.

At least as early as the first century B.C. handbooks were available giving summaries of philosophical doctrines. Arius Didymus, who taught the emperor Augustus, was the author of a compendium of Stoic and Peripatetic ethics which was used by Stobaeus about the fifth century A.D. The summary of Stoicism by Diogenes Laertius probably drew upon Arius Didymus and other similar collections. So too perhaps did Cicero, though he certainly went direct to some Stoic writers (e.g. Panaetius for the *De officiis*) as well. Cicero in fact is our oldest indirect evidence for Stoicism. The problem of discriminating between sources is a large one, and it may be best if I conclude this section by explaining the methodology which I shall adopt rather than treat the subject itself at greater length.

The phase of Stoicism most central to the purpose of this book begins with Zeno and ends with Antipater. It would be desirable to chart the contributions of individuals, but in many cases this cannot be done; we are in a better position to say, 'This was the general Stoic view of virtue', than 'Zeno put it thus' and 'Chrysippus' view was this'. In some cases where an innovation or divergent opinion is well documented I will indicate the fact. But my primary aim is to give an analysis of the basic Stoic doctrines. Within each section the material will be presented historically if that seems to be appropriate, and in this way some sense of the development within Stoicism during its first phase should emerge. Proper names will be used whenever this is justified by the evidence; otherwise I shall refer to 'The Stoics' meaning either a point of view which there is every reason to regard as common ground in early Stoicism or, what will usually come to the same thing, evidence attributed to the Stoics in general. In the fifth chapter the Middle Stoics, Panaetius and Posidonius, will be discussed, and that will also be the place to say something about the eclectic synthesis between Stoicism and certain doctrines of Platonism and the Peripatetics which was attempted by Antiochus of Ascalon.

II. STOIC PHILOSOPHY: SCOPE AND PRESENTATION

No part of philosophy is separate from another part; they all combine as a mixture (D.L. vii 40).

The Stoics followed the Platonist Xenocrates in treating philosophy under three broad headings: logic, physics and ethics (D.L. vii 39). These English terms, though each is derived from the Greek word which it conventionally translates, are all relatively misleading. By 'logic' the Stoics meant something which includes theory of know-ledge, semantics, grammar, and stylistics as well as formal logic. In Stoicism these elements of 'logic' are all associated with each other because they have *logos* as their subject-matter. *Logos* means both speech and reason; and speech can be considered both from a phonetic and from a semantic aspect. Or again, a Stoic will discuss under 'logic' both the rules of thought and valid argument—logic in the strict sense—and also parts of speech, by which thoughts and arguments are expressed. To know something in Stoicism is to be able to assert a proposition which is demonstrably true, and thus epistemology becomes a branch of 'logic' in the generous sense given to that term by the Stoics.

The subject-matter of 'physics' is *physis*, nature, and this too must be interpreted broadly enough to take in both the physical world and living things including divine beings as well as men and other animals. Thus 'physics' embraces theology in addition to subjects which might be loosely classified under natural science, and in no case is the approach to these subjects scientific in an exact sense. The early Stoics left it to men like Strato the Peripatetic and Archimedes to make advances which are more recognizably scientific. Stoic 'science' is speculative—philosophy of nature—though much of it is also rooted in the observation of particular phenomena.

Finally, ethics. Like Epicurus and other Greek philosophers the Stoics were practical and not merely theoretical moralists. They did offer an analysis of moral concepts; but this was preparatory to showing why such concepts are valid and what is as a matter of fact the foundation of human well-being, the best life which a man can lead.

These three subject headings, logic, physics and ethics, were adopted by the Stoics for the purpose of expounding their system, and I will adhere to their methodology in the following pages. But this division of philosophy must be interpreted purely as a methodological principle. It is not an affirmation of three discrete subjects of study. On the contrary, the subject-matter of logic, physics and ethics is *one* thing, the rational universe, considered from three different but mutually consistent points of view. Philosophy, for the Stoics, is 'the practice of wisdom' or 'the practice of appropriate science' (*SVF* ii 35, 36), and they explained the relationship of philosophy to its parts in a number of similes: 'Philosophy is like an animal in which the analogue of bones and sinews is logic, that of the fleshy parts ethics, and that of the soul physics.' In a second simile philosophy is compared to an egg which has logic as its shell, ethics as its white and physics as the yolk. And according to a third simile, philosophy resembles a fertile field in which logic corresponds to the surrounding wall, ethics to the fruit and physics to the soil or vegetation (D.L. vii 40).

Clearly the chief object of these curious analogies is to show that philosophy is something organic to which each of its so-called parts makes an integral and necessary contribution. They need not, and I would argue should not, be interpreted as illustrating a hierarchy of subjects. Logic and physics have fundamental ethical implications, and ethics itself is wholly integrated with physics and logic. In one sense of course the practical goal of 'living well' may be said to make physics and logic subordinate in Stoicism to ethics. But the Stoic view is that these latter subjects cannot be practised adequately unless one is a good or wise man, and conversely, being a good or wise man requires supreme competence at physics and logic. In its broadest sense ethics informs all the parts of Stoic philosophy. But as a sub-division of philosophy in Stoicism ethics refers to a series of subjects such as virtue, impulse and appropriate acts, which require an understanding of physics and logic as their basis (D.L. vii 84ff.).

This necessary relation between physics, logic and ethics has been admirably expressed by Émile Bréhier:

> They are indissolubly linked together since it is one and the same reason (*logos*) which in dialectic binds consequential propositions to antecedents, which in nature establishes a causal nexus and which in conduct provides the basis for perfect harmony between actions . . . it is impossible to realize rationality independently in these three spheres.[1]

The two fundamental concepts in Stoicism are *logos* (reason) and *physis* (nature). It is because nature as a whole is informed by reason that Stoicism seeks to unify all aspects of philosophy. Stoic philosophy, we might say, is designed to make for complete correspondence between language and conduct on the one hand and the occurrence of natural events on the other hand.[2]

Diogenes Laertius asserts that it was customary to combine the teaching of logic, physics and ethics (vii 40), and it must have been necessary to stress the interconnexions of subject-matter which I have just described. But he also says that Zeno and Chrysippus used to begin with logic, then pass to physics and end with ethics. This is probably too sharp a division to correspond precisely with early Stoic practice. Chrysippus is reported by Plutarch to have advocated logic as the subject which the young should study first, followed by ethics and finally physics (*Stoic. rep.* 1035a = *SVF* ii 42). The contradiction may be only apparent. Chrysippus made it absolutely clear that ethics depends upon an understanding of nature in the widest sense. He may then, in his lectures and written courses of study, have prefaced his treatment of ethics with some general consideration of natural philosophy, leaving to the last detailed problems which only advanced students may have been encouraged to pursue.

The scope of Stoic philosophy must have varied considerably according to the interests and abilities of its exponents. The moral goal of the system and the emphasis on exhortation and casuistry among later Stoics should not be taken to imply that early Stoic

---

[1] *Histoire de la philosophie* (Paris 1931) I p. 299.
[2] Chrysippus declared that the goal of man is 'to live in accordance with experience of natural events', D.L. vii 87.

philosophers devoted all their energies to inculcating practical morality. Chrysippus and Posidonius like Aristotle were deeply interested in theoretical problems. And there is no real discrepancy between theory and practice. Aristotle regarded the contemplative life as the activity in man of that which is best and most divine (*E.N.* xii 1177b24–1178a8). For a true Stoic the study of nature in any of its aspects cannot fail to contribute to the harmonious relationship between his own disposition and cosmic reason (D.L.vii 88).

III. STOIC LOGIC

The essential unity of Stoic philosophy creates considerable difficulties for anyone trying to write about it. If the general significance of details is continuously pointed out there is a danger of confusing the reader and boring him by repetition. Yet, if details are treated as if they were wholly self-contained a one-dimensional presentation of Stoicism will emerge which cannot be entirely satisfactory. This dilemma has been faced in different ways by modern scholars. Benson Mates and Martha Kneale have discussed the formal aspects of Stoic logic in an illuminating way.[1] But neither writer offers a comprehensive account of the subjects which constituted 'logic' for the Stoics, nor do they show the place of 'logic' in the system as a whole. I propose here to take a wider conspectus of the subject and to concentrate upon those topics which seem to throw most light upon the general character of Stoicism. Inevitably some things will be treated cursorily, and others not at all. But the notes to this section, with their references to further reading, are intended to make good some of its omissions.

The Stoics, probably from Chrysippus onwards, divided the subject-matter of 'logic' under two headings, rhetoric and dialectic (D.L. vii 41). To understand the significance of this subdivision a few historical comments are necessary. What has come to be called logic was determined for the philosophers of later antiquity by a group of Aristotle's works which they named *Organon*, 'instrument'. Aristotle did not classify these writings under a single title, but his commentators were proceeding quite sensibly when they did so. The *Organon* comprises the *Categories*, the *Topics*, the *De sophisticis elenchis*, the *De interpretatione*, and most importantly, the *Prior* and *Posterior analytics*. What unites all these works is Aristotle's concern with language, but

[1] Benson Mates, *Stoic Logic* (Berkeley and Los Angeles 1953); Martha Kneale in W. and M. Kneale, *The Development of Logic* (Oxford 1962) pp. 113–76.

this is also an important theme in the *Metaphysics* and more specifically, in the *Rhetoric* and the *Poetics*; likewise, metaphysics enters into the logical works, especially *Categories*. Logic, in our formal sense, is treated most fully in the *Analytics* where Aristotle sets out the principles of syllogistic reasoning. The *Topics* and the *De sophisticis elenchis* have 'dialectical reasoning' as their subject-matter. This is distinguished from 'demonstrative reasoning' (the subject of the *Analytics*) by reference to the premises from which it starts: dialectic for Aristotle means reasoning which takes men's convictions for its premises; the premises of the demonstrative syllogism are 'true and primary'. Semantics and problems about positive and negative statements are two subjects discussed in the *De interpretatione*, while the *Rhetoric* deals with the real or apparent means of persuasion. Aristotle posits a very close and un-Platonic connexion between dialectic and rhetoric. He asserts that both of these have to do with subjects that belong to human knowledge in general; hence neither of them is a science (*epistêmê*) which has any specific subject matter. Each is within its own province, a faculty for furnishing arguments (*Rhet.* i 1, 1–14).

If we think of all this as Aristotle's contribution to logic, then 'logic' is being used in a loose and extremely wide sense. But the problem is largely terminological. Language and reasoning are two fundamental properties of rhetoric, though the goal of rhetoric unlike that of demonstrative science is a practical one. The Stoics were therefore not aberrant when they classified rhetoric under 'logic'. On the contrary, in asserting 'logic' to be a *part* of philosophy they were proceeding more systematically than Aristotle himself. 'Logic' in Stoicism may perhaps be best described as 'the science of rational discourse'.

There are a number of extremely interesting differences between the Stoics' conception of dialectic and that of Aristotle. The essential point is that in Stoicism, as in Plato, dialectic is a science which has the real nature of things as its field of study. Not that dialectic means the same procedure in both systems. For Plato the dialectician is someone who arrives by a process of question and answer at true definitions, and who discovers in this way what things are. The Stoics recognized question and answer as one of the methods which dialectic uses, but for them this procedure seems to have been an educational device rather than the only proper way of doing philosophy. Dialectic in Stoicism is defined as 'knowledge of what is true, false and neither true nor false' (D.L. vii 42). As such it is the faculty which a philosopher must possess, and the Stoics claimed that the dialectician must be a wise man. Diogenes Laertius gives a brief statement of why this is so, and it forms the conclusion to his compendium of the logical doctrines.

After reporting that only the sage is a dialectician, Diogenes writes:

> For all things are intuited by means of investigation in language, both the subject-matter of natural science and that of ethics. . . . Of the two kinds of linguistic study which fall under virtue, the one considers what each thing is, the other what it is called (vii 83).

Words, things, and the relations which hold between them—that in a nutshell is the subject of Stoic dialectic. We must not forget that rhetoric, 'knowledge of how to speak well' (*SVF* i 491), was also treated as a subject of 'logic' in its broader sense. But the Stoic theories on figures of speech and the arrangement of an oratorical discourse will not be discussed here.[1] They are only of marginal philosophical interest from our point of view, though an ancient reader would have formed a different judgment.

(i) *Theory of knowledge*

Stoic 'dialectic' embraces two large topics, 'things which are signified', and 'things which signify' (D.L. vii 62). A most important class of things signified is the meaning of a term, phrase or sentence, what 'is said' by language, and we shall consider this in some detail shortly. But the Stoics did not confine the scope of 'things signified' to statements and the meaning of isolated words. They also treated under this heading sense-impressions and concepts, which may not be initially presented or signified by words. Indeed we are told that the Stoics gave the first place in their treatment of dialectic to 'impressions' (D.L. vii 49).

But what have 'impressions' to do with dialectic? The Stoic answer is that language and thought are not endowed with content *a priori*. The ability to speak and to think is something which develops over a long period in any individual man. At birth the mind is like a blank sheet of paper (*SVF* ii 83), well fashioned for becoming imprinted. The first imprinting is a consequence of sense-perception. External objects act upon the sense-organs (see p. 126) and cause an impression to occur in the mind. If this impression is 'cognitive', a condition which

---

[1] For a penetrating study cf. the last chapter of Karl Barwick's excellent monograph, *Probleme der stoischen Sprachlehre und Rhetorik* (Berlin 1957).

I will explain later, its occurrence constitutes perception, awareness of something that is real or actual. Impressions leave a record of their occurrence in the mind, and repeated records of the same thing or type of thing give rise to general concepts.[1] The Stoic theory at this point is virtually identical to the Epicurean 'preconception'. Some general concepts, however, are not direct derivatives of sense-perception. By various mental processes, 'resemblance', 'analogy', 'transposition', 'composition' and 'contrariety', other concepts may be formed (e.g. the concepts of a Centaur, of death, of space) and the Stoics, as this makes clear, did not confine the term 'impression' to awareness of sensible objects. In order to be aware of anything a man's mind must have something presented to it. His capacity to form general concepts is innate, but the realization of this capacity calls for experience, experience of the external world and self-consciousness, awareness of his own states of mind.[2] Intelligence is shaped and developed by the general concepts which a man 'naturally' builds up from his primary sense-experiences.

This seems to be a coherent and generally acceptable account of mental development, and to it must now be added a linguistic dimension which gives Stoicism a very modern ring in the light of transformational grammar.[3] Every living creature, they held, has its own governing-principle (*hêgemonikon*), and in man, when he is mature, the governing-principle is 'rational'. The full psychological implications of human 'rationality' need not be considered at this stage (see p. 175). What I wish to stress is that in Stoicism being 'rational' connotes the ability to speak articulately, to use language. This is not its only connotation: rationality is an extremely broad concept in Stoicism. But, in our present context, the important point is the notion that thinking and speaking are two descriptions or aspects of a unitary process (similarly, Plato, *Soph.* 263e). We may call this process articulate thought.

The relation of the doctrine of impressions to articulate thought is expressed very clearly as follows:

[1] On the ontological status of universals see p. 141.
[2] Cf. F. H. Sandbach, 'Ennoia and Prolepsis in the Stoic Theory of Knowledge' (*Class. Quart.* xxiv 1930, 45–51 =ch. 2 of *Problems in Stoicism* ed. A. A. Long, London 1971) for further discussion of concept-formation.
[3] The Stoics would be happy to agree with Noam Chomsky that 'the person who has acquired knowledge of a language has internalized a system of rules that relate sound and meaning in a particular way', *Language and Mind* (N.Y. 1968) p. 23.

Impression leads the way; then thought, which is able to speak, expresses in discourse what it experiences as a result of the impression (D.L. vii 49).

In this satement a sharp distinction appears to be drawn between a passive state, the awareness of something, and an active state, the interpretation of this impression by articulate thought. Certainly the impression is conceived as prior to articulate thought. But we should not suppose that this need always imply temporal priority. The Stoics would agree with other empiricist philosophers that in some sense there is nothing in the mind which was not previously in the senses. But it does not follow from this that every act of articulate thought is directly preceded by the occurrence of an impression. The priority referred to in our passage only implies that we cannot think articulately of something which is not present either as a sense-impression or as a memory-image or as something based upon prior experience. Impressions and articulate thought will normally be two aspects of a single mental process.

It will be well to dwell a little longer on this notion of articulate thought. The Stoics are arguing that the rational interpretation of experience requires language. A passage from Sextus Empiricus focuses upon this in a most illuminating way:

The Stoics say that man differs from irrational animals because of internal speech not uttered speech, for crows and parrots and jays utter articulate sounds. Nor does he differ from other creatures in virtue of simple impressions—for they too receive these—but in virtue of impressions created by inference and combination. This amounts to man's possessing an idea of 'connexion', and he grasps the concept of signal because of this. For signal itself is of the following form: 'If this, then that'. Therefore the existence of signal follows from the nature and constitution of man' (*Adv. math.* viii 275f.).

Here the relationship between impressions and articulate thought is set in a logical context. A man is a creature who possesses the capacity to see connexions (and to use language) as a natural endowment. To do this is to think articulately, to speak within oneself, to order the impressions of experience and to create new ideas from them. For the Stoics the whole world is the work of immanent *logos* or reason, and in his power of articulate thought a man is supposed to have the means to formulate statements which mirror cosmic events. Language is part of nature and provides man with the medium to express his relationship with the world.

We may pass next to the main question of this section: What is it in Stoicism to know something? According to Zeno (*SVF* i 68) to know something is to have grasped or apprehended it in such a way that one's grasp or apprehension cannot be dislodged by argument. The Greek term used by the Stoics to denote grasp is *katalêpsis*, and some aspects of this notion were considered in the last chapter with reference to criticism by the Academic Sceptics. Now it can be set in its proper Stoic context.

The Stoics analysed perception as a mental act in which we 'assent' to some impression. External objects cause disturbances to the material (air or water) which surrounds them, and under appropriate conditions these movements in the intervening material are conveyed to our sense-organs. They are then transmitted within the body to the governing-principle, which has its centre in the heart. The result of this process is an impression, which Chrysippus described as a 'modification' of the governing-principle (*SVF* ii 56). So far, perception is conceived as something in which the percipient himself is acted upon by external objects. Zeno illustrated this stage by the simile of an open hand. He then partly closed his hand, and so represented the response of the governing-principle to the impression: the mind assents to it. Having next made a fist he likened this to cognition ('grasping'). And finally, grasping his fist with the other hand he said: 'This is what knowledge is like' (Cic. *Acad.* ii 145).

It is the first two stages which concern us immediately. By distinguishing between the passive receipt of impressions and the mental act of assent the Stoics are drawing a distinction between mere awareness and noticing or perceiving or giving attention to something. Thanks to the stock of concepts which it has acquired through experience, the governing-principle is not normally limited in its reaction to registering awareness of the impression. It responds to the impression by interpreting and classifying it, seeing it as, say, a black dog and not merely as a shape of a certain colour and size.[1] Perception is rightly treated by the Stoics as a form of judgment: in assenting to the impression we are admitting that our sense-experience corresponds to some expressible fact, for instance, that what I see is a black dog.

But might I not be mistaken? The Stoics would concede this. The mere fact that I accept some impression as 'seeing a black dog' offers no guarantee that such an object actually exists outside my conscious-

[1] On this point and on the 'cognitive impression' in general cf. Sandbach, ch. 1 of *Problems in Stoicism*.

ness. Ill-health, hallucination, bad light, these and other conditions may distort my vision and make many perceptual judgments which I choose to make false. But the early Stoics claimed that there is one class of impressions on the basis of which I cannot form a false judgment (later Stoics qualified this claim, see below). The 'cognitive impression' is 'stamped and moulded out of the object from which it came with a character such as it could not have if it came from an object other than the one which it did come from' (Cic. *Acad.* ii 18, cf. Sextus, *Adv. math.* vii 402). Such impressions, as the careful definition asserts, are unmistakably trustworthy and in assenting to them we reach the third stage in Zeno's simile of the hand: we grasp something.

What is it that we grasp? Not merely the impression. The impression is something 'which reveals itself and its cause' (*SVF* ii 54). And its cause, in the case of a cognitive impression, is 'the real object'. So, in assenting to such impressions we also grasp the object which prompts them.[1] That is one way of expressing the Stoic theory, but in putting it thus we raise a difficulty which must now be faced. The words 'real object' are only an approximate translation of the original Greek. The Greek phrase is most literally rendered, 'that which is', and the word for 'is' (*hyparchei*) can be used with the sense 'exists' or 'is real' or 'is the case'.[2] We talk in English about objects existing or being real, and therefore since the cause of a cognitive impression is a physical object, it is reasonable to say that cognitive impressions enable us to grasp what exists or what is real (cf. Sextus, *Adv. math.* viii 85). But what we grasp is also 'that something is the case', for instance 'that I see a black dog'; indeed only in a metaphorical sense can we be said to 'grasp the object', for we do not physically take hold of it. We might put the Stoic position by saying: 'We assent to the impression *that* there really is a black dog' which we see.

The special characteristic of the cognitive presentation is that 'it can be grasped'. We are supposed to recognize this intuitively. Not that the cognitive impression by itself can provide all the information that we need to say 'This is a black dog'. Any statement of such a form also requires the prior acquisition of certain concepts. The cognitive impression guarantees that there is some actual object which corresponds precisely to itself. Our general concepts enable the assent

[1] cf. Sandbach, ibid.
[2] For a more detailed treatment of this point and what follows see my discussion in ch. 5 of *Problems in Stoicism*.

to a cognitive impression to be a recognition of *what* its corresponding object is.[1]

As we have seen, the Academic Sceptics attacked this representational theory of knowledge strongly. No impression, they argued, can guarantee its own reliability. The Stoics replied that unless some impressions are immediately trustworthy there can be no firm basis of knowledge. And they continued, some impressions just are of this kind. But how can we be absolutely certain that any particular impression necessarily corresponds to one particular fact or object? If the Stoics had stopped short of claiming 'necessary correspondence' they would have been able to fend off the main fire of the Sceptics. As it is, they defended a position which was always open to the rejoinder, 'How do you know this cognitive impression is cognitive?' Later Stoics, faced with such objections, conceded that even a cognitive impression might be misinterpreted owing to external circumstances; and they added to their specification of this criterion, 'provided that it has no obstacle' (Sextus, *Adv. math.* vii 253). When this extra condition is satisfied, 'being clear and striking the cognitive impression all but seizes us by the hair and drags us to assent' (ibid. 257).

This modified doctrine implies that the assent to a cognitive impression is normally instantaneous and not something calling for deliberate choice on our part. The 'obstacles' which these later Stoics had in mind are referred to by Sextus as 'external circumstances' (ibid. 254ff.): Menelaus returning from Troy received a cognitive impression of Helen, but failed to assent to it owing to a belief that Helen was still on his ship; in fact the Helen on his ship was a phantom fashioned by the gods to look like the real Helen. Now this example raises an important point. If our beliefs about a situation are mistaken we may see what is not there, or fail to see what is there. But suppose we say, as later Stoics apparently did (cf. Sextus ibid. 258), that if a man wants to grasp something as it really is, then he must take every step to obtain a 'clear and striking impression'. If he is in Menelaus' position his judgment will still go astray. The requirement of a criterion of truth is its power to establish certainty. But unless we know in advance, as Menelaus did not, when there are obstacles to our recognition of a cognitive impression, the doctrine loses all its original force. We shall need a further criterion to establish the fact that our impression is cognitive no matter how improbable this may seem at the time.

---

[1] Hence general concepts are also said to be a criterion of truth, *SVF* ii 473. cf. Gerard Watson, *The Stoic Theory of Knowledge* (Belfast 1966) ch. 2.

This concession therefore plays into the hands of the Sceptics, since it robs the cognitive impression of unconditional reliability. The later Stoics were in effect making the wholly unhelpful statement: 'A cognitive impression is a test of what is real if and only if it is recognized to be such.'

In the previous chapter the Stoics' distinction between knowledge and belief was noted. Belief, in philosophy, is typically regarded as something which may be either true or false, and the Stoics recognized this. But they expressed it in an odd way. For 'true' in reference to belief they used the term 'weak', classifying beliefs as acts of assent to something, which are either weak or false.[1] The point of this terminology seems to be primarily logical. Knowledge in Stoicism must be 'secure', and any cognitive state which lacks this property cannot be knowledge. The absence of knowledge is belief or ignorance, but beliefs are not monolithic. Some of them are patently false; others are acts of assent to what is true. But these latter lack the grip—one hand clasping another—by which Zeno characterized knowledge. 'Weak assent' describes the cognitive state of someone who has 'grasped' the object or what is really the case. But for Zeno this is still so far from constituting knowledge that he assimilated 'weak assent' to ignorance (Cic. *Acad.* i 41–2). As Arcesilaus saw, there is really no intermediate stage in Stoicism between knowledge and lack of knowledge. Unless you know something, you don't *know* it. That is the strict Stoic doctrine. But, obviously, a man who has grasped something however weakly is in a better position to aspire to knowledge than the complete ignoramus. We shall see later that the Stoics posited an equally exclusive disjunction between virtue and vice; but they also admitted that one man might progress further towards virtue than another.

What is required to convert weak assent into knowledge? Zeno's definition of knowledge has already been mentioned (p. 126), and knowledge is also described as 'a disposition in the acceptance of impressions which cannot be shaken by argument' (D.L. vii 47). These passages imply that there is something systematic about knowledge which makes it proof against refutation. From the fact that a man has assented to a cognitive impression that *p*, it does not follow

---

[1] Sextus Empiricus co-ordinates the predicates weak and false (e.g. *Adv. math.* vii 151) but Stobaeus correctly distinguishes an opinion which is 'assent to a non-cognitive impression' that is a totally 'false' opinion, from 'weak supposition' (*SVF* iii 548).

that he could defend *p* against every argument. Like the young slave in Plato's *Meno* he might assent correctly to all the steps of a geometrical proof; but the true opinion which he ultimately reaches needs to be 'tethered by reason' before it can count as knowledge. He must be able to show why the argument is valid. In claiming that knowledge must be irrefutable the Stoics were asserting that its possessor can prove what he knows by means of propositions that are necessarily true.

The Stoics drew a distinction which is curious at first sight between 'truth' and 'the true' (*Adv. math.* vii 38ff.).[1] It ties in however very neatly with their distinction between knowledge and belief (='weak assent'). 'The true' is said to be 'simple and uniform', and it is applied to any proposition which states what is the case. But 'truth' is something compound and a collection of many things. Unlike 'the true', 'truth' is peculiar to the wise man, and it is corporeal whereas 'the true' is incorporeal. The significance of the distinction between corporeal and incorporeal will require further consideration. But it is notable that 'truth' is cited alongside cause, nature, necessity and *logos* as things which refer to the same 'substance' (*SVF* ii 913). Each of these picks out an aspect of the universe. This cosmic 'truth' is also mentioned by Marcus Aurelius who calls it 'the first cause of all that is true' (ix 2). It seems to refer to the chain of necessary causes and effects. To know these is to know what must happen and therefore a set of necessary truths. That is the condition of the Stoic wise man. He never errs, never fails to grasp things with complete security. His knowledge is logically equivalent to 'truth', since it is based upon the causal nexus which controls cosmic events. Unlike the ordinary man who utters some true statements which he cannot prove against every attempt to overturn them, the wise man's judgments are infallible since he knows why each of them must be true.

This concept of knowledge and the wise man should be borne in mind throughout the chapter as further details of Stoicism are discussed. To the 'cognitive impression', which is its starting-point, the Stoics seem to have traced back any true statement (Cic. *Acad.* i 42). Most of our evidence places the cognitive impression in a treatment of perceptual judgments, and, as we have seen, it is perception which provides the foundation of all concepts. But the Stoics also recognized a class of 'non-sensible' impressions to which no physical object or single physical object would correspond. The impression that 'man

[1] See further *Problems in Stoicism*, ch. 5 pp. 98–101.

is a rational animal' or 'fifty is five times ten' falls under the category of rational or non-sensible impressions. From Sextus' criticism of the cognitive impression (*Adv. math.* vii 416–21, viii 85–7) it seems certain that the Stoics must have ultimately appealed to this doctrine to support such statements, and the same probably holds good for knowledge of moral concepts. That however is a problem which must be considered in the general context of Stoic ethics. For the present, further aspects of 'logic' require our attention.

(ii) Grammatical and linguistic theory

Although the Stoics treated 'impressions' as a species of 'things signified', this expression was also applied more narrowly to linguistic significance. What is language and what is it that language can be used to express? To these questions the Stoics devoted considerable attention. Unfortunately, the evidence which survives concerning their answers is seriously defective, and many obscurities might be removed if some of the linguistic books by Chrysippus and other Stoics had survived. But we know enough to see that their work in this field was of great interest and importance. The first ancient grammarian from whom a book is extant, Dionysius Thrax (second century B.C.), was strongly influenced by the Stoics, and the same is true for Varro, Priscian, and many others. In a loose sense language had been a subject of philosophical discussion since the Presocratics. Heraclitus' assumption that it is one and the same *logos* which determines patterns of thought and the structure of reality is perhaps the most important single influence upon Stoic philosophy. And we shall return to this point at the end of the section. The sophists, notably Protagoras and Prodicus, were interested in 'correctness of speech', and it was natural that the interpretation of poetry and the teaching of rhetoric, undertaken by the sophists, stimulated some discussion of semantics and grammatical forms.[1] Plato and Aristotle made a number of perceptive contributions, but their achievements in logic and the philosophical use of language are incomparably greater than their insights into its structure and form. In this latter subject the Stoics were pioneers. They helped to systematize much that was previously unsystematic, and they also established ways of analysing language some of which are still in use today.

---

[1] Much of the evidence on Greek language theory is now conveniently assembled and discussed by R. Pfeiffer, *History of Classical Scholarship* (Oxford 1968).

'The study of dialectic begins with the subject of voice' (D.L. vii 55). Distinguishing between human and animal utterances Diogenes of Babylon (a Stoic whose linguistic work was particularly influential) defined voice in its human sense as 'an articulate product of thought' (ibid.). From a physical point of view 'voice' is a 'vibration of air', and the Stoics regarded words in their phonetic aspect as material objects. This point is important because it marks a contrast with language in some of its semantic aspects: 'what is said' by a predicate or a sentence is 'incorporeal'.

The distinction between corporeal and incorporeal is a fundamental Stoic doctrine. It belongs to a metaphysical thesis that the only things which can be said strictly to exist are bodies. The test of something's existence, which they alone satisfy (see p. 153), is the capacity to act and to be acted upon. Air and voice meet this condition, but the meaning of a sentence does not. In order that something meaningful shall be said, certain material conditions must be satisfied: words of a particular kind must be uttered in a particular sequence, and this presupposes the existence of a rational being. In so far as he is thinking, and thinking or speaking in an articulate manner, something meaningful 'coexists' with his thought (Sextus, *Adv. math.* viii 70). But this meaning has no independent existence. In itself, it neither acts nor is it acted upon.

This notion of meaning as incorporeal will require further analysis, for I have given but the merest outline of its metaphysical implications. But a preliminary sketch must suffice until we have considered an apparently quite different dimension of Stoic phonetic and semantic theory. When philosophers first began to think seriously about language they were interested above all in the question, 'What is the relation between words and things—physical objects?' Or more strictly—for they had no word which corresponds precisely to 'word' —they formulated the question in terms of 'names': What is it that names stand for and why is, say, *anthrôpos*, the Greek name for man? Before problems about the meaning of phrases and sentences were properly formulated most thinkers would probably have adopted the naïve realist notion that the meaning of a name is the thing or physical object named; but there was no general agreement about how things come to have the names which men apply to them. In the fifth century B.C. the sophists raised important questions concerning the natural or conventional foundations of human social institutions. This debate focused particular attention upon the basis of moral values, but it was also extended to cover other matters including language. Plato's *Cratylus* introduces spokesmen for and against the view that names are natural in the sense that they represent in a linguistic form the actual properties of the things which they designate. Socrates in the dialogue shows some sympathy for the idea that the components of certain names have a natural appropriateness. But he also argues that convention as well as natural resemblance between name and name-bearer is an important principle in the constitution of names. Unlike Cratylus who wants to hold that to know the name is to know the thing named, and that names give the only valid form of instruction into the nature of things, Socrates argues that it is not from names but from things themselves that our learning should proceed (435d–439b).

The *Cratylus* makes a number of significant advances to the understanding of language. One of these, which was interpreted in different ways by Aristotle and the Stoics, is a distinction between 'names' and 'things said about them', a concept which in Plato adumbrates both the grammatical distinction between noun and verb and the logical distinction between subject and predicate. But Plato's most important legacy to the Stoics was the suggestion, about which he himself is equivocal, that some names and their components (letters and syllables) possess properties which are common to the things which they name. The longest section of the dialogue is a semi-serious demonstration by Socrates of onomatopoeia, which he backs up by a copious number of supposed etymologies: for instance, *anthrôpos* is explained as a transformation of an original sentence meaning 'that which looks up at what it sees' (399c). Socrates suggests that some names are 'primary' while others have been compounded out of these, and that 'representation' of things is the special function of the primary names (433d). He then raises objections to this theory, but the Stoics put it to positive use. Unlike Aristotle, who regarded all words as conventional signs, the Stoics held that 'the primary sounds imitate things' (*SVF* ii 146).

We have no Stoic list of these 'primary sounds', but it is clear from later grammarians that they comprised words for which an explanation by onomatopoeia is at least plausible. The writer of the *Principia dialecticae*, traditionally identified with St. Augustine, observes that the Stoics selected those words 'in which the object designated harmonizes with the sense of the sound'; and as Latin examples he cites *tinnitus*, 'jangling', *hinnitus*, 'neighing' etc. (ch. 6, *Patres latini* xxxii 1412). The analysis was extended to individual letters and syllables, and it may be these rather than the words compounded from them which the Stoics regarded as 'primary sounds' (cf. *SVF* ii 148). 'Some syllables', writes Varro (fr. 113 G), 'are harsh; others smooth . . . harsh ones include *trux, crux, trans*; smooth ones, *lana, luna*' (*crux* means 'cross' as signified in crucifixion, *lana* means 'wool'). This strict onomatopoeic interpretation of language was only held to apply to the 'primary sounds' or words. In the terminology of the *Principia dialecticae* this is the principle of *similitudo*, 'resemblance'. Other principles of word-formation are also asserted in this tract: *contrarium*, 'opposition', explains the word *bellum*, 'war', by opposition to *bellus*, 'beautiful'; *lucus*, a 'grove', is derived from *lux*, 'light', in the same way! The source of these etymologies is Stoic, and it was probably Diogenes of Babylon who first introduced the principles taken over by the grammarians. Fanciful and fantastic though some of them are they deserve notice for several reasons. In particular, some of the etymological principles noted in the *Principia dialecticae* correspond with Stoic ways of concept-formation which I have already described (p. 124). And this is no accident. If words and what they signify have a natural relationship to each other, it is reasonable to suppose that there is some correspondence between the ways in which words have been formed and the formation of concepts.

The attention which the Stoics paid to etymology proves that they regarded this as a key to understanding *things* as well as words. A bizarre example of this is Chrysippus' explanation of the first person singular pronoun, *egô*. In uttering the first syllable of this word the lower lip and chin point to the chest; Chrysippus, who held that the heart and not the brain is the centre of consciousness, used this 'etymology' of *egô* as an argument in support of this psychological doctrine (*SVF* ii 884). Such etymologies were not unnaturally treated with little respect by some ancient critics, but in smiling at them ourselves we should remember that the correct principles of morphology have only been grasped in modern times; and the etymology of many words is still obscure. Ancient critics of Stoic etymology were right to attack many of their efforts, but they had nothing positive to offer instead.

It is possible that Zeno and Cleanthes attempted to defend the natural relationship of language to things more rigidly and less self-critically than their successors. Zeno's general maxim was that a spade should be called a spade, a view which fits someone who holds that this is the naturally appropriate word to use (*SVF* i 77). Chrysippus however, like Plato, realized that language had changed in the course of time and that there can be no one to one relationship between a word and its meaning.' Every word', he argued, 'is naturally ambiguous since the same word can be taken in two or more senses' (*SVF* ii 152). He also drew attention to 'anomaly', the fact that two unlike words can be used with the same sense and that similar words can be used with unlike senses (*SVF* ii 151). From these observations it follows that we cannot establish what someone is saying merely by analysing the linguistic components of his utterance. And on the evidence of a papyrus fragment Chrysippus seems to have drawn a distinction between someone's thought or what he means to say, and the statement which a listener may take him to be making (*SVF* ii 298a p. 107 col. x).

In a recent study, 'Grammar and Metaphysics in the Stoa', A. C. Lloyd suggests that 'there is a latent and unacknowledged conflict between the Stoic theory of meaning and the Stoic theory of etymology'.[1] The conflict to which he refers is the apparent disparity between meaning as 'incorporeal', and the theory that the elements of language are naturally similar to things in the world. I too think that there is a conflict and indeed some confusion, but this is perhaps to be explained by two things: first, innovations by Chrysippus which were grafted on to earlier Stoic theories; secondly, a metaphysical analysis of objects and their properties to which language was required to conform.

The fundamental concept in Stoic semantic theory is something which they called the *lekton*. This term may be translated 'what is said' or 'what can be said', and 'meaning', 'fact', 'statement' or 'state of affairs' are English interpretations which fit many of its uses in Greek. I shall prefer here to leave it transliterated. Two kinds of *lekton* were distinguished: 'deficient', which are exemplified by the meaning of verbs lacking a subject, for instance 'writes' or 'loves', and 'complete' statements as expressed by a sentence such as 'Cato is walking' (D.L. vii 63). *Lekta* of the latter kind, and only they, are true or false. The complete *lekton* is compounded out of a predicate, say, 'is walking', and something termed *ptôsis* (D.L. vii 64). This latter term is often translated 'subject', but its literal meaning is 'grammatical case', nominative, accusative, etc.

Now, grammatical form and syntax are certainly necessary constituents of meaningful utterance, but they are not traditionally regarded as a part of what we mean. The Stoics postulate a very tight

[1] *Problems in Stoicism*, ch. 4.

relationship, which might even seem to be identity, between meaning and grammatical form. But we must remember their distinction between corporeal and incorporeal. As an arrangement of letters and syllables grammatical form is a material property, a property of the utterance. 'What is said' by a sentence is a *lekton*, something incorporeal, which requires for its expression words that are inflected and arranged in a definite way.

Words which have a *ptôsis* are nouns (and adjectives), and these are never said to signify 'deficient *lekta*'. They may be said to signify a *ptôsis*, a grammatical case, or to signify 'common or particular qualities', according as they are common nouns or proper names.[1] Qualities in Stoic theory are corporeal, arrangements or dispositions of matter. But *lekta*, as we have seen, are incorporeal. This confusing account can be clarified by the help of a passage from Seneca:

There are material natures, such as this man, this horse, and they are accompanied by movements of thought which make affirmations about them. These movements contain something peculiar to themselves which is separate from material objects. For instance, I see Cato walking; the sense of sight reveals this to me and the mind believes it. What I see is a material object and it is to a material object that I direct my eyes and my mind. Then I say 'Cato is walking'. It is not a material object which I now state, but a certain affirmation about a material object. . . . Thus if we say 'wisdom' we take this to refer to something material; but if we say 'he is wise' we make an assertion about a material object. It makes a very great difference whether you *refer* to the person directly, or *speak about* him (*Ep.* 117, 13).

As I understand this passage, Seneca is saying that the meaning of the isolated term 'wisdom' *is* a material object (the corporeal nature of mental and moral properties is orthodox Stoicism). And this fits in with the idea that nouns signify qualities. *Lekta* only come into play in actual discourse when we say something with the intention of ascribing some predicate to the subject of a sentence. In the complete *lekton* or statement, 'Cato is walking', we are not merely denoting some object; we are saying something about it. In the real world there are not two things, Cato and Cato's walking. The meaning of the word 'Cato' is an individual man. But in the sentence 'Cato is walking' we abstract from the real man something which has no independent existence (his walking) and refer to it by using a term

[1] Cf. Sextus, *Adv. math.* xi 29, D.L. vii 58, and my discussion on pp. 104ff. of *Problems in Stoicism*.

which denotes (Cato) and a term which 'says something' (is walking). It is not entirely clear why the complete *lekton* as a whole is incorporeal, since it does and must contain a designating term. But I would conjecture that the Stoics thought of nouns as fulfilling different functions depending upon whether they are used as mere names or as the means of signifying the subject of a sentence. In the latter case, noun and verb combine to form a sentence the meaning of which is not a thing but an abstraction—not Cato the man plus something else, but the statement 'Cato is walking'.

It was probably the Stoics' very strong presumption that only bodies can exist which led them to distinguish between merely denoting something and the making of statements. Statements cannot be thought of as having corporeal existence, whereas in fact many of the bearers of names are bodies. The metaphysical notion that all properties must be dispositions of matter and thus attached to some body is paralleled linguistically in the doctrine that descriptions have no status in themselves: they must be predicated of an actually existing subject if they are to say something about the world which is true or false. Most of the surviving Stoic etymologies are of nouns, and it is possible that the 'primary sounds' were considered to be solely nouns or components of nouns. As signifying actual entities, nouns might be regarded as naturally representational in a way which the Stoics could less easily defend for verbs and other parts of speech. But this is a speculation. The fundamental point is their recognition that the meaning of a sentence is what it is used to say; that this is something which cannot be reduced to any physical or psychological state of affairs, though it depends on both of these. As we shall also see in the next section, Stoic formal logic, which is a system of relations between statements, requires *lekta* as its subject-matter.

One of the most interesting features of Stoic semantic theory is the fact that it allows a distinction to be drawn between sense and reference.[1] This distinction, which was first formulated in a technical sense by the German logician Gottlob Frege, has been extremely fruitful and it is best illustrated by an example used by him. In the statement 'The morning star is identical with the evening star' we are describing the same thing by the words 'evening star' and 'morning star'—a particular heavenly body. But the statement is clearly different from 'The

---

[1] Mates was the first scholar to make this point in his *Stoic Logic*. G. Watson also has penetrating remarks on the Stoic theory of meaning, *The Stoic Theory of Knowledge*.

morning star is identical with the morning star'. Frege explained this difference by saying that 'morning star' and 'evening star' are proper names which have the same reference but different senses. A number of Stoic doctrines require us to make a similar distinction. It is one of their axioms that 'good' and 'profitable' can be asserted only of virtue and virtuous action (D.L. vii 94, 102). 'The good' and 'the profitable' have the same reference. But the sentence 'The good is the profitable' expresses a different sense (*lekton*) from 'The good is the good'. The Stoics used the former sentence not to express a tautology but to assert that whatever is denoted by 'good' is also denoted by 'profitable' and vice versa. This statement proved to be controversial not because of its sense but because of its denotation or reference to virtue. For it is undoubtedly controversial to say that virtue alone is profitable. But, returning to Frege, we should beware of assimilating his theory of meaning and the Stoics'. The Stoics have no term which corresponds clearly to Frege's use of *Bedeutung*, 'reference'. Its place in Stoicism is taken by 'bodies' (the thing referred to) or the 'grammatical subject' (*ptôsis*).

The Stoics made a number of acute and influential grammatical observations. By the time of Chrysippus, four 'parts of speech' had been distinguished: nouns—common nouns and proper names were given different terms—verbs, 'conjunctions', which included prepositions, and the 'article', which included pronouns and demonstrative adjectives.[1] Adjectives were classified under nouns, and later, adverbs were recognized as a 'fifth' part of speech. Two of the Stoics' greatest grammatical achievements were in the field of accidence. They recognized and named the five inflections of Greek nouns and adjectives, and the terms they used (nominative, accusative, etc.), have become canonical. Equally noteworthy is their analysis of tenses. Here too they fixed the terms which we use (present, perfect, etc.), analysing verbs as means of signifying different temporal relations. It was a Stoic doctrine that 'only the present is real' but the present is said to consist of past and future (*SVF* ii 509, 517). This is a way of saying that time is continuous, and can only be broken up into different relations by means of language. Time like *lekta* has no independent existence but is rather something which rational beings make use of in order to explain the movements of bodies.

Before we pass on to formal logic a general assessment of the

[1] The evidence is found in R. Schmidt, *Stoicorum Grammatica* (Halle 1839, reprinted Amsterdam 1967).

Stoics' linguistic theory may be helpful. Like their predecessors the Stoics failed to distinguish clearly between grammar and semantic or logical theory (the term *logos* does duty both for sentence and statement). But they laid admirable foundations for future investigation. Given the premise that language is naturally related to objective reality, it was consistent on their part to look for connexions between linguistic phenomena and features of nature. If this led the Stoics astray in etymology and prevented them from treating syntax as something to be studied in its own right, we should give them credit for a subtle theory of meaning and for noting correctly and systematically a number of fundamental points of grammar. Of course the Stoics were nothing if not systematic. That is both their strength and their weakness. In this short survey I have already alluded to details which belong to 'natural philosophy' rather than to 'logic', and it will be necessary to consider the method of definition and the so-called Stoic categories in later sections. It is easier from our point of view to treat these as metaphysical topics, but their linguistic implications will be readily apparent (see p. 162).

(iii) Statements, methods of inference and arguments

We come now to the most complex and controversial topic which the Stoics treated in their science of 'rational discourse'. The term 'logic' has a much broader reference in Stoicism than in modern usage, but the Stoics undoubtedly treated some aspects of logic in a recognizably modern sense. Sections 65–82 of Diogenes Laertius' summary discuss four main subjects: different kinds of statements; rules for deducing one statement from another; truth, possibility and necessity as applied to statements; and finally, methods of argument. The presentation of these matters is highly systematic, and the Stoics were clearly aware—as their nineteenth-century interpreters were not—that verbal precision and formal consistency are essential properties of logic. Benson Mates has shown the errors which can arise when Stoic formalism is not reproduced in translation, and his *Stoic Logic*, which takes account of modern logical theory, is a valuable contribution to the study of ancient philosophy. But while much of his work is authoritative, some scholars have recently argued that modern logic may not be the best key to understanding this or any other ancient logical theory.[1] The debate continues, and the main point to bear in

[1] See W. H. Hay, 'Stoic Use of Logic', *Archiv für Geschichte der Philosophie* 51 (1969) 145–57, and Charles H. Kahn, 'Stoic Logic and Stoic Logos', ibid.

mind is the ramification of Stoic logic into epistemology, linguistics, metaphysics and even ethics. This does not undermine the formal similarities to modern theories which Mates and others have noticed; but it does affect the interpretation of certain details and any general assessment of the Stoics' logical enterprises.

Formal logic in Stoicism takes its starting-point from the *lekton*, 'the meaningful description'. In its complete form the *lekton* has a subject and a predicate as its components, and the Stoics recognized nine types of assertion which fulfil this condition. These include questions, commands, prayers and oaths, but the all-important one is the *axiôma*, 'statement'. An *axiôma* (often translated 'proposition') is the *lekton* to which the predicates true or false can and must be applied (D.L. vii 65). The noun *axiôma* is formed from a verb which literally means 'to lay claim to'. And the force of the etymology is maintained in this Stoic sentence: 'One who says "it is day" seems to lay claim to the fact that it is day' (D.L. ibid.). Such claims are validated according to their correspondence with actual states of affairs.

The statement 'It is day' was classified by the Stoics as 'simple'. 'Simple' statements comprise three positive kinds: first, 'definite'— 'this man is walking'; second, 'categorical' (or 'intermediate')— 'Socrates' (or [A] 'Man') 'is walking'; third, 'indefinite'—'someone is walking' (D.L. vii 70). The significance of this distinction is metaphysical and epistemological rather than logical. In statements of the first type the subject is denoted by a demonstrative adjective, a term which serves to 'point', or rather, since terms cannot strictly point, 'this' is the linguistic equivalent of a gesture of pointing. In understanding the Stoics here we need to remember that 'impressions' registered by the senses are prior to statements made about them. The existence or reality of things is established not by logic but by the empirical criterion of 'cognitive impression'. 'The simple definite statement is true when the predicate, e.g. walking, belongs to the thing falling under the demonstrative' (Sextus, *Adv. math.* viii 100). The 'thing falling under the demonstrative' is a physical object disposed in a certain way, that is, moving one leg after another and so walking. This is what a 'cognitive impression' reveals—bodies disposed in different ways. The special status of the definite statement seems to be due to the fact that it makes ostensive reference to an actual

---

158–72. My 'Language and Thought in Stoicism' (*Problems in Stoicism*, ch. 5) is a further attempt to develop some of the general implications of Stoic logic.

thing. It is as if we were to say in English 'this here'. Other ways of denoting the subject involve increasing degrees of indefiniteness (*SVF* ii 204–5). Hence the truth of the categorical and indefinite statements is dependent upon the truth of a corresponding definite statement.

A true affirmative statement in Stoicism requires the existence of that which it describes: 'It is day is true', if it is day (D.L. vii 65). We see a curious implication of this in the Stoics' treatment of statements introduced by a universal term such as 'man'. Holding as they did that all existing things are particulars, the Stoics reduced universals to thoughts or concepts; they denied that there is any thing in the world corresponding to the general term, man. What then were they to say about the truth or falsity of a statement like 'Man is a two-legged rational animal'? Apparently for the Stoics, this is not a 'statement' in the strict sense; it is a meaningful utterance, but the evidence suggests that it is neither true nor false. The reference of this assertion is to the content of someone's thought, and not an externally existing thing. In order to make general statements which would not conflict with their metaphysics, the Stoics rephrased sentences of the form 'Man is . . .' as conditionals, 'If something is a man, then it is . . .' (Sextus, *Adv. math.* xi 8). Such an 'indefinite' antecedent has some individual existing thing hypothesized as its subject, and the Stoics are saying: 'If the predicate "is a man" is actually *instantiated* by something, then we can say of this "something" that it is a "two-legged rational animal".'

The subject of conditionals brings us to a further logical classification: compound statements, of which the Stoics recognized seven types. A quotation from Diogenes' summary (vii 71ff.) will give an idea of the way in which logic was set out in Stoic hand-books:

> Of statements which are not simple the 'conditional' . . . is constructed by means of the conditional connexion 'if'. This connexion asserts that the second part follows from the first, for instance, 'if it is day, it is light'. The inferential is a statement . . . constructed by means of the connexion 'since' . . . for instance, 'since it is day it is light'. The connexion asserts that the second part follows from the first and that the first is true. . . . The disjunctive is a statement which is disjoined by means of the disjunctive connexion 'or', for instance 'either it is day or it is night'. This connexion shows that one of the statements is false.

This truncated quotation shows clearly enough that the Stoics were interested in the *logical form* of certain statements. Modern logic has developed a system known as 'truth-functions' which the Stoics are often held to have anticipated. Very briefly, the system of truth-functions is a way of representing the truth conditions which govern statements of a particular logical form. The logical form of these statements is expressed by a combination of 'variables' and 'constants'. The variables, generally symbolized by letters, stand for a statement and other symbols are used for the constants, *not, and, or,* etc. The value of the system lies in its generality. P. F. Strawson writes: 'Any statement of the form "$p \vee q$" ("p or q"), is true if and only if at least one of its constituent statements is true, and false if and only if both its constituent statements are false.'[1] This expression of a logical rule in the truth-functional system bears some resemblance to the Stoics' definition of a disjunctive statement. But some of their definitions are not truth-functional, and import what we may call extralogical notions.[2]

There are similarities between the Stoics' account of formal reasoning and Aristotle's syllogistic logic, but the differences between the two systems are far more significant.[3] Like Aristotle the Stoics devoted great attention to patterns of argument in which, from the conjunction of two propositions which are laid down as premises, a third proposition can be inferred as conclusion. But Aristotle's logic is a system of establishing relationships between the terms which form the subject and predicate of the premises and conclusion: e.g. 'If all men are mortal [major premise], and Socrates is a man [minor premise], then Socrates is mortal [conclusion].' In this argument 'is mortal' is inferred as a predicate which applies to Socrates by means of the 'middle term' man. Aristotle uses letters to symbolize the variables in each mood of the syllogism, but the letters represent terms. Stoic logic is a system of establishing relationships between the propositions expressed by the sentences which form the premises and conclusion. Variables in Stoic logic, which they represented by numbers and not letters, are to be filled in by complete sentences, not terms. An example: 'If it is day it is light; it is day; therefore it is light'. This pattern of argument was expressed in the form: 'If the first, then the second; but the first; therefore the second' (e.g. Sextus, *Adv. math.* viii 227). Aristotle expressed the principles of the syllogism in conditional sentences,

[1] *Introduction to Logical Theory* (London 1952) p. 67.
[2] See W. and M. Kneale, *Development of Logic,* p. 148.
[3] For ancient disputes between the Stoics and the Peripatetics over their logical systems see Ian Mueller, *Archiv für Geschichte der Philosophie* 51 (1969) 173–87.

'If all men are mortal . . .', but the form of reasoning in the Aristotelian syllogism is not hypothetical. We can drop the 'if' without altering the syllogism's formal validity, and Aristotle specifically distinguished syllogistic reasoning from 'hypothetical argument' in which a proposition q is established on the hypothesis that q is true if p (*Pr. an.* i 44). Aristotle's successor, Theophrastus, may have already anticipated some of the Stoics' formalization of inference patterns for hypotheticals, but whatever he actually did was based upon the Aristotelian logic of terms. Only some Stoic argument forms employ conditional premises, but every Stoic argument is valid if the conditional proposition which has the argument's premises as its antecedent and the argument's conclusion as its consequent is true, where true is explained as: 'never has a true antecedent and a false consequent' (Sextus, *Adv. math.* viii 415ff.).

The most interesting feature of the Stoic theory of inference is a claim that all arguments can be reduced to five basic patterns. These patterns are 'undemonstrated' or 'indemonstrable', which was interpreted to mean that their validity is 'self-evident' (Sextus, *Adv. math.* viii 223). They are (using letters rather than numerals to symbolize propositions):

1. If p, then q; p; $\therefore$ q.
2. If p, then q; not-q; $\therefore$ not-p.
3. Not (both p and q); p; $\therefore$ not-q.
4. Either p or q; p; $\therefore$ not-q.
5. Either p or q; not-q; $\therefore$ p.

It appears from the titles of Chrysippus' logical works that he proved a large number of theorems for the analysis of complex arguments on the basis of these five inference patterns.[1] Unfortunately little evidence about these theorems survives. Ancient critics of the Stoics found fault with them for their fussiness about logical form and rigorous analysis. But it is these qualities which have earned the Stoics the admiration of modern logicians.

But the Stoics were not modern logicians and this fact, combined with a recognition of the very defective state of our evidence, is important. A number of studies have recently drawn attention to difficulties in Stoic logic, if this is considered purely as logic. One particular problem concerns the criteria for a true conditional proposition. It has been argued, probably rightly, that Chrysippus did not distinguish sharply (or at all) between logical and empirical

[1] See Mates, *Stoic Logic*, pp. 77–85; Kneale, *Development of Logic*, pp. 164–76.

compatibility of antecedent and consequent.[1] Carneades too, as we have seen (p. 103), was able to criticize Chrysippus for assimilating logical and causal relationships. But Chrysippus would no doubt have replied to Carneades along the following lines: in a universe governed by *logos* causal connexions are in a sense logical connexions and vice versa. It is the universal *logos* which is at work both in the connexion between cause and effect and between premises and conclusions. The Stoics were certainly interested in logical problems and are justly admired for their achievements. But a Stoic would not have given interest in pure logic as the reason for his logical studies. Logic is part of nature, and this is why the Stoic sage is required to practise logic. The Stoics themselves probably regarded the self-evidence of their undemonstrated inference patterns as something 'natural' rather than logical in a modern sense. The relation between cause and effect is *necessary* in Stoicism (it is sanctioned by universal *logos*) and there is no evidence that a different kind of necessity is involved in Stoic logic.[2] We may speculate that the inference patterns are natural laws applied to the explanation of relationships between statements.

If these thoughts are correct, they substantially affect the interpretation of Stoic logic. The Stoic universe is a world determined by law, by immanent *logos*. This is a fundamental concept in Stoicism, and it runs through all three aspects of their philosophy. After all, these are only aspects, ways of presenting something which in the last resort is a unity—Nature, the universe, or God. In language these different aspects can be picked out, abstracted from their coexistence in reality, and it was the need to distinguish the thing (i.e. the world) from what we say about it that led the Stoics to foreshadow the distinction between sense and reference. But as I understand the evidence, no statement can be true unless it accurately represents some real state of things. The 'true' is the propositional counterpart of the 'real'. The foundations of logic for the Stoics are embodied in the universe at large. They are not merely a system, something constructed by the human mind. Deductive inference is possible because of the way things are. The natural connexion of cause and effect is represented at the

---

[1] Josiah B. Gould, 'Chrysippus: on the Criteria for the Truth of a Conditional Proposition', *Phronesis* xii (1967) 156–61.

[2] Two texts may be cited out of many to illustrate this point: Stobaeus (*SVF* ii 913) observes that 'truth', 'cause', 'nature', 'necessity' and *logos* all refer to different aspects of the same 'substance' (i.e. the universe). Marcus Aurelius writes of 'one god, one substance, one law, common (or universal) *logos* and one truth' (vii 9), describing 'truth' as the first cause of all that is true (ix 2).

level of thought and language by man's 'concept of connexion'. The universe is a rational structure of material constituents. In natural events and in logic the consequent follows from the antecedent if and only if the connexion between them is 'true'. The 'truth' of all connexions is the work of Nature, God or cosmic *logos*.

(*iv*) *The Stoics and Heraclitus*

As they themselves acknowledged, the Stoics derived many ideas from Heraclitus. By examining some of these borrowings it will be possible to tie together some of the different threads examined in this chapter and to introduce the subject-matter of the next.

Here are three Heraclitean fragments which contain the word *logos*:

Listening not to me but to the *logos*, it is wise to agree (*homo-logein*) that all is one' (fr. 50 Diels-Kranz).

Although all things happen in accordance with this *logos*, men resemble people who have no aquaintance with it, even when they experience the words and doings which I set forth, distinguishing each thing according to its nature and pointing out how it is (fr. 1).

Although the *logos* is common, the many live as if they have a private understanding (fr. 2).

From these passages it is clear that *logos* is something which can be heard, which serves to explain things, which is common to all, etc.

Another fundamental Heraclitean concept is Harmony. He seems to have viewed the world as a collection of things unified and regulated by the *logos* which is common to them. And this notion is of great significance in Stoicism. For Heraclitus it is *logos* which makes the world an orderly structure, a *kosmos*. But the Milesian philosophers had assumed something similar when they attempted to explain all things in terms of transformations of some single material principle. The Greeks did not have to speak of a controlling *logos* in order to express the notion of order in nature. Heraclitus, though he certainly held that the world is an orderly structure, meant much more than this when he spoke of all things happening in accordance with the *logos*. In my opinion he was suggesting that there is a fundamental relationship between cosmic events and human thought or discourse; that if men would only but see it they have, in their own capacity to think and to speak, something which relates them to the world and which can provide clues to the true nature of things.

Heraclitus' own style reflects the antitheses and relationships which he held to be characteristic of the world itself. Perhaps the best example of this is fr. 48: 'The name of the bow (*bios*) is life (*bios*), but its work is death.' To Heraclitus the ambiguity of the word *bios* symbolizes an ambiguity in nature itself: the strung bow or lyre constitutes a unity or harmony, but it is a unity produced by tension or strife between the string and the frame. Just as language may be riddling, ambiguous, paradoxical, so in the world opposites coexist, unity is a product of diversity, harmony a consequence of strife. I am not suggesting that Heraclitus arrived at his theories about the world by thinking about the Greek language. But *logos-legein* in the sense 'meaningful discourse', must be relevant to his claim that *logos* controls all things. He held that the world is a unity of opposites, a harmony of opposing forces which can be signified by such statements as: 'God is day night, winter summer, war peace' (fr. 67); 'The road up and down is one and the same' (fr. 60). These conjunctions of contrary predicates were designed by Heraclitus to exemplify connexions in nature which everyday language had obscured.

The Stoics did not make much use of Heraclitus' notion of unity in opposition, though we find traces of this. But they took from him the concept of a *logos* which directs all things and which is shared by all men. Fire, the symbol or vehicle of the *logos* in Heraclitus, was also adopted by Zeno as the basis of Stoic physics. Above all, the Stoics systematically developed the linguistic and logical implications of a universe directed by *logos*. It would be fanciful to try to find specific influence of Heraclitus in all of this. But the Stoic notion of living *homologoumenôs*, consistently with *logos*, which stresses the relationship that should exist between man and the world, is Heraclitean in conception.

The assumption that the universe is an orderly structure is characteristic of Greek philosophy. And in Plato and Aristotle, as in Stoicism, the notion of order is combined with the notion of goal or purpose. But neither Plato nor Aristotle agreed with the Stoics that this order is an order of cause and effect perfectly represented both in terrestrial phenomena and the movement of the heavenly bodies. There is nothing in Stoicism corresponding to Plato's Forms, nor again to Aristotle's distinction between the celestial and sub-lunar realms. Stoicism does not set up Plato's degrees of reality, nor Aristotle's distinction between necessity and contingency. The objects of perception in Stoicism are all perfect examples of 'what exists', that is, bodies; and they exist necessarily given the causal nexus which determines all things.

Part of the difference between Platonic or Aristotelian methodology and Stoicism is due to the Stoic concept of *logos*. The unification under a single concept of the cause of all happenings and the instrument of thought and discourse led the Stoics to abandon certain modes of philosophical analysis which in their view had nothing real corresponding to them. Language and thought, being natural, must be matched up with natural phenomena. Universals, having no objective existence, cannot be a subject of philosophical study. As concepts they provide us with a convenient way of classifying things, but they do not define the structure of reality. Nature reveals to us particular objects not universals. The value of language to the philosopher is its capacity to describe the world. In a world governed by *logos* what is needed is to connect, to find the right description, the description which fastens upon the appropriate bit of Nature.

IV. THE STOIC PHILOSOPHY OF NATURE

Nature is an artistic fire going on its way to create (D.L. vii 156).

No particular thing however slight can come into being except in accordance with universal Nature and its rationality (*logos*) (Plutarch, *Stoic. rep.* 1050b, quoting Chrysippus).

The nature of the universe possesses voluntary movements, efforts and desires . . . and its actions accord with these just like ourselves who are moved by our minds and our senses (Cic. *N.D.* ii 58).

Stoic natural philosophy is a very large subject which can be approached from many different angles. The one from which I shall view it in this book is primarily conceptual. The historical background of Stoic physics and the Stoics' place in the history of science are topics which have deservedly aroused interest in recent years.[1] But for the purpose of this book they are less significant than the question: 'What is the conceptual structure in terms of which the Stoics tried to understand the world?' In seeking to answer this question I will mention a number of historical considerations, and one particular phenomenon—man—must be studied at the end. But in the interests of a comprehensive picture, many details of Stoic cosmology, meteorology, theology and other subjects will be passed over.

[1] See especially S. Sambursky, *Physics of the Stoics* (London 1959).

Logos is the concept which has so far received the bulk of our attention but the balance must now be redressed in favour of *physis*, 'nature' (Latin, *natura*). First, some examples of the use of the term in Stoicism: (1) the power or principle which shapes and creates all things (*SVF* ii 937); (2) the power or principle which unifies and gives coherence to the world (*SVF* ii 549, 1211); (3) fiery breath (or artistic fire) self-moving and generative (*SVF* ii 1132ff.); (4) necessity and destiny (*SVF* ii 913); (5) God, providence, craftsman, right reason (*SVF* i 158, 176, iii 323). The Stoics themselves ascribed two primary functions to Nature which subsume some of these uses: Nature, they said, is both that which holds the world together and that which causes things on the earth to grow (D.L. vii 148). But this statement does not bring out the functions of Nature signified in our fifth category. Nature is not merely a physical power causing stability and change; it is also something endowed with rationality *par excellence*. That which holds the world together is a supreme rational being, God, who directs all events for purposes which are necessarily good. Soul of the world, mind of the world, Nature, God—these terms all refer to one and the same thing—the 'artistic fire' going on its way to create.

To the 'artistic fire' we shall return. But next a word about the relation between Nature (*physis*) and the other key concept of Stoicism, *logos*. Nature and *logos* are often said to be the same thing in Stoicism, and it is certainly true that they often have the same reference— God, artistic fire, and so on. But they are not terms which have exactly the same sense. (Here again we have to distinguish, as the Stoics did, between the meaning of a word and the *thing* it refers to.) 'Nature is *logos*' is not a statement of identity, an empty tautology, and the Stoics, as one of the passages cited at the beginning of this section shows, could write of 'Nature *and its logos*'. Each term has its own connotations, and it does not forfeit these when applied to the same thing. The significance of this point can be clarified by an example from biology. Plants, so the Stoics argued, have *physis* (nature) as their governing principle; that of irrational animals is 'soul', and the principle in man is *logos*, 'reason' (*SVF* ii 714). Here we are considering three types of living thing as discrete objects. In fact, all three are governed by Nature, but Nature manifests itself in a different relation with respect to each type of thing. Nature itself is rational through and through, but that which governs a plant or an irrational animal is not rational so far as these individual living things are concerned.

Only in mature men is the rationality of Nature present to them as something which belongs to *their nature*. It is not the nature of plants to act rationally, but it is the nature of man so to act. Here we glimpse some of the ordinary connotations of the word 'nature' and the force of the Stoic conceptual relation between Nature and *logos*. Taken as a whole, as the governing principle of all things, Nature is equivalent to *logos*. But if we consider particular living things, though all have a 'nature' only some possess reason as a natural faculty.

The existence of God, or what comes to the same thing in Stoicism, the divinity of Nature, is a thesis which the Stoics devoted great energy to proving. They agreed with Epicurus that the strength and prevalence of human ideas of divinity provide evidence of the necessary existence of God or gods (Cic. *N.D.* ii 5), but they used many other arguments which have had a long theological history. Cleanthes, for whom theology was a dominant interest, accounted for religious beliefs by reference to many factors, four of which are recorded by Cicero: the validity of prophecy and divination, the benefits which men enjoy from the earth, awe inspired by phenomena such as lightning and earthquakes, and the beauty and orderly movement of the heavens (*N.D.* ii 13–15). Among a number of the arguments which Chrysippus put forward we may note the following:

If there is something in the world which human reason, strength and power are incapable of producing, that which produces it must be better than man. But the heavens and everything which display unceasing regularity cannot be produced by man. Therefore that by which those things are produced is better than man. And what name rather than God would you give to this? (*N.D.* ii 16).

Many Stoic versions of the argument from design are also recorded, all of which seek to show that this is the best of all possible worlds with divine purpose immanent in it and working for the benefit of rational beings.

Some of the difficulties which this optimistic theology engenders in Stoicism will be discussed later. Their strenuous defence of divine providence is a complete reversal of the Epicurean attitude. The Stoics also differ greatly from the Epicureans in their treatment of traditional Greek religion. They did not approve of its ceremonial aspects and rejected sacrifices, temples and images. But they found a place for the Olympian pantheon by interpreting the individual gods as names of natural phenomena (Hera or Juno is 'air') which are divine manifestations of the one ultimate deity, Nature, whose name is also Zeus. Fundamentally, Stoic theology is pantheist. The divinity of the stars and great heroes of the past represents the working of cosmic reason in its most perfect form.

(i) Historical background

In positing a cosmic principle which is not only intelligible but also intelligent the Stoics were sharply at variance with the Epicureans. But in the Greek philosophical tradition it is the Epicureans who stand out as exceptional. Most of the Presocratics, with the exception of the Atomists, found evidence of reason in natural phenomena. Anaxagoras posited Mind as the first cause of all things, and a slightly younger thinker, Diogenes of Apollonia, tried to explain the world by reference to air, assigning to air intelligence and identifying it with God. He held that air *pervades* and *disposes* all things, being itself subject to variations of temperature, moisture and speed (DK 64B5). Like Anaximenes, a hundred years his predecessor, Diogenes regarded the human soul as air and thus, on his principles, it is a 'portion' of God. In a fragment preserved by Simplicius he writes:

For without intelligence it would not have been possible for everything to be so distributed as to maintain the measures of all things—winter and summer, night and day, rains and winds and fair weather; and everything else one will find, if one is willing to reflect, disposed in the best possible way (DK 64B3).

Though their picture of the physical world is vastly more sophisticated than Diogenes', the Stoics have much in common with him. They too posited as their active principle an all-pervasive intelligent material which is identical to God and accounts for differences in particular things by differentiations of itself. Diogenes' air plays a similar biological and psychological rôle to Stoic fire or *pneuma* (fiery breath), and they also regarded the human soul as an 'offshoot' of God. Above all, they accepted like him that the orderliness of natural phenomena provides undoubted evidence of the world's excellence.[1]

One of the striking features of Stoic natural philosophy is its biological orientation. There is little doubt that the Stoics were influenced here by Presocratic modes of thought. But the Presocratics were only

---

[1] At *N.D.* ii 16–39 Cicero records a number of Stoic arguments for the world's excellence and rationality.

one influence on Stoic natural philosophy. This is not the retrogressive system that many earlier scholars have suggested. On the contrary, the Stoics drew on a wide range of material, including contemporary medicine, and there are notable similarities between their own natural philosophy and Platonic and Aristotelian concepts.

In late Plato we find many anticipations of Stoicism. Plato regularly appeals to the orderly movements of the heavenly bodies in support of his claim that the world is the product of intelligent direction. Whether he writes allegorically of a Craftsman, as in the *Timaeus*, or more literally of a 'world-soul' as in Book x of the *Laws*, Plato is convinced that the world is directed by intelligence for purposes which are good. One passage from the *Laws* is remarkably 'Stoic':

Let us persuade the young men by arguments that all things have been arranged by the overseer of the universe for the security and excellence of the whole; and the parts of the universe each act or are acted upon appropriately according to their capacity. Each of these parts down to the smallest feature of its condition or activity is under the direction of ruling powers, which have perfected every minutest detail. And you, you stubborn man, are one of these parts, minute though you are, which always contributes to the good of the whole. You have failed to see that every act of creation occurs for the sake of the universe, that it may enjoy a life of well-being; creation occurs not for your sake but you occur for the sake of the universe.... You are peeved because you fail to realize how what is best for you is best for the universe as well as yourself (903b–d).

This passage would be quite in place in Epictetus or Marcus Aurelius. Plato's distinction between part and whole is of central importance to Stoic ethics, and it has the same cosmic grounding. When Chrysippus wrote that ethics requires 'universal Nature' as its starting-point (Plut. *Stoic. rep.* 1035c) he was talking the language of *Laws* x. From a physical point of view there are of course great differences between Plato's universe and that of the Stoics. For Plato soul is something incorporeal like the Forms. The Stoics reject the Forms and make soul along with their 'artistic fire' a corporeal entity. But such differences do not undermine a fundamental common ground both in the attitude towards the universe and in its ethical implications.

The links between Stoicism and Aristotle's cosmology are rather different. Like the Stoics, Aristotle is a thoroughgoing teleologist, and his notion of 'nature' as a cause 'for the sake of something', expounded in *Physics* ii, has a superficial resemblance with Stoic *physis*. But Aristotle does not conceive nature as a rational agent; nature for him is that factor within each individual organism which accounts for its efforts to perfect itself. Though Aristotle sometimes speaks of nature as 'divine' he cannot in his mature system identify God and nature, since God is not 'in the world'. For Aristotle, God—the prime unmoved mover—is a pure Mind which acts upon the world not directly but through the mediation of the heavenly bodies whose movements are responsible for change in the terrestrial sphere. The precise relationship between Aristotle's self-absorbed Prime Mover and goal-directed processes on earth is one of the more obscure elements in his system. The Stoics, by setting Nature/God within the world, have united under a single principle functions which Aristotle kept apart. Stoic Nature resembles the Aristotelian Prime Mover in being a rational agent which is the ultimate cause of all things. But the Stoics also regard Nature as a material substance—'artistic fire'—which pervades all things and accounts for their persistence and their change.

It is interesting to note that the Aristotelian, Strato, who died about the same time as Zeno, reacted to Aristotle's cosmology in a quite different way. Instead of identifying God and nature Strato took the opposite step of denying any function to God in the explanation of the universe. In Strato nature becomes the ultimate cause of all phenomena, and it is conceived in mechanistic terms (Cic. *N.D.* i 35): nature is the interaction of opposing powers, fundamentally 'hot' and 'cold'. The Stoics are at the opposite end of this spectrum but only in one sense. They agreed with Strato in looking for the ultimate cause of change within the world and the Stoic concept of *pneuma* was very probably influenced by Strato's hot and cold.

Stoic natural philosophy looks radically different from Aristotle's cosmology in some respects. But in many details his influence is apparent. The Aristotelian distinction between 'matter' and 'form', and his notion of 'elements' which are transformed into one another, are two ideas which the Stoics incorporated with modifications into their own system. On neither theory is empty space acceptable. As advocates of a continuous and purposive universe Aristotle and the Stoics are at one against the Epicureans.

(ii) The structure of things: body, pneuma, *elements*
So much by way of general historical background. Nature, the concept with which we have been chiefly concerned thus far, refers in Stoicism to a kind of body, 'artistic fire' (or *pneuma*). Unlike the Platonists and Peripatetics the Stoics confined 'existence' to bodies (*SVF* ii 525).

Their position was justified by the assumption that for something to exist it must be capable of producing or experiencing some change, and that this condition is only satisfied by bodies—three-dimensional objects which are resistant to external pressure (*SVF* ii 359, 381). Zeno used this criterion of existence to refute claims of earlier thinkers concerning incorporeal entities (Cic. *Acad.* i 39). If the mind were such an entity, Zeno argued, it would be incapable of any activity. This is an interesting reversal of a Platonic argument in the *Sophist* (246a–247e). There the Eleatic Stranger argues against those who 'limit existence to what can be touched', who identify body and being, by turning the discussion to moral qualities. The materialists admit that there is such a thing as soul, and that souls may be just or unjust. The Stranger then elicits the admission that a just soul is one in which justice is present and that whatever can come to be present in (or absent from) something must be a real thing. The materialists, reluctant to abandon their position, are now said by Theaetetus to equivocate, neither accepting the inference that moral qualities (which are intangible) are unreal nor that they are bodies. The Eleatic Stranger next proposes that the materialists should abandon their previous criterion of existence in favour of a new 'mark of reality'—'that anything which really exists possesses some power of causing a change in something else or of experiencing change' (247e).

The Stoics, far from being embarrassed by Plato's mark of reality, accepted it and its consequences. They seized the nettle which Plato's materialists shrank from touching and boldly asserted that justice and all moral qualities *are* bodies like anything else which exists. An argument of Chrysippus' is quoted by Plutarch (*Stoic. rep.* 1042e) which implies the criterion of existence, 'power of acting or being acted upon', in discussing the perceptibility of virtue: virtue and vice are objects of sense-perception; we are able to see theft, adultery, cowardice, acts of kindness, and so forth. Therefore, we may interpolate, virtue and vice have the power to act upon our senses, and sensation requires physical contact between the percipient and the object.

But clearly, virtue or an act of kindness is not the same kind of thing as a man or a table. In order to see how the Stoics could intelligibly treat virtue as a corporeal entity we must turn to consider their two so-called 'principles' or 'starting-points' and the relation between them.

One of these 'principles' we have already encountered: the 'active principle' is Nature or God. But it is permanently related to a 'passive principle', termed 'matter' or 'substance without qualitative determination' (D.L. vii 134). Seneca gives a succinct description of these two principles: 'Matter is inert, a thing which is available for everything but which will be dormant unless something moves it'; the 'active principle' or 'cause' is 'reason which shapes matter and moves it whithersoever it wishes and fashions from it products of different kinds' (*Ep.* 65, 2). The Stoic concept of 'matter' was borrowed from Aristotle. In Aristotle's metaphysics 'matter' is the undefined substrate 'underlying' the form or properties which particular things possess; it is that 'out of which they come to be'. Considered just by itself matter in Aristotle is devoid of form, but it is never encountered in the world without some qualification: we know matter by analogy with the matter of particular things—the bronze of the statue, the wood of the bed. Similarly in Stoicism, matter and the active shaping principle never exist apart from one another. Together they constitute all that exists, and they can only be drawn apart for the purpose of conceptual analysis.

The physical relationship between the two principles or constituents of 'being' is mixture: 'God is mixed with matter, penetrates the whole of matter and shapes it' (*SVF* ii 310). This notion of one thing completely interpenetrating another is difficult, but for the present we may let it stand. A more pressing question is why the Stoics postulated two principles rather than one. No Stoic text provides an explicit answer, but the best clue is their criterion of existence as 'capable of acting or of being acted upon'. If body satisfies this condition then body must be analysable into active and passive components. For it could not simultaneously as a whole both act upon itself and be acted upon by itself. 'Matter' in Stoicism is therefore not equivalent to corporeality: it is rather one aspect of corporeality which in any particular body is conjoined with the active component.

Since matter is completely indeterminate it can become qualified by any form or disposition imposed upon it by the active principle. It is misleading to describe the Stoics as 'materialists'. Bodies, in the Stoic system, are compounds of 'matter' and 'mind' (God or *logos*). Mind is not something other than body but a necessary constituent of it, the 'reason' in matter. The Stoics are better described as vitalists. Their Nature, like Spinoza's God or Nature, is a thing to which both thought and extension are attributable.

Zeno and Cleanthes identified the *logos* with fire. Their reasoning was based upon the assumption that heat is something vital and active.

Cicero is drawing on Cleanthes when he presents this Stoic argument:[1]

It is a fact that all things which are capable of nurture and growth contain within themselves vital heat, without which they could not sustain nurture and growth. For everything which is hot and fiery is roused and moved by its own agency (*N.D.* ii 23).

Heat or fire was a fundamental concept in Presocratic thought, and its influence persisted in later times. Aristotle regarded heat as the cause of growth which is present in every seed, and the early Stoics extended this biological notion to explain movement and change in the whole universe. Nature is an artistic or creative fire; and the essence of this idea is expressed in the sentence: 'God is the "seminal" *logos* of the universe' (D.L. vii 136). Heat or fire never loses this pre-eminence in Stoicism. 'Fiery' is the one qualification which 'matter' is always endowed with by its association with *logos*.[2] But from Chrysippus onwards the Stoics identified the *logos* throughout each world-cycle not with pure fire but with a compound of fire and air, *pneuma*.

This modification of the earlier doctrine was almost certainly prompted by contemporary physiology.[3] *Pneuma*, which literally means 'breath', was regarded by medical writers as the 'vital' spirit transmitted via the arteries. Aristotle made use of this idea, and Zeno connected fire and breath in his definition of the soul ('hot breath'). The same reasoning which led to the identification of *logos* with fire was obviously applicable to breath as well, if both things are necessary to a vital principle. Chrysippus took this step, and made *pneuma* the vehicle of the *logos*.

The expression 'vehicle of the logos' is chosen because the active principle is not a simple chemical compound of air and fire. It is 'intelligent *pneuma*' (or 'artistic' fire in the earlier formulation), something which is both a physical component of the world and an agent capable of rational action. This ambiguity of function was characteristic of 'fire' in Heraclitus, but in Stoicism there is no conceptual confusion. *Pneuma* is a dynamic entity. Its continuous

---

[1] Not Posidonius, as has often been argued; cf. F. Solmsen, 'Cleanthes or Posidonius? The Basis of Stoic Physics', *Meded. der kon. Ned. Akad.* 24, 9 (1961).

[2] The *ekpyrôsis* ('conflagration') which ends each world-cycle is a resolution of all things into fire. During this phase the supreme deity, which is equivalent to *logos* or Nature, is 'wholly absorbed in his own thoughts', like Aristotle's Prime Mover (Sen. *Ep.* 9, 16).

[3] See Solmsen, 'The Vital Heat, the Inborn Pneuma and the Aether', *Journal of Hellenic Studies* lxxvii (part 1) 1957.

movement, which we must consider shortly, makes *pneuma* something more like 'force' or 'energy' than a material object, and the Stoics stressed the tenuity and fineness of its structure (*SVF* ii p. 155, 33f.). Perhaps 'gas' is the least misleading modern analogue.

In Heraclitus' cosmology the material constituents of the world are 'turnings' or modifications of fire (fr. 31). The Stoics were strongly influenced by this idea, but in their system there is a further concept unrecognized by Heraclitus, 'matter', and a qualitative theory of 'elements' which betrays Aristotelian ideas. In Chrysippus' account, the only 'element' which persists for ever is fire (*SVF* ii 413). But fire, being a dynamic disposition of 'matter', causes it to take on other qualifications besides hot, namely: cold, dry and moist. Matter so qualified becomes respectively air, earth and water. These four 'elements' (the traditional quartet of Greek philosophers) are thought of as constituting two pairs, one active (fire and air=*pneuma*) and the other passive (earth and water). Once the cosmic fire has given positive determination to air this derived element joins with fire to form the active component of body, while earth and water constitute its passive counterpart (*SVF* ii 418). Thus the conceptual distinction between active and passive or *logos* and matter is backed up by an empirical distinction between *pneuma* and the elements of earth and water. Of course, the latter pair is not mere matter, a logical abstraction, but a disposition of matter engendered by fire.

The two pairs of elements are differentiated in further ways. A property of *pneuma* is to 'give coherence', to 'hold together' the other pair of elements, earth and water (*SVF* ii 439f.). The universe itself is a sphere, and all its constituents tend to move towards the centre; but only earth and water actually possess weight (*SVF* i 99). The *pneuma*, unlike the passive elements, pervades the whole cosmic sphere and unites the centre with the circumference. It prevents the universe from collapsing under the gravitational pull of its heavy constituents by endowing the whole with coherence. This function of *pneuma* in the macrocosm is equally at work in every individual body. Organic and inorganic things alike owe their identity and their properties to the *pneuma*. Its two constituents, fire and air, are blended in different proportions in different things. One arrangement of *pneuma* is the soul of an animal; the structure of a plant is a further arrangement, and the coherence of a stone yet another (*SVF* ii 716). Whatever *pneuma* disposes it also holds together by the 'tension' which it establishes between the individual parts (*SVF* ii 441, 448).

Some obscurity attaches to the notion of 'tension'. It is a concept which the Stoics inherited from Heraclitus, though their interpretation of his 'back-turning' or 'back-stretched' harmony (Diels-Kranz fr. 51) no doubt goes beyond anything which he had in mind. 'Tension' in Stoicism describes a kind of 'movement', which is to be sharply differentiated from change of place. Alexander of Aphrodisias, who criticized the Stoics from an Aristotelian position, speaks of Stoic *pneuma* as 'simultaneously moving from itself and towards itself' (*SVF* ii 442). Likewise Nemesius writes: 'According to the Stoics there is a "tensional" movement in bodies, which moves simultaneously inwards and outwards; the movement outwards produces quantities and qualities, while that inwards produces unity and substance' (*SVF* ii 451). Sometimes tensional movement is described as an alternation of two opposite movements (*SVF* ii 450, 458), but this is probably a modification of the Stoics' own words prompted by the difficulty of attributing simultaneous contrary movements to the same thing.[1] In fact the problem of simultaneity is largely resolved if the movement of *pneuma* is analysed as a function of the movement of its two constituents.

Pneuma is a compound of fire and air, and the two directions of its movement are explained as a 'contraction' due to cold (air) and an 'expansion' due to heat (fire) (*SVF* ii 446). By virtue of its constituents *pneuma*, which is spatially continuous, is continuously active. It makes the universe into a dynamic continuum all the parts of which are interconnected, though they differ from one another individually according to the mixture and tension of the *pneuma* that pervades them. Matter is made coherent and stable by the balance of forces which act upon it through its association with *pneuma*. The world-picture which results from this concept of *pneuma* differs radically both from Epicurean and Aristotelian physics. The ultimate constituents of Epicurus' universe are empty space and atoms. All change is a consequence of the movement and other necessary properties of an infinite set of discontinuous indivisible bodies. The Stoic universe sets this system on its head. The movement and properties of individual bodies are a consequence of the dispositions of a single all-pervading dynamic substance. There is nothing like this in Aristotle's cosmology with its chain of movers of which the prime one, God, is not in any spatial relation to the universe. Movement for Aristotle requires the existence

---

[1] Galen put 'tensional movement' to interesting use as an explanation of muscular activity (*SVF* ii 450).

of a continuous spatial medium. But he does not attribute any active function to the medium itself.

A recent study of Stoic physics has pointed out some interesting analogies between the *pneuma* theory and modern scientific concepts.[1] Some of the functions served by Stoic *pneuma* were taken over by the ubiquitous aether postulated by scientists from the seventeenth century up to quite recent times. Or the *pneuma* may be compared with the notion of a 'field of force' activating matter. More generally, it is intriguing to notice two modern writers describing the nature of things in a manner which could not fail to have won the Stoics' approval:

Matter and energy are simply different aspects of the same fundamental reality and in all their manifestations obey ineluctable cosmic laws. . . . There exists a single unified system from one end of the cosmos to the other; in the last analysis, everything is energy [the Stoics would write 'pneumatic force']. Its larger spirals are the galaxies, its smaller eddies suns and planets, its softest movement the atom and the gene. Under all forms of matter and manifestations of life there beats the unity of energy according to Einstein's law. Yet this unified stuff of existence not only twists itself into the incredible variety of material things; it can also produce living patterns of ever greater complexity—from the gas bubble in the original plasma to . . . the crowning complexity of the human brain.[2]

From a conceptual point of view, the most interesting feature of the Stoic physical system is the reduction of all qualitative distinctions between objects and within objects to states or dispositions of *pneuma* interacting with matter. The Stoics were not exact scientists, but their theory would lend itself in principle to an expression of physical states in terms of a measurement of pneumatic movement and an analysis of pneumatic compounds. On one detail however, and it is a significant one, ancient and modern writers have noticed a fundamental difficulty. According to Chrysippus, *pneuma* interacts with matter by permeating it completely (*SVF* ii 473). But both *pneuma* and matter are corporeal, and it is an elementary principle of physics that two bodies cannot occupy the same space at the same time. How then is it conceivable that *pneuma* can completely permeate matter? The Stoics were aware of the difficulty, and they sought to overcome it by distinguishing between different modes of mixture.

[1] Sambursky, *Physics of the Stoics*, pp. 29–44.
[2] Barbara Ward and René Dubos, *Only One Earth* (Harmondsworth 1972) p. 83.

(iii) Mixture

Aristotle had already discussed mixture in the treatise *On coming to be and passing away* (i 10). There he distinguishes between two fundamental kinds of mixture: first, 'combination' (*synthesis*) is the state which results when, say, grains of barley and grains of wheat are 'mixed' together. For Aristotle this is not truly a mixture since the constituents retain their own properties. The Stoics followed Aristotle here, using the term 'juxtaposition' to refer to such mechanical combinations. Secondly, Aristotle distinguishes 'blending' (*mixis* or *krasis*): the characteristic of this is that the mixed components combine to form something homogeneous the properties of which are determined by the interaction between the mixed components. Thus bronze results from the mixture of copper and tin. But if one component is much larger than another, no new compound results: the 'weaker' component, say a drop of wine, does not mix with ten thousand measures of water; the wine loses its vinous property and becomes part of the total volume of water. The Stoics differed from Aristotle here by distinguishing two further modes of mixture.

One of these, 'complete fusion', is described by Alexander of Aphrodisias as follows:

> When bodies are destroyed together throughout their substance and component properties, as occurs in the case of drugs, the simultaneous destruction of the things which are mixed produces a new body (*SVF* ii 473).

Some of the examples of Aristotelian 'blending' would fall under 'complete fusion' though Aristotle's doctrine is based upon distinctions between potentiality and actuality which the Stoics did not recognize. But more important and more puzzling than the first two Stoic modes of mixture is the third. Here is Alexander's account:

> Certain mixtures occur when bodies are completely extended throughout the substance and properties of one another while maintaining their original substance and properties in this mixture. Chrysippus calls this specifically a 'blending' of mixtures (*SVF* ii 473).

Like 'juxtaposition' the components of this mixture can be separated since they retain their own properties throughout. But in 'blending', the components so 'extend' throughout one another that every particle among them shares in all the components of the mixture.

The Stoics defended this theory of the complete interpenetration of two bodies by empirical examples. The mixture of wine and water, they argued, is more than a juxtaposition of wine and water droplets. But it is not a complete fusion of these, since if one puts an oiled sponge into such a mixture the two components can be separated (*SVF* ii 472). The idea is clearly that no volume of such a mixture, however small, can be reached in which the constituents fail to exhibit the same properties and relationship to each other. So Chrysippus contradicted Aristotle's claim that a drop of wine cannot mix with a vastly greater volume of water (*SVF* ii 480). In the Stoic view the relative size or mass of two components is irrelevant to their potentiality for mixing. And here we see how the Stoics tried to defend a theory of the complete interpenetration of one body by another. The case in which they are acutely interested is the relation of *pneuma* to matter. Both of these are corporeal, but *pneuma* is a body of extreme tenuity. Matter is supposed to be pervaded through and through by the *pneuma*. And in order to explain this it was necessary to consider the different modes of mixture. The Stoics seem to have thought that the fineness of *pneuma* is such that a volume of it can simultaneously occupy the same space as a volume of matter. Their theory is made more plausible by the assumption that the quantity of *pneuma* within any compound will always be extremely small in proportion to the quantity of matter: 'If wholes completely extend through wholes and the smallest through the largest right up to the limits of extension, whatever place is occupied by the one will be occupied by both together' (*SVF* ii 477).

The Stoics could have avoided the consequences of this ingenious but untenable theory of mixture if they had emancipated the notion of physical force from the notion of body. Yet this would have required a complete revision of their basic principles, since *pneuma* possesses its power to act and to fashion matter in virtue of the fact that it is a corporeal entity. The Stoics did not recognize the possibility of action at a distance. The model behind their theory of causation is that of one thing touching and so acting upon another. But we may leave the problem of mixture at this point and examine in further detail the concept of qualitative differentiation which the Stoics based upon *pneuma*.

(iv) Categories

Simplicius and Plotinus are the chief sources of evidence for a Stoic theory of 'categories'.[1] Aristotle has a set of ten 'categories' and his

---

[1] See the texts in von Arnim, *SVF* ii 376–404. It is generally and probably rightly assumed that Chrysippus was the first Stoic to formulate the doctrine.

use of these straddles logical and linguistic analysis on the one hand and metaphysical analysis on the other. The same holds good in Stoicism but there are significant differences between the two category systems. Aristotle's categories are a supposedly exhaustive classification of the ways in which we talk about things: for instance, 'being of a certain size', 'being in a certain place', 'being at a certain time', 'acting', 'being acted upon'. The Stoic categories—four instead of Aristotle's ten—are more abstract. To put it briefly, they are a series of headings for analysing and describing the two constituents of reality, *pneuma* and matter, and their interrelations.

The first category is 'substrate' or 'substance', and this corresponds to 'matter'. But 'matter' in Stoicism never exists without some qualification since it is invariably permeated by *pneuma*. This fact accounts for the second Stoic category, 'qualified'. Anything in the world must be a substance, that is a material object, but it cannot exist as a material object without being qualified by *pneuma*. 'Substance' and 'qualified' are general predicates which must characterize anything that exists.[1] This applies macroscopically—the world is a single and unique qualified substance. But it also applies to all particular things. Since matter is continuous, particularity in Stoicism does not refer to discrete atomic objects. It refers to the shape or form which marks off one stretch of matter from another. The qualification which *pneuma* bestows upon matter as a whole is also the means of differentiating between different parts of matter. These different differentiations of matter are what we call individuals, this man, this horse. Each of them owes its individuality to *pneuma*, which so qualifies matter that each so-called individual possesses some characteristic shared by nothing else in the universe and which persists as long as it persists.[2]

Each qualified substance therefore has an 'individuating quality' (SVF ii 395). That is part of the analysis of what it is to be 'qualified'. But the Stoics also recognized that some of the properties possessed

---

For a detailed discussion see J. M. Rist, 'Categories and Their Uses', *Stoic Philosophy* (Cambridge 1969) pp. 152–72 = ch. 3 of *Problems in Stoicism*.

[1] As we have seen, incorporeals (*lekta*, time, void and place) do not exist, but they are not nothing; they can form the content of a thought and may be said to 'subsist'. The Stoics nominated a 'class' called 'the something' which embraces both substances (bodies) and incorporeals (*SVF* ii 117).

[2] The Stoics insisted that no two things are exactly alike, citing hairs and grains of sand as examples (Cic. *Acad.* ii 85). For their anticipation of Leibniz's principle of the identity of indiscernibles cf. Sambursky, *Physics of the Stoics*, pp. 47f.

by one individual can be classified under the same heading as those possessed by another individual. Socrates shares with Plato the property of being two-legged, rational and animal. These 'common qualities' are so badly documented in our sources that it is difficult to form any clear idea of what the Stoics said about them. But there can be nothing in the world which directly corresponds to them, for in nature only particular differentiations of substance exist. 'Common qualities' are probably concepts arrived at by generalization which provide a way of classifying the qualification of particular things. This ties in closely with the Stoics' discussion of nouns. Proper nouns signify the individuating quality; common nouns have the common qualities as their reference (see p. 136). What answers to the latter is not an individual, but something which belongs to many individuals.

The third Stoic category, 'being in a certain state', is generally translated 'disposition' (*SVF* ii 399–401). From one point of view the Stoics seem to have described any differentiation as *pneuma* or matter 'in a certain state'. But they also used this expression to distinguish relatively impermanent or accidental dispositions of individuals. The soul is '*pneuma* in a certain state' but it is essential for every animal to have a soul. Virtue and vice are also *pneuma* in a certain state, but not everything which has a soul is virtuous or vicious. These predicates only apply to mature men. What they refer to is a 'disposition' of the *pneuma* which is already in the state necessary to constitute soul. In its usage as a category, 'disposition' is a way of analysing not the specific and permanent characteristics of an individual but what it is about some individual which permits us to describe it as being somewhere, being at some time, acting, having a certain size, being coloured and so forth. Of course, any individual must at any time be in a condition where such things can be said about it. But men begin and cease to walk, they learn new things and forget other things, they undergo moral improvement or not as the case may be. Such descriptions are possible in the Stoic system because the *pneuma* which pervades anything is both the cause of its persistence in time and also the cause of its different states at different times. In the sentence 'Cato is walking' a disposition of a particular material object is described. Cato's walking is a certain state of the *pneuma* which makes Cato Cato. The disposition is not separable from the man himself; but in language we can draw a distinction between the subject of a sentence and what is said about it. Cato's walking refers to a physical reality; but his 'walking' is not something which can exist without Cato.

It describes the disposition of a material object at a certain time and place.

The fourth and final Stoic category is 'relative disposition' (*SVF* ii 402–4). The function of this is to classify properties which one thing possesses *in relation to* something else. Thus a man may have the property of being a father, but this differs from his, say, being white, in that being a father entails a relationship with something else, his child or children. Right and left, father and son—each one of these pairs 'needs something external if it is to subsist' (*SVF* ii 403). Relative disposition provides a category for analysing the extent to which what we can truly say about one thing is dependent upon something else. But the reasons which led the Stoics to posit this category are probably metaphysical rather than logical. All parts of the universe are related to one another by the *pneuma* which pervades them. Relative disposition offers a category for describing the working of cosmic 'sympathy', as it was called.

For this reason the fourth of the Stoic categories has the widest and most interesting implications. Where all things are interdependent, an idea which has today taken on a particular ecological significance, the concept of relationships is a fundamental one. In Stoicism, to be a good and happy man is to be related in a certain way to Nature or God. The psychological need to relate—to oneself, to one's society, to the world—was sensed acutely by the Stoics. Like William James, or Jung, or Fromm, they detected an all-inclusive desire to 'feel at home in the universe'. The Stoic philosophy of Nature provides a cosmic orientation for personal identity which, far from neglecting human relationships, makes them implicit in life according to reason. 'We have come into being for co-operation' (Marcus ii 1); 'The good of a rational being consists in communal association' (v 16). Individualism, in its Whiggish sense, was as antithetical to Stoicism as it is to many modern psychologists and philosophers.

(v) Causation: determinism, human action, cosmic evil.
This reference to social and ethical theories is no digression. For they are intimately bound up with the Stoic concept of Nature. But a more strictly physical dimension of relatedness remains to be considered. Nature connects and determines all things, and it was this conception of Nature which made the Stoics the first philosophers who maintained systematically the law of universal causation. What this law states has been expressed by Russell as follows:

There are such invariable relations between different events at the same or different times that, given the state of the whole universe throughout any finite time, however short, every previous and subsequent event can theoretically be determined as a function of the given events during that time.[1]

Now consider the following quotations:

Prior events are causes of those following them, and in this manner all things are bound together with one another, and thus nothing happens in the world such that something else is not entirely a consequence of it and attached to it as cause. . . . From everything that happens something else follows depending on it by necessity as cause (*SVF* ii 945).

If there could be any man who perceived the linking of all causes nothing would ever deceive him. For whoever grasps the causes of future events must grasp everything which will be. . . . The passage of time is like the unwinding of a rope, bringing about nothing new (*SVF* ii 944).

As these passages show, the Stoics held strictly to the view that for everything that happens there are conditions such that, given them, nothing else could happen. Chance is simply a name for undiscovered causes (*SVF* ii 967). All future events are theoretically predictable, and astrology and divination were appealed to as evidence for the validity of the causal nexus. Possibility exists to the extent that, but only to the extent that, men are ignorant of the causal connexion between events (*SVF* ii 959). A possible event is one 'which is prevented by nothing from occurring even if it will not occur' (ibid.). But there is something which prevents all non-events from occurring—the causes of those events which do occur. It is only human ignorance of causes which entitles men to assert the absence of any impediment to the occurrence of non-events.

The Stoics based their determinism on the proposition, every event must have a cause. Holding the universe to be a unified system they argued that any uncaused event would undermine its coherence (*SVF* ii 945). They also argued mistakenly, as we saw in the last chapter, that every proposition could not be true or false unless all things are a consequence of a fixed sequence of antecedent causes. But apart from such specific reasons, the Stoics were committed to determinism by the properties which they ascribed to Nature itself. As the all-pervading *pneuma* or *logos*, Nature is the intelligent director of everything. If some events were fortuitous or fell outside the scope of

[1] *Our Knowledge of the External World* (London 1914) p. 221.

Nature's power, the world could not be analysed entirely by reference to Natural Law. But it is fundamental to Stoicism that this should be possible. Further, divine providence, which the Stoics strenuously maintained, presupposes a capacity in God or Nature to bring about good works. The Stoics held that this is the best of all possible worlds; notwithstanding apparent imperfections here and there, Nature so organizes each part that harmony is present in the whole. The psychological and moral implications of this notion are constantly invoked by Marcus Aurelius, and it seems to be a fact that many men have found considerable comfort in the belief that, come what may, their lives contribute to some grand universal scheme:

> Nothing is harmful to the part which is advantageous to the whole. For the whole contains nothing which is not advantageous to itself. . . . As long as I remember that I am a part of such a whole I shall be well content with all that happens (x 6).

> Everything that is in tune with you, O Universe, is in tune with me. Nothing that is timely for you is too early or too late for me (iv 23).

William James was unwilling to classify such statements as descriptions of religious experience. But that may be a quarrel about a phrase. At the very least, Marcus' sentiments display something close to exaltation at being in harmony with Nature. The Stoic attitude was advocated by writers like Shaftesbury in the eighteenth century, and it is not one of blind resignation. They believed that the essential attribute of human nature, rationality, is derived from and an integral part of the active principle in the universe. This is something which will need to be borne in mind when we come to consider what they had to say about evil and the causes of human action.

The Stoics did not follow Aristotle in distinguishing different types of causal explanation (material, formal, efficient and final), but the single cause which they posited can be regarded as something which brings together in one substance his four causes. Seneca writes:

> We Stoics look for a primary and universal cause. This must be single because matter is single. We ask what that cause is? The answer is 'creative reason', that is God (*Ep.* 65, 12).

It is the 'creative reason' which ultimately accounts for all particular substances and all happenings. Like God in Spinoza's *Ethics*, the *logos* is the 'indwelling cause of all things'. A portion of the cosmic *pneuma* is present in each substance and thereby constitutes the substance as something particular, a stone, a man etc. But the environment in which each individual thing is situated is also accountable to *pneuma*. According to its different dispositions *pneuma* is both an internal cause and an external cause. This distinction between internal and external is crucial to Chrysippus' explanation of action. The detailed evidence which survives about his theory suggests that he was the first Stoic to explore the problem of causation in depth. He may have been persuaded to do so in order to answer the criticism that Stoic determinism did away with all human freedom of action. But the thesis which he advanced is also applicable to the movements of inanimate objects.

In elucidating his causal distinctions Chrysippus took as an example a rolling drum (Cic. *De fato* 39–44). We are probably to suppose that the drum is placed upon a flat surface. Its rolling according to Chrysippus must be accounted for by reference to two causes. First, some external agency: drums on flat surfaces do not start to roll unless something else gives them a push. But secondly, the drum would not roll unless it had a certain kind of shape. Square boxes do not roll however hard they are pushed. The drum's rolling is thus a consequence both of external pressure and its own intrinsic nature. Chrysippus termed the first type of cause 'auxiliary and proximate'; the second, the drum's capacity to roll, is a 'principal and perfect cause'. Neither cause is sufficient to bring about the effect unless the other is also present. But Chrysippus' terminology shows that he regarded the intrinsic properties of something as more significant for the purpose of causal explanation than external stimuli.

Chrysippus' distinction is clearly useful and important. If we are considering the movement of some physical object, say a motor-car, it is not a sufficient explanation of the engine's ticking over to say: 'Someone turned on the ignition and the self-starter.' The engine would not go without fuel, and it would not go unless it were a properly manufactured machine which has the capacity to convert the energy present in its fuel into rotary movement. When fuelled and driven it functions necessarily in a manner determined by the arrangement of its parts. Chrysippus argued that every natural substance has a structure which is a causal component of anything predicable of it. In order for anything to act some external stimulus is required. But the manner in which a natural substance reacts to such a stimulus is necessarily determined by its intrinsic structure (*SVF* ii 979).

Cicero (*De fato*) shows how Chrysippus applied this causal theory to the explanation of human actions.[1] The problem is to maintain some human autonomy within the causal nexus, and Chrysippus sought to achieve this by arguing that in every action we have to distinguish between the external stimulus and the mind's response. He seems to claim that external causes are responsible for the 'impressions' which present the mind with a possible course of action. But it is up to the man himself how he responds to the impression. The external causes are an expression of the working of destiny, but they are not sufficient to necessitate our actions:

Although an act of assent cannot take place unless it has been prompted by a sense-impression, yet . . . assent has this as its proximate not principal cause. . . . Just as someone who pushes a drum forward gives it a beginning of movement, but not the capacity to roll, so the visual object which presents itself . . . will mark its image on the mind; but assent will be in our power and . . . once it has been given an external stimulus it will move itself for the rest by its own force and nature (*De fato* 42-3).

This argument leaves a great deal that is obscure. It does not, for instance, elucidate what is meant by 'in our power', and clearly not all 'impressions' which prompt action have external causes. But other evidence makes it plain that 'in our power' means not referable to anything outside ourselves (*SVF* ii 1000). This leaves it open to ask whether a man at the moment when he assented to something was in fact free to act otherwise. The Stoic answer is no. The drum's capacity to roll belongs to the drum and nothing else, but it is a *necessary* constituent of the drum's structure. In the case of man his own nature determines the response to external stimuli. Nature here is a complex notion. It refers both to factors which are common to all men, for instance the faculty of assent, and also the character of the individual. All men respond to stimuli by giving or withholding assent, but the assent which any particular man gives or withholds is determined by the kind of man he is.

In explaining a deliberate act as the combination of an impression and an internal response Chrysippus is in line with the general position of Aristotle (*De an.* iii 10-11). Like Aristotle the Stoics did not look for a criterion of voluntary action in 'being free to act otherwise *now*'

[1] For a more detailed treatment of this subject see my discussion in ch. 8 of *Problems in Stoicism*, 'Freedom and Determinism in the Stoic Theory of Human Action'.

(*SVF* ii 984). Their test of human power is not freedom to act other-wise but acting deliberately. In spite of the distinction between internal and external causes, the character of the individual falls under the general causal law. For character is a consequence of heredity and environment. The capacities with which a man is born are 'the gift of destiny' (that is, cosmic Nature) which fashions each individual thing (*SVF* ii 991). Once a man is born he comes into contact with the environment, and the character which he acquires is shaped by the interaction between his innate capacities and external events.[1] In the last resort both of these are determined by one and the same thing since *logos* is all-pervasive. But that is only one perspective. From the subjective point of view the *logos* which determines the structure of each individual man is *his logos*. We might express this by saying that the universal causal principle takes on particular identity within each individual man. And since the individual's *logos* is his real self, the distinction between external and internal is a meaningful one. To say that a man's character is determined by *logos* is equivalent to saying that it is self-determined. Spinoza's concept of freedom may be com-pared with the Stoics': 'That thing is said to be Free which exists by the mere necessity of its own nature and is determined in its actions by itself alone' (*Ethics*, part i, def. vii).

The Stoic philosophy of nature is an attempt to provide a rational explanation for all things in terms of the intelligent activity of a single entity which is coextensive with the universe. The history of the universe is the history of one thing, which can be signified by many different names. Uncreated and imperishable Nature, God, *pneuma* or universal *logos*, exercises its activity in a series of eternally recurrent world-cycles. Beginning and ending as pure fire each world-cycle fulfils the goals of its active principle. Within each cycle Nature disposes itself in different forms, animal, vegetable and mineral. To one class of animals, men, Nature gives a share of its own essence, reason, in an imperfect but perfectible form. Because Nature as a whole is a perfect, rational being, all of its acts are ones which should com-mend themselves to other rational beings.

But, if 'the world is designed for the benefit of rational beings' is there nothing bad within it? The problem of evil tested Stoic ingenuity

---

[1] This comes out very clearly in *SVF* ii 1000. The Stoics laid great stress upon environment in explaining character development, and they traced the causes of moral corruption to the 'persuasiveness of external affairs' and 'communication with [bad] acquaintances' (D.L. vii 89, cf. *SVF* iii 229–36).

to the uttermost.[1] Chrysippus in particular offered a number of different explanations which are recorded and criticized by Plutarch.[2] On the one hand he argued that nothing is strictly bad except moral weakness, and the explanation of moral weakness raises its own problems, as we shall see (p. 181). But this confinement of evil to moral weakness provided no answer to questions about diseases, droughts, earthquakes and the like, none of which could be attributed to human depravity. Chrysippus did not deny that such things may legitimately be called bad in some sense, nor did he argue that they are caused by something other than Nature. But he claimed that they do not undermine Nature's providence:

> The evil which occurs in terrible disasters has a rationale (*logos*) peculiar to itself; for in a sense it too occurs in accordance with universal reason, and so to speak, is not without usefulness in relation to the whole. For without it there could be no good (Plut. quoting Chrysippus, *Comm. not.* 1065b).

Chrysippus, it should in fairness be said, was well aware of the difficulty of explaining away cosmic evil. The argument quoted above seems to be the best which he can put forward. From this it will follow that diseases and natural disasters are not *per se* the object of Nature's plan but an unavoidable consequence of the good things which are. An example of this which Chrysippus used is the fragility of the human head (*SVF* ii 1170). In order to fulfil its function the head is said to be fashioned out of very delicate and small bones. It is not a good thing for the head to be fragile, but better fragility and a good head than a bad but solid one. The illustration is well-chosen because it exemplifies the fact that Nature plays a double rôle in any causal explanation. To say of something that it is natural in Stoicism is to combine description with evaluation. Nature embraces both the way things are and the way they should be. It is important to remember that Nature is conceived as a 'craftsman' (artistic fire). To understand the work of a craftsman we need to know both what he is doing (e.g. planing a flat surface) and why he is doing it (e.g. to make a table). The craftsman works purposefully. Likewise Nature's works—which are matters of fact—are designed for a purpose, and because Nature has right reason its purposes are necessarily good. The Stoics regarded Nature's providence as something which it would be contradictory

[1] I have discussed the Stoic concept of evil in *Philosophical Quarterly* 18 (1968) 329–43.
[2] See especially *De Stoicorum repugnantiis* 32–7.

to deny: it is as natural as heat to fire or sweetness to honey (*SVF* ii 1118).

If Nature's providence is all-embracing then any event which causes injury or suffering has to be interpreted as something which, if all the facts were known, would be recognized as beneficial by rational men. As Pope, following Shaftesbury, wrote: 'All discord, harmony not understood, all partial evil, universal good.'[1] But all the facts cannot be known and therefore the supposed value of much that happens must be taken on trust. This optimistic attitude towards natural events, no matter how terrible they may seem, is one of the least palatable features of Stoicism. It is one thing to say that human vision is limited, unable to grasp the full cosmic perspective. But even at its noblest, in the writings of Epictetus or Marcus Aurelius, there is something chilling and insensitive about the Stoic's faith that all will turn out well in the end. They were the only Greek philosophers who tried to find a rationale for everything within their concept of a perfect, all-embracing Nature.

(vi) The soul and human nature

What is it about a man that distinguishes him from other physical objects? The traditional answer which philosophy has given is that a man has a mind. But what is the mind? To this question a bewildering variety of answers have been offered ranging from thoroughgoing mentalism on the one hand, which reduces body to mind, to thoroughgoing materialism, which reduces mind to body. Between these two extremes a large number of intermediate positions are to be found. Plato and Descartes regarded body and mind as two quite different kinds of thing, a theory which at once raises the problem of how one of them can act upon or be acted upon by the other. In his influential book *The Concept of Mind*, Gilbert Ryle set out to explode the 'Cartesian myth' by arguing that there is no internal substance which we are naming when we talk about the mind. To talk about the mind for Ryle is to describe a person's publicly observable dispositions to behave in various ways. More recently, attempts have been made to show that there are no good reasons for denying that mental processes are purely physical processes in the central nervous system.[2]

---

[1] Basil Willey has discussed the idea of Nature as a harmonious order proclaiming divine handiwork in *The English Moralists* (London 1964).

[2] A notable example is D. M. Armstrong's *A Materialist Theory of Mind* (London 1968).

These are just two notable examples of a continuing debate which, whatever its final outcome, is unlikely to produce much comfort for Platonists and Cartesians. The Stoics' theory of mind takes on a new interest in the contemporary philosophical climate.

Both behaviourist and materialist accounts of mind have affinities with Stoic ideas, but neither of these terms is an adequate description of their theory. In Stoic natural philosophy, as we have seen, mind and matter are two constituents or attributes of one thing, body, and this analysis applies to human beings as it does to everything else. A man is a unified substance, but that of which he consists is not uniform. A broad distinction can be drawn between his physical frame—flesh, blood, sinews—and his capacities to sense, to talk etc. In the last analysis all the attributes of a man are due to the interpenetration of matter by *pneuma*. But the Stoics applied their distinction between matter and *pneuma* to the traditional distinction between body and soul. The soul of man is a portion of the vital, intelligent, warm breath which permeates the entire cosmos (D.L. vii 156). That which it pervades, in the case of a man, is his body where body answers to matter.[1]

We should remind ourselves that *pneuma*, though it is the cause of all qualitative differentiations, does not endow everything with life. Life only arises for individual things if their *pneuma* has 'tension' of a certain kind, and the kind of life depends on the degree of tension. In those things which are alive *pneuma* disposes itself differently according as they are plants, animals or men; and only the two latter sets of living things have soul (*SVF* ii 714–16).

The Stoics spoke of parts, qualities or faculties of the soul. There are eight of these—the five senses, the faculties of reproduction and speech, and something called the 'governing-principle' (*hêgemonikon*) (*SVF* ii 827). This word is an adjective in grammatical form, used freely before the Stoics to mean 'capable of commanding'; but they were the first philosophers to form a noun from it which designates some component of the soul. As its name implies, the governing-principle is 'the most authoritative part of the soul' (D.L. vii 159), and it is situated, like the centralized sense faculty of Aristotle's *Parva naturalia*, in the heart. From the heart it dispatches the other parts of the soul as 'currents of warm breath' (*pneumata*) throughout the body,

---

[1] Most Stoics supposed that the soul, which is separated from the body at death, survives for a limited time. Cf. R. Hoven, *Stoïcisme et Stoïciens face au problème de l'au-delà* (Paris 1971).

governing them and through them the body itself. In one simile, Chrysippus portrays the governing-principle as a spider, with the threads of its web corresponding to the other parts of the soul (*SVF* ii 879). Just as a spider is sensitive to any disturbance of the web which it controls by its feet, so the governing-principle receives messages concerning the external world and internal bodily states by means of the air-currents which it administers.

The governing-principle is the seat of consciousness and to it belong all the functions which we would associate with the brain. One of these functions is what the Stoics called 'impulse', 'a movement of soul towards or away from something' (*SVF* iii 377). Impulse is a movement which the soul may initiate on receipt of some impression (*phantasia*). Together, impression and impulse provide a causal explanation of goal-directed animal movements.

But this is somewhat over-simplified. Granted that all animals exhibit goal-directed behaviour, why is it that they pursue some things and avoid others? The Stoics' answer to this question is most interesting. They argued that every animal is genetically determined to show just those preferences and aversions which are appropriate to its natural constitution (*SVF* iii 178–88). All creatures are so constituted by Nature that they are 'well-disposed towards themselves'. The word translated 'well-disposed' (*oikeios*) is commonly used in Greek to mean 'related/akin/belonging to'; but the Stoics are expressing a technical concept which can fairly be regarded as original, though Zeno, if Antiochus is to be believed, was influenced by the Academic Polemo (Cic. *Fin.* iv 45).[1] *Oikeiôsis* determines an animal's relationship to its environment, but that to which it is primarily well-disposed is itself (D.L. vii 85). Its self-awareness is an affective relationship, and all behaviour can be interpreted as an extension or manifestation of the same principle. Thus the direction of an animal's impulses is determined both by what it senses and by its innate capacity to recognize things which belong to itself. If we observe a dog making for a bone it is reasonable to infer that the dog has seen the bone and has an impulse to gnaw it. But the reason why it has impulses of this kind can be traced to a predisposition to recognize what belongs to itself as a dog.

A further factor is involved in the dog's behaviour. It has the sense-impression of a bone, but the source of this impression might have been a stone which looks like a bone. Suppose that the dog goes up to

[1] For a detailed discussion cf. S. G. Pembroke, *Problems in Stoicism*, ch. 6.

the stone and then turns away. This apparent change of intention is to be explained by a further faculty of the governing-principle, 'assent'. Our senses are reporting innumerable messages at any moment; we only attend to a fraction of these, namely those 'we assent to'. To assent to a sense-impression is to take note of a message and to identify its source. Hence assent is a necessary condition of impulse (*SVF* iii 171). We are not impelled or repelled by things which we fail to recognize as sources of advantage or harm. In going up to the bone-like stone the dog took what he saw to be a bone; he assented to the impression and experienced an impulse because of his predisposition to gnaw bones. A closer look was followed by a different response; the dog no longer assented to the stone's being a bone and his behaviour changed its pattern accordingly.

The faculties which have been described so far are common to animals and men alike (*SVF* ii 979, 991). The possession of a governing principle entails the capacity to select from the environment those things which are necessary for a creature's self-preservation. It does not necessarily entail the possession of reason.[1] Rationality is only characteristic of the governing-principle in mature men. The infant is 'not yet rational' (Sen. *Ep.* 124, 9) for *logos* takes seven (or fourteen) years to develop. Impulse, the primary determinant of animal behaviour, is also the faculty which governs human beings in their earliest years, so that their first thought is self-preservation. But gradually, as a child develops, its governing-principle is modified fundamentally by the accretion of reason, *logos*. In the words of Chrysippus, 'reason supervenes as the craftsman of impulse' (D.L. vii 86). The language is chosen deliberately to remind us that the universal causal principle is at work.

Reason, the late developer, is a faculty which shapes but does not destroy those faculties that precede its emergence. In the Stoic view of human development, innate impulses are so transformed by the flowering of reason that they cease to exist as an independent faculty. They are taken over by reason. Human nature is so constituted that it develops from something non-rational and animal-like into a structure which is governed throughout by reason. This conception is of the greatest importance in Stoic ethics. The development of rationality brings with itself a change in the direction of impulse. New objects of desire take precedence over the satisfaction of basic bodily needs.

[1] For the governing-principle of animals in general cf. Cic. *N.D.* ii 29; Sen. *Ep.* 121, 10.

Virtue is found to be something which 'belongs to a man' in a more fundamental sense than food, drink, shelter and so forth (Cic. *Fin.* iii 20ff.). But the processes at work are still the same, in the sense that man and beast alike act naturally when they seek out the things which 'belong' to them.

I leave over to our next section a full discussion of this 'natural' development towards a moral life. For it introduces a normative dimension which cannot be adequately grasped until we have completed the description of mental faculties. But facts and values cannot in the final analysis be kept apart from one another in Stoicism. This point emerges very sharply from a passage of Epictetus which is relevant to our immediate discussion:

> You will find many things in man alone, of which the rational animal had particular need, but also many things common to ourselves and non-rational creatures. Do they understand the relationship between events? Certainly not. Need and understanding are two quite different things. God had need of the animals to make use of impressions, and of us to understand the use of them. Therefore it is sufficient for them to eat, drink, to rest and procreate . . . but for us, to whom God has given the faculty of understanding, these things are no longer sufficient. Unless we act correctly and in an orderly way and each in accordance with his own nature and constitution we shall no longer attain our own goals. For the acts and goals of creatures vary with their different constitutions. . . . God has introduced man to be an observer of himself and his works, and not merely an observer but an interpreter too. Therefore it is shameful for man to begin and cease where the animals do; he should rather begin where they do and end at the point where Nature has ended with respect to us (i 6, 12–20).

The observations about human nature in this passage are largely non-empirical. What it means to be morally aware, to experience hope, joy, awe, regret, to recognize that the world is multi-dimensional, these are not facets of human nature which can be established in any ordinary scientific sense.[1] But they form so much a part of what it is to be a man that any comprehensive theory of human nature which failed to accommodate them would be worthless. The Stoics were sensitive to this point. Their concept of human nature is both descriptive and prescriptive. On the one hand it includes a number of mental faculties which account for human behaviour in a factual sense. But

---

[1] A suggestive book which develops this point is *A Rumour of Angels* (Harmondsworth 1969) by Peter L. Berger.

it also stipulates a mode of conduct which is the use of faculties for the purpose designed by universal Nature.

(vii) Human rationality and the passions

The attainment of rationality is conceived as something which alters the whole structure of a man's governing-principle. Human behaviour in orthodox Stoicism cannot be analysed in terms of three independent psychic components as the Platonic model lays down. According to Chrysippus, 'there is no such thing as the appetitive and the spirited elements, for the whole of the human governing-principle is rational' (*SVF* iii p. 115). At first glance this looks an odd and highly unplausible statement, and so it has been interpreted by ancients and moderns alike.[1] Posidonius rejected Chrysippus' theory, largely on the ground that it failed to take account of 'irrational' elements in human experience.[2] Plato had provided for this, so it seemed, by treating appetite as a component of the soul which is distinct from reason though capable of submitting to and rebelling against it. Many scholars have chided Chrysippus for his excessive intellectualism.[3] There is some point to these criticisms, but they have been made too hastily. Chrysippus was a philosopher of the first rank, and before one dismisses any of his theories as senseless it is essential to take them seriously.

Much of the difficulty has arisen because the word 'rational' (or in Greek, *logikos*) is an imprecise and often an emotive term. The main charge against Chrysippus is that he flouts common sense by denying a distinction between, say, desiring or fearing and calculating or deliberating. But is this so? The answer depends on what is meant by rational, and it is pretty clear what Chrysippus means. The rationality of the governing-principle can be analysed as follows: all human acts—perception, procreation, speech, desire—are causally affected by the fact that man is a creature who sees relationships between things and has the means of expressing these in articulate thought.[4] Now let us consider how this affects Chrysippus' treatment of desire or impulse.

---

[1] Galen, drawing upon Posidonius, criticizes Chrysippus at length, *De placitis Hippocratis et Platonis* Books iv–v.

[2] *Posidonius* vol. i ed. Edelstein and Kidd, frs. 31–5.

[3] For a more sympathetic treatment cf. Josiah B. Gould, *The Philosophy of Chrysippus*, pp. 181–96, and J. M. Rist, *Stoic Philosophy*, pp. 22–36.

[4] See for instance the passages cited on p. 125.

Apart from being 'a movement of soul towards or away from something' impulse can be described as 'an act of assent' and as 'the reason of man commanding him to act' (*SVF* iii 171, 175). The first description is a physical account of something which presents itself to consciousness as a command. For elucidating the two further descriptions an example will help. Any act of perception involves assent, taking what I see to be, say, an orange. But suppose that I not only see an orange but also seize it and begin eating it. Chrysippus' explanation of the second fact is that in assenting to my seeing an orange I also issue myself with an imperative to eat it. Why do I do this? Because I am a man who likes eating oranges. My act of assent to what I see is not in this case a mere act of perception (though it perfectly well could be); it also contains an appetitive element. The orange strikes me as 'something good for me', and this 'striking me as something good for me' means that I desire it. My impulse is an act of the governing-principle, and it is rational in the sense that it is an imperative implicit in a judgment *of the kind that moves to action*. That does not make my impulse only a bogus desire. To describe it as Chrysippus does is to analyse the notion of a desire. What will distinguish mere intellectual assent to the proposition 'X is good for me' from the proposition 'I desire X' is a movement of soul which follows in the latter case only.[1]

Chrysippus' doctrine of the passions follows similar lines.[2] A passion is defined as 'impulse' plus something else. Impulses become passions if they are 'excessive' (*SVF* iii 479), and their excess manifests itself in the movement of the heart (*SVF* ii 899). The 'excess' of a passion is comparable to the sense in which a man running 'exceeds' a man walking. Chrysippus also said that passions are false 'judgments' which have as their predicate very good or very bad (*SVF* iii 466, 480). Fear is 'judgment of an impending evil which seems to be intolerable'. In so far as passions involve value judgments they do not differ from impulses. The difference between them is analysed in terms of 'reason'. Passions, as distinct from mere impulses, are 'not-rational'.

[1] Impulse, unlike judgments in a wider sense, can only be prompted by something which has absolute or relative value, *SVF* iii 118–21. Although all impulses are acts of assent, there is no reason to suppose the Stoics thought all acts of assent are impulses.

[2] This paragraph does not take account of the so-called 'good emotional states'—joy, well-wishing, and discretion—which are concomitants of a perfectly rational governing-principle, *SVF* iii 431–42.

But here we seem to get a contradiction. If the human governing-principle admits of only rational dispositions how can passions as so described be possible? This difficulty is ostensibly resolved by distinguishing between 'right' reason and 'wrong' reason (*SVF* i 202). Anything which a man does is rational in some sense; this is an analytic truth since man is a 'rational animal'. But in another sense, the sage or good man is the criterion of rationality since he alone has 'right reason' (*SVF* iii 560). The soul admits of different degrees of tension, and any man whose *logos* is not consistently at the right degree of tension falls short of perfect rationality (*SVF* iii 473). To that extent his disposition is not-rational. He has an unsound *logos*. 'Passion is not other than *logos* nor is there dissension between two things, but a turning of the one *logos* to both aspects; this escapes notice because of the suddenness and swiftness of the change' (*SVF* iii 459). Here we have the Stoic explanation of the conflict between reason and passion. The difference from Plato is primarily a temporal one. As the Stoics would have it, a man is not simultaneously subject to the influence of two different forces. Rather, if he is not a sage whose life is on a consistently even keel, he is liable to sudden changes and fluctuations of his governing-principle. At one moment he may assent to the true Stoic proposition that pain is not a bad thing; but if this judgment is insecurely based it will not be strong enough to reject a contrary judgment, that pain is something very bad, which comes to mind and is accompanied by a bodily reaction as the dentist starts drilling his tooth. The Stoics distinguished good men from others by reference to the consistency of their *logos*. At worst a man might have a governing-principle which is never rational in the correct sense. But this is probably a very exceptional case. Most of us, Chrysippus would have said, are ruled by reason in a quasi-right sense part of the time; but we are also ruled by reason in its wrong sense part of the time and this absence of consistency with right reason marks us out as 'foolish' or bad men. We fluctuate between these two conditions and our desires may clash as one condition is followed by the other. Our moral progress is typified not by the extirpation of all emotion and desire, but by the occurrence of desires and feelings which are dispositions of a governing-principle increasingly consistent with right reason. The Stoics laid great emphasis upon the need to resist morbid emotions (see p. 206).

If the concept of 'right reason' strikes the reader as opaque, not to say arbitrary, it may be helpful, and would certainly be equally Stoic, to think in terms of mental health (*SVF* iii 278). This is a concept often in use today and most of us probably have some implicit criterion of normality with which we judge the behaviour of others. There is in our society a marked and probably increasing tendency to treat as personality defects dispositions which our grandparents would have termed morally reprehensible. A generation brought up on Freud and conscious of the damage which neglect can cause to a child's development is less confident in its ability to act as moral censor. Health and sickness are terms which have no necessary moral connotations. The Stoics, though they divided mankind into the two categories of wise and foolish, preferred this terminology to 'good' and 'bad'. Misunderstanding or ignorance not innate wickedness or sin is the characteristic of the foolish man, and the Stoics, as I have already mentioned, appealed to factors in the environment to explain the 'perversion' of reason. Equally, education and application can set a man on the road to virtue. No one is born a wise man, and there is no congenital elect. But human nature is such that a man can attain true well-being if he recognizes the full implications of his own rationality. Hints of these have already been given in our earlier pages, and they will be developed in the next section.

Clearly the Stoics' analysis of human nature may be faulted on several grounds. Their account of desire and passion, even if interpreted along the lines suggested, remains insensitive to aspects of human behaviour which cannot in any ordinary sense be reduced to rationality. One may also complain about the failure to describe mental faculties in language which is value-free. The second charge would also apply to Plato and, to a lesser extent, Aristotle. If we make it, we should recognize that we lack today anything which might be called a comprehensive theory of human nature. This may be a good thing, for theories of human nature have too often been used for purposes inimical to human welfare. But it is important to be aware of the fact that the special sciences of psychology, anthropology, sociology, biochemistry, along with philosophy and religion, are all attempting to say something about different aspects of the same thing, man. The Stoics, like other Greek philosophers, were able to be bolder than we dare to be. They did not suffer from the disadvantages of an ever-growing fragmentation of knowledge. In an exact scientific sense they knew extraordinarily little. But they certainly put what they knew to purposes which are still instructive.

V. STOIC ETHICS

The virtue of the happy man and a well-running life consist in this: that all actions are based on the principle of harmony between his own spirit and the will of the director of the universe (D.L. vii 88).

In one of the analogies which the Stoics used in order to illustrate the relationship between the sub-divisions of their philosophy ethics is compared to the 'fruit of a garden' (*SVF* ii 38). It is an apposite image. Logic and natural philosophy prepare the ground for ethics, and the reader will have noticed that moral doctrines have frequently been referred to in the treatment of the first two subjects. Nature, which the 'physicist' and the dialectician investigate from specific points of view, is also in Stoicism the ultimate source of everything which has value. So Chrysippus wrote: 'There is no possible or more suitable way to approach the subject of good and bad things, the virtues and happiness than from universal Nature and the management of the universe' (Plut. *Stoic. rep.* 1035c). Nature (God, *pneuma*, cause, *logos* or destiny) is a perfect being, and the value of anything else in the world depends upon its relationship to Nature. Accordance with Nature denotes positive value and contrariness to Nature the opposite.

(i) The part and the whole

But what is it for something to accord or fail to accord with Nature? This is clearly a fundamental question, and the analysis of it requires our making a number of distinctions. First of all, we need to specify what it is that we are talking about. If our subject is a plant then we know what it means to say that a plant flourishes. Similarly, it is relatively easy to distinguish among, say, a group of cats those whose condition is excellent and those whose condition is not. A plant or a cat accords with the nature of plants or cats when it grows and behaves in a certain way. That way defines what it is for something to be good of its kind, and by reference to this 'natural' norm things can be classified as appropriate or inappropriate for plants, animals and men. On this method of analysis, accordance with universal Nature is referred to the nature which is appropriate to the type of thing in question.[1] The concept of universal Nature is necessarily a complex one which has a diversity of references. Eating hay is natural to horses but not to men. It accords with universal Nature that horses should eat hay and that men should speak a language. But the former

[1] cf. the procedure in Cic. *N.D.* ii 120ff., Sen. *Ep.* 124, 7–24.

is inappropriate to men and the latter to horses. Universal Nature sanctions a norm for particular things—the nature of plants, animals and men—by reference to which they can be said to attain or not to attain their individual ends.

We may call this method of analysis the perspective of the part. But universal Nature accommodates all particular natures, and these can secondly be described and evaluated from the perspective of the whole.[1] It is an obvious fact that many creatures do not experience things which are appropriate to their particular nature. Disease, drought and famine create conditions which make it impossible for many individual living things to function successfully. Are such occurrences contrary to Nature? We have already noticed the Stoics' answer to this question. From the long-term point of view nothing of this kind is independent of Nature's ordering. If an event is considered independently of its relation to the cosmos as a whole it can be evaluated as natural or unnatural (or neither natural nor unnatural) to the creature affected by it. From the perspective of the part, poverty and ill-health are unnatural to mankind. But such an analysis is only made possible by abstracting human nature from universal Nature. From the perspective of the whole even such conditions are not unnatural, because all Natural events contribute to the universal well-being.

These two perspectives are brought together in many Stoic texts. 'Many external things can prevent individual natures from perfecting themselves, but nothing can stand in the way of universal Nature because it holds together and maintains all natures' (Cic. *N.D.* ii 35). The universe as a whole is perfect, but its perfection is compatible with and even requires a certain proportion of things which are unnatural if the perspective of the part alone is considered. Marcus Aurelius writes: 'Welcome everything which happens, even if it seems harsh, because it contributes to the health of the universe and the well-faring and well-being of Zeus. For he would not have brought this on a man unless it had been advantageous to the whole' (v 8). From the perspective of the whole nothing which befalls a man is disadvantageous either to himself or to the whole. Certain things can be called disadvantageous which are contrary to Nature from the perspective of the part. If Nature could have arranged a perfect world without such things this would have been done. Nature does not

---

[1] It is characteristic of Marcus Aurelius to analyse particular things from this perspective, viii 46, v 8 etc.

ordain suffering for its own sake, but it is necessary to the economy of the whole.

From what has been said so far it follows that 'unnatural' is an evaluation and description of events which can only be applied when Nature is referred purely to the faring of particular things. The Stoics seem to be committed to the claim that from the cosmic perspective everything which happens accords with Nature and is therefore right. But then nothing can be wrong (Marcus, ii 17). Yet the Stoics insisted most strenuously that the term 'bad' has a valid usage; that there is something which must on any analysis be judged contrary to Nature. Their attempt to resolve this apparent contradiction involves yet a further conceptual distinction, but before we study this some lines from Cleanthes' *Hymn to Zeus* will help to focus attention upon the dilemma.

> Nothing occurs on the earth apart from you, o God,
> nor in the heavenly regions nor on the sea,
> except what bad men do in their folly;
> but you know how to make the odd even,
> and to harmonize what is dissonant; to you the alien is akin.
> And so you have wrought together into one all things that are good and
>   bad,
> So that there arises one eternal *logos* of all things,
> Which all bad mortals shun and ignore,
> Unhappy wretches, ever seeking the possession of good things
> They neither see nor hear the universal law of God,
> By obeying which they might enjoy a happy life (lines 11–21, *SVF* i 537).

This point of view persists from the earliest to the latest Stoicism. Epictetus, writing almost four hundred years after Cleanthes, rephrases it:

> Zeus has ordained that there be summer and winter, plenty and poverty, virtue and vice and all such opposites for the sake of the harmony of the whole (i 12, 16).

Much can be written about the pre-Stoic background of these sentiments, but I cannot pursue that interesting subject here.[1] According to Cleanthes, everything does accord with Zeus (or Nature) with one

[1] See especially Heraclitus fr. 67 'God is day night, winter summer, war peace . . .'; fr. 102, 'To God all things are fair and right, but men have judged some things to be right and others wrong.' Hugh Lloyd-Jones, *The Justice of Zeus* (Berkeley, Los Angeles, London 1971) should be consulted for the early literary background.

exception. 'What bad men do in their folly' is contrary to the will of Zeus. But in the very next sentence Cleanthes qualifies this assertion. Out of disharmony Zeus creates harmony. So it seems that everything after all, including the actions of bad men, ultimately accords with Zeus (or Nature).

It is difficult to resist the conclusion that the Stoics' desire to attribute everything to a single principle has produced a fundamental incoherence at this point. But to this they would reply that the harmony of the universe as a whole is something which transcends any attempt to view the world from the perspective of a particular part. If we view Nature's activities as contradictory this is due to the limitations of human vision. Moreover, Nature does not will the actions of bad men. The harmonizing of dissonance, not the creation of dissonance, is Nature's work.

What does this last assertion mean? Chrysippus argued that virtue cannot exist without vice (*SVF* ii 1169f.), and one may comment that it is hard to see what use there could be for one of these terms unless the other is also applicable to something else. He also said that it is more fitting to live with the possession of a corrupt reason than not to live at all (*SVF* iii 760). These statements are essential to the understanding of Stoic ethics. Unlike all other natural beings, man alone is endowed by Nature with the capacity to understand cosmic events and to promote the rationality of Nature by his own efforts. But equally, he is the only natural being who has the capacity to act in a manner which fails to accord with the will of Nature. These antithetical capacities are what make man a *moral* agent, that is, someone of whose conduct and character 'good' or 'bad' can be said.[1] By endowing man with reason (*logos*) Nature has ensured that every man will be and do either good or bad. But Nature's own dispensation is not morally neutral. Man is naturally equipped with 'impulses to virtue' or 'seeds of knowledge', and this equipment is sufficient to direct human reason in the right direction (*SVF* i 566; Sen. *Ep.* 120, 4). But Nature itself does not go further than this.[2] The achievement of a good character calls for the most arduous efforts from any man and, as we have seen, external influences can (and generally do) prevent him from developing a rational disposition perfectly harmonious with Nature itself.

[1] For the thesis that *good* can only be realized in that which is rational, cf. Sen. *Ep.* 124, 13ff.
[2] Cic. *Leg.* i 27; Sen. *Ep.* 49, 11.

In order that virtue shall be attainable the potentiality for vice must also be granted. Nature has established these conditions and given man the status of a moral agent by making him a conscious participant in the rational processes of the universe. The effect of this is to set before the majority of men a task which they are too 'foolish' to fulfil just in the manner which Nature would have them adopt. But their 'badness' is not inimical to the ultimate purposes of the cosmos if these purposes are to include the offer of a life chosen deliberately to harmonize with Nature. As the Stoics look at the world it is better to be vicious and to have the opportunity of virtue than to be denied the latter possibility.

In giving man reason Nature makes him, from the perspective of the part, an autonomous agent (see p. 168). The character which a man develops, though it falls under the law of cause and effect, is his own character, not Nature's. For the environment in which a man finds himself he is not responsible. But the way in which a man acts in relation to his environment is attributed to him. The Stoics stressed the importance of aiming at rather than achieving a desirable result.[1] Moral judgments and human well-being are related to the agent's inner attitude, his state of mind. This distinction between external results and intentions was illustrated by the simile of a dog tied to a cart. The cart represents a man's external situation. He cannot act independently of this, but, so it is argued, the man himself and not his environment can determine whether he will run willingly or be dragged along. 'Guide me, O Zeus, and thou Destiny, whither I have been appointed by you. For I will follow freely; and if, grown bad, I prove unwilling, I shall follow no less' (Cleanthes, *SVF* i 527).[2]

But here of course we touch upon another crucial difficulty. Many of the things which befall a man during the course of his life cannot be isolated from his own intentions. The Stoics often write as if all external circumstances are beyond the individual's power to alter. But if the notion of an appointed life is to be compatible with moral judgment, then it only makes sense to regard a very limited set of circumstances as the dispensation of God or Nature. It would certainly be un-Stoic to regard an habitual criminal as a good man. The acts of a criminal cannot be explained as tasks appointed to him with which he should comply willingly, since they will occur in any case.

[1] See further, p. 198.
[2] I have discussed this passage and its moral implications in *Problems in Stoicism*, ch. 8 pp. 192f.

In advocating acceptance of the external situation the Stoics did not intend to prescribe passivity, nor did they regard the results of a good man's actions as equivalent in value to those of a bad man. But the possibility of inner freedom and the distinction between good and bad, which Nature as provident guarantees, cannot be squared easily with the factual necessities which Nature as destiny establishes. The Stoics tried to overcome this problem by stressing the importance of education. The initial potentialities of a man are supposed to be such that, with rigorous training, he can achieve a disposition to act in complete accord with the factual and moral order of things. But success or failure seems to depend on Nature and external circumstances rather than anything for which the individual can reasonably be praised or blamed.

Having now sketched some of the characteristics and problems of Stoic ethics I turn to details, following Stoic methodology as far as possible. It will not be possible to discuss their historical background here (see p. 111), but readers familiar with Socratic, Platonic and Aristotelian ethics will notice many points of contact with Stoicism.

(ii) From primary impulse to virtue

Diogenes Laertius tells us that from Chrysippus onwards the Stoics divided the 'ethical part of philosophy' into a number of sub-sections (vii 84). From the arrangement which he cites Diogenes exempts the names of Zeno and Cleanthes, though he observes that 'they did divide (i.e. classify) ethics, logic and physics'. The earliest Stoics differed from later ones in treating ethics 'less methodically'. We know too little about Zeno and Cleanthes to make a precise assessment of Chrysippus' own ethical innovations. It is not likely that he differed greatly from them over matters of substance. The refinement and systematization of Stoic moral philosophy was probably his primary object in this field. Most of the evidence from which I will draw over the next few pages is certainly or possibly derived from the teaching of Chrysippus. And it may reasonably be assumed that the majority of doctrines discussed here are those which a Stoic in the middle of the Hellenistic period would have espoused.

The division of ethics attributed to Chrysippus specifies three broad categories: first, 'on impulse'; second, 'on good and bad things'; third, 'on passions'.[1] The first category is sub-divided into 'virtue'

[1] This interpretation of the ethical categories is also adopted by Zeller, *Phil. der Griechen*, vol. iii 2 p. 206 n. 1.

and 'the goal of action'; the second has as its sections, 'primary value', 'moral action' and 'appropriate acts'. Finally, after 'on passions', Diogenes lists a topic 'suasions and dissuasions' which is probably to be regarded as an appendix giving prescriptions and proscriptions based upon the theory already laid down. Diogenes' own summary and to a lesser extent Book iii of Cicero's *De finibus* and Arius Didymus' compendium in Stobaeus, correspond fairly precisely to this arrangement of subject-matter. It is a reasonable assumption that the extant hand-books of Stoic ethics reflect the Stoics' own order of presenting the subject.

Of our summaries the most informative from a philosophical point of view is undoubtedly Cicero's. Who his source or sources were we do not know, but Cicero refers by name to all the leading early Stoics and to Chrysippus in particular. The most interesting formal characteristic of Cicero's book is its logical, or would-be logical, coherence. The quality of argument is uneven, but this and a number of obscurities may be due to Cicero rather than any Stoic writer. What is undeniable is the attempt to present a set of moral truths which are so related that the last is entirely consistent with the first. Throughout the book logical connectives abound—'from which it follows that', 'since . . . it is necessary that', 'if . . . it does not follow that', etc., and the work as a whole seems to be designed to exhibit through language the coherence which the Stoics claimed to be characteristic of Nature. The procedure, like some of the thought itself, reminds one of nothing so much as the *mos geometricus* of Spinoza. Spinoza is of course still more formal, but his practice of setting down one continuous chain of reasoning consisting of propositions, proofs and corollaries would have won the firm approval of Chrysippus. The resemblances are not accidental. Like Spinoza the Stoics sought to deduce ethical conclusions from premises describing the all-inclusive attributes of a Nature which is perfect.

The starting-point of Stoic ethics is the 'primary impulse' of a new-born creature. Diogenes Laertius' evidence on this deserves to be quoted in full:

The Stoics say that an animal has self-protection as the object of its primary impulse, since Nature from the beginning endears it to itself, as Chrysippus says in his first book *On goals*: 'The first thing which is dear to every animal is its own constitution and awareness of this; for it was not likely that Nature estranged the animal from itself, nor that, having made it, Nature gave it no attitude of estrangement or endearment. It follows then that having constituted the animal Nature endeared it to itself; thus it is that the animal rejects what is harmful and pursues what is suitable (or akin) to itself.'

The assertion that pleasure is the object of animals' primary impulse is proved to be false by the Stoics. For pleasure, they claim, if it really exists, is a secondary product when and only when Nature by itself has searched out and adopted the things which are suitable to the animals' constitution; as such pleasure is like the flourishing of animals and the bloom of plants. Nature made no absolute distinction between plants and animals, for Nature directs plants too, independently of impulse and sensation, and in us certain processes of a vegetative kind take place. But since animals have the additional faculty of impulse, through the use of which they go in search of what is suitable to them, it is according to Nature for animals to be directed by impulse. And since reason in accord with a more perfect prescription has been bestowed on rational beings, life according to reason rightly becomes in accordance with their nature; for reason supervenes as the craftsman of impulse (vii 85–6).[1]

Something has already been said in this book about the concepts of impulse and self-endearment which are made use of in this passage (p. 172). Arguments concerning them were set out with great detail in more technical Stoic treatises, as we can tell from the fragmentary remains of Hierocles' *Foundations of ethics* (see p. 116). The writer of this work was at pains to demonstrate that the first thing of which a creature is aware is not something in the external world but itself. Self-awareness, he argues, is the precondition of perceiving externals; but to be aware of oneself is at the same time to picture oneself in relation to something else.[2] The infant's self-awareness is manifested by its relation to the mother's breast. Its perception of the latter is thus an integral part of its perception of itself. And if we ask, 'What attitude does a creature have towards the image of itself?' the answer must be affection. For all creatures, up to the limit of their power, strive to preserve themselves and to avoid things which are harmful.

The last statement may be treated as an empirical observation, but in the quotation which Diogenes preserves from Chrysippus it is also described as the work of Nature. This means that an animal's primary impulse to preserve itself is not only an objective fact but also something ordained by the being which is perfect in all respects. The primary impulse, because it has Nature's sanction, provides the

---

[1] For a detailed logical analysis of this passage cf. my paper, 'The Logical Basis of Stoic Ethics', *Proceedings of the Aristotelian Society* 1970/1, 85–104. My translation is reprinted from this paper.

[2] See further S. G. Pembroke, *Problems in Stoicism*, ch. 6 pp. 118f.

logical starting-point for Stoic ethics. Their procedure is of the greatest interest and has every claim to be called original.

If human beings possessed no reasoning faculty, self-preservation along the lines initially sketched out by Chrysippus would be the only natural, and hence the right or appropriate thing, for them to pursue. Food-gathering, fending off enemies, procreation, these are activities which an irrational animal perceives as belonging to itself, and in engaging upon them it acts naturally—that is, in the manner designed by Nature. It preserves itself—that is to say, what it recognizes as constituting itself—by doing such things. But are not such activities also natural to human beings? The Stoic answer to this question is complex, and our best approach to it will be through an extended quotation from the *De finibus*:

> Let us proceed therefore, since we have left these starting-points of Nature behind, and what follows must be consistent with them. One consequence is this primary classification: the Stoics say that that has value which is either itself in accordance with Nature or such as to bring about that state of affairs; accordingly it is worthy of being selected because it possesses something of sufficient moment to be valued, whereas the opposite of this is not to be valued. We have then established as basic principles that those things which are in accordance with Nature are to be acquired for their own sake and their opposites are to be rejected. The first appropriate function of a creature is to maintain itself in its natural condition. The second, that it should seize hold of the things which accord with Nature and banish those which are the opposite. Once this procedure of selection and rejection has been discovered, the next consequence is selection exercised appropriately; then, such selection performed continuously; finally, selection which is absolutely consistent and in complete agreement with Nature. At this point for the first time that which can truly be called good begins to be present in a man and understood. For a man's first affiliation is towards those things which are in accordance with Nature. But as soon as he has acquired the capacity for understanding or rather, a stock of rational concepts, and has seen the regularity and harmony of conduct, he values this far higher than everything for which he had previously felt affection, and he draws the rational conclusion that this constitutes the highest human good which is worthy of praise and desirable for its own sake. In this harmony consists the good which is the standard of all things; and so virtuous action and virtue itself, which is reckoned the only good thing, though later in origin, is the only thing to be desired through its intrinsic nature and worth. And none of the primary objects of natural affiliation is desirable for its own sake (*Fin.* iii 20–1).

This passage encapsulates the fundamental doctrines of Stoic ethics. Knowledge of 'what can truly be called good' and virtuous action are treated as the culminating stage in the development of a rational being. From infancy onwards a pattern of behaviour is sanctioned by Nature as appropriate to man (and other living creatures), but the pattern changes as man matures from a creature whose responses are purely animal-like and instinctive into an adult fully endowed with reason. Each of the five stages traced by Cicero assigns a function to human beings which is appropriate to them at particular periods of their development. Human nature, as so defined, is an evolving phenomenon, a concept which gives distinctive character to Stoic ethics. Things which are appropriate at an early stage do not cease to be such later. But their relation to the function of a man changes as he changes. Each new stage adds something which modifies the immediately preceding function. The goal of the progression is life in accordance with mature human nature, that is, a life governed by rational principles which are in complete harmony with the rationality, goals and processes of universal Nature.

The stages sketched out here give a normative account of the development of human nature. The majority of men never fully attain to the final stage, and many of them do not reach even the fourth. If this were a purely descriptive statement of evolution from infancy to maturity foolish or bad men would not exist. They do exist because, as we have seen, the perfection of human nature is not determined independently of a man's own efforts, as are his primary instinctive impulses. But the ultimate goal or function of a man *is* the perfection of his nature.

'Function' is a word which has occurred several times in the last two pages, and it may seem odd to designate moral behaviour as a human function. The problem is Cicero's term *officium*, the Latin translation of a Greek Stoic term, *kathêkon*. About this concept more will need to be said shortly. I will just remark here that 'function' seems to me to be the least misleading translation of the term in our present context. *Officium* is an ambiguous word. Like its English derivative, 'office', *officium* is regularly used in Latin for the task, function, or duty of an official—a consul, a legionary commander, and so forth. A consul is bound or obliged by his office to fulfil certain duties, but one cannot speak of the duties of an infant, much less the duties of animals and plants to which the Stoics also ascribed *kathêkonta*. A mature man, according to the Stoics, does have duties and this is an appropriate interpretation of *officium* from stages three to five. But what makes them duties is the fact that they are functions of a rational being. Nothing in the moral sense obliges a non-rational creature to behave in a certain way. It is therefore best to translate *officium* by 'function' throughout, while remembering that it carries connotations which are determined by the nature of the creature whose functions are under consideration.

(iii) The good and the preferable (natural advantages)

So much by way of general discussion. Cicero's text also provides an excellent jumping-off point for the treatment of a number of fundamental details, and we may take these in the order of his text. He begins with a brief statement of what it is for something to have 'value', and this has proved a problematic concept in the interpretation of Stoicism, but some of the difficulties which have been found in it are more apparent than real.[1] As Cicero explains, the value of anything in Stoicism is defined by reference to Nature. By capitalizing this term I wish to signify Nature in its universal sense but, as has already been explained, Nature can and often must be analysed as the structure and behaviour appropriate to particular things—the nature of a plant, the nature of an animal and so forth. Anything which accords with the nature of a creature necessarily has positive value, and anything which is contrary to a creature's nature necessarily has negative value (I refrain from using the obviously simpler words 'good' and 'bad' for a reason which will be stated later). The *nature* of anything is simply that structure and pattern of behaviour which universal Nature has ordained as appropriate or in the interests of the creature concerned.

Although anything, and above all virtue, has value because it accords with Nature, orthodox Stoics from Zeno onwards used the expression, 'things according to nature', to designate a particular class of valuable objects, the opposites of which were called 'things contrary to nature' (*SVF* iii 140–6). The class of such objects was also divided in such a way that some of them are marked off as 'the primary things according to (contrary to) nature'. Let us take the latter first. The word 'primary' refers to chronological priority, and we have seen that every living creature is credited with a primary impulse to preserve itself. Those things which it is instinctively impelled to pursue and to avoid are according to or contrary to its nature in this primary sense, and they include food of a certain kind,

---

[1] I. G. Kidd gives an illuminating discussion, *Classical Quarterly*, new series v, 1955, 181–94 = *Problems in Stoicism*, ch. 7.

shelter, and parental affection. But human beings, as they develop, experience a natural affiliation towards a wider range of things than irrational animals. In a list of things according to and contrary to nature we find technical competence, health, beauty, wealth, high repute, nobility of birth and their opposites (*SVF* iii 127). This list could be considerably extended, but the examples show that it includes mental and physical attributes and external possessions all of which were popularly regarded in antiquity, like today, as 'good' things. It accords with the nature of man that he should regard these favourably and reject their opposites. Cicero's second stage, the acquisition of 'things according to nature' and the rejection of their opposites, describes this function as it would be appropriately exercised by a young child. We do not expect young children to discriminate carefully between items towards which they are favourably disposed. It is through trying out and rejecting things that a child learns what it means to select in a discriminating way.

Before we consider Cicero's third stage it should be noted that the method of classifying things according to Nature does not comprise everything in the world. It is a matter of total indifference whether someone gesticulates this way or that (*SVF* iii 118). Human nature is not so constituted that a man has any built-in preference or aversion towards this and comparable things.

A young child is 'not yet rational', but the development of rationality is a continuous process which must be assumed to be well under way, though not perfected, at Cicero's third stage. Things which it was the function of a young child to pursue and to avoid instinctively, and other objects which are *naturally* attractive to more mature human beings, now present themselves as material for rational selection and rejection. The word 'rational' does not occur in Cicero's text at this point, but other evidence entitles us to supply it. As a human being acquires rationality this modification of his nature prescribes a new mode of appropriate behaviour. The function of a man is now to perform 'appropriate acts' (*kathêkonta*) the starting-point of which is not mere impulse or instinct but reason (*logos*). An appropriate act is defined as 'that which reason persuades one to do' (D.L. vii 108), or 'that which when done admits of reasonable justification' (ibid. 107). Inappropriate acts are defined in the opposite way.

Diogenes Laertius (loc. cit.) gives examples of 'appropriate acts': honouring parents, brothers, and native land, taking proper care of one's health, exercising by walking, sacrificing one's property. The last of these is only appropriate in certain circumstances, whereas the proper care of one's health is said to be 'unconditionally appropriate'. But the appropriateness of all these things rests on the fact that they accord with the nature of a rational being. That is to say, a man from the onset of rationality is supposed to recognize that the performance of such acts is 'becoming' to him. As rationality develops within a man the range of actions which it is 'appropriate' for him to perform becomes considerably enlarged. Cicero reports the Stoic view that 'we have been bound together and united by Nature for civic association' (*Fin.* iii 66). The social principles of Stoic ethics are derived from this impulse implanted by Nature to form familial and extra-familial relationships (*De off.* i 12). But the principle determining such behaviour is not regarded as different in kind from that which prompts more obviously self-regarding actions. The starting-point of justice is *oikeiôsis*, that attitude of attraction towards things which belong to oneself (*SVF* i 197), see p. 172. In its simplest and most basic analysis, moral development for the Stoics is the recognition that community life and virtue are pre-eminently things which belong to human nature.

Are we then to say that anyone who performs an 'appropriate' act does well? The answer to this question is negative. Following the dictates of reason is the appropriate function of a mature man, but reason, as we have seen, admits of the predicates 'right' or 'wrong', 'healthy' or 'unsound'. Any man who takes steps to maintain his physical well-being does something which is defensible on rational principles. But the mere fact that he does this tells us nothing about his moral qualities. He might be keeping fit for the purpose of robbing a bank. Or again, a man might behave patriotically solely because he is after a knighthood. These of course are extreme cases, and it is doubtful whether the Stoics would have regarded such acts as appropriate in any sense. But they help to show why the selection of something according to nature by a rational being is only a midway point in the acquisition of moral knowledge. It is certainly a necessary condition of virtuous action. The good man does everything in his power to promote the welfare of his country; he too is favourably disposed to 'the things according to nature'. But about him much more can be said than the fact that he is a rational being who selects such things and rejects their opposites.

The good man's selection is 'continuous'. He does not seek to promote his health and honour his parents, but ignore the interests of his country. All his behaviour is a continuous series of appropriate selections and rejections. What begins as something intermittent and erratic has become a disposition to act continuously on the basis of Nature's rational promptings. But continuity does not guarantee absolute consistency for the future. The good man is 'in complete agreement with Nature', a stage beyond 'continuity'. This means in Cicero's formulation that his scale of values changes or takes on a new dimension. The ever-growing consistency of his selection of natural advantages (performance of appropriate acts) brings a recognition that there is something of far greater worth than any of these objects, singly or collectively. Virtue is not defined by the consequences in the world which it succeeds in promoting, but by a pattern of behaviour that follows necessarily from a disposition perfectly in tune with Nature's rationality. The disposition to behave in such a way is not inconsistent with earlier human functions. Like all men the Stoic sage is predisposed to look after his health and his property. But he does not regard such natural advantages as things which are desirable for their own sake. He selects them if and only if his reason dictates that this is the right thing to do. The right thing to do is that which accords with virtue, and this is equivalent to saying that it accords with the nature of a perfect rational being. Only virtue has absolute or intrinsic worth. Natural advantages can be used well or badly and the same holds good for natural disadvantages (*SVF* iii 123). The sage will make good use of poverty, if it comes his way; and a foolish man may use wealth badly. This does not undermine the objective fact that wealth is preferable to poverty. But wealth is not a constituent of virtue. The moral value of selecting wealth depends entirely upon the agent's principles and manner of acting.

The Stoics expressed this difference between the value of virtue and that of other things by a number of linguistic and conceptual distinctions. Both virtue and wealth accord with Nature, but they accord with it in different ways. Virtue accords with Nature in the sense that it is the special function or goal of a rational being to be virtuous (D.L. vii 94). This statement is not relative to circumstances. It applies absolutely and unequivocally to all mature men. Wealth accords with Nature in the sense that a rational being is naturally predisposed to prefer wealth to poverty if it is open to him to select either of these. Wealth is a state which is objectively preferable to poverty, but wealth is not something which it is the special function of a rational being to possess. The value of wealth is relative to poverty, but wealth has no value relative to virtue. Morally speaking, wealth and poverty are indifferent; for it makes no difference to a man's moral worth (or welfare) whether he is rich or poor (*SVF* iii 145–6). In order to make the value of virtue sharply distinct from that of natural advantages like wealth the Stoics confined the reference of the ordinary Greek words for 'good' and 'bad', 'advantageous' and 'disadvantageous', 'useful' and 'useless' to virtue and vice respectively. ['The good' and 'the profitable' are logically equivalent (see p. 138).] Everything else is indifferent so far as moral judgments are concerned. But within the category of 'indifferent' things, the natural advantages are marked off as 'preferred' or 'preferable' and their opposites are similarly classified as 'things to be rejected'. The same distinction is observed in other ways: only virtue is 'choiceworthy' or 'desirable'. Natural advantages are 'to be selected' or 'to be taken'.

Ancient critics of the Stoa regarded these as pettifogging and incoherent distinctions. But before we consider what can be said for and against them it will be useful to quote some passages which help to elucidate the Stoic point of view. The most Cynic of the Stoics, Ariston, refused to make judgments of value about anything apart from virtue and vice (*SVF* i 351–69). This unorthodox position is criticized in Cicero's *De finibus*:

> The next subject is a way of differentiating things without which life would be turned into utter confusion, as it is by Ariston, and no function or work for wisdom could be found. For (under Ariston's procedure) there would be absolutely no difference between those things which affect the conduct of life and it would not be incumbent on us to make any discrimination between such things. Thus, although it has been adequately settled that the only good thing is virtue and the only bad thing vice, yet the Stoics wished there to be something to differentiate those things which have no significance for the actual happiness or unhappiness of life, in such a way that some of them are to be valued positively others negatively, and still others neither positively nor negatively. . . . Suppose we imagine that the final goal of action is to throw a die in such a way that it stands upright; a die so thrown will possess something 'preferable' with respect to this goal, yet the goal itself is not affected by the die's 'preferability'; similarly, those things which are 'preferred' have reference to the goal of life, but they do not affect its own meaning and nature (iii 50–4).

A further analogy might express the point more clearly. Until now no man has set foot on the planet Mars, but scientists are working to make such an event practically possible. Their goal is to land a man on Mars, and some day this goal may be achieved. But the goal is what it is independently of anyone's achieving it. One can ask questions about whether the efforts in promoting the goal are worthwhile or not irrespective of anything that may result from success. The goal of life according to the Stoics is virtue and virtuous action, but in order to achieve this goal a man must aim at particular goals which can be specified precisely. The virtuous man, if he has the opportunity, will engage in political life, marry, rear children, take exercise, study philosophy, and so forth (D.L. vii 121f.). All these things are objectively 'preferable' to their opposites, and worth making effort to achieve. But in aiming at them the good man always has a more comprehensive goal than the object which defines his particular action.[1] His comprehensive or ultimate goal is consistently virtuous behaviour, and at this he can always be successful whether or not he achieves each particular goal. The comprehensive goal is achieved by the qualities of rational discrimination and effort which go into the attempt to secure particular goals. Natural advantages and disadvantages are not constituents of virtue. But they are a necessary condition of virtue for at least two reasons.

First, complete knowledge of that which is good (Cicero's fifth stage) presupposes and arises out of a disposition to select natural advantages and reject their opposites on the promptings of reason (*Fin.* iii 23, 31). Secondly, they provide the 'material' for the exercise of virtue or vice (ibid. 61). The objection to Ariston takes its force from this point. Any virtuous action must aim at bringing about some change in the external world, and merely to say that someone acted virtuously or from the best intentions tells us nothing about what he did or tried to do. The distinction between natural advantages and disadvantages is valid independently of an agent's intentions and it makes possible the specification of a set of 'intermediate' goals which will normally include anything aimed at by a good man (and many things aimed at by men who are not good). I say 'normally' because exceptional circumstances may justify the promotion of a goal which is not 'preferred'. Chrysippus had this in mind when he wrote:

So long as the succession of events is uncertain to me I always cling fast to the things which are better adapted for the attainment of natural advantages; for God himself has given me the capacity to select such things. But if I knew that sickness was ordained for me now, I would pursue sickness (*SVF* iii 191).

[1] Later Stoics used two different terms to distinguish the 'comprehensive' from the 'intermediate' goal. I have discussed this in 'Carneades and the Stoic Telos', *Phronesis* xii (1967) 78ff.

Universal Nature's ordinances for a man may include a large supply of things which are natural disadvantages. The good man, if he knows or has good reason to believe in advance that these are in store for him, will accept them gladly. But without such knowledge he will adhere to Chrysippus' principle. If his pursuit of health is unsuccessful, well and good. The moral worth of the action is not affected, and lack of success does not show that he was wrong to try. It is preferable to succeed but not morally more worthwhile.

Diogenes of Babylon, who was Chrysippus' successor as head of the Stoa, defined the goal of life in the formula: 'to act rationally [i.e. with right reasoning] in the selection of natural advantages' (D.L. vii 88). This prescription clearly sums up the general doctrine which has just been outlined, and it is possible that some of Cicero's Stoic material in the *De finibus* is expressed in Diogenes' formulations which may not always have been those used by Chrysippus. But there is no compelling reason to assume any divergence of opinion between these two Stoics on the relation of virtue to natural advantages.[1] Apart from the quotation of Chrysippus just referred to, we find Plutarch criticizing the Stoics in general for trying to have it both ways:

> By their actions they lay hold on natural advantages as if they are to be chosen and good, but in their terminology they renounce and revile them as indifferent, useless and of no weight with regard to well-being (*Comm. not.* 1070a).

Plutarch also attacks Chrysippus personally on the same lines in a number of places (e.g. *Stoic. rep.* 1042c–d). Diogenes' definition of the goal is an explicit statement of the orthodox Stoic position. Natural advantages have no moral value in themselves, but they provide the material or the means to exercise rational discrimination, which is morally good.

There were many in antiquity who shared Plutarch's contemptuous attitude. The fundamental criticism began with Carneades. He argued that the goal of engaging in any rational activity must be the actual attainment of something which is not contained in the activity itself (Cic. *Fin.* v 16): the Stoics have a good candidate for this, natural advantages, but they insist that the attainment of these is not the ultimate object of activities which are defined by reference to them.

[1] A similar view is taken by I. G. Kidd (cited on p. 189), who argues, to my mind convincingly, that the Stoics did not at any time differ significantly from one another on the status of natural advantages. For other opinions Kidd's paper should be consulted.

In fact, a formulation of the goal by Antipater, Diogenes' successor, does include the words, 'the attainment of natural advantages'. Antipater is credited with this formulation: 'doing everything in one's power to attain the primary natural advantages' (*SVF* iii Ant. 57). I have argued elsewhere that this formulation of Antipater's was prompted by Carneades' criticism of Diogenes' definition.[1] By substituting the expression 'efforts to attain' for Diogenes' 'rationally select', Antipater, as I understand him, accepted Carneades' insistence that 'the attainment of natural advantages' is implied as a goal by the Stoics. But he stipulated that the value of this goal is subordinate to the value of trying one's best to achieve it. It is probable that Antipater with this formulation did not intend to deviate from the doctrines of his predecessors. But as an answer to Carneades it played into the Sceptic's own hands and left the Stoa in an even more equivocal position. In Diogenes' formula, which Antipater also used (perhaps at an earlier stage of his career), the moral value of selecting natural advantages rests upon the opportunity this provides for exercising right reason. But Antipater's new formula makes no explicit reference to right reason. The natural inference which an opponent can draw from the words 'making continuous and infallible efforts to attain natural advantages' is the unqualified desirability of possessing such things. Antipater did not mean this, since he devoted three books to proving that virtue is sufficient on its own to provide well-being (*SVF* iii Ant. 56). But he could fairly be taken to imply it, and a fellow-Stoic, Posidonius, was later to object that the notion of 'life consistent with reason' should not be contracted into 'doing everything possible for the sake of the primary natural advantages' (*SVF* iii 12).

The distinction between 'the good' and 'the preferable' was also attacked from several points of view by the eclectic Academic philosopher, Antiochus of Ascalon. 'The good', so Antiochus argued, ought to include the satisfaction of those natural impulses from which it is supposedly derived (Cic. *Fin.* iv 25–8). He charged the Stoics with treating man as if he were a disembodied mind needing nothing from the physical environment. Why, Antiochus asked, are natural advan-

---

[1] In *Phronesis*, cited on p. 194. The relative dates of Diogenes and Carneades, along with Plutarch's reference to Antipater's being 'forced into verbal quibbling by the harassment of Carneades' (*Comm. not.* 1072f.), make it most unlikely that Diogenes' formulation was prompted by Carneades. For an interpretation of Antipater's definition which differs somewhat from my own cf. M. Soreth in *Archiv für Geschichte der Philosophie* 50 (1968) 48–72.

tages to be selected if the possession of them is not something 'good'? (ibid. 71f.). He was fully prepared to grant pre-eminent value to virtue (*Fin.* v 38). But virtue is not the only good thing, even if it outstrips the worth of everything else. There are bodily 'goods' which make a difference, however slight, to the sum total of human well-being (ibid. 71f.).

Was Antiochus right? Are the Stoics, as he held, to be interpreted as smuggling in a variety of 'goods' under a new terminology? Or is the distinction between 'the good' and 'the preferable' a coherent and valid one? The answer to these questions must depend to some extent on the critic's own moral theory. A Kantian will find different things to object to in Stoicism from a utilitarian. But any philosopher is likely to have difficulty with one Stoic concept about which little has been said so far. The Stoics claimed that virtue, the comprehensive goal of human nature, is wholly constitutive of *eudaimonia*, happiness, welfare or well-being: in order to fare well a man needs nothing but virtue, and as virtue is something absolute, welfare admits of no degrees (Cic. *Fin.* iii 43ff., D.L. vii 96). Compare this position with the more realistic view of Aristotle. He defined *eudaimonia* as 'activity of soul in accordance with virtue', but recognized that it also requires adequate provision of possessions, health and other 'goods'. The concept of welfare seems to be logically tied up with notions like useful, beneficial, profitable, and the Stoics themselves recognized this.[1] Virtue, which constitutes welfare for them, is profitable to its possessor. But once welfare has been admitted as 'the good for man', it seems to be arbitrary and false to assert that nothing except virtue identifies the content of welfare.

An even more serious difficulty arises if we turn to consider the welfare of others. Take the case of a child which is in danger of burning to death in its bed. The Stoics would recognize that a virtuous man will do everything in his power to avert this happening. In this case we might be prepared to agree with them that a man who so acted would in some sense fare well, if virtuous acts are beneficial to their agents. But part of the value of the action must consist in the external object which is its goal, the welfare of a child. The Stoics agree that the object has value, but it is something 'preferred' and not 'good'. Many will think that it makes far better moral sense to say that both the action and its external object were good. Good was done by the virtuous man's efforts to promote another's welfare; still more good

[1] cf. G. H. von Wright *The Varieties of Goodness* (London 1963) p. 87.

would have come from success. The Stoics recognized rightly that
the goodness of an intention or principle of action must be evaluated
independently of a man's achieving some desirable result, and their
emphasis on this point is one of the most important aspects of their
ethics. But their terminological distinctions may be thought to introduce more confusion than clarification. What makes motives or
intentions commendable is the good which the agent sought to produce. If we call that 'good' the 'preferable', following the Stoics, we
obscure the relation between the value of a morally good action and
the value of the change in the world at which it is aimed.

Furthermore, a man's moral worth, one could argue, is partly
demonstrated by the attitude which he has towards success or failure
at achieving morally desirable results. We would normally think less
well of a man who felt no sorrow or regret that he was unable to save
a child's life in spite of all his efforts to do so. The Stoics however
argued quite differently. The virtuous man, having done everything
in his power, does not feel pity or regret (*SVF* iii 450–2). He accepts
what happens without reacting emotionally. This seems such a strange
notion that it calls for a different approach to our problem. We shall
misunderstand the distinctions of value which have just been discussed
unless we place them in the context of Stoic ideas encountered earlier
in this book.

A man, as I have repeatedly stressed, is an integral part of the
Stoic universe. The external circumstances of his whole life are an
episode in the life of universal Nature, and they are 'in his power'
only to the extent that he can choose to accept them or not when they
occur. If he is a convinced Stoic he will accept them all gladly, on the
understanding that they contribute to the well-being of the universe
as a whole. But even a convinced Stoic is not omniscient. After something has happened he can say, 'Be it so', but not before. He is not a
mere spectator of events, but an active agent himself. Before he goes
to bed the Stoic will consider what may be the circumstances of
tomorrow, and in advance of their happening he is more favourably
disposed to some events than to others. He would prefer all manner
of things for other people and himself to their opposites, and so far
as he is able he seeks to bring about these preferable states of affairs.
His preferences are perfectly rational, that is, they fully accord with
an objective assessment of the relative merits of external things as
determined by Nature itself. But he does not regard the things which
he prefers as good, nor does he desire them. Why not? The answer to

this has been partly outlined already. Viewed as an event which forms part of Nature's universal harmony, anything that happens is good. But, in his imperfect knowledge, the Stoic may be perfectly justified in preferring something which does not happen. Yet it would have happened if Nature had determined that it should. Therefore it was not good that it should happen. Towards future events the Stoic maintains an attitude of preference or rejection. He is in no position to judge of their goodness, and therefore views the future with relative indifference. This is something of concern to Nature alone who embraces all things.[1]

For similar reasons, if the Stoic's own well-being is to be 'in his power' it cannot depend on the attainment of results which may not be realized. But something is in the Stoic's own power, namely his disposition as a rational man. Nature ordains that a man can and should attain well-being solely through what is in his own power. This means through virtue, the only good. Virtue is a 'consistently rational disposition' (*SVF* i 202), and its value is something different in kind from natural advantages. They are things which a man can take if he encounters them, but virtue is something he can choose irrespective of circumstances. Natural advantages supply a man with objective goals at which he can choose to aim, and the material for forming his own moral principles. They are necessary to virtue only as means by which it can be exercised, and not as things which it needs for their own sake.[2]

(iv) *The content of virtue: perfect and 'intermediate' actions*

Let us recall what has so far been said about virtue. First of all, it is the one thing to which 'good' belongs in a strict and necessary sense; nothing else, for example an action, can be good unless it 'participates' in virtue (*SVF* i 190, iii 76). In a definition of virtue with which the names of Zeno, Ariston, Chrysippus and Menedemus, a Cynic, are associated it is said to be a disposition and faculty of the governing-principle of the soul, 'or rather: reason itself, consistent, firm and unwavering' (*SVF* i 202). Secondly, virtue is the goal which Nature

---

[1] See further Victor Goldschmidt, *Le Système stoicien et l'idée de temps* (Paris 1969), who relates the Stoics' stress on the importance of each present moment to their idea that future consequences have no bearing on the virtue of an action, pp. 145–51.

[2] For a comparison of the Stoics' position and Aristotle's *vis-à-vis* external goods see my discussion in *Bulletin of the Institute of Classical Studies* 15 (1968) 74–6.

has laid down for man. Thirdly, the earlier stages of a man's development are necessary to virtue as providing patterns of appropriate behaviour out of which it can arise. But this is a very abstract account. Can we fill out the content of virtue and state more fully what it means to be virtuous?

Virtue is a kind of 'knowledge' or 'art' (*SVF* iii 256, 202). It is a unitary disposition of the soul which can be analysed into four primary virtues: practical wisdom, justice, moderation and courage.[1] Each of these is defined in terms of knowledge: for instance, courage is 'knowledge of things which should be endured' (*SVF* iii 285). To have this knowledge or the knowledge which belongs to any particular virtue it is necessary to have the knowledge constitutive of virtue as a whole. The influence of Socrates and Plato is plainly evident here.

The virtuous man's knowledge is grasped by his intellect, but as steps preliminary to its acquisition he uses the evidence of sense-perception. After sketching out the stages of man's moral development Cicero amplifies his account of 'knowledge of the good' in the following passage:

> After the mind by means of rational inference has climbed up from those things which are in accordance with Nature it arrives at the idea of the good. But we perceive the good and name it so not as a result of addition or growth or comparison with other things but through its own specific nature. Honey, though it is very sweet, is perceived to be sweet by its own taste and not through comparison with other (sweet) things; similarly that good, which is our subject, is something of the highest value, but this assessment is valid because of the kind of thing the good is, not because of its size (*Fin.* iii 33–4).

Cicero's language recalls the famous passage in Book vi of Plato's *Republic* (509c–511e) according to which the philosopher ascends to knowledge of the good by the help of 'hypotheses' about the objects of sight and intellect. Cicero seems to be describing a comparable methodology. The 'things which accord with Nature' serve as stepping-stones to reach a principle which is *sui generis* and cannot be inferred directly from them. They are the 'preferable' objects of instinctive and, later, rational selection. The fact that 'the good' is not intuited by a simple comparison with these natural advantages does not mean that 'the good' falls outside things which accord with Nature. Cicero's

---

[1] These primary virtues each admit of sub-divisions. For example, justice embraces piety, kindness, fellow-feeling and fair dealing (*SVF* iii 264).

illustration makes this clear. We can get a notion of sweetness by tasting a number of sweet things; but tasting an apple will not provide an idea of the sweetness of Turkish delight. Accordance with Nature takes the place of sweetness in the illustration. Different things can provide an idea of being in accordance with Nature, but 'the good' accords with Nature in a sense which is beyond anything else. Other things provide the mind with a ladder which can help it up to a position from which 'the good' is directly apprehended through its own nature. How are we to interpret this conception in practical terms? Clearly no account can be fully adequate. Only he who has seen 'the good' knows precisely what it is. But we can conjecture what it entails. To know 'the good' means discovering a principle of conduct which satisfies the general idea of 'accordance with Nature', formed by induction and introspection, and the particular facts of human nature— that man is a rational being with the capacity to understand and participate in the universal activities of Nature.

One of Seneca's letters allows us to be still more specific. Seneca poses the question: 'How do we attain our first concept of the good and virtue?' (*Ep.* 120). It is not an innate human endowment, and it would be absurd to suppose that man hit upon it by chance. Seneca next lays it down that the antecedents of moral knowledge are 'observation' and 'comparison' of repeated acts. Without explaining this statement he continues: 'Our school of philosophers claims that what is good and of moral worth is learnt by means of "analogy"', and this last term he does explain. By analogy with physical health, a (natural) condition which is familiar to us, we have inferred (*collegimus*) that there is such a thing as health of mind.[1]

There are certain acts of generosity, or of humanity or courage, which have amazed us. We begin to admire them as if they were perfect. But they conceal many faults which are hidden by their appearance of something brilliant; and we have overlooked these. Nature bids us to augment praiseworthy actions.... From them therefore we have derived an idea of remarkable goodness.

Seneca proceeds to illustrate his theory by examples. By analogy with bodily health we learn that there is such a thing as health of mind; but that is not sufficient to show what health of mind is. In order to give

---

[1] Seneca's account is consistent with the brief statement: 'something just and good is conceived of *naturally*' (D.L. vii 53). To reason by analogy is natural to man. It is also Plato's regular practice to describe conditions of the soul in terms of health and sickness, e.g. *Rep.* 444c–e.

content to our general concept observation is necessary: we form an idea of courage by observing and comparing the behaviour of individual men. Seneca then draws distinctions between 'prodigality' and 'generosity', 'courage' and 'foolhardiness'. 'The similarity between these forces us to take thought and to distinguish things which are related in appearance but are immensely different in fact. In observing men who have become famous through doing some outstanding act we begin to note the sort of man who has done something with magnanimity and great zeal, but once only.' We see men who show courage in war but not in other spheres of life. 'Another man, whom we see, is kindly towards his friends, unimpassioned towards his enemies, dutiful in his public and private behaviour.' This kind of man is 'always consistent with himself in every action, good not through policy but under the direction of a disposition such that he is able not only to act rightly but cannot act without acting rightly. In him we recognize that virtue has been perfected.'

According to this theory our general concept of virtue is refined by observation. We learn to distinguish isolated acts of quasi-courage from the conduct of a man who always shows fortitude. Does this mean that the moral concepts which men form are relative to their experience? The Stoics tried to avoid the problems of relativism by setting up the sage as a paradigm and giving detailed descriptions of his disposition and of the kinds of things that he does. Imitation of the sage or actual good men cannot ensure virtue, but it can certainly set a man on the right road to secure it. We might sum up by saying that all men naturally form general concepts of value. Nature's part is to give man the equipment to form such concepts and the ability to think analogically. But virtue or knowledge of what is truly good does not follow necessarily from these faculties. To know what is truly good a man has to consider what is involved in the performance of, say, a courageous action and to ask himself why a man who acts apparently well in one sphere can fail to do so in another. That is to say, he needs to grasp what is needed if a man is to act well in all spheres at all times. The conditions nominated by Cicero and Seneca alike are orderliness, propriety, consistency and harmony. To know what all of these are is to know what is good.

'The good' is prior in value to anything else, but so far as any individual man is concerned it is posterior in time to other valuable things. A man can only come to recognize 'the good' after he has learnt to select natural advantages and to reject their opposites in a regular and systematic pattern of action. We may remind ourselves that natural advantages include all those states of affairs which, though not constituents of virtue, are objectively (or Naturally) preferable to their opposites. In most circumstances natural advantages are the intermediate goals at which the good man aims, but it is not necessary to be a good man to aim at these things. On the contrary, the good man was aiming at them before he became good and all men do so to a lesser or greater degree. It is not the special mark of a good man to select natural advantages but to do so in a certain way and on the basis of certain principles (*SVF* iii 516). The changes in the world which the good man seeks to bring about are all prompted by virtuous motives. But viewed objectively or externally they do not differ necessarily from the goals of foolish men, the other category of mankind.

Suppose that we observe a man taking exercise. According to the Stoics this is an 'appropriate' thing to do, for good physical health is a natural advantage. But on the basis of our specific observation we cannot form a judgment about this man's moral character. Cicero makes a similar point taking the example of 'returning a deposit' (*Fin.* iii 58f.). This too is something appropriate; it is justifiable on rational grounds and to accomplish such a transaction is a 'preferable' state of affairs. But there is a great deal of difference between returning a deposit and doing this 'rightly'. The former is merely 'appropriate', whereas the latter is 'perfectly appropriate'. But both actions have the same 'intermediate' goal. The expression 'intermediate goal' was used earlier in our discussion to distinguish the sage's aim to select natural advantages from his comprehensive goal, virtuous action. But natural advantages stand as 'intermediate goals' in the further sense that they are 'neither good nor bad'.

If an appropriate action is considered independently of the character of its agent it must be judged 'intermediate'.[1] But in terms of the agent's character every action, whether appropriate or not, is either 'perfect' or 'faulty'. The 'faultiness' of an appropriate act can have nothing to do with its external object.[2] Only 'inappropriate' acts are

---

[1] cf. J. M. Rist, *Stoic Philosophy*, pp. 98ff.

[2] This should not be taken to mean that an appropriate act is faulty if it fails to secure the object aimed at. I. G. Kidd argues that 'the whole stress of *kathē-konta* lies in the object of the act being achieved' (*Problems in Stoicism*, p. 155), but no evidence seems to require this conclusion. It must in certain circumstances be sufficient to have tried but failed, though the efforts of a foolish man will be defective by comparison with those of a sage. My thinking on this point has been influenced by discussion with Professor P. A. Brunt.

faulty in this respect. But if an appropriate act is performed by someone who is not a sage it lacks the fundamental characteristic of fitting
into a pattern of actions all of which are completely harmonious with
each other. Of the man who has advanced to the point when he only
just falls short of wisdom or perfection Chrysippus wrote:

> He fulfils all appropriate actions in all respects and omits none; but his life
> is *not yet* in a state of well-being. This supervenes when these 'intermediate'
> actions acquire the additional property of firmness, consistency and their
> own proper co-ordination (*SVF* iii 510).

Here of course we have an extreme case. Most performers of appropriate acts will by no means fulfil all of them, and will thereby be
still further away from the absolute harmony characteristic of virtue.
In respect of *what* he does Chrysippus' man must be classified with
the sage, but in respect of his character he is to be judged still 'foolish'.[1]
In Stoic ethics a miss is as bad as a mile. There are no degrees of
goodness, though there are degrees of coming closer towards it. But
until a man is good he is bad (*SVF* iii 657–70). The minute element of
disharmony present in a man who has nearly reached the top is sufficient to disqualify anything that he does from the accolade of virtue.

This is a hard doctrine, and it is made all the harder by the Stoics'
own reservations on the actual existence of any man who has made the
grade. Chrysippus himself admitted the enormous gap which Stoicism
admits between theory and practical achievement:

> Wherefore on account of their extreme magnitude and beauty we seem to be
> stating things which are like fictions and not in accordance with man and
> human nature (*SVF* iii 545).

But if human nature is perfectible nothing short of its perfection can
be admissible as the ultimate goal. Stoic ethics is an epitome of idealism. The sage, to whom every commendatory epithet belongs, is not
found in everyday life. He is a perfect man, whose character mirrors
the perfection of Nature. Judged by the standards of the sage we are
all foolish or bad. But through assiduous effort and education the
theory is that we can progress to a condition which approximates to

---

[1] Seneca observes that 'precepts' can only lead to 'right actions' if a man's
character is compliant; they may tell one what to do but not *how* to live virtuously
(*Ep.* 95). It is of interest to compare the Stoics' view with W. D. Ross's claim in
The Right and the Good (Oxford 1930) that 'right' and 'wrong' refer entirely to
the thing done; 'morally good' and 'morally bad' to the motive of the agent, p. 7.

perfection. If virtue is to be something supremely worthwhile it deserves every effort on the part of man, and the ideal sage persists as a standard to which we may seek to conform ourselves.

The Stoics developed a radical political theory around this concept of the sage. I have already referred to Zeno's *Republic* in which the fundamental social and economic institutions of the Greek world are abolished (p. 110). In the ideal world the state withers away because each Stoic sage is self-sufficient and his own authority (*SVF* iii 617). But he is united with his fellows by the bond of friendship, for all wise men are friends to each other and it is only between them that friendship in its true sense can exist (*SVF* iii 625). A communal way of life which dispenses with all distinctions based upon sex, birth, nationality, and property—this is the pattern of social behaviour. The theory is utopian and was recognized to be such. But its interest lies in the criticism of contemporary society which it implies. Stoic political theory is not a blue-print for reform but a paradigm of the world as it might be if men could be united not by artificial ties but by the recognition in each other of common values and common purposes. Money, family, and hereditary status are all seen as divisive factors. They have nothing to do with being virtuous and virtue has everything to do with the ideal state.

Stoicism never lost its idealistic character. But over the years individual Stoic leaders gave increasing attention to the detailed analysis of practical moral principles for the guidance of day-to-day behaviour. The work which has proved most influential was done by Panaetius, but before we come to this it will be worthwhile to pause a little longer over the Stoic sage and his perfect actions.

(v) The Stoic sage: tests of virtue

The sage is defined by his moral expertise. He knows infallibly what should be done in each situation of life and takes every step to do it at the right time and in the right way. But suppose that we wish to form a judgment about the moral status of some man whom we are observing. Are there any tests which can be applied, independently of his own statements about himself, from which we may form a reasonable opinion? It is not sufficient that he should be seen to perform 'appropriate' actions, since these do not, on the Stoic concept of character or disposition, give any necessary indication of an agent's state of mind. Sextus Empiricus argues that the Stoics are unable to supply evidence from which the 'wise disposition' of the sage can be established (*Adv. math.* xi 200–6). He considers a further test, 'steadiness and orderliness', and claims that this too is illusory since the wise man must be always adapting himself to changing circumstances (ibid. 207–9). But this criticism misses the point. It is perfectly possible to act differently according to changing events and maintain steady and consistent moral principles. One characteristic of the sage which Sextus fails to mention is 'timely' behaviour.[1] The Stoics justified suicide on the grounds that such an act might in extreme circumstances be the rational thing to do.[2] Suicide cannot be formulated in a general rule, such as the appropriateness of maintaining one's health. The preservation of one's life is what accords with human nature in most situations. But many of the things which accord with human nature are not unconditionally appropriate. 'Good timing' in the Stoics' sense has been well described as 'the point at which the process of a man's actions meets and coincides with those events which are the result of a series of causes called Fate'.[3] Suicide is an extreme example of conduct inimical to a man's own interests in most circumstances which might be rationally defended in certain situations. If we were to observe a man whose conduct had always satisfied all general principles of appropriateness—he had looked after his health, his family, his property, and the interests of others—voluntarily submitting himself to unjust imprisonment, torture or public vilification, or even taking his own life or that of a relative suffering from a most painful and fatal disease, there would be reason to regard such a man as a possible candidate for being a sage. The Stoics' defence of cannibalism, incest and non-burial, under exceptional circumstances (*SVF* ii 743–56), is to be placed in this context of 'timely' action.

But there is a more important test which we could perform. The Stoic sage is free from all passion. Anger, anxiety, cupidity, dread, elation, these and similar extreme emotions are all absent from his disposition. He does not regard pleasure as something good, nor pain as something evil. Many of a person's pleasures or pains are things which he can keep to himself, but it is difficult to conceive of someone subject to anger, dread or elation who never revealed his state of mind to an outside observer. The Stoic sage is not insensitive to painful or pleasurable sensations, but they do not 'move his soul excessively'.

[1] *SVF* iii 630; the Latin word is *opportune*, cf. Cic. *Fin.* iii 61.
[2] J. M. Rist has a good discussion of Stoic attitudes to suicide, *Stoic Philosophy*, ch. 13.
[3] D. Tsekourakis, *Studies in the Terminology of Early Stoic Ethics*, Ph.D. dissertation of London University (1971) pp. 91–2.

He is impassive towards them. But he is not entirely impassive, contrary to the popular conception of a Stoic. As I noted earlier (p. 176 n. 2), his disposition is characterized by 'good emotional states'. Well-wishing, wishing another man good things for his sake; joy: rejoicing in virtuous actions, a tranquil life, a good conscience (Sen. *Ep.* 23, 2); and 'wariness', reasonable disinclination. Like Aristotle the Stoics regarded the emotional attitude which accompanies actions as an index of moral character.[1]

The absence of passion and the presence of the qualities just enumerated provide an objective measuring-stick for sorting out possible sages from other men. Added to the tests already mentioned, they set up a canon of excellence which could within limits be vouched for by an observer if any candidates were forthcoming. It is not surprising that Stoic philosophers themselves did not pass the examination and knew of none who had done so.

The starting-point of this long chapter was a quotation which spoke of the 'remarkable coherence' of Stoicism. Unlike Aristotle the Stoics did not regard ethics as a science the subject-matter of which is imprecise by contrast with that of metaphysics. As moral philosophers the Stoics sought to establish a set of values and principles of conduct which would be as securely based as the laws of Nature from which they were derived. The concept of 'consequence' or 'what follows from what' is the lynch-pin of their entire system. The laws of the universe are manifested by a strict causal nexus. As a natural philosopher the Stoic describes the effects of this system, as a logician he analyses what can be said about it and the truths which it sanctions, and as a moral philosopher he looks at its implications for human well-being and conduct. We have seen that the system is incoherent, or verges on incoherence, at certain crucial points. Two fundamental and related difficulties are first, the usage of Nature both to describe objective facts and to sanction values, and second, the concept of 'rational assent' as something 'in our power' at the level of subjective consciousness and yet apparently determined objectively by the necessary sequence of cause and effect. The Stoics showed considerable ingenuity in attempting to resolve these dilemmas, but the result is not ultimately satisfactory.

But, for all that we know at the present time, free will is nothing more than a phenomenon of human consciousness. Possibly human

[1] For a comparison between the two, cf. pp. 79–82 of the article cited in n. 2 p. 199. More generally, J. M. Rist, *Stoic Philosophy*, ch. 3.

actions are causally related to antecedent events in a manner which could in principle be fully explained by the laws of physics and chemistry. If this is the case, it might have a marked effect on our concept of moral responsibility. But the need to evaluate actions and to designate certain states of affairs as better than others would still exist. Part of the contemporary interest of Stoicism lies in its attempt to square a highly elaborated moral theory with objective facts, facts which take account of innate human drives, environmental influences and laws governing all natural phenomena.

There are many other details, some of which I have remarked, that bear upon modern interests. Yet, in the last resort, Stoicism defies any simple comparison with developments which come before or after it. The Stoics offer a complete world picture and in a sense, as they themselves observed, one must swallow the whole thing or none of it. Points on which they seem to agree with other philosophers must always be considered in the context of the total system. If we ask which moral philosopher of subsequent times comes closest to the Stoics two candidates are particularly worthy of mention. Kant, who was certainly influenced by them, is a strong contender.[1] His 'categorical imperative', something 'conceived as good *in itself* and consequently as being necessarily the principle of a will which of itself conforms to reason' (*Ethics* 38), looks very like the Stoic 'right reason'. The value which the Stoics placed upon the subjective content of a moral action, and the relation of this to objective necessity or universal law, can hardly be accidental points of resemblance with Kantian ethics. But for Kant welfare or happiness is not a constituent of moral goodness, whereas Stoic virtue constitutes something which is in the interests of man *par excellence*. *Pflicht* (duty) and *Wille* (will) have nothing in Stoicism which corresponds to them with any precision, yet they are fundamental Kantian concepts.

Another strong contender is Spinoza. Consider his proposition: 'In the nature of things nothing contingent is granted, but all things are determined by the necessity of divine nature for existing and working in a certain way' (*Ethics*, part I prop. xxix). Or, 'All ideas, in so far as they have reference to God [sc. or Nature], are true' (part II prop. xxxii). But Spinoza renounced the conventional meanings of virtue and vice. More rigorously determinist than the Stoics, he totally rejected the idea of any purpose which a person is designed to

[1] cf. W. Schinck, 'Kant und die stoische Ethik', *Kant Studien* xviii (1913) 419–75.

fulfil. Like the Stoics he regarded happiness as wholly dependent upon understanding Nature and man's place in it. And he also stressed, as they did, the necessity of grasping the causes of man's passionate love and hatred of objects which have no relevance to happiness. But the 'freedom' of mind which such understanding can bring, though strikingly similar to the state of the Stoic sage, is not a goal which Spinoza's Nature sets man to achieve. Spinoza would have nothing to do with final causes. Pleasure and prudence, not Nature's disposition for man's active promotion of the world's well-being, are the motives which inspire Spinoza's philosopher towards fortitude and nobility.

CHAPTER FIVE

Later Developments in Hellenistic Philosophy

THE establishment of the Roman empire by Augustus in 30 B.C. ends the third and last Hellenistic century. For the history of philosophy this date has a general rather than a specific significance. Throughout the next two hundred years and more, Stoicism, Epicureanism and, to a much more limited extent, Scepticism found their adherents. Marcus Aurelius, Diogenes of Oenoanda and Sextus Empiricus are three writers who bear witness to this fact. But if we except the Sceptic Aenesidemus, who may have lived after the Augustan principate (see p. 75 n. 1), the movements described in this book had no representatives in the Roman empire who were outstanding for original contributions to philosophy. This does not mean that Hellenistic philosophy came to a dead end. Stoicism in particular was a force to reckon with for many years to come. As a moral doctrine its influence was pervasive long after 30 B.C. Indeed, the names of prominent Romans who were Stoics are more numerous from the first century A.D. than in any other period. They could include men as diverse as Seneca, the epic poet Lucan, the satirist Persius, and opponents of the tyrannical regimes of Nero and Domitian—Thrasea Paetus, Helvidius Priscus, Musonius Rufus, and others. Philosophy in antiquity was never a purely academic discipline, and the influence of Stoicism on Roman literature and social life is of the greatest interest and importance.

But in intellectual vitality Hellenistic philosophy reached its zenith before the fall of the Roman Republic. During its later years however (150–50 B.C.), three men flourished whose work deserves a short discussion. Panaetius, Posidonius and Antiochus are names which have only figured intermittently so far. Cicero was personally acquainted with Posidonius and Antiochus, and he drew on the work of all three philosophers in his own writings.

(i) Panaetius

The career of Panaetius has already been briefly described (p. 114). In one modern work he is said to have been 'very influential in his day . . . but his period of great influence was short'.[1] This is a relative judgment. Panaetius is not often referred to by writers other than Cicero, and this may indicate that he was little read in later antiquity. But few classical texts from the Renaissance to the nineteenth century have enjoyed the renown and influence of 'Tully's Offices', that is, Cicero's *De officiis*. It is certain that Cicero based the first two books of this work upon Panaetius, and through Cicero Panaetius might fairly be regarded as the most influential of all Stoic philosophers.

Because our information about Panaetius is relatively scanty it is difficult to gain a clear impression of his philosophical activities as a whole.[2] But the evidence does not point to a man who advanced strikingly new theories. Panaetius' importance rests largely on the manner in which he approached and developed the practical side of Stoic ethics. In earlier Stoicism, as we have seen, logic, physics and ethics are brought together to constitute a single coherent system. Panaetius disapproved of 'logic-chopping' (fr. 55), and though he did not abandon the central Stoic concept of a rationally directed universe, the doubts which he expressed about a number of orthodox dogmas relating to physics suggest that the emphasis on this subject was weaker in his work. Human nature rather than universal nature was Panaetius' primary interest.

Before considering this in more detail we may briefly review some of the orthodox theories on which Panaetius pronounced himself sceptical, or which he rejected altogether. Like all Stoics he took the universe to be imperishable, but he doubted or denied that it is periodically subject to a state in which all things are reduced to fire (*ekpyrōsis*, frs. 64–9).[3] This probably implies, as Philo of Alexandria asserts (fr. 65), that he rejected the related notion of a perpetual recurrence of the same events in successive world-cycles. Cicero also tells us that Panaetius was the only Stoic who 'repudiated the forecasts of astrologers' (fr. 74).[4] Earlier Stoics argued that the gods could not be

[1] J. M. Rist, *Stoic Philosophy*, p. 173.
[2] The texts in which he is named have been collected by M. van Straaten as *Panaetii Rhodii Fragmenta* (ed. 3, Leiden 1962).
[3] Boethus of Sidon, a Stoic contemporary with Panaetius, also rejected this tenet and made a number of further modifications to the orthodox doctrine which show the influence of Aristotle. Evidence in *SVF* iii 265–7.
[4] In this he agreed with Carneades, Cic. *De div.* i 12.

interested, as they are, in human welfare unless they give signs of future events which men can interpret (*SVF* ii 1191–5). If the forecasts of diviners and astrologers are proved false, the fault lies with the forecasters and not with the dreams, meteorological phenomena, flights of birds, entrails, and other evidence from which the future can in theory be foretold (*SVF* ii 1210). The Stoic defence of such forecasting can easily seem ridiculous, but the principle itself was a fundamental feature of the system. Unless signs of what will happen are available in natural phenomena, the Stoic aim to live in accordance with natural events has no secure foundations. Moreover, all events are causally related to one another, and therefore anything that happens must in theory be a sign of some subsequent effect.

Does Panaetius' rejection of astrology imply an abandonment of these basic Stoic doctrines? Cicero also reports that he had doubts about divination (frs. 70–1), and other sources say he rejected it altogether (frs. 68, 73). But such attitudes are quite compatible with a belief in divine providence, a subject on which Panaetius wrote a book (fr. 33). Panaetius could hold that the world is arranged for the benefit of mankind, while denying that human beings as a matter of fact are able to find evidence of the future in stars and other phenomena. But he seems to have discarded astrology on stronger grounds than the limitations of human knowledge. Cicero, who claims to be drawing upon Panaetius, argues that the stars are too distant from the earth to sanction the causal relationship which astrology must postulate between celestial movements and human affairs (fr. 74). This certainly suggests that Panaetius was less committed than his predecessors to the necessary connexion between all events in the universe.

Panaetius' general attitude towards natural philosophy seems to have been more Aristotelian than that of earlier Stoics. At the beginning of the *De officiis* (i 11–20) Cicero, drawing on Panaetius, derives the four cardinal virtues from natural human impulses. This is a short-circuiting of the orthodox Stoic procedure rather than a positive modification of it, but Cicero proceeds to treat 'wisdom' as if its province were primarily a disinterested pursuit of knowledge. The other three virtues—justice, moderation and courage—are grouped together with the task of 'providing the foundations for moral conduct in the practical business of life'. Earlier Stoics gave purely moral definitions of wisdom. It is clearly not Panaetius' view that there is any sharp distinction between wisdom and the other virtues (*De off.* i 15 = fr. 103), but he did distinguish 'theoretical' from 'practical' virtue (fr. 108) and this is unorthodox. Panaetius' most obvious precedent is Aristotle's Nicomachean and other ethical treatises.

Aristotle regarded the moral virtues as dispositions of the appetitive and emotional element in human nature (*E.N.* i 1102a23ff.). Panaetius, if Cicero is reporting his views (*De off.* i 101 = fr. 87), said:

> Souls have a double capacity and nature; one of these is impulse which drives a man this way and that; the other is reason which instructs and explains what should be done and not done.

Panaetius' analysis of the virtues may have been designed to fit an account of the soul which was more Aristotelian or Platonic than early Stoic. But too much should not be based upon the 'double' nature of the soul, as Cicero describes this. Psychological dualism is superficially incompatible with Chrysippus' doctrine that 'impulse' is a function of reason. Yet we know from Galen that Chrysippus was quite capable of using the term 'impulse' as if it referred to something which was in some sense distinct from reason.[1] Posidonius certainly abandoned Chrysippus' conception of the soul. Panaetius quite possibly did so too, but the modifications *explicitly* attributed to him are of much less significance.[2]

When we come to ethics Panaetius' position emerges with more clarity, but assessments of his orthodoxy have varied considerably.[3] There is little doubt that Panaetius placed less emphasis than his predecessors on the perfect but unexampled Stoic sage. The *De officiis* takes as its subject not 'perfect virtue' but 'likenesses of virtue'. The latter can be manifested by men whose wisdom is imperfect, and Panaetius' work *On that which is appropriate* (Cicero's source) dealt with 'duties' which should be the 'intermediate' goals of all men whether perfect or not:

> Since life is passed not in the company of men who are perfect and truly wise but men who act well if they show likenesses of virtue, I think it must

---

[1] cf. Josiah B. Gould, *The Philosophy of Chrysippus*, p. 183.

[2] Panaetius nominated six 'parts' of the soul, thereby making speech a part of 'impulse' and reproduction a part of 'nature' (fr. 86), see p. 171. The significance of this point is not clear. It is often said that he totally denied any survival of the soul after death, but no Stoic postulated unlimited survival or immortality. Panaetius may have adhered to the orthodox view of survival for a limited duration, cf. R. Hoven, *Stoïcisme et Stoïciens face au problème de l'au-delà*, p. 57.

[3] I agree in general with the position of I. G. Kidd, *Problems in Stoicism*, ch. 7. In my opinion Panaetius' ethical innovations were less significant than J. M. Rist supposes, *Stoic Philosophy*, pp. 186–200.

be understood that no one should be entirely neglected in whom any mark of virtue is evident (*De off.* i 46).

Earlier Stoics also took account of those who are 'progressing towards virtue', and they may have handled this subject with greater detail and sympathy than our fragmentary evidence suggests. But the probability is that Panaetius' readiness to admit 'likenesses of virtue' represents a methodological concession which made Stoicism both less rigid and more humane. The rigidity of early Stoic ethics is typified in the so-called 'paradoxes': there are no degrees of virtue or vice; all men except the sage are insane; all acts of wrong-doing are equally wrong. Panaetius would have agreed with his predecessors that such statements are correct from the perspective of perfect virtue. But we may presume him to have argued that they are wholly unhelpful for the purpose of everyday life and moral education.

Such a conclusion is justified not only by the content of the *De officiis* but also by a number of assertions which Cicero makes about Panaetius. 'He shunned,' says Cicero, 'the gloom and harshness of other Stoics and did not approve of the severity of their attitudes' (*Fin.* iv 79 = fr. 55). In his speech in defence of Murena Cicero contrasts the 'softening' effect of Panaetius' company upon Scipio with Cato's obduracy. But he adds: 'Panaetius' discourse and doctrines were just the things which please you' [sc. Cato] (66 = fr. 60). This last statement could not have been uttered if Panaetius' ethics were clearly out of line with the orthodox Stoicism embraced by Cato. Panaetius did not reject the ideal of perfection, any more than Chrysippus and Zeno ignored the performance of 'duties' as a mark of progress.[1] The duties covered by Cicero's treatise spring from natural impulses which are also the basis of perfect virtue.[2] It is the orthodox doctrine, as we have seen, that knowledge of goodness presupposes the ability to recognize and do the appropriate thing at the right time and in the right way. The *De officiis* looks at appropriate behaviour from the vantage-point of one who lacks this knowledge in its perfect form but aspires to possess it. Panaetius does not suggest even at this second-best level that virtue rests on the thing done or the external goal aimed at. 'That virtue, which we are seeking, depends entirely

---

[1] Zeno thought interestingly that a man's dreams provide him with evidence of his progress, *SVF* i 234.

[2] 'To live in accordance with the impulses bestowed on us by Nature' is Panaetius' formulation of the *summum bonum* (fr. 96).

on the mind's effort and reasoning' (i 79).[1] But guide-lines to the attainment of virtue can be laid down in general terms. Justice prescribes two basic principles: first, do no injury to another man; and secondly, see that the public interest is maintained (i 31). A man who acts upon these principles will act appropriately or fulfil his duty. What he ought to do can be and should be derived from these principles. But perfect virtue is more than the adherence to such principles and the attempt to do one's duty. The truly good man acts on the basis of knowledge, which is not reducible to a set of specifiable moral rules.[2] But moral rules can set a man on the right road, and Panaetius devoted considerable pains to the analysis of those attitudes and actions which characterize a man who is on this road.

It is this emphasis on what a man can achieve here and now which marks Panaetius' specific contribution to Stoic ethics. An approving comment by Seneca makes the point very clearly:

I think Panaetius gave a neat answer to a young man who asked whether the sage would be a lover: 'As to the sage we shall see. Your task and mine, who are still a great distance from the sage, is not to fall into a state which is disturbed, powerless and subservient to another' (*Ep.* 116, 5=fr. 114).

The requirement to live free of passion is characteristically Stoic, but on the orthodox doctrine it distinguishes the sage from the rest of mankind. Panaetius, recognizing the fact of human imperfection, treats questions about the sage as irrelevant to life as we find it. He seems to have sensed the need for a criterion of moral judgment which was not satisfied by the orthodox dichotomy between sages and fools. Panaetius agreed with Zeno and other Stoics that the basis of moral conduct is man's rational nature (*De off.* i 107), but he also emphasized the fact that every man has particular attributes of his own. Self-knowledge, a concept which had a moral significance for the Greeks as early as the sixth century, was introduced by Panaetius as a criterion of 'propriety'. We should so act that our behaviour accords with human nature in general and our own nature in particular (i 110=fr. 97). The *De officiis* lays down general principles, and it also seeks to show how these have been appropriately applied by different kinds

---

[1] In *De off.* iii 13ff. Cicero again distinguishes perfect virtue from the knowledge of 'intermediate duties'. But he makes it clear that even these latter depend on 'goodness of disposition' (*ingenii bonitas*) and 'advancement in learning'. See further p. 203.

[2] Cf. Sen. *Ep.* 94, 5of. referred to by Kidd, p. 164, cited in n. 3 p. 213.

of men in different situations. None of this is inconsistent with earlier Stoicism, but the cosmic dimension has virtually disappeared. It reappears in Marcus Aurelius and Epictetus, though the latter succeeds in combining it with the more humanist approach of Panaetius.

Panaetius was undoubtedly a Stoic, but he had an independent mind and was not afraid to modify or give a different emphasis to the doctrines of his predecessors. His cultural interests were possibly more diverse than those of Chrysippus, and he wrote about the authenticity of Socratic dialogues, Greek history and perhaps other non-philosophical subjects (frs. 123–36). A number of sources speak of his indebtedness to Plato and Aristotle (frs. 55–9), and historians of philosophy have often regarded 'eclecticism' as the defining characteristic of this period. Both Panaetius and Posidonius were eclectic in the sense that they were prepared to welcome ideas advanced by other philosophers if this suited them. And Antiochus of Ascalon manifests the same tendency still more strongly. This loosening of the boundaries between philosophical schools has been explained in various ways. The introduction of philosophy to Rome is sometimes thought to have had the effect of making the subject more pragmatic and therefore less concerned with theoretical niceties. But it is difficult to see anything specifically Roman in the philosophy of Panaetius or Posidonius. It was men like Cato who made Stoicism a Roman ideal. Philosophical dissatisfaction with certain aspects of Stoicism is the most likely explanation of the changes introduced by Panaetius, Posidonius and other Stoic philosophers of this period. Carneades' criticism must have made many Stoics all too well aware of weaknesses in the system, and it was not necessary to be an official Sceptic to have doubts about the usefulness or validity of certain doctrines. Orthodox Stoicism could not unfairly be charged with offering a way of life which fully satisfied neither everyday needs nor the yearnings of those whose temperament inclined them towards mystical and religious experience. The revival of Pythagoreanism in the first century B.C. is a symptom of interest in an other-worldly philosophy, quite unlike the Hellenistic systems, which was eventually to give rise to Neoplatonism.

(ii) *Posidonius*
Posidonius (see p. 115) has sometimes been regarded as a precursor of Neoplatonism, but with little justification. The subject of innumerable speculations for over a hundred years, Posidonius has concealed his significance more successfully than any ancient thinker of major

stature.[1] We know that he was erudite, prolific, extraordinarily many-sided, renowned and influential. On some of his work, in history, geography and philosophy, we are quite well informed. But until 1972 there existed no authoritative and comprehensive collection of all the evidence in which ancient writers refer to Posidonius by name. That gap has now been filled, thanks to the invaluable work of the late Ludwig Edelstein, and of I. G. Kidd, who has completed what Edelstein began.[2] Yet this the latest addition to the Posidonian literature should ideally have been the basis of every previous detailed study. If it had existed in the nineteenth century we might have been spared the endless series of theories about this enigmatic figure. Instead, Posidonius has been found lurking behind countless statements in Cicero, Seneca, and many other writers who never mention his name. Not unlike Pythagoras, Posidonius has turned up to explain anything and everything. Stoic and Platonist, rationalist and mystic, superficial and penetrating, reactionary and original—these are but a few of the alleged contradictions which surround Posidonius.

Whether Posidonius as a philosopher had any highly original ideas is a question to which I would give a provisional negative. But firmer answers are best withheld until Mr. Kidd has published the commentary on Posidonius' fragments which he is now preparing. Even if my provisional answer should prove to be correct it would not undermine the influence and importance of Posidonius. Neither Francis Bacon nor Rousseau was a man who advanced fundamentally new theories of great significance, but few thinkers have exercised more influence on their contemporaries. Originality in any case is a quality which can be assessed in a vast number of different ways. A critical synthesis of existing knowledge may be highly original and a most fruitful source of new discoveries.

Posidonius was a Stoic but a most unusual one. The remarkable thing about him is not what he made of Stoicism but the range of his interests. He settled, as I have already mentioned, in Rhodes (p. 115), but he travelled widely over the Mediterranean world and took careful

---

[1] Marie Laffranque gives a useful survey of work on Posidonius in her *Poseidonios d'Apamée* (Paris 1964) pp. 1–44.

[2] *Posidonius: vol. i The Fragments* (Cambridge University Press). A second volume of commentary is in preparation. The only previous work which attempts to collect all the evidence was published by J. Bake in 1810. By modern standards this is a very defective collection, though valuable in its day. The fragments of Posidonius' historical and geographical work have already been edited by Felix Jacoby in *Die Fragmente der griechischen Historiker* 87 (Berlin 1926).

note of what he saw. Whether it was the social customs of the Celts in Gaul, the Atlantic tides at Cadiz, apes on the North African coast, rabbits on an island near Naples, Posidonius recorded his observations. Geography in the widest sense, vulcanology, astronomy, meteorology, mineralogy, oceanography, ethnography—he wrote and studied all of them. He compiled a huge series of 'historical' treatises, which will have included most of his geographical data, and the fragments cover events datable between 142 and 93 B.C. Posidonius is said to have started where Polybius left off (146 B.C.), but it is impossible to say how far the younger writer shared his predecessor's favourable attitude towards Roman imperialism. Add to all this Posidonius' work in the conventional subjects of Hellenistic philosophy—physics, logic and ethics—plus the fact that he was a mathematician competent enough to criticize and amend various points of Euclidean geometry, and we are left with the impression of a veritable polymath.

In the range of his studies Posidonius can be compared with Aristotle, Theophrastus and the great Alexandrian librarian, Eratosthenes. But these men flourished at a different time and under different social and political circumstances. Posidonius stands alone in the first century B.C. Why was he interested in so much? This may seem a foolish question but the facts oblige us to ask it. We must take it for granted that he was a man of prodigious ability and energy. But these qualities do not explain the universality of Posidonius' interests. Nor does the equally reasonable assumption that he was indefatigably curious. In Posidonius we find philosophy and science reunited as they had not been since the time of Theophrastus. Was Posidonius acutely conscious of the lack of rapport between Stoicism and the empirical sciences, which had developed so successfully in the early Hellenistic period? Can we say that his universalist procedure was motivated by a dissatisfaction with the narrowness and scholasticism of contemporary philosophy, above all, Stoicism?

I think that these questions are along the right lines. Strabo, himself a Stoic, contrasts Posidonius' interest in 'seeking out causes' with normal Stoic practice (T85). In the same breath Strabo describes Posidonius' activity as Aristotlizing, and adds that 'our school avoids this because of the concealment of causes'. Aristotle regarded 'knowledge of causes' as the basis of science, and Posidonius seems to have agreed with him. Both men devoted great energy to the collection and classification of factual data. But this was not characteristic of the Stoics. While insisting that nothing happens without a cause Chrysip-

pus argued that men cannot discover every cause (*SVF* ii 351; 973).[1]
Posidonius could with justification object that his Stoic predecessors
had used this as a pretext for not trying. He had no quarrel, so far as I
can see, with the basic axioms of Stoic cosmology, though he modified
a number of details.[2] Unlike Panaetius he defended astrology and
divination. But not without evidence. Posidonius' principle was that
theories must be seen to fit the facts, and he rejected orthodox Stoic
doctrines which seemed to him to conflict with this principle.

The case which is best documented is his quarrel with Chrysippus
over the structure of the soul and the causes of passionate emotion.[3]
As we have seen (p. 176), Chrysippus held that the passions are
'excessive impulses' and that there is no such thing as an irrational
faculty of soul. Posidonius objected that there must be such a faculty
if some impulses are 'excessive', for reason could not exceed its own
activity and limits (F34). This is not merely a logical objection.
Posidonius clearly thought that the facts of human behaviour can only
be adequately explained on the assumption that the soul does possess a
purely irrational faculty. If Galen is reliable, Posidonius preferred
Plato's tripartite psychology, with its clear distinction between
rational and irrational faculties, to Chrysippus' monistic conception;
and he also sought to show that Cleanthes and even Zeno were not
supporters of Chrysippus' doctrine (T91). Chrysippus had defended
his views by quotations from the poets and Posidonius cited counter-
instances (F164). He also argued that Chrysippus' psychology made it
impossible to account for human badness (F169). Unless this has its
source within our own nature, which Chrysippus denied, why are
men attracted to pleasure? Why do they experience excessive impulses?
Posidonius rejected Chrysippus' explanation of 'external influences'
and located the 'root' of badness within the soul. Man has 'natural'
affinities to pleasure and worldly success, which compete with his
natural affinity to virtue and knowledge (F160). This 'irrational' side of
human nature is the cause of our passions, and it must be made subservient to reason if man is to attain his goal (F148; 186).

[1] On this point and on Posidonius' methodology and ethics cf. I. G. Kidd,
'Posidonius on Emotions', in *Problems in Stoicism*, ch. 9. I am greatly indebted to
this study.
[2] The assessment of Posidonius' modifications to Stoic physics is a very
controversial subject. I can only say here that I ascribe even less significance to
them than J. M. Rist, whose account of Posidonius, *Stoic Philosophy*, ch. 11, is
more sober than most.
[3] Galen's *De placitis Hippocratis et Platonis* is our source, cf. Edelstein-Kidd,
especially frs. 156–69.

Posidonius recommended various 'irrational' procedures for 'curing' emotional disturbance which cannot be fully enumerated here.[1] They include music and poetry, and the basic assumption is that the 'irrational' can be purged and changed only by means which take account of the 'irrational', which appeal to our pleasures and sensuous experience. Reason itself has no competence to modify our passions. One is reminded forcefully of the place which Plato assigns to poetry, music and other arts in his educational curriculum of the *Republic*; Aristotle's claim that tragedy by the pity and fear which it rouses purges these emotions is equally relevant. Seneca's tragedies, for all their rhetoric and platitudes, may be regarded as a practical Stoic example of the poetic purgative which Posidonius had in mind.

There is much more to Posidonius' psychology and emotional therapy than I can deal with here. But I have said enough perhaps to justify a few general comments. Posidonius' criticism of Chrysippus undoubtedly focuses on a number of basic difficulties. And this tells us something important about Posidonius. Possibly he misinterpreted Chrysippus whose 'rationalism' can be viewed more sympathetically than Posidonius acknowledged (p. 175). But Posidonius was eminently justified in raising questions about it and offering an alternative theory which seemed to explain human behaviour more convincingly. The alternative theory does not appear in essentials to say anything that had not been said before. Plato's psychology seemed to Posidonius to provide a better basis for understanding behaviour than Chrysippus', and he adapted it to suit a framework of Stoic concepts and terminology. This is not eclecticism in any disparaging sense. Rather, Posidonius remains a Stoic, but a Stoic who is prepared to criticize his own school if necessary and to make use of extraneous ideas. We should not suppose that earlier Stoics did not criticize each other. Chrysippus criticized Cleanthes, and no doubt Diogenes of Babylon and Antipater criticized Chrysippus. But, so far as our evidence goes, we are justified in saying that Panaetius and Posidonius show an open-minded attitude towards orthodox dogmas which was not characteristic of earlier Stoicism.

Seneca reports that Posidonius credited wise men with the government of human society in its earliest phase and with technological discoveries in the broadest sense—house-building, metallurgy, weaving, husbandry, fishing and so forth (*Ep.* 90 = F284). The first point

[1] F168. cf. Kidd (cited on p. 219), pp. 205f.; Edelstein, *The Meaning of Stoicism* (Cambridge, Mass. 1966) pp. 56-9.

is acceptable to Seneca but he rejects the second: the sage has never engaged in such mundane matters. This critical observation brings us back to the universality of Posidonius' interests. If, as I have suggested, Posidonius did not amend the fundamental doctrines of Stoic physics, he certainly showed that a Stoic could advance the understanding of particular phenomena on a very wide front. Earlier Stoics did not share Posidonius' passion for astronomy, mathematics or geography. But he wanted more than vague generalizations. Measuring the size of the earth, calculating the sun's size and distance from the earth, classifying quadrilaterals, these are but a sample of the activities of Posidonius. Mathematics had always been the queen of the sciences in the Greek world and Posidonius' concern to reunite philosophy and science is surely demonstrated by his devotion to mathematics. A contemporary Epicurean, Zeno of Sidon, had attempted to overturn the principles of geometry, and Posidonius attacked him in 'a whole book' (F46). Galen tells us that he was 'trained in geometry and more accustomed than other Stoics to following proofs' (T83). Of course Chrysippus was passionately interested in logic but not, so far as we know, mathematical logic. Galen's intense dislike of Chrysippus may have helped him to emphasize Posidonius' achievement. But Galen was himself greatly interested in geometry, and we must presume that he found an ability in Posidonius which other Stoics had not shown.

Our evidence for Posidonius is extremely fragmentary and only a part of it has been described here. Did he hold some unitary conception of all departments of knowledge? Did he wish to show that all facts are worth ascertaining in a universe rationally determined by immanent providence? Such views a Stoic could hold and justify, and Posidonius was a Stoic first and foremost. One German scholar regarded cosmic 'sympathy' [i.e. the interaction and connexion between all things in the universe] as the unifying theme of Posidonius' philosophical and scientific enterprise.[1] The doctrine is not, as he sought to show, indicative of Posidonius' individuality. But the fact that other Stoics espoused it does not remove its importance in Posidonius. Cicero many times refers to Posidonius' efforts to establish divination: 'He supposes that there are signs in nature of future events' (*De div.* i 129=F110). 'That the dying foresee the future is established by Posidonius with this example: a Rhodian as he was dying named six of his contemporaries and said which of them would die first, second and so on' (ibid. 64=F108). Or, what is perhaps the most revealing

---

[1] Karl Reinhardt, *Kosmos und Sympathie* (Munich 1926).

passage, 'The Stoic Boethus and our own Posidonius have studied the causes of prognostications; and if the causes of these things were not discovered yet the facts themselves could be observed and noted' (*De div.* ii 47 = F109). Posidonius' dedication to the study of causes has already been discussed, and here it is related to prediction and the knowledge of facts.

The predictability of events and cosmic 'sympathy' go hand in hand. Posidonius, unlike Panaetius, was strongly committed to both of them. If we wish to find a concept which might explain Posidonius' multifarious activities, cosmic 'sympathy' is perhaps the best candidate. But even if this is correct—and I would not base a Posidonian *system* upon this concept—it does not warrant us in regarding this fascinating man as a mystic or, what would be even less true, as unscientific. The characteristics of mysticism are not attributable to Posidonius, and it is a defining mark of science to determine the causes of things. Undoubtedly Posidonius was too credulous in his commitment to astrology and divination. But he was hardly wrong to postulate a causal connexion between observable phenomena and future events. Like most forecasters however he studied material which was insufficient to establish the actual links.

By any standards Posidonius was one of the outstanding personalities of the Hellenistic world. He exercised influence on many areas of intellectual life for over a hundred years, and Cicero, Seneca and Strabo were all heavily indebted to him. Geminus, a Rhodian follower, wrote a summary of one of Posidonius' scientific works (F18). No doubt there were other disciples. What Aristotle was to Plato, so in a sense was Posidonius to the Stoics. These two men mark the beginning and the end of Hellenistic philosophy. It is unfortunate that we lack the evidence to make a true comparison of their achievements.

(iii) Antiochus

The third individual who must come within the purview of this chapter is Antiochus of Ascalon.[1] A Syrian like Posidonius, Antiochus (born *c.* 130 B.C.) is known to us chiefly through Cicero, who studied under him at Athens in 79/8 B.C., admired him and disseminated his views in the *Academica* and *De finibus*.[2] As a young man Antiochus

---

[1] Ancient texts in which Antiochus is referred to by name have been collected by Georg Luck, *Der Akademiker Antiochus* (Bern and Stuttgart 1953).

[2] For Cicero's presentation of Antiochus' views, cf. H. A. K. Hunt, *The Humanism of Cicero* (Melbourne 1954).

came to Athens where he attended lectures of the sceptical Academic, Philo of Larisa, and two Stoics, Dardanus and Mnesarchus, the latter of whom was a pupil of Panaetius (Cic. *Acad.* ii 69ff.). Under Philo's influence Antiochus became a Sceptic and a most rigorous proponent of the New Academy (Cic. loc. cit.). On the outbreak of the war against Mithridates in 88 Philo left Athens for Rome, and Antiochus probably went with him. If so, Antiochus then had an opportunity to become acquainted with Lucullus, an up-and-coming Roman statesman who owed his rise to the patronage of Sulla. In 87/6 Lucullus was in Alexandria as deputy-quaestor attempting to raise a fleet for Sulla, and according to Cicero (*Acad.* ii 11) Antiochus was with him there. This visit to Alexandria marks a turning-point in Antiochus' career. There he read for the first time two books by Philo which made him very angry (Cic. loc. cit.). They were so much at variance with Philo's earlier views that Antiochus found it difficult to credit their authorship. Philo had attempted in his new work to maintain that the distinction between the Old and the New Academy was erroneous (Cic. *Acad.* i 13f.). The details of his argument escape us, but it seems from Antiochus' reply (*Acad.* ii 13–18) that Philo tried to interpret the 'ancients'—Empedocles, Democritus, Socrates and Plato—as 'sceptics' in a sense compatible with the New Academy.

Why did this annoy Antiochus so much? The answer turns on Philo's reasons for assimilating the two Academies. Arcesilaus and Carneades had insisted that the true nature of things cannot be known. Philo, doubtless in the books which provoked Antiochus' wrath, claimed that 'things can be grasped as they really are' but not by the Stoic criterion of 'cognitive impression' (Sextus, *P.H.* i 235). How then do we grasp things? Philo, it seems, offered no criterion. But he apparently maintained that the absence of a criterion does not entail that things are by nature unknowable. In practice Philo defended the probabilist position of Carneades, but from a weaker theoretical basis. His support for the Old Academy is to be interpreted in this light. He can hardly have defended the positive doctrines of Plato, on the evidence of Antiochus' own mature standpoint. Rather, we must presume that Philo tried to defend his modification of Scepticism by appeal to the 'ancients'. Ignoring Plato's theory of Forms—which was of course challenged by Plato himself in the *Parmenides*—Philo no doubt invoked Plato's support for the view that knowledge is attainable in theory but not in practice (cf. *Acad.* i 46).

Antiochus objected to this on historical grounds. It did justice neither to the Old Academy nor to the New. Plato had a 'most excellent positive doctrine' (*Acad.* ii 15). The New Academy professed nothing of the kind. But Antiochus' renunciation of the New Academy cannot have been prompted by a purely disinterested desire for accurate history. If, as is likely, he had become disenchanted with Scepticism before the appearance of Philo's latest works, the feature which must have annoyed him most would be Philo's attempt to bring Plato and his predecessors under the Sceptical umbrella. Antiochus saw a very sharp distinction between the Old and the New Academy, and in the final stage of his life he devoted himself to restoring, at the expense of Scepticism, what he claimed to be the true Academic tradition.

The two fundamentals of philosophy, according to Antiochus, are the criterion of truth and the chief good or object of desire (Cic. *Acad.* ii 29). Theory of knowledge and ethics provide the basic subject-matter of his investigations. But the most interesting thing about Antiochus is not what he contributed to these topics but the sources of his ideas and his interpretation of the Academic tradition. He included as Academics not only Speusippus, Xenocrates, Polemo and Crantor but also the early Peripatetics, above all Aristotle himself (Cic. *Fin.* v 7). Even more strikingly, he claimed that the Stoics differed from the Peripatetics not in doctrine but in terminology (Cic. *N.D.* i 16), and that Stoicism, as founded by Zeno, was a 'correction' of the Old Academy rather than a new system (*Acad.* i 43). 'Zeno and Arcesilaus were diligent pupils of Polemo; but Zeno, who was older than Arcesilaus and an extremely clever dialectician . . . set out to remodel the system' (*Acad.* i 35).

Although Antiochus claimed to be an Academic, most of his doctrines conform to the 'remodelled system of Zeno's'. He took over and defended at length the Stoic theory of knowledge (Cic. *Acad.* ii 16–39). His ethics is primarily Stoic, though we shall observe a number of modifications in this field, and his philosophy of nature is more Stoic than anything else (*Acad.* i 26–30). How are we to evaluate Antiochus' conception of the Academic tradition? Cicero, who acts as the spokesman for the New Academy in his *Academica* ii, charges Antiochus with failing to follow his own 'ancestors' (Plato, Xenocrates, Aristotle) and never diverging a foot's length from Chrysippus (ii 142f.). The context is polemical—a Sceptical attack on dogmatic philosophers by reference to their disagreements—but history seems to be largely on Cicero's side. Neither Platonists nor Peripatetics defended a theory of knowledge based upon anything which resembles the 'cognitive impression'. This is a peculiarly Stoic doctrine. In ethics however Antiochus' main divergence from Stoicism, though less significant than his agreements, is compatible with one aspect of Peripatetic theory and also with a doctrine ascribed to Polemo.

The Stoics held that virtue by itself is sufficient to constitute happiness and nothing else makes any positive contribution to this goal. Antiochus, distinguishing in a non-Stoic manner degrees of well-being, argued that virtue is the necessary and sufficient condition of a happy life but not 'the happiest life' (Cic. *Tusc.* v 21ff.). As we have already seen, Antiochus rejected the Stoic distinction between 'the good' and 'the preferable' (p. 196). The value of good health, riches, reputation and so forth, though slight by comparison with that of virtue, is sufficient, in Antiochus' judgment, to make a virtuous life which is embellished by such things happier than one which lacks everything save virtue (*Acad.* i 22). Aristotle, similarly, observes that certain external goods disfigure happiness if they are absent (*E.N.* i 1099a31ff.). Some things, he writes, are needed as instruments for the performance of virtuous actions; others are 'adornments' which by their presence or absence can augment or detract from happiness. Subsequently Aristotle qualifies this assertion, and he can be read as adopting a position on external goods which is virtually equivalent to that of the Stoics.[1] But unlike them he regarded 'good' as a term which has multiple uses. Antiochus' claim that the Stoics and Peripatetics agree in substance and differ in terminology is superficially a fair comment on their respective attitudes towards external goods.

The position which Antiochus defended is also attributed to Polemo both in Cicero (*Fin.* iv 51) and elsewhere (Clement *Strom.* ii 22). This Academic philosopher, as I have already mentioned, is a most elusive figure (p. 112), and much of our meagre evidence about him is derived from Antiochus (cf. Cic. *Fin.* v 14). But there is no doubt that Zeno was personally acquainted with Polemo, and it is Polemo's specification of 'the natural starting-points' which, again on Antiochus' authority, Zeno is said to have inherited (*Fin.* iv 45). This statement may not be special pleading. In the *Academica* (i 19) Varro who is giving Antiochus' interpretation of Academic ethics says: 'They sought the subject-matter of good conduct from Nature and said that Nature must be obeyed, and that the ultimate good must be looked for in Nature

[1] I have discussed this point in *Bulletin of the Institute of Classical Studies* 15 (1968) 74–6.

alone. And they postulated that to have obtained all things which accord with Nature in mind, body and livelihood is the ultimate object of desire and the chief good.' This is Antiochus' position and what differentiates it from Stoicism is the characteristic assignment of positive value to bodily and external goods as well as virtue. As a summary of Platonic or Aristotelian ethics, as we understand these, it reads very oddly. But we cannot rule out the possibility that Polemo himself expressed such views as valid Academic doctrine. If he did, it would make the historical basis of Antiochus' interpretation and criticism of Stoic ethics more intelligible, though hardly sufficient to justify his view of the Stoa as simply an offshoot of the Academy. Cicero himself seems to have recognized the historical unreliability of such a thesis.

Historical reliability however is not the same thing as philosophical judgment. In order to appreciate Antiochus' interpretation of the Academic tradition we must remember that Stoicism had been a flourishing system for over two hundred years. For the same period the Academy had devoted itself to Scepticism. The Peripatetic school ceased to be influential after the death of Strato, whose devotion to science did not commend itself to Antiochus (*Acad.* i 34). In the first part of the first century B.C. Stoicism had more conceptual affinities with Platonism and Aristotelianism than any other philosophical movement. If Antiochus wished to combat Scepticism with the help of the current system which had most in common with the Academic tradition he had to turn to the Stoics. Under the guidance of Panaetius and Posidonius leading Stoics had begun to assimilate a number of Platonic and Aristotelian ideas. Platonism, as expounded by Plato's immediate successors, was dead. But interest in Plato's writings seems to have increased in the second century B.C., and a new stimulus to the study of the 'ancients' was to be provided, shortly after Antiochus' time, by the edition of Aristotle's treatises brought out by Andronicus of Rhodes.

Antiochus regarded the Stoics as the heirs of the Platonic and Aristotelian tradition. Within his loose terms of reference he was justified in doing so. But, as Cicero remarks, he was far more of a Stoic than a Platonist or Peripatetic. Whatever Antiochus knew of Plato, Aristotle and their immediate successors—and we must assume that he knew a good deal—he chose to make use of only those points which seemed to him clearly superior to the Stoics' views. His requirement that the highest good must take account of bodily well-being and things of material value is the most significant deviation from Stoicism, and he regarded the Stoics' 'indifference' to these as a contradiction of their own principles (Cic. *Fin.* iv 37–41). He also recognized correctly and seems to have disapproved of other 'innovations' by Zeno (*Acad.* i 35–9). The equality of all wrongful acts was 'most strenuously' rejected by him (*Acad.* ii 133), and he probably rejected the Stoics' rationalization of the passions and their refusal to admit an irrational faculty of mind.

In the realm of natural philosophy, judging from Varro's summary in Cicero (*Acad.* i 24–9), Antiochus interpreted the Academic tradition in almost exclusively Stoic terms. A passing reference to Aristotle's fifth element—the aether which is the material of the heavenly bodies—is the chief non-Stoic item, and it contributes nothing to the main train of thought. Later, Zeno is said, correctly, to have excluded the fifth element, and his rejection of incorporeal substances is also mentioned (39). But these play no overt part in the summary of 'Academic' physics.

The most puzzling subject is Antiochus' theory of knowledge. On the evidence of *Academica* ii he committed himself wholeheartedly to the Stoic doctrine of 'cognitive impression' and defended this, with some interesting arguments—many of them no doubt drawn from Stoic writers—against the criticism of the Academic Sceptics. Towards the end of the book, where Cicero is speaking as a Sceptic against Antiochus, he outlines a number of tests of truth advanced by various philosophers, concluding with Plato: 'Plato held that the entire criterion of truth and truth itself is independent of opinions and the senses and belongs to thinking and the intellect. Surely our friend Antiochus does not approve of any of these doctrines?' (142). Even if this is a rhetorical objection it does not undermine the fact that Antiochus' defence of the 'cognitive impression' commits him to the thesis that sense-perception can be distinguished as true or false, and that 'true impressions' are the basis of knowledge.

Yet in *Academica* i the Academics and Peripatetics are said to have regarded the intellect as the 'judge of things; because it alone perceives that which is always simple and just what it is' (30). Varro then adds: 'They call this "form", a name already given to it by Plato'; and he goes on to report Plato's distinction between the intellect and the senses, whose objects are always unstable. Here clearly we are a very long way from Stoicism. Subsequently, Aristotle is criticized for 'weakening' the theory of forms (33), and on the evidence of this context we would have every reason for supposing that Antiochus supported some version of this Platonic doctrine.

There seems to be a fundamental inconsistency, but it may not have been too great for Antiochus to swallow. The Stoics, as I have already noted, recognized 'rational' as well as 'sense' impressions. The 'general concepts', whose basis is sense-perception, are also included as a criterion of truth in Stoic theory. Further, the Stoics distinguished mere instances of accurate perception or 'grasping' from 'knowledge', which is 'secure and unshakeable'. And they also made their own use of Plato's distinction between knowledge and belief (p. 129). Antiochus himself, when defending the 'cognitive impression', speaks of the 'intellect itself as the source of sensations', and he seems to have regarded the acquisition of valid general concepts as a necessary condition of accurate perception (*Acad.* ii 30). I am not sure whether this can be called fully orthodox Stoicism. If Antiochus is describing what the Stoics called 'knowledge' then his emphasis on general concepts is orthodox. But as I understand the 'cognitive impression' in Stoicism, this does not require general concepts as a *test* of its validity (p. 128). Their function is to classify the objects of perception and to furnish material for the formation of non-empirical notions. However this may be, Antiochus' stress on intellect in his defence of the 'cognitive impression' is striking, and sufficient to suggest that he tried to marry up this Stoic concept with what he understood to be the Platonic theory of Forms. The Forms are not of course concepts, much less concepts derived from sense-perception. They are the ultimate realities which exist apart from our thoughts. But Seneca knew an interpretation of the doctrine which turned the Forms into the thoughts of God (*Ep.* 65, 7). Several scholars have suggested Antiochus as the source of this idea, and it is a promising hypothesis. The Stoics spoke of 'seminal principles' which God employs in his determination of the universe. Antiochus might well have interpreted these as Platonic Forms which men can intuit by their perception of particular objects.

Compared with Posidonius Antiochus was a thinker of minor stature.[1] His blend of the Stoic and Academic traditions lacks rigour, and it brings out the best in neither of them. But it would be a mistake to dismiss Antiochus as uninteresting or ineffective. As a renegade Sceptic he was well equipped to draw attention to theoretical and

---

[1] A much more detailed assessment of Antiochus will be found in J. Dillon's *The Middle Platonists*, a forthcoming volume in the Classical Life and Letters series.

practical difficulties in Scepticism. He succeeded in turning the Academy back towards a positivist philosophy, and when Scepticism was revived and supplemented by Aenesidemus (p. 75) it took the name of Pyrrhonism. Antiochus' criticism of Stoic ethics fastens upon genuine problems, and his recognition that human nature needs more than virtue for its perfect satisfaction is particularly important. More significant than his Academic teacher, Philo, Antiochus helped to prepare the ground however lightly for the revival of Platonism. This movement was to gather momentum over the next three hundred years until it culminated in the mystical and highly elaborate metaphysics of Plotinus.

(iv) Cicero

It would be inappropriate to conclude this discussion of later developments in Hellenistic philosophy without a further word about Cicero whose writings provide us with so much of our evidence.[1] Cicero never laid claim to any special expertise in philosophy, but no Roman of his time, with the possible exception of Varro, was better equipped to write about it. As a young man Cicero came into contact with leading Stoic, Epicurean and Academic philosophers who fostered in him an enthusiasm for philosophy which was by no means characteristic of ambitious Romans in the first century B.C. Rhetoric was the foundation of education for a young Roman with a public career to make, but Cicero combined the study of rhetoric with philosophy in the Greek fashion. With the help of his friends and voracious reading Cicero maintained his philosophical interests throughout a life crowded with activities of a very different kind. But it was not until 45 B.C., when he was over sixty, that Cicero took up philosophical writing on a large scale. These were the years of his greatest political disillusionment and personal unhappiness. Civil wars had finally destroyed the Republic and his beloved daughter, Tullia, was dead. In these circumstances Cicero found some personal consolation in a great burst of literary activity. The *Academica*, the *De finibus*, the *Tusculan Disputations*, the *De natura deorum*, the *De divinatione*, the *De fato*, the *De officiis*, and short popular works like *De amicitia* were all composed within less than two years.

As he makes plain on many occasions, Cicero had strong personal reasons for devoting this time to philosophy. But they were not his

---

[1] A. E. Douglas gives a helpful account of Cicero's philosophical writings in *Cicero*, Greece and Rome New Surveys in the Classics, no. 2 (Oxford 1968).

only motive. In the prefaces to his philosophical writings Cicero justifies his activity at some length. This extract from the *De natura deorum* may be taken as representative:

If anyone wonders why I am entrusting these reflections to writing at this stage of my life, I can answer very easily. With no public activity to occupy me and the political situation making a dictatorship inevitable, I thought that it was an act of patriotism to expound philosophy to my fellow-countrymen, judging it to be greatly to the honour and glory of the state to have such a lofty subject expressed in Latin literature (i 7).

Cicero was not a man who underrated his own achievements, but it would be a mistake to dismiss such references to patriotism as smug or insincere. Cicero genuinely believed that he was doing Latin speakers a service in making Greek philosophy available to them, and he was right. Before his time, it seems, Epicureanism was virtually the only philosophical subject which had attracted the attention of Roman writers and the works of the Epicureans, whom Cicero dismisses with such contempt (*Tusc.* iv 6–7), have vanished without trace. (Lucretius' poem, which Cicero never refers to in his philosophical writings, may not have been in general circulation at this time.) Cicero cast his net much wider. Professing to be an adherent of the moderate scepticism of Philo of Larisa, Cicero surveyed and criticized those doctrines of the Stoics, Epicureans and Antiochus of Ascalon which were probably most familiar to Greek readers and which he himself regarded as the most important. He is much less comprehensive than he claims to be. Ethics and theory of knowledge are treated in considerable detail. Physical theories are summarized only in broad outline and logic is scarcely handled at all. To some extent this reflects the activities of philosophers in the early first century B.C., but it is clear that Posidonius, to take only one example, had many speculative interests which find no mention in Cicero.

From a modern point of view Cicero's philosophical writings have other shortcomings. They are often verbose, sometimes obscure; and the subtlety of Greek thought tends to dissipate itself in his long periodic sentences. But we should judge Cicero by what he achieved and not what we should like him to have achieved. He had no expectations that the philosophically expert would read his work in preference to Greek originals. His philosophy is largely derivative and acknowledged to be so. But Cicero had far more understanding of the Hellenistic systems than he has sometimes been credited with, and he was quite capable of pursuing a difficult train of thought rigorously. The fact that he wrote in Latin was itself a very considerable achievement, for he had to find new means of expressing ideas for which Latin was naturally ill equipped. He could not overcome this problem with complete success, but he pioneered the way to the later development of Latin as a highly effective philosophical language. And the sceptical criticism which he directed against dogmatic theorists, however unoriginal it may be, marks a significant contrast with Seneca's approach to philosophy and that of later Roman writers.

It would however be wrong to give the impression that Cicero was a rigorous sceptic. As a jurist he was well fitted to set out the pros and cons of a particular position, but there can be no doubt that the humane Stoicism of *De officiis*, his most influential work, represents views which he himself approved. It is the bearing of philosophy on human conduct which matters most to Cicero. Nor should one overlook the importance of his earlier political writings, *De republica* and *De legibus*, in which the Stoic concepts of natural law and justice are expounded. It was largely due to Cicero that such ideas gained the support of Roman lawyers and the Roman Church Fathers who gave them a new foundation in western culture.[1]

[1] cf. Gerard Watson, 'The Natural Law and Stoicism', in *Problems in Stoicism*.

CHAPTER SIX

Hellenistic Philosophy and the Classical Tradition

CICERO'S influence on later antiquity and more recent times is just one aspect of the classical tradition to which Hellenistic philosophy contributed. The history of Stoicism, Scepticism and Epicureanism begins in fourth-century Greece, but it extends over the Mediterranean world through the Roman empire and into the Europe of the Renaissance and beyond. The influence of Plato and Aristotle has proved to be more profound and persistent, but in the widest sense less pervasive. Everyone has some notion of what it means to be stoical, sceptical and epicurean. First through Cicero and Seneca, later through Plutarch, Lucretius, Diogenes Laertius and Sextus Empiricus, the main ideas of Hellenistic thought were recovered in the Renaissance. These were the years when men looked to Hellenistic philosophy for moral guidance and for insight into the religious and scientific controversies of the time. The Middle Ages and the last two centuries, for clearly different reasons, are less noteworthy. But many of the ideas discussed in this book, especially Stoic concepts, have exercised a continuing rather than an intermittent influence.

The subject is so large and difficult to control that only an outline of some of its most significant features can be given here. It must be emphasized at the outset that an adequate critical and historical approach to the interpretation of Hellenistic philosophy has only been developed within the last hundred years. In this chapter I am concerned primarily with the writers and scholars who made Stoicism, Scepticism and Epicureanism a notable part of the classical tradition. We may take first the contribution of Hellenistic philosophy to thought and literature in the Roman empire, and second, its influence on the sixteenth and seventeenth centuries.

In the Roman world during the first two Christian centuries Stoicism was the dominant philosophy among educated pagans. The reasons for its success are not difficult to find. Stoicism was able to accommodate many traditional Roman attitudes about human excellence, and it also provided them with a theoretical basis in place of, or rather in addition to, custom and historical examples. The life and death of Cato the Younger showed what it might mean to be a Roman *and* a Stoic. Venerated by republicans for his patriotic suicide at Utica, Cato became the object of a long series of panegyrics. He was eulogized by Lucan in his epic poem *Bellum civile*, and undoubtedly helped to popularize Stoicism among Roman aristocrats during the first century A.D. The so-called Stoic opposition to the principate at this time has its sources in political conservatism and senatorial independence rather than moral theory. But it cannot be a coincidence that some of the most outspoken critics of the emperors were Stoics. Yet in the middle of the next century a Stoic, Marcus Aurelius, sat on the imperial throne. This is a remarkable development, though it must be admitted that Marcus was a Stoic as much by temperament as by conviction.

It is the Stoicism of Seneca, Epictetus and Marcus which has had greatest influence on later writers, and this is first and last a practical moral doctrine. 'The true philosopher,' writes Seneca, 'is the teacher of humanity' (*Ep.* 89, 13). In his best prose work, the *Moral letters to Lucilius*, Seneca sought to make good this claim by putting Stoicism to work in the moral education of his correspondent. The *Moral letters* are not a Stoic tract; Seneca frequently quotes an Epicurean maxim and he refers to other philosophers, most notably Plato. But the Stoics are *nostri*, 'our own philosophers', and Seneca deals in some detail with a number of central Stoic doctrines. Advice and exhortation, however, are his main concern. Stoicism is valued for the benefits which its principles can confer on a man's state of mind and the conduct of his life. Seneca has little time for logic and purely theoretical knowledge. 'To desire to know more than is sufficient is a form of intemperance. This pursuit of liberal studies makes men wearisome, wordy, tactless and complacent; they do not learn what they need because they have already learnt things which are superfluous' (*Ep.* 88, 37). Stoicism of course had always stressed the relevance of its subject-matter to practical ethics. But Seneca and the other Roman Stoics gave a more restricted and less rigorous interpretation to 'philosophy' than their Greek predecessors.

The process of toning down the rigid intellectualism of Stoicism had begun with Panaetius. Roman Stoics like Seneca and Epictetus followed his lead with their emphasis on progress rather than perfection, and concessions to human fallibility. Stoicism becomes warmer and more responsive to the emotional side of human nature. But it ceases to be an elaborate conceptual system. In the first century A.D. Stoics and Cynics came closer together. Cynicism seems to have been relatively insignificant during the second and first centuries B.C., but the literature of the early Roman empire indicates a strong revival of the movement. A Cynic called Demetrius, who castigated wealth and luxury, was admired by Seneca, and an idea of what it meant to be a genuine Cynic at this time—there were many charlatans—can be gained from some of the published speeches of Dio Chrysostom (A.D. 40–after 112). Dio began his life in prosperous circumstances, and won acclaim as an orator and sophist in Greece. Banished by Domitian for alleged complicity in a political conspiracy, he spent fourteen years wandering in the Balkans and Asia Minor before he was restored to favour by Nerva. He lived by taking menial work and perhaps also by begging. The themes of his speeches were the traditional Cynic programme, and Diogenes figures as a model in several of them. Dio saw his rôle as a spiritual doctor who cures mental ill-health by showing that happiness comes from self-sufficiency and strength of character, not property, reputation or bodily pleasure.

The mendicant way of life and the value which Cynics placed upon poverty and freedom of speech or, in some cases, squalid appearance and insulting manners, were frowned upon by the Stoics. But Epictetus, although he criticized the parade of 'shamelessness' in Cynicism, saw the 'true Cynic' as 'a messenger sent to men from Zeus to show them that they have gone astray over things which are good and bad' (iii, 22, 23). A Stoic like Epictetus did not adopt the external characteristics of Cynicism—preaching in the streets and travelling from town to town with staff and satchel—but the inner freedom which Cynicism sought to inculcate is one of his favourite themes. Equally Cynic is his emphasis on hardiness and asceticism.

It is not only the moral earnestness of Seneca and Epictetus which has influenced those who call Roman Stoicism a religion. The description imports some misleading connotations, but it would be insensitive to overlook the religious language and feeling in contexts of Seneca, Epictetus and Marcus where they speak of the 'universe' or 'nature' or 'god'. None of this is inconsistent with earlier Stoicism, and Cleanthes' verses show that the system could provide a basis for genuine religious experience. But among Stoics of the Hellenistic world Cleanthes stands out as exceptional, even allowing for the deficiencies of our evidence. Religious aspirations are notoriously difficult to define, but recorded pagan thought during the early Roman empire has a religious dimension which marks it off from philosophy in the Hellenistic world. Plutarch is typical of the later period in this respect. Stoics had traditionally attempted to harmonize their teaching on Nature and God with the divinities of Greek and Roman religion. But we find few traces of this in the writings of the Roman Stoics. Their conception of a supreme being is practically if not formally monotheist. Epictetus calls God the father of mankind. In Seneca God is a somewhat elastic conception, but he has no doubts about divine benevolence and the personal interest of God in humanity. 'God approaches men—no, the relation is closer: he enters men. Without God no mind can be good. In the bodies of men divine seeds have been scattered' (*Ep.* 73, 16). Such statements could not fail to make an impression on Christian writers, and there was much else in the Stoicism of Seneca and Epictetus which they found congenial and instructive.

The Stoa continued to exist formally until 529 when Justinian closed the four philosophical schools at Athens. Its effective life was over three centuries earlier. By this time Christianity was spreading rapidly throughout the empire, and the revival of Platonism among pagan intellectuals also threatened the survival of Stoicism as an independent philosophical movement. Plotinus (205–70) incorporated Stoic and Aristotelian concepts in his new interpretation of the Platonic tradition, and Neoplatonism became a significant rival to Christianity in the fourth century. But it was the Church which helped above all to keep Stoic ideas in circulation, and Stoicism in its turn had an important influence on the Christian Fathers, in association with the still more notable influence of Platonism.

To an early Father, like Clement of Alexandria (*c.* 150–216), it was essential to demonstrate the superiority of Christianity to Greek philosophy. But Clement's official denunciations of pagan philosophers are much less striking than the positive use which he makes of Stoic and Platonic doctrines. He assimilates Stoic *logos* to 'the word of God', approves of the suppression of emotional impulses, and while teaching salvation as the basis of ethics sees the life of the Christian as 'a collection of rational actions, that is, the invarying practice of the teachings of the Word, which we call faith' (*Paid.* i 102, 4 Stählin). The sinner, like the Stoic 'fool', is ignorant. And we find Clement using a Stoic style of argument to prove that man is loved by God (*SVF* ii 1123). Clement was steeped in Greek literature, and the Stoic doctrines which he refers to or incorporates are part of the orthodox tradition. Of all the Christian Fathers he is the most valuable as a source for Stoic theory.

Among the Roman Church Fathers the same equivocal attitude towards Stoicism recurs. Tertullian stresses the differences between a philosopher and a Christian, but he calls Seneca 'often one of us' (*saepe noster*). The legend of Seneca as a Christian convert probably developed only in the late Middle Ages, but he was sufficiently read and esteemed by Christians in the fourth century to make it seem reasonable that he knew and corresponded with St. Paul.[1] The letters which purport to be from Seneca are first cited by St. Jerome in 392. They greatly helped to propagate the notion of Seneca as a convert to Christianity. After Greek texts ceased to be widely available in the western part of the empire Cicero's *De officiis* also helped to keep knowledge of Stoic moral theory alive. Epictetus' *Manual* took the place of Seneca in the east, and traces of his work have been found in Arabic texts.

The fortunes of Epicureanism in the empire have already been briefly surveyed (pp. 17ff.). Up to the year 200 it probably remained the main rival to Stoicism, but its influence on literature and intellectual thought was very much weaker. Epicureanism was always an inward-looking movement in antiquity, and under the later empire it probably flourished more in the eastern provinces than the Romanized west. So far as our evidence goes, the school produced no individual at this time who stands comparison with Seneca or Epictetus. Throughout its history Epicureanism remained predominantly the philosophy of Epicurus himself, and his name is invoked by later writers far more frequently than Zeno, the founder of Stoicism. Knowledge of Epicurean doctrines was widespread, and the space which Diogenes Laertius allots to Epicurus in his *Lives and doctrines of the eminent philosophers*, though it does not prove Diogenes an Epicurean, suggests a third-century audience with considerable interest in the system. It is particularly noteworthy that Diogenes abandons his normal practice of chatty anecdotes or potted summary in recording three of Epicurus' own works along with the *Principal doctrines*.

Plutarch is the most voluminous pagan critic of Epicureanism and Stoicism alike. The Christian Fathers were also hostile to Epicurus, but less so than one might have expected. Both Lactantius and Augustine refer frequently to Epicurus, and they sometimes give him qualified

[1] cf. A. Momigliano, 'Note sulla leggenda del cristianesimo di Seneca', *Rivista storica italiana* 62 (1950) 325–44.

approval. Unlike most of the Renaissance critics of Epicureanism they understood enough of the system to realize that Epicurus was not an advocate of unbridled sensuality. But Epicurus' theology and his insistence on the mortality of the soul were sufficient grounds in themselves to rouse the opposition of the Church.

Intellectual life during the later Roman empire assumed very diverse forms. It is important to remember that scholarship existed alongside superstition, and that science was not suddenly ousted by religion. Galen, Ptolemy, Plotinus, Proclus, and the long line of distinguished commentators on Aristotle from Alexander of Aphrodisias to Simplicius—these were men whose writings helped to preserve and extend the classical heritage of Greek philosophy and science. But it was a tradition which never gained a firm hold in Rome, and from the fourth century A.D. the Byzantine world became the main repository of Greek learning and literature for the next thousand years.

The revival of Scepticism at Alexandria, which began with Aenesidemus (see p. 76) and culminated in the works of Sextus Empiricus about the end of the second century, must also be regarded as an episode in the intellectual history of the eastern empire. Sextus' detailed presentation of sceptical arguments and his criticism of the dogmatists implies a conception of philosophy which was very different from the moralizing preoccupations of Roman writers. Scepticism was never a popular movement in the ancient world, and Sextus Empiricus exercised far more influence in the later Renaissance than he seems to have enjoyed at any other time. But two of the Latin Fathers, Lactantius and Augustine, were familiar with Cicero's *Academica*, and it was largely from their very different assessments of Academic scepticism that men in the Middle Ages derived some knowledge of sceptical ideas. Lactantius found the Academic criticism of all positivist philosophy a valuable beginning for Christian belief. This position is expounded in the third book of his *Divinae institutiones*, and it prefigures the way in which many Renaissance thinkers used scepticism as a basis for fideism. St. Augustine on the other hand attacked scepticism in his *Contra academicos*, an early work written in 386. The answer to scepticism for Augustine was the Christian revelation, but his critical treatise, with its approval of Plato, does not conceal the fact that scepticism made a strong impression upon him as a young man.

Cicero, Seneca and the Latin Patristic writers were the principal sources through which western Europe in the Middle Ages attained some knowledge of Stoic moral thought. The number of ninth- and tenth-century manuscripts of Seneca gives a proof of the interest his work aroused, and many of Cicero's philosophical works were known at this time, though the great period of their influence began with Petrarch and other Italian humanists. William of Conches in the twelth century wrote a *Moralium dogma philosophorum* which he based largely on Cicero's *De officiis* and Seneca. These were the favourite ancient authors of Roger Bacon and some other notable medieval writers. But it was not until the Renaissance that Hellenistic philosophy reappeared as a major formative influence on western thought. By the beginning of the sixteenth century a combination of complex circumstances—they include the Reformation, the new humanist curriculum which emphasized rhetoric and moral philosophy rather than scholastic logic and theology, availability of printed editions, and the rediscovery of Plato and other Greek authors— contributed to more intense study of familiar writers such as Cicero and Seneca and the immediate popularity of many others who had been newly recovered: Epictetus, Plutarch and Diogenes Laertius are those most relevant to our main theme. The vogue of Lucretius and Sextus Empiricus came rather later.

Renaissance scholars were highly eclectic in their approach to ancient philosophy. Through Nicholas of Cusa, Marsilio Ficino and Pico della Mirandola Neoplatonism experienced a revival in Italy during the fifteenth century, and later, as we shall see, there were neo-Stoics, Epicureans and Sceptics. But it is generally misleading to apply such descriptions to sixteenth-century figures. They read Greek and Latin authors principally for moral edification, and Stoic, Platonic and Aristotelian ideas were frequently brought together and combined with Christian doctrine. In *The education of a Christian prince* Erasmus wrote: 'To be a philosopher and to be a Christian is synonymous in fact if not in name', and the philosopher might be Plato or Cicero, Seneca or Socrates.[1] Stoicism cannot be easily isolated from other constituents of Renaissance culture. But its importance at this time is conspicuous, and certain facts can be stated without undue danger of over-simplification.

Seneca enjoyed an enormous reputation, and the other principal sources of Stoic ideas were Cicero, Epictetus and Plutarch. Diogenes Laertius had been known through the Latin translation of Ambrogio

[1] Trans. L. K. Born (New York 1936) p. 150.

Traversari since the early fifteenth century,[1] but Diogenes' important summary of Greek Stoic doctrines was unpalatable compared with the rhetorical elegance and practical moralizing of the Roman Stoics. Erasmus, though he did not share Calvin's admiration for Seneca, published an edition in 1527, followed by a second two years later, which was reprinted several times before 1580. Calvin himself, who called Seneca 'a master of ethics', wrote a commentary on the *De clementia*. Epictetus was first edited complete by Trincavelli in 1535. The *Manual* was already widely known through Politian's translation, first published in 1495, and by 1540 it had been printed in Greek with Latin translation at Strasburg, Venice, Nuremberg, Basle, and Paris. The first edition of Marcus Aurelius appeared at Heidelberg in 1558.

The Stoics' emphasis on the rationality of human nature is frequently reflected by Renaissance writers. More's Utopians define virtue as life according to nature and the 'natural' life is interpreted in Stoic terms as one 'which in desiring and refusing things is ruled by reason' (pp. 121f. ed. Goitrim). Guillaume Budé drew on Seneca's *De tranquillitate animi* for his own work, *De contemptu rerum fortuitarum* published in 1520. Another sixteenth-century English work to which Stoicism made an important contribution is Richard Hooker's *Of the laws of ecclesiastical polity* (1594). But there were more notable attempts to harmonize Stoicism with Christianity. The Belgian humanist, Justus Lipsius, whose greatest scholarly work was an edition of Tacitus, projected a large commentary on Seneca which he did not live to complete. His interest in Stoicism had been declared in 1583 when he published *De constantia,* a work which proved extremely popular, and the completed parts of his Seneca commentary ran through five editions between 1605 and 1652. They include two essays on Stoicism, *Manuductio ad Stoicam philosophiam* and *Physiologiae Stoicorum*. In the latter work Lipsius gives an analysis of Stoic metaphysics and, where possible, he seeks to justify the Stoics by quoting biblical references. The *Manuductio* likewise is not an impartial account of Stoic ethics. Lipsius was concerned to show that Stoicism, by which he means chiefly the moral doctrines in Seneca and Epictetus, can be regarded as a valuable supplement to Christian faith. But in pursuing this aim Lipsius opened the door to natural religion

---

[1] R. Sabbadini refers to an earlier Latin version now lost which was in circulation from the tenth to the thirteenth centuries, *Le scoperte dei codici Latini e Greci* II (Florence 1914) pp. 262f. Mrs. A. C. Griffiths kindly drew my attention to this and several other points which I have incorporated in this chapter.

and secular morality. Holding as he did that a man imitates God by living in accordance with reason, Lipsius gave just the kind of rationalist interpretation of Christianity which men like Erasmus and Montaigne found objectionable.

Lipsius' Stoicism finds an interesting parallel in the work of a French contemporary, Guillaume du Vair. A lawyer by training, du Vair wrote three works designed to show the value of Stoicism as a philosophy of life: *La philosophie morale des Stoïques*, translated into English by Charles Cotton in 1664; *De la constance et consolation ès calamités publiques*, translated by Andrew Comt in 1602 with the title, *A buckler against adversitie*; and *La sainte philosophie*. Du Vair acknowledged that Stoic rationality must be augmented by faith and that perfection requires the help of God. But he traced the sources of moral error to false judgments, emphasized the need to free the soul of passionate emotions, and defined the good for man as 'a healthful reason, that is, virtue'.

Judging by printed editions of Seneca, Epictetus and Marcus Aurelius, Stoicism in the Renaissance was at its most popular in France, Germany and Italy between 1590 and 1640.[1] But its influence continued to be strong over the next hundred years. In his *Discourse of the pastoral care* (1692) Gilbert Burnet recommended the clergy to read Epictetus and Marcus Aurelius, whose works 'contain such Instructions that one cannot read them too often nor repass them too frequently in his thoughts'.[2] In England under the reign of Queen Anne a remarkable secular interest in Cato developed. Admiration for this Roman Stoic saint was nothing new. Through Plutarch's *Life* and other ancient sources Cato became one of the outstanding heroes of the Renaissance, but in early eighteenth-century England he was used as a symbol of political 'liberty' as well as moral virtue. Of Addison's tragedy, *Cato* (1713), Pope wrote to John Caryll, 'I question if any play has ever conduced so immediately to morals as this.'[3] Whigs and Tories alike claimed support for their principles from Cato, and Jonathan Swift seems to have consciously modelled himself on the Roman Stoic.[4] The English Augustan writers particularly admired the

---

[1] cf. J. Eymard d'Angers, 'Le Renouveau du stoicisme au XVI et au XVII siècle', *Actes du 7 Congrès Guillaume Budé* (Paris 1964) pp. 122–55.

[2] Quoted by M. L. Clarke, *Classical Education in Britain 1500–1900* (Cambridge 1959) p. 169.

[3] *Works* ed. Elwin and Courthope, vol. vi (London 1871) p. 182.

[4] cf. J. W. Johnson, *The Formation of English Neo-classical Thought* (Princeton 1967) pp. 101f.

Roman Republic and Cato provided a focus for their neo-classical ideals.

The philosophical influence of Stoicism, as I have already mentioned (p. 208), is evident in Spinoza and Kant. Two English philosophers whose work is worth studying from this point of view are the Earl of Shaftesbury and Bishop Butler.

Epicureanism had to wait longer than Stoicism for its own renaissance. The religious, moral and intellectual currents of the sixteenth century were largely against a philosophy which contained hedonism and empiricism as two principal features, and the usage of 'Epicure' to denote sensualist dates from this time. It is also worth observing that Lucretius unlike Seneca was virtually unknown in the Middle Ages. The oldest manuscript (Oblongus) dates from the ninth century, but it was Poggio's discovery of a text of Lucretius in 1417 which made the poet available to the Renaissance. The first printed edition appeared at Brescia in 1473, and Lambinus' important text and commentary was published in 1564. But it was not until 1675 that a Latin edition of Lucretius came out of England. Interest in Epicureanism and Lucretius grew more rapidly in Italy, France and Germany, but Laurentius Valla's sympathetic treatment (*De voluptate ac vero bono*, 1431) was exceptional before the seventeenth century, and Valla had not read Lucretius.

The man who did most to make Epicureanism respectable and who pioneered an important revival of interest in it was Pierre Gassendi. Gassendi (1592–1655) was a Catholic priest who ended his career as professor of mathematics at the Royal College in Paris. Like Descartes, Gassendi was a vigorous opponent of Aristotelian scholasticism, but the direction of his dissent was very different from Descartes'. In common with many of his French contemporaries Gassendi was influenced by ancient scepticism, and his 'Pyrrhonist' leanings helped to determine his search for a criterion of truth in the senses and not the rationalist's *cogito*.

In 1647 Gassendi published his *De vita et moribus Epicuri*, which he followed two years later with *Animadversiones in decimum librum Diogenis Laertii et philosophiae Epicuri syntagma*. The *De vita* was the most significant work of neo-Epicureanism. In it Gassendi sought to defend Epicurus' life and teaching against ancient and modern criticism. Most of the principal Epicurean doctrines were well understood by Gassendi and his commentary on the tenth book of Diogenes Laertius is a considerable work of scholarship. But Gassendi did not approach Epicurus as a disinterested scholar. Critical of Aristotle and Descartes alike, Gassendi found in Epicureanism a system which he could turn to good account in the dawning scientific enlightenment. As a Christian however he could not take over ancient Epicureanism without modification. The main changes which he introduced throw an interesting light on a man who was both a devout Catholic and a free-thinker. Gassendi rejected Epicurus' theology. The universe, on Gassendi's interpretation, is not a chance combination of atoms but an expression of divine goodness, and the atoms were created by God. Nor, as Epicurus claimed, is there an infinite number of atoms. Only God is infinite, and the movements of atoms reveal order and providence.

The actual effects of Gassendi's promotion of Epicureanism on seventeenth-century science cannot be assessed in this short survey. What is certain is his general influence upon an Epicurean revival which spread from France to England. Two years before the publication of the *De vita* another Frenchman, Jean François Saresin, brought out a work entitled *Discours de morale sur Epicure*, and these two books were drawn upon by Walter Charleton whose *Epicurus's morals* (1656) is the earliest surviving Epicurean publication by an Englishman. Charleton was a high-church medical doctor and his work gives a popular defence of Epicurean ethics. There was still however no English translation of Lucretius' complete poem. The diarist, John Evelyn, brought out a verse translation of the first book in the same year that Charleton's work appeared. But neither Charleton nor Evelyn provided the main stimulus to Epicureanism in England. The credit for this belongs to Thomas Creech, John Dryden and Sir William Temple.

Creech's importance rests on his translation of Lucretius which was published at Oxford in 1682. At last the most detailed account of Epicureanism was available in English, and Creech's translation in vigorous heroic verse was an immediate success. Creech concealed from his preface any overt sympathy for Epicurus. Like many who had previously written on Lucretius he professed that 'the best method to overthrow the Epicurean hypothesis . . . is to expose a full system of it to public view'. But the intellectual climate of Restoration England was for rather than against Lucretius and Epicurus. In 1685 Dryden included a selection of verse translations of Lucretius in his *Second miscellany*, and Dryden's reputation helped to stimulate still more interest in the Epicurean poet and his doctrines. Like Creech, Dryden was careful to distinguish between translating Lucretius and approving what he said. But in the same year, positive endorsement of Epicurean ethics came from the eminent and influential Temple. *Upon the Gardens of Epicurus; or, of Gardening, in the year 1685* is an odd mixture of Epicurean apologetics and a discussion of seventeenth-century gardening. The intention of Temple's apology can be shown by this enthusiastic quotation:

> I have often wondered how such sharp and violent invectives came to be made so generally against Epicurus whose admirable wit, felicity of expression, excellence of nature, sweetness of conversation, temperance of life, and constancy of death, made him so beloved by his friends, admired by his scholars, and honoured by the Athenians.[1]

For a short period, with the support of Charles II and his circle, a popular form of Epicureanism was fashionable in England. Shadwell's *The Virtuoso* contains praise of Lucretius. And the importance of distinguishing genuine Epicureanism from prevalent misconceptions is echoed in these interesting lines from Cowley's poem, *The Garden*:

> When Epicurus to the World had taught,
> That Pleasure was the chiefest Good,
> (And was perhaps i' the right if rightly understood) . . .
> Whoever a true Epicure would be,
> May find there [*sc.* in a Garden] cheap and virtuous luxurie.

But counter-attacks were soon forthcoming, including a turgid poem by Sir Richard Blackmore in 1712: *Creation: a philosophical poem demonstrating the Existence and Providence of God.*[2] Indirect references and influences are more difficult to detect. They have been postulated for many English writers from Hobbes to Gibbon, and John Stuart Mill regarded Epicureanism as an early, though inadequate, example of utilitarianism.

On the philosophical and literary influence of Stoicism and Epicureanism much work remains to be done. Ancient scepticism also enjoyed a considerable vogue in the Renaissance, and its direct influence on philosophy and religious thought has been demonstrated by Richard Popkin.[3] In the Hellenistic world it was the existence of conflicting

---

[1] *Works*, vol. iii (London 1757) p. 203.
[2] The French Cardinal, Melchior de Polignac, wrote a more distinguished verse polemic, *Anti-Lucretius*, published in 1745.
[3] *The History of Scepticism from Erasmus to Descartes* (Assen 1960).

positivist systems which provided conditions under which philosophical doubt could flourish. The sceptic solved the problem of judging between Stoics, Epicureans and others by developing arguments designed to show that certainty and truth were unattainable by any system. Later, as we have seen with Lactantius and Augustine, Christian thinkers asserted that the only adequate answer to scepticism lay in faith and revelation. But Lactantius unlike Augustine found it possible to approve scepticism for showing philosophical 'wisdom' to be illusory.

In the Reformation, which produced its own problem of the criterion of truth, scepticism was called upon, especially by Catholics, as a means of attacking the other side. Erasmus in *De libero arbitrio* (1524) gave a sceptical criticism of Luther's biblical interpretation advocating in its place a pious acceptance of the traditional Church doctrine. Luther's impassioned reaction in *De servo arbitrio* (1525) charged Erasmus with undermining Christianity: a Christian cannot be a sceptic; '*spiritus sanctus non est scepticus*'. What Popkin has called 'the intellectual crisis of the Reformation' gave a new interest and importance to ancient sceptical arguments. In *The praise of folly* Erasmus referred approvingly to the Academics,[1] but it was the Pyrrhonism of Sextus Empiricus, whose works only became widely known in the latter part of the sixteenth century, that proved particularly influential.

The first printed text of Sextus was a Latin translation of the *Outlines of Pyrrhonism* published by Henri Estienne (Stephanus) at Paris in 1562. Seven years later the French Counter-Reformer, Gentian Hervet, brought out a Latin edition of the whole of Sextus, which was printed at Paris and Antwerp. The Greek text was first printed in 1621 by P. and J. Chouet at Cologne, Paris and Geneva. This was not available to Montaigne who died in 1592, but the French essayist's familiarity with Pyrrhonist arguments is constantly evident in the work which had great influence on seventeenth-century scepticism, the *Apologie de Raimond Sebond*. Montaigne makes use of Pyrrhonism for its original purpose of casting doubt upon every objective criterion of judgment. He 'defends' Sebond in an oblique way by seeking to show that faith, not rational demonstration, is the basis of the Christian religion. Certainty is unattainable by theological reasoning and therefore Sebond's *Natural theology*, which had been criticized as unsound, could not be judged inferior to any other rational justification of Christianity. Two short extracts must suffice here to illustrate Mon-

[1] Trans. L. Dean (Chicago 1946) p. 84.

taigne's Pyrrhonism. The Pyrrhonist attitude of total doubt is approved because it

... presents man naked and empty, recognizing his natural weakness, fit to receive from on high any unknown force, stripped of human knowledge and all the more ready to accommodate the divine in himself, annihilating his own judgment to make greater room for faith.[1]

Here we see how Montaigne like Erasmus and other Catholics linked scepticism on the rational level with faith in religion, and saw the former as a means to the latter. Montaigne rehearses many of the traditional Pyrrhonist arguments against reliance upon sense-experience or scientific knowledge, and he concludes:

In order to judge appearances which we receive from objects we need an instrument of judgment; in order to verify this instrument we need demonstration; in order to verify demonstration we need an instrument: there we are, arguing in a circle.[2]

It was not only religious controversy which stimulated the 'new Pyrrhonists' of the next generation in France. Opposition to Aristotelian scholasticism, alchemy, astrology, and the mystical systems of men like Paracelsus, Pomponazzi and Giordano Bruno also gave birth to scepticism. There was nothing in the early seventeenth century which could count as a scientific orthodoxy. Modern science was in its infancy and no one at the time could foresee its eventual development. It is impossible to survey the influence of ancient scepticism on the French 'libertins erudits' in this chapter. We must simply note that Sextus Empiricus was a most important influence on the writings of François de la Mothe Le Vayer, Gabriel Naudé and Gassendi. In the second half of the seventeenth century a new generation of sceptics rose to attack the new dogmatists, especially Descartes. Pierre Bayle represents the culmination of this criticism, and these remarks from his article on Pyrrho in the *Dictionnaire historique et critique* (1697–1702), even allowing for irony, throw a fascinating light on Pyrrhonism two thousand years after its inception:

When one is capable of really understanding the tropes given by Sextus Empiricus, one feels that this Logic is the greatest effort of subtility that the human mind can make; but one sees at the same time that this subtility can give no satisfaction; it confounds itself: for if it were solid, it would prove that it is certain that one ought to doubt. There would then be some certitude,

[1] *Les Essais de Michel de Montaigne* ed. P. Villey (Paris 1922) p. 238.
[2] *Les Essais*, p. 366.

one would then have some Rule of Truth. . . . The reasons for doubting are themselves dubious. One must doubt if one must doubt. What chaos and what torture for the mind! It seems then that this unfortunate state is most proper of all for convincing us that our Reason is a way to Bewilderment, since when she deploys herself with the most subtility, she throws us into such an abyss. The natural consequence of this ought to be to renounce the guide and ask for a better one. This is the great step towards the Christian religion, for it wishes that we obtain from God the knowledge of what we ought to believe and do, it wishes that we make our understanding the obedient slave of faith.[1]

While Bayle attempted to undermine all rational explanations of the world, the laws of Nature were being proclaimed by Newton and his followers. The laws of Nature were the laws of reason, and to many in the eighteenth century the universe at large and the moral sense of the individual revealed the handiwork of a divine artificer. Deism, or natural theology, was a consequence of the contemporary scientific and religious situation, but it has very strong conceptual, if not historical, links with Stoicism. It was the Stoics whose concept of Nature as rational first sanctioned a clear connexion between physical causation and universal harmony on the one hand and moral well-being on the other. In the intellectual climate inaugurated by Newton this idea took on a new significance. Newton himself at the end of his *Opticks* wrote:

If natural Philosophy in all its Parts . . . shall at length be perfected, the Bounds of Moral Philosophy will also be enlarged. For so far as we can know by natural Philosophy what is the first cause, what Power he has over us, what benefits we receive from him, so far our Duty towards him, as well as that towards one another, will appear to us by the Light of Nature.[2]

The Stoics would equally have approved the sentiments expressed in this popular account of Newtonianism:

Our views of Nature, however imperfect, serve to represent to us, in the most sensible manner, that mighty power which prevails throughout, acting with a force and efficacy that appears to suffer no diminution from the greatest distances of space or intervals of time: and that wisdom which we see displayed in the exquisite structure and just motion of the greatest and subtilest parts. These, with the perfect goodness, by which they are evidently directed,

---

[1] Article 'Pyrrho', Rem. B, cited in Popkin, *Philosophy and Phenomenological Research* 16 (1955–6) 65. For the impact of Pyrrhonism on historiography, cf. A. Momigliano, *Studies in Historiography* (London 1966) pp. 10ff.

[2] *Opticks*, bk. iii, pt. i, qu. 31 (1st ed., 1704; reprint ed. E. T. Whittaker, 1931).

constitute the supreme object of the speculations of a philosopher; who, while he contemplates and admires so excellent a system, cannot but be himself excited and animated to correspond with the general harmony of Nature.[1]

Today such optimism seems out of place, but it was a reasonable attitude to hold in the eighteenth century and one which helps to show that Stoicism itself is of more than historical interest. The Stoics defended their system on rational grounds, but part of its attraction was aesthetic and emotional. The idea or ideal of an orderly universe to which men contribute as rational beings is one of its most important legacies to western culture.

The influence of Hellenistic philosophy on European literature and thought reached a high point between 1500 and 1700. Thereafter it becomes too diffused to be marked out briefly with any precision. The Roman moralists were still widely read up to the middle of the nineteenth century, but it was in the Renaissance that they were chiefly valued as guides to life. Epicurus and Sextus Empiricus helped to promote the development of modern empiricism, but this movement had acquired its own momentum by the early eighteenth century. For very good reasons academic interest in Plato and Aristotle increased, and the Hellenistic philosophers suffered by the comparison. In Germany, Hegelian idealism influenced the unfavourable assessment of Hellenistic philosophy given by Eduard Zeller in his *History of Greek Philosophy* (1st ed. 1844–52), and Zeller's authority determined many subsequent attitudes. But it was primarily German scholars, Zeller himself, Hermann Usener and Hans von Arnim in particular, who laid the foundations for a critical understanding of Stoicism and Epicureanism. A British scholar of distinction, A. C. Pearson, published *The Fragments of Zeno and Cleanthes* in 1891, twelve years before the appearance of Arnim's *Stoicorum Veterum Fragmenta*. And there were other notable British editions: J. S. Reid, Cicero's *Academica* (1885); Cyril Bailey, *Epicurus* (1926) and *Lucretius* (1947); A. S. L. Farquharson, *Marcus Aurelius* (1944). But in general, few British or American scholars who were active before the last war took a great interest in Hellenistic philosophy. Only two critical studies of lasting value were produced in Britain during this time: R.D. Hicks, *Stoic and Epicurean* (1910) and Bailey, *The Greek Atomists and Epicurus* (1928). Anglo-Saxon scholarship in this field

[1] Colin Maclaurin, *An Account of Sir I. Newton's Philosophical Discoveries* (quoted by C. L. Becker in *The Heavenly City of the Eighteenth Century Philosophers* (Yale 1932) pp. 62–3).

lagged behind the work which was being done in Germany, Italy and France.

The bibliography of this book, which concentrates on work in English, shows that the situation has changed during the last twenty years. British and American scholars have now done important new work on many aspects of Hellenistic philosophy, and as a result the subject has gained greater academic respectability in these countries. Under the aegis of cultural history Hellenistic philosophy has always commanded attention. But informed appreciations of its conceptual significance are still uncommon. More work is needed to illuminate unfamiliar topics and to demonstrate the intrinsic interest of Greek philosophy after Aristotle. Its limitations and achievements have much to tell us about ourselves.

Bibliography

THE principal ancient sources have been described briefly in the first part of Chapters 2, 3 and 4. Modern editions of these authors are listed in Part 2 of this bibliography, and some general works and background reading are referred to in Part 1. The rest of the bibliography is arranged according to the chapters of the book. Some works are cited here which are not referred to in the notes to chapters, and the bibliography is not designed to give details of every book or article mentioned in the notes. So far as possible the modern works which have been selected are in English, but some particularly valuable studies in other languages have also been included.

1. GENERAL

Philosophy and science
A. H. Armstrong (editor), *The Cambridge History of Later Greek and Early Medieval Philosophy* (Cambridge 1967); mainly devoted to Neoplatonism and later developments; good short treatment of the Academy and Lyceum in the Hellenistic period.

H. C. Baldry, *The Unity of Mankind in Greek Thought* (Cambridge 1965).

D. R. Dudley, *A History of Cynicism* (London 1937).

R. D. Hicks, *Stoic and Epicurean* (New York 1910); also deals with Scepticism; sometimes stimulating but also outdated in style and discussion of details.

W. and M. Kneale, *The Development of Logic* (Oxford 1962); very good discussion of Aristotelian and Stoic logic.

S. Sambursky, *The Physical World of the Greeks* (London 1956); includes an illuminating appraisal of Stoic and Epicurean physics.

E. Zeller, *Die Philosophie der Griechen*, vol. iii (5th ed., ed. by E. Wellmann, Leipzig 1923). An earlier edition translated by O. Reichel with the title, *Stoics, Epicureans and Sceptics* (London 1880); basically insensitive to the achievements of the Stoics, but still a useful synoptic work on Hellenistic philosophy.

History and cultural background

E. R. Dodds, *The Greeks and the Irrational* (Berkeley and Los Angeles 1951); includes a fascinating short account of philosophy and religion in the Hellenistic world which, in my judgment, does less than justice to the philosophers.

W. S. Ferguson, *Hellenistic Athens* (London 1911).

N. M. P. Nilsson, *Geschichte der griechischen Religion*, vol. ii (2nd ed., Munich 1961); the best book on Hellenistic religion.

R. Pfeiffer, *History of Classical Scholarship*, vol. i (Oxford 1968); a masterly work of synthesis on the scholars of the Hellenistic period.

W. W. Tarn, *Hellenistic Civilization* (3rd ed. revised by G. T. Griffith, London 1952).

T. B. L. Webster, *Hellenistic Poetry and Art* (London 1964).

2. PRINCIPAL ANCIENT AUTHORS

The editions specified include a full commentary unless otherwise indicated. Translations of most authors with facing Greek or Latin text are available in the Loeb Classical Library editions published by Heinemann and the Harvard University Press. Some more recent translations which have appeared in paperback are also mentioned.

Aurelius, Marcus (A.D. 121–80). *Meditations*, ed. and trans. by A. S. L. Farquharson, 2 vols. (Oxford 1944). Trans. in paperback by G. M. A. Grube, *The Library of Liberal Arts* (Bobbs-Merrill, Indianapolis and New York 1963).

Cicero (106–43 B.C.). *Academica*, ed. by J. S. Reid (London 1885).

— *De divinatione*, ed. by A. S. Pease (Urbana 1920–3).

— *De fato*, ed. by A. Yon, with facing French trans. (Paris 1950).

— *De finibus bonorum et malorum*, ed. by J. N. Madvig, with notes in Latin (3rd ed. 1876, Copenhagen; reprinted Hildesheim 1965). Books i and ii (summary and criticism of Epicurean ethics) ed. by J. S. Reid (London 1925).

— *De natura deorum*, ed. by A. S. Pease, 2 vols. (Cambridge, Mass. 1955–8). Trans. in paperback by C. P. McGregor, with introd. by J. M. Ross, Penguin Classics (1972).

— *De officiis*, ed. by H. A. Holden (3rd ed., Cambridge 1879).

— *De republica*, ed. by K. Ziegler (Leipzig 1960; critical text only).

— *Tusculan disputations*, ed. by T. W. Dougan and R. M. Henry

(Oxford 1905–34). Parts trans. by M. Grant in *Cicero on the Good Life* (along with *De amicitia* and other extracts), Penguin Classics (1971).

Diogenes Laertius (3rd century A.D.). *Lives of Eminent Philosophers*, ed. by H. S. Long, 2 vols. (Oxford 1964; brief annotation only). The best trans. is into Italian by M. Gigante (Bari 1962).

Epictetus (*c.* A.D. 55–135). *Discourses Recorded by Arrian*, ed. by H. Schenkl (2nd ed., Leipzig 1916; critical text only). Good Loeb trans. by W. A. Oldfather, 2 vols. (1925).

Epicurus, see Bibliography Part 3.

Galen (A.D. 129–*c.* 200). *De placitis Hippocratis et Platonis*, ed. by I. Mueller (Leipzig 1874; critical text only). No Loeb; Latin trans. in edition by C. G. Kühn (Leipzig 1821–33). A new edition is in preparation by Phillip de Lacy for the series, *Corpus Medicorum Graecorum*.

Lucretius (*c.* 94–55 B.C.). *De rerum natura*, ed. and trans. by C. Bailey, 3 vols. (Oxford 1947). Trans. in paperback by R. E. Latham, Penguin Classics.

Plutarch (*c.* A.D. 46–121). *De stoicorum repugnantiis* and *De communibus notitiis* have been edited along with Plutarch's anti-Epicurean treatises by M. Pohlenz in Plutarch *Moralia* vol. vi 2 (revised by R. Westman, Leipzig 1959; brief annotation only). Detailed discussion of the work *Against Colotes* (Epicurean) by R. Westman in *Acta Philosophica Fennica* VII (1955), written in German. The anti-Epicurean works are available in a Loeb edition by B. Einarson and Ph. De Lacy (*Moralia* XIV). A further Loeb edition of the anti-Stoic treatises is being prepared by Harold Cherniss.

Seneca (*c.* 5 B.C.–A.D. 65). *Epistulae morales*, ed. by L. D. Reynolds, 2 vols. (Oxford 1965; brief annotation only). A selection has been translated in a paperback edition by R. Campbell, *Penguin Classics* (1969).

Sextus Empiricus (second century A.D.). *Outlines of Pyrrhonism* and *Against the dogmatic philosophers*, ed. by H. Mutschmann and others (Leipzig 1914–54; critical text only). The Loeb trans. by R. G. Bury is sometimes seriously inaccurate. A selection of Sextus' writings trans. in *Scepticism, Man and God*, ed. by Ph. Hallie (Middletown, Conn. 1964).

3. EPICURUS AND EPICUREANISM

The standard collection of Epicurus' writings and other ancient evidence on his life and philosophy is H. Usener, *Epicurea* (Leipzig 1887, reprinted Stuttgart 1966). Usener arranged his material by subject-matter, beginning with Epicurus' own works, and the individual texts are numbered consecutively and referred to in this book as Us. 271 etc. No translations were given by Usener and he did not include fragments of Epicurus' works preserved in Herculaneum papyri. Much of the latter material has been incorporated in a collection by G. Arrighetti, *Epicuro Opere* (Turin 1960), who also gives an Italian translation and helpful annotation. This work, which is about to appear in a second edition, is a valuable supplement to Usener. The best text of the three *Letters* of Epicurus recorded by Diogenes Laertius is P. von der Muehll, *Epicurus: Epistulae tres et ratae sententiae* (Stuttgart 1923, reprinted 1966). A further text with translation and valuable commentary is C. Bailey, *Epicurus* (Oxford 1926).

General studies: the most authoritative work is C. Bailey, *The Greek Atomists and Epicurus* (Oxford 1928). N. W. de Witt, *Epicurus and his Philosophy* (Minneapolis 1954), and B. Farrington, *The Faith of Epicurus* (London 1967), are more stimulating but less reliable. J. M. Rist, *Epicurus: an Introduction* (Cambridge 1972), appeared after the first draft of this book was completed. It is a tougher work than its title suggests. For a bibliography of recent work and a collection of papers on many aspects of Epicureanism cf. *Actes du VIIIᵉ Congrès Association Guillaume Budé* (Paris 1969).

Some recent studies of particular topics: on Epicurus' theory of knowledge cf. D. J. Furley, 'Knowledge of Atoms and Void' in *Essays in Ancient Greek Philosophy*, ed. J .P. Anton and G. L. Kustas (N.Y. 1971) 607–19, and A. A. Long, 'Aisthesis, Prolepsis and Linguistic Theory in Epicurus', *Bulletin of the Institute of Classical Studies* 18 (1971) 114–33; on cosmology cf. F. Solmsen, 'Epicurus and Cosmological Heresies', *American Journal of Philology* 72 (1951) 1–23 and 'Epicurus on the Growth and Decline of the Cosmos', ibid. 74 (1953) 34–51; on indivisible magnitudes, a controversial subject, cf. G. Vlastos, 'Minimal Parts in Epicurean Atomism', *Isis* 56 (1965) 121–47 and D. J. Furley, *Two Studies in the Greek Atomists* (Princeton 1967) first study; on theology cf. A. J. Festugière, *Epicurus and his Gods*, trans. C. W. Chilton (Oxford 1955); and K. Kleve, 'Gnosis

Theon', *Symbolae Osloenses*, suppl. 19 (1963); on psychology cf. D. J. Furley, op. cit. second study and G. B. Kerferd, 'Epicurus' Doctrine of the Soul', *Phronesis* 16 (1971) 80–96; on pleasure cf. P. Merlan, *Studies in Epicurus and Aristotle* (Wiesbaden 1960) first study.

Individual later Epicureans. (*a*) Philodemus: much of the extant material is extremely fragmentary. The most important philosophical text is the *De signis* (On signs) which has been edited, translated and discussed by Ph. and E. A. De Lacy, *Philodemus: On Methods of Inference* (Philological Monograph of the American Philological Association, no. x, Pennsylvania 1941). Cf. also M. Gigante, *Ricerce filodemee* (Naples 1969). (*b*) Lucretius: the best study of his treatment of Epicureanism is by P. Boyancé, *Lucrèce et l'Épicurisme* (Paris 1963). (*c*) Diogenes of Oenoanda: critical text by C. W. Chilton (Leipzig 1967), trans. and commentary by the same author, *Diogenes of Oenoanda* (London, O.U.P. 1971). New fragments have been discovered and published by M. F. Smith, *American Journal of Archaeology* 74 (1971) 51–62, 75 (1971) 357–89, and *Journal of Hellenic Studies* 92 (1972) 147–55.

4. SCEPTICISM

The best comprehensive study is V. Brochard, *Les Sceptiques grecs* (2nd ed. Paris 1932, reprinted Paris 1959). Less detailed but more interesting philosophically is C. L. Stough, *Greek Skepticism* (Berkeley and Los Angeles 1969).

Individual Sceptic philosophers: (*a*) Pyrrho and Timon: see Brochard especially; (*b*) Arcesilaus: an excellent concise study by H. von Arnim in Pauly-Wissowa, *Real-Enzyklopädie*, vol. 2, no. 1, article on Arkesilaos; see also O. Gigon, 'Zur Geschichte der sogennanten neuen Akademie', *Museum Helveticum* i (1944) 47–64; (*c*) Carneades: notes by A. Weische in Pauly-Wissowa, suppl. 11, article on Karneades; see also A. A. Long, 'Carneades and the Stoic Telos', *Phronesis* 12 (1967) 59–90; (*d*) Aenesidemus: for a persuasive account of his philosophical development see J. M. Rist, 'The Heracliteanism of Aenesidemus', *Phoenix* 24 (1970) 309–19.

Other useful modern studies: R. Chisholm, 'Sextus Empiricus and Modern Empiricism', *Philosophy of Science* 8 (1941) 471–84; Ph. De Lacy, '*Ou Mallon* and the Antecedents of Ancient Scepticism', *Phronesis*

3 (1958) 59–71; R. Popkin, 'David Hume: his Pyrrhonism and his Critique of Pyrrhonism', *Philosophical Quarterly* 5 (1951) 385–407.

5. STOICISM

The standard collection of evidence for Early Stoicism (Zeno to Antipater of Tarsus) is H. von Arnim, *Stoicorum Veterum Fragmenta* (*SVF*), 4 vols. (Leipzig 1903–24, reprinted Stuttgart 1964). This work has proved its value over the years, but it is now in need of revision. Some of the material which Arnim included is of doubtful validity for establishing Chrysippus' views, and certain writers, especially Cicero and Seneca, are under-represented. In using this collection it is always necessary to consider the context and characteristics of each author who is excerpted.

In this book, texts which are relatively accessible such as Diogenes Laertius and Cicero are normally cited by reference to their authors. Material which is most easily consulted by using von Arnim is cited by the fragment number in his collection, for instance *SVF* iii 121, that is, volume 3 and the passage or passages included as fragment 121. The text translated is not always that of von Arnim.

General studies: E. V. Arnold, *Roman Stoicism* (Cambridge 1911); lucid and well-balanced, though somewhat over-simplified and now outdated; especially valuable for its many quotations in the original. J. Christensen, *An Essay on the Unity of Stoic Philosophy* (Copenhagen 1962); the most philosophically sophisticated short introduction. L. Edelstein, *The Meaning of Stoicism* (Cambridge, Mass. 1966); a stimulating little book which is sometimes misleading. M. Pohlenz, *Die Stoa* (3rd ed., Göttingen 1964) 2 vols.; the most comprehensive book on Stoicism, very fully annotated in the second volume.

Zeno: K. von Fritz, Pauly-Wissowa, *Real-Enzyklopädie* suppl. 10A, article on Zenon of Kition; a new study, particularly interesting on Zeno's philosophical background.

Chrysippus: E. Bréhier, *Chrysippe et l'ancien stoïcisme* (2nd ed., Paris 1950); a thoughtful and generally reliable book. J. B. Gould, *The Philosophy of Chrysippus* (Leiden 1971); some useful discussions but marred in part by rigidity in the selection of evidence.

Books which discuss specific topics in detail: Victor Goldschmidt, *Le Système stoicien et l'idée de temps* (2nd ed., Paris 1969). *Problems in Stoicism* (London 1971) ed. A. A. Long, with contributions by I. G. Kidd, A. C. Lloyd, A. A. Long, S. G. Pembroke, J. M. Rist, F. H. Sandbach and G. Watson. B. Mates, *Stoic Logic* (Berkeley and Los Angeles 1953). J. M. Rist, *Stoic Philosophy* (Cambridge 1969). S. Sambursky, *The Physics of the Stoics* (London 1959). G. Watson, *The Stoic Theory of Knowledge* (Belfast 1966).

Most of these works and a number of recent articles have been cited in the notes to Chapter 4. The following are also valuable: Ph. De Lacy, 'The Stoic Categories as Methodological Principles', *Transactions and Proceedings of the American Philological Association* 76 (1945) 246–63; R. P. Haynes, 'The Theory of Pleasure of the Old Stoa', *American Journal of Philology* 83 (1962) 412–19; M. E. Reesor, *The Political Theory of the Old and Middle Stoa* (N.Y. 1951) and 'Fate and Possibility in Early Stoic Philosophy', *Phoenix* 19 (1965) 285–97.

6. PANAETIUS, POSIDONIUS, ANTIOCHUS, CICERO

Source collections and some other works have been cited in the notes to Chapter 5.

Panaetius: the best comprehensive treatment is M. van Straaten, *Panétius, sa vie, ses écrits et sa doctrine* (Amsterdam 1946). He is rightly cautious about inferring Panaetius' views from texts in which the philosopher is not named. Apart from Panaetius' certain influence upon Cicero's *De officiis*, he was probably drawn on by Cicero for the *De republica* (cf. i 34).

Posidonius: a cautious and comprehensive study of M. Laffranque, *Poseidonios d'Apamée* (Paris 1964). Another useful work is 'The Philosophical System of Posidonius' by L. Edelstein, *American Journal of Philology* 57 (1936) 286–325. For a detailed bibliography Laffranque's book should be consulted. The Ciceronian works on which Posidonius' influence can be argued with some probability are *De divinatione* and *Tusculan Disputations*.

Antiochus: see the works cited in notes pp. 222–8 of Chapter 5.

Cicero: to Hunt and Douglas cited on pp. 222, 229 of Chapter 5 may be added: T. Petersson, *Cicero, A Biography* (Berkeley 1920); the introduction to J. S. Reid's edition of the *Academica* (London 1885) and the bibliographical surveys by S. E. Smethurst in *Classical World* li (1957), lviii (1964–5) and lxi (1967).

7. GENERAL AND LATER INFLUENCE

Good introductions to the Stoicism of Seneca, Epictetus and Marcus Aurelius in M. Pohlenz, *Die Stoa* (Göttingen 1964) and E. Zeller, *Philosophie der Griechen* vol. iii part 1, trans. by S. F. Alleyne as *A History of Eclecticism in Greek Philosophy* (London 1883). On the Roman Cynics cf. D. R. Dudley, *A History of Cynicism* (London 1937).

This list gives a short selection of books which deal with or touch on the influence of Hellenistic philosophy in antiquity and later:

E. Barker, *From Alexander to Constantine* (Oxford 1956).

M. L. Clarke, *The Roman Mind* (London 1956).

S. Dill, *Roman Society from Nero to Marcus Aurelius* (2nd ed., London 1905).

P. Gay, *The Enlightenment* (London 1967).

H. Haydn, *The Counter-Renaissance* (New York 1950).

J. W. Johnson, *The Formation of English Neo-classical Thought* (Princeton 1967).

P. O. Kristeller, *The Classics and Renaissance Thought* (Cambridge, Mass. 1955).

T. F. Mayo, *Epicurus in England* (New York 1934).

R. Popkin, *The History of Scepticism from Erasmus to Descartes* (Assen 1960).

C. B. Schmitt, *Cicero Scepticus: a Study of the Influence of the Academica in the Renaissance* (The Hague 1972).

M. Spanneut, *Le Stoïcisme des Pères de l'Eglise* (2nd ed., Paris 1969).

J. S. Spink, *French Free-Thought from Gassendi to Voltaire* (London 1960).

L. Zanta, *La Renaissance du Stoïcisme au XVI siècle* (Paris 1914).

Bibliographical Postscript 1985

THE book's original bibliography was unavoidably selective, and deliberately biased towards publications for English-speaking readers. As a part of the book's original scope and design that bibliography is retained here. The supplements which I now offer, by being placed separately, will help to show how Hellenistic philosophy has developed in the years since 1974. In choosing what to include, I have tried to incorporate all studies which seem to me to be of central importance, with a generous selection of those shorter publications that contribute to the philosophical issues that are being discussed most fruitfully.

During the past few years, several new periodicals have appeared which cater specifically for ancient philosophy: *Ancient Philosophy* (Duquesne University, Pittsburgh), *Cronache Ercolanesi* (Naples), *Cahiers de Philologie* (University of Lille), *Elenchos* (Naples), *Oxford Studies in Ancient Philosophy*, *Philosophia* (Athens), *Prudentia* (Auckland, New Zealand). All of these include articles on Hellenistic philosophy.

I. GENERAL

D. Babut, *La religion des philosophes grecs* (Paris 1974)
J. Dillon, *The Middle Platonists* (London 1977)
J. C. Fraisse, *Philia. La notion d'amitié dans la philosophie antique* (Paris 1974)
P. M. Frazer, *Ptolemaic Alexandria*, 3 vols. (Oxford 1972)
J. Glucker, *Antiochus and the late Academy* (Göttingen 1978), a mine of information on many aspects of the Hellenistic schools

W. Görler, *Untersuchungen zu Ciceros Philosophie* (Heidelberg 1974)

J. C. B. Gosling and C. C. W. Taylor, *The Greeks on Pleasure* (Oxford 1982)

H.-J. Krämer, *Platonismus und hellenistische Philosophie* (Berlin 1971)

G. E. R. Lloyd, *Greek Science after Aristotle* (London 1973)

J. Mejer, *Diogenes Laertius and his Hellenistic Background* (Wiesbaden 1978)

G. Reale, *Storia della filosofia antica*, III (Milan 1976)

D. N. Sedley, 'Diodorus Cronus and Hellenistic philosophy', *Proc. Cambr. Philological Soc.* NS 23 (1977) 74–120, a pioneering study on the background to Hellenistic dialectic

R. Sorabji, *Necessity, Cause and Blame. Perspectives on Aristotle's Theory* (London 1980)

R. Sorabji, *Time, Creation and the Continuum* (London 1983)

G. Striker, *Kritêrion tês alêtheias* [Criterion of truth], *Nachricht. der Akad. der Wiss. in Göttingen*, Phil.-hist. kl. 1974, 2, 47–110

II. TEXTS, TRANSLATIONS, COMMENTARIES

Alexander of Aphrodisias (fl. A.D. 200). *De fato, Alexander of Aphrodisias On Fate*, text, transl. and commentary, R. W. Sharples (London 1983)

De mixtione, Alexander of Aphrodisias On Stoic Physics, text, transl. and commentary, R. B. Todd (Leiden 1976)

Bion of Borysthenes (c. 335–245 B.C.). A Collection of the fragments with Introduction and Commentary, J. F. Kindstrand (Uppsala 1976)

Diogenes Laertius, transl. M. Gigante, 2nd ed. 2 vols. (Bari 1976)

Epictetus, *Epiktet von Kynismus*, M. Billerbeck (Leiden 1978)

Galen, *On the Doctrines of Hippocrates and Plato*, ed., transl. and commentary, P. De Lacy, *Corpus Medicorum Graecorum* V 4, 1, 2 (Berlin 1978)

Lucretius, Loeb Classical Library, M. F. Smith (London and Cambridge, Mass. 1975)

Plutarch, *Moralia XIII*, Loeb Classical Library, H. Cherniss, 2 vols. (London and Cambridge, Mass. 1976)

Sextus Empiricus, *Grundriss der pyrrhonischen Skepsis*, introd.
and transl., M. Hossenfelder (Frankfurt am Main 1968)

III. COLLECTIONS OF ARTICLES DEALING WITH MORE THAN ONE SCHOOL

M. Schofield, M. Burnyeat, J. Barnes, ed. *Doubt and
Dogmatism. Studies in Hellenistic Epistemology* (Oxford 1980)
J. Barnes, J. Brunschwig, M. Burnyeat, M. Schofield, ed.
Science and Speculation. Studies in Hellenistic Theory and Practice
(Cambridge and Paris 1982)
W. Fortenbaugh, ed. *On Stoic and Peripatetic Ethics. The Work
of Arius Didymus* (New Brunswick and London 1983)

IV. EPICURUS AND EPICUREANISM

Editions, commentaries, translations: G. Arrighetti, *Epicuro
Opere* 2nd ed. (Turin 1973). M. Isnardi Parente, *Opere di Epicuro*
(Turin 1974), includes principal testimonia and some works
of later Epicureans as well as all Epicurus' surviving writings
in translation. M. Bollack and his Lille colleagues have published editions with French translation and commentary of the
Letters to Herodotus, Menoeceus, and *Pythocles,* together with the
Kuriai Doxai and *Gnomologium Vaticanum: La lettre d'Épicure*
(Paris 1971), *La pensée du plaisir* (Paris 1975), *Épicure à Pythocles*
(Lille 1978). The text of these volumes is entirely based on
the three principal MSS whose virtually complete authority
the authors seek to defend without emendation. Diogenes Laertius' *Life of Epicurus,* 10. 1–34, is edited and commented on
by A. Laks, *Cahiers de Philologie* 1 (1976), 1–118. For studies
of the papyrus fragments of Epicurus *On nature,* cf. G. Arrighetti, *Cronache Ercolanesi* 1 (1971) 90–111 and 5 (1975) 39–51;
D. N. Sedley, 4 (1974) 89–92; and for editions of individual
books, cf. Arrighetti ('On time') *Cron. Erc.* 2 (1972) 5–46; Sedley ('Book 28') ibid. 3 (1973) 5–83; C. Millot ('Book 15') ibid.
9 (1979) 9–39. For ethics and ethical testimonia there is an
annotated edition by C. Diano, *Epicuri Ethica et Epistulae* 2nd
ed. (Florence 1974). H. Usener's word index and collection

of illustrative texts has been edited by M. Gigante and W. Schmid in *Glossarium Epicureum* (Rome 1977).

General studies and monographs: for a good introduction, cf. D. Pesce, *Introduzione a Epicuro* (Rome-Bari 1980), with very detailed bibliography. More specialised: E. Asmis, *Epicurus' Scientific Method* (Ithaca and London 1984); D. Clay, *Lucretius and Epicurus* (Ithaca and London 1983); B. Frischer, *The sculpted word: Epicureanism and philosophical recruitment in ancient Greece* (Berkeley and Los Angeles 1982); M. Gigante, *Scetticismo e Epicureismo* (Naples 1981); V. Goldschmidt, *La doctrine d'Épicure et le droit* (Paris 1977); D. Konstan, *Some Aspects of Epicurean Psychology* (Leiden 1973); D. Lemke, *Die Theologie Epikurs* (Munich 1973); A. Manuwald, *Die prolepsislehre Epikurs* (Bonn 1972); R. Müller, *Die epikureische Gesellschaftstheorie* (Berlin 1974). The writings of two eminent scholars are collected in C. Diano, *Scritti epicurei* (Florence 1974), and R. Philippson, *Studien zu Epikur und den Epikureern* ed. C. J. Classen (Hildesheim 1983).

Collection of articles, and critical bibliography of recent work: ΣΥΖΗΤΗΣΙΣ *Studi sull'Epicurismo Greco e Romano offerti a Marcello Gigante*, ed. G. P. Carratelli, 2 vols. (Naples 1983); many of these articles are in English.

On epistemology, cf. W. Detel, 'Aisthesis und Logismos, zwei Probleme der epikureischen Methodologie', *Archiv f. Gesch. d. Philos.* 57 (1975) 21–35; G. Striker, 'Epicurus on the truth of sense impressions', ibid. (1977) 125–42; V. Goldschmidt, 'Remarques sur l'origine épicurienne de la prénotion', *Les stoiciens et leur logique* [see section VI below] 155–70; C. C. W. Taylor, 'All perceptions are true', *Doubt and Dogmatism* [see section III above] 105–24; E. N. Lee, 'The sense of an object. Epicurus on seeing and hearing', *Studies in Perception*, ed. P. K. Machamer and R. G. Turnbull (Columbus, Ohio 1978) 27–55; D. K. Glidden, 'Epicurus on self-perception', *Amer. Philosoph. Quart.* 16 (1979) 297–306, 'Epicurean semantics', ΣΥΖΗΤΗΣΙΣ 185–226.

On physics, cf. A. A. Long, 'Chance and natural law in Epicureanism', *Phronesis* 22 (1977) 63–87; F. Solmsen, 'Epicurus on void matter and genesis', ibid. 263–81; D. Konstan, 'Problems in Epicurean physics', *Isis* 70 (1979), 394–418; B. Inwood, 'The origin of Epicurus' concept of void', *Classical Philology* 76 (1981) 273–85; D. N. Sedley, 'Two conceptions of vacuum', *Phronesis* 27 (1982) 175–93. On the swerve of atoms more specifically, cf. I. Avotins, 'Notes on Lucretius 2.251–293', *Harvard Studies in Classical Philology* 84 (1980), 75–9; K. Kleve, '*Id facit exiguum clinamen*', *Symbolae Osloenses* 15 (1980) 27–31; M. Isnardi Parente, 'Stoici, Epicurei e il motus sine causa', *Rivista Critica di Storia della Filosofia* 35 (1980) 23–31; D. N. Sedley, 'Epicurus' refutation of determinism', ΣΥΖΗΤΗΣΙΣ 11–51: D. Fowler, 'Lucretius on the *clinamen* and "free will"', ibid. 329–52.

On time, cf. M. Isnardi Parente, 'Chronos epinooumenos e chronos nooumenos in Epicuro', *La Par. d. Pass.* 31 (1976) 168–75; F. Caujolle-Zaslawsky, 'Le temps épicurien est-il atomique?', *Études philosophiques* (1980) 285–306. On theology, cf. K. Kleve, 'Empiricism and theology in Epicureanism', *Symbolae Osloenses* 52 (1977) 39–51 and 'On the beauty of God, a discussion between Epicureans, Stoics and Sceptics', ibid. 53 (1978) 69–83. On social theory, cf. N. Denyer, 'The origins of Justice', ΣΥΖΗΤΗΣΙΣ 133–52, and R. Müller, 'Konstituierung und Verbindlichkeit der Rechtsnormen bei Epikur', ibid. 153–83.

On Epicurus' philosophical background there are two important articles by D. N. Sedley, 'Epicurus and his professional rivals', *Cahiers de Philologie* 1 (1976) 121–59 and 'Epicurus and the mathematicians of Cyzicus', *Cron. Erc.* 6 (1976) 23–54.

Later Epicureans: work on Philodemus has proceeded splendidly in the pages of *Cronache Ercolanesi*. Studies that call for particular mention are the new edition of *Philodemus: On Methods of Inference* by P. and E. A. De Lacy (Naples 1978), and *Polistrato, Sul Disprezo irrazionale delle Opinioni popolari* by G. Indelli (Naples 1978). The arguments of Philodemus' book are discussed by D. N. Sedley in 'On signs', *Science and Speculation* [see section III above] 239–72. For Diogenes of Oenoanda,

M. F. Smith has now recovered a further large number of fragments, cf. *Class. Quart.* NS 22 (1972) 159–62, *Thirteen new fragments of Diogenes of Oenoanda, Denkschrift Akad. Wien* phil.-hist. kl. 117 (1974), *Hermathena* 118 (1974) 110–29, *Cahiers de Philologie* 1 (1976) 279–318, *Anatolian Studies* 28 (1978) 39–92 and 29 (1979) 69–89, *Prometheus* 8 (1982) 193–212. Cf. also A. Laks and C. Millot, 'Réexamen de quelques fragments de D. sur l'âme, la connaissance et la fortune', *Cahiers de Philologie* 1 (1976) 321–57.

V. SCEPTICISM

Editions, commentaries, translations: F. Decleva Caizzi, *Pirrone Testimonianze* (Napoli 1981). A new annotated text of the fragments of Timon of Phlius is included in *Supplementum Hellenisticum*, ed. H. Lloyd-Jones and P. Parsons (Berlin 1983). Cf. also A. A. Long, 'Timon of Phlius: Pyrrhonist and satirist', *Proc. Cambr. Philological Soc.* NS 24 (1978) 68–91. The ten Sceptic Modes are translated and interpreted by J. Annas and J. Barnes in *The Modes of Scepticism* (Cambridge 1985).

For a rich miscellany of articles, together with a comprehensive bibliography, cf. *Lo scetticismo antico*, ed. G. Giannantoni, 2 vols. (Naples 1981). This collection is discussed by M. R. Stopper in 'Schizzi Pirroniani', *Phronesis* 28 (1983) 265–97. Other important collections which include articles on ancient scepticism are *Doubt and Dogmatism* and *Science and Speculation* [see section III above] and *The Sceptical Tradition*, ed. M. F. Burnyeat (Berkeley and Los Angeles 1983), and *Philosophy and History*, ed. R. Rorty, J. B. Schneewind and Q. Skinner (Cambridge 1985).

General studies: J.-P. Dumont, *Le scepticisme et le phénomène* (Paris 1972); M. Conche, *Pyrrhon ou l'apparence* (Villers-sur Mer 1973); M. dal Pra, *Lo scetticismo greco* 2nd ed., 2 vols. (Rome-Bari 1975). Cf. also U. Burkhard, *Die angebliche Heraklit-Nachfolge des skeptikers Aenesidem* (Bonn 1973). On the latest phase of the sceptical Academy, see D. N. Sedley, 'The end of the Academy', *Phronesis* 26 (1981) 67–75, and H. Tarrant,

Scepticism or Platonism? The Philosophy of the Fourth Academy (Cambridge 1985).

Two fundamental studies by P. Couissin were accidentally omitted from the first printing of *Hellenistic Philosophy*: 'Le stoïcisime de la Nouvelle Académie', *Revue d'histoire de la philosophie* 3 (1929) 241–76 and 'L'origine et l'évolution de l'epochê', *Rev. Ét. Gr.* 42 (1929) 373–97.

An issue which has been keenly debated is the beliefs, if any, that a Pyrrhonist may consistently hold: cf. M. F. Burnyeat, in *Doubt and Dogmatism* 20–53 (repr. in *The Skeptical Tradition* 117–48); M. Frede, 'Des Skeptikers Meinungen', *Neue Hefte für Philosophie* 15/16 (1979) 102–29; J. Barnes, 'The beliefs of a Pyrrhonist', *Proc. Cambr. Philological Soc.* NS 28 (1982) 1–29; C. Stough, 'Sextus Empiricus on Non-assertion', *Phronesis* 29 (1984) 137–64.

Other articles: J. Barnes, 'Proof destroyed', *Doubt and Dogmatism* 161–81, 'Ancient skepticism and causation', *The Skeptical Tradition* 149–204; M. F. Burnyeat, 'Protagoras and self-refutation in later Greek philosophy', *Philosophical Review* 85 (1976) 44–69, 'Tranquillity without a stop: Timon frag. 68', *Class. Quart.* NS 30 (1980) 86–93, 'Idealism and Greek philosophy: What Descartes saw and Berkeley missed', *Philosophical Review* 91 (1982) 3–40, 'The Sceptic in his place and time', *Philosophy and History* 225–54; E. Flintoff, 'Pyrrho and India', *Phronesis* 25 (1980) 88–108; M. Frede, 'Stoics and Skeptics on clear and distinct impressions', *The Skeptical Tradition* 65–95, 'The Sceptic's two kinds of assent and the question of the possibility of knowledge', *Philosophy and History* 255–78; K. Janáček, 'Zur Interpretation des Photios-Abschnittes über Ainesidemos', *Eirene* 14 (1976) 93–100; A. A. Long, 'Sextus Empiricus on the criterion of truth', *Bull. Inst. Class. Stud.* 25 (1978) 35–49, 'Stoa and Sceptical Academy: origins and growth of a tradition', *Liverpool Classical Monthly* 5 (1980) 161–74, 'Aristotle and the history of Greek scepticism', *Studies in Aristotle* ed. D. J. O'Meara (Washington D.C. 1981) 79–106; I. Mueller, 'Geometry and scepticism', *Science and Speculation* 69–95; D. N. Sedley, 'The motivation of Greek skepticism', *The Skeptical*

Tradition 9–30; G. Striker, 'Sceptical strategies', *Doubt and Dogmatism* 54–83, 'Über den Unterschied zwischen den Pyrrhoneern und den Akademikern', *Phronesis* 26 (1981) 153–71, 'The ten tropes of Aenesidemus', *The Skeptical Tradition* 95–116.

VI. STOICISM

Editions, commentaries, translations: U. Egli, *Das Dioklesfragment bei Diogenes Laertius*, Sonderforschungsbereich 99 Linguistik (University of Konstanz, 1981). Under the same imprint K. Hülser has collected and translated *Die Fragmente zur Dialektik der Stoiker* in an introductory volume and 8 Bände. This collection, which completely eclipses the material on Stoic logic excerpted by von Arnim in *Stoicorum Veterum Fragmenta*, is a research tool of primary importance. Philodemus' fragmentary treatise on the Stoics has been edited by T. Dorandi, *Cronache Ercolanesi* 12 (1982) 91–133. For other recent work on individual authors see section II above.

Collections of articles: *Les stoiciens et leur logique* ed. J. Brunschwig (Paris 1978); *The Stoics* ed. J. Rist (Berkeley and Los Angeles 1978); *Spindel Conference 1984: Recovering the Stoics*, vol. XXIII, suppl. *The Southern Journal of Philosophy*, ed. R. H. Epp. This includes a bibliography of nearly 1200 items, compiled by R. H. Epp, and a critical survey of recent work, by J. M. Rist. See also *Doubt and Dogmatism*, *Science and Speculation*, *On Stoic and Peripatetic Ethics* [all section III above] and *The Skeptical Tradition* [section V above].

General books and monographs: most of the books published since 1972 have been specialist studies. An important exception is F. H. Sandbach, *The Stoics* (London 1975). Cf. also the 4th ed. of V. Goldschmidt, *Le système stoicien et l'idée de temps* (Paris 1979). Three books basic to the study of each of the three divisions of Stoic philosophy are: M. Frede, *Die stoische Logik* (Göttingen 1974); D. Hahm, *The Origins of Stoic Cosmology* (Ohio 1977); M. Forschner, *Die Stoische Ethik* (Stuttgart 1981).

More specialised: P. V. Cova, *Lo stoico imperfetto* (Naples 1978);

M. Dragona-Monachou, *The Stoic Arguments for the Existence and Providence of the Gods* (Athens 1976); A. Graeser, *Plotinus and the Stoics* (Leiden 1972), *Zenon von Kition. Positionen und Probleme* (Berlin 1975); B. Inwood, *Ethics and Human Action in Early Stoicism* (Oxford 1985); A. M. Ioppolo, *Aristone di Chio e lo stoicismo antico* (Naples 1980); F. H. Sandbach, *Aristotle and the Stoics*, Cambr. Philological Soc. suppl. 10 (1985); R. T. Schmidt, *Die Grammatica der Stoiker*, German transl. of the 1839 Latin ed. by K. Hülser with new introd. and bibliogr. by U. Egli (Wiesbaden 1979); D. Tsekourakis, *Studies in the Terminology of Early Stoic Ethics* (Wiesbaden 1974); A. J. Voelke, *L'idée de volonté dans le stoicisme* (Paris 1973).

Recent articles on particular topics:
On language and grammar, cf. M. Frede, 'Principles of Stoic grammar', *The Stoics* 27–76; U. Egli, 'Stoic syntax and semantics', *Les stoiciens* 135–54; A. Graeser, 'The Stoic theory of meaning', *The Stoics* 101–24; J. Pinborg, 'Historiography of linguistics', *Current Trends in Linguistics* 13 (The Hague 1975) 69–126. On formal logic, cf. J. Barnes, 'Proof destroyed', *Doubt and Dogmatism*, 161–81; J. Brunschwig, 'Proof defined', ibid. 125–60, 'Le modèle conjonctif', *Les stoiciens* 59–86; V. Celluprica, 'La logica stoica in alcune recenti interpretazioni', *Elencos* 1 (1980) 123–50; M. Frede, 'Stoic vs. Aristotelien Syllogistic', *Archiv f. Gesch. d. Philosophie* 56 (1974) 1–32; M. Mignucci, 'Sur la logique modale des stoiciens', *Les stoiciens* 317–46; I. Mueller, 'An introduction to Stoic logic', *The Stoics* 1–26; J. M. Rist, 'Zeno and the Origins of Stoic Logic', *Les stoiciens* 387–400; M. Schofield, 'The syllogisms of Zeno of Citium', *Phronesis* 28 (1983) 31–58.

On 'signs', cf. M. F. Burnyeat, 'The origins of non-deductive inference', *Science and Speculation* 193–238; D. N. Sedley, 'On signs', ibid. 239–72; G. Verbeke, 'La philosophie du signe chez les stoiciens', *Les stoiciens* 401–24. On the *sorites*, cf. J. Barnes, 'Medicine, experience and logic', *Science and Speculation* 24–68; M. F. Burnyeat, 'Gods and heaps', *Language and Logos* eds. M. Schofield and M. Nussbaum (Cambridge 1982) 315–38.

On epistemology, cf. J. Annas, 'Truth and knowledge', *Doubt and Dogmatism* 84–104; E. P. Arthur, 'The Stoic analysis of the mind's reactions to presentations', *Hermes* 111 (1983) 69–78; M. Frede, 'Stoics and Skeptics on clear and distinct impressions', *The Skeptical Tradition* 65–95; W. Görler, ''Ασθενὴς συγκατάθεσις: zur stoischen Erkenntnistheorie', *Wurzbürger Jahrbücher für die Altertumswissenschaft*, N.F. 3 (1977) 83–92; C. Imbert, 'Stoic logic and Alexandrian poetics', *Doubt and Dogmatism* 182–216; G. B. Kerferd, 'What does the wise man know?', *The Stoics* 125–36; A. A. Long, 'Dialectic and the Stoic sage', ibid. 101–24, 'The Stoic distinction between truth and the true', *Les stoiciens* 297–316, 'Stoa and Sceptical Academy: origins and growth of a tradition', *Liverpool Classical Monthly* 5 (1980) 161–74; M. Schofield, 'Preconception, argument and God', *Doubt and Dogmatism* 293–308; H. von Staden, 'The Stoic theory of perception and its "Platonic" critics', *Studies in Perception* eds. P. K. Machamer and R. G. Turnbull, (Columbus, Ohio 1978) 96–136; G. Striker [see section I above]; R. B. Todd, 'The Stoic common Notions, *Symbolae Osloenses* 48 (1973) 47–75.

On psychology, cf. A. A. Long, 'Soul and body in Stoicism', *Phronesis* 27 (1982) 34–57, and B. Inwood, 'Hierocles: theory and argument in the second century A.D.', *Oxford Studies in Ancient Philosophy* II (1984), 151–83.

On physics and metaphysics, cf. J. Barnes, 'La doctrine du retour éternel', *Les stoiciens* 3–20; A. Graeser, 'The Stoic categories', ibid. 199–221; D. E. Hahm, 'The Stoic theory of change', *Spindel Conference 1984* 39–56; M. Lapidge, '*Archai* and *Stoicheia*: a problem in Stoic cosmology', *Phronesis* 18 (1973) 240–78; A. C. Lloyd, 'Activity and description in Aristotle and the Stoa', *Proc. Brit. Acad.* 56 (1970) 227–40; A. A. Long, 'Heraclitus and Stoicism', *Philosophia* 5/6 (1975–6) 133–56, 'Astrology: arguments pro and contra', *Science and Speculation* 165–92, 'The Stoics on world-conflagration and everlasting recurrence', *Spindel Conference 1984* 13–38; D. N. Sedley, 'The Stoic criterion of identity', *Phronesis* 27 (1982) 255–75, 'Stoic metaphysics', *Spindel Conference 1984* 87–92; R. B. Todd, 'Monism and immanence; the foundations of Stoic physics', *The Stoics* 137–60.

On cause and determinism, cf. M. Frede, 'The original notion of cause', *Doubt and Dogmatism* 217–49; D. Frede, 'The dramatisation of determinism: Alexander of Aphrodisias *De fato*', *Phronesis* 27 (1982) 276–98; J. Moreau, 'Immutabilité du vrai, necessité logique et lien causal', *Les stoiciens* 347–60; M. Reesor, 'Necessity and fate in Stoic philosophy', *The Stoics* 187–202; R. W. Sharples, 'Aristotelian and Stoic conceptions of necessity in the *De fato* of Alexander of Aphrodisias', *Phronesis* 20 (1975) 247–74, 'Alexander of Aphrodisias *De fato*: some parallels', *Class. Quart.* NS 28 (1978) 243–66; 'Necessity in the Stoic doctrine of fate', *Symbolae Osloenses* 56 (1981) 81–97; C. Stough, 'Stoic determinism and moral responsibility', *The Stoics* 203–32; R. Sorabji, 'Causation, laws and necessity', *Doubt and Dogmatism* 250–82; P. L. Donini, 'Crisippo e la nozione del possibile', *Riv. d. Filol.* 101 (1973) 333–51, 'Fato e volunta umana in Crisippo', *Atti Acc. Torino* 109 (1974–5) 1–44.

On theology, cf. M. Dragona-Monachou, 'Providence and fate in Stoicism and prae-Neoplatonism', *Philosophia* 1 (1971) 339–78; J. Mansfeld, 'Providence and the destruction of the universe in early Stoic thought', *Studies in Hellenistic Religions* ed. M. J. Vermaseren (Leiden 1979) 129–188.

On ethics: for doxography, cf. A. A. Long, 'Arius Didymus and the exposition of Stoic ethics', with comments by N. P. White, *On Stoic and Peripatetic Ethics* 41–74. For foundations, cf. H. Görgemanns, '*Oikeiosis* in Arius Didymus', with comments by B. Inwood, ibid. 165–202; A. Graeser, 'Zirkel oder Deduktion', *Kant-Studien* 63 (1972) 213–24, 'Zur Funktion des Begriffes "gut" in der stoischen Ethik', *Zeitschrift f. philos. Forschung* 26 (1972) 417–25; A. M. Ioppolo, 'La dottrina stoica dei beni esterni e i suoi rapporti con l'etica aristotelica', *Rivista Critica di Storia della Filosofia* 29 (1974) 363–85; G. B. Kerferd, 'The search for personal identity in Stoic thought', *Bull. John Rylands Library* 55 (1972) 177–86; A. A. Long, 'Greek ethics after MacIntyre and the Stoic community of reason', *Ancient Philosophy* 3 (1983) 184–99; H. Reiner, 'Der Streit um die stoische Ethik', *Zeitschrift f. philos. Forschung* 21 (1967) 261–81; J. M. Rist, 'Zeno and Stoic consistency', *Phronesis* 22 (1977) 161–74; G. Striker, 'The role of *oikeiôsis* in Stoic ethics', *Oxford*

Studies in Ancient Philosophy 1 (1983) 145–64; N. P. White, 'The basis of Stoic ethics', *Harvard Stud. in Class. Philol.* 83 (1979) 143–78, 'The role of physics in Stoic ethics', *Spindel Conference 1984* 57–74.

For 'impulse', cf. B. Inwood, 'The Stoics on the grammar of action', *Spindel Conference 1984* 75–86, and G. B. Kerferd, 'Two problems concerning impulses', with comments by A. Preus, *On Stoic and Peripatetic Ethics* 87–106; A. A. Long, 'The early Stoic concept of moral choice', *Images of Man in Ancient and Medieval Thought. Studies Presented to G. Verbeke* (Louvain 1976) 77–92. For passions, cf. M. Daraki-Mallet, 'Les fonctions psychologiques du Logos', *Les stoiciens* 87–120; A. M. Ioppolo, 'La dottrina della passione in Crisippo', *Riv. Crit. Storia d. Filos.* 27 (1972) 251–68; A. C. Lloyd, 'Emotion and decision in Stoic psychology', *The Stoics* 233–46; J. M. Rist, 'The Stoic concept of detachment', ibid. 259–72.

Other aspects of Stoic ethics, cf. P. De Lacy, 'The four Stoic *personae*', *Illinois Classical Studies* 2 (1977) 163–72; I. G. Kidd, 'Moral actions and rules in Stoic ethics', *The Stoics* 247–58; H. Reiner, 'Die ethische Weisheit der Stoiker heute', *Gymnasium* 76 (1969) 330–57; M. Vegetti, 'La saggezze dell'attore, Problemi dell'etica stoica', *Aut Aut* 195/6 (1983) 19–41.

FORTHCOMING

Cambridge University Press will shortly publish A. A. Long and D. N. Sedley, *The Hellenistic Philosophers*. Vol. 1 Translations and commentaries, Vol. 2 Texts and notes. This work is intended as a source-book of the principal evidence for Stoicism, Scepticism and Epicureanism.

Index

Index 273